Recent Reviews of other Odyssey Guides...

"Thorough and beautifully illustrated, this book is a comprehensive—and fun—window into Afghan history, culture, and traditions. A must have for travel readers and a gripping read for anyone with even a passing interest in Afghanistan."
—Khaled Hosseini, author of *The Kite Runner*—

"...for coverage of Chongqing and the Gorges, and of the more placid and historically notable sites below Yichang and downriver to Shanghai, it is unrivalled..."
—*Simon Winchester*—

"It is one of those rare travel guides that is a joy to read whether or not you are planning a trip..."
—*The New York Times*—

"...Essential traveling equipment for anyone planning a journey of this kind..."
—*Asian Wall Street Journal*—

"If travel books came with warnings, the one for AFGHANISTAN: A COMPANION AND GUIDE would read, 'Caution: may inspire actual voyage.' But then, this lavishly produced guide couldn't help do otherwise—especially if you're partial to adventure."
—*TIME*, August 22nd 2005—

"Above all, it is authoritative and as well-informed as only extensive travels inside the country can make it. It is strong on the history. In particular the synopsis at the beginning is a masterly piece of compression."
—*The Spectator* (UK)—

"A gem of a book"
—*The Literary Review* (UK)—

"...Quite excellent. No one should visit Samarkand, Bukhara or Khiva without this meticulously researched guide..."
—*Peter Hopkirk, author of* The Great Game—

"The Yangzi guide is terrific"
—*Longitude Books*—

"...The bible of Bhutan guidebooks..."
—*Travel & Leisure*—

"...It's a superb book, superbly produced, that makes me long to go back to China..."
—*John Julius Norwich*—

"...Odyssey fans tend to be adventurous travelers with a literary bent. If you're lucky enough to find an Odyssey Guide to where you're going, grab it..."
—*National Geographic Traveler*—

MOSCOW,
ST PETERSBURG
&
THE GOLDEN RING

Moscow &

BY

Masha Nordbye

St Petersburg

Photography by
Patricia Lanza
Masha Nordbye

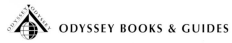 **ODYSSEY BOOKS & GUIDES**

Odyssey Books & Guides is a division of Airphoto International Ltd.
903 Seaview Commercial Building, 21–24 Connaught Road West, Sheung Wan, Hong Kong
Tel: (852) 2856-3896; Fax: (852) 2565-8004
E-mail: sales@odysseypublications.com; www.odysseypublications.com

Distribution in the USA by W.W. Norton & Company, Inc., 500 Fifth Avenue, New York, NY 10110, USA
Tel: 800-233-4830; Fax: 800-458-6515; www.wwnorton.com

Distribution in the UK and Europe by Cordee Books and Maps, 3a De Montfort St., Leicester, LE1 7HD, UK
Tel: 0116-254-3579; Fax: 0116-247-1176; www.cordee.co.uk

Moscow, St Petersburg & the Golden Ring, Third Edition
ISBN: 978-962-217-771-0
Library of Congress Catalog Card Number has been requested.
Copyright © 2007, 2004, 2003, 1999, 1995, 1991, 1990, Airphoto International Ltd.
Maps Copyright © 2007, 2004, 2003, 1999, 1995, 1991, 1990, Airphoto International Ltd.

Grateful acknowledgment is made to the following authors and publishers:

Peter Owen Ltd for *Adventures in Czarist Russia* by Alexandre Dumas, edited and translated by Alma Elizabeth Murch; Farrar, Straus and Giroux Inc. and Georges Borchardt Inc. for *In Plain Russian* by Vladimir Voinovich translated by Richard Lourie, translation © 1979 by Farrar, Strauss and Giroux Inc.; North Point Press for *The Noise of Time* translated by Clarence Brown © 1965 Princeton University Press; Princeton University Press for *The Road to Bloody Sunday: The role of Father Gapon and the Assembly in the Petersburg Massacre of 1905* by Walter Sablinsky © 1976 Princeton University Press; Random House Inc. and William Heinemann Ltd for *Among the Russians* © 1983 Colin Thubron; Penguin Books for *Dead Souls* by Nikolai Gogol, translation © 1961 David Magarshack; Chronicle Books for *White Nights* by Fyodor Dostoevsky © 1995.

Managing Editor: Helen Northey
Contributing Editor: Kevin Bishop
Design: Au Yeung Chui Kwai
Maps: On The Road Cartography 579, 587, 608–9, 613, 618
Index: Don Brech, Records Management International, Hong Kong

Cover photography: Keith Macgregor
Photography by Patricia Lanza
Additional photography/illustrations courtesy of Kevin Bishop 553, 561; Patrick Lucero 88, 96, 215, 222; Keith Macgregor 424, 425, 492–3, 496–7, 502, 512, 584, 589, 590, 594; Masha Nordbye 6–7, 26–7, 101, 103, 120, 121, 125, 129, 156, 166, 171, 183, 188, 190, 203, 220–1, 219, 230 (bottom left), 231 (bottom), 243, 244, 246, 247, 249, 250, 259, 274, 275, 282, 286–7, 292, 293, 294–5, 302, 308–309, 313, 317, 326, 331, 334, 438, 445, 448, 488, 489, 526, 542, 549, 550, 582, 591, 602, 605, 610, 611, 622, 627; Moscow History Museum & Interbook Business 99, 261; Trillium Studios (Cary Wollinsky) 23, 56–7, 136, 141, 146; Carolyn Watts 181

Production and printing by Twin Age Ltd, Hong Kong

E-mail: twinage@netvigator.com
Manufactured in China

Reading the safety information on these websites is advisable before travelling overseas:
US Department of State: www.travel.state.gov/travel warnings.html
UK Foreign and Commonwealth Office: www.fco.gov.uk/travel
Canadian Department of Foreign Affairs & International Trade: www.voyage.gc.ca/dest/sos/warnings-en.asp
Australian Department of Foreign Affairs & Trade: www.dfat.gov.au/travel/

SPECIAL ACKNOWLEDGMENTS

To SEBASTIAN—*Mein Spielzeugknabe, Meine Zuversicht*

and, lovingly, to Eleanor Nordbye, who gifted me the world.

We will preserve you Russian speech; keep you alive great Russian word.
We will pass you to our sons and heirs; free and clean, and they in turn to theirs.
And so forever.

Anna Akhmatova

After 25 years of journeying around Russia with many extraordinary experiences, a multitude of hosts and characters have blessed my path who have generously provided support and assistance, for which I am forever grateful.

I wish to especially thank my family and friends for all their help and humor during the many months of research and writing: Leonard Nordbye; Sandushka Johnson; Carlichka "Bogoliubsky" Gottlieb; Tommy & Target Campbell; Stuart & Mabel; Suzie, Annika & Kate; Todd Thompson; Mieke, Jim & Luka; Val Kountze; Beth Davidow; Lyoni Craven; Geri, Maya & Cupcake Sasha & Will Alexander; Phil Penningroth, Stacey & Claire; John Porterfield; Isabel Allende & Villie Gordon; Bob "The Great" Jones & Gudren; Misha Tunick for my writing pad; Demetria & Rock Newman; Bill Wood; Jane Brockman; Yanni Feist & Kate; Annette Sand; Andy Van Cleeve; Richard Neill; Manco computer wizards; the Roadside families; Gene Sawyer; Peggy Burns; David & Sue Ellen Boltski; Andy & Gank; Ari, Yuko & Aidan; Members of Sweetwater; Tom Sopko & the Lorchaks; Tanya, Andrei, Sasha, Max & *Malenkaya* Masha—the Frishkadelkamis; Dominque Jando & Lenichka; Dan in Moscow; Vladimir Uspensky; Dyadya AA Sonin, Natasha & The St Petersburg Circus & Museum; my first Russian language teacher, Alexandra Baker & Middlebury College; and a special hail to my Odyssey *tovarishi*, Magnus Bartlett, Cecilia Lee and Helen Northey.

To my mates on The Flying Trapeze: Great Master Ritchie Gaona, Tom "Sergei-Oleg" Moore and Tsar & Alexandra; Pampam & Ralph Ventura; Vendola & Rocky Balboa; Mercedes; Kristin; Brad & Catherine; Laura Faye & Bobby King; Anna; Crystal; catchers Alex G, Randy, Chobie & Colton; Tony Steele; Sami-sumbubba Keen; the Flying Cranes & Golovkos—Lena, Misha & Yulya.

In special memory of Mark Nordbye, Marieke Douridas; Uncle Murray, Ina Goff, Vita Uspenskaya, Papa & Mama Frish, Yuri Nikulin, Schneer, Robert Baker, Sam Orth, Milan, Helen Chaverini, Mek & Brud Morsey, Tom & Tina Roadside, Brian Seeholzer, Matt Valensic, and the Slavic-blooded Babushki Annas and Dyedushka Demetrius.

And a hearty *spasbo* to all those who helped throughout the many years in the ol' *Bolshaya Kapusta*.

Masha Nordbye

After defeating the Swedes in 1709, Peter the Great decided to build his Summer Palace, Peterhof, outside of St Petersburg, on the shores of the Gulf of Finland. The great Cascade Fountain in front of the palace has 17 waterfalls, 142 water jets and 39 gilded statues.

CONTENTS

INTRODUCTION 12

RECENT POLITICAL HISTORY ..25
PERESTROIKA 25
ELECTIONS AND ECONOMY 28
THE COMMUNIST PARTY 30
ATTEMPTED COUP OF AUGUST 1991 31
THE END OF THE SOVIET UNION 33
BORIS YELTSIN 34
THE FIRST MULTIPARTY ELECTIONS 35
THE EFFECTS OF REFORM.........................36
THE RESURGENCE OF THE COMMUNISTS 39
1996 PRESIDENTIAL ELECTIONS 40
THE LAST YEARS OF THE 20TH CENTURY......41
VLADIMIR PUTIN 44
RUSSIA TODAY...48

FACTS FOR THE TRAVELER...51
PLANNING YOUR TRIP 51
WHAT TO PACK 55
GETTING THERE 61
MONEY...64
VALUABLES...67
HEALTH AND EMERGENCIES 67
CRIME, SAFETY AND HAZARDS....................68
GETTING AROUND 70
BEING THERE..77
FOOD..87
SHOPPING 94
RUSSIAN LANGUAGE 96

MOSCOW..............102
RED SQUARE...114
THE KREMLIN 121
OLD MOSCOW 148
THE OLD MARX PROSPEKT 155
TVERSKAYA ULITSA 173
ULITSA VOZDVIZHENKA AND NOVY ARBAT...184
KUTUZOVSKY PROSPEKT.............................191
THE BOULEVARD RING..............................195
THE GARDEN RING 209
SPARROW HILLS 214
ALL-RUSSIAN EXHIBITION CENTER 226
DOWN THE MOSKVA RIVER.......................229

VICINITY OF MOSCOW......236

THE GOLDEN RING 264
SERGIYEV POSAD 273
ALEKSANDROV 281
PERESLAVL-ZALESSKY 283
ROSTOV VELIKY 288
NIKOLA-ULEIMA 297
UGLICH ON THE VOLGA..............................297
YAROSLAVL...299
TUTAYEV ON THE VOLGA 307
KOSTROMA 310
IVANOVO 314
PALEKH 315
VLADIMIR 321
YURYEV-POLSKY 335
SUZDAL 335

MOSCOW PRACTICAL
INFORMATION...................354

St Petersburg 422

History 427
Period of Perestroika 437
St Petersburg Today..............................437

Culture 444
Literature 444
Ballet..456
Music...463
Art...469

Getting Around 471

Sights 473
Peter and Paul Fortress........................473
Across the Kronverk Strait 477
Kirov Islands 479
The Strelka of Vasilyevsky Island 485
Palace Square..490
The Area of Senate Square 501
St Isaac's Square....................................507
Field of Mars..511
Mikhailovsky (Engineer's) Castle.........518
Nevsky Prospekt 520
Finland Station 539
The Smolny 544
Theater Square 548
Moscow Avenue.......................................555

Vicinity of St Petersburg...............565
Peterhof or Petrodvorets 565
Lomonosov or Oranienbaum 578
Kronstadt 581

West of the City (Northern Gulf)
Razliv..583
Repino..585

North of the City
Vyborg..586

South of the City
Tsarskoye Selo or Pushkin 588
Pavlovsk 599
Gatchina 604
Novgorod 606
Pskov 611

East of the City (Lake Ladoga Area)
Petrokrepost or Schlüsselburg 614
Staraya Ladoga 615
Valaam Island 617
Kizhi Island..619

St Petersburg Practical Information...................628

Useful Addresses 676
In the USA 676
In the UK 678
In Canada 679
In Hong Kong...680
In Australia 681
In New Zealand......................................681

Russian Language 684
Cyrillic Alphabet 684
Basic Russian Vocabulary......................685
Menu Vocabulary 690

Recommended Reading..696

WEIGHTS & MEASURES
CONVERSIONS 705

INDEX 708

SPECIAL TOPICS

CHRONOLOGY 18
FABERGÉ...145
THE RUSSIAN CINEMA 202
THE RUSSIAN CIRCUS 232
THE RUSSIAN ICON 329
THE TRANS-SIBERIAN RAILWAY 348
BANYAS...418
PETER THE GREAT 439
CATHERINE THE GREAT...............................513
YELISEYEV'S 540
LENIN AND THE RUSSIAN REVOLUTION 551
THE SIEGE OF LENINGRAD 559
ANNA AKHMATOVA......................................620
RUSSIAN ORTHODOX CHURCH HOLIDAYS
    AND FESTIVALS 682
GENEALOGY OF THE IMPERIAL FAMILY 706

LITERARY EXCERPTS

THOMAS STEVENS, *Traveling Through
    Russia on a Mustang* 86
JOHN REED, *Ten Days That Shook
    the World* 126
VLADIMIR VOINOVICH, *A Circle of
    Friends*...138
ALEXANDRE DUMAS, *Adventures in
    Czarist Russia*.....................................192
NIKOLAI GOGOL, *Dead Souls*....................208
LEO TOLSTOY, *War and Peace*..................255
PRINCE PETER KROPOTKIN, *Memoirs
    of a Revolutionist* 262
The Firebird..317
COLIN THUBRON, *Among the Russians*......435
OSIP MANDELSTAM, *The Noise of Time* 449

The Petition of January 9, 1905 454
MARQUIS DE CUSTINE, *Russia* 504
FYODOR DOSTOEVSKY, *White Nights* 536
ALEXANDER DYMOV, *Winter of 1942* 562
ALEXANDER PUSHKIN, *The Bronze
    Horseman* 625

MAPS

EASTERN EUROPE..11
MOSCOW...106–8
MOSCOW METRO 112–3
CENTRAL MOSCOW 116–7
VICINITY OF MOSCOW...........................238–9
SERGIYEV POSAD 277
PERESLAVL-ZALESSKY 284
ROSTOV VELIKY 290
YAROSLAVL...301
VLADIMIR 323
SUZDAL 343
PETER AND PAUL FORTRESS.......................475
ST PETERSBURG.....................................480–1
CENTRAL ST PETERSBURG 482
ST PETERSBURG METRO 483
VICINITY OF ST PETERSBURG 566
PETERHOF 569
ORANIENBAUM 579
VYBORG...587
TSARSKOYE SELO 592
PAVLOVSK 603
NOVOGROD 608–9
PSKOV 613
VALAAM..618

Eastern Europe

0   100   200   300 kms

0   100   800 miles

N

FINLAND

Valaam
Island

Lake Onega
Kizhi
Island

Helsinki

Lake
Ladoga

Stockholm

Gulf of Finland

St Petersburg

SWEDEN

Tallinn

Narva

ESTONIA

Novgorod

Pskov

Volga

Riga

Yaroslavl

LATVIA

Rostov

Baltic Sea

Dvina

Suzdal

Sergiyev
Posad

Vladimir

Kaliningrad

Neman

LITHUANIA

Moscow

(RUSSIA)

Vilnius

Smolensk

Oka

POLAND

Minsk

RUSSIA

Vistula

Bug

BELARUS

Dnieper

Desna

Warsaw

Brest

Pripet

Vistula

Dnieper

Kiev

Don

Lvov

Kharkov

SLOVAKIA

Bratislava

Dnestr

UKRAINE

Bug

Donets

Budapest

HUNGARY

MOLDOVA

Rostov-
on-Don

Siret

Kishinev

Dnieper

Zagreb

ROMANIA

Odessa

Sea of Azov

CROATIA

Sava

BOSNIA &
HERZEGOVINA

Belgrade

Bucharest

Yalta

Danube

Sarajevo

SERBIA &
MONTENEGRO

Sofia

Black   Sea

BULGARIA

Tirana

Skopje

F.Y.R.O.M.

ALBANIA

Istanbul

GREECE

TURKEY

© Airphoto International Ltd

INTRODUCTION

On with the journey!...
Russia! Russia!
When I see you... my eyes
are lit up with supernatural power. Oh, what a
glittering, wondrous infinity of space....What a
strange, alluring, enthralling, wonderful world!

Nikolai Gogol

Perhaps no other destination in the world has captured the traveler's imagination as much as Russia. Throughout the centuries, its visitors have reported phenomenal and fanciful scenes: from golden churches, bejeweled icons and towering kremlins to madcap czars, wild cossacks and prolific poets. Russia was, and remains, an impressive sight to behold. A travel writer in the early 20th century remarked that Russia's capital, Moscow, 'embodied fantasy on an unearthly scale... Towers, domes, spires, cones, onions, crenellations filled the whole view. It might have been the invention of Danté, arrived in a Russian heaven.'

By the 1600s, Russia was already the largest country in the world, stretching from Finland to Alaska. The massive conquests deep into the Siberian wilds by Ivan the Terrible and Peter the Great had created a territory larger than the Roman Empire with the richest resources on Earth. It was so vast that in 1856, when American Perry McDonough Collins arrived in Irkutsk to propose a railway line to link the country, it took him nearly a year to travel the 5,632 kilometers (3,500 miles) to St Petersburg. He had to change horses over 200 times.

After the 1917 Bolshevik Revolution, the countries bordering Russia fell into the Soviet Union's domain. The USSR became the world's largest nation with 15 republics stretching across 11 time zones and two continents, Europe and Asia. Its borders encompassed one-sixth of the planet's total land area with a population of 290 million speaking 200 languages and dialects.

On the historic day of December 21, 1991, after seven decades of Communist rule, the Soviet Union collapsed. The attempted coup in August 1991 was the catalyst that led to the dissolution of one of the most oppressive regimes in history. As one defender of a new and nontotalitarian government exclaimed: 'I have lived through a revolution, world wars, the Siege of Leningrad and Stalin, and I will not tolerate another takeover; let the people be in peace!' In its place was established the Commonwealth of Independent States (CIS), or the Soyuz Nezavysimeekh Gosudarstv (SNG).

Moscow is the Commonwealth's largest city and the capital of its largest state, the Russian Federation, which occupies 17,070,959 square kilometers (6,591,104 square miles), stretching to the eastern tip of Siberian Kamchatka. There are 1,064 cities, and over 80 percent of the population lives in European Russia to the west of the Ural Mountains. With nearly 150 million people and 130 nationalities and ethnic groups, Russia is truly the core of the Commonwealth. It is impossible to take in the diversity of the entire country during one, two or even three visits. However, there is no better way to learn about the Russian character and way of life than taking a trip to Moscow, St Petersburg and the area of the Golden Ring.

Moscow is the center of politics, industry and culture—the heart of this giant nation—and the source of the Russian spirit, or *dusha*. The Russian poet Alexander Pushkin wrote of his first trip to Moscow: 'And now at last the goal is in sight: in the shimmer of the white walls...and golden domes, Moskva lies great and splendid before us...O Moskva have I thought of you! Moskva how violently the name plucks at any Russian heart!'

The true enchantment of Moscow begins in the city center, where you can gaze upon the gilded domes of the palaces and churches of the former czars, rising up from within the old protective walls of the Kremlin. From the citadel, paths lead out to the fairy-tale creation of Ivan the Terrible, St Basil's Cathedral, which looms up from the middle of Krasnaya Ploshchad or Red Square. *Krasnaya* is an Old Russian word meaning both red and beautiful. The city, which marked its 860th anniversary in 2007, is also a place where frenzied consumerism is coupled with deep spirituality, and golden domes of long-closed churches are gleaming once again. In 1931, Stalin destroyed the immense Cathedral of Christ Our Savior, but in 1997 the next generation helped rebuild it with 360 million dollars collected in public funds. Shopping malls have even popped up alongside the Kremlin and in old KGB bunkers. Surely Lenin would not recognize the place—even though people (mostly foreign tourists now) still queue in front of Lenin's Mausoleum to view the Father of the Great October Revolution.

Like arteries from the heart of the city, long thoroughfares take one through various stages of Moscow's history. These roads, and ringroads, offer an abundance of sights and over 100 museums. The Arbat district, which celebrated its 510th anniversary in 2003, embodies both Russia's history and the changes currently sweeping the country. Here, *babushki* (grandmothers) amble along carrying bags filled with cabbages and potatoes, alongside tourists buying Russian souvenirs, while long-haired musicians jam on guitars and saxophones. The city offers a wealth of

(following pages) The Kremlin's Assumption Cathedral.
Its spacious interior is covered with exquisite frescoes and icons dating from the
15th century. The screen of icons on the front wall were painted in the mid-17th century
by monks of the Trinity-Sergius Monastery in the Golden Ring town of Sergiyev Posad.

breathtaking and poetic creations, as the famous Russian writer Anna Akhmatova remarked: 'As you stroll through the city, you'll find...all of Moscow is truly soaked with verses, saturated with meter, time after time.'

The towns and villages surrounding the city, known collectively as the Golden Ring, reveal a quieter and quainter lifestyle. This area is considered the cradle of Russian culture. The small towns, like Sergiyev Posad (the center of Russian Orthodoxy) and Suzdal (the most ancient Russian town), were built between the 10th and 17th centuries and are magnificently preserved. Antiquated villages, onion-domed churches, frescoes and icons by the 15th-century artist Andrei Rublyov, colorful wooden dacha (country homes) and endless groves of *beryoza* (birch trees) provide a delightful contrast to the bigger cities. These serene sites are reminiscent of a 19th-century Tolstoyan novel, a portrait of Russia's past.

Much more provincial than Moscow, St Petersburg is the legacy of Peter the Great. Images of this astoundingly beautiful city are reflected in the Neva River which winds around the many islands that comprise the area. A stroll along one of the many canal embankments takes in three centuries of ornate architecture glistening under the pastel northern lights. Sights abound: the Hermitage, one of the largest museums in the world; Peterhof Palace, rivaling Versailles in grandeur; Peter the Great's fortress; the golden-spired Admiralty; the statue of the Bronze Horseman; and scenes of numerous revolutions. Throughout the world, every time someone recites Gogol or Dostoevsky, or sees a performance of *Boris Godunov* or *Swan Lake*, St Petersburg's bounty flowers again. Liberated of the name Leningrad (and anything to do with Lenin) in 1991, the city's residents affectionately refer to their city simply as Pieter. They proudly celebrated St Petersburg's 300th anniversary in 2003.

It is now over a decade and a half since the fall of the Soviet Union and any visitor today will be astonished by the immense transformation that has swept across the land. Russia can rightfully claim that no other place on earth has made such radical changes in so short a period of time. After a thousand years of autocratic rule and 74 years of Communism, a new democratic market economy has, slowly but surely, spun into action for the first time in the country's existence.

Since Vladimir Putin was elected President to lead Russia into the 21st century, private enterprise has firmly taken hold of the economy. Today, over three quarters of the Russian economy is said to be in private hands. A whole new class of young *Noviye Russkiye* (New Russians), who do not even remember the Politburo, have ventured into *biznis* themselves. Government-run enterprises have given way to individual millionaires, state-owned land to real-estate moguls and ideological propaganda has shifted to billboards promoting products from around the world. Today an estimated three-quarters of the Russian economy is said to be in private hands.

If this is your first trip, or if you have not visited Russia in the past ten years, it is time to be truly flabbergasted at all the changes. Joint ventures between east and west have opened plush new hotels, internationally-stocked shopping malls and scores of new entertainment opportunities. Because of the whirlwind creation of new businesses and flood of consumer spending, Moscow has often been called the capital of *Deeky Vostok*, the 'Wild East.' But this country is just experiencing the growing pains of normal adolescence. Once it matures, economists predict that this large powerhouse, with its vast natural resources, new business-oriented generation, and immense desire for success, will become one of the most dynamic marketplaces in the world.

Many travelers still enter the country with an organized group, which includes hotels, meals and sightseeing tours. But, visitors can also enter on individual or business visas, and stay in Russian homes or apartments. Even though Moscow was recently listed as one of the most expensive cities in the world to visit, it also now offers a wide selection of places to stay (from 5-star to budget hotels) and thousands of eateries and food store options. For the more adventurous, a whole array of specialized tours are also offered, including biking, hiking, climbing and rafting.

Today, in many of the larger cities and towns, English is widely understood. If you do not read Cyrillic or speak Russian, take a Russian phrase book; a smile, some patience and the knowledge of a few Russian words is always well taken by the locals. So much so, that you may even find yourself invited to someone's home for *chai* (tea) or vodka, where you will quickly discover that Russians are among the warmest and most hospitable people you'll ever meet.

Do Svidanya!

A haze of legend will be cast
Over all, like scroll and spiral
Bedecking gilded boyar chambers
And the Cathedral of St Basil.

By midnight denizens and dreamers
Our Mother Russia most of all is cherished,
Here is their home, the fount' of all
With which this century shall flourish.

Boris Pasternak

CHRONOLOGY

700–882: The Vikings begin to leave Scandinavia and establish trading settlements with the Slavs in northwestern Russia. Kievan State in the south is formed and named after the Slavic Prince Kii. In 862, the Norseman Rurik defeats the important Slavic town of Novgorod and becomes one of the first Vikings to rule in Russia. In 880, Rurik's successor, Oleg, conquers the Slavic-ruled Kiev, unites the two states and makes Kiev his capital. The ruling class is known as 'Rus', (thought to be derived from the Viking word *ruotsi*, meaning rower or oarsman). This term is later applied to the people of Eastern Europe; eventually the areas are united into the Russian states.

977: Novgorod gains its independence from Kiev.

978–1015: Rule of Prince Vladimir, who introduces Byzantine Christianity into Russia in 988.

1015–1054: Rule of Yaroslav the Wise. Kiev becomes the first center of the Orthodox Church.

1113–1125: Rule of Vladimir Monomakh. The two principalities of Novgorod and Kiev are united again under his rule. The crown of Monomakh is worn by the later rulers of Russia. The decline of Kievan Rus begins after his death.

1147: Prince Yuri Dolgoruky 'Long Arms' founds Moscow. He builds a kremlin and defensive walls around the city.

1169: Prince Andrei Bogoliubsky transfers the capital from Kiev to Vladimir.

1223: First Mongol invasion of Russia.

1237: Batu Khan, grandson of Genghis Khan, invades Moscow and goes on to conquer many of Russia's other regions. The Mongol Tartars dominate Russia for the next 250 years.

1240: The Prince of Novgorod, Alexander Nevsky, defeats the Swedes in an important battle along the Neva River. Nevsky rules as grand prince in Vladimir from 1252–1263.

1299: The Church Metropolitan flees Kiev and takes up residence with the grand prince in Vladimir.

1325–1340: Reign of Ivan I, nicknamed Kalita 'Moneybags' because of his strong economic hold over the other principalities. Ivan is named grand prince in 1328, and chooses Moscow as his residence. The seat of the Orthodox Church is moved from Vladimir to Moscow. In 1337, St Sergius founds the Monastery of the Holy Trinity in Sergiyev Posad.

1353–1359: Reign of Ivan II. Plague wipes out one-third of Moscow population.

1362–1389: Reign of Dmitri Donskoi. In 1380, the grand prince defeats the Tartars in the Battle of Kulikovo on the Don, becoming the first Russian prince to win a decisive battle over the Mongol army. Two years later the Mongols burn Moscow to the ground.

1389–1425: Reign of Vasily I.

1425–1460: Reign of Vasily II. In 1445 a huge fire destroys much of Moscow.

1453: The Ottoman Turks conquer Constantinople, which releases the Russian Orthodox Church from Byzantine domination. Less than a decade later, the head of the Orthodox Church takes on the title of Metropolitan of Moscow and All Russia and receives his orders from the grand prince.

1460–1505: Reign of Ivan III (Ivan the Great). He marries Sophia, the niece of the last Byzantine emperor, in 1472 and adopts the crest of the double-headed eagle. Moscow is declared the Third Rome. During his rule, Ivan the Great rebuilds the Kremlin and annexes the city of Novgorod. He refuses to pay any further tribute to the Mongols and defeats their armies. Two centuries of Tartar oppression in Russia come to an end. Population of Moscow over 100,000.

1505–1533: Reign of Vasily III, father of Ivan the Terrible.

1533–1584: Reign of Ivan IV (Ivan the Terrible) who is crowned in 1547 in the Moscow Kremlin with the title of Czar (derived from Caesar) of All Russia. Moscow becomes the capital of the Holy Russian Empire. St Basil's Cathedral is built to commemorate the defeat of the Tartars in the far eastern provinces. He organizes the Oprichniki, a special bodyguard to prosecute the Boyars (noble-class landowners). In 1582, Russia loses the Livonian War and access to the Baltic. In the same year, Ivan also kills his son, Alexei, in a fit of rage. Upon his death, Moscovy is left in a state of political and economic ruin.

1584–1598: Reign of Fyodor I, son of Ivan IV. When he dies childless, so does the House of Rurik.

1591: The youngest son of Ivan the Terrible, Dmitri, mysteriously dies.

1598–1605: Reign of Boris Gudunov.

1605–1613: The Time of Troubles, an era of much instability, famine and unrest. In 1604, a false Dmitri (son of Ivan the Terrible), claiming to have survived the assassination attempt of 1591, turns up in Poland. With the help of Polish troops he seizes the Russian throne, but is murdered shortly thereafter. When a second false Dmitri, in 1605, then tries to gain the throne, the Russian army, headed by the Cossacks, emerge victorious.

1613–1645: Following the Time of Troubles and the defeat of Polish invaders, the 16-year-old Mikhail Romanov (related to Ivan the Terrible) is elected new czar of Russia on March 14, 1613. The Romanov dynasty continues to rule Russia until 1917; there were 18 rulers in all.

1645–1676: Reign of Alexei I, father of Peter the Great. Establishes Russia's first Law Code in 1649. Patriarch Nikon sets out to reform the Orthodox Church causing a major schism between the Reformers and the Old Believers. Nikon is deposed in 1660.

1676–1682: Reign of Fyodor III. When he dies, his feeble-minded brother, Ivan V, and half-brother, Peter (Peter the Great), are proclaimed joint czars. The Streltsy (marksmen) briefly gain control over the government. Sophia, Peter's half-sister, acts as regent until 1689.

1689–1725: Reign of Peter the Great. During his enlightened rule, Peter adopts the Julian calendar, transfers the capital from Moscow to St Petersburg, introduces Western culture and customs to his country and builds the first Russian fleet along the Baltic. In 1721, he dissolves the seat of the Patriarch and creates a governing church body known as the Holy Synod. That same year, after the end of the Great Northern War, he assumes the title of Emperor of All Russia. (See Special Topic on page 439.)

1725–1727: Reign of Catherine I, the widow of Peter the Great, who becomes czarina with the help of her guard Menschikov. Academy of Sciences founded in 1725.

1727–1730: Reign of Peter II, Peter the Great's grandson.

1730–1740: Reign of Anna Ivanova, daughter of Ivan V and niece of Peter the Great. In 1731, first opera performed in Russia.

1740–1741: Reign of Ivan VI.

1741–1761: Reign of Elizabeth, daughter of Peter the Great and Catherine I. In 1754, Rastrelli begins construction of Winter Palace. In 1755, the first university is founded in Moscow. In 1757, Academy of Arts founded.

1762 (for six months) Reign of Peter III. In 1744, Peter married Sophie of Anhalt-Zerbst. After his assassination, his wife, Catherine II ascended the throne.

1762–1796: Reign of Catherine II (Catherine the Great), German-born wife of Peter III. The first foreign woman to rule as czarina. She ushers in Russia's Golden Age (for more on Catherine the Great see Special Topic, page 513).

1796–1801: Reign of Paul I, son of Catherine the Great. Builds the Mikhailovsky Palace.

1801–1825: Reign of Alexander I, son of Paul I. In 1812, Napoleon's armies flee Moscow in defeat. Rise of the Decembrist movement, who petitioned for the end of autocracy.

1825–1855: Reign of Nicholas I, son of Paul I. On December 14, 1825 the Decembrists attempt to overthrow the czarist government and gain freedom for the serfs. The uprising was crushed and conspirators immediately hanged. Bolshoi Theater opens in 1825. In 1842, Gustav Fabergé opens his first jewelry shop in the capital. Marx and Engels publish the communist manifesto in 1848. In 1849, Petrashevsky Circle arrested. In 1851, the first railway opens between St Petersburg and Moscow.

1855–1881: Reign of Alexander II, son of Nicholas I. In 1861, Alexander signs a decree to emancipate the serfs.

1867: Sale of Alaska to the United States; Karl Marx's *Das Kapital* is translated into Russian and the first Marxist groups formed within the country.

1869: Tolstoy completes *War & Peace*.

1881: Alexander II is assassinated in a bombing by members of the Peoples' Will group—revolutionaries.

1881–1894: Reign of Alexander III. The brother of Lenin, Alexander Ulyanov, along with four others, attempt to assassinate the czar. All are hung in the Kronstadt Fortress.

1894–1917: Reign of Nicholas II. Nicholas marries the granddaughter of Queen Victoria; they have five children. In 1895, workers hold public rallies to celebrate May Day, day of worker solidarity. Nicholas dismisses a call for constitutional reform that provokes the founding of the Social Democratic Workers' Party. In 1903, this Party splits into two factions: Bolsheviks and Mensheviks. Russo-Japanese War 1904–05. The first revolution takes place in 1905 (known as the Bloody Sunday massacre) in St Petersburg. Romanov dynasty celebrates 300th anniversary in 1913. World War I breaks out in 1914. In 1916, Rasputin murdered by Count Yusupov. Second revolution begins in February 1917. Czar Nicholas abdicates on March 15, 1917 and a Provisional government is formed. The prime ministers of the new government are Prince Lvov (Feb–May) and Alexander Kerensky (May–Oct). Lenin and the Bolsheviks overthrow the Provisional Government in October 1917. In 1918, Nicholas and his family are executed in the Ural town of Sverdlovsk (present-day Yekaterinburg).

1918–1924: In 1918, Lenin moves capital from Petrograd to Moscow. Civil war erupts between 1918–20. The Socialist Soviet State is formed in 1922, and the first Soviet Constitution adopted. Switch to Gregorian calendar. The Communist Government nationalizes industry, introduces censorship of the press and forms the Cheka police force. Lenin introduces the New Economic Policy (NEP). When Lenin dies in 1924, St Petersburg (Petrograd) is renamed Leningrad. (see Special Topic on page 551).

1924–1953: Joseph Stalin. In 1927, Trotsky is expelled from the Party. In 1928, Stalin introduces the First Five Year Plan and Collectivization. A widespread famine sweeps the nation, eventually killing ten million people.

1934–1941: Stalin's assassination of Leningrad Party Chief Sergei Kirov signals the beginning of the Great Terror. Half the delegates of the 17th Party Congress are purged, along with 90 percent of the country's generals. Of approximately 20 million people arrested, seven million are shot immediately while the rest are sent to gulag camps for rehabilitation. In 1939, the Nazi-Soviet pack is formed. In 1940, Soviet Union annexes Baltic republics.

1941–1945: World War II. Hitler invades the USSR in 1941, and the siege of Leningrad lasts for 900 days until 1944. The Soviet Union suffers 20 million casualties.

1945–1953: World War II ends in 1945. Yalta and Potsdam conferences. Occupation of Eastern Europe.

(opposite) Tomb covering dating from 1630.

1953–1955: Georgi Malenkov is General Secretary of Communist Party.

1955–1964: Nikita Khrushchev becomes leader and founds the KGB, the committee for state security, in 1954. In 1956, at the 20th Party Congress, he denounces Stalin in a secret speech. Two-thirds of the Orthodox churches and monasteries are closed down. In 1961, the Soviets send the first man, Yuri Gagarin, into space, and the Congress votes to remove Stalin's body from its place of honor alongside Lenin in the Kremlin Mausoleum. Berlin Wall is constructed in 1961. In 1962, Cuban Missile Crisis fuels the Cold War.

1964–1982: Leonid Brezhnev forces Khrushchev's resignation, who immediately rescinds Khrushchev's Rule 25 restricting Party officials to 15 years in office. The discovery of large gas and oil reserves boosts the economy, but these benefits are undermined by poor planning and lack of incentives. Alcohol consumption quadruples in 20 years. Further repressions stimulate the dissident and Samizdat movements.

1968: Invasion of Czechoslovakia.

1979–1989: Occupation of Afghanistan.

1982–1984: Brezhnev succeeded by Yuri Andropov, former head of the KGB.

1984–1985: Andropov dies and is succeeded by Konstantin Chernenko, Brezhenev's 72-year old protégé, who dies one year later.

1985–1991: Mikhail Gorbachev (see History, page 25).

1991: December 21, the Soviet Union ceases to exist.

1992–1999: Boris Yeltsin, President of the Russian Republic, forms the 11-member Commonwealth of Independent States (see History, page 34).

2000–present: Vladimir V. Putin (see History, page 44).

RECENT POLITICAL HISTORY

PERESTROIKA

Mikhail Sergeyevich Gorbachev was born in 1931 in a small Cossack village within the Stavropol region. While in school, he worked as a combine operator's assistant, and by the age of 18, he had been awarded the Order of the Red Banner of Labor and had joined the Communist Party.

On March 11, 1985, 54-year-old Mikhail Sergeyevich Gorbachev was elected the new General Secretary of the Communist Party. Following in the footsteps of such past rulers as Ivan the Terrible, Peter the Great, Stalin and Brezhnev, Gorbachev inherited a stagnating economy, an entrenched bureaucracy and a population living in fear and mistrust of its leaders.

Gorbachev's first actions were to shut down the production and sale of vodka and ardently pursue the anticorruption campaign instituted by a former president, Yuri Vladimirovich Andropov. In 1986, Gorbachev introduced the radical reform policies of perestroika (restructuring), *demokratizatsiya* (democratization) and glasnost (openness), now household words. He emphasized that past reforms had not worked because they did not directly involve Soviet citizens. Perestroika introduced the profit motive, quality control, private ownership in agriculture, decentralization and multi-candidate elections. Industry concentrated on measures promoting quality over quantity; private businesses and cooperatives were encouraged; farmers and individuals could lease land and housing from the government, and keep the profits made from produce grown on private plots; hundreds of ministries and bureaucratic centers were disbanded. A law was passed that allowed individuals to own small businesses and hire workers so long as there was 'no exploitation of man by man'. In 2006, 75-year-old Gorbachev, published his book *To Understand Perestroika*. He also founded Green Cross International, devoted to improving the environment worldwide.

In a powerful symbolic gesture, Andrei Sakharov and other political prisoners were released from internal exile. (After winning the 1975 Nobel Peace Prize, Sakharov, the physicist and human rights activist, was banished for nearly seven years to the city of Gorky, the present-day Nizhny Novgorod. He died in Moscow on November 14, 1989.) One hundred Soviet dissidents from 20 cities were allowed to form the Democratic Club, an open political discussion group. Glasnost swept through all facets of Soviet life.

For the 40 million followers of the Russian Orthodox religion, and people of other religious beliefs, Gorbachev stated that 'believers have the full right to express their convictions with dignity'. On December 1, 1989, Gorbachev became the first

Soviet leader to set foot in the Vatican, where he declared: 'We need spiritual values; we need a revolution of the mind... No one should interfere in matters of the individual's conscience. Christians, Moslems, Jews, Buddhists and others live in the Soviet Union. All of them have a right to satisfy their spiritual needs—this is the only way toward a new culture and new politics that can meet the challenge of our time.'

As Peter the Great understood, modernization meant Westernization, and Gorbachev reopened the window to the West. With the fostering of private business, about five million people were employed by over 150,000 cooperatives. After April 1, 1989, all enterprises were allowed to carry on trade relations with foreign partners, triggering the development of joint ventures. Multimillion-dollar deals were struck with Western companies, such as Chevron, Pepsi, Eastman-Kodak, McDonald's, Time-Warner and Occidental.

At the 1986 Iceland Summit, Gorbachev proposed a sharp reduction in ballistic missiles, and in December 1987, he signed a treaty with US President Ronald Reagan to eliminate intermediate-range nuclear missiles. In January 1988, the Soviet Union announced its withdrawal from Afghanistan. Nine months later Andrei Gromyko retired and Gorbachev was also elected President of the Supreme Soviet.

During a visit to Finland in October 1989, Gorbachev declared: 'The Soviet Union has no moral or political right to interfere in the affairs of its Eastern European neighbors. They have the right to decide their own fate.' And that is what they did. By the end of 1989, every country throughout Eastern Europe saw its people protesting openly for mass reforms. The Iron Curtain crumbled, symbolized most poignantly by the demolition of the wall between East and West Berlin.

In December 1989, Gorbachev met with US President George H.W. Bush at the Malta Summit, where the two agreed that 'the arms race, mistrust, psychological and ideological struggle should all be things of the past'.

ELECTIONS AND ECONOMY

On March 26, 1989, there was a general election for the new Congress of People's Deputies—the first time that Soviet citizens had had the chance to vote in a national election. One thousand five hundred delegates were elected together with an additional 750, who were voted in by other public organizations. The 2,250-delegate body then elected 542 members to form a new Supreme Soviet.

Ousted a year earlier from his Politburo post for criticizing the reforms, the Congress candidate Boris Yeltsin won 89 percent of the Moscow district vote. As

(previous pages) In 1870, the Abramtsevo Estate, located north of Moscow, was purchased by wealthy merchant and art patron, Savva Mamontov, who turned it into a popular artist colony. Artist Viktor Vasnetsov designed this small wooden dacha, known as the 'Hut on Chicken Legs,' named after the headquarters of the witch Baba Yaga from a popular Russian fairy tale.

Moscow crowds chanted 'Yeltsin is a Man of the People' and 'Down with Bureaucrats', a surprising number of bureaucrats had, in fact, lost to members of such groups as the Church Metropolitan of Leningrad. Andrei Sakharov was also elected. An interesting aspect of the election rules was that even candidates who ran unopposed could lose if over half the votes polled showed a level of no confidence, a privilege not enjoyed by voters in most Western countries.

At the beginning of 1990, Soviet citizens once again headed to the polls to elect their own regional and district officials, this time with the additional opportunity of choosing candidates from other independent and pro-democracy movements. Scores of Communist Party candidates were defeated by former political prisoners, adamant reformers, environmentalists and strike leaders. Yeltsin was voted in as President of the Russian Federation, the Soviet Union's largest republic with more than half the country's population and Moscow as its capital. In June 1990, Yeltsin resigned from the Communist Party, declaring that 'in view of my...great responsibility toward the people of Russia and in connection with moves toward a multiparty State, I cannot fulfill only the instructions of the Party'.

Yeltsin's ascent underscored the fact that for all Gorbachev's unprecedented reforms and innovative policies, he had failed to bring the country's economy out of stagnation; because of this he lost his popularity at home. An extensive poll conducted throughout the Soviet Union revealed that more than 90 percent considered the economic situation critical. Some of the disheartened commented that 'glasnost has produced more copies of Solzhenitsyn than salami'. Food and fuel were in critically low supplies, and the population anticipated the worst food shortages since World War II. Ration coupons were issued for meat, sugar, tea and soap. After the launch of a probe to Mars, graffiti in Moscow appeared exclaiming: 'To Mars for Soap!'

Modernization still did not approach Western standards: there were few computers and most areas continued to use the abacus. It was estimated that 40 percent of the crops had been wasted because of poor storage, packing and distribution methods. Many Soviets felt that their living conditions had worsened: 'We live like dogs. The leash has become longer but the meat is a bit smaller, and the plate is two meters further away. But at least we can now bark as much as we want.'

Gorbachev was also faced with a budget deficit of over 100 billion rubles. The severe shortages boosted the black market, which provided goods for up to 85 percent of the population. On November 1, 1989, the government drastically cut the bank ruble exchange rate by 90 percent to curb black-market exchanges (up to 20 times the official rate) and bring the ruble closer to an open exchange on the world market. The prime minister stated that 43 million people (15 percent of the population) were living below the poverty level. There was also an estimated 23 million unemployed, the new paradox of this modern Soviet society.

Compounding failing measures and political contradictions, the nation was rocked by a series of disasters: Chernobyl, the earthquake in Armenia, ethnic unrest and extensive strikes in mines and factories across the country (a 1989 law legalized strikes). But Gorbachev remained confident and pressed on with perestroika: 'This is a turbulent time, a turbulent sea in which it is not easy to sail the ship. But we have a compass and we have a crew to guide that ship, and the ship itself is strong.'

In one of the most important changes in the country's political and economic system since the 1917 Bolshevik Revolution, Mikhail Gorbachev was elected by Congress as the Soviet Union's first executive president. This new post, replacing the former honorary chairmanship of the Supreme Soviet, had broader constitutional powers. The president now had the right to propose legislation, veto bills passed by Congress, appoint and fire the prime minister and other senior government officials, and declare states of emergency (with the approval of the republics).

Gorbachev himself summarized the results of all his policies: 'Having embarked upon the road of radical reform, we have crossed the line beyond which there is no return to the past... Things will never be the same again in the Soviet Union—or in the whole communist world.' Gorbachev's second revolution became one of the most momentous events in the second half of the 20th century.

THE COMMUNIST PARTY

> *If what the Communists are doing with Russia is an experiment, for this experiment I would not even spare a frog.*   Professor I P Pavlov (1918)

The Bolshevik Party, formed by Lenin, began as a unified band of revolutionaries whose 8,000 members organized the mass strike of the 1905 St Petersburg revolt. By October 1917, the Bolshevik Party (soon renamed the Communist Party) had over 300,000 members, many of whom became the leaders and planners of the newly formed Soviet State.

Before the fall of Communism, there were more than 20 million Party members, a third of them women. Membership was open to any citizens who 'did not exploit the labor of others', abided by the Party's philosophy and gave three percent of their monthly pay as dues to the Party. Members were also required to attend several meetings and lectures each month, provide volunteer work a few times a year and help with election campaigns. Approximately 200,000 of these members were full-time officials, *apparatchiks*, paid by the Party. The Komsomol, or Communist Youth Organization, had 40 million additional members, while 25 million schoolchildren belonged to the Young Pioneers. Eligibility for party membership began at age 18.

On February 7, 1990, after 72 years of Communist rule, the Soviet Communist Party's Central Committee voted overwhelmingly to surrender its monopoly on power. On March 15, 1990, the Soviet Congress of People's Deputies amended Article Six, which had guaranteed the Communist Party its position as the only 'leading authority' in government. In its revised form, Article Six stated that the Communists, together with other political parties and social organizations, had the right to shape State policy. During the 28th Party Congress, the Party voted to reorganize its ruling body, the Politburo, to include Communist Party leaders from each of the 15 republics, in addition to the top 12 Moscow officials. Instead of being selected by the Central Committee, the Party in each republic chose its own leaders, guaranteeing, at the time, a voice in the Party to even the smallest republic.

Other amendments revised the Marxist view that private property was incompatible with Socialism. Individuals could own land and factories as long as they did not 'exploit' other Soviet citizens. New economic policies replaced direct central planning, instituted price reforms, created a stock exchange and allowed farmers to sell their produce on the open market. Additional new laws decreed that 'the press and other mass media are now free; censorship of the mass media is forbidden', and that all political movements had access to the airwaves with the right to establish their own television and radio stations. The monopoly enjoyed by the Communist Party on State-run radio and television ended. Even advertising, long denounced 'as a means of swindling the people' and a 'social weapon of the exploiter's class', became acceptable. These momentous changes paved the way toward a multiparty democracy and a free-market economy.

By the end of August 1991, Boris Yeltsin stood in the Russian parliament building, the White House, and declared: 'I am now signing a decree suspending the activities of the Russian Communist Party!' All Communist newspapers such as *Pravda* were temporarily shut down. Gorbachev followed by issuing decrees to end Soviet Communist rule. These decrees dissolved the Party's structure of committees and policy-making, which included the Central Committee. Archives of the Party and the KGB were seized, and the government confiscated all of the Party's assets throughout the country. It would take two years before the Communist Party regained some of its powers.

ATTEMPTED COUP OF AUGUST 1991

Gorbachev's vision of a second revolution never included an attempted coup. During his last year in office, many of his actions contradicted all that he had worked toward. After strongly supporting accelerated reforms, Gorbachev suddenly rejected the 500-Day Plan, which proposed converting the sluggish centralized economy into a market-oriented one. Then, in December 1990, he appointed the conservative Boris Pugo as his Minister of the Interior.

On January 11, 1991, Lithuania announced its independence; two days later Pugo sent in troops. Soviet troops were also sent into Latvia to quell demonstrations. This prompted Eduard Shevardnadze, the Foreign Minister, to resign, stating: 'We are returning to the terrible past... reformers have slumped into the bushes. A dictatorship is coming.' During the Gulf War, the Chairman of the KGB, Vladimir Kryuchkov, charged that foreign governments were trying to destabilize Soviet society; the Russian military had become much more sensitive to the reactionary elements gathering force.

Gorbachev banned Yeltsin's rally of support in March 1991 and renewed censorship of the print and television media. The people in Moscow demonstrated anyway and troops were sent in. One of Gorbachev's aides said: 'March 28 was the turning point for Mikhail Sergeyevich. He went to the abyss, looked over the edge, was horrified at what he saw and backed away.' Gorbachev had to move closer to an alliance with Yeltsin to survive.

Those in the government became uneasy with the upcoming republics' treaty; much of Moscow's power would be usurped if it was signed. Leading bureaucrats realized they could lose their jobs and began planning ways to undermine Gorbachev's power. Even though he had created an unprecedented wave of changes, Gorbachev's popularity at home had now fallen to practically zero. After five years of promises, reforms had only made the living standards of average citizens worse. When prices had risen by over 50 percent, the population became increasingly reluctant to trade their goods for worthless banknotes—inflation rose to over 1,000 percent and the ruble collapsed. Despite a grossly dissatisfied population, disjointed government and repeated warnings of a plot against him, Gorbachev left for a vacation in the Crimea to work on the Union Treaty.

On the Sunday afternoon of August 18, 1991, Gorbachev was told that Yuri Plekhanov, a top KGB official, had arrived to see him. Gorbachev sensed something was wrong and tried to use the telephones; all five lines were dead. Then Valery Boldin, the Chief of Staff, entered the room, saying that Gorbachev had to sign a referendum declaring a state of emergency within the country. If he did not sign, the vice president would take over leadership duties. Since Gorbachev refused to go along with the conspiracy, thousands of troops were sent into Moscow. Ironically, the coup members failed to arrest Boris Yeltsin who, that morning, had just happened to rush off to his office in the parliament building 45 minutes earlier than usual.

The next morning, the coup leaders announced that Gorbachev, 'with serious health problems', could no longer govern. But it became obvious from the outset that the coup was ill-planned. None of the opposition leaders had been arrested. Yeltsin, holed up in the White House, was receiving calls from around the world (from a cellular phone slipped in by the manager of Pizza Hut) and ate take-out pizza. The coup was doomed to fail just from the attention created by all the international media connections. At one point, Yeltsin went outside and climbed on top of a tank in front of 20,000 protesters. He appealed for mass resistance and named himself the Guardian of Democracy. The crowd swelled to well over 100,000. By the end of the day, troops were switching to Yeltsin's side, and many of the elite commando divisions were now protecting the White House.

By August 20, the coup attempt was weakening; many of the planners stayed at home. Crowds of people raised the old white, blue and red Russian flag. The famous cellist, composer and conductor Mstislav Leopoldovich Rostropovich, a survivor of the Siege of Leningrad, even flew in from Paris and played music within the parliament building. Tank divisions descended upon the White House later in the day. Swarms of people blocked their way; after three were killed, the tanks retreated, refusing to fire on their own people.

Three days after the attempted coup, Yeltsin announced its failure. He sent officials to the Crimea to bring Gorbachev safely back to Moscow. The shaken president and his family (his wife, Raisa, later died of leukemia in 1999, at the age of 67) returned by airplane early the next morning. Seven members of the State Emergency Committee, also called the Gang of Eight, were arrested; the eighth, Boris Pugo, shot himself in the head.

The crowds cheered, not so much for Gorbachev's return, but for their savior, Boris Yeltsin. Communism had disintegrated with the attempted putsch. Thousands celebrated as the statue of 'Iron Felix' Dzerzhinsky, the founder of the secret police after the 1917 Revolution, was toppled from its pedestal in front of the KGB building. A Russian flag and crucifix were put in its place—a monument to the millions who had died in prison camps at the hands of the KGB. Unbelievably, a new era had begun.

THE END OF THE SOVIET UNION

The Soviet Union ceased to exist on December 21, 1991. The great ideological experiment began by Lenin's Bolshevik Revolution, constituted on December 30, 1922, ended nine days short of its 70th year. 'One State has died,' announced Russian television, 'but in its place a great dream is being born.' The birth was of the Commonwealth of Independent States. Four days later, Gorbachev, the eighth and final leader of the Soviet Union, submitted his resignation. He no longer had a Soviet Union to govern. Boris Yeltsin claimed his office in the Kremlin.

> *The patience of the Russian people was great, and it gave foreigners to believe that the Russian people were slaves at heart. Now the Russian people must show to the whole world that it is a truly free people. After this great turn of events the Russian man must rule himself.*
>
> Nikolai Berdyayev, from the journal *Narodopravstvo*, 1917–18

BORIS YELTSIN

Boris Nikolayevich Yeltsin was born into a poor family in Sverdlovsk in 1931. He went on to dismantle the entire Soviet empire. In an historic meeting in Alma Ata, the capital of Kazakhstan, Yeltsin convinced the leaders of the former Soviet republics to sign a new treaty forming the 11-member Commonwealth. In February 1992, Yeltsin officially put the Cold War to rest in a meeting with US President George H.W. Bush. He proclaimed a 'new era', in which the two nations would join as allies to seek 'an enduring peace that rests on lasting common values'.

By the time Yeltsin took control, the economy was in disarray. Without GOS-PLAN (the former central planning commission) and GOSNAB (the former central supply organization), factories everywhere had no idea what to produce or where to ship their goods. With the help of economic advisor Yegor Gaidar, Yeltsin announced the lifting of price controls. Gradually, over 600 commodities exchanges were formed and the Moscow Stock Exchange building returned to its original function. Russians received government vouchers redeemable for cash, or shares in businesses that were previously State-owned. People in private enterprises began to flourish, from street vendors to entrepreneurs. Newly rich businessmen (nick-named *Noviye Russkiye* or New Russians) operated with the latest technology and bought expensive cars. (Today Russia is the largest market in the world for luxury cars.) It was possible for some young people to make more money in one day than their parents had in months, or even years. But for many, especially the elderly, the new order meant standing in longer queues and spending hours in the cold trying to sell pitiful possessions to make ends meet.

Newspapers were also freed of censorship. Advertisements interrupted television programs. Soap operas were watched avidly—over 60 percent of the population tuned in to the Mexican series *The Rich Also Cry*. Western imports, including *MTV*, *Santa Barbara* and *Beverly Hills 90210*, deluged Russian television. And foreigners could now travel legally to once-restricted cities.

Yeltsin's biggest crisis since the attempted coup of 1991 arose after he dissolved the obstructionist Russian legislature at the end of September 1993, and moved to replace it with a new elective body. Yeltsin said he was acting to stem a 'senseless struggle that was threatening to lead Russia into a political abyss... the body is an outmoded Soviet-era institution sustained in office by a useless constitution'.

A growing animosity had been brewing between Yeltsin and his opposition, which had tried and failed to impeach him six months earlier in March 1993. Yeltsin had conducted a referendum in April in which Russian voters had expressed their preference for him and his policies. However, the Supreme Soviet instantly claimed Yeltsin's order to dissolve the legislature as null and void. Vice President Alexander Rutskoi, now a Yeltsin rival, was immediately elected acting president and Yeltsin was impeached on a 144–6 vote. The Parliament Chairman, Ruslan Khasbulatov, called on Russian trade unions to go on strike to protest Yeltsin's order. Communist and nationalist leaders appeared on the White House balcony and urged their supporters to stay on. Many were taken with the irony of the gathering, on the very site where Yeltsin, next to Rutskoi, had faced down the right-wing coup plotters in August 1991. But this time Yeltsin was the coup plotter. While both sides waged all-out political warfare, many Muscovites could not care less if there was a coup. One citizen stated: 'We are tired of the political battles and want to live a normal life and earn some decent mone; noone knows anymore what we're coup-ing for!'

About a week after this crisis began, parliament supporters smashed through police lines, stormed the mayor's office and attacked the headquarters of the State television company, which exploded into the worst political violence since the 1917 Bolshevik Revolution. 'There can be no forgiveness for attacking innocent people,' announced Yeltsin. 'The armed revolt is doomed.' Yeltsin then countered by creating a state of emergency and sending in armored personnel carriers, tanks and elite commando units, which fired upon the White House. A new military tactic was also employed—blasting pop group Dire Straits and Russian Rap from loudspeakers near the White House. Thirteen days later, the opposition leaders surrendered after a massive barrage by tanks and paratroopers. The battle left 187 people dead and the White House a blackened shell with nearly every window blown out. Half a year later, the arrested White House hard-liners, who had tried to topple the government in 1991 and 1993, were pardoned by the new Parliamentary Duma.

Yeltsin continued to promise that his struggling nation would not retreat from economic reform. To aid the reform process, many countries pledged financial support to Russia. In January 1994, US President Bill Clinton journeyed to Moscow for a summit with Yeltsin. In an historic meeting, the Ukraine also participated and signed an agreement to disarm all of the 1,800 nuclear warheads that had fallen to it after the collapse of the Soviet Union. Clinton told Yeltsin: 'You are in the process of transforming your entire economy while you develop a new constitution and democracy as well. It boggles the mind and you have my respect.'

THE FIRST MULTIPARTY ELECTIONS

Two years after Yeltsin had banned Communist activity on Russian soil, the constitutional court lifted Yeltsin's order, ruling that it violated the constitution. Thus, the Communist Party participated in the country's first true multiparty election on December 12, 1993. In the election, a new Russian constitution was also voted in, which gave the president more power and Parliament less. The constitution granted Russia's 149 million citizens many economic freedoms and civil liberties that had been stifled since the Bolshevik takeover. These included the right to own land, the right not to be wiretapped and the right to travel freely at home and abroad. It also provided for a new Parliament, known as the Federal Assembly, with the Federation Council as its upper chamber and the Duma as its lower. A month after the ballot, those elected assembled in Moscow to launch the new parliamentary democracy. Yeltsin stated: 'We must preserve this for the sake of national peace and to make sure dictatorship never returns to Russia.'

Even though they were no longer the only party, the Communists again became one of the largest political forces in the land. Taking part in the election were other hard-line groups, among them the Agrarian Party, the Centrist Democratic Party and the Women of Russia Party. The pro-reform parties included Russia's Choice, the Yavlinsky Bloc and the Russian Unity and Accord Party. The Beer-Lovers Party was one of many on the fringe. Some of those elected were reactionary journalist Alexander Nevzorov, weightlifting champion Yuri Vlasov, and the psychic healer Anatoly Kashpirovsky.

Although Yeltsin's opponents won the majority of the 450 seats in the Duma, they were forced to compromise with his supporters. The upper chamber, the 178-seat Federation Council, roughly equivalent to the US Senate, met under the new State symbol, the double-headed eagle, first adopted by Ivan the Great in the 15th century. First Deputy Prime Minister Vladimir Shumeiko, a close ally of Yeltsin, was elected as the first Speaker.

The ultranationalist Liberal Democratic Party, headed by Vladimir Zhirinovsky, shocked the world by beating Yeltsin's Russia's Choice Party in these first ever parliamentary elections. Zhirinovsky's party won nearly a quarter of the Russian vote, which many saw as a protest by a population feeling the pain of reform. In the three years that this obscure Moscow lawyer rose into the national spotlight, he rashly advocated party dictatorship, Russian military expansion, the expelling of millions of non-Russians and ending payments of foreign debt. Zhirinovsky also threatened to restore Russia's imperial borders, annex Alaska and invade Turkey and Poland. With this character climbing to the forefront of Russian politics, no wonder the world was greatly concerned for Russia's fragile young democracy and its vulnerability to irresponsible leadership.

THE EFFECTS OF REFORM

A few weeks after Parliament convened, Yegor Gaidar, the architect of Russia's free-market reforms and leader of Russia's Choice Party, unexpectedly quit his post as Economic Minister. As a result the ruble plummeted. (The Russian Central Bank had already pumped more than one billion dollars into the economy—more than a quarter of its hard currency reserves—to stabilize the monetary system.) Launched in January 1992, Gaidar's reforms had freed most prices from State control, privatized a third of State-owned enterprises and created a new class of entrepreneurs.

But since their introduction no more than ten percent of the population seemed better off, while over 50 percent complained of being worse off. The continuing credit squeeze created more unemployment, delayed pay checks and wiped out entire savings accounts of average citizens. The Russian comedian Mikhail Zhvanetsky joked about the economy: 'Much has changed but nothing has happened. Or is that much has happened and nothing has changed.' Many forecasted that nearly a century of suppressed initiative combined with a government-controlled lifestyle would take at least a generation to alter.

By 1993, inflation (2,600 percent in 1992 and 900 percent in 1993) became so rampant that savings of 20,000 rubles—that could once buy four cars—was now worth only a few pounds of sausage. One survey concluded that on his monthly salary, an average Russian could only pay rent, consume a daily ration of half a kilogram (one pound) of bread, half a liter (less than one pint) of milk, 100 grams (three-and-a-half ounces) of beef, and five cigarettes. Satire was commonplace: 'What was the nationality of Adam and Eve? Russian, of course—who else would think that being homeless, naked and splitting one apple between them was living in paradise.'

Russians began to augment their diets with vegetables grown in gardens or apartment window boxes. To supplement their incomes, many turned to vending sausages or cigarettes, pawning family goods, collecting bottles for recycling, or working as taxi drivers. An entire generation of educated people could barely afford to live. And one teacher wryly noted: 'We can't even afford to die.' (The cheapest funeral cost over $300, while the average pension was $50 per month—the official poverty level was set at $35). One retiree summarized, 'And what good is freedom to me now? Freedom to buy a pornographic magazine, openly complain all I want, or travel to Cyprus when I can't even afford to eat? I hope and believe that things will get better. But they will never be better for us. I'll simply not live to see those days.'

During the first years of transition, the World Bank estimated that one-third of the population, or nearly 50 million Russians, had an income below the minimum sustenance level. With prices for food, gasoline and consumer goods approaching US levels, average Russian salaries were still only one-tenth of those in America. Over one-quarter found themselves unemployed and a survey reported that only ten percent of Russian males were capable of fully supporting their families. Russia's life expectancy plummeted so fast in the first half of the 1990s that a British medical journal stated that it was 'without parallel in the modern era'. Due to the severe decline in living standards a Russian man's life expectancy fell to age 58, compared to 72 in neighboring Finland. The male incidences of heart disease, suicide and alcoholism are still among the highest in the developed world, and the mortality rate exceeds the birth rate. Alarmingly, if the trend continues, the population would be halved to 75 million by the middle of the next century, and in 1,000 years there would only be 150 people left in Russia!

For the first time in Russian history, investment and stock funds, quasi-banks, and joint-stock companies (without insurance protection) filled print advertising and the airwaves with the promise of large returns—in some cases up to 30,000 percent. In a few years alone, over 2,000 banks opened across the country. Many investors never saw their money again. One businessman stated that 'the average Russian is the most unprepared investor in the world. For 70 years all he did was put his money into State-owned banks and was raised to believe that whatever was told over TV or in the newspapers was true.' Scam operations and pyramid schemes flourished, and hundreds of thousands of victims were cheated out of their life savings in the new era of cowboy capitalism.

However, with the explosion of new commercial activities, a new class was created—that of the filthy rich or *Noviye Russkiye* (New Russians). About 60 percent of this group simply turned the socialist empires they managed into their own private companies. Others capitalized on the 'Wild East' state of mind, where practically everything was up for grabs. With both a penchant for entrepreneurship and greed, some became billionaires virtually overnight. Suddenly, the demand for office space, apartments, retail markets and shopping centers was enormous.

Consumption by the nouveaux riches is decadent even by Western standards. Protected by bodyguards, driving armor-plated Land-rovers, building villas in the French Riviera, sending their children to study abroad, wearing designer clothing, this elite class has built an enormous division between the haves and have-nots. One pensioner declared, 'We're back to having two classes again—the aristocrats and the peasants!' Many Russian nightclubs have no foreign customers—they simply cannot afford the prices.

It is often said that the collapse of Communism has fertilized the ground upon which gangsters and mafia thrive. But the word mafia has a different implication in Russia. It simply defines a broad range of group activity that was already flourishing under Socialism. Since much was illegal during this era—from owning a business to playing rock 'n' roll—most unsanctioned activities were commonplace; a survey in the 1980s indicated that the average Russian dealt daily with black marketeers who provided the economy with most of its goods. In turn, these types had no problem embracing capitalism and finding immediate ways to make money. Even though encountering mafia activity may be the price of doing business in Russia (the chances of experiencing any as a tourist are practically zero)—all in all, violent crime rates are still much lower than in the United States.

In 1994, after two decades of forced exile in the United States, Russia's greatest living writer Alexander Solzhenitsyn was allowed to return to his homeland. The winner of the Nobel Prize for Literature in 1970, Solzhenitsyn was banished by the former Soviet Government in 1974 for writing *The Gulag Archipelago*, which preserved the memory of the Soviet holocaust. (Also in 1994, the long-suppressed 1939 census was finally published: a quarter of the population, over 40 million people, had been lost in this Stalinist year to famine and purges.) But before Solzhenitsyn returned to his homeland, he first wanted to complete his four-volume epic *The Red Wheel*, a history leading up to the 1917 October Revolution that he had worked on for 20 years: 'Our history has been so hidden. I had to dig so deep, I had to uncover what was buried and sealed. This took up all my years.' The work totals over 5,000 pages.

After his exile, Solzhenitsyn declared: 'All of us in prison in the 1940s were certain that Communism would fail. The only question was when... In a strange way, I was inwardly convinced that I would someday return to Russia.' It was not until late 1989 that Gorbachev had finally given permission to publish Solzhenitsyn's works in Russia.

In 1993, a political poll in St Petersburg showed that 48 percent of the respondents wanted Solzhenitsyn as their president. In The First Circle, first published in the West in 1968 because it was banned in the Soviet Union, he described that in a tyranny a real writer is like a second government. In 2006, billboards across Russia advertised the 87-year-old Solzhenitsyn's TV adaptation of this fiercely anti-Soviet novel; and the 10-part mini-series, directed by Gleb Panfilov, became one of the nation's most watched programs. (Solzhenitsyn himself served eight years in the Gulag after criticizing Stalin in 1945.) The story chronicles three days in the lives of prisoners at Mavrino, a special prison set up in an old country estate outside Moscow in the aftermath of WW II. (The title is a reference to Dante's concentric circles of hell in "The Divine Comedy".) Even though Alexander Solzhenitsyn has returned home to live, he knows that there is a long road ahead: "If it took Russia 75 years to fall so far, then it is obvious that it will take more than 75 years to rise back up. I know that we are still faced with incredible hardships for years to come".

THE RESURGENCE OF THE COMMUNISTS

In February 1995, the Commonwealth of Independent States elected Yeltsin as its chairman and moved its headquarters from Minsk, Belarus to Moscow. After celebrating Victory Day, the 50th anniversary of World War II, in May, Yeltsin had to vigorously embark on his reelection campaign—for only six percent of the population approved of the job he was doing. The majority of Russians blamed Yeltsin for the social upheavals, deplorable living conditions and unpopular war in Chechnya. In addition, many civil servants, teachers, and pensioners had not received a government pay check in up to six months. Following his elevation to near sainthood after the 1991 coup attempt, Yeltsin now found himself with single-digit ratings, was in declining health and drinking heavily. He soon suffered two heart attacks and was confined to bed for four months.

But Yeltsin struggled on, stating: 'It is our task to prevent a Communist victory at the polls.' But, in the December 17, 1995 parliamentary elections, the Communists led the field of 43 parties. Gennady Zhuganov, who had taken charge of the reborn Communist Party in 1993, now even welcomed religious members. The Communists and Zhirinovsky's ultranationalists finished first and second, garnering 22 percent and 11 percent of the vote respectively. The astounded world questioned how a country so recently freed from socialist rule could so quickly choose a course back to renewed oppression. With a long tradition of not regarding freedom as a value, the average Russian experienced reform more as hardship than salvation. Even writer Ivan Turgenev expressed this notion after Alexander II agreed to free the serfs in 1861: 'And although you were freed from slavery, you do not know what to do with freedom.'

Foreigners find it difficult to comprehend how Russians can be skeptical of the transition to a Western-style democracy and economy. One must first understand that to them it may only be another short-lived phase in their country's history. So many promises in the past have proven hollow. Even Gorbachev warned: 'If reforms continue pushing people into a dead end, discontent could spring loose and extremism move in.'

1996 PRESIDENTIAL ELECTIONS

The architect of Russia's privatization program, First Deputy Prime Minister Anatoly Chubais, was dismissed in January 1996, but then called back in March to help with Yeltsin's presidential campaign. Yeltsin's daughter Tatyana Dachenko also played a major role. At 65, Yeltsin wanted to prove he was, indeed, capable of a comeback at the June 16 election. A few weeks before the ballot, on May 27, Yeltsin brought Chechen leader Yanderbiyev to the Kremlin to sign a peace treaty after 18 months of war that had left Chechnya ruined and over 40,000 dead. Boris Yeltsin was as determined as ever not to have the Communist Party win: 'Our responsibility to the memory of the millions who suffered in the camps and to our children and descendants is to prevent neo-Stalinists, fascists and extremists from coming to power in Russia. Russia must enter the 21st century without this filth.'

On June 16, 1996, an 11-man race took place for the presidency. Yeltsin captured 35 percent of the vote, and Zhuganov 32 percent. General Alexander Lebed, an ex-paratrooper and decorated hero of Russia's war in Afghanistan, received 15 percent. Zhirinovsky finished seventh with less than six percent of the first round vote. Since no candidate received over 50 percent a national run-off election was scheduled to take place on July 3. In a calculated move, Yeltsin appointed Lebed as his national security chief. Alexander Lebed was killed in a helicopter crash in 2002.

The Communist Party now faced a major identity crisis. People were just as uncertain of Zhuganov's politics as they were of Zhirinovsky's. Gennady Zhuganov, in his 1995 book *I Believe in Russia*, stated that 'if Stalin had lived longer, he would have restored Russia and saved it from the cosmopolitans'. Most of the population, especially the younger generation, were more interested in pay checks than politics. Many also feared that if Zhuganov won, the Communist party would not allow others to exist and would return to monopolizing the State. To the relief of the majority, the election resulted in a stunning victory for Yeltsin: he received 54 percent to Zhuganov's 40 percent.

On August 9, 1996, Yeltsin, with a stiff walk and slowed speech, swore an oath for his second term as president, with his hand held over a red-bound copy of the Russian constitution. By October Alexander Lebed was fired, accused of plotting a military coup. (Lebed was later killed in a helicopter crash in 2002.) A month later, on November 5, Yeltsin underwent a major coronary bypass operation; he had had another heart attack right before his reelection.

THE LAST YEARS OF THE 20TH CENTURY

By 1997, even though Russia was finally emerging from its post-Soviet economic slump, just six percent of Russians said they were content. Seventy-two percent felt their lives had changed little over the past five years, while 62 percent felt their lives would not get any better. A major role reversal had also taken place within the country. Instead of children having to live with parents (because of housing shortages), parents now found themselves living with their children out of economic necessity. The clash of extraordinary monetary achievement and oppressive backwardness continued to mar the road ahead.

In February 1998, as Russia journeyed through a seventh year of insecurity, Yeltsin felt that the 'nation needed a new strategy for upsurge', and fired three cabinet ministers along with his deputy prime ministers for failing to reverse Russia's economic and social ills. Yeltsin then pressured the Duma into voting in the 35-year-old Sergei Kiriyenko, then Minister of Oil and Energy, into the position of prime minister. Many regarded this merely as a political stunt to shift blame from Yeltsin's own sagging popularity. By May, thousands of striking coal miners, in massive protests, even blocked routes of the Trans-Siberian railway, demanding $600 million in back wages.

By 1998, Yeltsin's government had fallen behind by months, even years, with payments of State wages and pensions, which forced people in many areas to resort to barter and subsistence farming. It was estimated that nearly 70 percent of the population lived mostly off the produce grown in their small garden plots. Many villagers kept a cow, caught and dried fish from the rivers and grew cabbage, beets, potatoes and onions. The result was an almost cashless society where business was transacted and employees paid mainly by trading goods and services. Since most companies and citizens had no money, they could not pay their taxes (the government claimed that fewer than three percent of the population had filed income tax declarations the year before), meaning the state was constantly short of funds, and the deficit continued to grow.

In August 1998, the country experienced its worst economic crisis since the 1991 Soviet collapse. Overnight the ruble plunged to less than a quarter of its value, shutting down the nation's largest commercial banks, which in turn caused the nation to default on most of its debt. (It owed the IMF 17.5 billion dollars for the year and the country's GNP was estimated to be lower than Belgium's.)

Yeltsin responded by dismissing the Russian cabinet, the third time in little more than a year, replacing Prime Minister Kiriyenko with Foreign Minister Yevgeny Primakov, an ex-KGB head. He also assigned Vladimir Putin to head the former KGB, now known as the Federal Security Bureau. With Russia plunging into turmoil and also suffering from one of the worst harvests since 1953 (the last year of Stalinist rule), many accused Yeltsin of trying to shift blame away from himself. A new joke circulated in Moscow: 'For too long we have been standing at the edge of the precipice; now we are taking the great leap forward.'

By October 1998, millions of dissatisfied Russians across the country took part in rallies demanding Yeltsin's resignation. (Yeltsin and other Kremlin members were also being investigated for bribery and corruption.) At the end of the month, Yeltsin was admitted to a sanatorium for rest and treatment for what was termed neuropsychological asthenia. Although no one knew what this meant, the Kremlin announced that this condition forced the president to relinquish his day-to-day duties, which would be taken over by Primakov. The question asked by Russia and the world was how the country would survive without a strong leader and a solution to its dire economic crisis.

On May 12 1999, one day before impeachment hearings were to be held (the impeachment, supported by Communists, never came to pass), Yeltsin fired 70-year-old Yevgeny Primakov (many surmised because of Primakov's increasing popularity) replacing him with yet another revolving-door Prime Minister, the more youthful Sergei Stepashin. Yeltsin continued with his unpopular erratic decisions by subsequently replacing Stepashin three months later with Vladimir Putin. Then, on September 30, a few weeks after explosions in two apartment blocks in Moscow left over 200 dead (Islamic terrorism was suspected, but never proven), Yeltsin sent ground troops back into separatist Chechnya (Russia had pulled out in 1996), in what would become an ongoing bloodbath.

Even though Boris Yeltsin had inherited a decaying and corrupt Socialist empire and created the most democratic state in Russian history (in 1990, everything belonged to the state; by 1997, almost 75 percent of property was held privately) and in the eyes of the world had accumulated a list of major international accomplishments (he slashed the nuclear arsenal by 60 percent, halved the armed forces, helped broker a Serbian retreat from Kosovo and in October 1999, signed the order for the last Russian troops to exit the Baltic), this leader now found himself suffering the same fate as Gorbachev—ending his final days in office with only a two percent approval rating. With his health and mental acuity diminishing, many sadly compared him with the Communist leader Brezhnev, who, at the end of his term, served only as a weak puppet figure. But Yeltsin asserted, 'I am not going to resign. It's very difficult to remove me. And considering my character, it is practically impossible.'

So, when on December 31 1999, the 68-year-old Yeltsin appeared on television to give a New Year's address, no one expected him to take the world again by surprise. He announced his immediate resignation, although officially in office until the following June. 'I want to beg forgiveness for your dreams that never came true. And I also want to beg forgiveness for not having justified your hopes. I beg your forgiveness for having failed to jump, in one leap, from the gray stagnant, totalitarian past to the light, rich and civilized future.' Yeltsin, once hailed as the 'Father of Russian Democracy' by former US President Clinton, handed over power to 47-year-old Vladimir Putin as acting-President of the Russian Federation (thereby forcing early elections in March 2000). Yeltsin ended his speech by stating, 'Russia must enter the new millennium with new politicians, new faces, and new intelligent, strong and energetic people. We, who have been in power for many years, must go.'

During his Presidential campaign, Putin (and his newly formed Unity Party) were well ahead in the poles of the ten other candidates, which included Primakov, Yavlinsky, Zhuganov and Zhirinovsky. Yuri Luzhkov, re-elected Mayor of Moscow in December 1999 (and who had decided not to run for the national election), helped Putin gather votes in this region. On March 26, elections were held and Putin won a four-year term by garnering 53 percent of the vote; his inauguration was held on May 7 2000. Later in the year, he published the book-length conversation *First Person*. He had never before held an elective office.

VLADIMIR PUTIN

Vladimir Vladimirovich Putin, born October 7, 1952, grew up in a *kommunalka* communal apartment (today some 700,000 St Petersburgh residents still live in these) in Leningrad, Russia's most westward-looking city. The only child of factory workers (his father was the son of one of Stalin's cooks), the driven young Vladimir became the city's judo champion (he has a black belt) and he graduated from Leningrad State University with a Law Degree. During his studies, he was recruited by the KGB. In 1975, the year Putin joined up, the agency had already sent Noble Prize winner Andrei Sakharov into internal exile. A year earlier, another Noble Prize winner, Alexander Solzhenitsyn, was forced into exile abroad. As a special agent Putin received special Communist perks including free housing and travel opportunities. In 1983, he married Lyvdmilia and they had two daughters, Masha and Katya, Putin spent 16 years with the KGB, rising to the rank of lieutenant colonel, and was mainly stationed in Dresden, East Germany, where he witnessed the end of the Cold War.

As a young man, Putin spent the second half of the 1980s recruiting people to spy on the West. Working as a foreign intelligence operative, the goal was to steal Western technology. Fiercely patriotic, he later defended Soviet-era intelligence and said that he would 'never read a book by a defector, by someone who had betrayed the Motherland.' In 1989 (shortly after the fall of the Berlin Wall), Putin returned to Leningrad and soon rose to become the city's Deputy Mayor. For his toughness and dedication he earned the nickname 'Stasi,' after the East German secret police. With the break-up of the Soviet Union came the disintegration of the KGB, and Putin resigned from the agency in 1991.

In 1996, when St Petersburg mayor Anatoly Sobchak failed to be re-elected, Putin got a job in the Moscow Presidential Administration office. Then, two years later, the ex-intelligence officer found himself coming full circle when Yeltsin appointed him as head of the FSB (the Federal Security Bureau, what used to be the KGB). One of Putin's first moves was to try and obtain approval for the monitoring of e-mails and other Internet communications by requiring service providers to install equipment linking all their computers with the FSB. As can be imagined, critics harshly protested a return to old Soviet spying standards and the proposal never passed through the Duma. By 1999, Putin had become secretary of the Security Council, and in August of that year, he was appointed the last Prime Minister in Yeltsin's sea-sawing government.

Many Russians elected Putin because of his staunch no-nonsense, take-charge leadership which they felt necessary to tackle the country's enormous problems. One of the first things Putin did after becoming acting President was to fly to Chechnya on New Year's Day and hand out awards to Russian servicemen fighting there. He then fired Boris Yeltsin's daughter Tatyana from her Kremlin Post as 'image advisor.' (She was also under investigation for taking government kickbacks; Putin had granted Yeltsin immunity from prosecution.)

Introducing a new supply-side economic plan for the country, he also allowed for a simplified flat tax of 13 percent. There was also a sigh of relief from international residents and tourists. Moscow had been ranked the world's third most expensive city for travelers in 1998, now it had fallen to 34th place. St Petersburg had fallen from 83rd to 101st, making it one of the least costly destinations in Europe.

Five months after the election, 73 percent of Russia approved of Putin's presidency. This tough pragmatist appealed to the masses who were downright fed up with decades of inept leadership and rampant corruption. One Russian journalist noted that perhaps what Russians really yearned for was a nationalist father-cum-czar-like figure whom they could have faith in to restore order to this apparent state of cowboy capitalism. The double entendre of Ras-Putin, was not lost within circles of discussion. (In 2000 a national poll discovered that 79 percent of Russians regretted the demise of the Soviet Union, up from 69 percent in 1992.) In his first State of the Union address in July 2000, Putin promised Russians 'a solid country, strong and pure.'

Even though the rich tycoons had bankrolled Yeltsin's 1996 re-election campaign, Putin wanted them out of politics. (Many wondered how, during Yeltsin's term in office, a handful of Russian businessmen had ended up with a 30 percent share of one-seventh of the world's resources; The oils and metals tycoon, Roman Abramovich, became the world's richest man under 40.) Now Putin warned the country's wealthy oligarchs that he would not stand for anymore bandit capitalism, 'Those fishing in muddy waters will no longer be able to keep their catch.' Bank accounts were frozen, and two business and media barons, Boris Berezovsky (who had once been appointed as Executive Secretary of the Commonwealth) and Vladimir Gusinsky (chairman of the Media-Most empire, who had made his fortune in banking and real estate), were forced to flee the country. The latter's NTV channel, Russia's first privately-owned network, was taken over by the State gas monopoly Gazprom. Pressure was also put on the press to censor any negative stories about the new government. The world sat in wonder: was Putin really a new innovative breed or just another retainer from the old Communist-trained school?

In May 2001, Putin signed another decree that divided Russia into seven federal zones, each with its own Kremlin representative. All of Russia's 89 provinces were regrouped under the new system. Putin vowed that a 'strong central authority was essential to avoiding the breakup of the country.' The President also reinstated the Soviet-era music written by Stalin court composer Alexander Alexandrov (and first broadcast nationally on 1 January 1944) as the country's national anthem. This had been dropped by Yeltsin in 1990. (Many preferred Glinka's famous 1833 choral hymn march, Slavsya or Glory! or 'A Patriotic Song', but it was deemed too difficult to sing.) New words for the 'Unbreakable Union' were written by 87-year-old Sergei Mikhalkov, a popular children's poet, who, ironically, had written the original words, approved by Stalin, in 1943. The Soviet-era lyrics shifted from "Party of Lenin, the strength of the people/To Communism's triumph, lead us on..." to something more prosaic to better suit the modern era: "...You are unique in the world, inimitable. Native land protected by God!"

It did not seem to bother Russians much that Putin attempted to muzzle the media, tried to gain more authoritative power, fueled the ongoing war in Chechnya, and grossly mishandled the Kursk submarine disaster. (And later, there was a large public outcry against the government's mishandling of the Moscow Theater Chechen Siege, along with the Beslan School terrorist take-over, where over 200 people were killed. In addition, by severely underestimating the populace, Russia lost hold on the ex-Soviet states, from Central Asia to Georgia, Belorus and the Ukraine.) For, after nearly a decade of decline, the country was finally enjoying a mild economic boom thanks to higher oil export prices and a lower ruble exchange rate. The average monthly wage was rising, and citizens were finally getting paid on time. In addition, on September 20 2001, eight decades after Lenin had first banned private ownership of property, Russia's parliament voted to allow its citizens (and foreigners alike) to buy, sell and own land. (Since the elections, foreign investment had risen by 40 percent.) Putin was also the first Russian leader in a decade to enjoy a working majority in parliament, and the country had a balanced (and surplus) budget for the first time in post-Soviet history.

On the international scene, Putin was optimistically welcomed by leaders from around the world. Britain's Prime Minister Tony Blair commented that this Russian President, eager to forge closer ties with Europe, 'talks our language on reform.' During the Okinawa G-8 summit, Putin held his own with the heads of state of the world's leading industrial nations. And by attending the United Nations Millennium Summit in New York, Putin also assured his country's participation in the future of world events.

In May 2002, US President George W Bush traveled to a Moscow Summit to sign a ten-year accord with Putin to shrink the nuclear arsenals of both countries by two-thirds. President Bush commented that, 'this agreement liquidates the legacy of the Cold War.' He made another visit to Russia during St Petersburg's 300th anniversary.

In 2003, according to *Fortune* magazine, half of the world's top ten billionaires under 40 are now Russians. And the combined wealth of the country's top seven business tycoons totals nearly $18 billion—all earned in a little over a decade. In Russia today, just a handful of these oligarchs are said to control 85 percent of the value of the country's leading private companies.

With such an enormous concentration of Russia's wealth in the hands of a few, it is no small wonder that there is government concern. And when the prominent oil executive Mikhail Khodorkovsky (his oil conglomerate, Yukos-Sibneft, is said to contribute seven percent of Russia's total tax revenue; his personal worth is estimated to be at $8 billion) began to express major political ambitions, he was arrested by the Kremlin on October 25, 2003, at gunpoint on his plane in Siberia. What brought him down is far from clear. Whether pure political rivalry and an attempt by Putin to consolidate his power or real gross misconduct, the 40-year-old Khodorkovsky was charged with forgery, fraud and tax evasion. (The company's $15 billion in assets were later frozen and put up for auction. Khordorkovsky argued that his meteoric rise to wealth during the 1990s privatization of state assets occurred not because he did anything illegal, but because of poorly written laws. Now, resigned from Yukos, he still remains in jail, and faces up to ten years in prison.) But even after the cloudy arrest, Putin's approval rating remained high at 73 percent.

The December 7, 2003, parliamentary elections gave the pro-Kremlin and nationalist parties a landslide majority for the first time in post-Soviet history. The United Russia party, that merely ran on a loyalty to the President and 'Strong Russia' campaign, gained a majority 50 percent of the 450 Duma seats, while the nationalist Rodina or Homeland (which ran on a populist ticket of returning the riches to the people), got nearly ten percent of the vote.

One of the main dramas of the election was the demise of the Communist Party. Whether it is true that Putin ran a 'war of media extermination', as Communist Party leader Gennady Zhuganov claimed, or that the population split their traditionalist 'Red-White' views between the Homeland and United Russia parties, it was clearly shown that it was time for old-guard Communist ideology to move off the modern stage.

On the other side, liberals also struggled to survive, and found themselves ousted from parliament for the first time in a decade. Both Yabloko (mainly funded by Yukos-Sibneft) and the Union of Right Forces (SPS) failed to garner five percent of the vote needed to win a block of seats. One party member sadly reflected, 'The democrats no longer exist. The democratic movement has been enfeebled, decapitated and destroyed.' Since the administration this time around went out of its way to help conservatives rather then liberals, many worry that the Kremlin has inadvertently created a new strain of nationalism. One journalist wrote, 'Today, the authoritarian character of the political system has been exposed.'

After his first full term in office, Putin emerged with the dualistic reputation of being both a man of the future and a traditionalist, doing whatever was necessary to promote the stability and growth of his country, but his seemingly open embrace of democratic values, such as civil liberties and a free press, proved to be questionable. Some considered the schizophrenic standoffs of the two Putins worthy 'of the pen of a new Dostoevsky'.

On March 14, 2004, Vladimir Putin easily won a second term as President (he ran against five challengers) when he garnered well over two-thirds of the vote (of more than a 50 percent turnout), in an election widely criticized for heavy Kremlin censoring of all opposition. After this election, the government believes that Putin, now with a clear majority, has carte blanche to enforce his system of power, restore Russia's might on the world stage, and continue with economic reforms. The world can only trust that Putin will use this mandate to plow ahead with his campaign promise of 'managed democracy' to continue the nurturing of a Russia—stable, prosperous and linked to the West.

RUSSIA TODAY

Today, President Putin is reaping the benefit of a soaring economy, and his approval rating at home remains solid at 70 percent. This support has allowed Putin to brush off Western critics who accuse the Kremlin of tightening its grip on society, controlling all major television stations, and retaking control of many industries and natural resources, such as the gas giant Gazprom. In addition, with the cost of living rising each year, pensioners and war veterans across the country have staged massive protests against major cuts in long-standing social subsidies. (Welfare cuts wiped out free bus/metro travel and subsidized prescriptions. Russia has about 30 million retirees, who receive monthly pensions of $100 or less a month.) Good news indicates that the poverty level, according to the World Bank, has dropped from 41 percent in 1999 to 20 percent today. (More than half the population earns less than 5000 rubles—$185 a month.) And (with internal wars winding down), it was announced that the current mandatory two-year army terms will be cut to 18 months in 2007 and then to one year in 2008. Compared to the chaotic decade after the fall of the Soviet Union, and the unpredictable Yelstin-era, it appears that Russians are willing to trade some liberties for more stability and economic opportunities.

Most of Russia's economic activity is concentrated in Moscow and 80 percent of the nation's money has a foothold in the capital. The most successful businesses are those that never existed under Socialism, such as the restaurant and food industry, computer technology, and advertising. With oil prices high, Russia is awash in cash, and more of it is now trickling down to the middle class. Since Putin's election in 2000, the country has enjoyed single-digit growth, and this has fueled the consumer class and brought more prosperity to the hinterlands of the country. Even though millions continue to struggle, a middle-class lifestyle is reaching more Russians than ever before.

One of the most meaningful changes (that Westerners so often take for granted) is that a majority of Russians now have the opportunity to try and lead the life they could earlier only have imagined. Of Moscow's nine million citizens 25 percent are members of the new burgeoning middle class. These youthful professionals (who in the past may have been forced to live in communal flats) now have their own apartment with a television, VCR, computer (17 percent of the population is now online), car (sales of new foreign cars jumped 60 percent last year), and even a cell phone (mobile phone sales have soared from 12 for every 100 Russians in 2002 to 88 today). Even though inflation is running at about 12 percent and real-estate prices are soaring (Moscow is now one of the world's most expensive cities to live in), studies have estimated that 30 percent of the population lives a comfortable middle-class lifestyle on about $1,000 a month for a family of four. With more leisure time, the middle class can also relax at a summer dacha, vacation abroad and enjoy an entirely new world of entertainment opportunities (there are now more casinos in Moscow than in Las Vegas). With a more optimistic lifestyle, these are the people building Russia's future.

In few countries of the world are people under 35 playing such an important role in a nation's transformation. Unlike the elderly, they do not remember the state's promise of cradle-to-grave security and are willing to energetically take up challenges in the midst of much uncertainty. The formation of independently owned companies is increasing, and over 20 percent of business managers now have studied abroad. The most important turn round for the country is that these internationally educated youth actually choose to return to Russia. For example, the computer industry in Novosibirsk, Siberia, is so successful that the area has become known as the Silicon Taiga. The younger generation is excited to participate in creating a new and enterprising Russia.

Merely trying to graft Western models of democracy onto the largest nation on earth has not always been met with success. Today, the rich are getting richer and corruption and organized crime are still endemic. The rich still transfer billions of dollars annually out of Russia to foreign banks, much of it from the sale of the country's natural resources. Bank mortgages and loans are only just beginning, less than 10 percent of the population have checking accounts, and five percent have credit cards. The nation remains a cash and barter society, a 'Wild East' where conspiracies abound, extra judicial killings are probable and mafia-like squabbles are interwoven; text book cases include the late 2006 slaying of Moscow journalist, Anna Politkovskaya, and an ex-KGB agent living in London, Alexander Litvinenko, allegedly investigating her death, mysteriously poisoned by Polonium 210, a crime linked back to sinister, unidentified parties in Moscow.

Although things on the economic front might be looking up, the legal and health care systems are still abysmal. Within the courts, over 99 percent of those accused are convicted, and many sit in jail for years awaiting trial. When they do get one, the accused are made to sit in a cage, while the judge and two citizens (mainly pensioners) act as the jury to decide their fate. The country's health care has, in turn, collapsed with the country's health. Public hospitals and clinics are in dire need of funds, and doctors still earn very poor wages. And for many, homelessness, stress, and poverty (one-third of the population still live at subsistence level) are taking a mental and physical toll. Russia's suicide rate is among the highest in the world, three times that of the US.

Alarming recent statistics indicate (in Soviet times there were no accurate records) that today only ten percent of Russian babies are born healthy. Seventy percent of adolescents are said to suffer from some type of chronic illness. Russia has one of the highest rates of tobacco use in the world and two-thirds of deaths in men are alcohol related (life expectancy for men is down to 59.3 years, compared to 72.9 in the US). Over three million drug addicts are suffering without treatment, many hooked on the 300 tons of heroin that flow in each year from Afghanistan and Tajikistan. Because of the rise in prostitution and spread of dirty needles, one in 1,000 Moscovites are said to carry the HIV virus, the highest rate in Russia. Seventy-five percent of Russian women still rely on abortion to control family size. The twin trends of rising deaths and declining births are canceling out the growth for Russia's future. The population peaked in 1992 and in the next five decades the total is estimated to contract from its current 146 million to well below 120 million, where it was in 1960.

After a thousand years of monarchy or dictatorship, it cannot be easy for a population to re-adjust to an entirely new and novel nation-there is ample reason for both hope and despair. But, that Russia has so quickly transformed itself from an "evil empire" to a middle-income democracy in only fifteen years is an astounding achievement. In a recent poll, three-quarters said that they have now adjusted to the new economic reality. After enduring an already long and tumultuous history, the odds are that Russia can, yet again, survive another turbulent transition. Russians pride themselves on their own resiliency and uniqueness, and whatever the future brings, they are firmly determined in the 21st century to create a country of their own making. And not to be forgotten is the extraordinary, indefatigable resolve of the Russian spirit.

> *Russia is baffling to the mind,*
> *Not subject to the common measure*
> *Her ways—of a peculiar kind*
> *One must have faith in Russia...*
> *For she will prevail.*

Poet Fyodor Tyutchev, 1866

FACTS FOR THE TRAVELER
PLANNING YOUR TRIP

Traveling to and around Russia is not as easy as for most Western countries; it requires much more careful planning. Read some literature on your destinations and areas of interest and talk to people who have been there. Locate travel agents or other specialist organizations that have experience in dealing with travel to Russia.

GROUP TOURS

There are a multitude of package and special-interest group tours from which to choose. The advantage of a group tour—especially if it is your first trip and you do not speak the language—is that everything is set up for you. Most group tours have preset departure dates and fixed lengths of stay, and usually include visits to Moscow and St Petersburg. The group rate often includes round-trip airfare, visa-processing fees, first-class accommodation, up to three meals a day, transportation within Russia, sightseeing excursions and a bilingual guide. (If you are more of a free spirit, it may be cheaper to book with a tour and then abandon the group for a time once in Russia.) Special interest groups also offer trips that include some sightseeing, but otherwise focus on more specific areas, such as sports, ecology, the arts, citizen diplomacy, religion or world peace. Adventure tourism has also opened up a whole new array of opportunities, among them rafting, hiking, climbing, biking, kayaking, horseback riding, golfing and even trans-Arctic expeditions (see Useful Addresses p 676).

INDEPENDENT TRAVEL

Independent travel to Russia is still difficult. It is not quite as simple as going to a Russian embassy or consulate, filling out a visa form, and taking off. You must first provide proof of a hotel reservation, or business/family sponsorship. The official reason for this visa restriction is that hotel space in Russia is still fairly limited. Many hotels tend to be prebooked in high seasons, and the government does not want visitors to arrive with nowhere to stay. The good news is that the old monopoly of mediocre Intourist hotels has dissolved along with the Soviet Union, and today many new one- to five-star hotels, motels, hostels, bed-and-breakfasts and even campsites have sprung up. Independent travelers can also arrange homestays with a Russian family. Cheap accommodation is in big demand; try and book at least six to eight weeks in advance to guarantee space and the best rates. Today many higher-class hotels, hostels, host family organizations and travel agencies specializing in Russia can also provide visa invitations.

VISAS

Most travelers to the Russian Federation must have a visa. There are mainly three types: tourist, business and private visitor. Normally visas should be obtained in the country of residence (otherwise it may be more difficult to procure). Visas were issued by the Russian Foreign Ministry or MVD, but as of November 2002, this service was transferred to the Interior Ministry or OVIR. Over the past few years visa costs have gone up considerably and a tourist visa can now cost upwards of $100 for one obtained in ten business days, and over $300 for the same business day! As of 2003, Russian visas are now stamped into US passports. If staying more than three months, a medical certificate indicating an HIV negative status may be required.

TOURIST VISAS

If you are with a group or package tour, the company takes care of your visa application. There are several ways for independent travelers to procure a tourist visa. They can deal with a local travel agency that handles Russian visas, or collect a visa application at a Russian embassy or consulate. (If you telephone, a form can be mailed, e-mailed or faxed to you, along with specific instructions, and there is also a visa-information recording which explains what you need to do. This can also be done through the website.) A single or double-entrance tourist visa is good for up to 30 days.

There are seven basic steps to apply for a Russian Visa: 1) Complete the application form and sign it; 2) One passport-size photograph is required; 3) An original and valid passport needs to be included. (Note: The Russia visa stamp takes up two open pages, so make sure you have at least two blank pages remaining.); 4) If you are an American male between the ages of 16–45, an additional supplemental page must also be filled out; 5) If staying in a hotel, then you must include proof of a confirmed hotel reservation; it does not have to be pre-paid. (This reservation can be made through a travel agency, or faxed/e-mailed from a host hotel or other booking organization.) If you do not need to stay in a hotel (have friends or relatives, etc.), another way to get a tourist visa is to go through a travel agency that specializes in Russian visas and issues official invitations (see Useful Addresses p. 676). You must provide either an official invitation or proof of a hotel reservation; 6) Depending on how quickly you need the visa returned (a visa can be issued within a few hours), a corresponding processing fee is charged which you must include with your application. Try to give ample time—up to ten or 15 business days for processing; 7) It is recommended to include a self-addressed envelope and the proper postage for FedEx or express mailing.

By Russian law, you are required to register your visa within three business days of arrival in Russia (see Registration under Business Visas). When staying at a hotel, the reception automatically registers and stamps the visa upon check-in. When exiting the country, a registration stamp must appear on your visa, or you may have to pay a fine or not be allowed to depart.

A tourist traveler can also stay in a hotel for just one night, obtain a registration stamp, and then go on to stay elsewhere. Only one registration stamp is needed for the entire stay but the dates marked must include your entire stay in the country. As an alternative to hotels, you can also book a homestay with a Russian family; agencies coordinating stays can also help obtain a visa. Some of Russia's Youth Hostels are now affiliated with the International Youth Hostelling Association. RYH can help students and other members with visa processing, inexpensive hostels, travel tickets and other information. Some companies that provide Russian visas are www.travel2russia.com; www.gotorussia.com; www.visahouse.com; and www.russianvisa.ru. (See also Practical Information sections under Accommodation and Useful Addresses on page 676.)

BUSINESS VISAS

If a traveler is going to Russia on business or is just an independent tourist who would like a longer stay in the country to visit friends, rent an apartment, or even enter the country without hotel reservations, the best way is to apply for a business visa. The easiest way is to contact a Russian specialist travel agency near you (see Useful Addresses). These firms can also help find places to stay and take care of other travel needs. Many of these agencies can officially issue a letter of sponsorship for an added fee, and with this invitation and the application forms (see requirements under Tourist Visa), a one-month or three-month single- or double-entry business visa can be issued. You should give yourself at least 15 business days to get this visa for the standard processing fee, otherwise fees can be considerably higher. Multiple-entry business visas can also be issued that are good for three or six months, or one year. The processing time can take up to one month.

If sponsored by a Russian host organization, you can also receive a business visa. Have them send, fax or e-mail an invitation letter which contains the dates of your visit and mentions that they are responsible for all your needs, including a place to stay (have them contact OVIR for the current requirements). By giving this, along with your appropriate visa application forms to the Russian embassy or consulate, a business visa can be issued without needing proof of hotel reservations.

Most airlines check to see if passengers have a Russian visa before allowing them to board a flight to Russia.

Registration: With any business visa (or tourist visa when not staying in a hotel), you must personally register your address in Russia at an OVIR office within three working days of arrival. The agency that sponsors and issues your visa usually has their own contact office in Moscow, or at the airports and in other cities where it is easier to register—so do not forget to ask for an address. (In case they need to hold onto your passport for several days, always keep a xerox copy of passport

/visa with you.) The registration fee is approximately $20–30. Many Russian-based travel agencies can also register the visa for an added fee. If three business days are exceeded, a penalty may apply. On the other hand, if you are staying in the country less than three business days, a registration stamp is not required. Only one r egistration stamp is needed per stay. If you have a double- or multiple-entry visa, another registration stamp is needed for the next period of entry. If you try to exit without a registration stamp, passport control may require a penalty fine, or not permit departure. You must also exit the country before the visa expires. (If it has expired, report to a specialist travel agency or an OVIR office for an extension; you cannot get one at the airport.) There are numerous district OVIR offices in Moscow. One central agency is located at 42 Pokrovka Street (Metro Kurskaya), tel. 208-2091; open on Tuesdays and Thursdays 10am–6pm. Another office is at 11 Durasovsky Lane (Metro Kurskaya), tel. 917-4421; open Tuesdays/Thursdays 10am–6pm and Fridays/Saturdays 10am–4pm (closed 1–2pm).

In St Petersburg, 4 Saltykova-Shchedrina Street (Metro Chernyshevskaya), †el. 278-2481. Open 9am–6pm; closed weekends.

VISITOR'S VISAS

If hosted by a relative or friend, you can enter on a private visitor's visa. You must send your host a duplicate of your complete visa application form, not a photocopy. Upon receipt the host takes it to their travelers' organization, OVIR, which will issue a visitor's invitation. This you then send to the Russian embassy or consulate, This process can take up to several months. The person is only allowed to stay at the address designated on the visa, and must register in the city within three working days. Since you must make these arrangements so far in advance, you may prefer to obtain a tourist or business visa instead.

Do not panic if your visa has not arrived as your departure date nears. Russian embassies and consulates are notorious for issuing visas at the last minute. When applying, indicate with an enclosed letter that you absolutely need the visa delivered by a certain date, and follow up with a phone call. If a passport is lost in Russia, contact your embassy or consulate.

Beginning in 2002, for certain countries (such as the UK, Japan and Switzerland) a short-term (up to 72-hours) tourist entry visa can be issued (prior to entering Russia). You must check because terms for acquiring a short-term visa often change and the nationalities allowed to receive one remain limited.

If you are a student with proof of enrollment at an accredited Russian school, a student visa can be issued. You may also need separate visas (and transit visas) to travel to or through other Commonwealth states such as the Ukraine or Belarus, but US and UK citizens do not need visas for the Baltic States. Passport control may review other visas before allowing you to leave for the next destination.

WHEN TO GO

Hotel prices and itineraries of many tour programs change depending on the season. Peak season is from May to September. Alternatives are to go in the spring (April 1–May 15) or fall (September 1–October 31) when prices are lower and the cities less crowded. The summer White Nights in St Petersburg are spectacular, but at the same time the summer in Moscow can be humid and dusty. An Indian summer in the fall can be quite lovely. If you do not mind the cold and snow, the winter season is cheapest and accommodation most readily available (but the number of daylight hours are limited). The rainiest months for both cities are July and August.

TIME ZONES

Russia has 11 time zones. Moscow and St Petersburg are in the same zone. Moscow is 11 hours ahead of the US West Coast, eight hours ahead of the East Coast, three hours ahead of London, two of Central Europe, and one hour ahead of Helsinki. Russia changes its clocks the last Sunday in March (one hour forward) and last Sunday in October (one hour back). Moscow time is five hours behind Hong Kong, seven hours behind Sydney, and nine hours behind New Zealand.

WHAT TO PACK

For your convenience, travel as light as possible. Most airlines allow up to two pieces of luggage and one piece of cabin baggage. Luggage allowance tends to be very strict when exiting Russia. Often all bags are weighed, including your cabin baggage. You may be charged per additional kilogram (2.2 pounds) for overweight luggage. On most international flights, for example, two pieces of baggage are allowed, each weighing no more than 23 kilos (50 pounds). On internal flights each must weigh no more than 20 kilos (44 pounds). This goes for both economy and business class.

DOCUMENTS

Keep your passport, visa, important papers, tickets, vouchers, prescription medications and money in your hand luggage at all times! Also carry a photocopy of your passport and visa, and a few extra passport pictures. Bear in mind that you may need to show identification to get into certain places or exchange money, even if it is a xerox copy of a passport or visa. Know your credit card and pin numbers, and their emergency telephone numbers in case of loss or theft. Bring along a few personal checks; you may need one in order to get cash from a credit card, such as AMEX (see Traveler's Checks and Credit Cards, page 65).

(following pages) A large stone lion stands above the Neva by the Palace Bridge (Dvortsovy Most). The building across the river with the tower is the Kunstkammer (Cabinet of Curiosities), built in 1714 to house Peter the Great's private collections. It is now the Museum of Anthropology and Ethnography and the Lomonosov Museum. The columned building to the left is the Academy of Sciences.

CLOTHES

The season of the year is the major factor in deciding what to bring. Summers are warm, humid and dusty, with frequent thunderstorms, especially in Moscow—bring a raincoat or an umbrella. The White Nights of St Petersburg are delightful in the summer, but occasionally a pullover or light jacket is needed. Winters are cold and damp, with temperatures well below freezing. It can snow between November and April, when cold Arctic winds sharpen the chill. Be prepared with your warmest clothes—waterproof lined boots, hat, gloves, scarf and thermal underwear (surprisingly, it is often colder in Moscow than St Petersburg). Interiors are usually well-heated, so dress in layers. Bring slightly smarter attire for ballets and banquets. A must is a good pair of walking shoes that can get dirty. Wearing shorts or sleeveless shirts may prevent you from entering churches during services.

Even though numerous clothing stores have now opened throughout both cities, Western attire and brand-name fashion is much more expensive than at home, and Russian-made goods do not ensure quality. It is best to buy necessary clothing before you leave, but otherwise you should now be able to find almost anything, especially in Moscow and St Petersburg.

MEDICINE

Many more Western medicinal products are available in Moscow and St Petersburg now, but they cost more than at home. Bring along necessary prescription drugs (know generic names) and allergy medications, antibiotics (such as Cipro) and a course of antidiarrhea drugs (such as Lomotil), glasses and contact lenses. Also consider packing a small first-aid kit for cuts and bruises. If you take injections, bring your own needles and syringes. Even though you can now find many items in various Western-style supermarkets, they may not carry your preferred brands. To save time looking for them, bring some of these with you: aspirin, throat lozenges, cold formulas, vitamins, laxatives, lip salve, dental floss, travel sickness pills, water-purifying tablets, antibacterial handwash, handi-wipes, contact-lens cleaner, mosquito repellent/anti-itch spray and indigestion tablets. Luxury-class hotels usually have a resident nurse on hand. (See Practical Information sections for each city for listings of medical facilities, dentists and pharmacies.)

PERSONAL ARTICLES

One can now find most necessary travel articles that were always lacking in Russia—thus, no one really needs to pack an extra five kilograms of toiletries and toilet paper! Even though many products are available, consider bringing along preferred brands of cosmetics, shampoo, lotions, razors and shaving cream, toothpaste, sanitary towels or tampons, small packets of tissues for restrooms, a water bottle for long trips, money belt, washing powder, an all-purpose plug for bathtubs and sinks, earplugs, a sewing kit, pantyhose, adhesive tape, extra locks for suitcases, sunglasses, pens and note pads, plastic bags and a sturdy tote-style shopping bag. A small flashlight and whistle are good to carry at night. If you are a student bring a student ID—many places offer discounts on fares or admission charges. This also applies to senior citizens.

GADGETS

Voltage is 220V (and sometimes varies to 127V). Most of the major hotels have plugs for 220/110V. Pack a few adapters (Russia uses the European round two-pin plug). Duel voltage coils are useful for boiling water and brewing tea and coffee in your hotel room, but should be used with caution. A CD music player or IPod, as well as a small tape recorder may come in handy. Bring plenty of batteries for your camera, alarm clock and watch. Also useful is a Swiss army knife or penknife that has a bottle opener and corkscrew.

FILM AND PHOTOGRAPHY

Digital flash cards and film are available in both cities, but is more expensive than at home. Using a flash is prohibited in many museums and churches. If you can wait, it is advisable to have your photos printed at home. Also remember to take along extra camera batteries as these may not be available locally.

In the former Soviet Union there were many photographic restrictions, but these no longer apply. Some places still prohibit cameras (such as the Lenin Mausoleum), and others, such as museums and churches, may require a permit to be purchased. Many locals are still uncomfortable with having their picture taken. Understand that people are sometimes sensitive about foreigners photographing what they perceive as backward or in poor condition. Always remain courteous. When passing through airports, photographers with film, especially high-speed, should have it inspected by hand—Russian X-rays are not always guaranteed film-safe. (Before leaving home, purchase a film shield pouch—lead laminated; the bag protects your undeveloped film against airport X-rays.)

MISCELLANEOUS/SUNDRIES

A Russian phrase book and dictionary really come in handy. Try to master some of the Cyrillic alphabet before you leave. It is especially helpful in places like the Metro. Bring reading material and travel literature—Western books will be more expensive, and most of the Russian-published material is, surprise, in Russian! Gift-giving is part of Russian *gostyepriimstvo* (hospitality). Bring some specialty gift items from home—picture travel books of your country or city, postcards, T-shirts, sport pins or favorite music CDs are always appreciated. You can also purchase liquor and other gift items while in Russia.

GETTING THERE

INTERNATIONAL FLIGHTS

Most major airlines fly to Moscow (Sheremetyevo II) and St Petersburg (Pulkovo II), although some international airlines now fly into Moscow's Domodedovo airport. Moscow is connected to over 120 cities in Europe and 70 countries around the world. Inquire at travel agencies and telephone the different airlines to discover the best rates. The advance-purchase (14–21-day APEX) fares usually give the most value for money. Since flying from points outside Europe can involve large time differences, consider a stay in a European city for a day or two to recover from jet lag. Stopovers are often included or provided for a minimal extra charge.

Aeroflot is the largest Russian airline that flies to over 50 countries, carrying over six million passengers annually. The airline, which marked its 80th anniversary in 2003, flies to and from a multitude of destinations in North America, Europe, Asia (and a few in Africa) with stopovers in Moscow and other Russian cities. Since the fall of the Soviet Union, Aeroflot has immensely improved in-flight conditions. They acquired dozens of new Western-made planes, introduced a new menu and their new airport terminal in Moscow, Sheremetyevo III, should open by 2008. Today, Aeroflot no longer holds the monopoly on air travel within the country, but it operates nearly 70 percent of Russian international routes, and over a third of internal routes, connecting over 30 cities in Russia and the CIS. Check out the website www.aeroflot.ru (and click on 'English' in the upper right corner).

CONNECTING TRAINS

One pleasant way to travel is to take a train from a European city to Moscow or St Petersburg. In the USA, call Rail-Europe at (888) 382-7245, and in Canada at (800) 361-7245. (website: www.raileurope.com) Also try www.trainweb.com, www.trainsrussia.com, www.connectrussia.com and www.themoscowtimes.com/travel. For example, after a few relaxing days in Helsinki, you can then take the train to St Petersburg or Moscow. There are three daily trains that leave Helsinki to St Petersburg (445 kilometers/278 miles). They depart at 7.42am, 3.42pm and 5.42pm and arrive at Finland Station respectively at 2.30pm, 10.40pm and 1.35am. Prices range from $75 to $250. Trains depart St Petersburg at 5.51am, 7.28am, and 7.30pm. There is a one-hour time change. First class one-way costs approximately $125 (luxury class $240, second class sleeper $75). The Russian train number 33 departs St Petersburg at 7.24am and arrives in Helsinki at 12.30pm the same day. The Finnish train number 35 leaves at 5.12pm and arrives in Helsinki at 9.30pm.

Even during the cold winter months, people enjoy walking in Red Square. The distinctive onion domes of St Basil's Cathedral gradually evolved from the original Byzantine cube-shaped roofs to withstand heavy snowfalls. The Spasskaya Clock Tower overlooks Lenin's Mausoleum.

The Moscow train leaves each day from Helsinki at 5.42pm and arrives the next morning at 8.25am. A return train from Moscow departs at 10.50pm and arrives in Helsinki at 11.20am the next morning. (Make sure your Russian visa is good for this extra day.)

Remember to hide or secure your valuables and money, and lock your compartment door; unfortunately, thefts occur, especially on overnight trains. By reserving a lower berth, you can store your luggage in the compartment underneath it. (**A tip**: both the compartment door lock and second security lock can be opened from the outside. Use a short nylon cord, necktie or belt to tie the door handle at night when sleeping.)

One can also travel by rail from other European cities, such as Berlin (35 hours) or Warsaw (26 hours) which can take from one to two days. Another popular train route is from the Baltic States (Estonia, Lithuania and Latvia) to Moscow or St Petersburg. (Make sure to check if any countries you pass through require transit visas.) The famous Trans-Siberian, on its western run, starts in Beijing and routes through either Manchuria or Mongolia, then crosses Siberia (one is allowed to get off at various locations along the way) with Moscow as its destination; from here, one can also continue on to other cities in Western Europe. (See Special Topic on page 348.)

By Ferry And Bus

Ferries leave for Russia from numerous European countries, such as Sweden, Finland, Latvia and Germany. The journey takes about 14 hours; overnight cabins are available. Ferries arrive and depart St Petersburg from the Sea Passenger Ship Terminal on Vasilyevsky Island. Cruises are also offered that journey along inland waterways with destinations such as Kizhi Island in Lake Ladoga or Valaam Island in Lake Onega, or along the Volga River. Overland round trip bus excursions are also available to Moscow and St Petersburg from European countries, with frequent departures from Helsinki. (See Useful Addresses and Practical Information sections for more details on cruise and bus excursions.)

Driving

It is not recommended to drive to Russia in your own car. There are 25.6 million cars on Russian roads. Of these, 1 in 163 are in road accidents each year! The highways and border towns are filled with police and smugglers who both make a living out of extortion and theft. Definitely make sure you have proper insurance and contact a tourist information center before you leave to set up precise routes and learn of requirements and official procedures. Once inside Russia, unkept roads make targets for holdups, routes are poorly marked, parts are scarce or expensive and gas stations are often impossible to find.

Customs and Immigration

Visitors arriving by air pass through a passport checkpoint in the airport terminal. Those arriving by train do this at the border. Uniformed border guards check passports and stamp visas.

Russian custom declaration forms are usually issued during your flight or train journey, or you can pick them up from stands located near the baggage claim area in the airport. The form has both an arrival and departure page. (If entering with a tourist visa, make sure you do not check 'Commerce' for 'Purpose of Visit', even if you plan to do business.) Fill in both pages; the 'B Departure' section is handed in upon exiting the country. At Passport or Border Control, you are requested to hand over your passport/visa and both A and B sections. (Note: If you land at Moscow's Sheremetyevo II airport, expect long chaotic lines at passport control. If you have a connecting flight elsewhere within the country, tell an official who should move you to the front of a line.) Proceed to baggage claim. (If you see no luggage carts, ask for them. Often a lazy worker needs some prompting!) As of March 15, 2003, if you have less than $10,000 and have no other valuables to declare, proceed through the Green Channel. If you are carrying in more than $10,000, you must exit through the Red Channel and declare the amount. (If you declare money, you cannot exit the country with more than you entered with.)

If you arrive with expensive items (such as jewelry), these could be confiscated when departing if you have no proof that you brought them into the country. Any expensive cameras, videos, personal computers, musical instruments, etc., should also be declared on the customs form. If uncertain about any items, proceed through the Red Channel and double-check with a customs officer. Also note that once declared, you must then depart with these items (unless you have official permission to leave them behind) or you could be subject to a duty up to the full value of the goods in question.

If you are in Moscow and need to transit to another airport, such as the nearby Sheremetyevo I, go to the appropriate airline transit desk once you exit the customs area. You must carry your luggage to the next airport. Make sure you have at least three hours between arrival and departure times between I and II. The transfer process (and check-in at the local airport) takes considerably longer than expected. A complete revamp of most of Moscow's airline terminals is long overdue.

Drugs, other than medicinal, are highly illegal. Do not try to exit with items of cultural value, such as antiques (made before 1947), old icons, or very expensive works of art (even modern) unless you have an authorized certificate from the Ministry of Culture. The place of purchase can usually help obtain this. People charged with trying to export items of cultural significance without proper certification can face a prison sentence of three to seven years. Carry receipts so you can also prove their value if questioned. Caviar can also be confiscated (check—there may still be a two can limit). If something does get confiscated, and a friend staying behind is with you at the airport, give it to them for safekeeping; otherwise customs may keep it. If using a porter at an airport or train station, make sure to first ask how much is charged for each bag; it can cost up to 100 rubles (US$3) per bag.

MONEY

The Russian currency is the ruble, which became Russia's national currency in 1534. The new bank notes (first circulated in 1998) come in denominations of 10, 50, 100 and 500 rubles. In 2000, new R1,000, R5,000 and R10,000 notes were introduced. The front of the R1,000 note features the Yaroslavl coat-of-arms and the monument to Yaroslavl the Wise; other bills may follow. There are 1, 2, 5 ruble coins. There are 100 kopeks to the ruble, and they come in 1, 5, 10, and 50 kopek coins. As of 2006, the exchange rate has settled to about R27 to US$1; R34.4 to the Euro; R50.7 to one pound sterling; R24 to one Canadian dollar; R3.5 to one Hong Kong dollar; R20.5 to one Australian dollar; and R17.2 to one New Zealand dollar.

RUBLE HISTORY

The last ten years have seen a wide fluctuation in the value of the ruble. Before 1989 the Soviets set an exchange rate for the ruble within the country at about US$1.60. But on November 1, 1989, Gorbachev's government devalued the ruble by 90 percent. Soon after, the kopek coin was completely taken off the market, new notes were printed, and the ruble plummeted to less than one American cent. (Russians nick-named their currency 'wooden money', while the slang for American dollars, real money, became *kapusta* or cabbage.) The intention of devaluation was to bring the ruble closer to its actual value and discourage huge black-market activities. In 1992, the ruble was floated on the world market and on July 25, 1993, new denomination ruble notes were circulated to coincide with soaring inflation. All of these notes are now invalid. By 1997 the world market exchange had risen to 6,000 rubles to US$1. At the beginning of l998, Yeltsin's government decided to reissue new ruble tender notes, knocking off three zeros. During the country's economic crisis in the fall of 1998, the ruble plunged to over 20 rubles to US$1, falling to less than one third of its value. Check your change—make sure you receive the current ruble notes in your money exchange—any note marked prior to 1997 is probably not valid. Ruble notes with many zeroes are worthless!

CURRENCY EXCHANGE

For information on currency exchange rates (кур, pronounced 'kurs'), dial 008.

Cash is the most acceptable form of currency in Russia (the country still does not have a check system). Traveler's checks are not as widely accepted. You can convert foreign currency to rubles at the airport or in your hotel. In addition, hundreds of exchange kiosks (signs in Russian say **ОБМЕН ВАЛЮТУ**—*Obmyen Valyutoo*) also line the streets of big cities. Counterfeit US dollars have flooded Russia, so do not be offended if your dollars are carefully examined. Make sure all bills are in good condition; any torn, taped or marked bills may not be accepted. Also carry the newer US$100 Franklin notes, as older $100 bills may not be taken. The exchange rates are now fixed and there is really no reason to seek out black marketeers; besides, it can be risky and you could be tricked with out-of-date notes. Official exchange offices usually ask for ID, such as a passport or visa (showing a photocopy is acceptable), and they may want to stamp your customs declaration form. You can exchange unused rubles at the end of your trip in town, at the airport or border.

Most shops and restaurants take only rubles, though many now accept credit cards. (Note: by law, only rubles or credit cards are acceptable in most locations. Nonetheless, prices may be stated in Y.E., meaning conventional units (in dollars or Euros). Carry lower denomination bills, for many places cannot provide change for larger bills; they are also handy for tipping, cab fares, etc. Tipping is discretionary, depending on the service. Usually about ten percent is acceptable.

TRAVELER'S CHECKS AND CREDIT CARDS

Credit cards are now accepted at many banks, hotels, restaurants and some shops. However, except in banks, traveler's checks are not as widely accepted. Bear in mind that most shops, bars and cafés still only accept rubles, and if you can pay in foreign currency you will probably get change in rubles, so always have smaller denomination notes available. The most widely accepted cards are Visa, Mastercard and American Express.

Numerous ATMs (Automated Teller Machines) have sprung up in cities and can be used 24 hours per day. Many major banks and hotels have ATMs or can give cash advances against credit cards with a commission (about three percent) based on the amount (always carry your passport and a personal check). When using an ATM to get cash from your bank or credit card, you must know your international PIN number (and for use in Russia, it can only be 4 digits long). Most machines now allow you to select to receive cash in either dollars or rubles and have an English language guide.

At American Express offices, you can cash traveler's checks or get cash from your AMEX card (with an approximate 5 percent commission). You also need a personal check to get cash from a credit card. Make sure you can get the exchange in foreign currency and not all in rubles. They also have a full-service travel bureau. AMEX web-site: www.americanexpress.com (Also see Post and Mail, page 80.)

Moscow AMEX office: 17 Gazetny Lane, tel. 755-9900, 725-6572. Open Monday–Friday 9am–5pm. (Metro Okhotny Ryad). If a credit card or traveler's checks are lost or stolen, report the loss immediately to the United Card Service in Moscow, tel. 325-6135/6134, which can help cancel and replace the items.

St Petersburg AMEX office: 1/7 Mikhailovskaya St (in Hotel Grand Europe). tel. 329-6060. Open Monday–Friday 9am–5pm. (Metro Nevsky Prospekt). The Industry –Construction Bank at 38 Nevsky Prospekt and the Central Exchange Center at 1 Nevsky also cash traveler's checks and handle credit cards.

Many Russian banks can now receive international money transfers. Western Union money transfer offices are also located in both cities.

BEWARE OF DUAL PRICING

Basically a foreigner in Russia can still expect to pay anything from double to ten times more than locals at cultural sites such as museums and theaters. (The good news is that prices for hotels, transportation, air and tram tickets should now be the same for everyone.) The dual pricing is understandable—the average Russian earns less than $200 per month—but visits to the many musuems can really add up. One way to avoid being charged the higher price is to have a Russian friend, or a friendly local, buy the ticket for you; enter with them (just do not speak; often the ticket taker will purposely ask a question in Russian to see if you understand). If you know any Russian, you can also try buying the cheaper ticket yourself. (Note: the price for foreigners is often posted in English, and the lower price in Russian.) It is easier to get away with this in St Petersburg and other smaller towns. But in Moscow, those *babushki* (grandmothers) working in the ticket booths have sharp ears and eyes and can easily recognize any slight accent and a western-dressed foreigner. But, you have nothing to lose by trying. A photography/video permit is usually an extra fee. Showing some type of international Student ID can also get you up to a 50 percent discount.

Another way to save money is to go on a Russian group excursion. Russian tour buses tend to be cheaper than the bus excursions organized for foreigners. If you do not understand Russian, then just bring a guidebook with you. (The cost could be only $5 for the local tour compared to $50 for a tour for Westerners.) Buying excursion or theater tickets at specially marked street *kassas* can also be much cheaper than purchasing them through your hotel.

VALUABLES

Hotels usually have safe deposit boxes by the front desk. It is advisable to lock up your valuables, money, passport and airline tickets—thefts have been reported from hotel rooms. In case of loss or theft, notify the service bureau at your hotel immediately. Always put your money in a safe place, carry bags tightly around your shoulder and make sure backpacks are secured. Buy a money belt, so you can carry your money discreetly. Unfortunately, over the last few years the number of crimes against tourists has risen—pockets are picked and bags stolen. Take extra care when in large crowds and markets, or if a band of Gypsies or street urchins approaches. Take the same precautions as you would in any large metropolis.

HEALTH AND EMERGENCIES

To call an ambulance in Russia, dial 03 (this will change to 112 by 2008). Since a Russian ambulance may take time to arrive, also try calling one of the Western clinics immediately.

Immunizations are not required unless you are coming from an infected area. Russia does not have many health risks, but the main areas of concern are the food, water and cold weather. Some people may have trouble adjusting to Russian cuisine, which can include heavy breads, thick greasy soups, highly salted and pickled foods, smoked fish and sour cream. In the smaller towns familiar vegetables and fruits are often in short supply. (If you do not have an iron constitution, bring indigestion or stomach disorder remedies.) If you are a vegetarian or require a certain diet, consider bringing some packaged freeze dried or specialty foods and vitamins along. A vegetarian can always find potatoes and cabbage—ethnic restaurants such as Georgian and many Western-style cafés serve nonmeat fare.

DO NOT drink the tap water, especially in St Petersburg, where a virulent parasite *Giardia lamblia* can cause miserable bouts of fever, stomach cramps and diarrhea. If you feel ill, get checked by a doctor. For *Giardia,* some prescribe Metronidazole (available in Russia as Trikapol) 200mg three times per day for two weeks. Local juices or flavored sugar water, along with iced drinks, cannot always be trusted. (Most five-star hotels now have their own water-purifying systems, but you are advised to check.) Stick to bottled mineral water (some old brands of Russian water can be quite salty). In winter be prepared for a cold, and in the spring and summer months possible allergy attacks or mosquito bites.

If staying in Russia longer than a few months you may need to present a negative HIV test. If illness occurs, see Practical Information sections under Medical for hospital/pharmacy/dental locations. Many of these Western clinics can also organize air evacuation in the event of an emergency. It is advisable to purchase travel medical insurance before the trip. In the USA, try Travel Insurance Service, tel. (800) 937-1387; web-site: www.travelinsure.com, or International SOS Assistance (tel. (215) 942-8226. The latter has a local office in Moscow 937-6477.

CRIME, SAFETY AND HAZARDS

To call Police, dial 02 (this will change to 112 by 2008). The reports of crime in Russia have, for the most part, been overly dramatized by both Russian and Western press. Statistically, Russian streets are as safe as in Paris, London or New York. Even though some areas of Russia are experiencing unrest, it is considered safe to walk around Moscow or St Petersburg at any time during the day or evening, though, as in any big city, use common sense and take care of your valuables. It is highly unlikely for the average tourist to ever cross paths with Russian mafia or organized crime.

As a foreigner, you are automatically assumed to have money. Do not flaunt expensive jewelry and watches or wads of cash, and try to dress inconspicuously. Never exchange a large amount of money at a currency kiosk while walking alone on the street. Pickpocket gangs, often using children to distract their targets, work areas around major hotels, popular restaurants and tourist attractions (thieves come in all denominations—from the well-dressed or the elderly to pretty young women). As one gets your attention, another may try to pick your pocket, cut the strap off your shoulder bag, snatch your camera or open your backpack. If all valuables are secure, then nothing can be stolen. Carry rubles in one place, and dollars in another; place the bulk of foreign cash in yet another safe area. It has been known for thugs to follow big winners home from a casino, or an intoxicated foreign couple leaving a restaurant. Late at night, do not walk alone down poorly lit back-alleys or in neighborhoods you are not familiar with. It is safe to ride the Metro, but from the station, make sure you do not have to wait long for a bus or walk a long way to get home. The biggest nuisance is usually inebriated Russians, but aside from a few incoherent mumbles, their incapacitation renders them relatively harmless.

In addition, do not flag down a taxi or private car late at night and ride by yourself to the outskirts of town; if more than two people are in the vehicle and you are alone, do not get in. If staying with friends, never give the driver, or any other stranger for that matter, the entire address. If you should experience a mugging, do not resist—the gun is probably real. It is a good idea to place a small sum of money in one pocket and hide the rest; this way, you can pull out the smaller amount, and say it is all you have. The GAI or Militsia Police wear blue or gray uniforms with red epaulettes and cap bands. Their vehicles are usually navy blue and white. If robbed, report the incident to the police; your hotel can direct you to the nearest police station (you will probably need an official report to file an insurance claim). If something major occurs, also report it to your embassy or consulate.

As an added twist, in the past few years incidents have occurred where officials, looking like policemen, have pulled over tourists to question their documents and then tried to extract money. (As an example, a policeman may ask you to step inside a van and ask to see your passport. He will then remark that your documents/visas are not in order and you need to pay a $100 cash fine to get your passport back.) In Moscow, this has more frequently occurred around Red Square, and in St Petersburgh along Nevsky Prospekt. If you are suddenly questioned by police and asked to pay out money, this could well be a scam. Demand to call your embassy or consultate first. Always carry a photocopy of your passport and visa with you at all times (just say that you do not have your passport with you). In this way, if questioned, you can just hand over the photocopy.

Do be aware of the fact that due to the 2002 Moscow Chechnen hostage attack and recent bombings more police are now stationed outside, particularly at Metro stations, train stations and bus stops, and they are allowed to stop anyone and ask for their documents. (A more ethnic-looking is usually singled out for spot-checks.) In Russia, it is required that a foreigner carry identity documents on them at all times.

If someone tries to pick you up in a bar, restaurant, or hotel, remember both men and women work as prostitutes (they now frequent virtually all of Moscow's hotels). Think twice—not only is AIDS (and hepatitis and other venereal diseases) on the rise, but there are many reports of victims being drugged and robbed (prostitutes often work with criminals to target guests). Hotel guests should also never open their doors for unexpected callers. Russia has now become one of the major routes to Europe from the Golden Triangle. Do not even think of purchasing drugs or using them—Russian jails and prisons are awful; remember this country created the gulags.

Beware of fake art works, especially icons and lacquer boxes. A seller will try to charge a foreigner as much as possible. If you think the price is high and you cannot tell an antique from a modern imitation, do not buy it—scams abound. For example, white fish eggs have been blackened with shoe polish to look like expensive black caviar and resealed in official looking cans. This also happens with vodka—homemade brew or *samogon* is poured into empty bottles and resealed with a brand label. Do not buy vodka and caviar off the street or from some alley kiosk; purchase them in larger stores.

If in need of a public toilet, first try finding one in a hotel, restaurant or museum. Otherwise, look on the street for the sign WC or **ТУАЛЕТ** (*tyalet*)—they are hard to find and most are not in good condition. The men's toilet is marked with an M (women should go to the door marked Ж). Most train stations now have automated toilets. At the entrance, you may need to pay a small fee to an attendant. Sometimes, a few squares of toilet paper are provided; learn to carry small packets of tissues, they can be very useful.

Do not jaywalk—cross only at appropriate crossings or lights. Drivers do not care what is in front of them (practically no one has car insurance), and many streets are too wide to cross quickly (use underground crossings). Also be cautious when walking on sidewalks. There are many construction sites or deteriorating areas filled with deep holes, uncovered manholes or other hazards.

The hot water supply is often interrupted in summer months, especially in smaller towns. Central power stations usually close down for repairs and cleaning for several weeks during the year. If you arrive and there is no hot water, this may be the reason. Ask for a samovar or tea pot for your room in which to boil water; take a sponge bath or go to one of the numerous local saunas or *banya*. When in Rome...!

Smoking has reached epidemic proportions in Russia. While tobacco companies are being hounded in the United States, they are welcomed with open arms in Russia where cigarette sales are a goldmine business and advertising abounds. Smokers are everywhere, in restaurants, hotels, trains and museums, and it is legal. A recent survey reported that 57 percent of Russia's adult men and 48 percent of adult women smoke.

If you are susceptible to allergies, springtime can be a problem, especially in Moscow where pollen from trees and plants is a wheezer's anathema; at times, white fuzzy blossoms from poplar trees, called *pukh*, accumulate like snow drifts throughout the city.

GETTING AROUND

Sheremetyevo II, Moscow's main international airport, is located 30 kilometers (19 miles) northwest of the city. A new $300 million-dollar terminal, Sheremetyevo III, is scheduled to open by 2008. A few international airlines are now also operating out of Domodedovo Airport, located 52 kilometers (32 miles) southeast of Moscow. Express trains run from this airport to Paveletsky Station.

St Peterburg's Pulkovo II, 17 kilometers (11 miles) south of the city, was completely renovated in 1997. A new terminal, Pulkovo III, is currently under construction.

When arriving in Moscow or St Petersburg, group travelers should automatically be taken by bus to their hotel. When booking a hotel, check if they provide airport or train station transfers. If you are arriving as an independent traveler, try to arrange someone to meet you at the airport. Otherwise, most airport taxis are controlled by a local cartel of drivers who monopolize the service. Thus, rides from the airport into town can cost up to five times more than they cost in the opposite direction.

From Moscow's Sheremetyevo II a taxi may try to charge up to $150 for the 40-minute ride. They may even show you an official-looking price list. Since it only costs $50 (or less) to take a taxi from the Kremlin to the airport, try negotiating the price. Try offering to share a ride with other passengers into town and split the cost. Or you may be able to find a private driver moonlighting (just use your own safety sense). A visitor can also pre-order a taxi for pick up upon arrival at the airport. Numerous travel agencies can arrange this, as well as local Russian taxi companies who have reasonable rates. Try *Capital Cabman*, and book at www.citytaxi.ru (press ENG on the website for English) and www.enjoymoscow.com. They also make airport to airport transfers. If you have very little baggage, upon exiting the terminal, walk down to the right, to the overhead sign with a black bus. Here you can find minibuses or *marshrut* that go the nearest Metro (in the northern part of the city) and cost about 30 rubles or US$1. On the front of the vehicle, in Russian, is the name of the Metro destination—Aeroport, Planernaya or Rechnoi Vokzal. From here, you can catch a taxi or ride the Metro further to your destination. These minibuses seat 15 people with minimal space for baggage—a big suitcase is too much. (Minibuses return from these Metro stations to the airport, but there are often very long queues.) For transportation to and from other airports, see page 359.

To return to the airport, your hotel can help arrange a ride or find a taxi for a realistic fare. Or you can call a taxi to pick you up at your address. (See page 354 for taxi listings.) Moscow's Aerovokzal, 12 kilometers northwest of the city, near Metro Aeroport, also provides bus rides to all airports.

From St Peterburg's Pulkovo II airport, taxis can charge up to $50 for a 30-minute ride into town. So try to negotiate. A taxi from the city center to the airport only costs about $15–20. Local minibuses outside the terminal also make runs to the nearest Metro station. The airport's city bus No. 13 runs to Moskovskaya Metro station and Hotel Pulkovskaya. To get from town to the airport, bus No. 13 runs every 20 minutes from Moskovskaya Metro, and Group Taxi No. 213 leaves from Sennaya Square.

You can now order taxis, limos, minivans, trucks, even a private jet, on the Internet at www.taxi.ru. The site services major cities and features screens in both Russian and English. For telephone numbers, see page 354.

Remember to reconfirm your departure flight. This can be done through a hotel service desk or by telephoning the airlines directly. Reconfirm internal flights as well, as they tend to be overbooked. Always arrive at the airport at least two hours in advance for international flights—boarding sometimes closes 40 minutes before departure.

TRAVEL BETWEEN CITIES

If on a group tour, most of your itinerary has been booked before your arrival. If traveling independently and you would like to extend your visa, make other hotel, train or plane reservations, or simply book a sightseeing excursion within a city or travel to another town, such as in the Golden Ring area, always inquire first at your hotel. If they cannot handle something for you, they will be able to recommend travel organizations that specialize in your area of interest. As these arrangements can take time, never wait until the last minute to make travel plans.

BY AIR

The airports used for internal flights are much more crowded and chaotic than the international airports, so try to arrive several hours before departure. Passports and visas are required to be presented at check-in. (Take care, often even carry-on luggage is weighed, and any overweight is charged. If this is the case, have someone discreetly take your hand luggage aside when you check in.) Boarding passes are issued, either with open seating or with seat numbers, and rows written in Cyrillic! Remember that Russians are quite assertive and can push vigorously to get on the plane which is usually not boarded by row numbers—one general announcement for boarding is made, often just in Russian. If the flight has open seating, do not be last on the plane—the airlines frequently overbook. On internal flights, there is often just one class of seating. Sometimes the only meal consists of soda water, and bread and cucumber sandwiches. Consider taking some drinks and snacks along. Airport departure tax is usually included in the price of the ticket. You can reserve and buy Aeroflot (and other Russian airlines) tickets at most major hotels, or you can go directly to an Aeroflot office.

You can also reserve and buy airline tickets on foreign airlines at their representative offices (see Practical Information sections for Moscow and St Petersburg airline office locations).

BY TRAIN

Trains are much more fun, efficient and cheaper than flying. The commercial trains between Moscow and St Petersburg are a splendid way to travel. Traveling during daylight hours affords wonderful views of the countryside (it is also cheaper), or board the sleeper at night and arrive the next morning for a full day of sightseeing.

In 1850, when the Moscow–St Petersburg rail road was being built, Czar Nicholas I drew a straight line on a map to indicate the construction path between the two cities. The story goes that the Czar's finger caused a bump in the ruler line and resulted in a detour in the route, which is still known as the 'Czar's Finger.' However, the Ministry of Railways recently straightened this five-kilometer portion of the line.

There are about 15 daily trains that run the Moscow--St Petersburg route. Regular trains (that run both day and overnight) take between 7 and 8 hours (with stops) to cover the distance. (An average first-class, four-berth compartment now costs between $60–110; and other classes from hard seats to luxury can run between $40 and $395.) Trains for St Petersburg leave from Moscow's Leningradsky Station, and to Moscow from Petersburg's Moskovsky Station.

The Nevsky Express makes no stops, and can reach speeds up to 200 km/hour. It departs Moscow daily (except Sundays) at 6.28pm and arrives in St Petersburg 11.15pm. The return from St Petersburg departs daily (except Saturdays) also at 6.28pm.

The slightly faster ER–200 express departs both Moscow and St Petersburg on Mondays, Wednesdays and Fridays. From Moscow at 7.10pm and arrives in St Petersburg at 11.46pm. From St Petersburg at 7.08am and arrives in Moscow at 11.50am.

Another fast train is the daily Aurora Express, departing Moscow at 4.30pm and arriving in St Petersburg at 10pm. It leaves St Petersburg at 4pm and arrives in Moscow at 9.30pm. (Express train classes cost between $100–$261).

The Grand Express is Russia's first privately-owned luxury-passenger train, offering daily overnight service between Moscow and St Petersburg. Prices range from $170 to $450. Trains depart both cities at 11.24pm and arrive at 8.26am.

Express trains also run from Moscow to Kaluga, Tula and Vladimir in just two and a half hours.

Since there are several train stations in each city (eight in Moscow alone), make sure you know which one you depart from. In Moscow, trains for St Petersburg leave mostly from the Leningradsky Vokzal (Leningrad Station). In St Petersburg they leave from the Moskovsky Vokzal (Moscow Station). (The word *vokzal* stems from London's Vauxhall Station.) Large boards listing time schedules and track numbers are posted at each station. Trains always leave on time with a single five-minute warning broadcast before departure—so pay attention!

There are three classes for long-distance travel. Luxury or *lyuks* (SV) has two soft berths to a compartment (and often a personal bathroom); first or *coupé* class has four soft berths; *platskart* has either six hard berths or standard seats (try to avoid the latter for overnight travel). Your ticket will indicate the train, wagon (*vagon*), compartment (*kupé*) and berth (*myesto*) number. The lower the wagon number, the closer it is to the front of the train on departure. A personal car attendant (*provodnik*) offers tea, brewed in the car's samovar, and sometimes a boxed meal, and wakes you up in the morning. Remember to turn off the radio at night or it may blast you awake at 6am.

If you are traveling on an overnight train and can afford it, try buying the entire compartment to ensure both privacy and safety. If you share the compartment with strangers, secure your valuables and sleep with money, passport, etc. on your person. Reserve a lower berth, where you can place luggage and other valuables in the storage compartment underneath. During the night, compartment locks can be opened from the outside. If you are alone, consider securing both locks before retiring to sleep by using cord, belt or necktie to tie around them as an extra precaution. The compartments are not segregated. If there is a problem, the attendant can usually arrange a swap—it is safe traveling alone as a woman. (Carry earplugs in case of snorers!) A minimal fee may be charged for sheets and towels (which you are expected to fold up on arrival). Tickets are collected at the beginning of the trip and returned at the end.

Even though a dining car is usually available (though often crowded), it is fun to bring along your own food, drink, and spirits to enjoy in your compartment (remember a knife, fork and bottle opener). Also bring clothes to sleep in, slippers and toilet paper. Toilets on most trains are without supplies and never cleaned during trips, thus not always a pleasant experience. In summer months, it can be quite hot as compartment windows are sealed shut; hallway windows can be opened. Porters (*nosilshchiki*) are available, but they may try to charge a foreigner more; negotiate a per bag price before starting out (find out from a local what this is). In stations, always keep a watchful eye on your bags and valuables. Do not let just anyone carry your bag—it may be the last you see of it.

The easiest way to purchase train tickets is through your hotel service desk, or an appropriate travel agency. Your passport and visa are supposed to be checked with your ticket when boarding the train, so it is best not to buy a scalper's ticket (especially for a long-distance trip) which will be in a different name. Students sometimes get discounted fares. Foreigners and locals are now supposed to be charged the same fares.

To purchase a ticket on your own, go to the appropriate ticket counters at the station. Make sure you have sufficient rubles and your passport and visa. Same day tickets can be purchased at the station of departure. Moscow has four main rail ticket centers. Tickets up to 45 days in advance can be purchased at 5 Komsomolskaya Sq (Metro Komsomolskaya); open daily from 7am. The Central Railway Booking office is at 6 Mal. Kharitonevsky Lane (Metro Chistye Prudy); open Mondays– Saturdays 8am–7pm. (Credit cards can now be used to purchase tickets at these two stations.) Other offices are at 15 Petrovka St (Metro Kuznetsky Most) and 24/7 Myasnitskaya (Metro Turgenevskaya). In the future, Russian railways plans to extend credit card purchase to all major train stations. Rail information for Moscow stations, tel. 266-9006. Also dial 266-8333 to order tickets in advance; they are delivered to a home or office after two or three days, payment upon delivery. (Try also www.trainsrus-sia.com for train schedules and bookings.)

Besides ticket centers located in each of the five train stations, St Petersburg also has a rail ticket office at 24 Griboyedov Canal. One can also make an on-line reservation at www.express-3.ru.

Local commuter trains, known as *prigorodnye* (suburban) or *elektrichka*, serve the suburbs of both cities and some Golden Ring towns. They usually have only hard wooden benches (some have softer first class seats), poor amenities (toilets are dirty), and can be quite crowded on weekends and in summer months. The advantage is that they are cheap and leave frequently. Tickets can be bought the same day at the station of departure; ID is not usually required. Make sure you keep your ticket—you may need it to both enter and exit the station turnstiles, especially in Moscow—this is a measure to catch 'hares', or ticketless passengers.

Take note that many train and plane schedules are still listed throughout the country using Moscow time which does make things confusing. If you are traveling in a time zone other than Moscow's, always check to see what time (Moscow or local) is actually indicated on your ticket.

BY BUS AND COACH

Group tourists are shown around Moscow and St Petersburg by coach. Often the buses are not air-conditioned, but all are heated during winter. If you are an individual traveler, you can sign up through a hotel or local travel agency for city sightseeing excursions. Comfortable coach tours are also offered to Golden Ring towns. Always take notice of your bus number, as parking lots tend to fill quickly. For longer rides bring along some bottled water and snacks.

LOCAL BUSES, TRAMS AND TROLLEYS

Local transportation operates from 5.30am to 1am and is charged by either a flat rate or by distance. The front and back of each vehicle is marked in Russian with its destination, and the number of the route. To find a bus or trolley stop (A for *autobus* or T for *trolleybus*), look for numbered route signs on sidewalks. For trams, signs hang on wires by the street adjacent to the tram stop or over tramlines in the middle of the road. As you board, look for a sign near the door which indicates the cost of a ride (seven to ten rubles on average). Tickets can be bought from the driver, or an attendant who patrols the aisles. You can also prepurchase transportation cards, called *talony*, on the bus or at many kiosks and Metros. Special ticket machines are mounted throughout the vehicle where you punch your ticket (newer vehicles have card scanners). A monthly combined bus and Metro card can also be purchased. Inspectors sometimes make spot checks and fine ticketless passengers. If the bus is crowded, try to anticipate your stop and inch towards the door. You may hear a voice behind asking, *Vi Vikhoditye?* (Are you getting off now?). If locals think you are not alighting, they may push by; the *babushka*, especially, are superb shovers! Similarly, if trying to board a crowded bus, you may find yourself pushed from the back and packed in like a sardine. Just make sure the door does not close on you. Long-distance buses have their own terminals within each city. Minibuses or *marshrut* also stop along bus routes. They make fewer stops but charge more.

METRO

The Metro is the fastest and cheapest way to get around Moscow and St Petersburg. More than eight million people ride the Moscow Metro daily. Trains run every 90 seconds during rush hour. Central stations are beautifully decorated with chandeliers and mosaics. Metro stations are easy to spot—entrances on the street are marked with a large M. Even the long escalator rides are great entertainment. Metro maps are posted inside each station, or use the ones in this book (see pages 112–3 for Moscow and page 483 for St Petersburg). To ride the Metro, first purchase a magnetic-strip card at the underground *kassa* booth. (In St Petersburg, some stations may still use tokens or *zheton*) Alas, the cost has risen with inflation from $0.03 (5 kopeks) to about $0.25, but it is still a flat rate regardless of where you ride to or, with transfers, how long you remain underground.

Insert the card into the turnstile and wait for the green light before taking your ticket and passing through (some turnstiles are still archaic and can shut violently). All station and transfer areas are clearly marked, but in Russian. If you do not read Cyrillic, have someone write down the name of your destination. People are always helpful and are glad to point you in the right direction. Even though transferring to another station underground can be especially confusing, never forget to relish the adventure and marvel at the beauty of the stations. (see also page 110.)

TAXIS

You can order a taxi from the taxi desk located in the lobby of most hotels, or call a taxi to come to a specific location; a minimal service fee may be charged. For some telephone numbers of taxi companies, see the Practical Information section for the relevant city. Officially two hours notice is required, but taxis can arrive within minutes. If in a hotel, it may be easier to just go outside and flag one down (the ride is made cheaper by walking a few blocks away from the hotel). There are official and private taxis (which are required to display ID registrations) and private cars. Unlike most other countries, a Russian taxi ride is not as simple as it would seem. Even hailing a taxi can be a problem. Stand with your arm held out, palm slightly down. If a taxi stops, the driver may ask where you want to go before deciding if he wants to take you. If there is no meter, you need to negotiate a price. Be aware that the wealthier you appear, the higher he may bid. Often you can bring the price down by saying it is too much and pretending to walk away. Always carry small bills as the driver often says he has no change.

Many of the official taxis now have meters, but because of inflation and constant monetary devaluation, these may not have kept up with the changes. Taxi fees can be higher in the evening. It is wise to find out the average cost of your journey before you start bargaining. (By law you should pay in rubles, but a driver never usually refuses dollars.) If the driver seems to take a circuitous route, and the meter is running, ask—the driver may not be trying to cheat you. Often more direct roads may be closed and under construction.

Hitching is quite common—taxis are not always available and drivers of private cars are often eager to earn some extra cash by picking up paying passengers. Because of recent crime, evaluate the taxi or car before you get in, and never take a ride late at night, especially to an outlying area. If you do not have a good feeling about the driver, do not get in; always use common sense. Never get into a vehicle already occupied by two people, or let your taxi stop to take another passenger en route.

CAR HIRE

Many hotels offer a car hire service with a driver, and a guide can also be hired for the day. There are now both Russian and Western car services where automobiles, jeeps, mini-vans and buses can be rented, but usually only with an accompanying driver. If new to the city, it is recommended not to drive on your own; public transportation is actually much safer and more convenient. If you do plan on driving, check with your insurance company before leaving home; often Russia is not covered on a policy. If you want to tour an area, many private cars and off-duty taxi-drivers are often open to suggestions. Some can be hired for the day to take you around. Make sure to agree on the amount and payment terms beforehand; gasoline costs are usually extra. ALWAYS wear your seatbelt.

BEING THERE
HOTELS

Intourist, the old Soviet travel dinosaur, no longer monopolizes the Russian hotel system and the *dezhurnaya*, that hawk-eyed hall attendant, is also nearing extinction. Travelers who may have visited during Socialist days, will not believe the changes— hotel staff are actually friendly and most speak English. From foreign-owned luxury palaces and restored privatized State-run hotels to hip hostels and bed and breakfasts, there is something for everyone's budget. Bohemian suites, moderate motels and bargain beds are available in every area of town. However, it is best to find a location as close to the center as possible; taxis can be expensive and public transportation a time-consuming experience. Many establishments also provide visa and other travel services. Check to see if your hotel provides airport or train station transfers. To prevent crime, hotel doormen may require to see a hotel card before allowing you to enter. If you are stopped, state in English that you are staying in the hotel and have forgotten your card, or wish to eat at the restaurant— once recognized as a foreigner, the guards should let you in. (To find out how to book hotel rooms, check Facts for the Traveler/Visas, page 52, and Practical Information sections under Accommodation for more details.)

Hotels in Russia accept rubles, dollars (or other foreign currency), and major credit cards and traveler's checks. (Remember to check if VAT and city tax charges are included in the quoted room rates.) Many have restaurants and bars (breakfast is often included in the price), business and fitness centers, shops, post offices and service bureaus, which book travel, sightseeing excursions, theater tickets, train reservations, etc. If you cannot afford to stay in a more expensive hotel, you can still use its amenities—their spa centers usually offer special day-rates, or have an expresso in the coffee shop while reading the *Herald Tribune* to recharge! Especially during low seasons, bargaining for special rates can be attempted.

COMMUNICATIONS
INTERNATIONAL CALLS
Communication has become substantially easier since the Soviet era when placing an international call would take days. Today there are a number of ways of making an international call. For example, if you have an AT&T or Sprint Express telephone card, dial the appropriate access number and an operator can provide direct service to the US or elsewhere abroad.

You can also direct dial to the United States and other countries abroad (including areas in the CIS) from a home or business phone. First dial 8 and wait for second dial tone, then dial international code 10, and then the country code and phone number.

A telephone service is also available from most major hotels but this can be very expensive. (Always check prices and service charges before calling.) It may be easier and cheaper for somebody to call you from abroad if they know your contact number.

Yet another way is to use the numerous international (*Mezhdunarodny*) phone booths throughout both cities. You can pay with either a credit or phone card (that can be bought at city kiosks and Metro stations). Always check the costs before you call; some satellite phone booths may also have a three-minute minimum charge.

Several long-distance telephone centers are also located in each city and town. Go to the international desk and give the attendant your telephone number. When the call goes through, you are directed to a numbered booth to take the call.

Afterward the charge is usually paid in rubles, but some now take dollars or credit cards. In Moscow, the main communications centers are at the Central Telephone & Telegraph, 7 Tverskaya Ulitsa and 2 Novy Arbat. In St Petersburg, one is at 3/5 Bolshaya Morskaya Ulitsa. All are open daily from 9am–9pm.

To save costs make phone calls over a Web gateway or IP Telephony in Russia sells pre-paid telephone cards, and their rates are much lower than regular lines. Cell phones can also be rented in Moscow and St. Petersburg. Americans can rent a special phone from their cellular provider (or buy a local SIM-card), and some European cell phones (such as GMS) work in Moscow. It is now illegal to use a mobile phone while driving in Russia unless using a hands-free device.

Internet cafés are now found in cities and larger towns and most major hotels provide fax and computer/Internet services.

CALLS WITHIN RUSSIA

One can direct dial most cities in Russia from a hotel, home or office phone. From your hotel phone, first dial 8 and wait for a second dial tone. Now dial the city code and then the phone number. As of 2006, many of the region's area codes were changed; see page 354 for a complete listing. If you do not know the area code, ask your hotel service desk to find out for you, or dial 07 for an intercity operator. You can also place calls from main telephone centers or special telephone street booths, called *Mezhdugorodny* (as opposed to the *Mezhdunarodny* mentioned on page 78). Unless marked as such, regular pay phones cannot make city to city calls. Most of these phone booths now use plastic phone tokens or cards, which are sold in stores, kiosks and Metro stations around the city (same card as for local calls).

LOCAL CALLS

It once cost only two kopeks to make a local call, but now the thousands of telephone booths located about the cities are operated by pre-paid phone cards which can be purchased at hotels, shops or street kiosks. These cards can be used for international, inter-city, and local calls—but you have to call from the correct phone booth. To work the phones in some of the older booths, first lift the receiver and make sure there is a dial tone. To display English press the button above the green one, then follow the instructions on how to insert the card. Dial the number and as soon as the party answers press the right-hand button that displays the speaker symbol, otherwise the call may not go through.

Do not lose your telephone numbers! Russia has still not compiled a telephone directory with resident phone numbers and addresses. For directory assistance, dial 09; you may need the person's full name, including patronymic and address. For information in other cities, dial 07. A number of business directories are now available. Two excellent editions in English and Russian are: *The Traveller's Yellow*

Pages for Moscow and *The Traveller's Yellow Pages for St Petersburg.* (To order a copy in the US, see Recommended Reading section, page 697.)

POST AND MAIL

Russia's main post office centers take care of postal service, telegrams, and phone calls. Outbound mail to the US and Europe takes about three weeks. Inbound mail can take longer. You can buy postage stamps at most hotels which also provide mail boxes; some even have their own post offices. To send an international or local package, you may have to first show the contents for inspection. It is then wrapped for you. There are now several express mail services, such as Federal Express and DHL. (See Practical Information sections for locations. See pages 354, 628) If staying over a longer period of time, letters can be addressed directly to your hotel or other address, or to a poste restante at a post office which holds mail for up to two months. Never send anything of importance. Notice that addresses are written backwards in Russian with country and zip code first and name last.

The address for the main post office (*glavpochtamt*) in Moscow is: 103009, Moscow, 26/2 Myasnitskaya Ulitsa, Poste Restante (in Russian *Pochta do Vostrebovaniya*), your name. (Open daily 8am–7.45pm.) The St Petersburg main post office is: 19044, St Petersburg, 9 Pochtamskaya Ulitsa, Poste Restante (*Pochta do Vostrebovaniya*), your name. (Open 9am–7.30pm Monday–Saturday; 10am–5.30pm Sundays.) These Moscow companies offer more reliable incoming mail services: PXPost, tel. 956-2230; www.pxpost.com, or IPS Independent Postal Service, tel. 250-4272 or 251-7487.

American Express card holders can have their mail (letters only) sent to them c/o the American Express office in Moscow and St Petersburg. It takes about four days, via Helsinki, to arrive from the US. (For locations, see Facts for the Traveler/ Traveler's Checks and Credit Cards, page 65.)

MEDIA

The best places to find newspapers and magazines in English are at news shops in major hotels. Some street kiosks and stores also carry foreign literature. Pick up a free copy of the *Moscow Times* in English, distributed through many restaurants, stores and hotels. Listings in the Friday and Saturday sections, especially, give up-to-date information on concerts, theaters, nightclubs, films, art events, etc. This newspaper is also distributed in St Petersburg. The *St Petersburg Times* is also a good newspaper to check.

There are now numerous national and cable TV channels in Moscow and St Petersburg (with satellite TV, up to 100 channels). Russia's three dominant TV stations are RTR, ORT and NTV. Compared to Soviet TV (consumed by boring propaganda news and war musicals), contemporary TV is filled with everything from talk and game shows to New Age healers and soap operas. Many foreign films are broadcast in their original languages or shown with subtitles. To get an idea of how the culture is changing, try watching some TV during your stay. (Most large hotels also subscribe to foreign cable networks, such as CNN, BBC and MTV.) The video format in Russia is SECAM, which is not compatible to NTSC.

A few Russian radio stations broadcast in English, along with airing Voice of America and BBC World Service. Some good FM music stations, such as Moscow's Europa Plus, Ekho Moscovy or Radio Rox, broadcast daily.

Many Russian Internet sites now have English language sections, including gazeta.ru, lenta.ru and moscowtimes.ru.

ADDRESSES
No other place in the world has harder addresses to locate than in Russia. If you are presented with the following address, for example, this is how to decipher it: Tverskaya Ul Dom 33, Korpus 2, Etazh 3, Kvartira 109, (Kode 899). Firstly, street numbers are poorly marked. Once you have found 33 Tverskaya Ulitsa (Street), there may be several different buildings using this one address, which are separated by their *korpus* or block numbers. (One often enters the buildings from the back.) Once you locate Block 2, look for a list of apartment numbers usually indicated on the outside of each building. Make sure your *kvartira* or apartment number is listed; if not, it may be located in a different block. When you enter the security code of 899, the door should open. (If it does not work, a *dezhurnaya* or attendant may live on the ground floor, or wait for someone to enter or exit, or just shout!) Once you are inside, proceed up to the third floor or *etazh* and look for apartment 109. (109 does not mean it is on the first floor!) The passage to the apartment may be blocked by yet another door that secures the hallway. Look for the appropriate apartment number by this door and ring the buzzer. If there is no answer the buzzer may be broken, so try ringing some of the others so someone else can let you in. Most Russians also have a double door leading into the apartment; and if you knock they will not hear, so ring the bell. Ideally you should make sure somebody knows you are coming so they can look out for you.

Additionally, many apartment block elevators are old and run down and may not be operating; be prepared to walk up. (On a humorous note: during Soviet times, the primo apartment was considered to be on the first floor and not the penthouse. On the first floor, a tenant was assured of getting hot water and not having to rely on the elevator!) One last point concerning addresses: 3-ya 55 Liniya means 55 Third Liniya Street, for example; this also means that there is a First and Second Liniya Street indicated by 1-ya and 2-ya.

ETIQUETTE

Often Russians appear very restrained, formal or downright glum. But there is a dichotomy between their public (where for so many generations they dared not show their true feelings) and private appearances. In informal and private situations or after friendship has been established, the Russian character is charged with emotional warmth, care and humor. They are intensely loyal and willing to help. Arriving in or leaving the country merits great displays of affection, usually with flowers, bear hugs, kisses and even tears of sorrow or joy. If invited to someone's home for dinner, expect elaborate preparations. Russians are some of the most hospitable people in the world. If you do not like drinking too much alcohol, watch out for the endless round of toasts!

The formal use of the patronymic (where the father's first name becomes the child's middle name) has been used for centuries. For example, if Ivan names his son Alexander, he is known as Alexander Ivanovich. His daughter Ludmilla's patronymic becomes Ivanovna. Especially in formal or business dealings, try to remember the person's patronymic (although the formal patronymic is used less by the younger generation these days). As in the West, where Robert is shortened to Bob, for example, Russian first names are also shortened once a friendship is established. Call your friend Alexander 'Sasha', Mikhail 'Misha', Ekaterina 'Katya', Tatyana 'Tanya' and Mariya 'Masha', or even use the diminutive form 'Mashenka'.

CUSTOMS AND SUPERSTITIONS

Here are some customs and superstitions that may be useful to remember if you are visiting a Russian home:

- Never shake hands over a threshold, it can lead to an argument or misunderstanding.
- Never whistle indoors, it will blow your money away.
- Never light a cigarette from a candle, it brings bad luck.
- Bring only an odd number of flowers, even numbers are for funerals.
- If invited to a Russian home, always try to bring a small gift such as food or drink.
- While in a Russian home, expect to remove your shoes and wear the traditional *tap'pechki* (slippers).
- Do not overly admire a household item, often it will be gifted to you upon departure.
- Before departing it is expected to do one last sit down with friends or associates, it is a good luck gesture for your return.

COMPLAINTS

Even today rules, regulations and bureaucracy still play a role in Russian life, with many uniformed people enforcing them. People here are not always presumed innocent until proven guilty. When dealing with police or other officials, it is best to be courteous while explaining a situation. For example, police in the streets can randomly pull over vehicles to spot-check the car and registration. If you are pulled over, it does not mean you have done anything wrong. If you are kept waiting, as in restaurants, remember everyone else is waiting too. Be patient and remember that you are in a foreign country. Polite humor can often work well. Do not lose your temper, mock or laugh when inappropriate. Should you be arrested, you have the right to immediately contact your embassy or consulate.

A few commonly used words are *nyet* and *nelzya*, which mean 'no' and 'it's forbidden'. The Russian language uses many negations. If people tell you something is forbidden, it may mean that they simply do not know or do not want to take responsibility. Ask elsewhere.

WOMEN AND MINORITIES

There have been reports of some Russian groups, such as skinheads, targeting Asian and African students living in Moscow. These student groups are mainly from Vietnam, Laos or the African continent. An attack on a foreign tourist is very rare. If of Asian or African origin, or a woman, use proper conduct and common sense as you would to ensure your safety in any big city. Do not walk late at night (especially alone) in unfamiliar neighborhoods or get into cars or taxis you are unsure about. (Carry a whistle, flashlight, penknife.) During the day, you may be hassled by the usual array of souvenir-sellers or street urchins pretending to sell something. Secure all valuables, and keep pockets empty. Do not leave purses or backpacks open, or carry money or cameras in obvious view. If nothing is visible, and you are not wearing expensive-looking clothing, then you are unlikely to be targeted. Women should avoid being alone and dressing provocatively, otherwise they might be mistaken for a prostitute.

In the evenings, the only real threat are the numerous intoxicated locals who may try to pick you up or get your attention in a hotel, restaurant, nightclub, or on the street. Even though a nuisance, they can barely focus let alone cause any harm. If they are in a larger group, do not provoke anybody; politely get out of the area. A Russian escort, now drunk, may insist on seeing you home. If uncomfortable with any situation, just say *NYET*! (See Crime, Safety and Hazards on page 68.)

GAYS AND LESBIANS

One of the last revolutionary fronts formed was the Gay Rights Association. In the early 1990s, Article 121 of the penal code was finally repealed. Under this code any type of homosexual conduct, even among consenting adults, was punishable by up to five years in prison or a stay in an asylum. The Russian slang for homosexual is *goloboy* (blue boy) and lesbian, *lesbianka*. Even though gay rights have made enormous strides, there is still prejudice, especially among male heterosexuals who have been known to be aggressive. However, many prominent figures, especially in the art world, are now having the courage to come out and take a stand for homosexual rights. Gay clubs (that include transvestites) have opened in both cities, along with organized special 'gay nights' throughout the year. (See Practical Information sections.)

VISITORS WITH DISABILITIES

Sadly, Russia has never paid special attention to its disabled. (It is rare to see a handicapped person or, for that matter, anyone using a wheelchair or crutches.) It is nearly impossible to use public transportation, and there are no street access elevators to get down to a Metro station. Street curbs are not built for wheelchairs. It is really only the new international hotels who offer any assistance for disabled people.

WEIGHTS AND MEASURES

Russia operates on the metric system for weights and measures. For some useful conversion tables, see page 705.

MAJOR HOLIDAYS

New Year's Day: January 1st

Russian Orthodox Christmas: January 7th (The Orthodox Church still goes by the old calendar, which differs from the Gregorian by 13 days.)

Day of the Defender's of the Fatherland (Army Day): February 23rd (Voted as a holiday by Russian lawmakers in 2002.)

International Women's Day: March 8th (Established after the Second International Conference of Socialist Women in Copenhagen in 1910)

Orthodox Easter (*Pas'kha*): Falls in April or May

Labor Day/May Day: May 1st, 2nd (Even though no longer celebrated as International Workers' Solidarity Day, it still retains a festive nature with parades on Moscow's Red Square and St Petersburg's Palace Square. Much of the country shuts down for the first two weeks in May.)

Victory Day: May 9th (Parades are held at war memorials, such as the Piskarov-skoye Cemetery in St Petersburg, to celebrate VE Day, the end of WWII in Europe.)

Russian Independence Day: June 12th

Day of National Accord and Reconciliation (formerly known as the Day of the Great October Revolution): November 7th

Constitution Day: December 12th

Even before Boris Yeltsin took power, Russia celebrated 31 official holidays (*prazd'niki*) and festivals, today there are over 70—about one every five days!

January 27th is the anniversary of the complete liberation of Leningrad in 1944.

The second week in March is **Maslenitsa** or Blini Day. This stems from an old Pagan tradition of making blini pancakes (representing the sun) to honor the coming of spring. The **Moscow Stars Musical Festival** is May 5th-13th. **St Petersburg Day** is celebrated on May 27th.

During the summer months, some of the other celebratory holidays include: **Radio Day**, May 7th (to celebrate Alexander Popov, inventor of wireless telegraphy and, as Russians regard, also the co-inventor of Radio along with Marconi); **International Day for the Protection of Children**, June 1st; **World Environmental Protection Day**, June 5th; **Pushkin's Birthday**, June 6th; **Memory & Sorrow's Day**, June 22nd; **St Petersburg White Nights Festival**, June 21st–July11th; **Day of Youth**, June 27th; **International Day of Small Business**, July 1st; **Police (GAI) Day**, July 3rd; **Day of Russia's Military Glory**, July 10th (in commemoration of the Poltava battle in 1709); **Day of Russian Mail**, second Sunday in July; **Navy Day**, last Sunday in July (in St Petersburg the fleet usually parades along the Neva River); **Day of Railway Troops**, August 6th; **Day of Russia's First Sea Victory** (by Peter the Great over the Swedes), August 9th; **Air Force Day**, August 15th; **Russian Flag Day**, August 22nd; **Russian Cinema Day**, August 27th; **Miner's Day**, August 29th.

In addition, the **Seige of Leningrad Day** (special ceremonies in St Petersburg mark the end of the 900-day seige during WWII) falls on September 8th, and **Moscow Day** on September 19th.

Mother's Day is on November 30th, and the **Russian Winter Festival** is celebrated from December 25th to January 5th, with special events held throughout Moscow, St Petersburg and Golden Ring towns.

Name Days: Many calendar dates have a corresponding name day. Russians love to celebrate their own name day.

Moscow and St Petersburg have many other art, music, and sports festivals during the year. Every odd year in summer, Moscow hosts the **Moscow International Film Festival**. Every August, the **Moscow International Marathon** is run through the city.

For Church Holidays and Festivals, see page 682.

RED SHIRTS AND BLACK BREAD

We plunged into plebeian Moscow, the world of red-shirted workmen and cheap frocked women; low vodka shops and bare, roomy traktirs, where the red-shirted workmen assemble each evening to gossip and swallow astonishing quantities of tea, inferior in quality and very, very weak.

Here was Moscow's social and material contrast to the big houses, with sleeping Dvroniks, and of the silent street of painted house fronts, curtained balconies and all the rest. Though day had not yet dawned for other sections of Moscow, it had long since dawned for the inhabitants of this. Employers of labor in Moscow know nothing of the vexed questions as to eight-hour laws, ten-hour laws, or even laws of twelve. Thousands of red shirts, issuing from the crowded hovels of this quarter, like rats from their hiding places, had scattered over the city long before our arrival on the scene; other thousands were still issuing forth, and streaming along the badly cobbled streets. Under their arms, or in tin pails, were loaves of black rye bread, their food for the day, which would be supplemented at meal times by a salted cucumber, or a slice of melon, from the nearest grocery.

Though Moscow can boast of its electric light as well as gas, it is yet a city of petroleum. Coal is dear, and, in the matter of electric lights and similar innovations from the wide-awake Western world, Moscow is, as ever, doggedly conservative. So repugnant, indeed, to this stronghold of ancient and honourable Muscovite sluggishness, is the necessity of keeping abreast with the spirit of modern improvement, that the houses are not yet even numbered. There are no numbers to the houses in Moscow; only the streets are officially known by name. To find anybody's address, you must repair to the street, and inquire of the policeman or drosky driver, who are the most likely persons to know, for the house belonging to Mr. So-and-so, or in which that gentleman lives. It seems odd that in a country where the authorities deem it necessary to know where to put their hand on any person at a moment's notice, the second city of the empire should be, in 1980, without numbers to its houses.

Thomas Stevens, Through Russia on a Mustang, 1891

FOOD

Russian cooking is both tasty and filling. In addition to the expected borsch and beef stroganov, it includes many delectable regional dishes from the other Commonwealth states, such as Uzbekistan, Georgia or the Ukraine.

The traditions of Russian cooking date back to the simple recipes of the peasantry, who filled their hungry stomachs with the abundant supply of potatoes, cabbages, cucumbers, onions and bread. For the cold northern winters, they would pickle the few available vegetables and preserve fruits to make jam. This rather bland diet was pepped up with sour cream, parsley, dill and other dried herbs. In an old Russian saying, peasants described their diet as *Shchi da kasha, Pishcha nasha* (cabbage soup and porridge are our food). The writer Nikolai Gogol gave this description of the Russian peasant's kitchen: 'In the room was the old familiar friend found in every kitchen, namely a samovar and a three-cornered cupboard with cups and teapots, painted eggs hanging on red and blue ribbons in front of the icons, with flat cakes, horseradish and sour cream on the table along with bunches of dried fragrant herbs and a jug of *kvas* [a dark beer made from fermented black bread].'

Russians remain proud of these basic foods, which are still their staples today. They will boast that there is no better *khleb* (bread) in the world than a freshly baked loaf of Russian black bread.

In 2006, the Russian samovar celebrated its 260th birthday. Stemming from *sam* (self) and *varit* (to boil), the samovar came to represent the warmth of the Russian soul and was even given a place of honor in the household. Samovars were made mainly from copper, silver, platinum and porcelain, and decorated in the style of the times. One made from gold (fashioned as a rooster) won a grand-design prize at the Vienna's World Fair in 1873. Samovars were used to boil up water for the favorite national pastime—drinking a cup of *chai* or hot tea. It was popular to sip tea through a cube of sugar held between the teeth (known as *vpriskusku*) rather than mixing the sugar directly into the tea (*vnakladku*). As Alexander Pushkin wrote, 'Ecstasy is a glass full of tea and a piece of sugar in the mouth.' It was customary, in the 1700s, to pour the hot tea directly into the saucer, from which cooler mouthfuls could be taken. By the 1800s, Russians enjoyed sipping their steaming tea from a tall glass placed in a *podstakan'nik* (metal holder).

The introduction of tea to Russia is said to have been in 1638, when Czar Mikhail Romanov was gifted a foreign herb from the Mongolian Altun Khan. He tried to chew the bitter herb and the Khan's emissary finally had to instruct the court how to brew the tea in hot water. The tea drinking habit caught on and by the turn of the 20th century, Russia's tea consumption ranked second in the world. A recent survey discovered that half of the Russian population enjoy at least five cups of tea a day (prefering *chyorni* or black tea) and 82 percent still prefer loose tea to tea bags. Many artists painted scenes of samovars and tea drinking, such as Boris Kustodiev's *Kupchikha* (Merchant's Wife) *Drinking Tea* (1916) and *Moscow Traktir* (1916), and Kuzma Petrov-Vodkin's *By the Samovar* (1926).

The potato has long been a staple food of most Russian families. Legend has it that Peter the Great brought back the potato (*kartosh'ka*) from Holland and ordered it planted throughout Russia; it was called 'ground apple'. During these times, so many changes were being implemented upon the peasantry that many, particularly Old Believers, refused to eat what they considered the 'devil's apple'. But, by 1840, after the government decreed that peasants had to plant the potato on all common lands, this 'second bread' soon became the staple food for most of the poorer population. During the lean times of revolution and war, potatoes fed entire armies. Since soldiers did not have time to cut and clean them, they would first boil the potato whole and then eat them with the skin. To this day, unpeeled cooked potatoes (with grated cheese, mayonnaise, or minced garlic added) are known as 'Potatoes in Uniform'. Raisa Gorbachev once presented Nancy Reagan with a cookbook containing hundreds of potato recipes.

Russians love to hang out in their kitchens where they drink chai *(tea) and snack on freshly baked* khleb *(bread).*

Peter the Great also introduced French cooking to his empire in the 18th century. While the peasantry had access only to the land's crops, the nobility hired its own French chefs, who introduced eating as an art form, often preparing up to ten elaborate courses of delicacies. Eventually, Russian writers ridiculed the monotonous and gluttonous life of the aristocrats, many of whom planned their days around meals. In his novel *Oblomov*, Ivan Goncharov coined the term 'Oblomovism' to characterize the sluggish and decadent life of the Russian gentry. In *Dead Souls*, Nikolai Gogol described a typical meal enjoyed by his main character in the home of an aristocrat:

> On the table there appeared a white sturgeon, ordinary sturgeon, salmon, pressed caviar, fresh caviar, herrings, smoked tongues and dried sturgeon. Then there was a baked 300-pound sturgeon, a pie stuffed with mushrooms, fried pastries, dumplings cooked in melted butter, and fruit stewed in honey... After drinking glasses of vodka of a dark olive color, the guests had dessert... After the champagne, they uncorked some bottles of cognac, which put still more spirit into them and made the whole party merrier than ever!

As an old Russian saying goes: 'There cannot be too much vodka; there can only be not enough vodka!' Vodka has always been the indispensable drink of any class on any occasion. Whether rich or poor, no Russian is abstemious. Anton Chekhov wrote of a group of peasants who, 'on the Feast of the Intercession, seized the chance to drink for three days. They drank their way through fifty rubles of communal funds...one peasant beat his wife and then continued to drink the cap off his head and boots off his feet!' The writer also added: even though 'vodka is colorless...it paints your nose red, and blackens your reputation!'

The year 1998 marked the 600th anniversary of vodka. Genoese monks are credited as the first to come up with the distillation process. They were said to have begun shipping distilled grain spirits (then called *aqua vitae* or water of life) to Lithuania in 1398. Soon after, Russia embraced this new spirit with gusto. The word vodka stems from *voda*, meaning water; *vodka*, means dear or little water. Rye was the favored distilling ingredient, followed by barley, wheat or potatoes. Ivan the Terrible built the first *kabak* (tavern) for his palace guard in Moscow near the Kremlin, on the Balchug (where the five-star Hotel Baltschug stands today). Czar Alexis (Peter the Great's father) allowed the building of one *kabak* in every town (but three in Moscow), and instituted the famous Law Code of 1649 which decreed that all revenues from vodka sales went directly into royal coffers; this state monopoly lasted over 300 years. Only home brewing, or the making of *samogon*, was permitted without government control. Even today, 100 percent proof amateur spirits are still known as *speert* or *samogon*.

Between national consumption and international sales, the income from vodka was enormous. By the late 1800s, nearly 40 percent of all state revenue came from liquor sales alone, and a typical Russian family spent up to 15 percent of its annual income on alcohol. In 1865, it was the famous scientist, Dmitri Mendeleyev (the inventor of the Periodic Tables) who first recommended from his own studies that the human body could best assimilate alcohol in the proportion of 40 percent spirit. It was during this time that a new reform removed the State's monopoly on vodka supplies. Over the next three decades (before the government again took control), Pyotr Smirnov took advantage of the drinking craze and was able to strike it rich with his enterprising new brand of *Smirnov* vodka. By the end of the 19th century there were already over 100 different flavored vodkas sold in Russia. During World War II, Russian soldiers even received a daily commissar's ration of *narko-movskiye sto gram*—an allotted 100 grams (three-and-a-half ounces). Distilling factories had opened everywhere by the 20th century; the most famous was the Moscow State Warehouse No. 1. Built in 1900 on the banks of the Yauza River over three artesian wells, the factory now produces the *Yuri Dolgoruky* brand and the elite label of *Kristall* vodka—a vodka double-distilled in a process that takes five times longer than ordinary vodka.

A typical Russian breakfast or *zavtrak*, consists of tea, coffee, eggs, *kasha* (hot cereal), cheese, cold meats or sausage and a plentiful supply of bread and butter. Most hotels now offer either a Russian or Continental-style breakfast. A Russian *obyed* (lunch) consists of soup, bread, salad and usually a choice of meat, chicken or fish with potatoes, a pickled vegetable and a sweet dessert of cakes or *morozhnoye* (ice cream). Over 170 tons of ice cream are consumed in Moscow and St Petersburg each day. Salads or vegetables include cucumbers, tomatoes, cabbage, beets, potatoes and onions (a Russian 'salad' often does not contain lettuce). *Smetana* (sour cream) is a popular condiment—Russians like it on everything— some even drink a glass for breakfast. *Oozhiin* (dinner) is similar to lunch, except vodka, wine, champagne or cognac will usually be served.

Gone are the days when a tourist spent hours searching for something to eat, waited in long lines, or bribed a way into a State-run restaurant. The good news is that both Moscow and St Petersburg are teeming with restaurants, cafés, fast-food centers and food markets. The service has improved so much that it is practically unrecognizable from the old Soviet mediocrity and inefficiency. But, as a sign of the times, prices have also risen. Russians joke that under socialism they had money and there was nothing to buy; but now with democracy, they have practically everything at their disposal, but no money to buy it with. First-class restaurants charge the same as they would in New York, Paris or Tokyo. In one private club, I watched as a large table, filled with Russian *biznissmeny*, charged up $5,000 in appetizers alone! (Beware of menus that have no prices.) But there are restaurants to suit every budget, and to locate a place to dine check the listings in the Practical Information sections for each city. There are also plenty of restaurant guides available in the city, or just have a local recommend one of their favorite spots. Take a stroll and see what you can find; practically every corner now offers something edible, and there are also plenty of food markets that offer all sorts of groceries at reasonable prices.

Hundreds of eating establishments operate throughout both cities—from typical old-style Russian fare to ethnic cuisines from Georgian, Chinese, Japanese and Italian to fast-food and take-out, for any price and palate. (By the way, *bistro* originates from the Russian word *biistra*, meaning fast. During the 1815 Russian occupation of Paris, cossack soldiers were known to scream out '*biistra, biistra!*' to restaurant waiters; soon the bistro opened—a place where one could get served quickly.) Most establishments in larger cities accept credit cards. Tipping is 10–15 percent (check to make sure a service charge has not already been added to your bill). Most menus are printed in both Russian and English; if you cannot read it, the waiter can usually translate it for you. For more popular places, making a reservation is advisable.

DINING AND DRINKING

The first point to remember when dining out is that most Russians still consider eating out an expensive luxury and enjoy turning dinner into a leisurely, evening-long experience. Many restaurants provide entertainment, so do not expect a fast meal. (Russians can spend a few hours savoring appetizers—if your waiter is not prompt with bringing your entrée, this may only be for a cultural reason.) It is also customary for the waiter to take your entire order, from soup to dessert, at the beginning. Different parties are often seated together at the same table, an excellent way to meet locals and other visitors.

Most restaurants (in Cyrillic **Ресторан**, pronounced 'restoran') are open daily from 11am to 11pm, and close for a few hours in the mid-afternoon. Nightclubs and casinos can stay open all night and also be expensive. For fast foods other than pizza, burgers or hot dogs, be on the look out for specialty cafés, such as *shashliki* (shish kebabs), *blinnaya* (pancakes), *pelmennaya* (dumplings), *pirozhkovaya* (meat and vegetable pastries) and *morozhnoye* (ice cream and sweets). Try to drink only bottled water and beware of iced drinks, homemade fruit juices and *kompot*, fruit in sugared water, which are often made with the local water.

If invited to a Russian home, expect a large welcome. Russians love hospitality, which means preparing a large spread. If you can, take along a bottle of champagne or vodka. Remember, a Russian toast is followed by another toast and so on. This usually entails knocking back your entire shot of vodka each time! Since toasts can continue throughout the evening (and if you want to be able to stand up in the morning), you may want to consider diluting the vodka with juice or water, or just giving up—to the chagrin of your host. Some popular toasts are: *Za Mir I Druzhbu* (To Peace and Friendship), *Do Dnya* (Bottoms Up) and, the most popular, *Na Zdoroviye* (To Your Health). Gorky, in a memoir about his boyhood on the Volga, wrote, "people drank for joy and they drank for sorrow; the Russian soul is versatile."

ON THE MENU

(See pages 690–695 for a useful selection of Russian food and drinks vocabulary.) The Russian menu is divided into four sections: *zakuski* (appetizers), *pervoye* (first course), *vtoroye* (second course) and *sladkoe* (dessert). The order is usually taken all together, from appetizer to dessert. *Zakuski* are Russian-style hors d'oeuvres that include fish, cold meats, salads and marinated vegetables.

Ikra is caviar: *krasnaya* (red from salmon) and *chornaya* (black from sturgeon). The sturgeon is one of the oldest fish species known, dating back over 30 million years. Its lifespan is also one of the longest. No sturgeon is worth catching until it is at least seven years old and *beluga* are not considered adult until after 20 years. The best caviar is *zernistaya*, the fresh unpressed variety. The largest roe comes from the *beluga*, a dark gray caviar appreciated for its large grain and fineness of skin, and the most expensive. Caviar from the *sevruga* is the smallest and has the most delicate taste.

Caviar is usually available at Russian restaurants and can be bought in city stores. It has long been considered a health food in Russia. Czar Nicholas II made his children eat the pressed *payushnaya* caviar every morning. Since they all hated the salty taste, their cook solved the problem by spreading it on black bread and adding banana slices. The caviar-banana sandwich became the breakfast rage for many aristocratic families. Russia is still the largest producer of caviar in the world, processing over 1,000 tons per year; 20 percent of the catch is exported.

Many varieties of Russian soup are served, more often at lunch than dinner. *Borsch* is the traditional red beet soup made with beef and served with a spoonful of sour cream. *Solyanka* is a tomato-based soup with chunks of fish or meat and topped with diced olives and lemon. *Shchi* is a tasty cabbage soup. A soup made from pickled vegetables is *rasolnik*. *Okroshka* is a cold soup made from a *kvas* (weak beer) base.

Russian meals consist of *mya'so* (meat), *kur'iitsa* (chicken) or *rii'ba* (fish). *Bifshtek* is a small fried steak with onions and potatoes. Beef stroganov is cooked in sour cream and served with fried potatoes. *Kutlyeta po Kiyevski* is Chicken Kiev, stuffed with melted butter; *Kutlyeta po Pajarski* is a chicken cutlet; *Tabak* is a slightly seasoned fried or grilled chicken. The fish served is usually *lososina* (salmon), *osetrina* (sturgeon), *shchuka* (pike) or *seld* (herring). Russians are not big vegetable eaters, but *kapus'ta* (cabbage), *kartosh'ka* (potatoes) and *gribii's smyetan'oi* (mushrooms and sour cream) are always available. Georgian dishes include *khachapuri* (hot bread), *baklazhan* (eggplant), *chakhokhbili* (steamed dumplings) and *tolma* (meat and rice in vine leaves). Desserts include *vareniki* (sweet fruit dumplings topped with sugar), *tort* (cake), *pon'chiki* (sugared donuts) and *morozhnoye* (ice cream).

Chai (tea) comes with every meal. It is always sweet; ask for *biz sak'hera*, for unsweetened tea. Many Russians stir in a spoonful of jam instead of sugar. Coffee is not served as often. Alcoholic drinks consist of *pivo* (beer), *kvas* (weak beer), *shampanskoye* (champagne), *vino* (wine) and vodka. *Kvas* was the second favorite drink of Russia for centuries. Brewed mainly from rye, it is then spiced with everything from berries to horseradish. *Kvas* trucks used to be found all around the streets selling glasses of the warm fermenting drink for mere kopeks, but nowadays soft drinks seem to be overtaking tradition. Alcoholic drinks are ordered in grams; a small glass is 100 grams and a normal bottle consists of 750 grams or three quarters of a liter. The best wine comes from Georgia and the Crimea. There are both *krasnoye* (red) and *beloye* (white) wines. The champagne is generally sweet. The best brandy comes from Armenia—*Armyanski konyak*. *Nalivka* is a fruit liqueur. Vodka is by far the favorite drink and comes in a number of varieties other than Stolichnaya, Moskovskaya or Russkaya. These include *limonnaya* (lemon vodka), *persovka* (with hot peppers), *zubrovka* (infused with cinnamon, lemon and bison grass), *ryabinovka* (made from ash berries), *tminaya* (caraway flavor), *starka* (apple and pear-leaf), *Okhotnichaya* (Hunter's vodka flavored with port, ginger, pepper, cloves, coffee, juniper berries, star anise, orange and lemon peel, and roots of angelica—it was once customary for hunters to toast with it after returning from a kill), and *zveroboy* (animal killer!). One of the strongest and most expensive is *Zolotoye Koltso*, the Golden Ring.

If you see a Russian smile at you, while flicking the middle finger off his thumb into the side of his neck, your invitation to drink (and drink) has arrived. Normally Russians follow a shot of cold pure vodka (it is, of course, sacrilegious to dilute it with any other liquid) with a mouthful of *zakuska* or hors d'oeuvres, such as smoked salmon, caviar, herring, salami or even a slice of hearty Russian *khleb*, bread. Remember, Russians love to follow toast with toast—*dushá v dúshu*—heart to heart (so make sure you eat something while you drink!). They are quite capable of drinking *do beloi goryachki*—into 'a white fever of delirium' and *na brovyakh*—up to their eyebrows. Their equivalent of 'drinking one under the table' is *napeetsya do polozheniya riz*—literally, drinking till one is positioned very low beneath the icon frame. Never forget that Russians have a millennium of drinking in their blood. In 986, Prince Vladimir rejected Islam as the Russian State religion (he chose Byzantine Christianity) because it prohibited the drinking of alcohol. He reputedly said, 'For the people of *Rus*, drinking is joy; we cannot be without it!' Today, Russians drink more spirits than any other nationality—the equivalent of one 80–proof shot a day for every citizen.)

One note of caution when buying liquor, especially vodka, in Russia. These days, many imitations are being passed off on the market, such as homemade *samogon* poured into brand-name vodka bottles. (If it is *samogon*, you will immediately know the difference!) Do not buy vodka from small kiosks or off the street. Check to make sure the seal is secure and the label not suspiciously attached (horizontal glue lines usually mean factory-produced). Many Russians can tell genuine vodka just by the way bubbles move around in the bottle. Recently the government ruled that bar codes needed to be stamped on all labels, but these are already being faked.

SHOPPING

Since the fall of the Soviet Union the country has yet to be transformed into a shopper's paradise, but it has come an amazingly long way from the previous offering of half-empty shops and State-run *Beriozka* stores. The market economy, especially in Moscow, is booming, and stores are full of both Russian and Western goods. Pre-perestroika, a traveler had to bring along essential supplies, but today almost anything can be found, from peanut butter to prescription drugs. Not only are there department stores, galleries and boutiques, but the streets are also lined with small shopping kiosks with salespeople hawking everything from T-shirts and videos to condoms and cologne. Specialty shops for antiques, arts and crafts, and other souvenirs also exist for any budget, and flea markets are especially fun for bargain hunters. Farmer's markets offer a wide selection of foods at cheaper than store prices.

Traditional and popular Russian souvenirs include the *matryoshka* (the painted set of nested dolls), *khokkhloma* (lacquerware), *dymkovo* (earthenware), *gzhel* (china ornaments), *platki* (shawls), *shapki* (fur hats), wood carvings, jewelry made from amber or malachite, linen, samovars, balalaikas, art books and *znachki* (small pins). Painted lacquer boxes vary in style and price according to which Golden Ring town they were made in. The craftsmen of Palekh, for example, use tempera paint to illustrate elongated figures distinguished by the colors red, black and gold. An authentic box takes up to three months to complete, with the smallest details painted using brushes made from squirrel or mink hair. Many fakes are pasted with colored decal scenes which are not painted—check to make sure you have an original before buying.

LOCAL STORES

Some of the store (*magazin*) designations are: *univermag* (large department store), *kommissioniye* (commission or second-hand store), *co-op* (cooperative), *rinok* (farmer's market) and *kiosks*. The opening hours of most local stores vary widely, but they usually have a one-hour afternoon break sometime between 1pm and 3pm, and are shut during holidays. Many of the larger department stores and food stores are open 12 hours a day and also on Sundays. Expect to pay in rubles for your purchases (make sure you carry some smaller notes—changing large bills can be a hassle), though some also accept credit cards.

SHOPPING TIPS

If you see something you would really like, buy it! Otherwise, the item will probably be gone by the time you return for it. Remember to take along an empty bag—in places such as farmer's markets, you are expected to provide your own. (Otherwise you will be emptying the strawberries into your own pocket!) Some provincial stores may still use the three-line purchasing system (along with the abacus). Firstly, locate the desired item and find out its price. Secondly, go to the *kassa* (cashier's booth) and pay. Thirdly, take the receipt back to the salesgirl, who then wraps and hands over your purchase. If you are buying a number of items, ask or gesture for the salesgirl to write the total amount down (if you are wrong—it is back to the *kassa* all over again!). At times you may still have to stand in a long line or force your way to the counter. If you have any questions, do not be afraid to ask; many Russians know some English and are happy to help. It is illegal to take any item made pre-1947 out of the country. Customs officers are especially on the look-out for antiques and icons, and will confiscate things at the airport (even caviar—there is a limit on the amount that can be taken out). When you buy a more expensive painting or work of art, check to see if you need an exit permit from the Ministry of Culture. The gallery owner or artist can often help with this. Always save receipts to show at customs. Beware of the many fakes, especially icons and lacquer boxes. For more information on shoping and markets, see the listings in the Practical Information sections of each city.

First appearing in Russia in the 1890s, matryoshka *dolls represented peasant girls.
Today they are still painted in traditional Russian dress with* sarafan *jumpers, embroidered
blouses and* kokoshniki *headdresses, and are one of Russia's most popular souvenirs.*

RUSSIAN LANGUAGE
HISTORY

In the late 9th century, two Greek brothers Methodius and Cyril (both renowned
scholars from Macedonia) converted vernacular Slavic into a written language so
that teachings of Byzantine Orthodoxy could be translated for the Slavs. Many
letters were derived from the Greek—the Slavic alphabet was called Cyrillic, after
Cyril. When Prince Vladimir brought Christian Orthodoxy into Kievan Rus in the
10th century, Slavonic became the language of the Church. Church Slavonic, written
in the Cyrillic alphabet, remained the literary and liturgical language of Russia for
over seven centuries.

In 1710, Peter the Great simplified Church Cyrillic into the 'civil alphabet'
(*grazhdansky shrift*), a written form used in secular books. The two types of writing,
the older script of the Church and Peter's revised version, were both employed in

The interior of GUM Department Store on Red Square. Built in 1893, it is Russia's largest store and has a large glass roof and ornate bridges that lead to over 200 shops on three levels.

Russia up to the time of Lomonosov and the poet Pushkin, who were largely responsible for combining the two into a national language for the Russian people. The alphabet that is used today was further simplified after the October Revolution.

LETTERS AND WORDS

Since Russian is not a Romance language, it is more difficult to pick up words compared to French or Spanish. Before leaving for your trip, try to spend some time learning some of the Cyrillic alphabet, in which there are 33 letters compared to the English 26. Most Russian sounds are similar to English, but are just expressed with a different character symbol. For example, a Russian C is pronounced 's', and W is a 'sh' sound. Thus Masha is spelled Mawa and Sasha spelled Cawa. Once you start to recognize letters of the Russian alphabet, it is easy to sound out familiar words posted on the street, such as **METPO** (Metro), **Кафе** (café) and **Ресторан** (restaurant). Besides, it is fun to walk down the street and decipher many of the signs and shop names, and you will feel much more at ease in the new environment.

Once you can recognize Cyrillic letters, work on Russian vocabulary and phrases. As with learning any new language, first try memorizing a few common words, such as 'hello', 'goodbye' and 'thank you', and to count from one to ten. Granted, even though Russian is not an easy language to learn (there are six cases of declensions compared with four in English—these are nominative, accusative, dative, genitive, instrumental and prepositional—and the nouns and adjectives are all declined differently based on their case in the sentence and their masculine, feminine or neuter forms), you will discover that its native speakers appreciate any effort made in using their language and are delighted to help out. Even a few gestures and simple Russian expressions can go a long way and bring smiles to many faces! Purchase an English-Russian dictionary and phrasebook that can be shown to Russian-speaking people when you meet. Before your trip, you may also try one of the numerous Russian language courses for beginners and listen to its audio lessons to get a feel for the pronunciation.

See the Russian Language section on page 684 for a more comprehensive selection of useful everyday vocabulary.

Москва.
Moscou,

Третьяковскій проѣздъ.
Tretiakowski proiesd

An early 1900's scene of central Moscow's Tretyakovsky Passage. In 1871, the wealthy merchant Sergei Tretyakov, who founded the Tretyakov Art Gallery, created a passage through an old part of the Kitai Gorod wall to gain quicker access to the banks along Okhotny Ryad. Today, the passage, known as Moscow's Fifth Avenue, is filled with many upscale shops.

MOSCOW

MOSCOW

Come to Moskva!!!
I am hopelessly in love with Moskva.
Whoever gets used to her
Will never leave her.
I will love Moskva forever.

Anton Chekhov

For centuries Moscow has been an inseparable part of the life of Russia. Moscow's history dates back to 1147, when Prince Yuri Dolgoruky established a small outpost on the banks of the Moskva River. The settlement grew into a large and prosperous town, which eventually became the capital of the principality of Moscovy. By the 15th century Moscow was Russia's political, cultural and trade center, and during the reign of Ivan the Great, it became the capital of the Russian Empire. Ivan summoned the greatest Russian and European architects to create a capital so wondrous that 'reality embodied fantasy on an unearthly scale', and soon the city was hailed as the 'New Constantinople'. In the next century Ivan the Terrible was crowned the first czar of all Russia in the magnificent Uspensky Sobor (Assumption Cathedral) inside the Kremlin. The words of an old Russian proverb suggest the power held by the Kremlin: 'There is only God and the center of government, the Kremlin.' People from all over the world flocked to witness the splendors in the capital of the largest empire on earth.

In 1712, after Peter the Great transferred the capital to St Petersburg, Moscow remained a symbol of national pride. Many eminent writers, scientists, artists and musicians, such as Pushkin, Tolstoy, Lomonosov, Repin and Tchaikovsky, lived and worked in Moscow, which never relinquished its political significance, artistic merit and nostalgic charm. Even when Napoleon invaded in 1812, he wrote: 'I had no real conception of the grandeur of the city. It possessed 50 palaces of equal beauty to the Palais d'Elysée furnished in French style with incredible luxuries.' After a terrible fire destroyed Moscow causing Napoleon's retreat, Tolstoy wrote that:

> *It would be difficult to explain what caused the Russians, after the departure of the French in October 1812, to throng to the place that had been known as Moscow; there was left no government, no churches, shrines, riches or houses—yet, it was still the same Moscow it had been in August. All was destroyed, except something intangible, yet powerful and indestructible... Within a year the population of Moscow exceeded what it had been in 1812!*

(opposite) St. Basil's Cathedral, Red Square, Moscow.

Moscow symbolized the soul of the empire, and Tolstoy later observed that Moscow remains eternal because 'Russians look at Moscow as if she is their own mother.' The name Moskva is said to derive from the Finnish words *maska ava*, meaning mother bear.

Moscow has also played an important role in the country's political movements: the revolutionary writers Herzen and Belinsky began their activities at Moscow University; student organizations supported many revolutionary ideas, from Chernyshevsky's to Marx's; and Moscow workers backed the Bolsheviks during the October Revolution of 1917 and went on to capture the Kremlin. In 1918, after more than two centuries, Moscow once again became Russia's capital. But this time, the city would govern the world's first socialist state—the Soviet Union. Trotsky, Lenin's main supporter, wrote:

> ...*finally all the opposition was overcome, the capital was transferred back to Moscow on March 12, 1918... Driving past Nicholas' palace on the wooden paving, I would occasionally glance over at the Emperor Bell and Emperor Cannon. All the barbarism of Moscow glared at me from the hole in the bell and the mouth of the cannon... The carillon in the Savior's Tower was now altered. Instead of playing 'God Save the Czar', the bells played the 'Internationale', slowly and deliberately, at every quarter hour.*

In 1993, Moscow Mayor Yuri Luzhkov readopted the historic figure of St George as the capital's official coat-of-arms; St George also features on the city's flag. You will notice the dark red shield emblem throughout the city: Georgy Pobedonosets— St George the Victorious, wearing a blue cloak and riding a silver horse, strikes a black dragon with his golden spear. (In 1380, Prince Dmitri Donskoi carried the icon of St George to victory over the invading Mongols, and in 1497, Ivan III had St George's image engraved on Moscow's great seal.) In 2007, Moscow celebrated its 860th anniversary and today is the largest city in the country with a population of 10.4 million.

Today, the new Moskva of the 21st century is not only the center of the Commonwealth, but also the capital of the Russian Federative State. And this capital city is the source of the country's industry, politics (the Kremlin remains the seat of government) and culture. With the formation of the Commonwealth of Independent States and the collapse of communist Russia, Moscow is now the hub of an enterprising new metropolis. (Even Alexander Solzhenitsyn, who had lived in exile in the United States for 20 years, returned to live in Moscow in 1994.) The last 15 years of democratic development has created a wealth of business opportunities for the city's entrepreneurs. The once non-existent advertising sector is now a billion-dollar-a-year industry. And Moscow Mayor, Yuri Luzhkov, proudly acknowledges that 'corporate advertising in Moscow is increasing nearly 50 per cent each year, a clear indication that foreign companies are flooding into the market.'

If you have not been in Moscow for ten years or more, and remember it as a dull and drab façade of crumbling communism with no fun or food, it is time to be truly astonished at the sight of well over 1,000 eating establishments—from Internet coffee cafés and fast-food franchises to the most elegant restaurants in old palaces and ritzy hip clubs. There are more casinos here than in Las Vegas. However, the opportunities and changes have created many new extremes, unheard of in old Soviet society, but long familiar to the West: from the unemployed to multi-millionaires, the homeless to real-estate moguls, poor borrowers to rich bankers, and destitute pensioners to enterprising youth. Moscow is still adjusting to a new reality that virtually occurred overnight. Even though the city has been compared to Chicago of the 1920s, rife with mafia and rampant corruption, a traveler is not likely to encounter any of this. Moscow remains as safe or safer for a visitor than most other world cities.

Luzhkov, at 67, was re-elected to a third term in 2003 with nearly 80 percent of the vote. (This term shall be his last; and the Mayor maintains that he will not run for President in 2008 when Putin steps down). No other man in the new era has reshaped Moscow like him, and Luzhkov clearly delights in being the *khozyain* or boss, presiding over the capital's rebirth. Over the past decade, the ambitious mayor's construction blitz has completely reshaped Moscow's cityscape. But critics argue that his power has become so absolute that there is virtually no control over the rapid growth. Over 500 historic buildings were torn down to give way for modern hotel, apartment and hi-rise office buildings. And many monuments were erected with no public decision-making. Luzhkov has been compared to the brash, dynamic and iron-willed Peter the Great—and Luzhkov allowed the 50-meter tall statue of this Czar, considered an eyesore, placed on an island in the Moscow River. But, the mayor declares that "everyone is praising the new Moscow phenomenon. Ancient Moskva is transforming into a vibrant modern metropolis and it's common knowledge that today's capital is the most dynamically developing region of the Russian Federation."

Today, Russia has over 30 billionaire citizens, and almost all of them work and live in and around Moscow. (Yuzhkov's wife, Yelena Baturina's construction empire is valued at $1.4 billion). Even though Moscow is now rated as one of the world's most expensive cities, tourists continue to flood in with more accommodation and travel choices than ever before; and the mayor asserts that there has never been a more exciting time to visit or do business in the nation's capital. (Note, in 2005 Moscow's area code changed from 095 to 495.) Whether a visitor has a few days or several weeks, there is plenty to do and see. Moscow has over 2500 monuments and historical sites, 50 theaters and concert halls, 70 museums and over 4,500 streets and passages, visited annually by over 16 million people from 150 countries. Moscow is also rich in history, art and architecture. One of the most memorable experiences of your trip to Russia will be to stand in Red Square and look out on the golden magnificence of the cathedrals and towers of the Kremlin and St Basil's Cathedral.

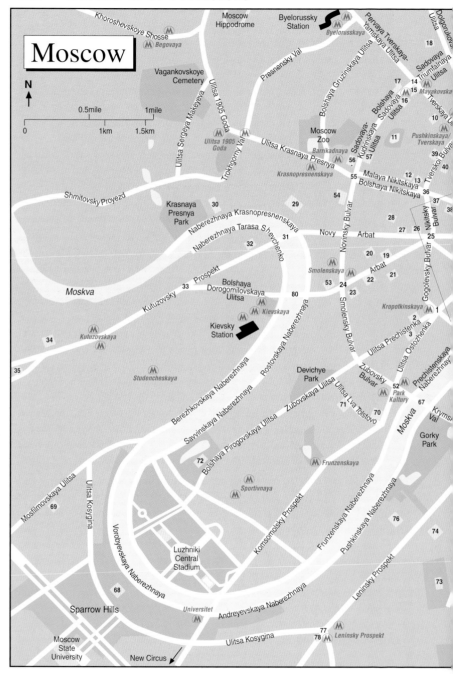

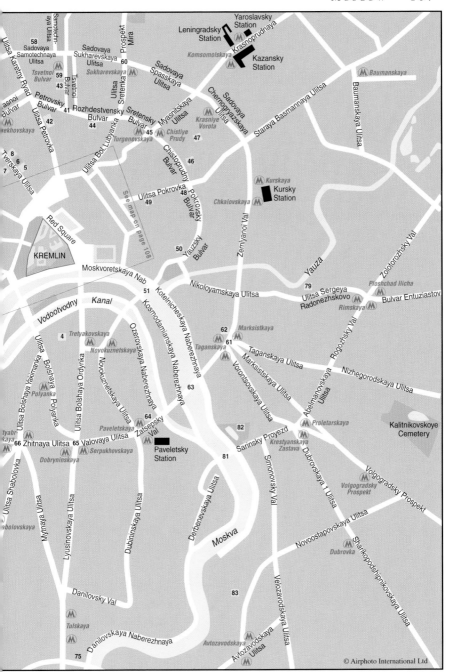

Key for Moscow Map:

1 Kropotkinskaya Ploshchad
2 Alexander Pushkin Museum
3 Leo Tolstoy Museum
4 Tretyakov Art Gallery
5 Aragvi Restaurant
6 Tverskaya Ploshchad
7 Moscow City Council
8 Yeliseyev's
9 Pushkin Square
10 Modern History of Russia Museum
11 Patriarch's Pond
12 Gorky House Museum
13 Alexei Tolstoy House Museum
14 Triumfalnaya Ploshchad
15 Tchaikovsky Concert Hall
16 Satire Theater
17 Pekin Hotel
18 Glinka Music Museum
19 Vakhtangov Theater
20 Skryabin Museum
21 Melnikov House
22 Pushkin House
23 Ministry of Foreign Affairs
24 Smolenskaya Ploshchad
25 Arbatskaya Ploshchad
26 Church of Simon Stylites
27 Dom Knigi
28 Lermontov Memorial House

29 The Former White House
30 Mezhdunarodnaya Hotel & Sovincenter
31 Novoarbatsky Most
32 Ukraina Hotel
33 Hero City of Moscow Obelisk
34 Battle of Borodino Panorama Museum
35 Triumphal Arch
36 Nikitskaya Ploshchad
37 Mayakovsky Theater
38 Tchaikovsky Conservatory Grand Hall
39 Pushkin Drama Theater
40 Gorky Theater
41 Trubnaya Ploshchad
42 Petrovsky Monastery
43 Old Circus Nikulin
44 Convent of the Nativity of the Virgin
45 Turgenevskaya Ploshchad
46 Eisenstein's House
47 Vasnetsov Memorial Apartment
48 Apraksin Mansion
49 Church of Saints Cosmas & Damian
50 Church of Saints Peter & Paul
51 Bolshoi Ustinsky Most
52 Krymskaya Ploshchad
53 Belgrad Hotel
54 US Embassy
55 Kudrinskaya Ploshchad
56 Planetarium

57 Chekhov House Museum
58 Obraztzov Puppet Theater
59 Tsentralny Rinok
60 Sukharevskaya Ploshchad
61 Taganskaya Ploshchad
62 Taganka Theater
63 Bolshoi Krasnokholmsky Most
64 Bakhrushin Theater Museum
65 Serpukhovskaya Ploshchad
66 Kaluzhskaya Ploshchad
67 Krymsky Most
68 Trinity Church
69 Mosfilm Studios
70 Church of St Nicholas at Khamovniki
71 Leo Tolstoy Country Estate Museum
72 Novodevichy Convent & Cemetery
73 Donskoi Monastery
74 Church of the Deposition of the Robe
75 Danilovsky Monastery
76 Academy of Sciences
77 Gagarinskaya Ploshchad
78 Yuri Gagarin Monument
79 Spaso-Andronikov Monastery
80 Borodinsky Most
81 Novospassky Most
82 Novospassky Monastery
83 Simonov Monastery
84 Church of the Intercession in Fili

Key to symbols and Russian terms:

Ⓜ = *Metro Station*
Ulitsa = Street

Bulvar = Boulevard
Ploshchad = Square

Pereulok = Lane
Proyezd = Passage

Most = Bridge
Naberezhnaya = Embankment

Other attractions include the Novodevichy Convent, which dates from 1514, and the Andronikov Monastery, which houses the Andrei Rublyov Museum of Old Russian Art, including the famed iconist's masterpieces. Moscow's galleries and museums, such as the Tretyakov Gallery and Pushkin Museum of Fine Art contain collections of Russian and foreign masters. There are also the fascinating side streets to explore, little changed since the time of Ivan the Terrible. The nighttime reflections of the Kremlin's ancient clock tower and golden onion domes on the Moskva River bring to mind the lyrics of one of Russia's most popular songs: 'Lazily the river like a silvery stream, ripples gently in the moonlight; and a song fades as in a dream, in the spell of this Moscow night.' Moscow has an eternal enchantment that can be felt in the early light of dawn, in the deepening twilight, on a warm summer's day or in the swirling snows of winter.

ARRIVAL

Most international travelers arrive at Sheremetyevo II International Airport (Sheremetyevo III Terminal is currently under construction, and the Domodedovo airport is in the southeast part of town). The route from Sheremetyevo II into the city center winds along the Leningradsky Highway (Leningradskoye Shosse), linking Moscow with St Petersburg. About 23 kilometers (14 miles) from the airport are large antitank obstacles, **The Memorial to the Heroes** who defended the city against the Nazi invasion in 1941; notice how close the Germans came to entering the city. The highway becomes Leningradsky Prospekt at a place that used to mark the outer border of the city. Here the street was lined with summer cottages. **The Church of All Saints** (1683) stands at the beginning of the prospekt at number 73A. Other sights along the route are Peter the Great's Moorish-Gothic-style **Petrovsky Palace**, built in 1775, and the 60,000-seat **Dynamo Sports Complex**. At number 33 is the **Palace of Newly-weds**, where marriage ceremonies are performed. As you approach the center of Moscow, the Byelorussky Railway Station is on your right. Trains run from here to destinations in Western and Eastern Europe. This station marks the beginning of one of Moscow's main thoroughfares, Tverskaya Ulitsa (Street). A road map of Moscow is made up of a series of rings. The Kremlin and Red Square lie at the center. Five concentric rings circle Red Square, each marking an old boundary of the city, showing its age like a cross-section of a tree. A sixth ring road is currently being built.

Centuries ago each ring was fortified by stone, wooden or earthen ramparts, which could only be entered through a special gate. The area around the Kremlin, once known as Kitai-Gorod, formed the original border of the city in the 15th and 16th centuries. Many of the streets and squares in this area carry their original names: Petrovskaya Vorota (Peter's Gate), Kitaisky Proyezd (Kitai Passage), Ulitsa Varvarka (St Barbara Street) and Valovaya Ulitsa (Rampart Street).

The second ring is known as Bulvarnoye Koltso (Boulevard Ring). The city's suburbs were placed beyond this ring in the 17th century. The Sadovoye Koltso (Garden Ring) is the third ring that runs for 16 kilometers (ten miles) around the city. This is also connected by the Koltso Metro line that stops at various points around the ring. The fourth ring, which stretches for 40 kilometers (25 miles) around the city, was known as the Kamer-Kollezhsky Rampart; it served as a customs boundary in the 18th and 19th centuries. The fifth ring is the Moscow Circular Road, marking the present boundary of Moscow. The area past this ring is known as the Green Belt, a protected forested area where many Muscovites have country and summer houses, known as dacha.

METRO

One of the quickest, easiest and cheapest ways of getting around Moscow is by Metro. It is also the most popular method of transportation—up to nine million people use the Metro daily, more than in New York or London. Construction began in 1931 under Stalin. Many Soviet and foreign architects and engineers spent four years building the deep stations, which served as bomb shelters during World War II. The cost was enormous. In 1934 alone, over 350 million rubles were spent on the metro (compared to 300 million rubles on consumer goods for the entire Soviet Union during the first Five Year Plan).

The first line was opened on May 15, 1935. Today, ten major lines and 170 stations connect all points of the city. The Metro, with almost 425 kilometers (264 miles) of track, operates daily from 5.30am to 1am; the trains are frequent, arriving every 60 to 90 seconds during rush hour. (In contrast, St Petersburg has 58 stations on four lines, and is open from 5.45am to midnight.)

Many of the older stations are beautifully decorated with mosaics, marble, stained glass, statues and chandeliers, and are kept immaculate. Some of the more interesting ones are: Okhotny Ryad, Teatralnaya, Kievskaya, Byelorusskaya, Novoslobodskaya, Mayakovskaya and Komsomolskaya; the latter two even won Grand Prix design awards at the New York International Expositions in 1938 and 1958, respectively. Ploshchad Revolutsii, which features 76 bronze statues of workers and revolutionaries, is even on the list of UNESCO's world heritage sites. In 2003 the world's deepest Metro station opened in Moscow—Park Pobedy. The escalators are 125 metres long and the station is 80 metres underground. It was decorated by Zurab Tseretelli with panels celebrtating Russia's victories over Napoleon and the Nazis. The Moscow **Metro Museum** is at 36 Khamovnichesky Val; above Sportivnaya Metro station (open Thursdays only 9am–4pm; tel. 222-7309), exit towards the Yunost Hotel and at the top of the escalator go through the passsage maked with the blue Militsia sign and continue up to the third floor. Tours of the Metro can also be booked through local travel agencies. If you can read Cyrillic, take a look at www.metro.ru.

The Metro is easy to use by looking at a map. All the color-coded lines branch out from a central point, and are intersected by the brown Koltso (Circle) line. Entrances above ground are marked by a large M. Take the long and fast escalators down to the station. Maps are located before the turnstiles. From 1935 to 1991, the Metro cost only five kopeks; now the price keeps pace with inflation. By 2000, the Metro system had completely phased out the use of the token, in favor of a card with a magnetic strip. Buy a card (using Russian currency only) at the ticket booth, *kassa* (**касса**), inside. Insert the card into one of the turnstile machines, the automatic gates open once the card is registered. (Wait for the green light, or the gates can close right on you!) It is the same fare (R7) for any length trip (whether you make one or two transfers), as long as you do not exit to the street. You can save money by purchasing metro cards for 2, 5, 10, 20, or 60 trips. A monthly pass (70 rides), three-month or a yearly pass can also be purchased. Also available is a monthly bus/Metro pass. Each time you pass the card through the turnstiles an 'M' is stamped on the back, so you can keep track of the number of trips.

Since many station names are still written only in Russian, ask somebody to write down the name of your destination or you can use the Metro map in this book (pages 112–3) to compare the Cyrillic. If you have trouble finding your way, show it to the attendant, who usually stands at the entrance, or ask: people are very helpful to strangers and many understand some English. The trains can be crowded and commuters push to get to where they are going. Stand near a door as your stop approaches. Maps of the route (in Cyrillic and Roman alphabet) are also posted inside each train car. The loudspeaker announces '*Ostorozhno, dveri zakrivayutsya*' (Look out, the doors are closing), '*Slyeduyushaya stantsiiya ...*' (the next stop is...). The doors open and close automatically. Changing lines at major stations can be confusing. Look for the word **Переход** (*Perekhod*—Transfer) followed by a list of stations written in Cyrillic (this is usually a blue sign with a stick figure running up the stairs). Try to locate your destination and proceed in that direction to a different train line. If exiting the station locate the sign **ВЫХОД В ГОРОД** (*Vwykhod v Gorod*—Exit to Town) and take an escalator up to street level.

Even since the fall of Communism, Muscovites still display a proprietary pride in their Metro; it is clean and graffiti-free, with reserved seats at the front of each carriage for the elderly and disabled. Passages to underground stations, once dark and empty, are now teeming with stores, cafés, money changing kiosks, hawkers, beggars and musicians.

Moscow Metro

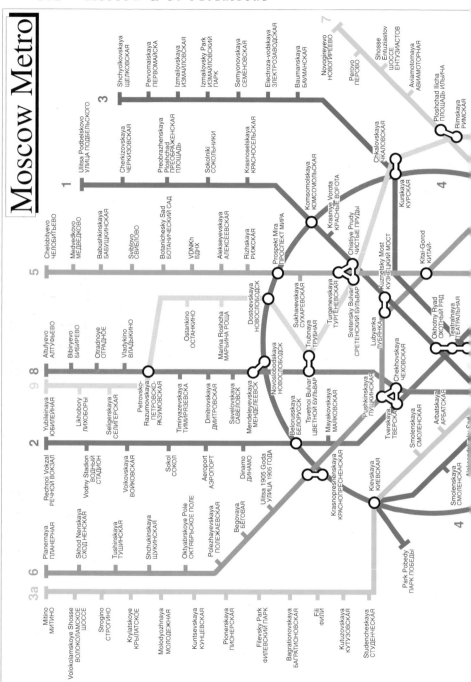

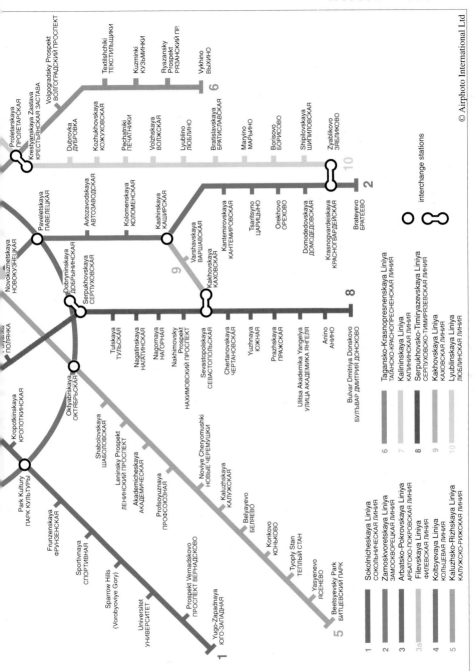

Proletarskaya ПРОЛЕТАРСКАЯ
Krestyanskaya Zastava КРЕСТЬЯНСКАЯ ЗАСТАВА
Volgogradsky Prospekt ВОЛГОГРАДСКИЙ ПРОСПЕКТ
Textilschiki ТЕКСТИЛЬЩИКИ
Kuzminki КУЗЬМИНКИ
Ryazansky Prospekt РЯЗАНСКИЙ ПР.
Vykhino ВЫХИНО
6

Dubrovka ДУБРОВКА
Kozhukhovskaya КОЖУХОВСКАЯ
Pechatniki ПЕЧАТНИКИ
Volzhskaya ВОЛЖСКАЯ
Lyublino ЛЮБЛИНО
Bratislavskaya БРАТИСЛАВСКАЯ
Maryino МАРЬИНО
Borisovo БОРИСОВО
Shipilovskaya ШИПИЛОВСКАЯ
Zyablikovo ЗЯБЛИКОВО
10

Novokuznetskaya НОВОКУЗНЕЦКАЯ
Paveletskaya ПАВЕЛЕЦКАЯ
Avtozavodskaya АВТОЗАВОДСКАЯ
Kolomenskaya КОЛОМЕНСКАЯ
Kashirskaya КАШИРСКАЯ
Kantemirovskaya КАНТЕМИРОВСКАЯ
Tsaritsyno ЦАРИЦЫНО
Orekhovo ОРЕХОВО
Domodedovskaya ДОМОДЕДОВСКАЯ
Krasnogvardeiskaya КРАСНОГВАРДЕЙСКАЯ
Brateyevo БРАТЕЕВО
2

interchange stations

Dobryninskaya ДОБРЫНИНСКАЯ
Serpukhovskaya СЕРПУХОВСКАЯ
Varshavskaya ВАРШАВСКАЯ
Kakhovskaya КАХОВСКАЯ
9

Тульянка ПОЛЯНКА
Oktyabrskaya ОКТЯБРЬСКАЯ
Tulskaya ТУЛЬСКАЯ
Nagatinskaya НАГАТИНСКАЯ
Nagornaya НАГОРНАЯ
Nakhimovsky Prospekt НАХИМОВСКИЙ ПРОСПЕКТ
Sevastopolskaya СЕВАСТОПОЛЬСКАЯ
Chertanovskaya ЧЕРТАНОВСКАЯ
Yuzhnaya ЮЖНАЯ
Prazhskaya ПРАЖСКАЯ
Ulitsa Akademika Yangelya УЛИЦА АКАДЕМИКА ЯНГЕЛЯ
Anino АНИНО
Bulvar Dmitriya Donskovo БУЛЬВАР ДМИТРИЯ ДОНСКОГО
8

Kropotkinskaya КРОПОТКИНСКАЯ
Shabolovskaya ШАБОЛОВСКАЯ
Leninsky Prospekt ЛЕНИНСКИЙ ПРОСПЕКТ
Akademicheskaya АКАДЕМИЧЕСКАЯ
Profsoyuznaya ПРОФСОЮЗНАЯ
Noviye Cheryomushki НОВЫЕ ЧЕРЕМУШКИ
Kaluzhskaya КАЛУЖСКАЯ
Belyayevo БЕЛЯЕВО
Konkovo КОНЬКОВО
Tyoply Stan ТЕПЛЫЙ СТАН
Yasenevo ЯСЕНЕВО
Beetsyevsky Park БИТЦЕВСКИЙ ПАРК
5

Park Kultury ПАРК КУЛЬТУРЫ
Frunzenskaya ФРУНЗЕНСКАЯ
Sportivnaya СПОРТИВНАЯ
Sparrow Hills (Vorobyoviye Gory) ВОРОБЬЁВЫ ГОРЫ
Universitet УНИВЕРСИТЕТ
Prospekt Vernadskovo ПРОСПЕКТ ВЕРНАДСКОГО
Yugo-Zapadnaya ЮГО-ЗАПАДНАЯ
1

1 Sokolnicheskaya Liniya СОКОЛЬНИЧЕСКАЯ ЛИНИЯ
2 Zamoskvoretskaya Liniya ЗАМОСКВОРЕЦКАЯ ЛИНИЯ
3 Arbatsko-Pokrovskaya Liniya АРБАТСКО-ПОКРОВСКАЯ ЛИНИЯ
3a Filevskaya Liniya ФИЛЕВСКАЯ ЛИНИЯ
4 Koltsyevaya Liniya КОЛЬЦЕВАЯ ЛИНИЯ
5 Kaluzhsko-Rizhskaya Liniya КАЛУЖСКО-РИЖСКАЯ ЛИНИЯ

6 Tagansko-Krasnopresnenskaya Liniya ТАГАНСКО-КРАСНОПРЕСНЕНСКАЯ ЛИНИЯ
7 Kalininskaya Liniya КАЛИНИНСКАЯ ЛИНИЯ
8 Serpukhovsko-Timiryazevskaya Liniya СЕРПУХОВСКО-ТИМИРЯЗЕВСКАЯ ЛИНИЯ
9 Kakhovskaya Liniya КАХОВСКАЯ ЛИНИЯ
10 Lyublinskaya Liniya ЛЮБЛИНСКАЯ ЛИНИЯ

RED SQUARE (KRASNAYA PLOSHCHAD)

Most visitors begin their acquaintance with Moscow in Krasnaya Ploshchad, Red Square, the heart of the city. It was first mentioned in 15th-century chronicles as the Veliky Torg, the Great Marketplace and main trading center of the town. From the time of Ivan the Great the square was used as a huge gathering place for public events, markets, fairs and festivals. Many religious processions came through the square led by the czar and patriarch of the Orthodox Church. It was also the scene of political demonstrations and revolts, and the site of public executions. The square received its present name in the 17th century from the old Russian word *krasny*, meaning both red and beautiful. From the Middle Ages it was a popular open-air market and it remained so until GUM, the shopping arcade, was completed in 1893 and the traders moved under cover. The first Victory Parade was held in the square on June 24, 1945.

This magnificent square encompasses an area of over 70,000 square meters (almost 84,000 square yards) and is bounded by the Kremlin walls, St Basil's Cathedral, the Lenin Mausoleum, the Historical Museum and the GUM Department Store.

Today national celebrations are still held here, especially on May Day when it is filled with huge parades and festivities. The closest Metro stop is Okhotny Ryad.

ST BASIL'S CATHEDRAL

Red Square's most famous and eye-catching structure is St Basil's Cathedral. This extraordinary creation was erected by Ivan IV (the Terrible) from 1555 to 1561, to commemorate the annexation to Russia of the Mongol states of Kazan and Astrakhan. Since this occurred on the festival of the Intercession of the Virgin, Ivan named it the Cathedral of the Intercession on the Moat (there used to be a moat around it). The names of the architects were unknown until 1896, when old manuscripts mentioning its construction were found. According to legend, Ivan the Terrible had the two architects, Posnik and Barma, blinded so they could never again create such a beautiful church. However records from 1588, a quarter of a century after the cathedral's completion, indicate that Posnik and Barma built the chapel at the north-east corner of the cathedral, where the holy prophet Basil (Vasily) was buried. Canonized after his death, Basil the Blessed (known as a *Yurodivy*, or 'Fool in Christ'; a *Yurodivy* was a half-wit, thought to have a direct connection to God) died the same year (1552) that many of the Mongol Khannates were captured. Basil had opposed the cruelties of Ivan the Terrible, and since most of the population also despised the czar, the cathedral took on the name of St Basil's after Ivan's death. It was later, in the 17th century, that the church was given its more colorful appearance.

The cathedral is built of brick in traditional Russian style with colorful, asymmetrical, tent-shaped, helmet and onion domes situated over nine chapels, each dedicated to a saint on whose feast day the Russian army won a victory. The interior is filled with 16th- and 17th-century icons and frescoes, and the gallery contains bright wall and ceiling paintings of red, turquoise and yellow flower patterns. Locals often refer to the cathedral as the 'stone flower in Red Square'. The French stabled their horses here in 1812 and Napoleon wanted to blow it up, and later Stalin tried to destroy it after he had demolished the Savior Cathedral. Luckily, both never succeeded.

The interior, now open to the public, has been undergoing a very slow restoration. Inside is a branch of the Historical Museum that traces the history of the cathedral and Ivan IV's campaigns. Under the bell tower (added in the 17th century) is an exhibition room where old sketches and plans trace the architectural history of St Basil's.

The museum is open daily 11am–6pm (in summer) and 11am–4pm (in winter), except Tuesdays, and every first Monday of the month. In 1991, the cathedral was given back to the Russian Orthodox Church to celebrate Russian New Year and Easter services; Yeltsin attended the first Easter service. On May 24, 2003, Sir Paul McCartney gave his first musical performance in Russia on Red Square. His encore was *Back in the USSR*, the backdrop the newly-restored St Basil's.

In front of the cathedral stands the bronze **Monument to Minin and Pozharsky**, the first patriotic monument in Moscow built from public funding. It originally stood in the middle of the square. Sculpted by Ivan Martos in 1818, the monument depicts Kozma Minin and Prince Dmitri Pozharsky, whose leadership drove the Polish invaders out of Moscow in 1612. The pedestal inscription reads 'To Citizen Minin and Prince Pozharsky from a grateful Russia 1818.'

Near the monument is **Lobnoye Mesto**, the Place of Skulls. A platform of white stone stood here for more than four centuries, on which public executions were carried out. Church clergymen blessed the crowds and the czar's orders and edicts were also announced from here.

THE LENIN MAUSOLEUM

By the Kremlin wall on the southwest side of Red Square stands the Lenin Mausoleum. Inside, in a glass sarcophagus, lies Vladimir Ilyich Lenin, who died on January 21, 1924. Three days after his death, a wooden structure was erected on this spot. Four months later, it was rebuilt and then replaced in 1930 by the granite, marble and black labradorite mausoleum, designed by Alexei Shchusev. 'Lenin' is inscribed in red porphyry. For more than 80 years Russians and foreigners have stood in the line that stretches from the end of Red Square to the mausoleum to view the once idolized revolutionary leader and 'Father of the Soviet Union'. Two

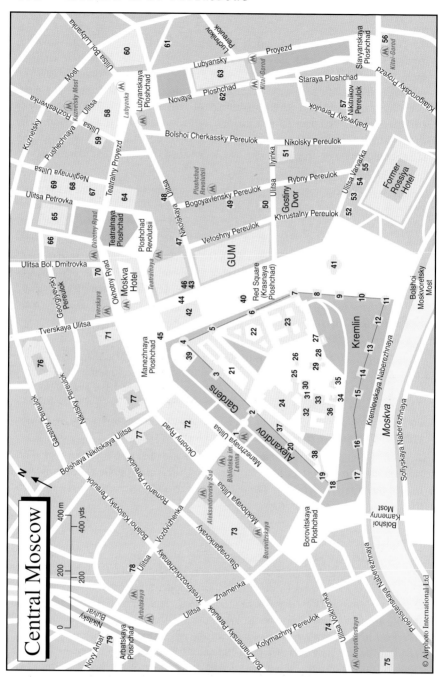

Central Moscow

400 m
400 yds
0   200   200   400 m

Ulitsa Bol. Lubyanka

Most
Rozhdestvenka
Kuznetsky Most
Kuznetsky
Ulitsa
Pushechnaya Ulitsa
Neglinnaya Ulitsa
Ulitsa Petrovka

60
61
Lubyanka Pereulok
Lubyansky
Proyezd
Lubyansky
63
Ploshchad
Novaya
Ploshchad
62
Staraya Ploshchad
Slavyanskaya Ploshchad
56
Kitai-Gorod
Kitai-Gorod
Kitaigorodsky Proyezd

58
59
Lubyanka
Lubyanskaya Ploshchad
Bolshoi Cherkassky Pereulok
Nikolsky Pereulok
Nikitnikov Pereulok
57
Ipatyevsky Pereulok
51
Ulitsa Ilyinka

69 68 67
Teatralny Proyezd
64
48
Ploshchad Revolutsii
Ploshchad Revolutsii
Bogoyavlensky Pereulok
49
50
Rybny Pereulok
Gostiny Dvor
52 53 54 55
Ulitsa Varvarka
Khrustalny Pereulok
Ulitsa
Former Rossiya Hotel

65
66
Ulitsa Bol. Dmitrovka
70
Okhotny Ryad
Teatralnaya Ploshchad
Ploshchad Revolutsii
47
Vetoshny Pereulok
GUM
Teatralnaya

Georgiyevsky Pereulok
Tverskaya
Moskva Hotel
Okhotny Ryad
Teatralnaya
46 43
44
42
40
6
Red Square (Krasnaya Ploshchad)
7 8 9 10 11
12
Kremlin
13
Bolshoi Moskvoretsky Most

71
Tverskaya Ulitsa
45
Manezhnaya Ploshchad
5
4
39
3
21
22
23
26 27
24
25
31 30
29 28
32
36
33
34 35
14
15
16
17
Kremlevskaya Naberezhnaya

76
77
Bolshaya Nikitskaya Ulitsa
Nikitsky Pereulok
Gazetny Pereulok
72
Okhotny Ryad
Manezhnaya Ulitsa
Manezhnaya Ulitsa
Biblioteka im. Lenina
1
2
37
20
Alexandrov Gardens
38
19
18
Moskva
Softiyskaya Naberezhnaya

77
Romanov Pereulok
Bolshoi Kislovsky Pereulok
Vozdvizhenka
Starovagankovsky
73
Borovitskaya
Mokhovaya Ulitsa
Aleksandrovsky Sad
Borovitskaya Ploshchad
Bolshoi Kamenny Most

78
Ulitsa
Krestovozdvizhensky
Arbatskaya
Nikitsky Bulvar
79
Novy Arbat
Arbatskaya Ploshchad
Znamenka
Ulitsa
Bol. Znamensky Pereulok
Kolymazhny Pereulok
Ulitsa Volkhonka
74
Ulitsa Lenivka
Kropotkinskaya
75
Prechistenskaya Naberezhnaya

N

© Airphoto International Ltd

Key for Central Moscow Map:

1 Kutafya Tower
2 Troitskaya (Trinity) Tower
3 Srednaya Arsenalnaya (Middle Arsenal)
4 Corner Arsenal Tower
5 Nikolskaya Tower
6 Senate Tower
7 Spasskaya Tower (Savior)
8 Tsarskaya Tower (Czar)
9 Nabatnaya Tower (Alarm)
10 Konstantino-Yeleninskaya Tower
11 Beklemishevskaya Tower
12 Petrovskaya Tower
13 2-Bezymyannaya Tower (2nd nameless)
14 1-Bezymyannaya Tower (1st nameless)
15 Tainitskaya Tower (Secret)
16 Blagoveshchenskaya Tower (Annunciation)
17 Vodovzvodnaya Tower
18 Borovitskaya Tower
19 Oruzheynaya Tower (Armory)
20 Kommendantskaya Tower (Commandant)
21 Arsenal
22 Senate
23 Presidium and Kremlin Theater
24 Patriarch's Palace
25 Church of the Twelve Apostles
26 Emperor Cannon
27 Kremlin Hill

28 Emperor Bell
29 Ivan the Great's Bell Tower
30 Cathedral of the Assumption
31 Church of the Deposition of the Robe
32 Terem Palace
33 Palace of Facets
34 Cathedral of the Annunciation
35 Cathedral of the Archangel Michael
36 Grand Kremlin Palace
37 Amusement Palace
38 Armory Palace
39 Tomb of the Unknown Soldier
40 Lenin's Mausoleum
41 St Basil's Cathedral
42 Historical Museum
43 Kazan Cathedral
44 Iberian Resurrection Gates
45 Statue of Marshal Georgy Zhukov
46 Old Royal Mint
47 Zaikonospassky Monastery
48 History and Archives Institute
49 Cathedral of Bogoyavlensky
50 St Ilyia Church
51 Moscow Stock Exchange
52 Church of St Varvara
53 Old English Inn
54 Church of St Maximus

55 Znamensky Cathedral
56 Church of All Saints on Kulishki
57 Church of the Holy Trinity in Nikitniki
58 Detsky Mir
59 Savoy Hotel
60 Former KGB Building
61 Mayakovsky Museum
62 History of Moscow Museum
63 Polytechnical Museum
64 Metropole Hotel
65 Bolshoi Theater
66 Bolshoi Sister Theater
67 Maly Theater
68 Ararat Park Hyatt Hotel
69 TsUM
70 Dom Soyuzov
71 National Hotel
72 Central Exhibition Hall
73 Russian State Library
74 Pushkin Museum of Fine Arts
75 Cathedral of Christ Our Savior
76 Central Telegraph Building
77 Moscow State University
78 House of Friendship
79 Prague Restaurant

Key to symbols and Russian terms:

(M) = *Metro Station*
Ulitsa = Street

Bulvar = Boulevard
Ploshchad = Square

Pereulok = Lane
Proyezd = Passage

Most = Bridge
Naberezhnaya = Embankment

guards man the entrance but there is no longer a changing of the guard. Photography is prohibited and cameras are not allowed to be taken inside—guards carry metal detectors. Any large bags and cameras should be left at the baggage check near the Kutafya Tower in the Alexandrov Gardens (tucked in below the pavilion steps leading up to the excursion booths). Once inside, visitors are not allowed to pause for long. The mausoleum is usually open 10am–1pm; closed Mondays, Fridays, and is free of charge.

Once in a while some die-hard Communists and Lenin loyalists will gather at the mausoleum to honor the former leader. In 1994, a German executive tried to purchase the body and take it on a world tour with a final resting place in a Cologne museum. Today there is still a movement within the country to remove Lenin's body from the mausoleum and rebury him elsewhere (he had requested to be buried in St Petersburg). Ironically though, with the new wave of capitalism, Lenin souvenirs are now more popular than ever, and Lenin's formaldehyde experts are offering their eternal Lenin Delux preservation techniques for a price of just over a quarter of a million dollars.

Marble viewing stands on both sides of the mausoleum hold up to 10,000 spectators on national holidays. Atop the mausoleum is a tribune, where the heads of the former Soviet Government and Communist Party once gathered on May and Revolution days.

Behind the mausoleum, separated by a row of silver fir trees, are the remains of many of the country's most honored figures in politics, culture and science, whose ashes lie in urns within the Kremlin walls. They include Lenin's sister and his wife, Sergei Kirov, Maxim Gorky, A K Lunacharsky, the physicist Sergei Korolyov and the cosmonaut Yuri Gagarin. Foreigners include John Reed and William Hayword (USA), Arthur McManus (England), Clara Zetkin and Fritz Heckert (Germany), and Sen Katayama (Japan). There are also the tombstones of previous leaders of the Communist Party: Sverdlov, Dzerzhinsky, Frunze, Kalinin, Voroshilov, Suslov, Brezhnev, Chernenko, Andropov, and Stalin, who was buried next to Lenin in the mausoleum from 1953–61. Nearby are the granite-framed common graves of 500 people who died during the October Revolution of 1917.

THE HISTORICAL STATE MUSEUM

At the opposite end of the square from St Basil's is a red-brick building, decorated with numerous spires and *kokoshniki* gables. This houses the Historical Museum. It was constructed for Alexander II by Vladimir Sherwood between 1878 and 1883 on the site where Moscow University was founded in 1755 by the Russian scientist Mikhail Lomonosov. When it opened in 1883, the museum had over 300,000 objects and was supported by private donations. Today the government museum contains over four million items in 48 halls that house the country's largest archeological collection, along with manuscripts, books, coins, ornaments and works of art from the Stone Age to the present day. These include birch-bark letters, clothing of Ivan the Terrible, Peter the Great's sleigh, Napoleon's saber and the Decree on Peace written by Lenin. The museum is open daily from 11am–6pm; closed Tuesdays and the first Monday of the month. Within the building, the restaurant Red Square offers sumptuous old-style traditional food.

GUM

Next to the Historical Museum, stretching across the entire northeastern side of Red Square, is the three-story State Universal Store, known as GUM. It is the largest shopping center in Russia, with a total length of 2.5 kilometers (1.5 miles), selling half a million items to almost a quarter of a million Russians and 100,000 foreigners every day. GUM's 110th anniversary was celebrated in 2003. The initials GUM stood for Gosudarstvenny Universalny Magazine, the Government Department Store, until 1990, when the Moscow city government turned it into a joint stock company owned mainly by the employees. The initials now stand for Glavny Universalny Magazine, the Main Department Store.

It was designed in 1893, in neo-Russian style, by Alexander Pomerantsev to replace a market destroyed by one of Napoleon's fires in 1812, as his troops were attempting to occupy Moscow. When it was built it was known as the Upper Trading Stalls. It was a showcase for goods and one of the world's most modern commercial areas, built of steel and concrete with ornate glass roofing and even electrical and heating systems. Today the building has been thoroughly renovated, and over 100 shops, both Russian and foreign, along with numerous cafés, line the first and second floors. The grand ceremonial entrance on Red Square, closed since the Bolshevik Revolution, was reopened in 1992. It is well worth visiting to view the interiors of preserved old Russian shops, ornate bridges, ornamental stucco designs and the large glass roof. It is open daily from 8am–8pm; 11am–7pm Sundays.

Exiting GUM at the northwest corner (towards the History Museum) brings you to the **Kazan Cathedral**. The original church was built in 1625 by Prince Pozharsky (whose statue stands in front of St Basil's) in tribute to the Virgin of Kazan icon, whose power was thought to lead Russia in victory over the invading Poles. Stalin had it destroyed in 1936. After the fall of the Soviet Union, private contributions led to the reconstruction of the cathedral. In 1990, a procession led by Boris Yeltsin, the Orthodox Patriarch Alexis II and the Moscow mayor left the Kremlin to lay the foundation stone. The structure was consecrated by the Orthodox Church in 1993. Religious services are conducted. Open to visitors from 8am–7pm daily.

The red-brick State Historical Museum on Moscow's Red Square was constructed for Alexander II. When it opened in 1883, the museum contained over 300,000 objects; today it exhibits over 4 million items. In front, stands the Statue of Marshal Georgy Zhukov, a WWII hero, who gazes from his horse over Manezh Square.

Exiting Red Square to the north takes you through the **Iberian Resurrection Gates**. The original main entrance gateway and white towers, first built in 1680, were torn down by Stalin in 1931 to create more room for mass parades and machinery to enter. The gates were reconstructed as a copy of the original in the early 1990s. On the other side of the arch stands the small **Gate Church of the Iberian Virgin**, also rebuilt. It was once customary for the czar to pray here before he entered the Kremlin.

THE ALEXANDROV GARDENS

The entrance to these charming gardens is opposite the Historical Museum at the Kremlin's wrought-iron Corner Arsenal Gate. On your way there take note of the **Statue of Marshal Georgy Zhukov**, a World War II hero, who gazes proudly from his horse onto Manezh Square. Russia celebrated the 100th anniversary of Zhukov's birth on December 1, 1996. The Alexandrov Gardens were laid out on the banks of the Neglinnaya River by Osip Bovet from 1819 to 1822 for Alexander I. They later became Moscow's first public garden. The river was later diverted by a system of pipes to flow beneath the park. An eternal flame burns before the **Tomb of the Unknown Soldier**, who died for his country during World War II. It was unveiled on May 8, 1967, on the eve of Victory Day.

It is a tradition for newlyweds on their wedding day to lay flowers on the tombstone, on which is inscribed: 'Your name is unknown, your feat immortal. To

(opposite) A scene of the Moscow Kremlin and interior buildings along the Moscow River.

the fallen 1941–45.' Along the alley in front of the tomb are blocks of red porphyry that hold earth from 'Hero Cities' designated after World War II, including Moscow and St Petersburg. Also in the gardens are a memorial to the War of 1812 and a granite obelisk with the names of the world's great revolutionaries and thinkers. The latter was originally erected in 1913 to commemorate the 300th anniversary of the Romanov dynasty. On Lenin's orders in 1918, the double-headed eagle was replaced by the obelisk. Now, with the spacious underground Manezh shopping mall located nearby, more people than ever enjoy a promenade within the gardens. The sculptures, fountains and tree-lined paths create a charming spot in the heart of the Russian capital.

The central alley of the Alexandrov Gardens leads to the Troitsky Bridge that approaches the entrance to the Kremlin.

THE KREMLIN

The earth, as we all know, begins at the Kremlin. It is the central point.

Mayakovsky

The Moscow Kremlin, an outstanding monument of Russian history, winds around a steep slope high above the Moskva River, enclosing an area of over 28 hectares (70 acres) next to Red Square. The Russian word *kreml* was once used to describe a fortified stronghold that encased a small town. A Russian town was usually built on a high embankment, surrounded by a river and moat, to protect against invasions. The word *kreml* may originate from the Greek *kremnos*, meaning steep escarpment. The medieval kremlin acted as a fortress around a town filled with palaces, churches, monasteries, wooden peasant houses and markets. The Moscow Kremlin was built

between the Moskva River and Neglinnaya River (the latter now flows underground). The walls are about one kilometer (half a mile) long, up to 19 meters (62 feet) high and 6.5 meters (21 feet) thick, with 20 towers and gates. Over ten churches and palaces lie inside. The Kremlin is open 10am–6pm (in winter 10am–5pm); closed Thursdays. The closest Metro stations are Okhotny Ryad (for Red Square) and Borovitskaya and Aleksandrovsky Sad (for the Gardens and Kremlin museum entrances). See page 124 for ticketing information.

HISTORY

The Moscow Kremlin has a fascinating eight-century history, and is the oldest historical and architectural feature of Moscow. The first written account of Moscow comes to us from a chronicle of 1147, which describes Prince Yuri Dolgoruky of Suzdal receiving Grand Prince Svyatoslav on Borovitsky (now Kremlin) Hill. Nine years later, Dolgoruky ordered a fort built on this same hill, which later became his residence. In 1238, the invading Mongols burned the fortress to the ground. By 1326 the Kremlin had been surrounded with thick oak walls and Grand Prince Ivan I had built two stone churches in addition to the existing wooden ones. During this time the metropolitan of Kiev moved the seat of the Orthodox Church from Vladimir to Moscow. In 1367, Prince Dmitri Donskoi replaced the wooden walls with limestone ones to fortify them against cannon attack; Moscow was then referred to as Beli Gorod (White Town). The Mongols invaded again in 1382; they razed everything and killed half the population. Within 15 years the Kremlin walls were rebuilt and the iconists Theophanes the Greek and Andrei Rublyov painted the interior frescoes of the new Cathedral of the Annunciation.

Ivan III (1460–1505) and his son Vasily III were responsible for shaping the Kremlin into its present appearance. When the Mongols no longer posed a threat to the city, the leaders concentrated more on aesthetic than defensive designs. Ivan the Great commissioned well-known Russian and Italian architects to create a magnificent city to reflect the beauty of the 'Third Rome' and the power of the grand prince and metropolitan. The white stone of the Kremlin was replaced by red-brick walls and towers, and the Assumption and Annunciation cathedrals were rebuilt on a grander scale. During the reign of Ivan IV the architecture took on more fanciful elements and asymmetrical designs with colorful onion domes and tall pyramidal tent roofs, as embodied in St Basil's—a style now termed Old Russian. The Patriarch Nikon barred all tent roofs and ornamental decorations from churches when he took office in 1652, terming the external frills sacrilegious. By 1660 though, the reforms of Nikon had created such schisms in the Church that he was forced to step down. Immediately the old decorative details were again applied to architecture.

Catherine the Great drew up plans to redesign the Kremlin in the new neo-classical style, but they were never carried out. During the War of 1812, Napoleon quartered his troops inside the Kremlin for 35 days. Retreating, he tried to blow it up, but townspeople extinguished the burning fuses, though three towers were destroyed. In the mid-1800s the Kremlin Palace and Armory were built. In 1918, the Soviet Government moved the capital back to Moscow from St Petersburg and made the Kremlin its permanent seat. Lenin signed a decree to protect the works of art and historical monuments and ordered the buildings restored and turned into museums. The Kremlin remains the center of Russian government today. See also www.kremlin.ru/eng.

VIEW FROM RED SQUARE

Ruby-red stars were mounted on the five tallest towers of the Kremlin in 1937, replacing the double-headed eagle. The towers of the Kremlin were named after the icons that used to hang above their gates. The most recognizable tower is the 67-meter-high (220-feet) **Spasskaya (Savior) Clock Tower**, which stands to the right of St Basil's. It used to serve as the official entrance of the czars, who had to cross a moat over an arched stone bridge to reach the gate. It is now the main entrance of government officials, who pull up in Russian-made, black limos or foreign SUVs. (In 1934, a Soviet magazine wrote that the *Zavod imeni Stalina* (Stalin Auto Plant) had begun production on the ZIS-101 automobile, built only for Communist Party bosses, so they could be driven in luxurious, domestically-produced cars. The ZIS-101 was a copy of the 1940 Packard. Later, Stalin was driven around in the ZIS-115; this bullet-proof car weighed 7 tons, and sheets of 6-millimeter steel armor were hidden inside the body panels. Later, after Stalin's death, the auto plant's name changed to Likhacheva, and thus the ZIL was born.)

The Savior Icon once hung above the Spasskaya Gate. Inscriptions in Latin and Old Russian name the Italian Solario as the tower's builder in 1491. In the middle of the 17th century, the Scottish architect Christopher Galloway mounted a clock on its face; this clock was replaced in 1918. Like Big Ben in London, the chimes of the Spasskaya Tower are broadcast over the radio to mark the hour.

The tower behind Lenin's Mausoleum is known as the **Senate Tower**; it stands in front of the Senate building. To the right of the mausoleum stands the **Nikolskaya Tower**, where the Icon of St Nicholas was kept. In 1492, Solario built a corner tower next to a courtyard used by Sobakin Boyars. The Sobakin Tower is now called the **Corner Arsenal Tower**, where munitions were stored.

GAINING ENTRANCE TO THE KREMLIN

Only group tours are allowed within the Kremlin grounds. It is highly recommended to book a group tour through your hotel (they are conducted in different languages), or a Russian travel agency (see p. 411). Check to see if the tour includes the Armory.

If you arrive as an independent tourist at the Kremlin without a ticket, it can be a daunting task to get in. Go to the Kutafya Tower; the excursion ticket pavilions are at the top of the steps nearby. (Note: underneath the steps is a baggage-check facility. A tourist cannot enter the Kremlin with large bags. Cameras are permitted, but not in Lenin's Mausoleum.) However, a foreigner is not really allowed to purchase a ticket here. The north pavilion sells group tickets for Russian-citizens only. Even if you speak some Russian, your accent will be checked when buying a ticket. Guards are now relentless in weeding out foreigners. Unless a Russian friend buys the tickets, do not attempt to stand in this line. The south pavilion, even with signs in English, is for guides and translators only. Try looking for English-speaking guides near this pavilion —they often try to gather enough independent travelers to form a small group. Arrive here before the scheduled group tours at 10am, 12pm, 2pm and 4pm. The official guide will then purchase a ticket for you and must escort you in. (The approximate cost is US$25 for two hours.) If this does not include entrance to the Armory, ask the guide to show you where to buy an Armory ticket once within the Kremlin grounds (see page 143). Most group tours enter through the Borovitskaya tower.

PALACE OF CONGRESSES

As you enter the Kremlin through the Kutafya and Trinity towers, the modern Palace of Congresses is on your right. Khrushchev approved the plans for this large steel, glass and marble structure. Built by Mikhail Posokhin, it was completed in 1961 for the 22nd Congress of the Communist Party. When no congresses or international meetings are in session, the palace is used for ballet and opera performances. Sunk 15 meters (49 feet) into the ground so as not to tower over the Kremlin, the Palace contains 800 rooms and the auditorium seats 6,000.

THE ARSENAL

The yellow two-story building to the left of the entrance tower was once used as the Arsenal. Peter the Great ordered its construction in 1702 (completed in 1736), but later turned it into a Trophy Museum. Along the front of the arsenal are 875 cannons and other trophies captured from Napoleon's armies in 1812. Plaques on the wall list the names of men killed defending the arsenal during the Revolution and World War II. It now houses the Kremlin Guard.

The 15th-century Assumption Cathedral in Moscow's Kremlin was modeled after the cathedral of the same name in the Golden Ring town of Vladimir. To its right stands the imposing Bell Tower of Ivan the Great, built in 1505 and once the tallest structure in Russia.

THE BROTHERHOOD GRAVE

*L**ate in the night we went through the empty streets and under the Iberian Gate to the great Red Square in front of the Kremlin. The church of Vasili Blazhenny loomed fantastic, its bright colored, convoluted and blazoned cupolas vague in the darkness. There was no sign of any damage.... Along one side of the square the dark towers and walls of the Kremlin stood up. On the high walls flickered redly the light of hidden flames; voices reached us across the immense place, and the sound of picks and shovels. We crossed over.*

Mountains of dirt and rock piled high near the base of the wall. Climbing these we looked down into two massive pits, ten or fifteen feet deep and fifty yards long, where hundreds of soldiers and workers were digging in the light of huge fires.

A young soldier spoke to us in German. 'The Brotherhood Grave,' he explained. 'Tomorrow we shall bury here five hundred proletarians who died for the Revolution.'

He took us down into the pit. In frantic haste they swung the picks and shovels, and the earth-mountains grew. No one spoke. Overhead the night was thick with stars, and the ancient Imperial Kremlin wall towered up immeasurably.

'Here in this holy place,' said the student, 'holiest of all Russia, we shall bury our most holy. Here where are the tombs of the Tsars, our Tsar—the People—shall sleep...' His arm was in a sling from the bullet wound gained in the fighting. He looked at it. 'You foreigners look down on us Russians because for so long we tolerated a medieval monarchy,' he said. 'But we saw that the Tsar was not the only tyrant in the world; capitalism was worse, and in all the countries of the world capitalism was Emperor... Russian revolutionary tactics are best...'

As we left, the workers in the pit, exhausted and running with sweat in spite of the cold, began to climb wearily out. Across the Red Square a dark knot of men came hurrying. They swarmed into the pits, picked up the tools and began digging, digging, without a word.

So, all the long night volunteers of the People relieved each other, never halting in their driving speed, and the cold light of the dawn laid bare the great square, white with snow, and the yawning brown pits of the Brotherhood Grave, quite finished.

We rose before sunrise, and hurried through the dark streets to Skobeliev Square. In all the great city not a human being could be seen; but there was a faint sound of stirring, far and near, like a deep wind coming. In the pale half-light a little group of men and women were gathered before the Soviet headquarters, with a sheaf of gold-lettered red banners, and the dull red—like blood—of the coffins they carried. These were rude boxes, made of unplaned wood and daubed with crimson, borne high on the shoulders of rough men who marched with tears streaming down their faces, and followed by women who sobbed and screamed, or walked stiffly, with white, dead faces. Some of the coffins were open, the lid carried behind them; others were covered with gilded or silvered cloth, or had a soldier's hat nailed on the top. There were many wreaths of hideous artificial flowers.

All the long day the funeral procession passed, coming in by the Iberian Gate and leaving the square by way of the Nikolskaya, a river of red banners, bearing words of hope and brotherhood and stupendous prophecies, against a background of fifty thousand people—under the eyes of the world's workers and their descendants for ever...

John Reed, Ten Days That Shook the World, 1919

After graduating from Harvard University, Reed traveled to Russia to support the Bolshevik Revolution. He was such an ardent supporter of socialism that Lenin penned the introduction to his book.

SENATE BUILDING

Directly in front of the Arsenal stands the three-story triangular building of the former Council of Ministers. Catherine the Great had it built in the classical style by Matvei Kazakov in 1787. After Lenin moved the capital from Petrograd (St Petersburg) to Moscow in 1918, the Soviet Government and the Bolshevik Party took up residence in the building. It is now used by the Senate; its large green dome is topped by the national flag. The plaque on the front wall shows Lenin's portrait and the inscription: 'Lenin lived and worked in this building from March 1918 to May 1923.'

The Central Committee of the Communist Party once met in **Sverdlov Hall**. The hall's 18 Corinthian columns are decorated with copies of bas-reliefs portraying czars and princes (the originals are in the Armory). Lenin's study and flat are in the east wing. Special objects stand on his desk, such as the Monkey Statue presented to him by Armand Hammer in 1921. The study leads to a small four-room apartment that Lenin shared with his wife and younger sister.

Across from the Senate, near the Spasskaya Tower, is the **Presidium** and the **Kremlin Theater**, built between 1932 and 1934. The building has also served as a military school and the former residence of the president of the USSR. To make room for these buildings, Stalin gave permission to tear down the 14th-century Monastery of the Miracles and Ascension Convent, where female members of the royal family lived and were buried. After the convent was destroyed, the bodies were transferred to the Cathedral of the Archangel Michael. Today these buildings can only be visited with special permission—they function as the offices of the President of Russia.

PATRIARCH'S PALACE

Opposite the Senate is the four-story Patriarch's Palace and his private chapel, the **Church of the Twelve Apostles** (with the five silver domes), which now house the **Museum of 17th-Century Life and Applied Art** with over 1,000 exhibits. Patriarch Nikon commissioned the palace for himself in 1635. After Nikon banned elaborate decorations on church buildings, he had the architects Konstantinov and Okhlebinin design the structure in simple white Byzantine fashion. The palace was placed near the main cathedral and the Trinity Gate, where clergy formally entered the Kremlin. The vaulted **Krestovskaya Chamber**, the Hall of the Cross, built without a single support beam, was used as a formal reception hall. Every three years the chamber was used for making consecrated oil for the Russian churches. In 1721, Peter the Great gave the palace to the Church Council of the Holy Synod. The museum has an interesting collection of rare manuscripts, coins, jewelry, furniture, fabrics, embroidery and table games. Vestments worn by Patriarch Nikon and the 17th-century golden iconostasis from the Monastery of the Miracles (destroyed to build the Senate) are also on display. The books include an ABC primer written for

The 40-ton Emperor Cannon is the world's largest cannon still in existence.
Designed in 1586 to protect the Savior's Gate on Red Square, it was never fired—
probably because each cannon ball weighed one ton.

the son of Peter the Great. Two of the halls are decorated to look like a 17th-century house. Some of the displays in the Church of the Twelve Apostles are wine coffers and ladles, on which Bacchus is carved. These objects belonged to the society of the Highest and Most Jolly and Drunken Council, founded by Peter the Great to make fun of (nonprogressive) Church rituals. The museum is closed on Thursdays.

EMPEROR CANNON

Beside the Church of the Twelve Apostles is the 40-ton Emperor Cannon. Its 890mm bore (35 inch caliber) makes it the world's largest cannon still in existence. It was cast in 1586 by Andrei Chokhov and never fired. (The largest was smelted at an arms factory in Perm in the 1530s and used to defend Russia against the Tartars; it was fired over 300 times.) A likeness of Fedor I is on the barrel. The decorative iron cannon balls (weighing one ton each) were cast in the 19th century.

Across from the cannon in the southeastern corner of the Kremlin lie the **Tainitsky (Secret) Gardens**. Winter fairs are held here for children during New Year celebrations. A statue of Lenin used to stand on the highest spot, known as **Kremlin Hill**, but was removed in 1997 (see picture on page 553). Nearby is the **Cosmos Oak**, which cosmonaut Yuri Gagarin planted on April 14, 1961. This vantage point affords a good view of the Kremlin and Spasskaya Tower. The **Tsarskaya (Czar's) Tower** stands to the right and is decorated with white-stone designs and a weathervane. A wooden deck used to stand on top of the tower, from which Ivan the Terrible supposedly watched executions in Red Square. The next tower is the **Nabatnaya (Alarm) Tower**; the bell that used to hang here is on display in the Armory Museum. Farther to the south is the **Konstantino-Yeleninskaya Tower**, which honors St Constantine and St Helen. In earlier days it was also referred to as the Torture Tower, since it housed a torture chamber. The corner tower is called **Moskvoretskaya**, built in 1487 by Marco Ruffo. It was known as Beklemischevskaya, named after Ivan Beklemisch, whose home stood next to it in the 16th century; his spirit is said to have haunted it. The Mongols broke through this tower to enter the Kremlin in the 17th century.

EMPEROR BELL

The largest bell in the world stands on a stone pedestal by the Secret Gardens. The bell is six meters (20 feet) high and weighs 210 tons. The surface bears portraits of czars and icons. It was designed in 1733 by Ivan Matorin and his son Mikhail for the empress Anna Ivanova, and took two years to cast. An 11.5-ton fragment broke off during the fire of 1737, when water was thrown on it. After the fire the bell was returned to its casting pit, where it lay for a century. The architect Montferrand raised the bell in 1836. It has never been rung.

The square between the Spasskaya Tower and the bell was known as Ivan's Square, along which government offices were located. Here criminals were flogged and officials read the czar's new decrees.

BELL TOWER

Behind the Emperor Bell stands the three-tiered Bell Tower of Ivan the Great. Built between 1505 and 1508, the tower contains 21 bells that hang in the arches of each section, the largest of which is the Uspensky (Assumption) Bell, weighing 70 tons; it traditionally rang three times to announce the death of a czar. The Old Slavonic inscription around the gilded dome notes that it was added to the belfry in 1600 by Boris Godunov. This was once the tallest structure (81 meters, 266 feet) in Moscow and was used as a belfry, church and watchtower. When the enemy was sighted, the bells signaled a warning. The upper tent-roof section, built in the 17th century, was rebuilt after Napoleon partially blew it up. A small exhibition hall is on the ground floor of the belfry showing items from the Armory Museum.

CATHEDRAL OF THE ASSUMPTION

In front of the bell tower stands the Kremlin's main church, the Assumption Cathedral or Uspensky Sobor. It faces the center of Cathedral Square, the oldest square in Moscow, built in the early 14th century. In 1475, Ivan the Great chose the Italian architect Aristotle Fioravante to design the church. He modeled it on the Cathedral of the Assumption in the Golden Ring town of Vladimir (see page 325).

This church, also known as the Cathedral of the Dormition of the Virgin, was built on the site of a stone church of the same name first constructed by Ivan I in 1326. For two centuries this national shrine stood as a model for all Russian church architecture. Within its walls czars and patriarchs were crowned. It also served as the burial place for Moscow metropolitans and patriarchs.

Combining Italian Renaissance and Byzantine traditions, the cathedral is built from white limestone and brick with *zakomara* rounded arches, narrow-windowed drums and five gilded onion domes. The ornamental doorways are covered with frescoes painted on sheet copper; the southern entrance is especially interesting, decorated with 20 biblical scenes in gold and black lacquer.

The spacious interior, lit by 12 chandeliers, is covered with exquisite frescoes and icons that date back to 1481. The artists Dionysius, Timofei, Yarets and Kon wove together the themes of heaven and the unity of Russia's principalities, symbolizing the 'Third Rome'. Some of these can still be seen over the altar screen. The northern and southern walls depict the life of the Blessed Virgin. In 1642, more than 100 masters spent a year repainting the church, following the designs of the older wall paintings. These 17th-century frescoes were restored after the

(above and top right) The Kremlin's gilded nine-domed Annunciation Cathedral
was built in 1482 by Ivan the Great. Once the private church of the royal family,
it is now open year-round for visitors.

(bottom right) Built in 1479, the Assumption Cathedral was formerly the coronation church of the czars. Guarding the czar's doors are frescoes of the archangels Michael and Gabriel, and above them stands a row of bishops. The virgin and child at the top symbolizes the virgin's assumption into heaven to which the cathedral is dedicated.

Revolution. Frescoes were painted in colors prepared from local clays and minerals mixed with water and bound by using egg-yolk and vegetable glues. Russian frescoes were painted by artists applying colors onto the still wet plaster. Sometimes others were executed in the Italian tempera manner—painting done on dry plaster. This cathedral contains both types of frescoes.

The elaborate five-tier iconostasis (altar screen) dates from 1652. Its upper rows were painted by monks from the Trinity-Sergius Monastery in Sergiyev Posad in the late 1600s. The silver frames were added in 1881. To the right of the royal gates are two 12th-century icons from Novgorod: St George and the Savior Enthroned. A 15th-century Rublyov-school copy of the country's protectress, the Virgin of Vladimir, also lies to the left. The original, painted in 12th-century Byzantium, was first hung in Kiev. In 1155, Grand Prince Andrei Bogolubsky carried it to Vladimir to save it from the invading Mongols. Later, in 1395, Grand Prince Vasily I, son of Dmitry Donskoi, brought it to Moscow and placed it in the original Assumption Church. After the Revolution, it was placed in the Tretyakov Gallery. The icons, *Savior of the Fiery Eye*, the *Trinity*, and the *Dormition of the Virgin*, were specially commissioned for the cathedral in the 14th and 15th centuries. Napoleon's armies used some of the icons as firewood and tried to carry off tons of gold and silver. Most of it was recovered—the central chandelier, Harvest, was cast from silver recaptured from the retreating troops.

The Metropolitan Peter (cofounder of the cathedral) and his successor are buried in the southern chapel. The 15th-century fresco *Forty Martyrs of Sebaste* separates the chapel from the main altar. Other metropolitans and patriarchs are buried along the northern and southern walls and in underground crypts. Metropolitan Iov is buried in a special mausoleum, above which hangs the icon of Metropolitan Peter, the first Moscow metropolitan. The gilded sarcophagus of Patriarch Hermogenes (1606–12) stands in the southwest corner covered by a small canopy. During the Polish invasion Hermogenes was imprisoned and starved to death. After Patriarch Adrian, Peter the Great abolished the position and established the Holy Synod. The patriarch seat remained vacant until 1917. In 1991, Patriarch Alexei was voted in by Church elections. Only after 1991 was the Russian Orthodox Church, headed by the patriarch, allowed to govern itself again.

Ivan the Terrible's carved wooden throne stands to the left of the southern entrance. Made in 1551, it is known as the Throne of the Monomakhs. It is elaborately decorated with carvings representing the transfer of imperial power from the Byzantine Emperor Monomakh to the Grand Prince Vladimir Monomakh (1113–25), who married the emperor's sister. The patriarch's throne can be found by the southeast pier; the clergy sat upon the elevated stone that is decorated with carved flowers. The *Last Judgment* is painted over the western portal. Traditionally the congregation exited through the church's western door. The final theme portrayed was the Last Judgment as a reminder to people to work on salvation in the outside world.

In October 1989, for the first time in over 70 years, the Soviet Government under Gorbachev allowed a Russian Orthodox service to be conducted within the cathedral. This was a significant act of tolerance, since only three decades earlier Khrushchev had over 10,000 churches closed. In 2006, a 15-minute ceremonial changing of the guard was created for Cathedral Square on Saturdays at noon from May to October. The guards are dressed in uniforms styled after 1913 czarist times, and the choreography is accompanied by flutes and drums played by the presidential orchestra, which has played in the Kremlin since 1938. Tickets are available at the Kremlin ticket booth one-hour prior to the ceremony.

CHURCH OF THE DEPOSITION OF THE ROBE

To the west of the Assumption Cathedral is the smaller single-domed Church of the Deposition of the Virgin's Robe, built by Pskov craftsmen from 1484 to 1485. It once served as the private chapel of the patriarch and was linked by a small bridge to his palace. It later became a court chapel in 1653. The iconostasis was executed by Nazari Istomin in 1627. The interior wall frescoes, some dating back to 1644, are devoted to the Blessed Virgin. The northern gallery displays an exhibition of wooden handicrafts. It is closed on Thursdays.

TEREM PALACE

In the small courtyard west of the church are the Terem Palace and the **Golden Palace of the Czarina**, which served as the reception site for czarinas in the 16th century. The Terem Palace resembles a fairy-tale creation with its checkerboard roof and 11 golden turrets. It housed the children and female relatives of noblewomen, and was built for Czar Mikhail Romanov, whose private chambers on the fourth floor were later occupied by his son Alexei. At this time, women and their daughters were secluded in a *terem* (the word is derived from the Greek word *teremnon*, meaning 'special quarters'). Many State functions took place here and in the **Hall of the Cross**. The czar received petitions from the population in the Golden Throne Room. Only the czar's wife, personal confessor and blind storytellers were allowed into the private chapel and Royal Bedchamber, which is whimsically decorated. All the chapels of the Terem were united under one roof in 1681, including the churches of the Resurrection, Crucifixion, Savior and St Catherine.

The Terem Palace was built by Czar Mikhail Romanov to house the children and female relatives of noblewomen. Only the czar's wife, personal confessor and blind storytellers were allowed into the czar's private quarters and royal bedchamber on the top floor.

The adjoining Golden Palace of the Czarina at the eastern end was built in 1526 by Boris Godunov for his sister Irina, who was married to Czar Fedor I. This was her own private reception hall. When Fedor died, Irina refused the throne (the last son of Ivan the Terrible had died earlier in an epileptic attack); her brother Boris Godunov became the first elected czar. Admission to the Terem is by special permission only.

PALACE OF FACETS

Facing the bell tower and on the west side of Cathedral Square, is the two-story Renaissance-style Palace of Facets, one of Moscow's oldest civic buildings, onstructed by Ruffo and Solario between 1487 and 1491. It took its name from the elaborate stone facets decorating its exterior. State assemblies and receptions were held here—Ivan the Terrible celebrated his victory over Kazan in 1532 in this palace, and Peter the Great celebrated here after defeating the Swedes at Poltava in 1709. After Ivan III, all wives including the crowned czarinas were barred from attending State ceremonies and receptions in the Hall of Facets; a small look-out room was built above the western wall, from which the women could secretly watch the proceedings. The **Red Staircase**, which led from the Assumption Cathedral to the palace's southern wall, was reconstructed in 1994; it had been destroyed in the 1930s under Stalin. Peter acquired his dislike of Moscow when the Streltsy (palace guards) revolted in 1682, and the future czar (then only aged ten) witnessed the murder of family members who were hurled off this staircase onto sharpened pikes below. In 1812, Napoleon also watched his attempted burning of Moscow from here. Today the Hall is used for State occasions. Entrance to the Palace of Facets is by special permission only. Both this and the Terem Palace have recently undergone a 300-million-dollar renovation.

CATHEDRAL OF THE ANNUNCIATION

This white-stoned cathedral, with its nine gilded domes, and jasper floors (a gift from a Persian shah), stands directly south of the Palace of Facets. It was built from 1484 to 1489 by Pskov craftsmen, commissioned by Ivan the Great, as the private chapel of the czars. (It is on the site of the first wood and stone church built in 1397 by Grand Prince Vasily.) After a fire destroyed it in 1547, Ivan the Terrible rebuilt the cathedral in 1564 with four additional chapels that included the Archangel Gabriel Chapel. After Ivan's fourth marriage, the Orthodox Church barred him from entering a church, so he had this chapel built through which he could view services. In 1572, a new porch, known as the Steps of Ivan the Terrible, were also added to the southeast corner. In 2001, a late 15th-century Moscow-school copy of the *Virgin of Vladimir* icon was returned from the Tretyakov Gallery to the Chapel of St

THE MAN IN THE WINDOW

*T*he building stands behind the high red-brick wall known to the entire
world. There are many windows in that building, but one was
distinguished from all the others because it was lit twenty-four hours a
day. Those who gathered in the evening on the broad square in front of the
red-brick wall would crane their necks, strain their eyes to the point of
tears, and say excitedly to one another: "Look, over there, the window's
lit. He's not sleeping. He's working. He's thinking about us."

If someone came from the provinces to this city or had to stop over
while in transit, he'd be informed that it was obligatory to visit that
famous square and look and see whether that window was lit. Upon
returning home, the fortunate provincial would deliver authoritative
reports, both at closed meetings and at those open to the public, that yes,
the window was lit, and judging by all appearances, he truly never slept
and was continually thinking about them.

Naturally, even back then, there were certain people who abused the
trust of their collectives. Instead of going to look at that window, they'd
race around to all the stores, wherever there was anything for sale. But,
upon their return, they, too, would report that the window was lit, and just
try and tell them otherwise.

The window, of course, was lit. But the person who was said never to
sleep was never at that window. A dummy made of gutta-percha, built by
the finest craftsmen, stood in for him. That dummy had been so skillfully
constructed that unless you actually touched it there was nothing to indicate that it wasn't alive. Its hand held a curved pipe of English manufacture,
which had a special mechanism that puffed out tobacco smoke at
pre-determined intervals. As far as the original himself was concerned, he
only smoked his pipe when there were people around, and his moustache
was of the paste-on variety. He lived in another room, in which there were
not only no windows but not even any doors. That room could only be
reached through a crawl-hole in his safe, which had doors both in the
front and in the rear and which stood in the room that was officially his.

He loved this secret room where he could be himself and not smoke a pipe or wear that moustache; where he could live simply and modestly, in keeping with the room's furnishings—an iron bed, a striped mattress stuffed with straw, a washbasin containing warm water, and an old gramophone, together with a collection of records which he personally had marked—good, average, remarkable, trash.

There in that room he spent the finest hours of his life in peace and quiet; there, hidden from everyone, he would sometimes sleep with the old cleaning woman who crawled in every morning through the safe with her bucket and broom. He would call her over to him, she would set her broom in the corner in business-like fashion, give herself to him, and then return to her cleaning. In all the years, he had not exchanged a single word with her and was not even absolutely certain whether it was the same old woman or a different one every time.

One strange incident occurred. The old woman began rolling her eyes and moving her lips soundlessly.

"What's the matter with you?"

"I was just thinking," the old woman said with a serene smile. "My niece is coming to visit, my brother's daughter. I've got to fix some eats for her, but all I've got is three roubles. So it's either spend two roubles on millet and one on butter, or two on butter and one on millet."

This peasant sagacity touched him deeply. He wrote a note to the storehouse ordering that the old woman be issued as much miller and butter as she needed. The old woman, no fool, did not take the note to the storehouse but to the Museum of Revolution, where she sold it for enough money to buy herself a little house near Moscow and a cow; she quit her job, and rumor has it that to this day she's still bringing in milk to sell at Tishinsky market.

Vladimir Voinovich, A Circle of Friends, 1969

Vladimir Voinovich, who turned 70 in 2002, is Russia's greatest living satirist. His other works include Life and Extraordinary Adventures of Private Ivan Chonkin, Ivankiad and the comic masterpiece Moscow 2042.

Nicholas-the-Miracle-Worker, where it originally hung. The three stars on the veil symbolize virginity, while the robed child represents Christ Emmanuel. Distinguishing it from the 12th-century Byzantine original are the placement of the hands, the tilt of the head and the direction of the Virgin Mary's gaze. (See Special Topic on The Russian Icon on page 329.)

Inside, frescoes that date back to 1508 include themes from the Book of Revelation, Moscovy princes and Byzantine emperors. Portraits of Greek philosophers and poets, such as Plato, Homer, Aristotle, Virgil, and Socrates, holding scrolls upon which are written their sayings, can also be found on the pillars and in the galleries. Old chronicles state that several tiers of the iconostatis, dating back to 1405, were painted by Theophanes the Greek (from left to right, on the largest right-hand deesis row are: *The Virgin, Christ Enthroned, St John the Baptist, Archangel Gabriel, Apostle Paul* and *St John Chrysostom*). Prokhor of Gorodets and Andrei Rubylov also painted icons on the second and third tiers, including Rublyov's *The Annunciation* and the *Archangel Michael*. The lovely iconostasis frame is made out of repoussé gilt bronze, and the Heavenly Gates, leading to the altar, are of chased silver. The multi-tiered chandeliers date back to the 17th century. The first clock in Moscow was supposedly hung beside the cathedral at the prince's court in 1404.

CATHEDRAL OF THE ARCHANGEL MICHAEL

The third main cathedral of the Kremlin is the five-domed Cathedral of the Archangel Michael (1505–08), which served as the burial place of the czars; the Archangel Michael was considered the guardian of Moscow princes. It stands directly east across from the Annunciation Cathedral. Ivan the Great commissioned the Italian architect Alevisio Novi to rebuild the church that stood here. Novi combined the styles of Old Russian and Italian Renaissance; notice the traits of a Venetian palazzo. The surviving frescos date from 1652 and depict aspects of Russian life. A large iconostasis (1680) is filled with 15th- to 17th-century icons, including the *Archangel Michael* by Rublyov. Nearly 50 sarcophagi line the walls of the cathedral, containing grand princes and czars and some of their sons. All czars and Moscovy princes were buried here up to the 18th century (except for Boris Godunov whose body lies in Sergiyev Posad). White tombstones give their names in Old Slavonic. The first grand prince to be buried here was Ivan I in 1341, who built the original church. After Peter the Great moved the capital to St Petersburg, the czars were buried in the Peter and Paul Fortress, except for Peter II, who died in Moscow. The cathedral is closed on Thursdays.

Two Persian war masks from the 16th-century (above)
and a pair of decorative breastplates, on display in the Armory Palace.

Behind the cathedral stands **Petrovskaya (Peter's) Tower**, named after the first Moscow metropolitan. The fourth unadorned tower from the corner is the **Tainitskaya (Secret) Tower**, which had an underground passage to the Moskva River. The next one over is the **Blagoveshchenskaya (Annunciation) Tower**, which contained the Annunciation Icon. The round corner tower is called the **Vodovzvodnaya, the Water-Drawing Tower** (1633), in which water was raised from the river to an aqueduct that led inside. This is Russia's first pressurized system; it was used for pumping water to the royal palaces and gardens.

GRAND KREMLIN PALACE

Built from 1838 to 1849, the Grand Palace, behind the Annunciation Cathedral, was the Moscow residence of the imperial family. Nicholas I commissioned Konstantin Thon to erect it on the site of the former Grand Prince Palace. There are 700 rooms and five elaborate reception halls; two of these, along the southern wall overlooking the river, were combined to form the Meeting Hall of the Russian Federation. The long gold and white St George Hall has 18 columns decorated with statues of victory. The walls are lined with marble plaques bearing the names of heroes awarded the Order of St George (introduced by Catherine the Great) for service and courage. The six bronze chandeliers hold over 3,000 light bulbs.

This hall is now used for special State receptions and ceremonies; cosmonaut Yuri Gagarin received the Golden Star Hero Award here in 1961. The **Hall of St Catherine** served as the Empress' Throne Room. In October 1994, Britain's Queen Elizabeth II made her first visit to Russia (her grandfather called Nicholas II 'Cousin Nicky') where she met with Boris Yeltsin in the gold and cream splendor of this hall. The Hall of Vladimir connected the Palace of Facets, the Golden Palace of the Czarina and the Terem Palace. The ground floor rooms used to contain the imperial family's bedchambers. Entrance is by special permission only.

AMUSEMENT PALACE

The Poteshny (Amusement) Palace, situated along the west wall behind the Terem Palace, was acquired from a Boyar family in 1652 by Czar Alexis, who turned the building into a residence for his father-in-law. When he died, Alexis turned the palace into the court's first theater. Later, Stalin lived here with his wife and two children. (They had married in 1918 when Stalin was 39 and Nadezhda only 17.) When his wife Nadezhda committed suicide in November 1932 (disillusioned with her husband's ways), the children were moved to other quarters, and Stalin lived separately in another Kremlin apartment.

ARMORY PALACE

The Oruzheinaya Palata (Armory Palace) is the oldest museum in the country which houses one of the greatest collections of its kind in the world. In 1485, Grand Prince Vasily III, son of Ivan the Great, constructed a special stone building on the edge of the Kremlin grounds to house the royal family's growing collection of valuables. It also contained the czar's workshops and a place to store armor and weapons. In the late 1600s Peter the Great converted it into a museum to house the art treasures of the Kremlin. The present building, designed and erected between 1844–1851 by Konstantin Thon, has nine exhibition halls that trace the history of the Kremlin and the Russian State. It also houses a magnificent collection of Western European decorative and applied art from the 12th to 19th centuries.

Hall I (Halls I–IV are on the first floor) exhibits a huge collection of armor and weaponry from the 13th to 18th centuries. The oldest item is the iron helmet of Yaroslavl the Wise, father of Alexander Nevsky. Hall II has displays of gold and silver from the 12th to 17th centuries, including jewelry, chalices (one belonging to Yuri Dolgoruky), bowls, watches and the Ryazan Treasure collection. Hall III contains gold and silver jewelry from the 18th to 20th centuries, including fabulous Fabergé eggs and jewelry. Hall IV has a collection of precious fabrics and vestments, including a robe of the first Metropolitan Peter, Peter the Great, and a coronation robe of Catherine the Great. One robe presented to the metropolitan by Catherine contains over 150,000 semiprecious stones. A silk *sakkos* vestment was embroidered for Patriarch Nikon in 1654; it consists of so many pearls and precious stones that it weighs over 22 kilograms (50 pounds)!

Hall V (Halls V–IX are on the ground floor) exhibits many of the foreign gifts of silver and gold from the 13th to 19th centuries from England, France, Sweden, Holland and Poland. Hall VI is known as the Throne and Crown Room and contains ancient royal regalia. The oldest throne, carved from ivory, belonged to Ivan the Terrible. A Persian shah presented Boris Godunov with a throne encrusted with 2,000 precious stones in 1604, and the throne of Czar Alexei Romanov contains over 1,000 diamonds. The most interesting is the Double Throne used by Peter the Great and his half-brother Ivan, when they were proclaimed joint czars. Peter's older half-sister Sophia acted as regent and used to sit in a secret compartment in the throne behind Peter to advise him. The Crown of Monomakh, decorated with precious stones and sable (first worn by Grand Prince Vladimir Monomakh in 1113), was used by all grand princes and czars until Peter the Great. The room also contains Catherine the Great's petite silver wedding dress, embroidered with imperial eagles (note the size difference between this and Catherine's later gowns). The coronation gowns of Alexandra (worn in 1896), the last Romanov empress, and Empress Elizabeth, are also on display. Halls VII and VIII contain saddles, bridles and sleigh covers. Hall IX is the Carriage Room, containing the world's largest collection of carriages dating back to Boris Godunov. The most elaborate is the coronation coach presented to Empress Elizabeth by Count Razumovsky. It is the Bourinhall carriage made in 1757 in Paris. The carved gilt wood is made to represent the sea and breaking waves. The paintings on the panels are by François Boucher. The most absurd is the miniature coach made in 1675 for young Peter the Great; it was pulled by ponies, and dwarves served as coachmen. The Diamond Fund Exhibit is a collection of the crown jewels and precious gems. These include the Orlov Diamond (189 carats) that Count Orlov bought for his mistress, Catherine the Great. Catherine the Great's coronation crown is covered with pearls and 4,936 diamonds. A new section of the Armory displays gifts to the former USSR from foreign countries.

The Armory is one of the most interesting museums in Moscow and should definitely be visited. Buying an entrance ticket to the Kremlin by the Kutafya Tower is often not good for entrance to the Armory. (It is recommended to book a group tour through your hotel or a Russian travel agency, see page 411.) Only groups are allowed to enter during four separate one-and-a-half-hour daily tours (except Thursdays) at 10am, 12pm, 2.30pm and 4.30pm, conducted in different languages. Trying to purchase a ticket as an individual traveler is extremely frustrating. The *kassa* for Armory tickets is at the Borovitskaya Tower and are sold for the same day only. Before you queue, try to check with a guard that Armory tickets are still available—they can often be sold out. For any chance of securing a ticket, get there early. Large bags musted be checked-in at the Kutafya pavilion. If entering for a Kremlin tour with a guide, they can show you where to purchase an Armory ticket —buy one immediately upon entering. Tickets to view the Diamond Fund (open 10am–5pm) are on sale near the second Armory entrance; sometimes it is only open with special permission. Some Moscow travel agencies such as Capital Tours, provide Kremlin and Armory (and Moscow sightseeing) excursions. tel. 232-2442, www.capitaltours.ru for bookings online.

FABERGÉ

In 1842, during the reign of Nicholas I, Gustav Fabergé founded the first Fabergé workshop in St Petersburg. His son Peter Carl later extended the French family business to the cities of Moscow, Kiev, Odessa and London. These workshops produced a wealth of exquisite jewelry, clocks, cut glass, and other decorative objects made from gold, silver and semiprecious stones.

For over a century Fabergé crafted unique art objects for the imperial court. Master craftsmen like Mikhail Perkhin, Erik Kollin, Henrik Wigström and Julius Rappoport had their own Fabergé workshops and sometimes spent years designing and crafting a single piece of art.

The fabulous Fabergé eggs were a favorite gift presented by the Romanov family and other members of the aristocracy. The first Fabergé Easter egg was commissioned in 1885 by Alexander III. When Carl Fabergé proposed creating an Easter gift for the Empress Maria Fedorovna, the czar ordered an egg containing a special surprise. On Easter morning, the empress broke open what appeared to be an ordinary egg, but inside, a gold yolk contained a solid gold chick with a replica of the imperial crown and a tiny ruby egg. (The crown and egg are now lost.) The empress was so delighted by the egg that the czar ordered one to be delivered to the court each Easter. Alexander's son Nicholas II continued the Fabergé tradition and ordered two eggs each Easter, one each for his wife and mother.

On Easter morning 1895, Nicholas gave his mother a Fabergé egg decorated with diamonds, emeralds and a star sapphire. Hand painted miniatures depicting Danish scenes known to the dowager empress (the former Princess Dagmar of Denmark) were hidden inside what became known as the Danish Egg. By 1896, the year of the coronation of Nicholas II, virtually all the State's royal gifts came from Fabergé . (At the height of the firm's success, Fabergé had four shops in Russia, one in London, over 500 employees, and an additional catalog business). In 1900, Fabergé presented the imperial family with a silver egg that contained a golden replica of the Trans-Siberian Railway. The surface of the egg is engraved with a map of the route. The compartment windows are made of crystal, and the headlamp on the locomotive is a ruby. Every detail is correct down to the destination boards and the labels on special compartments reserved for passengers. The train actually moves and can be wound with a tiny golden key. It is now kept in the Kremlin Armory.

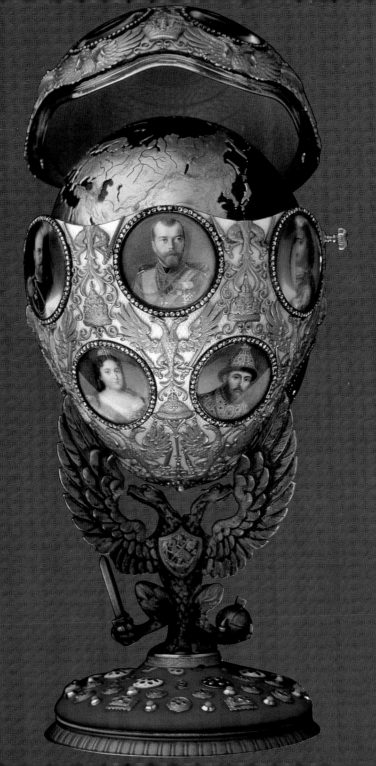

The last work by Mikhail Evlampiyevich Perkhin (who died in 1903) was an egg composed of clover leaves and stems, constructed of diamonds and rubies. In 1909, Wigström and Nikolai made a crystal egg with two pear-shaped pendants set at each end. The interior contained a gold model of the royal yacht *Standart*, set inside a turbulent sea of rock crystal.

In 1911, eggs were presented for the royals' 15th anniversary. Alexandra received an egg decorated with scenes of the coronation, and the dowager empress was presented with an orange tree egg complete with a golden feathered bird that sang at the press of a button. Another egg is designed to look like a vase in rock crystal (which appears to be filled with water) with a pansy decoration. By pressing a button on the stem, its petals flowered revealing miniature portraits of Nicholas II's children.

When the Russian Exhibition was held in Moscow in 1882, Carl Fabergé received the Gold Medal (in 1887, a Moscow workshop was opened on Kuznetsky Most); later, in 1900, at the Exposition Universelle in Paris, he won the Grand Prix award along with the Legion of Honor. By 1915, there were more than 150,000 Fabergé pieces in circulation around the world; and by 1917 Fabergé had created 54 Imperial Eggs; today 47 survive. Forced to close the company after the Revolution, Carl Fabergé fled Russia and died in Switzerland in 1920. Today, one of the most extensive Fabergé collections in the world can be seen at the Armory Museum in the Moscow Kremlin. In 2004, oils and metals magnate, Viktor Vekselberg, paid over $100 million to a private collector for nine Fabergé eggs, and giftd them bacl to Russia and the Kremlin Armory Museum.

Today, one can pay a visit to the salon of the Russian jeweler Andrei Ananov, considered Fabergé's contemporary heir. The showroom is located at 31 Nevsky Prospekt with items available for purchase. Website: www.ananov.com.

(opposite) In 1908, Henrik Wigström made a nephrite egg whose interior was a model of Tsarskoye Selo's Alexander Palace in St Petersburg. The surface of the egg is encrusted with elegant gold garlands, decorated by miniature portraits in frames made out of small diamonds.

OLD MOSCOW

The area to the east of the Kremlin is known as **Kitai-Gorod**. *Kitai* is derived from either the Mongolian word for central or the Old Russian *kiti* meaning bundle of stakes. These protective palisades surrounded the area. (One small fragment remaining from the original 16th-century wall is near the northern entrance of the Rossiya Hotel.) *Gorod* is the Russian word for town. (In modern Russian, *Kitai* means China.) Foreign settlements were later established in this area. In the 14th century the central town was surrounded by a protective earthen rampart and served as the central *posad* (market and trade area), where merchants and townspeople lived. Beyond the rampart lay the forest. Later Ivan the Terrible constructed a larger fortified stone wall. The original area of Kitai-Gorod (which formed Moscow's second ring) stretched in the form of a horseshoe from the History Museum on Red Square, along the back of GUM Department Store, and east down to the banks of the Moskva River. On each side of GUM are the small streets of Nikolskaya and Ilyinka.

On the opposite side of the square, the Iberian Gates (Iverskiye Vorota) served as the main entrance to Red Square. The Chapel of the Iberian Mother of God once stood atop the gates and contained the Virgin of Iver Icon, said to possess miraculous powers. The gates were also the access route from Kitai-Gorod (China Town) to the Beli Gorod (White Town). Before setting out on long journeys, Muscovites also stopped here to pray.

NIKOLSKAYA ULITSA (STREET)

This street, which begins at the northeastern corner of Red Square, runs along the side of GUM, and ends at Lubyanskaya Square. After the Revolution until 1991, its name was 25th of October Street, commemorating the first day of the 1917 Revolution. In the 17th century the area was nicknamed the Street of Enlightenment; Moscow's first learning academy, printing yard and bookshops lined the passage. The street was originally named after the nearby Nikolsky Monastery.

The first corner building as you leave the square was the Governor's Office, where the writer Alexander Radishchev was held before his exile to Siberia (by Catherine the Great) in 1790. His book, *A Journey from St Petersburg to Moscow*, described the terrible conditions of serfdom. Behind the Kazan Cathedral stands the **Old Royal Mint** inside the small courtyard. An inscription on the gates shows it was built by Peter the Great in 1697. When he later moved it to St Petersburg, the vice-governor had his office here.

Down the street from the Royal Mint, at number 7, are several buildings that remain from the **Zaikonospassky Monastery** founded by Boris Godunov in the early 1600s. The name means 'Icon of our Savior'; the monastery used to make and sell icons. The red and white **Savior's Church** was built in 1661. The church and adjoining buildings housed the **Slavic-Greek-Latin Academy**, Moscow's first and largest academy for higher education, which operated from 1687 to 1814. Among the first students were the poet Kantemir, the architect Bazhenov and Mikhail Lomonosov (1711–65), who became a renowned poet, historian and educator. Known as the 'Father of Russian Science', Lomonosov established Moscow University under Empress Elizabeth in 1755. (See also St Petersburg pages 444 and 487.)

At number 15 was the first Printing Yard, now the History and Archives Institute. Ivan the Terrible brought the first printing press to Russia in 1553. Still hanging on the Gothic-style aquamarine and white building are the emblems of the old printing yard, a lion and unicorn, together with a sundial, mounted in 1814. The thick black gates lead to the colorfully tiled **Building of the Old Proofreader**, where Ivan Fedorov spent a year printing Russia's first book. Ivan the Terrible visited Fedorov daily until *The Acts of the Apostles* (now in the State Public Library) was completed on March 1, 1564. The first Russian newspaper, *Vedomosti*, was printed here on December 16th 1702. The present building was constructed in 1814 and was used as the printing center for the Holy Synod, the council established by Peter the Great that regulated church affairs.

At number 19 was the **Slavyansky Bazaar**, one of Moscow's oldest and most popular hotels (it later closed due to fire damage). When the restaurant opened in the 1870's, it became a popular meeting place for Moscow merchants who negotiated deals over the delicious *blini* pancakes. The hotel was also a favorite hangout of Anton Chekhov when he lived in Moscow. (The hotel appeared in Chekhov's "The Lady with the Lapdog".) On June 21, 1897, the playwright and theater critic Vladimir Nemirovich-Danchenko just happened to be seated at a restaurant table with actor Konstantin Stanislavsky (the creator of the Stanislavky Method). They sat and talked about the dire state of Moscow theater; while drinking and eating, over the course of 18 hours, they hammered out plans for the creation of the legendary Moscow Art Theater, which later staged Chekhov's plays.

Opposite the Printing House is the former **Chizhov Coach Exchange**. The Chizhov family hired out horse-drawn carriages and carts as taxis. The Coach Exchange was popular year-round, when Moscow streets were either muddy or frozen. In winter Muscovites could hire a Chizhov troika, or sled (see excerpt from Nicholai Gogol's *Dead Souls* on page 208 for a wonderful description of a troika ride). Next door is the one-domed **Church of the Dormition**.

The small passage known as **Tretyakov Proyezd** links Nikolskaya Street with Okhotny Ryad. The wealthy merchant Sergei Tretyakov knocked this passage through the Kitai-Gorod wall in 1871 to gain quick access to the banks along Okhotny Ryad. It is now known as Moscow's Fifth Avenue, with stores from Tiffany to Gucci. At its front entrance stands the **Monument to Ivan Fedorov** (1510–83), the first Russian printer.

Halfway down Nikolskaya Street, take a right on Ilyinka Proyezd. Near the corner, on Bogoyavlensky Pereulok, stands the baroque red-brick 17th-century **Cathedral of Bogoyavlensky** (Epiphany), once part of a monastery established in the 13th century by Prince Daniil in order to protect inhabitants of the then unwalled city. The cathedral stands on the site of Moscow's first stone church, built by Ivan I. Many of the sculptures that were in the church are now on display in the Donskoi Monastery. The wealthy Boyar Golitsyn family had their burial vaults here until the mid-18th century; they were transferred to the Donskoi Monastery outside of the city when a cholera epidemic prohibited burial in the city center.

The pharmacy shop at number 21 is over a century old. The first pharmacy, for members of the czar's family, was set up in the Kremlin by Ivan the Terrible in 1581. Beginning in the 1600s, pharmacies sold medicinal herbs in Moscow. Many of the herbs were grown in the area of what is now the Alexandrov Gardens near the Kremlin. The first public pharmacies opened in 1721.

The passage is still lined with small bookshops; a popular one is Knizhnaya Nakhodka at number 23.

ULITSA ILYINKA (ILYINKA STREET)

Ilyinka Proyezd (Passage) leads into this street, which begins on Red Square and continues past the southeast side of GUM. It was once the main thoroughfare of Kitai-Gorod. In 1497, Ivan the Great gave a parcel of land on this street to 500 Novgorod merchant families to establish the Moscow-Novgorod Trade Exchange, at a time when Novgorod was still independent of Moscovy. The wealthy merchants erected **St Ilyia Church**, recognizable by its single dome and *zakomara* gabled arches. From 1935 to 1991 this street was named after the popular revolutionary figure Kuybyshev. The passage was once the busy thoroughfare of Moscow's bank and financial district. At number 6 the classical building of the **Moscow Stock Exchange** or Birzha (1838), with its large Ionic columns, once again bustles with commercial activity.

The wealthy merchant Pavel Riabushinsky commissioned Fedor Shekhtel to build the Riabushinsky Bank in 1904. Shekhtel also designed the nearby Moscow Merchants Building in 1909. Riabushinsky was a highly respected spokesman for the merchant class and chairman of the Moscow Stock Exchange.

As Ilyinka Passage continues across the street of the same name, it becomes Ribny Pereulok (Fish Lane), where many food stalls were once set up. From 1795 to 1805 the Italian architect Quarenghi built the Old Merchant Arcade, **Gostiny Dvor**, which occupied an entire block. This Corinthian-columned white structure now serves as a shopping plaza.

ULITSA VARVARKA (VARVARKA STREET)

Ribny Pereulok leads into Ulitsa Varvarka, which starts near St Basil's and continues past the Rossiya Hotel. Near the hotel are the remains of the 16th-century brick rampart walls that surrounded Kitai-Gorod; this wall was over 2.5 kilometers (one and a half miles) long and six meters (20 feet) high. One entered Kitai-Gorod through the Vladimirsky Gates; all that remains is a red gate built in 1871. After the Revolution until 1991 the street was known as Razin, named after Stenka Razin, a popular cossack rebel who was executed in Red Square in 1671.

This area used to lie beyond the old marketplace on the outer fringes of Red Square. In Old Russian *zariadi* means 'beyond the trading stalls'. The large **Rossiya Hotel** (once the world's largest hotel), which had been located behind St Basil's Cathedral since 1967, was demolished in 2006. A large retail and entertainment complex is planned for the 30-acre site.

The salmon and white **Church of St Varvara** (Barbara) stands at the beginning of the street, which is named after this saint. The 16th-century church was rebuilt in the 18th century by the architect Matvei Kazakov. Services are held daily at 5pm. This passage once stretched from the Kremlin, along the old trade route, to the towns of Vladimir and Kolomna. Prince Dmitri Donskoi used this route to return home after his victorious battle with the Mongols in the Battle of Kulikovo in 1380.

The small cube-shaped and five-domed **Church of St Maxim** stands nearby. Built in 1698 by Novgorod merchants, it held the remains of St Maxim, an ascetic prophet who died in 1433. It now houses branches of the Society for Environmental Protection and the Nobility League Art Salon, which sells souvenirs to do with the last royal family.

Between these two churches, at 4 Varvarka, is the **Old English Inn**, a white-washed house with tiny irregularly placed windows and a steep wooden roof. It originally belonged to a wealthy Russian merchant until, in 1556, Ivan the Terrible presented it to Sir Richard Chancellor, an English merchant who began trade relationships with Russia. Ivan even proposed marriage to Queen Elizabeth I, but she declined and instead offered Ivan asylum in England whenever he might need it. Later the inn was used by English merchants for their stores and living quarters, and English diplomats also stayed here. It has recently been restored and is open 10am–6pm, 11am–7pm Wednesdays and Fridays; closed Mondays.

Up the street, at number 8, is the **Znamensky Cathedral**, built in the 1680's, all that remains of the Nunnery of Our Lady of the Sign. It now houses a small concert hall (with 250 seats), a chapel (which holds services), and an icon workshop. At number 12 is the **Church of St George on Pskov Hill**. The colorful church, with red walls and a blue belfry (1818), was erected by Pskov merchants in 1657. Open daily 11am–7pm.

Near the Cathedral, at number 10, is the **House of Boyars Romanov**. Built in 1547, it's the oldest surviving private house in Moscow. It is now a branch of the State History Museum (also known as the Zaryade Museum) that has displays of life from the 17th-century Boyardom. The rich Boyar Nikita Romanov had his home in the center of Kitai-Gorod. Nikita's sister, Anastasia, was married to Ivan the Terrible. Nikita's grandson Mikhail, who was born in the house, was later elected to the throne in 1613 and began the reign of the Romanov dynasty. The house was restored in the 19th century and is furnished to look like an early noble household. Open 10am–6pm, Sundays 11am–5pm; closed Tuesdays.

The street ends at Slavyanskaya Square. Heading south on Kitaigorodsky Proyezd, by the Moskva River, is the **Church of the Conception of St Anne-in-the-Corner**. The church stood at the corner of the Kitai-Gorod wall and was named after the Virgin's mother, St Anne. The barren wife of Grand Prince Vasily III, Solomonia (whom he later divorced), often prayed here.

KITAI-GOROD

Varvarka Street leads east to Slavyanskaya Square and the Kitai-Gorod Metro station. Kitai-Gorod (China Town) is where the foreign merchants used to live. Following the Bolshevik Revolution, the area was known as Nogin Square, after the revolutionary figure Viktor Nogin. In 1991 it reverted to its original name. The **Church of All Saints on Kulishki** stands on the south side of the square.

After Prince Dmitri Donskoi defeated the Mongols at Kulikovo in 1380, he erected a wooden church on the *kulishki*, marshy land. It was replaced by the stone church in the 16th century, which has been restored. To the left of the church are the gray buildings of the **Delovoy Dvor**, the business chambers. Built in 1913, they were used for the business operations of the city.

Near the square are the **Ilyinsky Gardens**, with a monument to the Russian Grenadiers who died in the Battle of Plevna against Turkey in 1877. Along the small side street called Staraya (Old) Ploshchad, are buildings that were once used by the Central Committee of the Communist Party. A few minutes' walk west, at 3

The Church of St George on Pskov Hill was built in 1657 from donations given by the community of Pskov merchants who were living in Moscow. The golden Byzantine Orthodox crosses mounted on golden onion domes is a Russian design that dates back to the 15th century.

Nikitnikov Pereulok, is a 'jewel of merchant architecture', the Byzantine five-domed **Church of the Holy Trinity in Nikitniki.** In 1620, Mikhail Romanov hired a wealthy merchant from Yaroslavl, Grigory Nikitnikov, to work in the financial administration; and, he later became the only merchant authorized to trade with China. Nikitnikov named the street after himself, and later (with all his profits from importing tea and silk) built this church (1635-53) on the site of the wooden Church of St Nikita (his family saint), which burned down. The oldest icon is St Nikita, which Nikitnikov supposedly rescued from the burning church. The icon of the Trinity can be found on the iconostasis, carved in 1640. There are many unique frescoes and wood carvings on the walls.

The burial chapel of the Nikitnikovs lies to the right of the altar (Grigory was the first merchant to be buried inside a Russian Orthodox Church). Part of the church now functions as the **Museum of 17th-Century Architecture and Painting.** Open 10am–5pm, 12–7pm Wednesdays and Thursdays; closed Tuesdays. Church services are also held here.

Nearby, Staraya Ploshchad becomes Solyanka Ulitsa (Street). *Sol* means salt, and the old saltyards were along this street in the 17th century. At this time the area was considered the countryside of Moscow; Ivan the Great had a summer palace near the

In Moscow's Church of the Holy Trinity women donate their time to polish the golden iconostasis in preparation for an Orthodox service.

Convent of St John. Farther up the street is the **Church of St Vladimir-in-the-Old Gardens**. Solyanka intersects with Arkhipova Ulitsa, named after the artist who lived here in 1900. Many middle-class artisans lived in this part of the city. The **Moscow Choral Synagogue** is at 8 Bolshaya Spasoglinishhevsky Pereulok. The building went up in 1891, but did not open for another 15 years because the Moscow governor had expelled Jews from the city. But, it remained open after the Revolution. Today, it is the most important temple for Moscow's estimated 200,000 Jews. The synagogue serves kosher food in its café 'Na Gorke' on the first floor. The complex is open to the public 10am–6pm except on Saturdays and Jewish holidays (tel. 924-2424).

THE OLD MARX PROSPEKT

In 1991, Prospekt Marxa, the city's busiest avenue, was officially divided into three different streets. From Lubyanka Square to Teatralnaya Square, it is Teatralny Proyezd (past the Bolshoi Theater). From Teatralnaya Square to Pushkinskaya Street it is Okhotny Ryad (which leads from the Bolshoi Theater to Tverskaya Street and the National Hotel). The rest of the thoroughfare that runs alongside the Kremlin is now called Mokhovaya Street.

LUBYANSKAYA PLOSHCHAD (LUBYANKA SQUARE)

Teatralny Proyezd (Theater Passage) begins at this square, where a bronze statue of Felix Dzerzhinsky (1877–1926), a prominent revolutionary leader and founder of the Cheka (the All Russia Extraordinary Commission for Combating Counter-Revolution, Sabotage and Speculation), once stood in the center (earlier called Dzerzhinsky Square). The statue was pulled down by crowds on the night of August 22, 1991, after the attempted coup. (It now stands in the Park of the Fallen Idols on the grounds of the State Art Gallery near Gorky Park.) Various graffiti, coup memorabilia and an occasional Orthodox cross decorate the pedestal, which now commemorates all those killed by the KGB. For a century a charming fountain of cherubs, designed by Giovanni Vitali, had stood in the center of the square; in 1932, it was moved to the Academy of Sciences on Leninsky Prospekt. The Dzerzhinsky Monument was erected in its place 26 years later. (There is a current movement to bring back the statue to its original place.) In 1991, the square was given back its historical name of Lubyanka. In the 15th century, new settlers from Novgorod named the area Lubyanitsa, after a place in their native city. On the southeastern side of the square is the great stone from the northern Solovetsky Islands in the White Sea (an infamous 1930s gulag camp) laid in October 1990 by the Memorial Society. It bears an inscription commemorating the victims of the Soviet period.

Standing in Moscow's Lubyanka Square is the infamous former KGB building, used by Felix Dzerzhinsky to house the Cheka police after the Revolution. (His statue, which stood in the middle of the square, was pulled down by crowds on the evening of the August, 1991, attempted coup.) With the collapse of the Soviet Union, the KGB was disbanded; today, the building is still occupied by current Intelligence Services.

The Lubyanka Metro station exits on to the square. Original Kitai-Gorod walls were demolished to provide room for the Metro station, designed by Nikolai Ladovsky and opened in 1937. The large department store on one corner is **Detsky Mir** (Children's World), built in 1957, the largest children's store in Russia. More than half a million shoppers visit daily. Behind it is the **Savoy Hotel**. To the north, the street becomes Ulitsa Bolshaya Lubyanka.

Standing on the northeast side of Lubyanka Square is the infamous former **KGB Building**, constructed in the early 1900s as the headquarters of the Rossiya Insurance firm. It was built on the site of the Royal Secret Dispatch Office, where a dreadful prison was kept in the cellars during the reign of Catherine the Great. After the Revolution, Dzerzhinsky took the building over to house his Cheka police. In the 1930s the building was reconstructed; a new façade was erected, two floors were added and a massive underground prison complex, known as the Lubyanka, was built in the original cellars. (Under Stalin, in five years alone, the secret police or NKVD—People's Commissariat of Internal Affairs—executed over one million people. They also created the labor camp system.) In 1954, after the secret execution of Beria, Khrushchev founded the Committee for State Security—the KGB—to establish party control over the secret police after Stalin. At its height, the KGB employed an estimated 400,000 people.

On the left stands another (gray and black) KGB structure, built in 1980, and reputed to have many floors hidden underground. When the Communist Party was banned, the KGB tried to improve its image and even held a Miss KGB contest. With the fall of the Communist government, the organization of the KGB was disbanded; it was split into five agencies which included the Foreign Intelligence Service (SVRR) and the Federal Counterintelligence Service (SVR). The SVRR handled all intelligence gathering outside of Russia, including the former Soviet republics. Both divisions handled counterterrorism, illegal arms sales, drug trafficking and smuggling of radioactive materials. It is now forbidden to use substances (such as poisoned umbrella tips) that could damage human health or to blackmail people into cooperation. After the 1991 attempted coup against Gorbachev, many of the KGB leaders were purged and the agency was turned into the Federal Security Bureau (FSB). In his decree, Yeltsin harshly spelled out every acronym that the secret police had used since the Bolshevik Revolution: 'The system of the organs of the Cheka OGPU-NKVD-MGB-KGB-MB turned out to be unreformable.' (The Cheka OGPU was formed in 1922; NKVD in 1934; NKGB in 1943; MGB in 1946; and the KGB in 1953.)

Today the agencies are paralyzed with budget crises, massive reorganizations, a 30 percent staff cut, and a severe and disorienting change in mission since the end of the Cold War. At one point, a paper shortage in the country forced agents to type reports on the back of old documents; many offices still do not have computers and people are forced to share typewriters. It is now not only difficult to recruit foreigners as (secret) Russian agents, but native Russians as well. The American CIA and FBI were even called in to help revamp their computer systems. The goal of building Communism and the Great Motherland has been usurped by capitalist ideology, and the brightest no longer consider it prestigious to work for intelligence; registration at the Andropov Red Banner Institute, which trains intelligence recruits, has dropped by more than 75 percent. With Vladimir Putin, an ex-KGB agent, in office, many are still suspicious of where the intelligence organisations are heading.

Three interesting museums are nearby the square. The **Mayakovsky Museum** is on the corner of Myasnitskaya Ulitsa and Lubyansky Proyezd. The popular poet Vladimir Mayakovsky (1893–1930) lived at this address for over a decade, but then, disillusioned with socialism, committed suicide here in April 1930. Many of his works and personal items are on display. Films of Mayakovsky are also shown, along with recordings of him reading his work. The museum is open 10am–5pm, 1pm–8pm Thursdays (when literary readings are held in the evening); closed Wednesdays.

At 12 Novaya Ploshchad (New Square) is the **History of Moscow Museum**, founded in 1896. Since 1939, it has been housed in the Church of St John the Divine 'Under the Elm', built in 1825. It has photographic displays of early Kremlin settlements to World War II reconstructions, archeological finds (many from the early 1990s Kremlin Manezh Square excavations for the underground shopping center; other explorations of the Kremlin's honeycomb of tunnels and city sewer systems are also under way) and a waxworks exhibition. The gallery has paintings and prints for sale. Open 10am–6pm, 11am–7pm Wednesdays and Fridays; closed Mondays.

Opposite, at 3/4 Novaya Ploshchad, is the **Polytechnical Museum**. Opened in 1872, it was one of Moscow's first museums. The current building, completed in 1907, has 60 halls containing over 100,000 exhibits that trace the history of Russian science and technology. In the basement is a fabulous collection of old Russian automobiles; the first Russian car was the Pobeda (Victory), manufactured after World War II. Henry Ford also exported his cars to Moscow (through Armand Hammer) until Lenin's death in 1924. On the top floor is an interesting collection of Russian space capsules and an exhibition on the life of the first Soviet cosmonaut Yuri Gagarin. The library has over three million volumes.

The Polytechnical building was also a popular center for local meetings; writers such as Akhmatova, Gorky and Mayakovsky gave readings here, and Lenin often presented lectures. In 1967, the longest telepathic experiment in history took place between the museum and Leningrad. The sender Yuri Kamensky sent telepathic messages from here to the psychic receiver Karl Nikolayev at Leningrad University. From the 1950s until the 1980s, the Soviets vigorously studied parapsychology and aspects of psychic warfare. Today the Central Hall is run by the Znaniye (Knowledge) Society, and lectures and readings are still staged. The museum is open from 10am–6pm; closed Mondays.

TEATRALNAYA PLOSHCHAD (THEATER SQUARE)

The main section of the old Prospekt Marxa opens onto Teatralnaya Ploshchad (Theater Square). From 1919 until 1991 it was known as Sverdlov Square, after the first president of Soviet Russia, Yakov Sverdlov (1885–1919). The statue of Karl Marx, inscribed with the words 'Workers of All Countries Unite!' stands in the middle of the square. The Metro station is Teatralnaya. From Theater Square to Red Square, the street is now known as Okhotny Ryad (Hunter's Row—the street once led to the countryside and a popular hunting ground).

On the corner, at 1/4 Teatralny Proezd, is one of Moscow's finest and most expensive hotels, the **Metropol**. In the late 1880s, the Chelyshy Hotel stood on this spot. The Chelyshev family sold it to the St Petersburg Insurance Society for over one million rubles and the company then rebuilt the site, renaming the hotel Metropol, the Greek word for 'mother-city.' The head of the Society was Savva Mamontov, a Russian railroad tycoon and art patron, who in 1899, chose to stage a design contest for the building's façade. At first, the Russian Lev Kekushev was deemed the winner for his 'style-moderne.' But Mamontov pushed for a design by William Walcott, who had a more innovative approach with his art-nouveau design, entitled 'Women's Head.'

The first cornerstone of the hotel was laid in November 1898. After a disastrous fire ruined construction in December 1901, the hotel was finally completed in early 1905. Newspapers called it the 'Tower of Babylon of the 20th Century.' Costing over seven million rubles to build, it had hot water, electric elevators and even a state-of-the-art ventilation system. The mosaic panels and classical friezes were designed by Russian artists such as Mikhail Vrubel (*The Princess of Dreams*) at the western façade and Alexander Golovin and Nikolai Andreev (*The Four Seasons*) on the fourth floor. The hotel proved an enormous success. Fyodor Shalyapin sung here and many other famous artists, writers and musicians had work residences in the hotel. Rasputin even once had his headquarters here. Now, for nearly a century, the hotel has hosted thousands of international VIPs. Mstislav Rostropovich met his wife, Galina Vishnevskaya, in the restaurant, and in an irony of fate both John F Kennedy and Lee Harvey Oswald stayed at the hotel at different times. From 1986–91, the hotel was closed to transform its 370 rooms into the city's first five-star hotel. Inside are restaurants, bars and coffee shops, some with excellent all-you-can-eat breakfast and lunch buffets. Next door to the hotel is a fascinating antique shop. Facing the hotel to the right are walls of the 16th-century Kitai-Gorod.

Until 1919 this area was known as Theater Square, because two of Moscow's most prominent theaters were built here, the Bolshoi (Big) and the Maly (Small). One of the world's most famous theaters, **the Bolshoi** was built in 1824 by Osip Bovet and Alexander Mikhailov to stage performances of ballet and opera. It was constructed on the original site of the Royal Peter Theater, built in 1780. After a fire in 1856, the Bolshoi was rebuilt in neoclassical style by Albert Kavos to coincide with Alexander II's coronation. The stately building, with its large fountain in front, is crowned by the famous four bronze horses pulling the chariot of Apollo, patron of the arts. This is the work of sculptor Peter Klodt. The theater's gorgeous interior boasts five tiers of gilded boxes, whose chairs are covered with plush red velvet. The chandelier is made from 13,000 pieces of cut glass. The theater premiered compositions by Tchaikovsky, Glinka, Mussorgsky and Rimsky-Korsakov. After *perestroika*, it even premiered the Orthodox Church's *Millennium of the Baptism of Rus*.

The Bolshoi is currently closed until March, 2008, for a $700 million restoration. Additional rooms will also provide much needed space to store the company's 30,000 costumes and set pieces. The plush red-and-gold interior will be renovated, and the famous gold-threaded hammer-and-sickle curtain replaced with one featuring symbols of the Russian empire.

The Bolshoi Theater stands on Moscow's Theater Square. Built in 1824 to stage performances of opera and ballet, it premiered compositions by some of Russia's greatest composers; (above) Peter Klodt sculpted the four bronze horses that crown the roof; they pull the chariot of Apollo, patron of the arts.

Meanwhile, the Bolshoi's new 'Sister Theater,' standing directly across the street, had its grand opening in September 2002 (after six years of construction) for the start of the Bolshoi's 227th season. Tickets can be bought in advance at www.bolshoi.ru. Scalpers are also usually selling tickets outside before performances. Unfortunately, in the last few years prices have gone up considerably.

Across Petrovka Street from the Bolshoi is the pale-yellow **Maly Drama Theater**. At its entrance stands the statue of Alexander Ostrovsky (1823–86), the outstanding Russian playwright. The theater is nicknamed the Ostrovsky House. Many classic Russian plays are staged here. Nearby is the Central Children's Theater, formed in 1921. Across the street from the Maly is the old Mostorg, or Moscow Trade. In 1907, when the building was completed, it housed the English department store Muir and Murrilies.

Before continuing along the avenue, some old and interesting side streets off Theater Square merit exploration.

ULITSA PETROVKA (PETROVKA STREET)

Ulitsa Petrovka is a small side street that begins in front of the Maly Theater. The street has long been a popular shopping district with stores selling *podarki* (gifts), *bukinisti* (secondhand books) and *almazi* (diamonds). Next to the Maly, at number 2, is the gray four-story neo-Gothic-style building that houses TsUM, the **Central Universal Store**, open daily 9am–8pm; till 6pm Sundays. The Russkiye Uzory (lace) sells handicrafts, and at number 8 is Zolotoy Klyuchik, one of Moscow's favorite watch stores. At number 10 is **Petrovsky Passazh**, a popular shopping arcade. The Society of World Art had its first exhibition at number 15, displaying the work of Alexander Benois. The writer Anton Chekhov lived at number 19 for several years. (He also lived by the Garden Ring, at 6 Sadovaya-Kudrinskaya, now the Chekhov House Museum, see page 211)

At number 25 (nearer the Chekhovskaya Metro), is the capital's first **Museum of Contemporary Art**, housed in an old 18th-century residence. Opened in 1999 by artist Zurab Tseretelli, it displays international works, including many from Tseretelli's own private collection which include paintings by Chagall, Picasso and Dali. The **Literary Museum**, at number 28, traces the history of Russian and Soviet literature. Open 11am–5.30pm; 2pm–6pm Wednesdays and Fridays; closed Mondays and Tuesdays.

Three centuries ago, the passage was named after the Monastery of **St Peter-on-the-Hill**, which also served as a protective stronghold and entrance to the town. (It is situated right on the corner of Petrovka and Petrovsky Bulvar; open daily 9am–7pm.) The monastery was built by Prince Dmitri Donskoi to honor the Mongol defeat in the Battle of Kulikovo in 1380. In 1682, the future Peter the Great escaped here with his mother, Natalya Naryshkina, during the bloody Streltsy revolts. Today it serves as the Patriarch's Department for Religious Education and contains three churches. The **Church of the Virgin Icon of Bogoliubovo** (1685) was built over the graves of Ivan and Afanasy Naryshkin, killed in 1682 by the Streltsy. The octagonal-drum and helmet-domed **Cathedral of Metropolitan Peter** was reconstructed between 1514 and 1517. The baroque-style Refectory **Church of Sergius Radonezhsky** (founder of Sergiyev Posad Monastery) was commissioned by Peter the Great at the beginning of his reign in 1690; religious services are held here.

A **Monument to Wit** was erected in 2002 on the nearby boulevard; shaped as a stone pyramid fountain, each side represents the different moods of man. Before it stands a bronze statue dedicated to Moscow's most beloved clown, Yuri Nikulin, who died in 1997. The **Hermitage Gardens**, north of the boulevard, at 3 Karetny Ryad, have been here for over a century; open daily 9am–11pm. The Maly Concert Hall is located in the gardens.

KUZNETSKY MOST

Ulitsa Petrovka leads to Kuznetsky Most, a small lane intersecting it. As far back as the 15th century, the area was the popular residence of Moscow's blacksmiths, who lived along the banks of the Neglinnaya River, which at the time flowed through here. Kuznetsky Most means Blacksmith's Bridge.

Almost every building along this steep passage has a fascinating story related to it. It became a highly respected shopping district in the 19th century; items were stamped with 'Bought in Kuznetsky Most'. At number 9 was an ornate and popular restaurant called Yar, which Pushkin and Tolstoy mention in their writings. It was famous for its Gypsy dancers and drunken revelry; Rasputin was thrown out of the restaurant after he got involved in a brawl. Tolstoy listened to one of the world's first phonographs in the music shop that was at number 12, and he wrote of Anna Karenina shopping at Gautier's at number 20. The House of Fashion and many airline agencies are also located along this narrow street.

ULITSA NEGLINNAYA (NEGLINKA STREET)

Kuznetsky Most intersects Ulitsa Neglinnaya, which runs parallel to and east of Petrovka Street to Trubnaya Ploshchad (Square) on the Boulevard Ring. This street also sprang up alongside the banks of the Neglinnaya River, where many popular shops were located. *Neglinnaya* means without clay. Catherine the Great ordered that the river be diverted underground. In the 19th century, it was redirected to a larger aqueduct where it flows underground to the Moskva River.

The revolutionary Nikolai Schmit had his furniture store at the corner of Kuznetsky Most. The Moorish-style building of the **Sandunovskiye Baths** at number 14 was frequented by Chekhov. This is one of the grandest *banya* in town. The building was bought by the actor Sila Sandunov, who turned it into sauna baths in 1896. The *banya* is still a marbled and gilded extravaganza where one can steam, sweat and swim; open 8am–10pm. Another popular *banya* is the **Presnya Banya** at 7 Stolyarny Pereulok. Open 8am–10pm; closed Tuesdays; near Ulitsa 1905 Goda Metro station. Try to bring along your own towel, but buy a bunch of birch leaves usually sold seasonally outside; Russians love to swat each other with these while sweating! (See Special Topic on page 418 and Practical Information listings).

Also on Ulitsa Neglinnaya, at number 4, is Moscow's oldest sheet music shop, Nota, opened in 1911, and the Central Bank. At number 29 is the popular Uzbekistan Restaurant, open noon to midnight.

OKHOTNY RYAD

The continuation of the Prospekt from Theater Square to the Kremlin is now known as Okhotny Ryad (Hunter's Lane) the name of the old local markets. The main markets of Moscow spread from here to Red Square.

At the western end of the street once stood the **Moskva Hotel**, built in constructivist and Stalinist-empire style between 1932 and 1935. The top left of the building's façade was different from the right. In the 1930s, when the architects designed two different fronts for the hotel, the story goes he asked Stalin, 'Which one do you like best?' 'Yes,' replied Stalin. Afraid to question the Soviet leader again, the architect built the structure asymmetrically, including both designs. A new five-star hotel, to be built according to the initial 1930s' plans of Soviet architects Shchusev, Saveliev and Stapran, is currently underway.

Across from the Hotel is **Dom Soyuzov** (House of Trade Unions) on the corner of Dmitrovka and Tverskaya streets, at number 10. Built in 1784 in Russian classical style by Matvei Kazakov, it used to be the Noble's Club. Its Hall of Columns and October Hall hosted social functions. In 1856, Alexander II addressed the nobility on his desire to abolish serfdom, and the playwright George Bernard Shaw was even honored here on his 75th birthday in 1931. Also past leaders such as Lenin, Stalin and Brezhnev lay in state here before their burials. Next door is the City Duma or Parliament building.

Located in front of the hotel, in Manezh Square, is the 350-million-dollar **Okhotny Ryad Underground Shopping Complex**, which was opened in 1997. Spot the stained-glass domes and proceed down the bronze-banistered stairwell into the new commercial heart of Moscow. The three-story underground atrium, complete with indoor fountain, holds 86 shops, 26 restaurants, banks,and an Internet café; open daily 10am–10pm. It is amazing to view this enterprising area, considering it was once the center of Bolshevik and Communist activities (which forbade any Western influences). The closest Metro station is Okhotny Ryad.

Crossing the prospekt, via the underpass, brings you out in front of the grandly restored five-star **Hotel National**. Opened in 1903 (the cornerstone was laid on June 15th 1900), it is still one of Moscow's finest hotels, with 184 rooms and 37 suites. The famous French restaurant, Maxim's, is located on the ground floor. Immediately after the Revolution, the House of Soviets expropriated the hotel and turned it into the House of Soviets No.1. Lenin stayed in Suite 107; his green desk is still preserved in this room. Other Bolshevik leaders, such as Dzerzhinsky, Sverdlov and Stalin also lived here. In 1931, the building was returned to its hotel status. From 1991–95, the National was completely restored to its original design and decoration.

MOKHOVAYA ULITSA (STREET)

Running south from the National Hotel to the end of the prospekt at Borovitskaya Ploshchad is Mokhovaya (Moss-Grown) Street. In the center, in Manezhnaya Ploshchad, stood the Manége, the former imperial riding school. Built in 1817 to commemorate Russia's victory over Napolean, the 7,500-square-meter building later served as the country's largest exhibition hall. Designed by Osip Bove, the city's general architect who helped rebuild the city after the Great Fire of 1812, the building was considered innovative for its system of wooden girders, which allowed the roof to stand unsupported by internal walls. After a fire destroyed the structure, used as an Exhibition Hall, in 2004, the mayor promised to rebuilt it. At number 6 is the **Kalinin Museum** (open 10am–6pm; closed Mondays), the former mansion of Prince Shakhovsky, built in 1821. Opened on June 30, 1950, the museum traces the life of Party leader Mikhail Kalinin.

On the corner of Bolshaya Nikitskaya Ulitsa, stands one of the oldest buildings of Moscow University, recognizable by its columned portico and small dome. It was built in classical style, between 1786 and 1793 by Matvei Kazakov. A statue of Lomonosov, who founded the university in 1755, stands in the courtyard. Next door a newer building dating from 1836 now houses the Student Union. In the courtyard are two statues of graduates, Nikolai Ogarev and Alexander Herzen.

Mokhovaya ends a few minutes' walk farther down by the **Russian State Library** (formerly the Lenin Library), the largest library in Russia with 36 million books. Between 1784 and 1786, the governor of Siberia, P Pashkov, built his neoclassical mansion (to designs by Vasily Bazhenov) with beautiful exotic gardens filled with peacocks that wandered the hills around the Kremlin. It is still referred to as the **Pashkov Dom** and stands on the corner of Mokhovaya and Znamenka streets. Later in 1861, the building housed the famous Rumyantsev collection of over one million books and manuscripts. When Lenin died in 1924, it was renamed the Lenin Library. When the Metro was built in the 1940s, many books were moved into the larger building next door. In 1993, its name was changed once again after extensive restoration. For Moscow's 850th Birthday in 1997, a 3.7-meter-high bronze statue of great Russian novelist Fyodor Dostoeyevsky (1821–1881) was unveiled. Sculpted by Mikhail Posokhin, there was quite a local stir over the $1 million price tag. The closest metro station is Biblioteka Imeni Lenina.

VOLKHONKA AND PRECHISTENKA STREETS

Ulitsa Volkhonka begins at the Kremlin's Borovitsky Tower and runs into Ulitsa Prechistenka at the Boulevard Ring. The **Pushkin Museum of Fine Arts** is at 12 Volkhonka, and is a highly recommended stop during your visit. The neoclassical-style building was constructed in 1898 by Roman Klein to house a collection of fine art, which opened in 1912. The museum was initially named after Alexander III, but renamed after Pushkin during the poet's centenary year in 1937. After the Revolution, paintings belonging to two great collectors, Sergei Shchukin (1854–1937) and Ivan Morozov (1871–1921) were nationalized by the State. By 1914, Shchukin had more than 220 French impressionist artworks displayed at his house, the former Trubetskoi Mansion in Moscow. Rooms were filled with Matisse, Gauguin, Cézanne and Picasso. In his mansion at 21 Prechistenka Street, Morozov exhibited more than 100 impressionist paintings and 450 other works by Russian artists, including Marc Chagall. They both fled the country after the Revolution and, until 1948, their paintings were exhibited at Morozov's Mansion, known as the Museum of Western Art. After this was closed down by Stalin, their collections were kept in storage in the Pushkin Museum. Only after Stalin's death in 1953 were the paintings gradually put back on display. Today the museum boasts one of the world's largest collections of ancient, classical, Oriental and Western European art, with over half a million works. Open 10am–7pm; closed Mondays. Metro Kropotkinskaya.

The museum has also expanded to include the **Museum of Private Collections**, located next door at number 14, in the green and white palace. This was once the palace of the aristocratic Golitsyn family, and Catherine the Great stayed here during her coronation in 1762. Today its three floors exhibit private collections, many donated to the state. Open 12–7pm; closed Mondays and Tuesdays.

Behind the museums, at 3/5 Maly Znamensky Lane, is the **Roerich Museum** (open 10am–5pm; closed Mondays), with paintings by artist Nikolai Roerich (1874–1947), an avid Buddhist and mystic. He traveled extensively throughout the Himalayas, India, Tibet, and Mongolia, and created more than 7,000 paintings which are on display in Moscow's Tretyakov Gallery and Oriental Art Museum, and other major museums around the world. Roerich traveled across America in the early 1920s and founded a museum in New York which still operates today on West 107th Street in Manhattan. In 2006, in a Sotheby's auction, Roerich's 'Lao-tze' fetched $2.2 million, the most-ever for a Roerich work.

Standing beside Kropotkinskaya Ploshchad (Square) is the magnificent and newly reconstructed **Cathedral of Christ Our Savior**. Its history is both long and unbelievably tragic. Founded in honor of the famous Russian victory over Napoleon, it took 45 years to build, but only one day to destroy. Alexander I stipulated that the cathedral was to express the scale of the czar's gratitude to Christ for the country's protection, and selected the site on the bank of the river. But it was not until 1830, under the rule of Nicholas I, that serious planning began. Designed by Konstantin Thon, the czar's favorite architect, its construction then continued through the reigns of yet two more rulers. Alexander III was present during its consecration on May 26, 1883. With a capacity of 15,000, the cathedral was the country's largest and most lavishly decorated shrine, symbolizing the glory of the Russian empire. The cathedral was over 30 stories high, bedecked with over half a ton of gold, and its walls made from 40 million bricks, Altai marble and Finnish granite. The gigantic roof cupola was composed of 176 tons of copper, topped by a cross three stories high. Fourteen bells hung in the four belfries, one weighing 27 tons. The central iconostasis was decorated with bejeweled icons, which reflected

thousands of beeswax candles. Hundreds of frescoes were painted along the upper stories, and the lower portion was covered with 177 marble plates, each engraved with particular places, dates and heroes of the battles of Russian armies. This enormous shrine dedicated to the Son of God stood for 48 years; three years longer than it took to build.

Then, in 1931, to perpetuate the glory of the Soviet regime, Stalin decided to build his own glorified House of Soviets and selected the cathedral as its site. (Imagine if Mussolini had ordered St Peter's Basilica in Rome to be razed.) On July 18, 1931, workmen began removing thousands of priceless artifacts; they had four months to complete their assignment. (During this time, ten million would starve to death in the Ukraine, and Stalin started his first purges and labor camps.) Then began the demolition. Finally, on December 5, 1931, after one last detonation, a huge smoking mountain of rubble was all that remained of this wondrous accomplishment.

The final blueprints of 1933 had the planned House of Soviets higher than any American skyscraper at 420 meters (1,380 feet), topped with a 70-meter (230-foot) statue of Lenin (taller than the Statue of Liberty)—130 stories in all. The monument to Socialism was to look like an enormous multitiered wedding cake. But it turned out that the swampy mound of floating bedrock could not support the proposed building. Stalin died in 1953, and in the end it was Khrushchev in 1959 who ordered a pit dug for a swimming pool utilizing the bemired foundation (by then a garbage dump), all that remained of the demolished cathedral. Until 1994 this remained the Moskva Open-Air Pool Complex. With the fall of the Soviet Union, the new government allocated nearly 360 million dollars, underwritten by private donations and nongovernmental funds, to construct a near-replica of the original cathedral. It opened in 1997 after only two years of construction.

The interior walls are bedecked in white marble and covered with many golden icons. A gallery in the lower church holds a souvenir shop and an exhibit of the reconstruction process; open daily 10am–6pm. For a group tour, an elevator ride to the roof is given with a panoramic view of the city. The cathedral is open daily 8am–8pm. It stands beside Kropotkinskaya Metro station.

South, across the river from the cathedral looms the controversial bronze monument **Statue of Peter the Great**, erected in 1998 on an island near the Krymsky Bridge at a cost of $20 million. Mayor Yuri Luzhkov hired Georgian-born Zurab Tsereteli (many have nicknamed him the mayor's court sculptor) to create a statue in honor of the Russian navy's 300th anniversary. The 50-meter-high (164 feet) statue depicts Peter the Great in Roman attire standing on the prow of a

Moscow's original Cathedral of Christ Our Savior was built by Alexander I to commemorate Russia's 1812 victory over Napoleon. It was the country's largest and most lavishly decorated cathedral, which took 45 years to build. In 1931, Stalin ordered it razed to the ground. With the fall of the Soviet Union, the government allocated funds to construct a near-replica of the original cathedral, opened in 1997.

sailing ship. (Ironically, Peter hated Moscow and moved to St. Petersburg.) Shortly after its unveiling a few critics tried to blow it up; seven bombs planted in the base of the monument were discovered and diffused. It is still guarded daily. Yeltsin even called it a 'colossal eyesore.'

A recipient of the prestigious Lenin Prize, Tseretelli (who turned 70 in 2004) was awarded the entire former West German Embassy (on Bolshaya Gruzinskaya Street) by Mayor Luzhkov as his private home and studio. A prolific artist, he helped design the Okhotny Ryad Underground Shopping Mall and the Cathedral of Christ Our Savior. His works can also be viewed worldwide. His 39-foot-high sculpture, *Good Defeats Evil*, stands outside the United Nations Building in New York, a 1990 gift from the former Soviet Union. Tseretelli also has his own art gallery located a few blocks southwest of the cathedral. As François Mitterand left his mark on Parisan architecture, so too does Mayor Luzhkov feel driven to embellish his own city. Luzhkov and Tseretelli now have a project in the works to build a Crystal Chapel near the Kremlin they deem the 'Eighth Wonder of the World.'

From the Revolution until 1991, Prechistenka Street was called Kropotkinskaya (the Metro station still is), named after the revolutionary scholar, Pyotr Kropotkin (1842–1921), who lived nearby at 26 Kropotkinsky Pereulok. For centuries the street had been known as Prechistenka (Holy), after the Icon of the Holy Virgin kept in Novodevichy Convent. Many aristocratic families built their residences along this street. In the 18th and 19th centuries the area was one of the most fashionable places to live in Moscow. At number 10 lived Count Mikhail Orlov, a descendant of Catherine the Great's lover, Grigory; the mansion now houses the Peace Commission. Note the outside plaque commemorating the Jewish Committee which worked diligently for the Russian war effort against the Germans. They were later arrested and sent off to gulags by Stalin in 1952. The poets Zhukovsky and Davydov also lived on this street at number 17. At 9 Mansurovsky Pereulok (near the Palace of Fine Arts), in the yellow wooden house, another writer, Mikhail Bulgakov (1891–1940) lived for a while in the basement apartment. It is here that, in his famous novel *The Master and Margarita*, the master catches a glimpse of Margarita. (See Patriarch's Pond section on page 167 for more on where Bulgakov also lived.)

The mansion at 12 Prechistenka Street was built by Afanasy Grigorev. It now houses the **Alexander Pushkin Museum**, containing over 80,000 items connected with the celebrated poet. Open 10am–6pm, 11am–7pm Wednesdays and Thursdays; closed Mondays and Tuesdays. Across the street, at number 11, is the **Leo Tolstoy Museum**, which includes a collection of the beloved writer's manuscripts, book editions, literature on his life, a documentary ('Tolstoy Alive') and recordings of his voice. At the entrance is a portrait of Tolstoy by Ilya Repin, painted only a year before the writer's death. Open 11am–5pm; closed Mondays.

In 1862, Leo Tolstoy (known as Lev Tolstoy in Russian) married Sofya Andreyevna with whom he fathered 13 children. Between 1863 and 1869 he wrote *War and Peace* (his wife hand-copied it over seven times), and between 1874 and 1876 *Anna Karenina*. Two years later, Tolstoy published *Confession*, views on his newly embraced Christian moralities and commitment to individual rights and nonviolence (he even received interested letters from Mahatma Gandhi). The estate-museum, where Tolstoy lived from 1882 to 1901, is at 21 Ulitsa Lva Tolstovo (Leo Tolstoy Street); open 10am–5pm (in winter 10am–3.30pm); closed Mondays. Metro Park Kultury. (See also Yasnaya Polyana, page 254.)

The **Russian Academy for Arts**, at number 21, was once the residence of Prince Dolgorukov. In 1998, a statue honoring Vasily Surikov (1848–1936) was placed in front of the academy to honor the 150th anniversary of the artist's birth. An entire gallery of busts of outstanding Russian artists will soon join Surikov.

During their brief marriage in 1922, the famous American ballet dancer Isadora Duncan and her husband, Russian writer Sergei Yesenin, lived across the street at number 20. (He spoke no English, she no Russian.) Yesenin, yet another poet who became disillusioned with socialism, committed suicide by hanging himself in 1925, aged 30. He penned his final words in his own blood, 'In this life, there's nothing new in dying.' Isadora was strangled two years later in the south of France when her long scarf wrapped itself around the wheel of the car she was driving. The **Yesenin Museum** is at 24 Bolshoi Strochenovsky Lane; open 11am–5pm; closed Mondays and Tuesdays. Metro Serpukhovskaya.

Prechistenka Street ends at the Garden Ring by a statue of Engels. The next street south of Prechistenka, running parallel, is Ostozhenka, one of Moscow's oldest streets dating from the 16th century. In those times, meadows of haystacks or *ostozhye* covered the area. During the era of Ivan the Terrible, many noble families lived in this area; and the side lanes or *pereulok* still carry their names, such as Lopukhinsky, Khilkov and Yeropkinsky. Walking east down from the Garden Ring, the three buildings of the former **Provisions Warehouses** still stand. The structures were designed by Stasov, and built by Shestakov in 1829–35. By the Park Kultury Metro (one of city's first stations) is the Diplomatic Academy of Russia's Foreign Ministry, once a lyceum school. At number 49 is the empire-style mansion once owned by noblemen (the coat of arms is of the Loshakovsky-Vzevolzhky families), and later by the revolutionary, Bakunin. Whenever the writer Ivan Turgenev (*Fathers and Sons*) visited Moscow, he stayed at the gray-blue wooden *dacha* at number 37 with his mother, Varvara Petrovna. Here the writer observed scenes that he later described in his famous story *Mumu* about a deaf-mute janitor who drowned his dog *Mumu* on the orders of his eccentric and cruel landlady (based on his mother). This tiny structure is affectionately known as the *Mumu* House. Across the street, at number 38 is a classical palace, designed by architect Kazakov. It once belonged to General Yeropkin, who was famous for his many luxurious parties and banquets; the young Sasha Pushkin even attended a ball here. In 1806, it was bought by the Merchants' Society, and future author Goncharov (*Oblomov*) studied here in 1822–30. Today, the building houses the Moscow State Linguistic University. The mansion, at number 21, was built in 1901 in Art Nouveau style by the architect Kekushev for his family. A big lion once adorned the front façade. Located back off the street are the remains of the **Zachatyevsky (Conception) Nunnery**, founded in 1584. The interior ensemble and Church of St Anne were demolished during Stalinist times. The outside walls and Above-the-Gate Church (1696) have survived. The area is under restoration, and some nuns now live in the convent. Turning down 2nd Obydensky Lane towards the river brings the visitor to the **Church of Elijah Obydenny**, constructed in one day (*obydenny*), and later rebuilt in 1702. The Church is famous for never having closed down, not even during wars or purges. The 17th-century icons *Savior Not Made By Hands* and *The Icon of Our Lady of Kazan*, both painted by Simon Ushakov, still hang in the church's interior. Continue to 3rd Obydensky Lane onto Soymonovsky Passage which leads to the **Pertsov House** at 1 Kursovoy Lane. It was built in 1901 (to the drawings of Malyutin—creator of the Matryoshka doll), for P. Pertsov, a notable collector and entrepreneur. The fairy-tale house has decorative panels of colored majolica depicting mythical characters, such as Yarilo (Sun), Serin birds, dragons and stars. It is now the home to the Russian Diplomatic Corps (GlavUpDK) who have meticulously restored the site.

Jump on the Metro and travel east across the river to Tretyakovskaya station. At number 10 Lavrushinsky Pereulok is the newly renovated **State Tretyakov Gallery**, which turned 150 in 2006. In 1856, the Moscow merchants, Pavel and Sergei Tretyakov, avid art patrons, began to collect works of Russian artists. In 1892, after the death of his brother, Pavel Mikhailovich founded Russia's first public museum of national art and donated their collection of 3,500 paintings, drawings & sculptures to the city. The Tretyakovs also helped fund the artists of the *Peredvizhniki* (Itinerants) Movement of realist artists, and purchased works by Kramskoi, Perov and Repin. After Pavel's death in 1898, the Tretyakov mansion was transformed into the museum. Today, the gallery houses one of the world's largest Russian and Soviet art collections from the 12th to the 20th centuries with well over 140,000 works displayed in 62 rooms. These include the famous 12th-century Byzantine icon *Virgin of Vladimir* (church-museum), Rublyov's Old Testament Trinity icon (room 60), Ilya Repin's *Ivan the Terrible and His Son* (room 30), Vasily Surikov's *Morning of the Execution of the Streltsy* (room 28), and the largest painting in the gallery, Alexander Ivanov's *The Coming of Christ* (room 10). The shop inside has a collection of guidebooks, art posters and postcards for sale. It is open 10am–7pm (church-museum noon–4pm); closed Mondays. A new branch of the

Master icon painter Andrei Rublyov painted the Apostle Paul in the early 15th century. Its elongated proportions make the three-meter-long figure look slender and weightless. The blue lapis lazuli was a favorite color used by Rublyov. In 1918 it was discovered in a shed in the town of Zvenigorod where it once hung within the Assumption Cathedral's iconostasis. It now hangs in Moscow's Tretyakov Gallery.

Tretyakov (also closed on Mondays) has opened at 10 Krymsky Val. This is opposite Gorky Park near Oktyabrskaya Metro station.

This area is still known as Zamoskvarechiye—Across the Moskva River. A few blocks east of the Tretyakov Gallery is Bolshaya Ordynka Ulitsa. The medieval name stems from *orda*, which refers to the Mongol Golden Horde. This route once led to the Khan's southern headquarters. Moscow once boasted over 500 churches, and today the city's largest concentration of churches (over 15) is located within this small area. The **Church of Virgin of All Sorrows**, at 20 Bolshaya Ordynka, dates from 1790. When the church was destroyed in the fire of 1812 (which destroyed 80 percent of the city), Osip Bovet designed a new one with a yellow rotunda in empire style in 1836; the Icon of the Virgin is in the left chapel. Orthodox services are held on Sunday mornings.

At number 34 Bolshaya Ordynka is the **Convent of Saints Martha and Mary**, built by the sister of Empress Alexandra in 1908. After her husband Grand Prince Sergei was assassinated, the Grand Duchess Yelizaveta decided to retire to a convent of her own creation. The main Church of the Virgin Intercession was built by architect Alexei Shchusev in 1912, who later designed Lenin's mausoleum on Red Square. The interior frescoes were painted by Mikhail Nesterov; an icon restoration workshop is still on the grounds. After the Revolution Yelizaveta Fedorovna, along with other Romanov family members, was exiled to the Urals. In 1918, they were murdered by Bolsheviks in Alapaevsk (they were thrown down an old mine shaft and grenades were thrown in after them) a day after the royal family's execution in nearby Yekaterinburg. In 1992, the convent reopened in a nearby building.

At 17 Bolshaya Ordynka is the **Anna Akhmatova Museum**, where the famous poet once lived. Open Thursdays 3–6pm and Fridays 11am–3pm. (See Special Topic, page 620.)

At number 39 Bolshaya Ordynka a small church now houses the **Art Moderne Gallery** with exhibits by contemporary artists (closed Mondays). The **Church of St Catherine**, at number 60, was also reconstructed after a fire. Catherine the Great had Karl Blank build this church on the original site in 1767. One block west, at number 10 Shchetininsky Pereulok, look for the **Tropinin Museum** (open 12–6pm, weekends 10am–4pm, closed Tuesdays and Wednesdays). It houses works by 18th-century serf-artist, Vasily Tropinin, as well as other painters who studied at the Academy of Arts. Exhibits include landscape portraits and watercolors of old Moscow. Other churches can be found along the neighboring streets of Pyatnitskaya (numbers 4, 26, 51) and Vtoroy Kadashovsky, where at number 2 stands the five-domed Moscow Baroque **Church of the Resurrection**, built between 1687 and 1713, and funded by donations made from neighborhood weavers.

One block east, at 9 Malaya Ordynka Ulitsa and behind the whitewashed five-domed **Church of St Nicholas in Pyzhi** (built in 1670), is the **Ostrovsky House Museum** (open 12–7pm; closed Mondays), where one of Russia's best-known playwrights was born on March 31, 1823. The small wooden house is filled with photographs and pictures that document Moscow's theatrical history, especially from the Maly Theater where Alexander Ostrovsky worked from 1853 until his death in 1886. A statue of him stands outside the theater. Further east, on the corner of Novokuznetskaya and Vishnyakovsky streets stands the **Church of St Nicholas the Blacksmith** (1681). Rebuilt in the 19th century, it is known as St Nicholas of the Miracles because of its wonder-working icons; many people continue to faithfully pray before them. Running south, Novokuznetskaya ends at the Garden Ring and **Paveletsky Railway Station**, where trains lead to the Ukraine and lower Volga regions.

TVERSKAYA ULITSA

In the 18th century, Tverskaya Ulitsa was the main street of the city; today it is still one of the busiest in Moscow. The passage was named Tverskaya because it led to the old Russian town of Tver 256 kilometers (160 miles) north; from there it continued to St Petersburg. From 1932 until 1990, the street was called Gorky, after Maxim Gorky, a famous writer during the Stalinist period. In 1990, the Moscow City Council voted to restore the street's old name. From the Kremlin to the Garden Ring, the thoroughfare is known as Tverskaya, and from the Garden Ring to Byelorussky Train Station it is called Tverskaya-Yamskaya (in the 17th century the Yamskaya Sloboda, or settlement, appeared outside the city's ramparts). From the train station it becomes Leningradsky Prospekt, which leads to the international airport, Sheremetyevo II.

In prerevolutionary days the street, once winding and narrow, was known for its fashionable shops, luxurious hotels and grandiose aristocratic mansions. The first Moscow trams ran along this street, and the first movie theater opened here. In 1932 (after being renamed Gorky), the thoroughfare was reshaped and widened, and now retains little of its former appearance.

It takes about an hour and a half to stroll the length of Tverskaya Street. You can also ride the Metro to various stops along it—Pushkinskaya, Mayakovskaya and Byelorusskaya—to shorten the time.

Tverskaya Street begins in front of Red Square at the **Manezhnaya Ploshchad**, known as the 50th Anniversary of the October Revolution Square from 1967 to 1990. The czar had his riding school, the *manège*, in this area. Okhotny Ryad Metro station is at the beginning of the street. On the corner is the newly renovated, elegant **National Hotel** with a splendid view of Red Square. Lenin lived here during the Revolution. In March 2002, developers began demolition of Moscow's 30-year-old Intourist Hotel. Developers replaced the 22-story building with an 11-story, five-star hotel, the **Ritz-Carlton**.

Since the early 1990s many new shops have opened on Tverskaya, including foreign clothing and cosmetic outlets (many now accept credit cards), along with other Russian stores which accept rubles only.

Continuing along the street is the **Yermolova Drama Theater**, named after a famous stage actress, Maria Yermolova. Founded in 1925, the theater moved into the present building at number 5 in 1946. The Meyerhold Theater occupied the building from 1931 to 1938. It has staged everything from *Mary Poppins* to *Heartbreak House*. (For the Yermolova House Museum see page 197.) The **Central Telegraph Building**, with its globe and digital clock, is on the corner of Gazetny Pereulok. The building, designed by Ilya Rerberg in 1927, is open 24 hours a day. Telegrams, faxes, and long-distance calls can be made here.

Across the street at 3 Kamergersky Pereulok is the **MKhat Moscow Arts Theater** (today known as the Chekhov Moscow Artistic Academic Theater), established by Stanislavsky and Nemirovich-Danchenko in 1896. Here Stanislavsky practiced his 'method-acting' and staged many plays by Gorky and Chekhov (see Chekhov House Museum on page 211). After *The Seagull*, the bird was put on the outside of the building as its emblem. Plays such as *The Three Sisters*, *The Cherry Orchard*, *Anna Karenina* and *Resurrection* marked a new epoch in the theater. In 1987, the building was reconstructed and now seats 2,000. Today the theater's repertoire includes such plays as *Uncle Vanya*, *Bondage of Hypocrites* and *Tartuffe*. Next door at 3A is the Moscow Arts Museum, founded in 1923. Another building of the Moscow Arts, known as Gorky Theater (under different management) is at 22 Tverskoi.

The Aragvi Restaurant (once part of the Dresden Hotel, a favorite of Turgenev and Chekhov), specializing in Georgian cuisine, is on the next corner of Pereulok Stoleshnikov, at 6 Tverskaya. Stoleshnikov became Moscow's second pedestrian lane (the Arbat is already pedestrianized). Craftsmen embroidered tablecloths for the czar's court in this lane over 300 years ago (stoleshnik means tablecloth in Old Russian).

At an early age, the famous writer, Vladimir Gilyarovsky (1853–1935) ran away from home to experience adventure and real life (at one time, he even worked as a burkak—a man who pulled boats by rope up the Volga). He eventually became a journalist (known as the 'King of Reporters'), who would write about the common people. His real-life stories (as investigating Moscow's Khitrov market, one of the city's most criminally-infested areas) became best-selling thrillers. Gilyarovsky also wrote the popular Moscow and the Muscovites (1924); he lived across the street at number 9 for over half a century. The Stoleshniki Café, at number 6, is decorated in Old-Russian style. It is affectionately known as U Gilyarovskovo (At Gilyarovsky's) in tribute to the popular writer who was a regular here. Two rooms have been renovated in the café's 17th-century cellars: the Reporter's and Moscow and Muscovites halls. Here Gilyarovsky medals are awarded annually to the writers of the best articles about Moscow. At number 11, the pastry shop still uses old-fashioned ovens built into the walls, and has some of the best cakes in the city. The lane leads to Petrovka Street, a popular shopping area.

The southern side street Bryusov Pereulok leads to the terracotta-yellow Church of the Resurrection on Yeliseyevsky Lane. The church is said to have been built on the spot where Mikhail Romanov welcomed his father's return in 1619 after Polish imprisonment. It was reconstructed in 1629, and the church even remained open during Soviet years. Its interior is filled with icons, including a 16th-century copy of the Virgin of Kazan (believed responsible for the Russian 1613 victory over the Poles) and the icon of St George, the symbol of the city.

Tverskaya Ploshchad is marked by the equestrian Statue of Yuri Dolgoruky, founder of Moscow. It was erected in 1954 to mark the 800th anniversary of the city. The building behind the square, in the small garden, holds Party archives of the Marxism-Leninism Institute. The archives contain more than 6,000 documents of Marx and Engels and over 30,000 of Lenin. In front is a granite statue of Lenin by Sergei Merkurov.

Directly across the street stands the large red-brick and white-columned **Moscow City Council**, the city's legislature (and Mayor's office). The architect Matvei Kazakov designed the building as the residence for the first governor-general, appointed by Catherine the Great in 1782. Two of Moscow's governors were Prince Dmitri Golitsyn (1820–44), who paved the streets and installed water pipes, and Vladimir Dolgorukov, a descendant of Yuri Dolgoruky. In 1946, the building was moved back 14 meters (46 feet) and two more stories were added.

Stoleshnikov also leads to the octagonal-drum and small-cupola Church of Saints Cosmas and Damian (patron saints of blacksmiths), rebuilt in stone in 1626. Once a factory, it is now slowly being restored.

Further up Tverskaya is the Tsentralnaya Hotel at number 10, built in 1911 as the Hotel Liuks. In the same building is the most famous bakery in Moscow, formerly known as Filippov's. Next door is another popular food store, Gastronom Number 1, which recently reverted to its original name of Yeliseyev's (see Special Topic on page 540). Beautiful white sculptures and garlands line the shopfront, and the gilded interior is filled with stained glass and colorful displays. It is worth a visit just to see the interior. At 14 Tverskaya is the Ostrovsky Humanitarian Museum, open 11am–6.30pm; closed Mondays. Nikolai Ostrovsky (1904–1936) wrote How the Steel Was Tempered. The Soviet author's house (where he lived from 1935 to 1936) is now a museum exhibiting his books, photographs and letters. Also in the building is the Tetris Wax Museum, open 11am–7pm; closed Mondays. On display are wax figures that include Alexander Nevsky, Ivan the Terrible, Napoleon, Nicholas II and Stalin.

Down the southern side street, at 6 Leontevsky Pereulok, is the **Stanislavsky Memorial Museum**, open weekends 11am–3pm; Wednesday and Friday 2pm–7pm; Thursdays 11am–5pm; closed last Thursday of the month and every Monday and Tuesday. The theater director lived here from 1922 until his death in 1938. On display are the living quarters of Stanislavsky and his wife, the opera hall and collections of books, costumes and theatrical props. The ballroom was converted into a theater; the first production was Tchaikovsky's *Evgeny Onegin*. It is open 11am–5pm, Wednesdays and Fridays 2pm–8pm; closed Mondays and Tuesdays. (A museum to Stanislavsky's partner, **Nemirovich-Danchenko**, is located at 5 Glinish-chevsky Pereulok (on the north side of Tverskaya), open 11am–4pm Tuesdays to Fridays.) Opposite, at number 7, is the **Folk Arts Museum** which exhibits Russian national crafts and decorative art, and has souvenirs for sale. In 1900, the building was bought by art patron Savva Morozov specifically to house this museum. Open 10am–5pm; closed Sundays and Mondays. At 17 Tverskaya is the **Konenkov Memorial Studio**, open 11am–6pm; closed Mondays and Tuesdays. It displays marble and wooden statues by famous sculptor Sergei Konenkov (1874–1971), who lived here from 1947 until his death.

As Tverskaya crosses the Boulevard Ring, it opens into **Pushkin Square** (Pushkinskaya Ploshchad). In the 16th century the stone walls of the Beli Gorod (White Town) stretched around what is now the Boulevard Ring; they were torn down in the 18th century. The Strastnoi Convent used to stand on what is now Pushkin Square—the square was originally called Strastnaya (until 1931), after the Convent of the Passion of Our Lord. The convent was demolished in the 1930s and in its place was built the Rossiya Movie Theater and the Izvestia building. In the center of the square stands the **Statue of Alexander Pushkin**, by the sculptor Alexander Opekulin. It was erected in 1880 with funds donated by the public. Pushkin lived over a third of his life in Moscow, where he predicted, 'Word of me shall spread across the Russian land.' Dostoevsky laid a wreath on the statue at its unveiling. Today it is always covered with flowers and is a popular spot for open-air readings and political rallies. In 1999, to celebrate the 200th anniversary of Pushkin's birth, over 100 historical locations connected with the poet's life and work were restored throughout the city. Under the square are the three Metro stations: Tverskaya, Pushkinskaya and Chekhovskaya.

Behind the square is the 3,000-seat Pushkinsky Cinema, built in 1961 for the 2nd International Moscow Film Festival (the festival is held in Moscow every odd

(opposite) Statue of the famous writer Alexander Pushkin (1799–1837) which stands on Moscow's Pushkin Square.

year). This area is also Moscow's major publishing center. Here are the newspaper offices of *Izvestia*, *Novosti* (*APN*) and *Moscow News*. Walking up Malaya Dmitrovka Ulitsa (behind *Izvestia*) leads to the white-green tent-roofed **Church of Nativity of Our Lady in Putniki**, built between 1649 and 1652. Legend has it that a noble-woman gave birth in her carriage as she passed this spot and later commissioned a church to honor the Nativity. When it burned down, Czar Alexei Romanov donated money to have it rebuilt, along with a chapel dedicated to the icon that prevented fires, Our Lady of the Burning Bush, which is in the chapel. Behind it was once a resthouse where travelers or *putniki* stayed.

Across the street from Pushkin Square is the world's largest and busiest **McDonald's** fast-food outlet, with 800 seats, 27 cash registers and 250 employees serving up to 50,000 people a day (open daily 8am–midnight). When the restaurant opened, Russians automatically stood in the longest queue—in Russia a longer queue was indicative of better quality merchandise. Brochures had to be distributed explaining that each queue gave the same service and food. The chain has opened 20 restaurants in Moscow, and over 60 throughout Russia. As part of an agreement with the Moscow City Council, McDonald's was required to purchase or produce its raw materials in Russia, resulting in a vast production and distribution complex on the outskirts of the city. After decades of waiting hours in long lines, the country enthusiastically embraced fast food. Each month on average Russian customers of McDonald's restaurants consume 1.2 million servings of French

fries, 700,000 Big Macs, and 600,000 milk shakes. In 1996, McDonald's opened Moscow's first drive-through restaurant, called McAuto, at 63 Leningradskoye Highway on the way to the international airport.

To give an idea of the extent of business enterprise developing in the early 1990s, there was even a black market for hamburgers. Entrepreneurs would stand in line for hours to purchase eight Big Macs each (the maximum allowed per person), eat one, and then sell the rest at a huge profit to those not willing to wait. They earned more in one day than a physicist did in a month. Today black-market burgers are bust and the long lines gone.

On McDonald's yellow-brick building can be seen a small bust in tribute to Soviet cinema star Lyubov Orlova (1902–1975), who was a film cultural icon in the 1930s and 40s. In 1936, she received a State prize for her role in *Circus* as US circus artist Marion Dixon. But it was her role as the postwoman, Dunya, in the comedy *Volga-Volga* in 1938 (one of Stalin's favorite films), that made her a star. Her last apartment was in this building.

The grounds surrounding the restaurant are a popular meeting place; small kiosks abound and you can have your picture taken next to cardboard copies of Russian leaders. Bands play here and there are many young people amusing themselves on skateboards and roller blades.

The **Modern History of Russia Museum** is at 21 Tverskaya. This mansion was built for Count Razumovsky in 1780 by the architect Manelas. In 1832, it was rebuilt by Adam Menelaws after a fire, and was bought by the Angliisky (English) Club, formed in 1772 by a group of foreigners residing in Moscow. The club's members (all men) were made up of Russian aristocratic intellectuals and included the best minds in politics, science, art and literature. One member of the wealthy Morozov family gambled away one million rubles in a single evening. Tolstoy once lost 1,000 rubles in a card game in the 'infernal' room. Pushkin wrote of the club in his long poem *Evgeny Onegin*. When Tatiana arrived in Moscow, Evgeny described 'the two frivolous-looking lions' at the gates. The last *bolshoi* gala at the club was a banquet thrown for Nicholas II to celebrate the 300th anniversary of the Romanov dynasty in 1913. The museum, opened in 1924, exhibits over a million items from the 1905 and 1917 revolutions. It also displays materials on the country's history dating back to 1861. It was called the Central Museum of the Revolution until 1992. A new hall has opened displaying items from the August 1991 coup attempt. The gun outside was used to shell the White Guards in 1917. Also on display here is a tram that burned during the 1991 attempted coup. The museum is open 10am–6pm, closed Mondays. Next to the museum, at number 23, is the **Stanislavsky Drama Theater**. Behind it is the Young Spectator's Theater for children. Next door is the Stanislavsky Restaurant with a nightly disco.

PATRIARCH'S POND—BULGAKOV'S HAUNT

Turn south off Tverskaya by McDonald's and into Bolshaya Bronnaya Ulitsa. This leads to Malaya Bronnaya—turn right and at number 30 you will find Patriarch's Pond, one of the oldest and most charming residential areas of Moscow. This land was once known as Patriarskaya Sloboda, the Russian Orthodox patriarch's land in the 17th and 18th centuries. The pond was dug to provide the dining tables with plenty of fish. Later it was occupied by artisans—the *bronnaya* (armorers) and the *kozia* (wool spinners). The writer Mikhail Bulgakov (1891–1940) set his well-known masterpiece *The Master and Margarita*, in this neighborhood. (The novel begins with "...at the hour of sunset, on a hot spring day, two citizens appeared in the Patriarch's ponds park...") Completed in 1938, and about the Devil's influence on corrupt Soviet authorities, it was not allowed to be published until 1966.

In 2002, at the intersection of Bolshaya and Malaya Bronnaya streets, a monument to Russia's famous Jewish writer Sholom Aleichem (nom de plume of the writer Sholom Rabinovich) was unveiled. The column of the statue features some of the favorite characters from his novel *Errant Stars* (basis for the musical *Fiddler on the Roof*).

Between 1921 and 1924, Bulgakov, who was voted by Russians as one of their most influential 20th-century writers, lived just around the corner in Bolshaya Sadovaya Ulitsa—in the beige building between numbers 8 and 14. (He describes in his novel, 'it was painted cream, and stood on the ring boulevard behind a ragged garden fenced off from the pavement by a wrought-iron railing.') Go left at the back of the yard and notice the graffiti written by fans on the stairwell—a memorial to the writer who died in disgrace in 1940 and was described in the *Soviet Encyclopaedia* as a 'slanderer of Soviet reality'. A monument to the author and his characters stands near the pond. A popular TV series version of *The Master and Margarita* has been made and aired throughout the country.

A monument to Ivan Krylov (1769–1844), a popular children's fabulist, stands in the square. In winter, there is ice-skating and in summer boating. Across the street from the pond, at number 28, is the popular Café Margarita. The **Moscow Drama Theater** is at 4 Malaya Bronnaya. Formed in 1950, the theater seats 850.

A few blocks south on Ulitsa Spiridonovka is the newly restored **Morozov Mansion**, a magnificent structure with an incredible history. In April 1893, Zinaida Morozova, wife of prominent businessman Savva Morozov bought this nobility compound in the upmarket section of the old Arbat. Savva, the grandson of a serf-peasant, became a millionaire textile merchant and popular patron of the arts. (Morozov funded Stanislavsky's Moscow Arts Theater.) The Morozovs commissioned the famous architect Fedor Shekhtel to redesign their house in medieval

Gothic style, which was completed in 1898. The attention to detail is astounding—gargoyles, griffins, stone carvings and cast-iron railings decorate the exterior. For the interior, Mikhail Vrubel created enormous stained-glass windows. Pavel Schmidt contributed hand-carved wooden staircases and furniture, and great sandstone fireplaces and crystal chandeliers came from the Zakharov and Postnikov workshops. The mansion was frequented by the Moscow elite. Savva Morozov, a member of the Old Believer sect, backed the socialists. He even hid revolutionaries within the many corners of his home and secretly funded Lenin's newspaper *Iskra* (The Spark). After the bloody consequences of the 1905 Revolution, Savva Morozov could no longer live with the conflicts—bouts of industrial strikes in his factories coupled with his promotion of reforms—he committed suicide by shooting himself in the head.

In 1909 his wife sold the house to Mikhail Riabushinsky, who added art works by artist Konstantin Bogarevsky. The Riabushinsky family was forced to flee to America in 1918. Under Stalin, the mansion became the People's Commissariat for Foreign Affairs. In 1995, a large fire broke out, and many parts of the structure were severely damaged. For two years the Russian diplomatic firm UpDK painstakingly restored the entire building. Today it serves as the House of Receptions for the Ministry of Foreign Affairs.

Continuing south down Spiridonovka leads to Malaya Nikitskaya and the **Gorky House Museum** at number 6. Maxim Gorky (1868–1936), known as the 'Father of Soviet Literature', lived here for five years before his death. It was Stalin who gave Gorky this house as a meeting place for the union of writers and artists, but the writer felt uncomfortable here, 'like a bird in a golden cage'. The writer's real name was Alexei Maximovich Peshkov; he later adopted the pen name Gorky (meaning bitter). Orphaned in childhood, Maxim was put to work at the age of 11, and attempted suicide eight years later in 1887. He became widely known after writing his 1899 *Sketches and Stories*, and the poem *Song of the Stormy Petrel* in 1901. He followed with the plays *The Lower Depths* (centered in Moscow's destitute Myasnitskaya or Butcher area) and *Summer Folk*. In 1906, to avoid postrevolution crackdowns (he had already been exiled to Siberia in 1901), Gorky journeyed to the United States supported by Mark Twain. While there, he wrote his most famous work, *Mother*, the first example of socialist realist literature. Although it is suspected he was poisoned on Stalin's orders, the dictator still honored Gorky by placing his ashes in the Kremlin wall.

In 1902, the architect Shekhtel was commissioned by a member of the Riabushinsky banking dynasty, Stepan Pavlovich, to design the house in art-nouveau style; it was completed four years later. Encompassing style-moderne themes of nature and fluidity, the mansion was given stained-glass windows, a glass roof and flowered bas-reliefs. The exquisite staircase resembles a giant crashing

Modern graffiti art on Malaya Bronnaya Ulitsa in the Patriarch's Pond district. Since this was the home of Mikhail Bulgakov, who wrote the famous novel The Master and Margarita, *the colorful mural is entitled* Margarita *and depicts scenes from the story.*

wave which spills out onto the parquet floors. Today the library has over 10,000 volumes and the parlor looks as it did when Gorky lived here. A superb collection of carved ivory is in the bedroom, and many of the writer's books and letters are on display. The museum is open 10am–4.30pm, Wednesdays and Fridays 12–6pm; closed Mondays, Tuesdays. (The Gorky Literary Museum is at 25 Povarskaya Ulitsa, near Arbatskaya Metro station.)

Next to the Gorky House, at 2/6 Spiridonovka, is the **Alexei Tolstoy House Museum**. This is not the Leo Tolstoy of *War and Peace*, but a distant relative. This Tolstoy wrote *Ivan the Terrible*, *Peter the Great*, and the well-known trilogy about the Revolution, *The Road to Calvary*, completed in 1941; a year later it was awarded the Stalin Prize. His granddaughter Tatyana Tolstaya is a well-recognized contemporary author. Open Thursdays and weekends 11am–5pm, Wednesdays and Fridays 1–6.30pm; closed Mondays and Tuesdays.

On the other side of Gorky House stands the white Empire-style **Church of the Grand Ascension**, on the western side of Nikitskiye Vorota Square. It was here in February 1831 that Alexander Pushkin married Natalia Goncharova (who later was the cause of the St Petersburg duel in which Pushkin was killed). It is said that during the ceremony a crucifix fell from a wall and candles mysteriously blew out; an omen not taken lightly. The church, still in the process of being restored, is open for worship. At 12 Malaya Nikitskaya stands the 18th-century classical **Bobrinsky Mansion**, originally built by the Dolgoruky family and inhabited by Catherine the Great's illegitimate son with Grigory Orlov. Bobrinsky's descendants lived here up until the Revolution.

TVERSKAYA-YAMSKAYA ULITSA

At the intersection of Tverskaya and the Sadovoye Koltso (Garden Ring) is **Triumfalnaya Ploshchad**. In the 18th century the square was marked by triumphal arches used to welcome czars and returning victorious armies. On the corner of the square stands a large building with ten columns—the **Tchaikovsky Concert Hall** (built for Meyerhold's Theater in the 1930s), where orchestras and dance ensembles perform. The Moscow Stars and Winter Festivals also take place here. The Mayakovskaya Metro station is in front of the Hall. Directly behind it, at number 2, is the circular-domed building of the **Satire Theater**, founded in 1924, whose productions have ranged from *The Cherry Orchard* to the *Three-Penny Opera*. Across the street is the **Peking Hotel**, housing the very first Chinese restaurant in Moscow.

A statue of the poet Vladimir Mayakovsky (1893–1930) stands in the square at Mayakovskaya Metro station. At number 43 is the House of Children's Books, and at number 46 the Exhibition Hall of Artist Unions. A ten-minute walk northeast to

From Moscow's large, 120 year-old Byelorussky Railway Station, trains journey to points west in Europe. Additional local elektrichki trains run to the suburban areas of Borodino and Zvenigorod. Moscow has nine major train stations within the city.

4 Ulitsa Fadeyeva is the **Glinka Music Museum**, opened in 1943. The museum has a large collection of musical instruments, rare recordings and unique manuscripts of famous composers, such as Tchaikovsky, Shostakovich and Glinka; open 11am–7pm; closed Mondays.

Three streets east around the Ring, at 3 Delegatskaya Ulitsa, is the **Decorative and Folk Art Museum** with displays of Russian jewelry, applied art and handicrafts. Open 10am–6pm, closed Fridays.

Tverskaya-Yamskaya Street ends at Byelorusskaya Ploshchad, also called Zastava (Gate) Square, which was the old site of the Kamer-Kollezhsky gates on the road to Tver. At the center of the square is a **Monument to Maxim Gorky** (1868–1935), erected in 1951. Trains from the 120-year-old **Byelorussky Railway Station** journey to points west, including Warsaw, Berlin, Paris and London. The Byelorusskaya Metro station is in front. Here Tverskaya-Yamskaya Street turns into Leningradsky Prospekt, which runs all the way to the international airport, Sheremetyevo II. On the next side street are the offices of the newspaper *Pravda*, whose circulation was once ten million. After the 1991 attempted putsch, the offices were shut down for the first time in its history. There was no money to continue operations (Communist Party funds had been frozen). A few months later the newspaper was back in business, but it was asking for investments and the price of the paper had increased.

Along Begovaya Ulitsa (Running Street) is the **Moscow Hippodrome**, a race course. It was built a century ago in Empire style and frequented by the Russian aristocracy. Equestrian sports were very popular in Czarist Russia. By 1905, over 2,000 horses were competing in over 50 hippodromes, and the total prize money reached the sum of 3 million rubles, equal to the value of two tons of gold. Today, the Hippodrome is open three or four times weekly, drawing up to 20,000 people for the nine daily races. It annually hosts the International President's Cup equestrian tournament. During off hours, horses can be hired. The **Casino Royale** is now located in the Hippodrome's Central Hall. This was the idea of renowned eye-surgeon Svyatoslav Fyodorov, who developed the famous daisy-wheel operating room technique—operating on up to 10 patients in one room at a time. In nearby Begovaya Lane, find the small archway designed by Klodt, who also crafted the famous horse sculptures on St Petersburg's Anichkov bridge. A little farther up, at 32 Leningradsky, is the Hotel Sovietskaya and the **Romany Gypsy Theater**. Seating over 800, the theater focuses on gypsy national culture. The Moscow Chamber Musical Theater is at 71 Leningradsky Prospekt.

From here you can take the Metro or a bus to return to the city center.

ULITSA VOZDVIZHENKA AND NOVY (NEW) ARBAT

In 1991, Kalinin Prospekt was divided into two different streets. Vozdvizhenka Street (the name stems from the 16th-century Krestovozdvizhensky or Church of the Exaltation) runs from the Kremlin's Kutafya Tower (by the Alexandrov Gardens) to Arbatskaya Ploshchad (Arbat Square). Novy Arbat begins at Arbat Square and continues to

The Old Arbat is one of the most popular shopping areas in Moscow. Everything from antikvariant *antique stores and portrait painters to McDonald's are found along this pedestrian thoroughfare.*

the Novoarbatsky Most (Bridge). Here Novy Arbat becomes Kutuzovsky Prospekt and later the Minsk Highway.

The old route was known as Novodvizhenskaya; it stretched from the Kremlin to the outer walls of the city. A new thoroughfare was built along this former road

and from 1963 to 1991 it was named Kalinin, after a leader of the Communist Party, Mikhail Kalinin. The old section of the prospekt runs from the Kremlin to the Boulevard Ring, where the more modern part begins.

The road starts by a large gray building off Mokhovaya—the Russian State Library (see page 156). At number 5 is the **Shchusev Architectural Museum** exhibiting the history of Russian architecture; open 11am–6pm, weekends 11am–4pm, closed Mondays. The first part of the street still contains a few 18th-century buildings. At number 7 is the former **Monastery of the Holy Cross**. The house at number 9 belonged to Tolstoy's grandfather, Count Volkonsky, upon whom he based a character in *War and Peace*. At the corner of Romanov Pereulok is an early 18th-century mansion that belonged to a member of the wealthy Sheremetyev family. Across the street at number 5 is an old mansion of the Tolyzin estate, built by Kazakov. Many prominent Soviet officials also lived along this street, such as Frunze, Voroshilov, Kosygin and Khrushchev. The nearest Metro station is Alexandrovsky Sad.

At number 16 is the white, medieval former mansion of the merchant Arseny Morozov who, in 1899, hired his friend, the designer Mazyrin, to model his residence after a 16th-century Moorish castle they had seen while visiting Portugal; each room was decorated in a different style from Greek to English Gothic. After the Revolution it was turned over to the Union of Anarchists. In 1959, it became the **House of Friendship**, where delegations of foreign friendship societies meet. Nearby, the eight-story building with one turret was built in the 1920s as the first Soviet skyscraper in constructivist style. Near the Arbatskaya Metro station, on the square, is a **Monument to Nikolai Gogol**, standing in front of the house where the writer lived.

STARY (OLD) ARBAT

On the southwest corner of Arbat Square is the Prague Restaurant, marking the entrance to one of the city's oldest sections, the **Arbat**. Long ago the Arbat Gates led into Moscow. *Arbad* is an old Russian word meaning beyond the town walls. Alternatively, some believe the word could stem from the Mongol word *arba*, a sack to collect tributes; the ancient 'Arab' settlements ("rabat" meaning suburban outskirts); or the Latin *arbutum*, cherry, because of the cherry orchards that were once in the area. There is one other proposed origin: a creek named Chertory, the Devil's Creek, once meandered or 'hunchbacked' through the vicinity, which was quite damp and boggy. When a small one-kopek candle started a fire in the All Saints Church and burnt it and the rest of Moscow to the ground in 1365, many thought the area cursed. The Russian word *khorbaty* means hunchbacked place.

The area was first mentioned in 15th-century chronicles. It lay along the Smolensk Road, making it a busy trade center. Many court artisans lived here in the

16th century; in the 19th century many wealthy and educated people chose to live in the Arbat. Today the street is a cobbled pedestrian thoroughfare about one kilometer (two-thirds of a mile) long, and one of the most popular meeting and shopping spots in Moscow. Along with its shops, cafés, art galleries, concert and theater halls and a museum tracing the history of the area, are portrait painters, performance artists and even demonstrators. It is also a frequent site for festivals and carnivals. At its eastern end, notice the Wall of International Friendship, composed of hundreds of individually painted tiles. Chekhov once said that 'the Arbat is one of the most pleasant spots on Earth'. It is definitely worth a stroll.

The colorful buildings lining the pedestrian mall and its side streets have a rich and romantic history. Many poems, songs and novels, such as Anatoly Rybakov's *Children of the Arbat*, have been written about this area. The czar's stablemen once lived along Starokonivshenny (Old Stable) Lane. An old church stood on the corner of Spasopeskovsky Pereulok (Savior-on-the-Sand Lane). Other small streets have the names Serebryany (Silversmith), Plotnikov (Carpenter) and Kalashny (Pastrycook). After a leisurely stroll, you will better understand the lyrics to a popular song: 'Oy, Arbat, a whole lifetime is not enough to travel through your length!'

At 7 Arbat is the Literary Café, a favorite of both Mayakovsky and Isadora Duncan's husband, the Russian poet Yesenin, in the 1920s. The niece of Tolstoy, Countess Obolenskaya, lived at number 9; it is now an antique store. Several other *antikvariant*, souvenir shops and book stores are located along the street. After passing the 1,000-seat **Vakhtangov Theater** (founded in 1921), at number 26, turn right up Bolshoi Nikolopeskovsky Pereulok. At number 11 is the **Skryabin Museum**, home of the Russian composer and pianist from 1912 to 1915. Here he composed his symphonies "Divine Poem" and "Prometheus". His concert programs, photographs and books are on display, along with recordings of his music; there is also a chamber concert hall. Open 10am–4.30pm, 12–6.30pm Wednesdays and Fridays; closed Mondays and Tuesdays. Walking a few short blocks west to Spasopeskovsky Pereulok leads to the **Spaso House**, residence of the US ambassador (since 1933); it was originally built in neo-Empire style by banker Vtorov in 1913. Along this street notice the **Church of the Savior-on-the-Sand**, built in 1711, and currently under restoration. The artist Polenov depicted its bell tower in his famous painting "Moscow Courtyard".

Crossing the Arbat, continue a block south down to 10 Krivoarbatsky Pereulok and the **Melnikov House**. In 1927, the renowned architect Konstantin Melnikov built this house in constructivist style for his family, and lived here until his death in 1974. (Melnikov designed Lenin's glass sarcophagus.) The exterior consists of two honeycombed concrete cylinders cut into each other and connected by hexagonal windows, and the inside stories are linked by a spiral staircase. Today his

Moscow's old Arbat district, an area dating back to the 15th century, is, today, one of the most popular meeting and shopping spots in the capital. The one-kilometer long cobbled pedestrian thoroughfare is filled with shops, cafes, theaters and galleries.

son is restoring the house, and is planning to open it as a museum. One block further south leads to the **Herzen Museum** at 27 Pereulok Sivtsev Vrazhek (*vrazhek* means gully—once the River Sivtsev ran through a gully in this location). The writer Alexander Herzen (1812–70) lived here from 1843 to 1846. Here he wrote *Dr Krupov*, *Magpie and the Thief* and his famous novel *Who is to Blame?* For these revolutionary views he was exiled in 1847. From London, Herzen wrote his radical political magazine *Kolokol* (The Bell) and smuggled copies into Russia. His *Letters on Nature*, according to Lenin, put him alongside 'the most prominent thinkers of his time'. (Herzen was born in the house at 25 Tverskoi Boulevard.) The museum is open 11am–6pm, 1pm–6pm Wednesdays and Fridays; closed Mondays.

At 53 Arbat is the blue and white stucco **Pushkin House Museum**. Here, in this Empire-style mansion, in 1831, the famous writer lived with his new bride Natalia Goncharova. (Across the street is a gilded statue of the couple by Zurab Tseretelli.) Exhibits are on his marriage and Moscow activities. (Tchaikovsky also lived here in 1875.) Open 11am–5pm; closed Mondays and Tuesdays. In connection with the 200th anniversary of Alexander Pushkin's birth in 1999, the city created a 'Pushkin Path' that leads from this house to the Pushkin Museum on Prechistenka Street.

Another native of the Arbat was popular poet and singer Bulat Okudzhava, who coined the word arbatstvo or the Arbat spirit. "The Arbat to me is not just a street. It is a place that embodies Moscow and Russia." A monument in tribute to Okudzhava was put up on the corner of Plotnikov Lane, next to the house where the poet was born.

The Arbat ends at the Garden Ring Road and Smolenskaya Ploshchad where one of Stalin's seven Gothic skyscrapers stands, now the MID or Ministry of Foreign Affairs.

NOVY ARBAT

The avenue from Arbat Square on the Boulevard Ring to the Novoarbatsky Bridge is known as Novy (New) Arbat, the main western thoroughfare of the city. The shops and flats in this area were built during Khrushchev's regime in the 1960s; they were designed by Moscow's chief architect Mikhail Posokhin. Across the street from the Prague Restaurant (one of the oldest in Moscow) is the **Church of Simon Stylites** with colorful *kokoshniki* gables. It was here in 1801 that Prince Nikolai Sheremetyev married serf-actress Praskovia Zhemchugova-Kovalyova. Theirs is one of Russia's most romantic love stories. She, a daughter of a serf blacksmith, worked as an actress on the Sheremetyev estate in Kuskovo. They fell in love in 1789 and ten years later Nikolai granted her freedom. Sadly, two years after the marriage, Praskovia died in childbirth. Today the church has an exhibition hall, and is open for worship.

Heading north, down the side street behind the church, leads to the **Lermontov Memorial House** at 2 Malaya Molchanovka. Mikhail Lermontov (1814–41) lived here with his grandmother from 1829 to 1832, and while studying at Moscow University wrote about 100 poems and plays. He is best known for the 1840 prose-novel *A Hero of Our Time*; the main character Grigory Pechorin is one of the great romantic heroes in modern literature. For a poem criticizing the court's connivance in the death of Pushkin, Lermontov was exiled to the Caucasus by Nicholas I. Like Pushkin, Lermontov also died in a duel—over a trivial quarrel with a fellow infantry officer—he was shot through the heart on July 15, 1841. The museum is open 11am–4pm, 2pm–5pm Wednesdays and Fridays; closed Sundays and Mondays.

Next to the church, at 8 Novy Arbat, is **Dom Knigi** (House of Books), the city's largest bookstore (open 10am–7pm, closed Sundays). Here books, posters, and even antiques and icons (for rubles only) are for sale. The Malachite Casket Jewelry Shop is also in this building. On the same side of the street is the Melodia Record Shop and the 3,000-seat Oktyabr Cinema at number 24.

A series of shops and cafés line the left side of Novy Arbat. On the second floor of number 19 is the **Irish House**, where you can find most Western food products and the **Shamrock Bar**. The block ends at the 2,000-seat Metelitsa entertainment complex (open 24 hours, with loud music, floor shows and a casino).

Novy Arbat crosses the Garden Ring at Novinsky Bulvar (Boulevard) and ends at the river. The **White House** or Beli Dom, once headquarters of the Russian Parliament, stands to the right. It was the famous scene of two coup attempts. In August 1991, a number of conservative plotters tried to overthrow the Gorbachev government while

Virtually no visitor returns from Russia without a painted wooden souvenir reflecting 17th-century 'Khokloma' folk art. Originating in the Golden Ring village of Khokloma, its tradition is based on poetic floral and geometrical patterns and a rich variety of lacquered colors. After the 1889 Paris Exhibition, the art became recognized around the world.

he was vacationing in the Crimea. Boris Yeltsin, who became the nation's hero, climbed atop a tank in front of the building and rallied thousands of demonstrators to oppose the coup's collaborators. The events of these days led to the fall of the Soviet Union four months later. Then two years later, in September 1993, after Yeltsin suspended the constitution for three months, Parliament mutinied and Yeltsin's deputy Alexander Rutskoi declared himself 'acting president'. For eleven days, Rutskoi and his 300-member unofficial entourage took control of the White House until army tanks shelled them into submission. After the building's restoration, the Moscow patriarch came by and blessed it. It has since been turned into an office block.

Further west, on the same side of the river, is the Sovincenter and the **Mezhdunarodnaya (International) Hotel**, built with the help of Armand Hammer and used by foreign firms. It has a number of restaurants, cafés and shops, a health center with sauna and pool, a pharmacy, an Aeroflot ticket office and a food store on the second floor. Next door, in the **Sovincenter** office building (also known as the World Trade Center), are many other airline offices and Federal Express is on the ground floor.

KUTUZOVSKY PROSPEKT

After crossing the Novoarbatsky Bridge, Novy Arbat becomes Kutuzovsky Prospekt, named after the Russian General Mikhail Kutuzov (1745–1813), who fought against Napoleon. The building on the right with the star-spire is the **Ukraina Hotel**, which celebrated its 50th birthday in 2007. It has a large Ukrainian restaurant with other European-style cafés, a jazz club and disco. (This was the last of Stalin's 'seven sisters' skyscrapers to be built.) A statue to the Ukrainian poet Taras Shevchenko stands in front. On the next corner south of the hotel is the **Hero City of Moscow Obelisk**. Troops left from this point in 1941 to fight the advancing German army.

The obelisk stands at the junction with Bolshaya Dorogomilovskaya, along which is the **Kievsky Railway Station** (with a Metro station). Kievsky, which celebrates its 90th anniversary in 2008, was once the largest station in Europe (this honor is now held by Moscow's Kazansky Station), and is still considered the city's most beautiful. The train terminal handles up to 35,000 passengers a day.

Stalin's dacha was in this area, where he died in 1953. At number 25 Kutuzovsky, a plaque marks the 30-year residence of Leonid Brezhnev; Yuri Andropov also lived here. The prospekt ends at the **Triumphal Arch** in **Victory Square** (Ploshchad Pobedy), designed by Osip Bovet in 1829 to honor Russia's victory in the War of 1812. It originally stood in front of the Byelorussky Train Station and was reconstructed on

MOSCOW BURNING

N*arye at lunch next day—the Moscow Chief of Police, Schetchinsky by name. Before we had been more than 10 minutes at table a wild-looking police officer rushed in unannounced and uttered one word— "Pajare!"—"Quick!" The Chief of Police sprang from his seat while Narychkine and Jenny, with one voice, exclaimed: "A fire? Where?" A fire is no rare event in Moscow and is always a serious matter, for of the 11,000 houses in the centre of Moscow only 3,500 are of stone, the rest are of wood. Just as St. Petersburg counts its disasters in floods, Moscow numbers the fires that have reduced great stretches of the city to ashes, the most terrible being, of course in 1812, when barely 6,000 buildings remained standing.*

I was seized with a sudden urge to see this fire for myself.

"Can I come with you?" I begged the Chief of Police.

"If you promise not to delay me a single second."

I seized my hat as we ran together to the door. His troika, with its three mettlesome black horses, was waiting. We jumped in and shot off like lightning while the messenger, already in the saddle, spurred his own mount and led the way. I had no conception of how fast a troika can move behind three galloping horses, and for a moment I could not even draw breath. Dust from the macadamised country road billowed up in clouds above our heads; then, as we skimmed over the pointed cobbles of Moscow's streets, sparks struck by our flying hooves fell around us like rain and clung desperately to the iron strut while the Chief of Police yelled: "Faster! Faster!"

As soon as we left Petrovsky Park we could see smoke hanging like an umbrella—fortunately there was no wind. In the town there were dense crowds, but the messenger, riding a horse's length ahead, cleared a path for us, using his knout on any bystanders who did not move fast enough to please him, and we passed between ranks of people like lightning between clouds. Every moment I feared that someone would be run over, but by some miracle no one was even touched and five minutes later we were facing the fire, our horses trembling, their legs folding beneath them. A whole island of houses was burning fiercely. By good fortune the road in front of it was fifteen or twenty yards wide, but on every other side only narrow alleys separated it from neighbouring dwellings. Into one of these alleys rushed M. Schetchinsky, I at his heels. He urged me back—in vain. "Then hold fast to my sword-belt," he cried, "and don't let go!" For several seconds I was in the midst of flames and thought I would suffocate. My very lungs seemed on fire as I gasped for breath. Luckily another alley led off to our right. the Chief of Police ran into it, I followed and we both sank on a baulk of timber. "You've lost your hat," he laughed. "D'you feel inclined to go back for it?"

"God! No! Let it lie! All I want is a drink."

At a gesture from my companion a woman standing by went back in to her house and brought out a pitcher of water. Never did the finest wine taste so good! As I drank, we heard a rumble like thunder. The fire-engines had arrived!

Moscow's Fire Service is very well organised, and each of the 21 districts has its own engines. A man is stationed on the highest tower in the area, on the watch day and night, and at the first sign of fire he sets in motion a system of globes to indicate exactly where smoke is rising. So the engines arrive without losing a second, as they did on this occasion, but the fire was quicker still. It had started in the courtyard of an inn, where a carter had carelessly lit a cigar near a heap of straw. I looked into that courtyard. It was an inferno!

To my amazement, M. Schetchinsky directed the hoses not on the fire itself but on the roofs of the nearby houses. He explained that there could be no hope of saving the houses that were actually burning, but if the sheets of iron on neighbouring rooftops could be prevented from getting red hot there might be a chance of saving the homes they covered.

The only source of water in the district was 300 yards away, and soon the engines were racing to it to refill their tanks. "Why don't the people make a chain?" I asked.

"What is that?"

"In France, everyone in the street would volunteer to pass along buckets of water so that the engines could go on pumping."

"*That's a very good idea! I can see how useful that would be. But we have no law to make people do that.*"

"*Nor have we, but everyone rushes to lend a hand.* When the Théâtre Italien *caught fire I saw princes working in the chain.*"

"*My dear M. Dumas,*" *said the Chief of Police,* "*that's your French fraternity in action. The people of Russia haven't reached that stage yet.*"

"*What about the firemen?*"

"*They are under orders. Go and see how they are working and tell me what you think of them.*"

They were indeed working desperately hard. They had climbed into the attics of the nearby houses and with hatchets and levers, their left hands protected by gloves, they were trying to dislodge the metal roofing sheets, but they were too late. Smoke was already pouring from the top storey of the corner house and its roof glowed red. Still the men persisted like soldiers attacking an enemy position. They were really wonderful, quite unlike our French firemen who attack the destructive element on their own initiative, each finding his own way to conquer the flames. No! Theirs was a passive obedience, complete and unquestioning. If their chief had said "Jump in the fire!" they would have done so with the same devotion to duty, though they well knew that it meant certain death to no purpose.

Brave? Yes, indeed, and bravery in action is always inspiring to see. But I was the only one to appreciate it. Three or four thousand people stood there watching, but they showed not the slightest concern at this great devastation, no sign of admiration for the courage of the firemen. In France there would have been cries of horror, encouragement, applause, pity, despair, but here—nothing! Complete silence, not of consternation but of utter indifference, and I realised the profound truth of M. Schetchinsky's comment that as yet the Russians have no conception of fraternity as we know it, no idea of brotherhood between man and his fellows. God! How many revolutions must a people endure before they can reach our level of understanding?

Alexandre Dumas, Adventures in Czarist Russia, *1960*

this spot in 1968, when Tverskaya Street was widened. It is decorated with the coats-of-arms of Russia's provinces. Here on Poklonnaya Hill, Napoleon waited for Moscow's citizens to bow to him and relinquish the keys to the city. From the hill is a magnificent view of Moscow—Anton Chekhov once said, 'Those who want to understand Russia should look at Moscow from Poklonnaya Hill.' Between Kutuzovskaya Metro station and the arch is the **Statue of Mikhail Kutuzov** by Nikolas Tomsky and an obelisk that marks the common graves of 300 men who died in the War of 1812.

The large circular building at number 38 is the **Battle of Borodino Panorama Museum**, (ticket *kassa* open 10am–4.45pm), closed Fridays and the last Thursday of the month. A five-minute walk from the Kutuzovskaya Metro. The 68 cannons in front were captured from Napoleon. In 1912, to commemorate the 100th anniversary of the war, Franz Rouband was commissioned to paint scenes of the Battle of Borodino, which took place on August 26, 1812 (September 7 on the new calendar). The large murals are displayed in the museum, which was constructed in 1962 to honor the 150th anniversary. Behind is the **Kutuzov Hut**. Here on September 1, 1812, as the French invaded Moscow, Kutuzov and the Military Council decided to abandon the city. The actual site of the Battle of Borodino is about 120 kilometers (75 miles) outside of Moscow (see Borodino in Vicinity of Moscow section, page 241).

About 1.5 kilometers north of the museum is the **Church of the Intercession** in Fili. From Fili Metro station, walk five minutes north on Novozavodskaya and the red and white baroque-tiered towers come into view. Built between 1690–93 by Peter the Great's uncle, the boyar Naryshkin, it is a superb example of 'Naryshkin-style' architecture—using non-traditional proportions and white-stone fretwork. The upper-story summer Church of the Savior (open from May 15 to October 15) has a magnificent golden iconostasis with icons painted by renowned artists of the Czar, Kirill Ulanov and Karp Zolotarev. The lower, winter church is open daily 11am–6pm, closed Tuesdays, Wednesdays and the last Friday of each month.

From here, Kutuzovsky Prospekt becomes the Mozhaiskoye Chausee, the Minsk Highway, which leads south to the city of Minsk in Byelorussia.

THE BOULEVARD RING

During the 16th and 17th centuries, the stone walls of the Beli Gorod (White Town) stretched around the area now known as the Boulevard Ring. During the 'Time of Troubles' at the end of the 17th century, Boris Godunov fortified the walls and built 37 towers and gates. By 1800 the walls were taken down and the area was planted with trees and gardens, divided by a series of small connected boulevards. Ten *bulvari* make up the Bulvarnoye Koltso, the Boulevard Ring, actually a horseshoe shape that begins in the southwest off Prechistenka Street and circles around to the back of St. Basil's Cathedral on the other side of the Kremlin. Some of the squares still bear the name of the old gate towers. Frequent buses run around the ring, stopping off at each intersecting boulevard.

THE TEN BOULEVARDS

The first bears the name of the writer Nikolai Gogol. **Gogolevsky Bulvar** stretches from the Cathedral of Christ Our Savior to Arbat Square. It was known as the Immaculate Virgin Boulevard (Prechistensky Bulvar) until 1924; the first square is still called Prechistenskiye Vorota (Gates) with the Kropotkinskaya Metro station nearby. The right side of the street is lined with mansions dating back to the 1800s. In the 19th century the aristocratic Naryshkin family had their estate at number ten. At number 14 is the Central Chess Club. Chess is popular in Russia and the country has produced many world champions. In 1994, Anatoly Karpov set a world record by becoming the first international chess player to win 100 tournaments.

The next square is Arbatskaya, which leads into the Old Arbat district (see page 174). A side street leading to the Kremlin is Znamenka, which dates back to the 13th century. It means 'the sign', taking its name at the time from the Church of the Virgin Icon. In the 17th century the czar's apothecary was nearby; medicinal herbs were planted on Vagankovsky Hill.

Nikitsky Bulvar extends from Novy Arbat to Bolshaya Nikitskaya Ulitsa. Until 1992, it was named after the famous Russian army commander Alexander Suvorov, who lived at the end of the thoroughfare. The Nikitskiye Gates used to stand at the junction of the boulevard and Bolshaya Nikitskaya Ulitsa, which is named Nikitskaya Ploshchad after a monastery that was in the area. Gogol lived at number seven, now the **Gogol Memorial House** (open 1–5pm, closed Tuesdays and Fridays). Increasingly despondent in his later years, Gogol burned the second volume of his novel *Dead Souls* in this house and died here in 1852. A monument to Nikolai Gogol, upon which characters from his books are depicted, stands in front. The Union of Journalists, opened in 1920, is at number eight. The General Lunin House, at number 12, was built by Gilliardi in Russian-Empire style with eight Corinthian columns (1818–22). It is now the **Oriental Art Museum**, open daily 11am–7pm, closed Mondays. The museum exhibits Asian art, Siberian shaman artifacts and works by Nikolai Roerich (1874–1946), who studied and traveled in the Himalayas.

Bolshaya Nikitskaya extends from the Kremlin's Manezhnaya Square to the Boulevard Ring. In the 15th century, this was the route to the town of Novgorod. At number 19 is the **Mayakovsky Theater**, home to Meyerhold's Theater of the Revolution in the 1920s. (Meyerhold was later arrested in the 1930s and died in prison.) At number 13 is the **Tchaikovsky Conservatory Grand Hall**, the country's largest music school. The conservatory was founded in 1866 by Nikolai Rubinstein. (His brother Anton founded the St Petersburg Conservatory in 1862.) Tchaikovsky taught here and pupils included Rachmaninov, Skryabin and Khachaturian. The building also has two concert halls; the annual International Tchaikovsky Piano Competition is held in the larger one. A statue of Tchaikovsky stands in front (sculpted by Vera Mukhina in 1954). Notice the musical notes on the cast-iron railings—they come from the famous opus *Glory to the Russian People* from the Glinka opera *Ivan Susanin*. This was once the mid-18th century Moscow home of Princess Ekaterina Vorontsova-Dashkova, a close friend of Catherine the Great's; the czarina made her head of the Russian Academy of Arts and Sciences in 1783.

Nearby, at number 12 Gazetny Pereulok (Lane), is the **Menschikov Mansion**. Popular architect Matvei Kazakov designed the blue and white porticoed residence for Prince Sergei Menschikov (grandson of Alexander, Peter the Great's prime minister). It was restored after the great 1812 fire in Empire style.

Back on Bolshaya Nikitskaya, at number six, is the **Zoological Museum**. Founded in 1791 as a natural history project of Moscow University, it is one of Moscow's oldest museums. It was opened to the public in 1805; the present building was completed in 1902. The museum has a collection of over 10,000 species of animal, bird, fish and insect from around the world. Open 10am–5pm; closed Mondays.

Tverskoi Bulvar begins with the Monument to Kliment Timiryazev, a prominent Russian botanist. Built in 1796, it is the oldest boulevard on the ring, and was once a very fashionable promenade. Pushkin, Turgenev and Tolstoy all mentioned the Tverskoi in their writings. At number 11, where the great Russian actress Yermolova lived during the last half of her life, is now the **Yermolova House Museum**. Maria Yermolova (1853–1928) was the first person in the Soviet era to be awarded the title of 'Peoples' Artist'. The theater hosts a salon where small concerts are also performed. The museum is open 12–7pm; closed Tuesdays. At number 23 is the **Pushkin Drama Theater**, and across the street the **Gorky Theater**, built in 1973. The Literary Institute, at number 25, was started by Maxim Gorky in 1933. (The revolutionary Alexander Herzen was born in this building in 1812.) Tverskoi ends at Pushkin Square and the Pushkinskaya Metro station.

The Strastnoi (Passion) Monastery used to be in the area of the **Strastnoi Bulvar**, which begins with the Statue of Pushkin. On Pushkin's birthday, June 6, many people crowd the square to honor the poet. Chekhovskaya Metro station is close to the square. Strastnoi is one of the shortest and widest parts of the Boulevard Ring. It was Catherine the Great who ordered the city's original walls taken down from around the ring area. The city's Catherine Hospital, with its 12 Ionic columns, is at number 15. It was originally built by Matvei Kazakov as a palace for the Gagarin princes, and later housed the English Club from 1802 to 1812.

About one and a half kilometers (one mile) to the north at 2 Ulitsa Dostoevskovo is the **Dostoevsky Apartment Museum**, where the pensive writer lived from 1823–37. The events surrounding this ground floor apartment would greatly affect his later writings—Fyodor's father worked as a surgeon at the Hospital for the Poor next door; his mother contracted consumption and died here. Their windows also faced onto a route that prisoners took on their way to Siberia. The three rooms are open 11am–6pm, 2pm–8pm Wednesdays and Fridays; closed Mondays and Tuesdays.

The Petrovskiye Gates used to stand at what is now the beginning of **Petrovsky Bulvar**, which runs from Ulitsa Petrovka to Trubnaya Ploshchad. It is one of the few areas on the ring whose appearance has hardly changed since the 1800s. Some buildings still remain from the 14th century, such as the **Petrovsky (St Peter's) Monastery**, which still stands on the Neglinnaya River (see Ulitsa Petrovka on page 153). Trubnaya originates from the Russian word *truba*, meaning pipe; the river was diverted through a pipe under this square. Many of the old mansions on this boulevard were converted into hospitals and schools after the Revolution. At the end of Petrovsky stands the building of the former Hermitage Hotel; its restaurant was once the most popular in Moscow—Turgenev, Dostoevsky and Tchaikovsky all ate here. After the Revolution it became the House of the Collective Farmer and today is a theater. At 3 Karetny Ryad (Carriage Row) are the Hermitage Gardens.

Branching off north from Petrovsky is Tsvetnoi Bulvar, named after the flower (*tsveti*) market that used to be here. At number 13 is the **Old Circus**, also known as *Tsirk Nikulina na Tsvetnom Bulvare* or Nikulin's Circus on Tsvetnoi Bulvar (closed Tuesdays). It was established by Salamonsky for his private circus, the first in Moscow. After the Revolution it was turned into the State Circus. In the late 1980s a new circus was built on the site to match the original building. The 'new' Old Circus was reopened in 1989 under independent management. When Russia's most beloved clown, Yuri Nikulin (who also managed this circus), died in 1997, it was named after him. A statue of Nikulin stands out front. Tickets can be purchased at the building itself (daily 11am–7pm, closed 2–3pm for lunch) or at your hotel's service desk. Some kiosks on the street and in the nearby Metro station also sell tickets. Take the Metro to Tsvetnoi Bulvar. Make sure you buy tickets for the Old Circus (Stary Tsirk) since the New Circus (Novy Tsirk) is near Moscow University. (In summer tent circuses are set up in Gorky and Izmailovo parks.) Next to the Old Circus is the Tsentralny Rinok (Central Market), the best stocked *rinok* in the city; open daily.

Rozhdestvensky (Nativity) Bulvar ends at Ulitsa Sretenka, a popular shopping area. On the south side are the 14th-century walls of the **Convent of the Nativity of the Virgin**. It was founded in 1386 by the wife of Prince Andrei Serpukhovsky, son of Ivan I, as a place for unmarried women and widows to take refuge. The Church of St John Chrysostom was built in the mid-17th century. The white single-domed Cathedral of the Nativity (1501–05) houses the Icon of the Virgin which hangs on the left of the iconostasis; it was discovered in the 1980s by a priest cleaning an old door. The Refectory Church once housed exhibitions, but the Church is now taking control of the building. Other structures are also used as a refuge by the homeless. Closed in 1922, it was returned to the Church as a monastery in 1992.

On the corner of the boulevard and Sretenka Street stands the **Printer's Assumption Church**, built with money donated by the printers who lived in the area.

The **Statue to Nadezhda Krupskaya** (1869–1939), Lenin's wife, marks the beginning of **Sretensky Bulvar**, the shortest boulevard with a length of 215 meters (705 feet). The Old Russian word *vstreteniye* means meeting. In 1395, the Vladimir Icon of the Mother of God was brought to Moscow and was met here at the gate of the White Town on its way to the Kremlin. Lining the sides of the boulevard are early 20th-century homes, distinguished by their original façades. In 1885, Moscow named its first public library, located here, after the writer Turgenev. The boulevard ends on Turgenevskaya Ploshchad with a Metro station of the same name.

A statue of the writer Griboedov (1795–1829) marks the beginning of **Chistoprudny Bulvar**. Its name, Clear Pond, comes from the pond at its center, which offers boating and ice-skating in winter. (The Rachka River was diverted underground.) To the right, in Arkhangelsky Pereulok, one can make out the tower of the Church of the Archangel Gabriel. Prince Alexander Menschikov ordered it built on his estate in 1707; he wanted it to be taller than the Kremlin's Ivan the Great Bell Tower. In 1723, the archangel at the top was struck by lightning, so for a while the tower was the second largest structure in Moscow. It was rebuilt in 1780 without the spire, and today it is topped by a golden cupola and known as the **Menschikov Tower**. Next door is the 19th-century neo-Gothic **Church of St Fyodor Stratilit**, used as a winter church. The Sovremennik (Contemporary) Theater (called the Moscow Workers' Theater of the Prolekult in the 1930s) is at number 19. It was originally built as a cinema in 1914. Nearby at 23 Ulitsa Makarenko lived the renowned master of Russian cinema, Sergei Eisenstein. (See Special Topic on page 202.)

Pokrovsky (Intercession) Bulvar begins at Ulitsa Pokrovka. The 18th-century buildings to the east used to serve as the Pokrovsky barracks. The highly decorative rococo-style house at number 14 was known as the Chest of Drawers. Built in 1766, the façade is decorated with many strange beasts and birds. Ulitsa Pokrovka is distinguished by many well-preserved old churches and aristocratic residences. North of the ring, at number 22, is the baroque-style **Apraksin Mansion**, built in 1766. At the south corner of Pokrovka and Armyansky Pereulok stands the classical-style **Church of Saints Cosmas and Damian**, built between 1791–93 by Matvei Kazakov. A Colonel Khlebnikov commissioned the church, and also lived across the street in the palace located behind what is now the Belarus Embassy.

Another palace, at 11 Pokrovka, was built in 1790 by Prince Ivan Gagarin, a famous naval captain. Stroll down Armyansky Lane to find the Armenian Embassy at number 2. The wealthy Armenian businessman Lazar Lazaryan came to Moscow from Persia during the reign of Catherine the Great and built this residence. The Lazaryan family later bequeathed the buildings to the Armenian community.

Across the street at number 3 is an old 17th-century manor house which now houses the **Lights of Moscow Museum** with exhibits on the history of Moscow's street lighting from 1730 to present day. Open 10am–5pm weekdays. The city's first kerosene lamps were installed on Tverskaya Street in 1861 (prior to this oil and alcohol-burning street lamps were used), which were soon followed by new gas lights around 1865. In 1883, the invention of electric lights (known as Yablochka's 'electric candle') was put to use during the coronation of Alexander III. The square of the Cathedral of Christ the Savior was lit by these special arc lights. Filament lamps soon followed. The last gas lamp was removed from Moscow in 1932, marking the end of an era—prior to the 18th century, Moscow was draped in winter darkness for over 15 hours a day.

Yauzsky Bulvar is the last and narrowest section of the Boulevard Ring. This ends by Yauzsky Gate Square, where the Yauza River joins the Moskva River. A few 18th-century mansions remain in this area. Branching off to Petropavlovsky Pereulok brings you to the 18th-century baroque **Church of Saints Peter and Paul**. The 17th-century **Trinity Church** is located to the south in Serebryanichesky Pereulok (Silversmiths' Lane), named after the jewelers' quarter. Across the river lies Moscow's old Zayauzye district, once home to artisans and tailors. Continuing along the banks of the Moskva, past another of Stalin's Gothic skyscrapers, leads you to the back of the Kremlin. One of the best views of the Kremlin is from the **Bolshoi Kamenny Most** (Large Stone Bridge), first constructed in 1692 and rebuilt in 1936.

The czars often took Pokrovsky Boulevard to their estate in **Izmailovo**, now a popular 3,000-acre park in the northeastern part of the city. The estate, situated on an artificial island, dates back to the 14th century and was the property of the Romanovs. Later Peter the Great staged mock battle maneuvers in Silver Pond. The 17th-century baroque-style Churches of the Nativity and Protecting Veil survive along with some of the gates and three-tiered bridges. The **Izmailovo Flea Market** is well worth a visit (open daily 9am–6pm). Ride to Izmailovo Park Metro station. It is a good 20-minute walk north (past the Hotel Izmailovo), or take Minibus number 1 to the last stop. The entrance to the flea market is on the left, through the wooden rampart towers (admission R10). (The market on the right is more for locals.) The Flea Market is laden with every imaginable Russian souvenir and bargaining is a necessity. (Beware of fake icons and antiques, and pickpockets!) To reach the old estate, head southeast across the river onto the moated island.

A short walk from the Semyonovskaya Metro stop is the **Nikolsky Old Believers' Commune**. In 1652, the newly appointed Patriarch Nikon sought to reform the Church and remove any traditions from the service that did not follow the original Byzantine beliefs. Many people felt these reforms as an attack on the true Russian Church they had come to honor. Thus, a great schism broke out between Nikon's Orthodoxy and the groups who called themselves the Old Believers. They were even ready to go into exile for the sake of continuing to cross themselves with two fingers instead of with the newly prescribed three. The schism so weakened the independence and wealth of the Church that, after Nikon's death, Peter the Great placed the Church under the governing control of the Holy Synod. When Catherine the Great in 1771 granted Russia's citizens freedom to worship as they pleased, many Old Believers returned to Moscow from as far away as Siberia and continued to live together in community compounds. They still maintain old forms of Orthodox worship, such as the wearing of beards. The Old Believers established this residence in 1790; the red and white Gothic-style **Intercession Church** was soon filled with valuable icons and other works of art contributed by wealthy patrons. In the 1800s many aristocratic families such as the Riabushinskys and Morozovs belonged to the Old Believers' sect and are buried in the **Rogozhskoye Cemetery** located by the **Church of St Nicholas**. The compound is open 9am–6pm, closed Mondays.

Another two Metro stops toward the city is Baumanskaya. Outside on the building to the right is a mosaic that depicts scenes from the Nyemyetskaya Sloboda or German Quarter where, in the 16th and 17th centuries, most foreigners were required to live outside the city walls (so as not to so easily spread Western ideas to the population). It was in this area that Peter the Great was first introduced to his lover Anna Mons by his Swiss friend Franz Lefort, after whom the nearby prison, Lefortovo, is now named. A few minutes walk away is the **Yelokhovsky Cathedral**, at 15 Spartakovskaya Ulitsa. From 1943 to 1988 the complex was the seat of the Russian Patriarchy when it was then transferred to Danilovsky Monastery. The five-domed aquamarine structure, also known as the Church of the Epiphany, was rebuilt between 1837 and 1845 in an eclectic style. The poet Pushkin was baptized in the earlier church. The interior is filled with golden iconostases, and a few Church Patriarchs are buried in the chapel; Patriarch Alexei, who died in 1971, is buried in front of the main iconostasis. Open daily 8am–8pm with services held. At number 11 is Razgulyay Restaurant, a colorful Russian-style cellar eatery with Gypsy music on weekends; open daily 12–11.30pm.

THE RUSSIAN CINEMA

In May 1996, Russia celebrated the centennial of the first movies ever shown in the country. The first motion picture or Cinématographe-Lumière in Russia was shown in St Petersburg on May 4, 1896, at the Aquarium Gardens (now St Petersburg Film Studios). Three weeks later it also opened at Moscow's Hermitage Pleasure Garden. (The first Cinéma, created by the Lumiére brothers, had been shown in Paris on December 28, 1895.) In May 1896, the coronation of the last czar, Nicholas II, was filmed at the Kremlin and Red Square by a team of Parisian filmmakers; the motion picture they produced is regarded as the world's first newsreel. Russia's first feature film, *Stenka Razin* (a popular Russian hero who led a cossack uprising in 1670), premiered on October 15, 1908, and was seven and a half minutes long. Even at this time Russian films were censored by the czar; thus the subject matter focused mainly on mystical dramas or historical costume pieces, such as *The Death of Ivan the Terrible*. The most popular film of 1915 was *Song of Triumphant Love* with silent film legend, Vera Kholodnaya. Opening in Moscow on October 24, 1917 (and for only one day), *The Silent Ornaments of Life* was about the lives of aristocrat Prince Obolensky and two of his sweethearts. By the next day the Bolshevik Revolution had changed the course of history, along with the future of Russian cinema.

The world's first film school opened in the budding Soviet Union, and the new government recognized the propaganda value of filmmaking, turning out films such as *Tractor Driver*, *The Song of Russia* and *Volga-Volga*. In 1923, film student Lev Kuleshov incorporated his 'Kuleshov technique'—the first pioneering montage effects—in his film *The Strange Adventures of Mr West in the Land of the Bolsheviks*, a satire about an American visitor to Russia. Even after the Revolution, Russia put forth some of the world's most memorable cinematic classics: Pudovkin's *Mother* (1925), Donskoi's *Gorky's Childhood* (1938) and Dovzhenko's *Earth* (1930) were at the core of the silent cinema. Vertov's *The Sixth Part of the World* (1926) and *Man with a Movie Camera* (1929) became the forerunner to cinéma vérité.

The master of the Golden Age of Russian Cinema was Sergei Mikhailovich Eisenstein, born in 1898 to a Jewish family in Riga, Latvia. In 1914 he moved to Petrograd in order to study architecture and civil engineering. When his authoritarian father joined the White forces in 1918,

Sergei rebelled by serving in the Red Army where he studied arts and theater and worked as a poster artist in the psychological action division. By 1920 he was attending classes with leading stage director Vsevolod Meyerhold and working with avant-garde theater groups. As part of a theater production, Eisenstein made his first film in 1923, called *Glumov's Diary*, a five-minute interlude for a play by Alexander Ostrovsky. A year later he followed with his first feature, *Strike*, a criticism of czarist times. Here, the filmmaker created his own form of dramatic montage effects called shocks.

Eisenstein settled in Moscow's Chistoprudny District and lived at 23 Makareno Street, near the Sovremennik Theater. By the age of 27, Sergei had created one of his masterpieces, *Battleship Potemkin*, about the 1905 revolutionary events and mutiny of the battleship crew which culminated in the famous massacre scene on the Odessa steps. (At the Brussels Exhibition in 1958, this classic was voted the Best Film of All Time by a jury of film critics.) *Oktober* was made to celebrate the tenth anniversary of the 1917 Revolution. Supported completely by the government, *Oktober* became the Soviet Union's first film epic; thousands of extras and nearly 50,000 meters of film were used. But upon completion so many political changes had

The giant of Soviet cinema, Sergei Eisenstein, wrote, produced, directed and edited many film classics. He wrote in his A History of the Close Up (1942–46): 'A branch of lilac. White. Double. In lush green of the leaves... it becomes the first childhood impression I can recollect. A close up!'

occurred that Eisenstein had to re-edit the film. When it premiered on March 14, 1928, the new version was only 2,800 meters long. A year later, the first sound-film theater (now Znaniye Cinema at 72 Nevsky Prospekt) was opened in Leningrad on October 5, 1929.

In 1930, Eisenstein traveled to Europe and then America where he lived in Hollywood, met Charlie Chaplin and pitched ideas to Paramount Film Studios. American novelist Upton Sinclair offered to help finance Eisenstein's movie about Mexico, *Que Viva Mexico*. In 1932, when Sinclair's wealthy wife broke off their deal with Eisenstein, the director was forced to stop filming with only one episode remaining. (The first version of the Mexican film was edited in 1954, and finally reconstructed in 1979.) After returning to Moscow and suffering the strict confines of Soviet-Realism, Eisenstein suffered a nervous breakdown. For the next few years he was only allowed to make *agitkas*, or propaganda films. Then, after his first sound-speaking film, *Bezhin Meadow*, Eisenstein followed with his brilliant classic, *Alexander Nevsky*, (with Russian star Nikolai Cherkasov as Nevsky), about the Russian hero who, in 1240, defeated invading Teutonic knights. (The famous battle on the ice was shot outside Moscow in summer with artificial snow and ice.) Luckily Stalin liked the film (released in 1938 on the eve of World War II), with its anti-German tones and dramatic musical score by Prokofiev. Eisenstein fell back into favor and received the Order of Lenin. But, over the next three years (a period of Stalin's anti-Semitic stances and ruthless purges), Eisenstein was once again forbidden to practice his craft.

Finally, in 1942, the gifted filmmaker was permitted by ministers Zhdanov and Molotov to begin production on *Ivan the Terrible*, a three-part film epic. (Stalin felt a kinship with Ivan the Terrible and his Opritchniki police forces.) Part one was to be about Ivan IV's rise to power and proclamation as the first czar of all Russia. Filmed during the war years at a special studio in Central Asia, the movie was a triumphant success when it opened on January 16, 1945, and Eisenstein was awarded the Stalin Prize. But later, during the filming of part two, *The Boyars' Plot* (the last sequence was shot in color with Agfa film confiscated from the Germans at the end of the war), the mercurial Stalin staged vicious attacks and forbade the release of the film, demanding reshoots (the picture was not to be screened publicly until 1958). Under terrific strain, Eisenstein died of a heart attack on February 9, 1948, at the age of 50. Stalin allowed him to be buried in Moscow's Novodevichy Cemetery with honors. In 1998 Russia celebrated the centenary of his birth.

After World War II, one of the few themes that could pass by the censor boards of Goskino (Government controlled cinema) was that of the patriotic military. The best films of this genre usually involved the adventures of a hero struggling within the larger context of battle. Other popular films included Mikhail Kalatozov's *And the Cranes are Flying* (1957, winner of the Grand Prix at Cannes); Sergei Bondarchuk's *This Man's Destiny* (1959); Grigory Chukhrai's *Ballad of a Soldier* (1959); Naum Birman's *Chronicle of the Nose-diving Bombardier* (1968); Anorei Smirnov's *Belorussky Railway Station* (1971); Aleksei Gherman's *The Great Patriotic War* (1965) and Andrei Tarkovsky's *Ivan's Childhood* which won the Grand Prix at the Venetian Film Festival in 1962. (Tarkovsky went on to make many other classics such as *The Passion According to Andrei Rublyov* (1966), *Solaris*, *The Mirror* and *Nostalgia*. His last film *The Sacrifice* was shot in 1985.)

During the mid-1980s, another war film, *A Battlefield Romance* by Pyotr Todorovsky, was nominated for an Oscar (Best Foreign Film). It was only after perestroika that Todorovsky's next film, *Encore, Encore,* was permitted to paint a depressing portrait of Soviet military life. In 2004, his *In the Constellation of Taurus* was set in 1942 in the outskirts of Stalinigrad. Todorovsky's son, Valery, also a filmmaker, directed the hits *Love* (1992), *Moscow Nights* (1995), and the cult film *The Country of the Deaf*, examining life in modern Russia against the backdrop of a Mafia gang. One of the last successful war genre films was Sergei Bodrov's 1997 *Prisoner of the Caucasus*, a realistic portrayal of the war in Chechnya—as a reinterpretation of the short story by Tolstoy, and Alexander Rogozhkin's *Kukushka* (Cuckoo) set in August, 1944, when Finland signed an armistice agreement with the Soviet Union. In 2006, Dmitry Meskiev's wartime film *Svoit* (Ours), set in 1941, won a Russian Oscar for 'Best Film'.

Voted "Russian Viewers Most Loved Film" was *White Sun of the Desert* made in 1969 by maverick film director Vladimir Motyl (it was then considered "ideologically shaky" with its Western-style plot lines). The movie is about the adventures of Red Army officer, Fyodor Sukhov, who is trying to return home across Central Asia's Turkestan territories after the Civil War. In addition to the popular song, "Your Nobility Mrs Luck" by Bulat Okudzhava, the customs officer in the movie utters one of Russian cinema's most famous lines: "I take no bribes. *Za derzhavu obidno*—I just feel sorry for the country." (Former general, Alexander Lebed, who ran against Yeltsin for President in 1996, entitled his autobiography, *I Feel Sorry for the Country*.) The movie was Russia's first mega-hit, seen by over 100 million people within the first year of its release. When Brezhnev made a trip to the United States, he brought *White Sun* as one of Russia's five best classics to be shown at Carnegie Hall. For over 25 years Russian cosmonauts have made it a ritual to view the film before launching into space, and during the Soyuz-Apollo flight a video of White Sun was taken for the participating American astronauts to watch.

After the fall of the Soviet Union, long-banned films were released to packed houses, including Tengiz Abuladze's *Repentence* (about Stalinist horrors); Alexander Askoldov's *The Commissar*; Alexei German's *My Friend Ivan Lapshin*; and Panfilov's *Tema*, whose hero (a censored writer forced to work as a gravedigger to earn a living) utters the memorable line, 'Death is living in a country where one cannot practice the craft that gives one life!'

Once the film censor board was disbanded, scores of realistic films flowed from the studios: *Is It Easy to Be Young?*; *Solovki Power* (about Stalin's Siberian prison island) and *The Humiliated and the Offended* (a dramatized version of Dostoevsky's classic novel with Nastasia Kinsky as the heroine). Other popular films included *Little Vera*, a candid portrayal of a young woman and her family in a small industrial town. Andrei Konchalovsky shot *The Inner Circle*, about Stalin's projectionist, and Yevtushenko made *Stalin's Funeral*. Konchalovsky's half-brother, Nikita Mikhalkov won a 1995 Best Foreign Film Oscar for *Burnt by the Sun*. His other films include *Oblomov* (after a novel by Ivan Goncharov), *Urga, Black Eyes* (with Marcello Mastroanni) and *The Barber of Siberia*. Five other Russian films have also won an Academy Award for Best Foreign Film: the first was *Route of the German Troops* (1942); Mark Donskoi's *Rainbow* (1944); Sergei Bondarchuk's *War and Peace* (1968; nearly ten hours long, it took six years to film, using over 100,000 soldiers from the Soviet army who were mobilized to re-enact the battle of Borodino); the Soviet-Japanese production directed by Akiro Kurosawa, *Dersu Uzala* (1976); and Vladimir Menshov's *Moscow Does Not Believe in Tears* (1981). Foreign ventures also came to Russia to produce such feature and television projects as *The Russia House, The Saint* and *Rasputin*. In 2002, Konchalovsky's *House of Fools* won the Grand Jury Prize at the Venice Film Festival. It is based on the true story of a psychiatric hospital located near the border during the 1996 Chechen war with Russia.

Another 2002 phenomenon was Alexander Sokurov's *Russian Ark*. This 90-minute film was the first ever full-length feature ever shot in one single, uninterrupted take. The story has actors traveling through history as it unwinds through the vast halls of the Czar's Winter Palace and Hermitage Museum. It took eight months of rehearsal to prepare 2,000 actors and extras, three live orchestras and 22 assistant directors. The movie was shot in winter—there was only one shooting day and four hours of existing light. It's a must-see, and now is available with English subtitles.

Today, Russia's young directors and producers are forging a new film industry for the 21st century. In 2003, *The Return*, about the harrowing reunion of a father and his sons after a 10-year absence, won Venice Film Festival's top prize by first-time director, Andrei Zvyagintsev. *The Stroll*, a love triangle between three young Russians as they walk through the streets of St Petersburg, opened Moscow's International Film Festival. In Aleksei Balabanov's stylish gangster film, *Brother*, the former Leningrad becomes a lawless frontier town in the post-Soviet era. *Bumer*, the tale of four friends on the run in a stolen BMW, broke Russian box office records. The colorful slang or *fenya* spoken by the characters, along with the slick editing techniques and hip soundtrack from St Petersburg rocker, Sergei Shnurov, labeled the young director, Pyotr Buslov, the Russian Quentin Tarantino. In 2006, the sequel to the 2004 blockbuster *Night Watch* was released. In *Day Watch* (Dnyevnoi Dozor), the main character spends his evenings fighting witches and vampires on the streets of Moscow, while trying to manage the balance between the forces of Dark and Light. The trilogy (the third part is to be produced in English) is based on material by the popular Russian fantasy writer Sergei Lukyanenko.

Many new films and TV productions are also based on previously banned Soviet literature. In 2005, the 10-part TV miniseries of Mikhail Bulgakov's *The Master and Margarita*, directed by Vladimir Bortko, debuted with a quarter of the Russian population tuning in. (In Pskov, the book quickly disappeared from all bookstore shelves.) In 2006, another TV mini-series, *The First Circle*, based on the famous book about Russian *gulags* by Alexander Solzhenitsyn, was directed by Gleb Panfilov; it starred Dmitry Pevtsov in the role of Innokenty Volodin. Other films include *Notes from the Underground*, based on Dostoevsky's novel, depicting a more modern reflection of the nameless 19th-century St Petersburg clerk, and *His Wife's Diary*, the story of an intricate love triangle involving Nobel Prize winning Russian author, Ivan Bunin and his young lover, the poet Galina Plotnikova. It vied for an Oscar nomination for 'Best Foreign Film.'

After the lifeless Soviet era, today's Russian film and television industry has gained a more solid and exciting footing, driven by new and talented independent producers. The St Petersburg film studio, Lenfilm, produced only one film in 1996; now it produces about five feature films and 30 TV serials a year. On average, Russians go to the cinema five times more often than people in the West; and at any one time, over 100 features play in Moscow alone. Moscow and St Petersburg are now full of American-style multiplexes, with comfortable seats, Dolby sound and even popcorn. Every alternate summer, Moscow hosts a popular International Film Festival.

THE TROIKA RIDE

Selifan sat up and, flicking the dappled-grey on the back with his whip a few times and making him set off at a trot, then flourishing the whip over all the three horses, he cried out in a thin, sing-song voice: 'Gee-up!' The horses roused themselves and pulled the light carriage along as though it were a feather. All Selifan did was to wave his whip and keep shouting: 'Gee-up, gee-up, gee-up!', bouncing smoothly on the box, while the troika flew up and down the hillocks scattered all along the highway that sloped imperceptibly downhill. Chichikov only smiled as he bounced lightly on his leather cushion, for he was very fond of fast driving. And what Russian does not love fast driving? How could his soul, which is so eager to whirl round and round, to forget everything in a mad carouse, to exclaim sometimes, 'To hell with it all!'—how could his soul not love it? How not love it when there is something wonderful and magical about it? It is as if some unseen force has caught you up on its wing and you yourself fly and everything with you flies also; milestones fly past, merchants on the coachman's seat of their covered wagons fly to meet you, on each side of you the forest flies past with its dark rows of firs and pines, with the thudding of axes and the cawing of crows; the whole road flies goodness only knows where into the receding distance; and there is something terrible in this rapid flashing by of objects which are lost to sight before you are able to discern them properly, and only the sky over your head and the light clouds and the moon appearing and disappearing through them seem motionless. Oh, you troika, you bird of a troika, who invented you? You could only have been born among a high-spirited people in a land that does not like doing things by halves, but has spread in a vast smooth plain over half the world, and you may count the milestones till your eyes are dizzy. And there is nothing ingenious, one would think, about this travelling contraption. It is not held together by iron screws, but has been fitted up in haste with only an axe and chisel by some resourceful Yaroslav peasant. The driver wears no German top-boots: he has a beard and mittens, and sits upon goodness only knows what; but he has only to stand up and crack his whip and start up a song, and the horses rush like a whirlwind, the spokes of the wheels become one smooth revolving disc, only the road quivers and the pedestrian cries out as he stops in alarm, and the troika dashes on and on! And very soon all that can be seen in the distance is the dust whirling through the air.

Nikolai Gogol, Dead Souls, 1842

THE GARDEN RING (SADOVOYE KOLTSO)

After much of Moscow burned in the great fire of 1812 (80 percent of the city and over 7,000 buildings were destroyed), it was decided to tear down all the old earthen ramparts and in their place build a circular road around the city. Anyone who had a house along the ring was required to plant a *sad* (garden); thus the thoroughfare was named Sadovoye Koltso (Garden Ring). It is Moscow's widest avenue, stretching for 16 kilometers (ten miles) around the city, with the Kremlin's Bell Tower at its midpoint. It is less than two kilometers (just over one mile) from the Boulevard Ring. Each of the 16 squares and streets that make up this ring has a garden in their name, such as Big Garden and Sloping Garden. Buses, trolleys and the Koltso Metro circle the route. Along the way, 18th- and 19th-century mansions and old manor houses are interspersed among the modern buildings.

Beginning by the river, near the Park Kultury Metro station and Gorky Park, is Krymskaya Ploshchad (Crimean Square), surrounded by very old classically designed provisional warehouses, built by Stasov between 1832 and 1835.

Zubovsky Bulvar ends at Zubovsky Square, near Devichye Park (Maiden's Field) where carnivals were held and maidens danced to Russian folk tunes. To the north, Prechistenka Street leads to the Kremlin. The area between the Boulevard and Garden rings was once an aristocratic residential district; many old mansions are still in the area. Bolshaya Pirogovskaya (named after Nikolai Pirogov, a renowned surgeon) leads southwest to Novodevichy Monastery. Many of Moscow's clinics and research institutes are located in this area. At number 18 Zubovsky Bulvar is the former estate of the wealthy merchant Morozov.

On **Smolensky Bulvar** (formerly called Sennaya, the Haymarket) is the tall Ministry of Foreign Affairs. The Belgrad Hotel is at number 8.

Novinsky Bulvar begins at Smolenskaya Ploshchad. The great singer Fyodor Shalyapin (1873–1938) lived at number 25 from 1910 to 1922; it is now the **Shalyapin House Museum**. Open 10am–6pm Tuesdays and Saturdays, 11.30am–6.30pm Wednesdays and Thursdays, 10am–4pm Sundays; closed Mondays and Fridays. Fyodor wrote in his autobiography *Pages From My Life* that his childhood was a mixture of beatings, poverty and hunger. At the age of 17, he was taken under the wing of Tbilisi Imperial Theater artist Dmitry Usatov to learn the art of singing. He would soon perform operas in St Petersburg and Nizhny Novgorod where he met Savva Mamontov, who later became his patron. After marrying the ballerina Iola Tornagi, Shalyapin began the 1896 Moscow operatic season as Susanin in *A Life for the Czar*. By training his incredible basso voice, utilizing expressive gestures, exerting strong stage control and using dramatic face make-up, Shalyapin was attracting the attention of the West by the end of the century. After performing on the stages of the Paris Grand Opera and La Scala in Milan, he also continued to tour throughout Russia and played every role imaginable. Later, severely disillusioned with the new Soviet regime, Shalyapin left Russia on July 29, 1922, on a foreign tour which lasted 16 years, until the singer's death. In his other book *The Mask and The Soul* Shalyapin wrote that he was a free man and wanted to live freely; he could not adapt his art to the confines of Soviet realism. Many decades later, upon the request of Shalyapin's five children, their father's remains were transferred from Batignoles Cemetery in Paris and reburied, on October 29, 1984, in Moscow's Novodevichy Cemetery (see page 218).

The boulevard ends at Kudrinskaya Ploshchad, named after the local village of Kudrino. Up until 1992, it was called Vosstaniya (Uprising) Square, named after the heavy fighting that took place here during the revolutions of 1905 and 1917. The US Embassy is just south of the square at 19–23 Novinsky Bulvar.

Povarskaya Ulitsa, heading southeast from the square, was once one of the most fashionable areas of the city. It was named centuries ago, when the czar's servants and cooks lived in this area; *povarskaya* means cook. (Over 150 court cooks were employed to prepare 3,000 daily dishes for royalty and guests.) Other side streets were Khlebny (Bread), Nozhevoy (Knife), and Chashechny (Cup). The two lanes Skaterny (Tablecloth) and Stolovoy (Table) still branch off the street. In *War and Peace*, Tolstoy described the Rostov's estate at 52 Povarskaya Ulitsa, where there is now a statue of Tolstoy. Next door is the Writer's Club, named after the Soviet writer Alexander Fadeyev. The **Gorky Literary Museum** at number 25, recognizable by the statue of Gorky at the front, chronicles the life of the Russian writer who lived here before his departure abroad in 1921. It is open 10am–4.30pm, 12–6.30pm Wednesdays and Fridays; closed weekends; Metro Arbatskaya. Gorky also spent his last years (1931–6) in a house on the neighboring street of Malaya Nikitskaya, at number 6, which is also a museum. (See page 180.)

On the other side of Kudrinskaya Ploshchad is Barrikadnaya Ulitsa with a Metro station of the same name. The Planetarium and Zoo are in the area. In May 1996 the **Moscow Zoo** was reopened after major reconstruction designed by Zurab Tseretelli; open daily 10am–8pm (winter 10am–4pm). The zoo first opened in 1864 and is one of the oldest in the world with a collection of over 5,000 animals. It receives over 1,500,000 visitors each year.

Barrikadnaya leads into Krasnaya Presnya, once a working-class district and the scene of many revolutionary battles. Nearby, at number 4 Bolshoi Predtechensky Pereulok is the **Krasnaya Presnya Museum** which traces the history of the area and revolutions in Russia up to the present day. Open 10am–6pm; closed Mondays.

The famous writer Anton Chekhov lived from 1886 to 1890 along the next boulevard, **Sadovaya-Kudrinskaya**, in the small red house at number 6. It is now the **Chekhov House Museum**. Open 11am–5pm, 2–6pm Wednesdays and Fridays; closed Mondays. Chekhov was not born into nobility; his grandfather had, only a generation before, purchased the family's freedom from serfdom, and in 1876 the family moved to Moscow. By 1879 Chekhov had entered the Moscow University medical school and supported the family by writing humorous fiction. During his first seven years of literary activity, he published over 400 stories, novellas and sketches, and in 1883 received the Pushkin Prize in Literature. His first full-length play *The Seagull* failed miserably in its 1896 St Petersburg première. However, two years later, under the guidance of Stanislavsky at the Moscow Arts Theater, the production was a triumphant success. The company took the image of a seagull as its symbol, and Chekhov became, in the words of Stanislavsky, 'the soul of the Moscow Arts Theater'. He followed with *Uncle Vanya* in 1899, and while in Yalta wrote *The Three Sisters* (1901) and *The Cherry Orchard* (1903). In 1901, he married Olga Knipper, a leading actress with the Moscow Arts Theater. Chekhov died of tuberculosis on July 2, 1904, at the age of 44. Both Chekhov and Stanislavsky are buried in Moscow's Novodevichy Cemetery (see page 218).

Bolshaya Sadovaya Ulitsa (Great Garden Street) once had a triumphal arch through which troops returned to Moscow. The next boulevard, **Sadovaya-Triumfalnaya Ulitsa**, is followed by **Sadovaya Karetnaya** and then **Sadovaya-Samotechnaya Ulitsa**. At number 3 is the **Obraztsov Puppet Theater**, named after its founder. The puppet clock on the front of the building has 12 little houses with a tiny rooster on top; every hour, one house opens. At noon, all the boxes open, each with an animal puppet dancing to an old Russian folk song.

Branching off to the south is Tsvetnoi (Flower) Bulvar, with the Old Circus (see page 186) next to the Tsvetnoi Bulvar Metro station, and popular **Tsentralny Rinok** (Central Market).

To the north of the Garden Ring, in Frunze Central Army Park at number 2 Ulitsa Sovetskoy Armii, is the **Armed Forces Central Museum** with exhibits of the Russian Army during the 1918–22 civil war and World War II. Open 10am–5.30pm; closed Mondays and Tuesdays. Novoslobodskaya is the nearest Metro station. At number 12 Ulitsa Sovetskoy Armii is the **Children's Theater Museum** with exhibits on the history of puppets. Open 10am–6pm weekdays.

The next street and square returned to their original names of **Sukharevskaya** in 1992; they are named after Sukharov, a popular commander of the czar's Streltsy guards who were quartered here. After the Revolution the street and square were called Kolkhoznaya (Collective Farm). Peter the Great opened Russia's first navigational school in the center of the square where the Sukharov Tower had stood.

Several blocks north, off Meschanskaya, at 13 Vasnetsova Lane, is the **Viktor Vasnetsov Museum**, open 10am–5pm, closed Mondays; Metro Sukharevskaya. A contemporary of the painter Ilya Repin, Vasnetsov exhibited in traveling art exhibitions and enjoyed painting themes of Old Russia. His art can be found in the Tretyakov Gallery. Vasnetsov (1848–1926) lived in this log house for more than 30 years. The museum of his artist brother, Apollinary (1856–1933), is at 6 Furmanny Lane, near Metro Chistiye Prudy; closed Sundays and Mondays.

Prospekt Mira (Peace Prospekt) leads north to the **All-Russian Exhibition Center** (see page 207). Prospekt Mira's original name was Meshchanskaya Sloboda, Commoners' Quarters; immigrant settlements were concentrated here. At 5 Prospekt Mira is the Perlov House, the former home of an old tea merchant family of the same name. At number 18 is the **Wedding Palace**, an 18th-century structure designed by Bazhenov. Opposite the palace are the headquarters of Vyacheslav Zaitsev, one of Moscow's top fashion designers. At number 26 are the **Aptekarsky Botanical Gardens**, the city's oldest gardens. They were started by Peter the Great as medicinal gardens for the court. Today they are still filled with medicinal herbs, along with thousands of types of bushes and trees. Open daily 9am–5pm. Also near the Prospekt Mira Metro station is the Olympic Sports Complex, built in the late 1970s.

Returning to the Garden Ring, the next square, **Lermontovskaya**, is named after the Russian poet Lermontov, who was born in a house near the square on October 3, 1814; a plaque on a building marks where the house stood. The plaque is inscribed with Lermontov's words: 'Moscow, Moscow, I love you deeply as a son, passionately and tenderly.' The square was known as Krasniye Vorota (Red Gate) because red gates once marked the entrance to the square. The Metro station was given this name.

Zemlyanoi Val (Earthen Rampart) is the longest street on the ring, once named after the pilot Valeri Chakalov, who made the first nonstop flight over the North Pole from the USSR to America in 1936. At numbers 14 to 16 lived the poet Marshak, the composer Prokofiev and the violinist Oistrach. Tchaikovsky once lived at number 47. At number 57 is the **Sakharov Museum**, opened in 1996, with exhibits on the life and works of the Nobel prize-winning physicist and dissident during the Soviet period. The museum is dedicated to Sakharov's legacy, and regularly showcases events on human rights. In 2003, while exhibiting paintings and sculptures, entitled "Caution! Religion', members of a Russian Orthodox Church entered the hall and defaced many of the provocative 45 works with spray paint, terming them 'sacrilegious'. The perpetrators were arrested; but later the State Duma passed a resolution condemning the museum's organizers. (One sculpture was of a church made with vodka bottles, a reference to a tax exemption the church received in the 1990s to sell alcohol. Another depicted Jesus on a Coca Cola Advertisement, saying "This is my blood".) The furor over the exhibition thrust the two groups-artists and religious believers—both of whom suffered during the Socialist era, into opposition. One artist expressed that "...we have freedom of speech and religion in our Constitution, but do they only exist on paper?"

Behind the Kursky Railway Station is an 18th-century stone mansion, the Naidyonov Estate. Gilliardi and Grigorev built the estate, whose gardens stretch down to the Yauza River; it is now a sanitarium. After crossing the Yauza River, the ring reaches Taganskaya Ploshchad (with a Metro station of the same name), where the popular avant-garde theater **Taganka** is located.

The **Vysotsky Museum and Cultural Center** is located at 3 Nizny Tangansky, off Verkhnaya Radishchevskaya Street; open 11am–5.30pm, closed Sundays and Mondays. Known as the 'Russian Hamlet with a guitar,' the Moscow-born Vladimir Vysotsky (1938–1980), was one of Russia's most talented and popular bards. His songs defined the realities and hardships of Soviet times (he was barred by the government from officially recording them). He also achieved fame by acting in feature films and, at the Taganka Theater, he played such roles as Shakespeare's Hamlet and Brecht's Galileo. When Vysotsky died at the age of 42 (presumably of a heart attack—nothing was announced in the Soviet press), over 300,000 people followed his coffin from Taganka Square to Vagankovo Cemetery, where a bronze statue of his likeness stands over his grave. (In 1995, a second statue of him was unveiled at the intersection of Petrovka Street and Strastnoi Bulvar.) A few days before his death he wrote a poem for his wife Marina Vlady:

I'm half my age—a little way past forty.
I'm living thanks to God and you, my wife.
I have a lot to sing to the Almighty.
I have my songs to justify my life.

Across the Bolshoi Krasnokholmsky Most (Bridge) that spans the Moskva River and just off Zatsepsky Val, our next stop on the Garden Ring is the **Bakhrushin Theater Museum** at 31 Ulitsa Bakhrushina. Established by merchant Alexei Bakhrushin in 1894, the museum displays over 200,000 items (though not well organized) which illustrate the history of Russian theater and ballet from the classics to the avant-garde. The basement floor is dedicated to the opera singer Fyodor Shalyapin and the art patron Savva Mamontov. Open 12–7pm; closed Tuesdays. The Paveletskaya Metro station is nearby.

Serpukhovskaya Ploshchad was, until 1992, named Dobryninskaya Square after the 1917 revolutionary. The next square, Kaluzhskaya, leads to the entrance of **Gorky Park** (see page 220), with two large Ferris wheels. The nearby chocolate factory of Krasny Oktyabr (Red October) has been making chocolate here for over 125 years. Across from the park, at 10–14 Krymsky Val, is the **Tretyakov Art**

Gallery; open 10am–7pm; closed Mondays. On the grounds is the evocative **Park of the Fallen Idols**, the graveyard of revolutionary figures. The statue of Felix Dzerzhinsky, toppled during the 1991 attempted coup, is here along with the statues of Lenin, Kalinin, Sverdlov, Khrushchev and Stalin. Krymsky Val (Crimean Rampart) is the last section of the ring. It crosses the Moskva River by way of the Krymsky suspension bridge. Back, in the river, the immense Peter the Great statue can be seen.

When strolling along the Garden or Boulevard rings, pay attention to the traffic. Even 150 years ago, Nikolai Gogol wrote: 'What Russian doesn't like fast driving?' (See Literary Excerpt on page 190.) And this is just as true today. Traffic accidents have multiplied; cars often use sidewalks as passing lanes and headlights are not normally used at night. Many *yama* (potholes) are left unrepaired, so that getting splashed while walking, with rain and mud during a rainfall is likely. In 1986, there were only 650,000 cars on the road in Moscow. Today there are nearly three million. Because of a 30-year-old road system, the city is now constructing a new, third ring road, an eight-lane highway with only 50 percent above ground.

SPARROW HILLS (VOROBYOVIYE GORY)

The Sparrow Hills are situated in the southwestern part of the city; they were given this name in the 15th century. From 1935 to 1992, the area was referred to as Lenin Hills. Peter I and Catherine the Great had their country palaces in this area, and today many dachas, or country homes, are still situated here. It remains a favorite place for recreational activities like hiking, picnicking and swimming in summer, and ice-skating, sledding and skiing in winter. This spot is the highest point in Moscow and provides one of the most spectacular views of the city. The Metro runs to Universitet, pass the Sparrow Hills station which goes above ground and crosses the Moskva River. After leaving the Metro, stand and face the river; in good weather even the golden domes of the Kremlin are visible. It is customary for wedding parties to have photographs taken by this spot.

In the opposite direction you can see a massive 36-story building. This is Lomonosov University, more widely known as **Moscow University**, founded in 1755 by Russian scientist Mikhail Lomonosov. This university building was erected between 1949 and 1953 on the highest point of Sparrow Hills by Stalin, who had six other similar Gothic-style skyscrapers built throughout the city. (In 2001, the centenary of architect Dmitry Tchechulin's birth was celebrated. He was appointed Stalin's chief architect in 1945 and designed Moscow's seven *vysotki* (skyscrapers). He also designed several Metro stations, the Tchaikovsky Concert Hall, Pekin and

A large variety of items are for sale at the popular weekend Izmailovsky Flea Market, including contemporary cartoons and old religious icons.

Rossiya hotels and in 1980, one year before his death, he completed his last work, the White House.) This is the tallest of the seven at 240 meters (787 feet). The top of the university's main tower is crowned by a golden star in the shape of ears of corn. It is the largest university in Russia, with students from over 100 countries. The campus comprises 40 buildings, including sports centers, an observatory, botanical gardens and a park. The Gorky Library has over six million volumes. Gorbachev graduated from Moscow University with a degree in law, and his wife Raisa with a degree in Leninist philosophy. Recently Moscow University became independent from the Ministry of Education. Within the campus stands the green-domed **Trinity Church**, built in 1811 and open for worship.

A few blocks to the east, between Vernadsky and Lomonosovsky prospekts, is the circular building of the **New Circus** (*Novy Tsirk na Vorobyovykh Gorakh* or New Circus on Sparrow Hills); closed Mondays and Tuesdays. The circus is one of the most popular forms of entertainment in Russia, and the Moscow Circus is famous throughout the world. This circus building, opened in 1971, seats 3,400. Its ring has four interchangeable floors that can be switched in less than five minutes. One is the regular ring, another a special ring for magicians, and the others are a pool for the aquatic circus and a rink for the ice ballet. The Universitet Metro station is directly behind the New Circus. The other main circus of Moscow is the **Stary Tsirk** (Old Circus) at 13 Tsvetnoi Bulvar (see page 198).

In front of the New Circus is the former Moscow Palace of Young Pioneers, sometimes still referred to as **Pioneerland**. This is a large club and recreational center for children. Before the Communist Party lost its supreme power in 1991, children who belonged to the Communist Youth Organization were known as Young Pioneers. Older members belonged to the Young Komsomol League. During the last years of Communist rule, there were over 25 million Young Pioneers, and over 39 million in the Komsomol. The 400 rooms in the palace include clubs, laboratories and workshops. It also has its own concert hall, sports stadium, gardens and even an artificial lake for learning how to row and sail. There are over 35 youth house branches in Moscow. The entrance to the palace is marked by the Statue of Malchish-Kibalchish, a character from a popular children's book. On the corner is the **Children's Music Theater**. A monument to the theater's musical director, Natalya Satz (1909–93) was unveiled in 2000; her father, Ilya Satz, scored the famous ballet *Bluebird*.

A few minutes' drive away along Mosfilmovskaya Ulitsa is **Mosfilm Studios**, dating from 1927. Here worked many of the great Russian film directors like Pudovkin, Dovzhenko, Eisenstein and Tarkovsky (see Special Topic on Russian Cinema, page 202).

Across the river from the Sparrow Hills are the white buildings of the **Luzhniki Central Stadium** (the largest in Moscow). The complex consists of the stadium (seating 100,000), the Palace of Sport, the swimming and tennis stadiums, the Friendship Hall and the Museum of Physical Culture. Many events of the Moscow 1980 Olympics were held here. The Olympic Village was built behind the University on Lomonosov Prospekt. Glancing to the left of the stadium, you can make out the golden domes of the Novodevichy Convent.

Beyond the stadium, at 2 Lev Tolstoy Street (Ulitsa Lva Tolstovo), is the five-domed and colorfully tiled **Church of St Nicholas at Khamovniki**, built between 1676–1682; services are still conducted here. In the past weavers lived in the area and their guild paid for the construction of this church; the old Russian word for weavers is *khamovniki*. A copy of the Virgin Icon Helper of all Sinners (credited for working a few miracles) rests in the iconostasis left of the royal gates; to the right is an Icon of St Nicholas. Farther along the street, the whitewashed building with steep roof was once the Weaver's Guild House, where material was woven.

Also along this street, at number 21, is the 18-room **Tolstoy Country Estate Museum** where the writer lived from 1882 to 1901, the year he was excommunicated from the Orthodox Church. After this act by the Holy Synod, Tolstoy moved to his estate at Yasnaya Polyana (see page 254). A few of the works he wrote while living in this house are *Power of Darkness, The Death of Ivan Ilyich, The Kreutzer Sonata* and *Resurrection*. The opening hours in summer are 10am–5pm, and in winter 10am–4pm; closed Mondays and last Friday of the month. (Tolstoy's family would often stop by the beer factory next door, which has been brewing for over a century!) Another Tolstoy Museum is located at Ulitsa Prechistenka, see page 168.

NOVODEVICHY CONVENT

From Universitet Metro station, take the train towards Bol. Pirogovskaya across the river to Sportivnaya and get off in front of the stadium. Walking a short distance to the northwest brings you to one of the oldest religious complexes in the city, Novodevichy (New Maiden) Convent, a baroque-style complex of 15 buildings and 16 gilded domes dating from the 16th and 17th centuries. Grand Prince Vasily III founded the convent in 1514 to commemorate the capture of Smolensk from Lithuania, which had controlled the area for over a century (the convent was built on the road to Smolensk). It was also one in a group of fortified monasteries that surrounded Moscow. Novodevichy served mainly as a religious retreat for Russian noblewomen. Peter the Great banished his half-sister Sophia and first wife Evdokia to the convent and forced them to wear the veil. Boris Godunov was crowned here in 1598. Napoleon tried to blow up the convent before he fled the city, but a nun pulled out the fuses. The convent was converted into a museum in 1922.

The white-stone five-tiered **Virgin of Smolensk Cathedral** (1524) was the convent's first stone building and lies at its center. It was dedicated to the Virgin of Smolensk, a much revered 16th-century icon, and modeled on the Kremlin's Uspensky Cathedral. Many 16th-century interior frescoes portray the life of Vasily III (the father of Ivan the Terrible). A copy of the Icon of Our Lady of Smolenskaya hangs over the altar, and many of the icons were painted by Simon Ushakov. The beautiful gilded five-tiered iconostasis (1683–86) was presented by Sophia; its wooden columns, decorated with climbing grapevines, are made out of whole tree trunks. Ivan the Terrible's daughter Anna, Sophia and Evdokia are some of the noblewomen in the burial vault.

The baroque **Transfiguration Gate Church** (1687–9) stands above the main northern entrance. To its right are the two-story **Lopukhina Chambers**, where Peter the Great's first wife Evdokia Lopukhina lived. The next building along the wall, in front of the **Pond Tower**, houses **Sophia's Chambers**. Sophia's chamber-prison is where Peter the Great incarcerated his half-sister (until her death) when he deposed her as regent and took the throne at the age of 17. To further punish Sophia for leading the 1689 Streltsy revolt against him, Peter ordered that the dead bodies of revolt members be strung up outside her cell. The **Miloslavsky Chambers** are named after Sophia's sister, Maria Miloslavskaya, who also lived here until her death. The **Gate Church of the Intercession** (1688) tops the southern entrance, and west of the cathedral is the **Church of the Assumption** (1687), which has been open for worship for over three centuries (a choir sings during Sunday services). Behind it is the 16th-century **Church of St Ambrose**. Next to the church, along the southern wall, stands the small Irina Godunova Palace, where Irina Godunova lived out her last days. She was the sister of Boris Godunov and the wife of Fyodor I. When the czar died in 1598, Irina refused the throne and her brother Boris was elected ruler during the Time of Troubles. Other structures include the **Refectory Church** (1685–7), the six-tiered octagonal baroque bell tower (1690), small exhibit halls and four nun's residences (in 1994, Novodevichy was permitted its first resident nun since 1922).

Many notable Russian personalities are buried in the Novodevichy's two cemeteries. Within the convent grounds are the graves of princes, wealthy merchants, clergymen and war heroes. Behind the southern wall (the entrance is on the east side), the 19th- and 20th-century cemetery has been the burial site of many of Russia's most prominent statesmen, artists and scientists. These include Chekhov, Eisenstein, Gogol, Khrushchev, Mayakovsky, Prokofiev, Scriabin, Serov, Shalyapin, Shostakovich, Stanislavsky and Stalin's wife Nadezhda Alliluyeva, who committed suicide in 1932. The beloved clown Yuri Nikulin, who directed the Old

Zakomara gold trim decorates the plain walls of a small chapel in Moscow's Novodevichy Convent.

Circus, was buried here in 1997. A monument was erected over his grave in 2000; the sculpture, by Alexander Rukavishnikv, is of Nikulin sitting on the edge of a circus arena next to his favorite dog. Raisa Gorbacheva, the wife of Mikhail Gorbachev, who died of leukemia in 1999 aged 67, is also buried in the cemetery. A bronze monument was unveiled on the first anniversary of her death. A map of the graves can be bought at the entrance kiosk. The complex is open 10am–5.30pm; closed Tuesdays and the last Monday of the month. Guided excursions (in Russian) start from the entrance ticket kiosk every Sunday at noon and visit most of the buildings.

Nearby, at 4 Novodevichy Pereulok, is **Restaurant U-Pirosmani** with delicious Georgian food and paintings on the wall by famous Georgian painter Pirosmani, along with other artists.

GORKY PARK

Gorky Park lies a few minutes walk over the Moskva River from Park Kultury Metro station in the Frunze district. It can also be reached from the other side of the river, from Oktyabrskaya Metro station. A large archway marks the entrance to the park. Named after popular Soviet writer

Novodevichy Convent was built in 1524 by Vasily III, and became part of the city's outer defensive ring. In 1598, Boris Godunov was crowned czar in the five-domed Smolensk Cathedral.

Maxim Gorky, the area was commissioned as a Park of Culture and Rest in the 1920s. Today there are Ferris wheels and amusement rides, restaurants, boats for hire and the Zelyoni (Green) open-air theater. In summer the park is teeming with strollers, performance artists and circus performers of the tent circus. In winter the popular ice-skating rink (there are skates for rent) is in operation (made famous by

the book *Gorky Park*), along with cross-country skiing. The park is open daily 10am–10pm. Also in the park are the Neskuchny Sadi (Not-Boring Pleasure Gardens), originally part of the Trubetskoi Estate and later bought by Nicholas I in 1826; it is now used by the Academy of Sciences. The estate is part of the Main Botanical Gardens (with a collection of over 16,000 varieties of roses) that stretch as far as the river.

A youthful audience gathered at a
rock 'n' roll concert in Moscow's Gorky Park.

DONSKOI MONASTERY

South of Gorky Park, and a 20-minute walk from the Shabolovskaya Metro station, is the Donskoi Monastery. Heading west along Donskaya Street leads directly to the monastery walls. This monastery and seven churches were founded by Czar Fyodor I and Boris Godunov in 1591, on the site of the Russian army's line of defense against the invading Mongols. Legend claims that the city was protected by the Donskaya Virgin Icon, the icon that Prince Donskoi took for protection against the invading Tartars during the 1380 Battle of Kulikovo near the River Don. The monasteries were connected by an earthen rampart, today's Garden Ring. By the 18th century, this monastery was one of the most prosperous in all of Russia and owned over 7,000 serfs. After the Revolution, the Donskoi Monastery was opened to the public as a government architectural museum. In the early 1990s the complex was returned to the Orthodox Church and is now a working monastery.

The red and white **Old Cathedral of the Donskaya Virgin** (1591) was the first building of the monastery. (This was one of the few churches allowed to conduct services throughout the Soviet period.) The cube roof and onion domes are topped with golden half-moon crosses that symbolize the Christian victory over Islam. A copy of the Donskaya Virgin Icon is on the eight-tiered iconostasis; the original is in the Tretyakov Gallery. Patriarch Tikhon, who was appointed the head of the Orthodox Church on the eve of the October 1917 Revolution, is buried in a marble tomb at the southern wall.

The Naryshkin baroque-style **New Cathedral of the Donskaya Virgin** was commissioned by Peter the Great's half-sister Sophia in 1684. The interior frescoes were painted by the Italian artist Antonio Claudio between 1782 and 1785. At the southwestern corner of the monastery is the classical **Church of the Archangel Michael**, built between 1806 and 1809. The church served as a memorial chapel for the Golitsyn family. Mikhail Golitsyn (1681–1764) was Peter the Great's star general who began his career as a service drummer. Fourteen Golitsyns are buried here, including Dmitri and his wife Natalia, who is the subject of Pushkin's novel *Queen of Spades*. Some of the people buried in the cemetery are Turgenev, the architect Bovet, and Zhukovsky, the father of Russian aviation. Other baroque buildings include the **Tikhvin Gate Church** (1713), the Abbot's residence, a bell tower and the 20th-century Church of St Seraphim, now a crematorium. Outside the gates is the Church of Rizpolozhenie, whose priests also conduct mass in the Old Cathedral on Sundays and holidays. Only the main cathedral and icon shops are open during the week, otherwise the full grounds are open at weekends, 10am–4pm.

At 20 Donskaya Ulitsa is the Moscow baroque **Church of the Deposition of the Lord's Robe**, built in 1701. The Church is filled with interesting cherubs and contains a copy of the Icon of the Deposition of the Lord's Robe under a gilded canopy. In 1625, an envoy of a Persian shah presented Czar Mikhail Romanov and the Patriarch Filaret with a fragment of Jesus' robe. Filaret had an icon painted and declared a new Church holiday. The icon shows Romanov and Filaret placing the gold box, containing the piece of cloth, on the altar of the Kremlin's Uspensky Cathedral. The original icon is now in the Tretyakov Gallery.

DANILOVSKY MONASTERY

The Danilovsky Monastery, off Danilovsky Val, is a 5-minute walk northeast of Tulskaya Metro station. The grounds are open daily 8am–8pm. It was founded in 1276 by Prince Daniil, the youngest son of Alexander Nevsky, who was the only Moscow prince to be canonized by the Russian Church. The monastery's thick white walls served as part of the southern defenses of the city. During Stalin's rule the monastery was closed and later served as an orphanage, electronics factory and juvenile prison. Restoration work began in 1983 when the government returned the complex to the Orthodox Church. Two years later the buildings were reconsecrated for religious use. In 1988, to celebrate the Millennium of the Baptism of Rus, Patriarch Pimen chose St Daniil Monastery for the celebrations. It is now the residency of the Patriarch of all Russia, Alexei II, along with the administrative bodies of the Holy Synod.

The whitewashed **Cathedral of the Holy Fathers of the Seven Ecumenical Councils**, along the eastern side, was built by Ivan the Terrible in 1565 on the original site of St Daniil's church. Only a few of the 17th-century frescoes remain. St Daniil is buried here within a golden coffin. Services are usually held daily in the mornings and early evenings. Within the building is also the Church of the Protecting Veil, added in the 17th century. The largest, central structure in the complex is the yellow neo-classical **Trinity Cathedral**, designed in Moscow classical-style by Osip Bovet in 1833. Standing over the monastery entrance is the pink and white **Belfry Chapel of St Simon Stylites** (1730). New bells were placed in the tower during restoration; the old ones toll at Harvard University. The monastery also has an icon-painting workshop.

The Moscow patriarch even has its own hotel on the southern grounds at 5 Starodanilovsky Lane. The modern-style **Danilovsky Hotel Complex** has a restaurant, café and bar, and even a swimming pool.

Leninsky Prospekt runs past the Donskoi Monastery and leads out of the city and into Moscow's modern southwestern district, which consists mostly of residential housing. Beginning at Oktyabrskaya Metro station the prospekt passes the Academy of Sciences, formerly Neskuchny Castle, and Gagarinskaya Ploshchad (Gagarin Square). The square (at Leninsky Prospekt Metro station) features a titanium monument of Yuri Gagarin, who made the first manned space flight. At the base of the monument is a replica of the space capsule Vostok (East) in which Gagarin traveled on April 12, 1961. (Gagarin, trained as a test pilot, died in a plane crash in 1968; his ashes lie in the Kremlin Wall in Red Square.) This square used to mark the city limits in the 1950s. The prospekt continues past many department stores to the Lumumba People's Friendship University, with 6,000 students from around the world. It eventually becomes the Kievsky Highway and ends at the Vnukovo local airport.

SPASO-ANDRONIKOV MONASTERY

This monastery, at 10 Andronevskaya Ploshchad, is situated along the Yauza River, a tributary of the Moskva, in the eastern part of the city, a five-minute walk from Ploshchad Ilicha Metro station. It was founded in 1359 by the Metropolitan Alexei during the reign of Prince Donskoi and has quite an interesting history. After Alexei was confirmed by the Byzantine Patriarch in Constantinople in 1353, a heavy storm occurred at sea during his return journey. Alexei promised God that if he should live he would build a monastery dedicated to the saint whose feast day was celebrated on the day of his safe arrival in Moscow. Alexei returned on August 16, the Savior Day, or Vernicle. When the Mongol Khan suddenly summoned Alexei to help his ailing wife in the south, the metropolitan appointed Andronik, a monk at Sergiyev Posad's Trinity-Sergius Monastery, to oversee the complex's construction in his absence. The monastery was named the Spaso-Andronikov after the Savior and its first abbot. It later became the stronghold of the Old Believers.

This is the oldest architectural complex in Moscow after the Kremlin. The white helmet-domed **Cathedral of the Savior** was built between 1420 and 1427, and is considered the oldest building in Moscow. The master iconist Andrei Rublyov, who also trained as a monk at the Trinity-Sergius Monastery, painted many of the interior frescoes (it was here that Rublyov painted his famous Old Testament Trinity icon, now in the Tretyakov Gallery); he is said to be buried somewhere in the grounds of the monastery. The baroque **Church of the Archangel Michael** (1691–1739) was commissioned by Ustinia Lopukhina in 1694 to celebrate the birth of her grandson Alexei, son of Peter the Great, and her daughter Evdokia. Peter later banished Evdokia to Novodevichy Monastery (a form of divorce in those days) and the Lopukhinas to Siberia. The church is now an icon restoration studio.

The **Andrei Rublyov Museum of Old Russian Art**, opened in 1960, is housed in three separate buildings in the monastery. They are located immediately beyond the main gate. The former Seminary Building contains many 15th- and early 16th-century icons by Rublyov and his students (many now copies of the originals). Some of the icons include St Sergius, St George, John the Baptist and the Almighty Savior. Many of the icons found in the Monks' Quarters (behind the Savior Cathedral) were painted in Moscow, Rostov, Tver and Novgorod from the 13th to 17th centuries. Nearby is a new Exhibition Hall of mainly 17th- and 18th-century icons that include Our Lady of Tikhvin. There are also displays of other paintings, sculpture, embroidery, old books and chronicles. The museum complex is open 11am–6pm; closed Wednesdays and the last Friday of the month. Andrei Tarkovsky filmed many of the scenes for his well-known film *Andrei Rublyov* here at the complex.

ALL-RUSSIAN EXHIBITION CENTER

An utopian exhibition of economic achievements was first conceived of and built on this site in 1939. The Volga Pavilion was constructed to look like a river cascade, topped by Vasily Chapayev, a Civil War hero, on a rearing horse. Nothing remains of these original complexes. During the reconstruction of the exhibitions in 1954, many buildings were re-created to resemble their predecessors. The Exhibition of Economic Achievements or VDNKh was opened in 1956, just a few days before the 20th Communist Party Congress (that denounced Stalin's personality cult). Nearly 100,000 objects, representing the latest in Soviet achievements in science, industry, transport, building and culture were exhibited in 300 buildings and 80 pavilions which spread out over an area of 220 hectares (545 acres). Now called the All-Russian Exhibition Center, this huge park is siutaed on the opposite side of the street from the **Kosmos Hotel** at the end of Prospekt Mira, near VDNKh Metro station. One enters through the triumphal arch, crowned by a sculpture of a tractor driver and female collective farm worker. Opposite is the Main Pavilion that used to house the "The Triumph of Lenin's Ideas." All are now shops, ironically full of kitschy items and electronics for sale. The large Friendship of Nations Fountain (symbolizing the 15 republics and now dried up) includes golden statues of women dancing in a ring. The first monument that comes into view is the 96-meter high (315-feet) titanium **Sputnik Rocket** (the first Sputnik satellite was launched on October 4, 1957). The Soviet-realist **Monument to the Worker and Collective-Farm Girl** was sculpted between 1935 and 1937 by Vera Mukhina, who created it for the World Exhibition in Paris. Since 1937, it has stood at the entrance to the Exhibition Center; and in 2003 underwent restoration. (There was a problem figuring out how to re-assemble it so it may still not be up and standing). In 1998, a Hollywood firm offered to purchase the statue (it has long been a symbol of Mosfilm Studios, as the lion is to MGM), but the government refused the sale. Mukhina is also known as the designer of the *granyony staken*—the 12-sided glass tumbler created for the working class. They were used throughout the country from *stolovayas* (cafeterias) to *kommunalkas* (communal-living flats); and by the mid 1980s, half a billion were being produced, costing 7 kopeks each.

At the base of the Sputnik rocket is the **Cosmonautics Memorial Museum**. It has exhibits and old films on the history of Soviet space exploration. Open 10am–6pm, closed Mondays and the last Friday of the month.

Pavilions include the **Atomic Energy, Agriculture and Culture Pavilions**. There is also a giant ferris wheel and the roller-coaster, *Tsarskaya Gorka* (Tsar's Hill), which opened to celebrate the 250th anniversary of the attraction that Empress Elizabeth built as a 400-meter long sledding hill.

Since many of these halls never exhibited much of interest anyway (the Pig Pavilion had one pig from each of the Soviet republics), many have now been converted into shopping centers, and hundreds of small shop and food kiosks line the wide footpaths. The most interesting hall, located at the end of the park, is the **Kosmos Pavilion**. In front of it stands a replica of the Vostok rocket that carried Yuri Gagarin into space in 1961. Inside used to be displays of rockets and space capsules, including the first Sputnik, Lunnik and Soyuz rockets, and Salyut space stations. A display also honored Konstantin Tsiolkovsky, the father of the Russian space program. He invented the first wind tunnel and outlined the principle of the reactor rocket; he once said, 'This planet is the cradle of the human mind, but one cannot spend one's life in a cradle.' Today, sadly, the buildings are slowly crumbling in testament to the collapse of Soviet achievement only to be replaced by palaces of consumerism (many are now in the process of being restored). The pavilion is now filled with TVs and vacuum cleaners for sale. The first joint US–USSR space mission, Soyuz–Apollo, was undertaken in July 1975. The first Russian cosmonaut flew in the American Space Shuttle in February 1994 and in 1998, Russians and Americans flew together in the Mir Space Station.

The cosmonaut, Valery Polyakov, holds the world record for the longest space mission at 438 days, completed in Mir during 1994–95. Then in February 2001, after 15 years in space (it was originally designed to last for only five), the Mir was allowed to leave its orbit—the government could no longer afford to fund it. The 136-ton Mir's planned destruction marked the end of the world's longest running space-station which orbited the earth nearly 100,000 times, hosted more than 100 people and survived more than 1,500 breakdowns.

Later, in 2001, a Russian Soyuz space capsule and two cosmonauts took the world's first space tourist for a visit to the first International Space Station. The American tycoon, Dennis Tito, trained at Star City outside Moscow and paid a reported $20 million for the eight-day trip. In 2002, a Russian-US joint-venture announced plans for a 'space-plane' that would give an adventurer the chance to experience an hour-long ride, culminating in three minutes of zero gravity on the edge of space for $100,000. Over 100 people immediately booked a seat on the Cosmopolis-XXI (C-21) suborbital plane. In 2003 the first ever marriage from space took place when Russian cosmonaut Yuri Malenchenko married his sweetheart on earth, taking their vows via a live video link from the international space station.

Other buildings include an open-air theater, small zoo, amusement park, shopping centers, and restaurants. The Circorama circular movie theater was built in 1959. Documentaries were projected by 11 movie cameras, fixed on stands, onto 11 screens simultaneously. When not under renovation, the theater (standing-only) still shows films. You can hire boats and go fishing in the ponds; fishing tackle can be rented from booths along the bank. In winter, especially during the Winter Festival, there is plenty of entertainment, including ice skating and troika rides. The park is open on weekdays 10am–10pm, and on weekends 10am–11pm; the shopping pavilions are open from 10am–7pm. A half-hour tour of the park can be taken on electric trams.

OSTANKINO

Not far from VDNKh Metro station, at 5 Pervaya Ostankinskaya Street, is the **Ostankino Palace** (walk west from the station, cross the intersection and take tram number 11 or 17 to the last stop). It was built by serf-architect Pavel Argunov between 1792 and 1797 as the summer residence of Nikolai Sheremetyev on the grounds of the family's estate. The pink-classical palace was built of wood, but painted to resemble bricks and stone. Interesting rooms are the Blue Room, Egyptian Ballroom, Italian Reception Room and the Picture Gallery and Theater, which had over 200 serf actors, dancers and musicians. The palace also houses the **Museum of Serf Art**. The beautiful serf-actress Praskovia Zhemchugova-Kovalyova later became the count's wife (see page 250). The red-brick **Trinity Church** (1678) adjoins the palace. A beautiful English-landscaped park and gardens are also on the grounds, and a theater often holds evening concerts. The museum is open daily, apart from Mondays, Tuesdays and when the humidity is over 80 percent, from 10am–6pm; closed from October 1 to May 18; tel. 283-4645; www.museum.ru/museum/ostankino.

The 540-meter (1771-foot) high **Ostankino TV Tower** looms nearby at Akademinika Korolyova Street. The tower, which surpassed the Empire State Building as the world's tallest freestanding structure when it was built in 1967, has an observation deck and a rotating restaurant called Sedmoye Nebo (Seventh Heaven). Open 9am–8.30pm; closed Mondays.

DOWN THE MOSKVA RIVER

The Moskva River is 500 kilometers (300 miles) long, of which 77 kilometers (48 miles) wind their way through Moscow. Fourteen road bridges cross the river. Boat cruises leave at regular intervals (April to October) from various locations on both sides of the river; one of the popular embarkation points is near the Kievsky Railway Station—take the Metro to Kievskaya, not far from the Ukraina Hotel. The boat pier is located on the Berezhkovskaya Naberezhnaya (Embankment) near Borodinsky Most (Bridge). The *Rocket* hydrofoils also leave from beside Gorky Park and the Bolshoi Ustinsky Most where the Yauza and Moskva rivers meet, and continue eastwards down the river to the Novospassky Most. The full, round-trip cruise takes about two hours, but you can leave the boat at any point. Some sites along the way are the Kremlin, Rossiya Hotel, Cathedral of Christ the Savior, Novodevichy Monastery, Sparrow Hills, Moscow University, Gorky Park, Strelka Rowing Club, Ostankino TV Tower, and many estates, palaces and churches.

The tour ends at the **Novospassky Monastery**, founded in the 15th century by Ivan the Great (nearest Metro is Proletarskaya; open daily 7am–5pm). The 17th-century **Cathedral of the Transfiguration of the Savior** became the burial site of the czar's relatives; the inner vaults were painted by masters from the Kremlin armory. The bell tower, gates and stone walls also date from the 17th-century. Today the **New Monastery of the Savior** is again a working monastery. Also lying on the banks of the Moskva River are the 17th-century **Krutitskoye Metropolitans' Residence** (*krutitsy* are small hills), and the **Simonov Monastery**, founded in the 14th century by the nephew of St Sergius of Radonezh who was named Simonov, after a nobleman who had donated the land. It was built as a defensive fortress to protect the southern end of Moscow from the invading Mongols. Today, only a few buildings and a church remain (closed Tuesdays). Another architectural ensemble is the **St Andrew Monastery** with a 17th-century Church painted like a peacock's tail. Founded by Fyodor Rtishchev, a cultural advisor to Czar Alexis (father of Peter the Great), the monastery set up Moscow's first school, and the monks also translated books from foreign languages. Today, it houses the Library of the Synod, the central repository of the Russian Orthodox Church.

Boats leaving from the same piers also run westward to Kuntsevo-Krylatskoye in Fili-Kuntsevo Park, with a river beach and the swimming island of Serebryany Bor. This trip lasts about an hour.

(main picture) The Zapashny family is considered
a circus dynasty after performing with elephants
and tigers for four generations; (above right) the
circus always has a variety of acts, such as this bird
act performed by a female Lilliputian; (right) a
poster shows the face of a young Alexander Popov,
known as the Sunshine Clown, one of Russia's most
famous clowns; (left) Popov (in blue jacket) as he
is today. After performing in the circus for nearly
40 years, he prefers to continue working. 'What
happens,' he reflects, 'is that a fine speck of sawdust
enters your bloodstream and stays there for life.'
(far left) the audience discovers that circus magic
never ends.

THE RUSSIAN CIRCUS

'Oh, how I love the circus,' bellows Alexander Frish, a charismatic and eccentric clown, who has been clowning around in the Russian Circus for over 20 years. Frish believes that 'the circus is the universal language of joy and laughter that lets us all become children again'.

The Russian Circus is a world of vibrant artistry, precision and grace. Throughout the country the circus is a highly respected art form taken as seriously as classical ballet. As one of the country's most popular forms of entertainment half the population of more than 140 million people attend at least one circus performance a year. Today over 50 permanent circus buildings (more than in the rest of the world combined) in as many cities across the country, from Moscow to Siberia. The Russian State Circus (Rosgostsirk) oversees 40 circus collectives, 15 tent circuses, nine animal circuses, circuses on ice and the Circus of Lilliputians, employing over 3,000 artists who perform throughout Russia and more than 30 countries each year. Spectators are truly astounded by the levels of artistry that take place within the traditional one-ring theater.

The early traditions of the circus go back over three centuries. The first formalized circus was created in England in 1770 by an ex-cavalry officer and showman named Philip Astley. It consisted mostly of trick riding, rope dancers, tumblers and jugglers, staged within a circular ring. In 1793, one of Astley's horsemen and later competitor Charles Hughes introduced this novel form of entertainment to Russia, with a private circus for Catherine the Great in the Royal Palace at St Petersburg. (In the same year, Hughes' pupil John Bill Ricketts introduced modern circus to American audiences in Philadelphia.)

Russia's first permanent circus building was built in St Petersburg in 1877 by Gaetano Ciniselli, an equestrian entrepreneur from Milan. The Ciniselli Circus was the center of performance activitity up to the Revolution, and this classic building still houses today's St Petersburg

Circus. The second oldest circus was the Old Circus in Moscow (a new Old Circus has been built on the site where the original once stood). Moscow also boasts the New Circus and summer tent circuses. Nowhere in Europe were circus performers as politically active as in turn-of-the-century Russia. The circus became a sort of political sanctuary where sketches depicting the tumultuous state of Russia were tolerated. The clowns, especially, took every opportunity to satirize the czars, landowners and merchants. Many of the performers participated in active demonstrations with organized parades through the cities. Lunacharksy, the head of the Circus House that organized performers, encouraged their participation: 'Here it will be possible to have fiery revolutionary speeches, declarative couplets and clowns doing caricatures on enemy forces.' The artists performed on small flatbed stages that were rolled through the streets of Moscow. Vladimir Durov, with trained animals, joined the merry cavalcade, as did the most popular clown of the era, Vitaly Lazarenko, on stilts! Taking up the Bolshevik cause, the acts were now catalysts for social reform. The circus had become a political hotbed.

The poet Mayakovsky wrote for the circus. In one of his most famous skits, Moscow Burning, he wrote: 'Proud of the year 1917/Don't forget about 1905/A year of undying glory and fame/When the dream of the land came alive.../Comrade Circus, where's your grin?/Here's a sight to tickle us/Look and see who's trotting in/The Dynasty of Czar Nicholas !!!'

During these years of intellectual and political intensity, some of Russia's finest writers and directors, such as Gorky, Chekhov and Stanislavsky, turned their attention to the circus. In one of his short stories, Maxim Gorky wrote: 'Everything I see in the arena blends into something triumphant, where skill and strength celebrate their victory over mortal danger.' Later, even Lenin took time off from the Revolution to nationalize the circus—on September 22, 1919, the world's first government circus began its operations.

In order to provide a consistently high standard of training in the circus arts, the government founded the first professional circus school in 1927. Today at scores of circus schools throughout the country, students train for up to four years, studying all facets of circus life. During the final year, the student creates his own act and utilizes the services of circus producers, directors and choreographers. Once approved by a circus board, the performer's professional career begins.

Sadly, on August 21, 1997, the heart of Russia's most beloved clown, Yuri Nikulin, stopped beating. He had performed in the circus for over 30 years and had acted as the director of the Old Circus since 1984. Nikulin always tried to overcome hard times with the help of humor. He had accumulated more than 10,000 jokes since he started collecting them in 1936, which filled two volumes of his books Anekdoti I & II. The circus has been renamed Nikulin's Circus on Tvsetnoi Bulvar. He is buried in Novodevichy Cemetery where there is a bronze sculpture of him sitting on the edge of a circus arena with his favorite dog.

'Laughter is beneficial to the human body,' he wrote. 'When smiling, giggling, bursting into laughter (until you drop) a person, without even suspecting it, keeps himself healthy.'

The emblem of the Russian Circus depicts a circus performer reaching for the stars. The language of the circus is without words, as beauty, courage and skill bridge the gap between generations and nationalities. The circus is the universal language of the heart.

(opposite) The famous Flying Cranes trapeze act, produced by Vilen Golovko, chalk up before a performance. Considered one of the finest aerial acts of our time, the ten flyers rehearsed more than five years together before a single performance was given. They combined extraordinary trapeze and acrobatic skills and performed a breathtaking aerial ballet to classical music. The act was first inspired by a Russian song commemorating the spirits of the fallen soldiers who turn into white cranes and fly away, their souls released to heaven. The sole female performer, Lena Golovko, played the last of the fallen cranes, who is courageously rescued so that peace may prevail. "When I appear.. My soul is in it," After performing for more than 20 years, a new generation of Flying Cranes continues its soaring magic throughout the world.

VICINITY OF MOSCOW

Strewn throughout the Moscow suburbs are the beloved dacha or 'country homes'. From czarist through Stalinist times, the *dacha* was a privilege granted for loyalty or special service. (The name derives from the verb *dat*,—"to give".) Later, ordinary Russians began to build their own modest country houses, often from scrounged materials. These suburban retreats into nature were enjoyed as a re-connection to the Russian soul. In warmer months, families gathered wild mushrooms and berries in the forest, grew potatoes, tomatoes and cucumbers in their small garden plots, and socialized with neighboring *dachniki*.

Today, a whole new breed of country home, the *"kottedzhi"* is evolving with the richer "New Russians," who are changing the landscape of suburbia into gated communities. Many wealthy are now building luxury country palaces, surrounded by high brick fortress walls; and, understandably, the regular dacha dwellers are upset with the change. Today, it is now common to see million-dollar mansions go up next door to wooden shacks. A new trend is also developing where country-club settlements have everything from community swimming pools to kindergartens. In the new prestigious locations around Rublyovo-Uspenskoye or Dmitrovskoye Highways and Serebreny Bor, huge houses can rent from $5,000 up to even $50,000 per month. The market for the simple traditional Russian *dacha* is giving way to new symbols of affluence and excess.

In the 18th- and 19th-centuries, the privileged classes of Russia also built their summer residences in the countryside around Moscow. Many of these palaces and parks have been preserved and converted into museums. Here are 13 spots that can easily be reached by Metro, train or inexpensive *elektrichka*, bus or car. There are also group excursions (day or overnight) to some of these areas; check at the Service Bureau in your hotel for more information.

ABRAMTSEVO ESTATE MUSEUM (Абрамцево)

The **Abramtsevo Estate Museum** is located along the M8 Yaroslavskoye Highway (a few kilometers west of the 61k signpost) near the town of Sergiyev Posad, about 65 kilometers (40 miles) north of Moscow. Local buses run to and from Sergiyev Posad, or it is about an hour's journey by train from the Yaroslavsky Railway Station. (At Abramtsevo, cross the tracks and turn left at the road. Turn right at the crossroads and after crossing the Vorya river continue along the dirt path alongside the main road. The estate will appear on the right—about a 20-minute walk from the station.) If driving, try the Russkaya Skazka Restaurant at 43 Yaroslavskoye Highway, tel. (095) 584-3436. Otherwise bring food from Moscow for a picnic lunch, or there is a small restaurant next to the museum.

Chronicles dating back to the 16th-century remark on the region's *obramok* or forested hills flanked by a river. The name of the area became Obramkovo and later in the 18th-century it was softened to Abramtsevo. In 1843, the Russian writer Sergei Aksakov bought the country estate (built in the 1770s); over the next 15 years it was frequented by many prominent writers, such as Gogol, Tyutchev and Turgenev. Here Gogol gave a reading of the first chapter from his second volume of *Dead Souls*, which he later burned at his home in Moscow. (His portrait hangs on the wall of the central mansion.) The writer Ivan Turgenev often came here to hunt and was mentioned in Aksakov's popular *Hunting Almanac*. In 1847, Aksakov wrote his famous book, *Notes on Fishing*. In 1870, the railway and textile baron and art patron, Savva Mamontov, bought the estate and turned it into a popular meeting place and artist colony. Art, theater, writing, carpentry and pottery workshops were held, and Serov, Vrubel, Repin, Shalyapin and Stanislavsky all lived and worked here. Serov's famous portrait *The Girl with Peaches* (1887) hangs in the dining room (the original can be found in the Tretyakov Gallery); it is of Mamontov's daughter Vera, who is buried on the estate. Also gracing the walls are Repin's portraits of Mamontov and his wife Elizaveta. The traditional long timber-framed house with fancy lacework gable was said to be the model for Chekhov's manor house in *The Cherry Orchard*. Mamontov also opened a school for peasant children and taught their parents traditional folk crafts.

Standing in the park, the white **Church of the Savior-Not-Made-By-Hands** was designed by artist Viktor Vasnetsov and built in 1882. It was based on the Novgorod 12th-century-style Church of Savior in Nereditsa and other architectural schools. The interior icons were painted by Repin, Polenov and Vasnetsov. Valentin Serov painted the lovely *Winter in Abramtsevo, the Church*, as well as *Winter in Abramtsevo, a House*, both in 1886. The ceramic tiles that decorate the exterior were produced at the estate's own ceramic workshop. In 1891, a small chapel was added to the northern side to commemorate the tragic death of Mamontov's son, Andrei. Both Mamontov, who shot himself shortly after the Revolution in 1918, and his son are buried here. Vasnetsov also dreamed up the *Izbush'kha na Kur'nikh Nozhkakh'* (Hut on Chicken Legs), the headquarters of the witch Baba Yaga in a popular Russian fairy tale.

The countryside is filled with birch groves, colorful gardens and woods, and greatly inspired the landscape artist Isaac Levitan, who often visited the estate. Abramtsevo is now a museum and displays the rooms as they were used by Aksakov and Mamontov. Paintings and other art work executed on the estate, including many by Vrubel, are exhibited in the art studio. The museum is open from 10am–5pm, closed Mondays, Tuesdays and the last Thursday of the month. (Sometimes the estate is closed during the months of April and October, so check first, tel. 584-5533.) If the weather is pleasant, take a stroll about a kilometer north

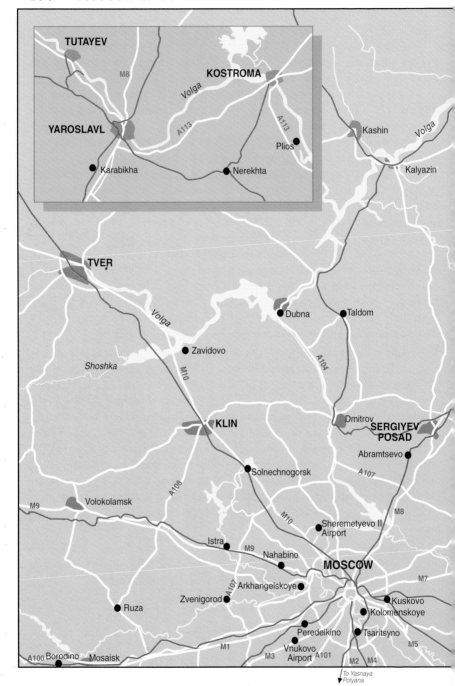

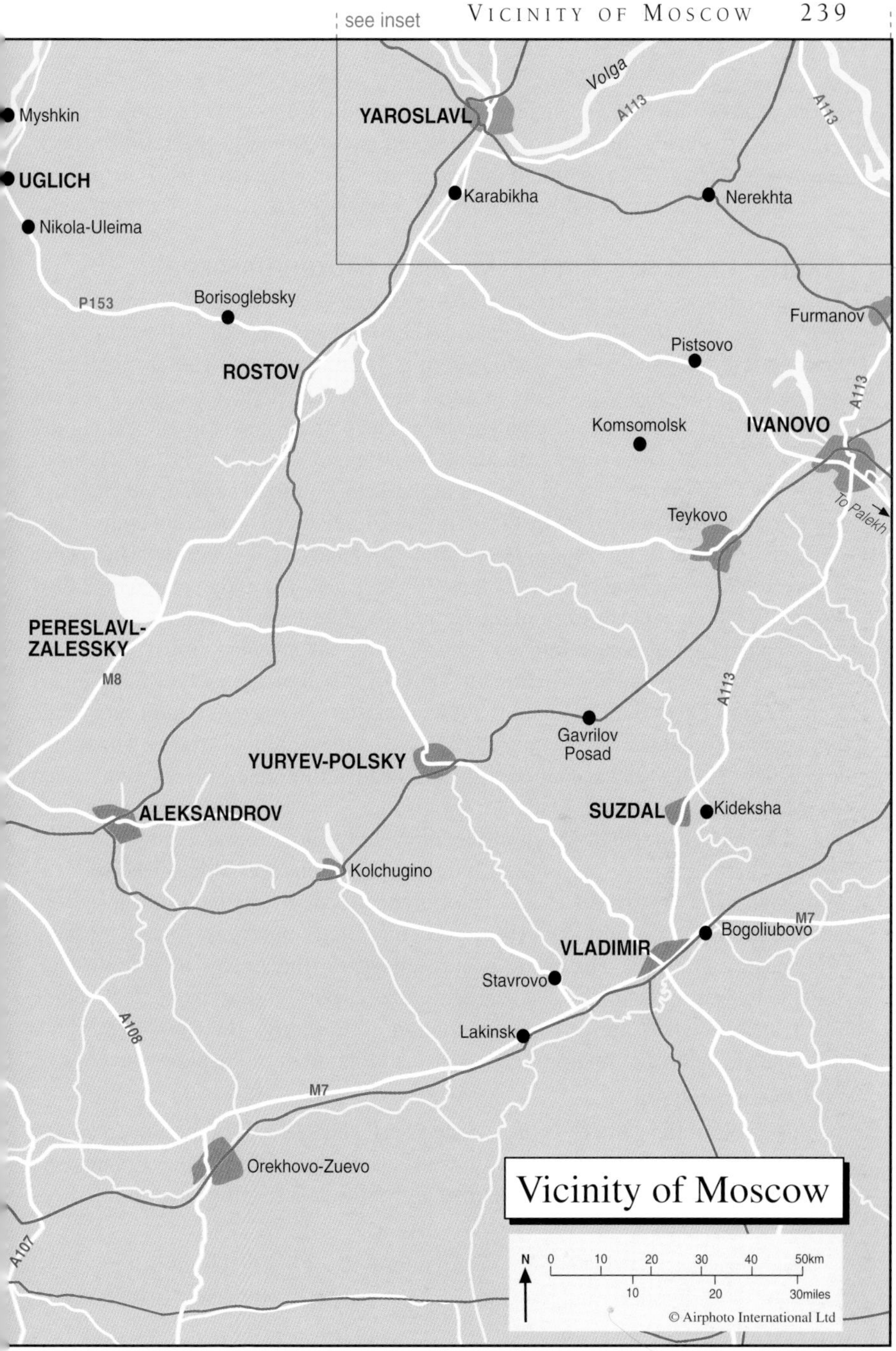

Myshkin

UGLICH

Nikola-Uleima

YAROSLAVL

Volga

A113

A113

Karabikha

Nerekhta

P153

Borisoglebsky

Furmanov

Pistsovo

ROSTOV

Komsomolsk

IVANOVO

A113

Teykovo

To Palekh

PERESLAVL-
ZALESSKY

M8

A113

Gavrilov
Posad

YURYEV-POLSKY

SUZDAL

Kideksha

ALEKSANDROV

Kolchugino

Bogoliubovo

M7

VLADIMIR

Stavrovo

A108

Lakinsk

M7

Orekhovo-Zuevo

Vicinity of Moscow

A107

N 0   10   20   30   40   50km

    10   20   30miles

© Airphoto International Ltd

to the village of **Khotkovo**, where a convent was founded in 1308 (destroyed in the 17th century during the Time of Troubles and later restored in the 18th-century). The recently restored Cathedral of the Intercession holds the remains of the parents of St Sergius who founded the monastery at Sergiyev Posad.

ARKHANGELSKOYE ESTATE MUSEUM (Архангельское)

This museum lies in the village of Arkhangelskoye, 16 kilometers (ten miles) west of Moscow. Take the M9 Volokolamskoye Highway and then the left road toward Petrovo-Dalniye. The closest Metro station is Tushinskaya; exit station right, turn right around the corner, and take minibus number 549 eight stops. It lets you off across the street from the museum entrance. The grand estate is situated along the banks of the Moskva River and took 40 years to complete. Prince Golitsyn originally founded the estate at the end of the 18th-century. The mansion and park were designed in French style by the architect Chevalier de Huerne and built by serf craftsmen. In 1810, the estate passed into the hands of the wealthy landowner Prince Yusupov (a descendent of one of the Khans—not the one who killed Rasputin) who was the director of the Hermitage Museum and Imperial Theater. He turned the classical palace into his own personal art museum. Today the palace (often closed for renovation) contains works by such artists as Boucher, Hubert Robert, Roslin and Van Dyck and the Italian master, Tiepolo. As rumor has it, the palace once contained the portraits of each of Yusupov's 300 mistresses. The rooms and halls are beautifully decorated with antique furniture (many pieces were owned by Marie Antoinette and Madame Pompadour), marble sculptures, tapestries, porcelain and chandeliers; much of the china and glassware was produced on the estate. The oldest structure is the **Church of the Archangel Michael** (1667); the **Holy Gates** link it with the estate. The **Colonnade**, originally built on the eastern side as the Yusupov Mausoleum (but never completed), now hosts a small museum and musical concerts. The estate is surrounded on three sides by a multi-level Italian-style park, lined with classical sculptures, arbors, and pavilions that include the **Tea House** and **Caprice Hall**. The **Temple to Catherine the Great** depicts her as Themis, Goddess of Justice. There is also a **Monument to Pushkin** who enjoyed visiting the grounds.

Just west of the gardens is the wooden **Serf Theater**, exhibiting theatrical and original set designs by Pietro Gottardo Gonzaga. Built in 1819 by the serf-architect Ivanov, the theater, which seated 400, had one of the largest companies of serf actors in Russia.

Arkhangelskoye's ticket *kassa* is open 11am–4.30pm; weekends until 3pm; closed Mondays and Tuesdays and the last Friday of each month; tel. 561-9660/2231;

www.arkhangelskoye.ru. A local restaurant is the **Russkaya Izba** (Russian Cottage) Restaurant, fashioned after Russian peasant rooms. The cooking is Old Russian; the menu offers bear meat and venison along with *kvas*, mead and tea served from a bubbling samovar. Call ahead to make reservations (tel. 561-4244); open daily 12–10pm; at 1 Naberezhnaya St, in Ilyinskoye village. As an additional dining choice, try the **Arkhangelskoye Restaurant** (tel. 562-0328), located across from the estate's main entrance, open 12pm to midnight. It has Russian and European dishes and wines, and a dining terrace is open in summer months (live music Thurs–Sun after 7pm).

BORODINO (Бородино)

Borodino, site of the most famous battle in the War of 1812, lies on the M1 Moscow –Minsk road, 120 kilometers (74 miles) southwest of Moscow. *Elektrichka* commuter trains run from Moscow's Byelorussky Railway Station and take about two hours. Today, it is the site of the Borodino Battlefield Museum and Nature Preserve.

In the late spring of 1812, Napoleon led his massive army of more than half a million men into Russia. Presented with no other option but a bloodbath, the generals of Alexander I's armies ordered a humiliating retreat. But, in August, the czar appointed 67-year-old Prince Mikhail Kutuzov as commander-in-chief to stop Napoleon invading Moscow. On August 26 1812, the Russians took on the French at Borodino. Napoleon's army numbered over 135,000 soldiers with 600 guns and the Russians, 150,000 soldiers with 640 guns. Remarkably, after 15 hours of fighting (and 80,000 dead from both sides), Napoleon was forced to retreat; the Battle of Borodino marked the turning point of the war. (Kutuzov remarked that "this was the bloodiest combat ever seen in modern times.") Kutuzov's generals, including Barclay de Tolly, wanted to stage another battle with Napoleon before Moscow, but Kutuzov wanted to save his armies from yet another bloody encounter. He argued, 'Moscow will be the sponge that will suck him in.' Meeting no resistance, Napoleon's remaining troops entered the gates of Moscow on September 2 at Poklonnaya Gora (Hill of Greeting) and waited for a formal surrender. No one arrived and the French found Moscow nearly deserted. As Napoleon slowly marched towards the Kremlin, immense fires broke out throughout the city; eventually over 80 percent of Moscow would burn to the ground. By mid-October, with winter approaching and no supplies at hand, Napoleon was forced to abandon Moscow and undertake a long march home during one of the worst winters on record. When he finally released his army only 25,000 Frenchmen remained alive. To celebrate Russia's triumphant victory, Alexander 1 ordered the Cathedral of Christ the Savior built in Moscow 'in the name of the fatherland to express our thanks and gratitude to all our loyal subjects, true sons of Russia.'

In 1912, to mark the battle's 100th anniversary, 34 monuments were erected throughout the battlefield. The polished granite obelisk (1966) crowned by a bronze eagle is dedicated to Field Marshal Kutuzov. Leo Tolstoy visited the battlefield in 1876 while writing *War and Peace*. Other memorials commemorate World War II battles that took place here in 1941. Every year, during the first Sunday in Septmber, the anniversary of the 1812 battle is celebrated by a Borodino Field Day, when the battle is actually reenacted. People playing the French and Russian soldiers dress in period uniforms, cannons roar and smoke rises from the battlefield. A religious ceremony is held after the battle to give thanks for Napoleon's defeat.

Filmmaker Sergei Bondarchuk's four-part nine-hour epic *War and Peace* was Russia's longest and most expensive film ever made. Taking five years to produce, it encompassed some of the most spectacular battle scenes ever seen on film. During the recreated Battle of Borodino over 120,000 extras were used from the Soviet army. The **Borodino Military History Museum**, with exhibits of the Battle of Borodino, is open 10am–5pm; closed Mondays. (Another Battle of Borodino Museum is in Moscow at 38 Kutuzovsky Prospekt, by the Triumphal Arch, see page 195.) Hotels can be found in nearby Mosaisk.

If you have time for a local side-trip while in Borodino, visit the **Spaso Borodinsky** (Borodino's Savior) **Convent** in the Village of **Tuchkovo**. It was established by Margarita Tuchkova, widow of the famous General Alexander Tuchkov, who died in Borodino defending positions against the French. In 1820, Alexander I donated 10,000 rubles for Margarita (she was of the noble Naryshkin family) to construct a church in honor of her husband and those who fell in battle. Inside the church is a marble cross inscribed with the words, 'Remember, O Lord, in Thy Kingdom, Alexander, killed in battle.' Later, Margarita moved to Borodino from Moscow and became a nun in 1840. Czar Nicholas I made further donations to the site and was present at the convent's consecration. Up until her death in 1852, Margarita (now Mother Superior Maria) provided shelter to homeless, abused and elderly women. Until 1917 it was the model for all other convents across the country. In a twist of fate, when the Nazis invaded during WWII the buildings were used as a concentration camp. In the 1990s, the convent underwent massive renovation work and today the churches and refectory (with its splendid iconostasis) are open to the public. The convent was renown for its beautifully sewn icons, where the women embroidered on silk, satin and velvet, with gold and silver threads. It also houses the exhibit "Leo Tolstoy and the battle of Borodino", with some of his original draft notes made on the battlefield. An *elektrichka* train runs from Borodino to the nearby Tuchkovo stop.

(opposite) Church Patriarch Nikon, who began construction of the New Jerusalem Monastery in 1656, designed the site after the churches in the Holy Land. The Resurrection Cathedral is modeled after Jerusalem's Holy Sepulcher Church.

ISTRA RIVER MUSEUM OF WOODEN ARCHITECTURE (Истра)

The museum is located 56 kilometers (34 miles) west of Moscow, along the M9 or Volokolamskoye Highway. *Elektrichka* trains also run from Moscow's Rizhsky Railway Station (the Prigorodniye *kassa* and trains are at the very end of the building) and take about an hour. The **Museum of Wooden Architecture**, in the park along the Istra River, contains a 17th-century wooden church and farmstead, cottages, granaries and windmills brought in from nearby areas. Both Istra and the New Jerusalem Monastery grounds are open 10am–5pm; closed Mondays and the last Friday of the month.

The Novoyarusalimsky or **New Jerusalem Monastery** (now returned to the Orthodox Church) is situated a few kilometers to the west of Istra (one train stop further, then by bus no. 22, or a 20-minute walk; tel. 994-5646). Patriarch Nikon, who caused the great Orthodox schism, began construction of the monastery in 1656, designing the site after the grounds and churches in the Holy Land. (Ironically, he was later stripped of his position by the czar and exiled here until his death in 1681.) During World War II the Germans blew up the grounds, but today much has been restored. The **Resurrection Cathedral** (1656–85) is modeled after Jerusalem's Holy Sepulcher Church, and the surrounding fortress walls represent the city of Jerusalem with its Zion and Damascus Towers. Many parts of the church (still under restoration) are named after the Stations of the Cross, and are extensively covered by tiles and colorful plasterwork. The most intriguing spot is the Golgotha Chapel

where an artificial fissure (representing the earthquake that shook the world when Christ died) cuts across a 17th-century wooden iconostasis with figures of the crucifixion. Nikon is buried beneath in the Chapel of St John the Baptist. A collection of Russian paintings, icons, furniture and porcelain and military uniforms is on display in the refectory and other buildings, including the Nativity Church, behind the cathedral.

North of the monastery, in the Gethsemane Park, is a small museum of wooden architecture as well as the original meditation house of Nikon. www.istra.ru/museum.

A number of small hotels are situated in the Istra District, including Ognikovo, tel. 737-7637, 994-5967, in Dukhanino and Vysotka Hotel, tel. 994-5408, in Buzharovo Village (see www.istra.ru/museum).

KLIN (Клин)

The old Russian town of Klin, founded on the banks of the Sestra River (a tributary of the Volga) in 1318, is located 80 kilometers (50 miles) northwest of Moscow along the M10 Highway. *Elektrichka* trains also run from the Leningradsky terminal, on the way to Tver, and take about two hours. Continue to the estate by local bus no. 5. Get off at Bolnitsa (hospital). The museum is across the street.

The town was the ancestral home of the Romanov dynasty; today only two Naryshkin baroque-style churches remain of the monastery. Klin is more widely known as the home of the great Russian composer Peter (Pyotr) Tchaikovsky (1840–93). The composer who said, 'I find no words to express how much I need the charm and quiet of the Russian countryside', bought the estate in 1885. (Tchaikovsky also yearned for peaceful isolation after the public rebuffed him for his homosexuality, and a number of friends had criticized some of his earlier works.) In the gray-green timber-framed house, at 48 Tchaikovsky Street, the composer went on to score some of his most popular works: the ballets *The Nutcracker* and *Sleeping Beauty*, and his Fifth and Sixth Symphonies. Not long after the première of his *Pathétique* (Sixth) Symphony in St Petersburg, Tchaikovsky died of cholera after ignoring a warning not to drink the water during an epidemic. (Some consider that he committed suicide.) Inside his dacha, portraits of famous musicians hang in the living room, along with a photographic picture of Tchaikovsky's father in the study. On his birthday, May 7, and day of his death, November 6, winners of the Moscow Tchaikovsky International Competition and other virtuosi play works on his grand piano. Concerts are also given year-round in a hall on the grounds.

For the first Tchaikovsky International Competition (held in March 1958 and chaired by Dmitri Shostakovich), the surprise winner of the Gold Medal (this was

(opposite) In the town of Istra, west of Moscow, an old 17th-century church is exhibited in the Museum of Wooden Architecture, surrounded by beryoza or birch trees.

during the height of the Cold War under Khrushchev) was a 23-year-old Julliard-trained pianist named Van Cliburn, a tall blonde Texan, who flawlessly performed Rachmaninov's Third Piano Concerto and Tchaikovsky's Piano Concerto No. 1. The Russian pianist, Lev Vlasenko, came second. Van Cliburn won the substantial sum of $6,000 (25,000 rubles) and was honored with a ticker tape parade in New York. On his 60th birthday in 1994, Van Cliburn performed with the Moscow Philharmonic in Los Angeles. Today, Moscow's annual Tchaikovsky Competition ranks among the most prestigious in the world, with a first-prize of $20,000.

The **Tchaikovsky Memorial House** and estate-museum is open 10am–6pm (ticket *kassa* closes at 5pm); closed Wednesdays and Thursdays, and the last Monday of each month, tel. (9624) 539-8196.

*The famous Russian composer, Peter Tchaikovsky lived for eight years
(up until his death in 1893) in this charming timber-framed house in the quaint town of Klin.
Here he scored many of his most popular works, such as* The Nutcracker *and* Sleeping Beauty.

KOLOMENSKOYE MUSEUM PRESERVE (Коломенское)

This large preserve is situated about ten kilometers (six miles) southeast of Moscow on the banks of the Moskva River, at 39 Andropova Street. It is well worth taking a day's excursion to the outer suburbs for a visit. Drive south of the city along the Kashirskoye Highway or take the Metro to the Kolomenskaya (accent on 'lo') station and it is only about a ten-minute walk from there. Head east along Novinki Street and then south on Bolshaya which turns into Shtatnaya Sloboda and leads to

Today, the Kolomenskoye Museum Preserve, outside Moscow,
is a four-square kilometer open-air museum of 16th-and 17th-century architecture
which includes many elaborately decorated Russian Orthodox churches.
The area was used by Peter the Great and Ivan the Terrible as their country estates.

the northern entrance gate. In summer, some Moscow River cruises also stop at the ferry landing by the eastern gate. Kolomenskoye was once the country estate of numerous Russian princes and czars, including Ivan the Terrible and Peter the Great. The name of the area dates from the 13th-century, when villagers fleeing Mongol attacks on the town of Kolomna settled here. Some of the oldest trees in Moscow can be found in the preserve, many over 400 years old.

The area is now a four-square-kilometer open-air museum of 16th- and 17th-century architecture. Visitors enter the park through the northern, whitewashed **Savior Gate**, which stands on the grounds that were once Czar Alexei's orchards.

The czar (father of Peter the Great) was passionate about hunting, and also helped train falcons; more than 300 birds of prey and 100,000 doves were said to have been raised on his estate. Between 1666 and 1667, workers for Alexei constructed a large wooden palace known as the Jewel-Box, complete with 250 rooms, 3,000 windows of glittering mica, and elaborate *kokoshniki* gables. The czar's throne was flanked with a pair of large gilded lions who could roar and roll their eyes with a pull on a hidden mechanism. In 1768, Catherine the Great had the palace torn down and a new one built near the Ascension Church. (A model replica of Czar Alexei's throne room is on display in the museum.) Alexei's royal palace was joined by a passageway to the 17th-century baroque-style **Church of the Kazan Virgin**; it stands on the left as you walk through the gates. A copy of the famous icon the Virgin of Kazan is located in the main iconostasis. (After the Revolution the original icon disappeared.) Today the church is a busy place of worship, and services are held daily.

On the south side of the complex, rising high on the banks of the river stands the tent-shaped and elaborately decorated **Ascension Church**. The brick structure was built in 1532 to celebrate the birth of Vasily III's first son, Ivan the Terrible. The building was also the highest structure in all of Moscow at 60 meters (197 feet) and served as a watchtower. It was the first church to reproduce the design of wooden churches in brick and it is believed to be the forerunner to St Basil's Cathedral, built a quarter of a century later. From an upper window Ivan the Terrible could observe his soldiers fighting the invading Mongols. Alongside stands the 16th-century **St George Bell Tower**, all that remains of the Church of St George the Victorious. Other structures of interest are the Dyakovskaya Church, the water tower (which brought water up from the river), a Siberian watch tower (1631) and a gatehouse whose clock has been working since the time of Peter the Great. A museum housing religious and royal artifacts is situated within the eastern **Palace Gatehouse**, built in 1673, and its adjoining building; it was founded in 1923. Of particular interest is the replica of Czar Alexei's wooden palace, made by the carver Smirnov in the 19th century. Follow the wooden steps southwest through the forest to the fived-domed **Church of St John the Baptist**, built in 1529. Moscow's St Basil's Cathedral is said to be modeled on this.

From the 1930s to 1950s, monuments of Russian architecture were brought to the park from different regions of the country. These buildings, located in the northwestern side of the park, in the older palace area, now exhibit 16th- to 19th-century Russian applied and decorative art, including collections of paintings, ceramics, woodcarvings and clocks. The only building opened here is **Peter the Great's cabin**. He lived in this six-room cottage in 1702, while supervising the building of his navy in the northern city of Arkhangelsk. It is a favorite area for picnics, shaded by oaks, elms and poplars; one of the ancient oak trees is thought to date back to the 14th century, during the rule of Ivan Kalita. Russian film director Sergei Eisenstein also shot some of the famous scenes of his film *Ivan the Terrible* here at Kolomenskoye. The complex grounds are open daily 7am–10pm April to October, winter months 9am–9pm, ticket offices open 10.30am–5pm and the museums until 5.30pm; closed Mondays. In summer, some weekend river cruises stop at the ferry landing. Each year a festival of Sacred Music takes place in the Ascension Church and, around the last Sunday in May, there is a parade to celebrate Peter the Great's birthday. To check museum times or book excursions, tel. 115-2309 or 112-0414. www.museum.ru/kolomen. Every year (end February/March) during the *Maslenitsa* (Butter Week) holiday, a huge festival takes place on the grounds, where *blini* pancakes are served to celebrate the return of the spring sun.

KUSKOVO PALACE MUSEUM (Кусково)

This estate-museum is located within the city limits, 12 kilometers (eight miles) to the southeast and can be easily reached from the Ryazansky Prospekt Metro station. From the station, it is a 20-minute walk or short bus ride (six stops on bus number 133) to 2 Yunost Street. The lands of Kuskovo were in the Sheremetyev family since the early 17th century. (Boris Sheremetyev fought with Peter the Great against the Swedes in the Battle of Poltava in 1709.) The Sheremetyevs were incredibly wealthy with over three million acres of land holdings and 200,000 serfs. (Today, Moscow's main airports, built on land that belonged to their estates, take the Sheremetyev family name.) When Boris' son Pyotr Borisovich married the Romanov princess Varvara Cherkassova in 1743, they decided to built a summer estate at Kuskovo, where as many as 30,000 guests could be entertained in a single day; it was soon nicknamed the Moscow Versailles. The pink and white wooden **Mansion** (1769–75) was designed by Karl Blank and the serf-architects Alexei Mironov and Fyodor Argunov. It is faced with white stone and decorated with parquet floors, antique furniture, embroidered tapestries and crystal chandeliers; notice the carved initials PS over the front door. The mansion also houses an excellent collection of 18th-century Russian art; a portrait of Catherine the Great hangs in the Raspberry Drawing Room and the White Ball Hall is decorated with rich bucolic scenes painted by Sheremetyev serfs.

Exiting the palace, and walking right in a counter-clockwise direction, leads to the Estate **Church** (1739) and **Belltower** (1792) and then on to the large **Kitchen** wing and **Coach House**; in front stands the **Grotto**, where five small pink-white

The Kuskovo Mansion (1769–75), faced with white stone, has the initials PS (for the owner Peter Sheremetyev) carved above the front door. The estate has its own small church with a colorful iconostasis.

When the wealthy merchant, Peter Sheremetyev, married a Romanov princess in 1743,
he built a lavish summer estate at Kuskovo, nicknamed the Moscow Versailles.
They lived in this pink and white mansion, which now houses a collection of 18th-century
Russian art. On the estate grounds are other colorful pavilions, cottages and theaters.

menagerie pavillions are situated around the pond. (Pyotr Sheremetyev loved to stage mock military battles on the lake for his friends.) Above them stands the white **Italian House** (1755), which also displays a collection of 18th-century paintings and sculpture. Walking up past the wooden-framed **Bird Pavillion** brings you to the famous **Open-Air Theater** (1763), where the celebrated company of Sheremetyev serf-actors performed weekly plays. One of the most popular actresses was Praskovia Zhemchugova-Kovalyova (1768-1803), the daughter of a serf blacksmith. In 1789, when she caught the eye of Nikolai Sheremetyev, son of Pyotr, one of Russia's most romantic love stories developed. Creating a major scandal, Nikolai granted her freedom in 1798, and went on to marry the commoner in 1801. To get away from increasing social gossip, they moved to a palace at Ostankino (see page **228**). Sadly, Praskovia died two years later of consumption after giving birth to a son. In the neighboring **Orangerie**, a small display tells their love story and the **Ceramics Museum** exhibits a fine collection of Russian and European porcelain, faience and glass. Continuing around brings you to the **Manager's House** (1810) and the **Large Stone Conservatory** (1763). Walking down through the **Sculptures in the Park** (over 50 are placed throughout the grounds), leads past the yellow, neoclassical **Hermitage**, designed by Karl Blank in 1765; the brick-façade **Dutch Cottage** (1749); and the brick and wooden-tiered **Swiss House** built in 1864 by Nikolai Benois.

The estate and museums are open 10am–4pm (ticket *kassa* closes at 3pm) from November to March (if the weather is particularly cold or humid the estate is often closed). From April to October it is open 10am–6pm (*kassa* closes at 5pm). It is closed Mondays and Tuesdays and the last Wednesday of each month; tel. 375-5252 or 370-0160. The palace stages chamber music concerts in the Hall of Mirrors on summer evenings.

In the vicinity, at no. 6 Topolyovaya Alleya, is **Kuzminki**, the country estate of Baron Stroganov. Closed Mondays and the last Friday of the month.

MOSCOW COUNTRY CLUB (Нахабино)

The 142-hectare (350-acre) Moscow Country Club, at Nahabino, with Russia's first 18-hole championship golf course, is located about 30 kilometers (18 miles) northwest of Moscow in the Krasnogorsk district (a 40-minute drive from the city center along the M9 Volokolamskoye Highway (by the 31 kilometer marker) or by train from Moscow's Rizhsky Railway Station. Designed by renowned California golf architect Robert Trent Jones II, the course is rated as one of the top ten golf courses in Europe and has an 18-hole, 6,735-meter (7,000-plus-yard) par-72 championship course. The club is owned by GlavUpDK, Russia's Diplomatic Service Administration, and managed by Le Meridien Hotels. tel. 926-5927.

The golf course construction began in 1987, and took over six years to complete. The first Russian Golf Association was established in 1992. A year later, Moscow held its first Golf Open Championship at Nahabino; the first winner in Russian history was American Steve Schroeder. In September 1996, the club hosted Russia's first international golf tournament as part of the PGA European Challenge Tour, with 100 tour-ranked members, including 20 professionals from 26 countries; ten of the participants were Russian, playing for the first time on home soil.

It took over two decades to negotiate and build Russia's first golf course. The first joint venture planning began in 1974 between Robert Trent Jones Senior and Junior, Armand Hammer and GlavUpDK. Many interruptions (some serious, others wildly amusing) occurred during periods of the Brezhnev stagnation and Afghanistan War.

The golf course was designed to be a very traditional parkland course. From the back tees, it has sufficient length and difficulty to host any type of championship tournament. The deep Russian forest with large evergreens, birch and native wildlife and song birds is a magnificent setting. The concept is classic strategy with hazards placed to create risks and rewards and exciting, enjoyable golf for beginners and proficient golfers of all ages and abilities.

Robert Trent Jones, Jr.

When Trent Jones II submitted some of his first course plans to the US Commerce Department (a mandatory requirement when doing business in Russia at the time), the US Defense Department wanted to immediately halt the progress when they noticed that 'bunkers' had been incorporated into the design! (Later, while building the course in Moscow, Jones' employees actually came across foxholes, dug during World War II as protection against invading Germans.) Russia has come a long way—no golf terminology existed in their language: 'Fore' started out as *Ostarozhno* or 'Look Out!' Today the Reds on the greens now make up over one-tenth of club members and many Russian children come out as part of school curriculums to practice their golf swing. There are also numerous junior and amateur tournaments.

On the grounds, there is also a driving range, practice greens, and a clubhouse with an extensive restaurant menu and full bar service, and pro-shop, complete with locker room facilities and a computerized golf simulator. The club has a hotel complex and conference center, a multi-million dollar spa and sports club which provides an indoor pool, tennis, squash, basketball, gymnasium, aerobics and fitness training, plus a health spa and beauty salon. Outside, there is also a lakeside beach area, water sports, boating and fishing. Individual luxury homes, modeled on 18th-century wooden dachas, are arranged around a central garden area. In colder months one can try cross-country skiing, snowmobiling, and winter golf.

The 5-star Le Meridien Hotel (with four restaurants and bars) is open year-round to tourists. In Moscow tel. 926-5911, fax 926-5921 for reservations; website www.mcc.co.ru. Spa and golf facilities are available for nonmembers. Daily *elektrichka* trains run to Nahabino from Rizhsky station.

PEREDELKINO (Переделкино)

Take an *elektrichka* train from Moscow's Kievsky Railway Station for the half-hour ride southwest to Peredelkino in the Solntsevo district. From the station, either take a bus to the end of Pavelyenko Street, or walk 20 minutes to the village. (If driving, take the Mozhaiskoye Highway to the Minskoye Highway and at the 21 kilometer signpost, turn left for Peredelkino.) For decades the Soviet Government granted the Writers' Union land in this area to build resident dachas for their members. Peredelkino became a name synonymous with a writers' and artists' colony. Even Anna Akhmatova and Alexander Solzhenitsyn lived here at one time; the latter lived in a spare room of a writer friend after he had smuggled out *The Gulag Archipelago* to the West. Here you can also visit the estate and grave of the great Russian writer and Nobel laureate Boris Pasternak, who wrote *Dr Zhivago*. (For this novel the disillusioned writer was expelled from the Writers' Union and forced to decline his 1958 Nobel prize.) In 1960, Pasternak died at his dacha, now the **Pasternak House Museum**. (Open 10am–4pm; closed Mondays, Tuesdays and Wednesdays.)

Pasternak wrote of Moscow:

> *For the dreamer and the night-bird*
> *Moscow is dearer than all else in the world.*
> *It is at the hearth, the source*
> *Of everything that the century will live for.*

Above the railway station stands the 15th-century **Church of the Transfiguration**, whose interior is decorated with a multitude of saints and a fine iconostasis. Following the path to the left of the church brings you to Pasternak's grave (the headstone bears his profile), bordered by three pines and usually covered with flowers. Other prominent writers are also buried in the cemetery. It is a lovely place to stroll through the countryside; bring a picnic. Nordic skiing and ice fishing are also possible in winter months.

Near the railway station, at 2a Pervaya Chubotovskaya Alley, and housed in what was formerly Brezhnev's daughter's dacha, is the ten-room **Villa Peredelkino Hotel** (tel. 435-8184/1478) **and Restaurant** serving Italian food (tel. 435-1478), open 12pm–midnight (last train to Moscow is at 12.30am). **Setun Restaurant**, at 1 Pervaya Chubotovskaya, also has Russian food. Open 12–11pm; tel. 439-0429.

TSARITSYNO (Царицыно)

Tsaritsyno Estate lies 21 kilometers (13 miles) south of Moscow at 1 Dolskaya Street. To get here, drive via the Kashirskoye Highway or take the Zamoskvoretskaya Liniya to Orekhovo Metro station. (Note the line splits at Kashirskaya. If coming from the city center, make sure the destination posted on the front of the train reads Krasnogvardeiskaya/Promzona, not Kakhovskaya.) Once there, head west towards the park.

In the 16th-century Irina, wife of Czar Fyodor Ioannovich, lived at her country estate here and had the Tsaritsyno (Czarina) ponds dug. Later it was the favorite of the Golitsyn princes; in 1712, Peter the Great presented the estate to a Moldavian count.

After Catherine the Great remodeled the Winter Palace and Hermitage in St Petersburg, she turned her attention to Moscow. In 1775, she bought the estate in the wooded countryside south of Moscow, complete with a palace and miniature opera house. It was known as Chornaya Gryaz (Black Mud); Catherine renamed it Tsaritsyno. Her architect Vasily Bazhenov was commissioned to transform the main building into a Moorish-Gothic-style palace, and the 6,200 acres into English-style formal gardens. After ten years of work, Catherine came down from St Petersburg to inspect it. She commanded that all work be stopped and the main palace torn down. In 1786, Bazhenov's pupil and main rival, Matvei Kazakov, was asked to redesign the property; these are the buildings we see today. Some speculate that Catherine had the original palace torn down because she had had it constructed in two parts—one for herself and one for her son Paul—connected by a common corridor. After a decade, however, she had come to abhor her son, who held equal contempt for her, so she no longer wanted anything to do with him. She also came to dislike the Freemasons and hated all freemasonry motifs. The rebuilding was halted at the resumption of the Turkish wars and stopped altogether upon her death in 1796.

Intended as the main entrance to the palace, the **Figurny Bridge** (with stone Maltese crosses—motifs of the Freemasons) separates Tsaritsyno's two lakes. The main building, through the **Grapevine Entrance** gates, looks more like a cathedral than a palace. Its windows are broken and the roof is crumbling—in the 19th century, a local factory needed roofing materials and raided the roof. At one time it was also used for mountaineering training, and crampon holes can still be seen in the walls. The **Palace** has never been lived in and has stood empty for more than two centuries.

The palace is bordered by the **Bakery** (Khlebny Dom) and, on the other side, by the **Small Palace** (Maly Dvoretz). Next door is the restored **Opera House** with a small exhibit of porcelain, sculptures and paintings; musical concerts are also held here. The path in front of the palace leads to the octagonal **Octahedron** and the **Church**, originally constructed in 1765. The strange deserted buildings are fun to explore, and strolling around the grounds is delightful; bring a picnic. (There is talk of restoration and plans for the buildings to house a gallery of modern art.) Boats are available for hire in summer. In winter it is fun to ice-skate, sled or cross-country ski in the area (you need to bring your own equipment).

In 1988, the Russian Church was allowed to build a church in the town of Tsaritsyno to commemorate the Millennium of the Baptism of Rus; it was the first church allowed to be built in Moscow during the Soviet era. The **Museum of History, Architecture, Art and Nature** is open 11am–5pm; weekends 11am–6pm; closed Mondays and Tuesdays and the last Wednesday of the month. To check times and information, tel. 321-6366. Concerts are usually held on Saturday and Sunday, tel. 325 4844.

To dine try the **Usadba (Country Estate)** at 10 Polskaya Ulitsa, with live evening music. It is located in an elegant old mansion built by Catherine the Great, open daily noon–midnight (tel. 343-3837). Metro Orekhovo. Nearby, at 47 Shipilovsky, is the three-star **Hotel Tsaritsino**, with luxury apartments, restaurant and bar (tel. 343-4343/45; fax. 343-4363; www.all-hotels.ru/moscow/tsaritsino).

YASNAYA POLYANA (Ясная Поляна)

The town lies some 200 kilometers (125 miles) south of Moscow along the M2 Simferopolskoye Highway (about a three-hour drive). A high-speed train now runs between Moscow and Tula that leaves daily at 5:27pm and arrives at 8pm. A train returns to Moscow at 7:19am. Other long-distance (three hours) and surburban (over four hours) trains also depart Moscow's Kursky Station for Tula. From the Tula station, take bus number 114 on Lenin Prospekt, marked Shchyokino, for the 14-kilometer drive south. From the Yasnaya Polyana stop, it's a one kilometer walk

THE CONQUEROR

*A*t ten in the morning of the second of September, Napoleon was standing among his troops on the Poklonny Hill looking at the panorama spread out before him. From the twenty-sixth of August to the second of September, that is from the battle of Borodino to the entry of the French into Moscow, during the whole of that agitating, memorable week, there had been the extraordinary autumn weather that always comes as a surprise, when the sun hangs low and gives more heat than in spring, when everything shines so brightly in the rare clear atmosphere that the eyes smart, when the lungs are strengthened and refreshed by inhaling the aromatic autumn air, when even the nights are warm, and when in those dark warm nights, golden stars startle and delight us continually by falling from the sky.

The view of the strange city with its peculiar architecture, such as he had never seen before, filled Napoleon with the rather envious and uneasy curiosity men feel when they see an alien form of life. By the indefinite signs which, even at a distance, distinguish a living body from a dead one, Napoleon from the Poklonny Hill perceived the throb of life in the town and felt, as it were, the breathing of that great and beautiful body.

Every Russian looking at Moscow feels her to be mother; every foreigner who sees her, even if ignorant of her significance as the mother city, must feel her feminine character, and Napoleon felt it.

"A town captured by the enemy is like a maid who has lost her honor," thought he, and from that point of view he gazed at the oriental beauty he had not seen before. It seemed strange to him that his long-felt wish, which had seemed unattainable, had at last been realized. In the clear morning light he gazed now at the city and now at the plan, considering its details, and the assurance of possessing it agitated and awed him.

Leo Tolstoy, War and Peace, *1869*

(or taxi ride) west to the estate. Daily buses also run to Tula from Moscow's Shchyolkovsky bus station (next to Metro Shchyolkovskaya), in the northeast part of the city. A group excursion can also be booked in Moscow. The **Moska Hotel** stands right outside the Tula train station at Moskovskaya Vokzala Square tel. (487) 208-952/295-780.

The great Russian writer, Count Lev (Leo) Nikolayevich Tolstoy, was born in Yasnaya Polyana (Clear Glade) on August 28, 1828, and lived and worked here for over 60 years; he inherited the property in 1847. Everything on the estate, situated in a pastoral setting of birch forests and orchards, has been preserved as he left it— his living room (Tolstoy was born on the leather sofa), library (with 22,000 volumes), and parlor (where his wife Sofya Andreyevna meticulously copied his manuscripts). On the Persian walnut desk in the study, Tolstoy wrote *War and Peace* (1863–69; Sofya claimed to have copied the entire manuscript —more than 3000 pages—seven times, when not busy bearing his 13 children!) and *Anna Karenina* (1873–77), and chapters of *The Resurrection*. Portraits by Ilya Repin and Valentin Serov decorate the walls. Today the manor house functions as the **Tolstoy House Museum**. The writer also opened a school for local peasant children, and this now houses the **Literary Museum**. Peasants and other followers would gather outside under the Tree of the Poor to ask his advice.

The 445-hectare (1,100-acre) Yasnaya Polyana was the main source of creative inspiration for Tolstoy, and the location is reflected in many of his works. Here he wanted to create a miniature of Russian society. Tolstoy also developed a philosophy of Christianity so potent that the Russian Church excommunicated him. He also became a vegetarian, enjoyed wearing simple peasant attire and worked in the fields alongside his serfs. Tolstoy wrote: 'It is difficult for me to imagine Russia without my Yasnaya Polyana.' On October 28, 1910, at the age of 82, Tolstoy decided to renounce all his possessions and left the estate with his youngest daughter, Alexandra and his doctor to embark on a journey. When they arrived at Astapovo Railway Station almost 320 kilometers (200 miles) away, Tolstoy was stricken with influenza. The great writer died in the station master's hut on November 7; his last words were said to be: 'Search, always go on searching...'

Three years after the death of his mother, when Lev was 5, his 10-year-old brother, Nikolai, proudly created the Ant Brotherhood and claimed to have discovered "the way for all men to... become continuously happy." Nikolai said that he wrote the answer to the secret of garnering earthly happiness on a green stick, which he buried at the edge of a gorge on the family estate. Tolstoy spent much of his life searching for the secret of happiness for all mankind. Upon his death, in accordance with his wishes, he was buried at the spot where his brother had assured him

The great Russian writer Count Leo Tolstoy was born at Yasnaya Polyana, south of Moscow, in 1828. He inherited the estate in 1847 and lived and worked here for more than 60 years. Today this 19th-century estate is known as the Leo Tolstoy Museum where everything of the writer's has been preserved, including the 22,000 tome library and study. (see www.yasnayapolana.ru)

At the Persian walnut desk, inherited from his father, Tolstoy penned his novels Anna Karenina and War and Peace (see Literary Excerpt on page 233).

contained the green stick. A short walk down a well-worn path leads to Tolstoy's simple grave-a small mound of earth with no headstone. Tolstoy's wife, and then his daughters, managed the estate until 1956, when it was placed under Soviet control. Today, Tolstoy's great-great grandson Count Vladimir Tolstoy (over 200 relatives are scattered around six countries) presides over the daily management. In the future he wants to develop a 'living 19th-century estate,' complete with a hotel tourist complex. Yasnaya Polyana is open 10am–5pm (House Museum 11am–3pm); Russian and foreign language tours are usually given between 10am and 2pm. The estate is closed Mondays and Tuesdays, and the last Wednesday of the month, tel. (487) 339-832. Excursion service (487) 339-118. Special one- or two day group itineraries around Tula area (487) 393-599.

In Moscow you can also visit two other Tolstoy Museums (see pages 168 and 217). Also note the Tolstoy reading list in the Recommended Reading Section.

ZAVIDOVO (Завидово)

At the confluence of the Volga and Shoshka rivers, 120 kilometers (74 miles) northwest of Moscow (off the M10 Highway north of Klin), is the resort village of Zavidovo. It is managed by Russian firm GlavUpDK (who own the Moscow Country Club and the prestigious apartment/office complex Park Place in southwest Moscow). The year-round moderately priced resort has hotel and cottage accommodation, a health spa, swimming pool and shooting range. Sports include tennis, squash, horse riding, windsurfing, water skiing and other water activities. In winter there is even skiing, skating and ice fishing. Hunting and fishing excursions are also available and a golf course is currently under construction. For information in Moscow tel. 937-9955/9944`; website www.zavidovo.ru. From here an excursion to nearby Klin can easily be made.

Thirty kilometers further north along the Volga from Zavidovo is the city of **Tver**, (formerly Kalinin), once one of Moscow's chief rivals in earlier centuries. Since it was on the Moscow–St Petersburg road, Catherine the Great popularized the destination by resting here on route. With many museums, old churches and markets, Tver is another interesting area to explore on a day trip from Zavidovo or Klin. Trains leave from Moscow's Leningradsky Station and take two to three hours. From Tver, there are daily trains to St Petersburg and buses to Novgorod.

ZVENIGOROD (Звенигород)

Zvenigorod lies about 55 kilometers (33 miles) west of Moscow along the M1/A105/A107 routes. *Elektrichka* trains also run from Moscow's Byelorussky Railway Station and take about an hour. (Buy your ticket at entrance 2, marked Prigorodniye—you will need it to enter and exit the train station. Departure times are posted on boards inside the ticket hall.) At Zvenigorod, bus 23 runs to the museum complex.

Zvenigord, founded in 1339, later became the powerful religious center of Czar Alexei, father of Peter the Great. Today, the picturesque town, situated on a hill that overlooks the Moscow River, is known as Moscow's Switzerland. The operating monastery contains numerous old churches and buildings, many of which are historical museums.

Zvenigorod, standing atop a hill that overlooks the Moskva River and founded in 1339, is known as Moscow's Switzerland. The heart of the town, known as "Gurodok" (citadel) is a former earthen fortress. Up in the hills stands the 14th-century single-domed **Cathedral of the Assumption**, built by the son of Dmitri

Donskoi; morning services are usually held here. The monk Savva, a disciple of St Sergius, began construction on the **Monastery of Savva-Storozhevsky** in the 14th century. It became the favorite religious retreat of Czar Alexei in the mid-17th century; his white palace is situated across from the cathedral's porch. Over the centuries the monastery grew to one of the richest and most powerful in Russia. Monks led a local revolution against the Bolsheviks in 1918; but a year later the monastery was shut down by the new government. The monastery has now been returned to the Orthodox Church.

The 15th-century **Cathedral of the Nativity**, decorated with *kokoshniki* and stone carvings, is open for religious services. The interior iconostasis towers from floor to ceiling. Next to the multi-tiered bell tower (which you can climb) is the **Transfiguration Church**. The 17th-century **Trinity Church** is nearby with the attached Kazan Refectory. It was here that one of Russia's greatest film directors, Andrei Tarkovsky, staged much of his classic film on the life of the famous icon painter Andrei Rublyov, whose icons were discovered within the church in 1918 (These include the "Savior", "Apostle Paul" and "Archangel Michael", now exhibited in Moscow's Tretyakov monastery). Lining the left-hand wall of the fortress is the red and white **Czaritsa's Chambers**, used by the Polish wife of Czar Alexei. On the outside porch, notice the carved double- and single-headed eagles, emblems of Russian and Polish rulers. The **History Museum** is now located within the chambers, and another museum, exhibiting paintings, ceramics and wood carvings by local contemporary artists, is in the nearby two-story monks' quarters. Museums are open 10am–5pm; closed Mondays and the last Friday of the month; tel. 592-9464.

In summer, bring food from Moscow to picnic by the river and have a swim. Take a stroll through the Old Town (uphill from the center), and get swept back a century as you pass old wooden dachas, intricately carved and colorfully painted. In 1884, the writer and physician Anton Chekhov worked in a hospital here and later wrote the story *Ward 6* about a doctor who goes mad. During the Soviet era, KGB and military officers kept summer homes here and frequented the nearby health resort.

Hotels in town are inexpensive. There is the Hotel Zvenigorod on Lermontov Street, tel. (095) 338-4124, and the Izobretatel on Oktyabrskaya, tel. (095) 597-1072. Outside of town is the three-star Pokrovskoye Hotel, tel. (095) 592-9312.

*An early 19th-century view of the Moscow Kremlin from the Stone Bridge;
this scene is exhibited in Moscow's State Historical Museum.*

THE OLD ARISTOCRACY

W*ealth was measured in those times by the number of "souls" which a landed proprietor owned. So many "souls" meant so many male serfs: women did not count. My father, who owned nearly twelve hundred souls, in three different provinces, and who had, in addition to his peasants' holdings, large tracts of land which were cultivated by these peasants, was accounted a rich man. He lived up to his reputation, which meant that his house was open to any number of visitors, and that he kept a very large household.*

We were a family of eight, occasionally ten or twelve; but fifty servants at Moscow, and half as many more in the country, were considered not one too many. Four coachmen to attend a dozen horses, three cooks for the masters and two more for the servants, a dozen men to wait upon us at dinner-time (one man, plate in hand, standing behind each person seated at the table), and girls innumerable in the maid-servants' room—how could anyone do with less than this?

Besides, the ambition of every landed proprietor was that everything required for his household should be made at home by his own men.

"How nicely your piano is always tuned! I suppose Herr Schimmel must be your tuner?" perhaps a visitor would remark.

To be able to answer, "I have my own piano-tuner," was in those times the correct thing.

"What a beautiful pastry!" the guests would exclaim, when a work of art, composed of ices and pastry, appeared toward the end of the dinner. "Confess, prince, that it comes from Tremblé" (the fashionable pastry cook).

"It is by my own confectioner, a pupil of Tremblé, whom I have allowed to show what he can do," was a reply which elicited general admiration.

As soon as the children of the servants attained the age of ten, they were sent as apprentices to the fashionable shops, where they were obliged to spend five or seven years chiefly in sweeping, in receiving an incredible number of thrashings, and in running about town on errands of all sorts. I must own that few of them became masters of their respective arts. The tailors and the shoemakers were found only skillful enough to make clothes or shoes for the servants, and when a really good pastry was required for a dinner-party it was ordered at Tremblé's, while our own confectioner was beating the drum in the music band.

That band was another of my father's ambitions, and almost every one of his male servants, in addition to other accomplishments, was a bass-viol or a clarinet in the band. Makar, the piano-tuner, alias under-butler, was also a flautist; Andrei, the tailor, played the French horn; the confectioner was first put to beat the drum, but misused his instrument to such a deafening degree that a tremendous trumpet was bought for him, in the hope that his lungs would not have the power to make the same noise as his hands; when, however, this last hope had to be abandoned, he was set to be a soldier. As to "spotted Tikhon", in addition to his numerous functions in the household as lamp-cleaner, floor-polisher, and footman, he made himself useful in the band—today as trombone, tomorrow as bassoon, and occasionally as second violin...

Dancing-parties were not infrequent, to say nothing of obligatory balls every winter. Father's way, in such cases, was to have everything done in good style, whatever the expense. But at the same time such niggardliness was practised in our house in daily life that if I were to recount it, I should be accused of exaggeration. However, in the Old Equerries' Quarter such a mode of life only raised my father in public esteem. "The old prince," it was said, "seems to be sharp over money at home; but knows how a nobleman ought to live."

Prince Peter Kropotkin, Memoirs of a Revolutionist, *1899*

THE GOLDEN RING (ZOLOTOYE KOLTSO)

The ancient towns of the Golden Ring, built between the 11th and 17th centuries, are the cradle of Russian culture. During Russia's early history, the two most important cities were Kiev in the south and Novgorod in the north. They were both situated in what is now western Russia and lay along important commerce routes to the Black and Baltic seas. The settlements that sprang up along the trade routes between these two cities prospered and grew into large towns of major political and religious importance. From the 11th to 15th centuries, the towns of Rostov, Yaroslavl, Vladimir and Suzdal became capitals of the northern principalities, and Sergiyev Posad served as the center of Russian Orthodoxy. In the 12th-century Moscow was established as a small protective outpost of the Rostov-Suzdal principality. By the 16th century Moscow had grown so big and affluent that it was named the capital of the Russian Empire. These prominent towns that lay in a circle to the northeast of Moscow became known as the Golden Ring. Each town is a living chronicle documenting many centuries in the history of old Russia.

THE RUSSIAN TOWN

Up to the end of the 18th century, a typical Russian town consisted of a kremlin, a protective fortress surrounding the site. Watchtowers were built in strategic points along the kremlin wall and contained vaulted carriageways, which served as the gates to the city. The timber town within the kremlin contained the governmental and administrative offices. The boyars, or noble class, had homes here too that were used only in time of war—otherwise they lived outside the town on their own country estates, where the peasants or serfs worked the land. The *posad* (earth town) was the settlement of traders and craftsmen. The *posad* also contained the *rinoks*—the markets and bazaars, as well as the storage houses for the town. The merchants and boyars used their wealth to help build the churches and commissioned artists to paint elaborate frescoes and icons. The number of churches and monasteries mirrored the prosperity of the town. The rest of the townspeople lived in settlements known as the *slobody* around the kremlin. The historical nucleus and heart of the town was known as the *strelka*. The regions were separated into principalities with their own governing princes. The ruler of the united principalities was known as the grand prince and later czar. The head of the Orthodox Church was called the metropolitan or patriarch.

The Golden Ring area provides an excellent opportunity to view typical old Russian towns, which are still surrounded by ancient kremlins, churches and monasteries. The towns of Rostov, Vladimir, Suzdal and Pereslavl-Zalessky retain much of their original layouts. Outside Suzdal and Kostroma are open-air architectural museums—entire wooden villages built to typify old Russian life. All the towns of the Golden Ring have been well-restored, and many of the buildings are now museums that trace the history of the area that was the center of the Golden Age of Rus.

RELIGION AND THE CHURCH

Before Prince Vladimir introduced Byzantine Christianity to the Kievan principality in AD 988, Russia was a pagan state; the people of Rus worshipped numerous gods. Festivals were held according to the seasons, planting and harvest cycles, and life passages. Special offerings of eggs, wheat and honey were presented to the gods of water, soil and sun. Carved figures of mermaids and suns adorned the roofs of houses. When Prince Vladimir married the sister of the Byzantine Emperor and introduced Christianity, Russia was finally united under one God and Kiev became the center of the Orthodox Church. (According to the Primary Chronicle—the first recorded history of Kievan Rus, written by monks in the eleventh century—emissaries of Vladimir's, whom he had dispersed on a fact-finding mission to locate the 'true faith', were so enamoured with the capital of Byzantium that they exclaimed, "We knew not whether we were in heaven or on earth, for surely there is no such splendor or beauty anywhere else".) But it took almost a century to convert the many pagan areas, especially in the north. Early church architecture (11th-century) was based on the Byzantine cube-shaped building with one low rounded cupola on the roof bearing an Orthodox cross facing east. The domes gradually evolved into helmet drums on tent-shaped roofs. In the 17th century Patriarch Nikon banned the tent-shaped roof because it appeared too similar to the design of Western Lutheran churches. Thus the onion-shaped dome (also more suitable for the heavy snowfalls) became the distinctive design of the Orthodox Church. Nikon also decreed the assembly of five domes (instead of the usual one); the central higher dome symbolized 'the seat of the Lord', while the four lower ones, the four evangelists. The next two centuries witnessed classical and baroque influences, and the onion domes became much more elaborately shaped and decorated. During your tour of the Golden Ring, try dating the churches by the shapes of their domes.

The outer walls of churches were divided into three sections by protruding vertical strips, which indicated the position of the piers inside. A few centuries later churches expanded considerably and were built from white stone or brick instead of wood. (Unfortunately, many of the wooden buildings did not survive and stone churches were built on their original sites.) The main body of the church was tiered into different levels and adjoined by chapels, galleries and porches. A large tent-shaped bell tower usually dominated one side.

With the new era of religious freedom, many artists practice the trade of fresco restoration and also paint religious art for the many new churches now under construction.

During the two and a half centuries of Mongol occupation (beginning in the mid-13th century), Russia was cut off from any outside influence. Monasteries united the Russian people and acted as shelters and fortresses against attacks. They became the educational centers and housed the historical manuscripts, which monks wrote on birch-bark parchment. During this period Russian church architecture developed a unique style. Some distinctive features were the decorative *zakomara*, semicircular arches, that lined the tops of the outer walls where they joined the roof (see picture on page 205). The *trapeza* porch was built outside the western entrance of the church and other carved designs were copied from the decorations on peasant houses. Elaborate carved gables around doors, windows and archways were called *kokoshniki*, named after the large headdresses worn by young married women. Through the years, even though the architecture took on European classical, Gothic and baroque elements, the designs always retained a distinctive Russian flair. Each entrance of the kremlin had its own Gate Church. The most elaborate stood by the Holy Gates, the main entrance to the town. Many cathedrals took years to build and twin churches were also a common sight—one was used in winter and the other, more elaborate, for summer services and festivals.

The interior of the church was highly decorated with frescoes. Images of Christ were painted inside the central dome, surrounded by angels. Beneath the dome came the pictures of saints, apostles and prophets. Images of the patron saint of the church might appear on the pillars. Special religious scenes and the earthly life of Christ or the Virgin Mary were depicted on the walls and vaults. The Transfiguration was usually painted on the east wall by the altar and scenes from the Last Judgment and Old Testament were illustrated on the west wall, where people would exit the church. The iconostasis was an elaborate tiered structure, filled with icons, that stretched behind the altar from the floor toward the ceiling. The top tiers held Christ, the middle the saints and prophets, and the lower tiers were reserved for scenes from church history.

Fresco painting was a highly respected skill and many master craftsmen, such as Andrei Rublyov and Daniil Chorny, produced beautiful works of art. The plaster was applied to the wall of the church and then the artists would sketch the main outline of the fresco right onto the damp plaster. The master supervised the work and filled in the more intricate and important parts of the composition, while the apprentices added the background detail.

The building of elaborate churches and painting of exquisite icons and frescoes reached its zenith in the prosperous towns of the Golden Ring. Even cathedrals in the Moscow Kremlin were copied from church designs that originated in Rostov, Vladimir and Suzdal. Today these churches and works of art stand as monuments to an extraordinary era of Russian history.

RELIGION AFTER THE REVOLUTION

For nearly 1,000 years the Russian Orthodox Church dominated the life of Russia and, as Tolstoy observed, for most of the Russian people 'faith was the force of life'. But after the 1917 Revolution, when Marx proclaimed that 'religion is the opium of the masses', all churches were closed to religious use and their property confiscated and redistributed by the government—even though Article 124 of the Soviet Constitution stated that 'Church is separate from State' and provided 'freedom of worship for all citizens'. (Trotsky also scathingly condemned the superstitious, backward Russia of "icons and cockroaches.") Before the Revolution, Russia had almost 100,000 churches and monasteries; Moscow alone had more than 500. By the time of the purges in the 1930s, the capital had lost over a third of its glorious churches, and less than 100 still functioned officially in the entire Soviet Union. Churches were turned into swimming pools, ice-skating rinks, and atheist museums. Moscow's Danilovsky Monastery was used as a prison. The Church of St Nicholas became a gas station.

In 1988, the Millennium of Russian Christianity was officially celebrated throughout the former Soviet Union, and government decrees provided a new legal status for the Orthodox Church and other religions. The Russian Orthodox Church remained headed by the patriarch and assisted by the Holy Synod, whose seats are in Sergiyev Posad and Moscow respectively. But the government continued to control and dictate the moves of the Church, while the topic of religion was discussed in meetings of the Supreme Soviet. Positive signs of increased religious tolerance and freedom slowly emerged and a small number of churches were eventually given back for religious use.

During the period of perestroika, the process of renewal of Soviet society brought about major changes in the relations between Church and State and believers and nonbelievers. On April 29, 1988, the eve of the Millennium of Russian Orthodoxy, Gorbachev received the Patriarch of Moscow and All Russia and members of the Synod in the Yekaterinsky Hall in the Kremlin. Gorbachev stated: 'Believers are Soviet people; they are workers and patriots and they have a full right to adequately express their convictions. The reforms of perestroika and glasnost concern them also without any limitations.' On October 13, 1989, a Thanksgiving Service was held in the Kremlin's Assumption Cathedral, the first service to take place there in 71 years. The last Mass held there had been at Easter in 1918. The government also returned the Danilovsky Monastery which became the seat of the Orthodox Church in Moscow. In 1988 alone some 900 buildings were returned to the Church, and religious figures were even elected to the Congress of Peoples' Deputies. On December 1, 1989, Gorbachev became the first Soviet leader to set foot in the Vatican.

One well-respected St Petersburg rector of the Orthodox Church and city seminary (who was allowed to visit Rome for an audience with the Pope during perestroika) remarked, 'I am an optimist. People are not only interested in bettering themselves economically, but also morally and spiritually. The powers of the Communist State could never extend to the soul. And in these uncertain times, we would like to help the new generation find its way.'

Since the collapse of the Soviet Union, the Patriarch of All Russia is now the head of the Russian Orthodox Church and the Church is separate from the State. Since the establishment of Christianity in Russia, the form of Church leadership has changed several times. From AD 988 until 1589, the Church was headed by a metropolitan and from 1589 until 1721, by a patriarch. Peter the Great then dissolved the seat of patriarch and created a governing Church body known as the Holy Synod, a group of 11 of the highest-ranking priests. In November 1917, the Bolshevik government decided to restore the patriarchate; that is, leadership by one supreme individual rather than by a collective body.

In 1992, Boris Yeltsin became the first Russian leader since the 1917 Bolshevik Revolution to attend Easter ceremonies in an Orthodox Church. Yeltsin, who was baptized, told Patriarch Alexei, 'It is time for Russia to return to her strong religious heritage.' On November 4, 1993, Yeltsin attended the consecration of the newly restored Kazan Cathedral in Red Square. During the stand-off siege of 1993 in the White House, the patriarch was called in to help arbitrate between the hard-liners and Yeltsin. Another battle was also being waged: to determine whether the government, museums or the Church owned the religious art. In 1993, Yeltsin signed orders to transfer two famous icons by Andrei Rublyov in the Tretyakov Gallery to the Orthodox Church.

After the fall of the Soviet Union more than 10,000 churches were reopened for religious activities. Today the Orthodox Church claims 80 million followers, or more than half of Russia's population (another 40 percent are indifferent to religion and five percent are committed atheists). St Petersburg has over 30 places of worship and Moscow supports over 130 active churches. More people, especially the younger generation, are attending religious services and being baptized. Ever since the 11th-century Orthodox Russians have worshiped in the same way. There are no pews, and the congregation remains standing throughout the long service. The priest, bedecked in heavy embroidered vestments while gently swinging incense censers, leads the worshippers through the familiar liturgy. Theological seminaries are training monks and priests, and Church charity organizations are now permitted to help the new classes of homeless, poor and unemployed. The Russian Orthodox Church has also embraced the capitalist spirit. Many churches have their own shops, and priests are earning money by blessing businesses and apartments, even cars, bars and casinos.

With Moscow's new 360-million-dollar Cathedral of Christ Our Savior (rebuilt on the spot where Stalin destroyed the old one), the Orthodox Church and its patriarch find themselves back at the apogee of political power in the new Russia. During the presidency of Boris Yeltsin a strong partnership, which had not existed for centuries, was formed between the Orthodox Church and the Russian State. While State officials attended Christmas and Easter services, the patriarch was invited to the Kremlin to attend secular ceremonies and treaty signings.

In 1997, to fully cement its dominance, the Orthodox Church sponsored a bill in an attempt to restrict all other faiths in the country. Patriarch Alexei II commented: 'A law on religion is needed to protect Russians from destructive pseudo-religious cults, and foreign false missionaries.' (Ironically, the bill was supported by the Communists.) On September 26, 1997, Yeltsin signed the Freedom of Conscience and Religious Association Acts, which state that only those churches that collaborated with the regime during 1917–91 are recognized by the Russian Government; others may still pray and worship, but only in their homes. (Any religious denomination that had failed to secure a new registration was effectively banned from practicing in Russia.) Many consider that this new State supervision of religion in Russia is directed as much at internal as well as external enemies of the Russian Orthodox Church. Others cannot miss the irony that the Church, appearing more intent at gaining political power than promoting faith, is not much better than Stalin's old government which conducted devastating campaigns of persecution against Christians and other religions. Today, clashes continue between post-Soviet Church conservatives, members of other religious groups and State reformists. In 2003 a Russian Orthodox priest was defrocked for marrying two men in the Church's first gay marriage.

Also in 1997, the Council of Archbishops of the Russian Orthodox Church bestowed sainthood on metropolitans Pyotr and Sarafim, and Archbishop Faddei, who were all subjected to repression by Stalin in 1937. Even though an official St Petersburg burial was permitted for the last czar Nicholas II and his family (in July 1998), the Chairman of the Holy Synod refrained from canonizing them. In July, 1998, an official St Petersburg burial was permitted for the last czar, Nicholas II, and his family. In 2000, Nicholas and Alexandra were beatified by the Church.

A monk stops to chat with a member of his congregation in front of the Assumption Cathedral in Sergiyev Posad, one of the major centers of the Russian Orthodox Church.

Today, even after all the transitions, most religious groups are enjoying a new period of openness. There are one and a half million officially registered Jews (given as their nationality), four million Roman Catholics, five million Uniates (Catholics of Eastern Rite), 800 Protestant congregations, over one million Baptists and two million Lutherans. An estimated 20 million persons are of the Islamic faith, or about one in seven Russians. There are also half a million Buddhists and about one million Old Believers, a sect resulting from the 1666 schism of the Orthodox Church. The current Patriarch of the Orthodox Church, Alexei II, observes that 'religion in Russia is enjoying a renaissance; more than 13,000 churches have been built or rebuilt in the last ten years alone.' No matter what ecclesiastical precedences are established, it is well worth recognizing that as Russia heads into the 21st century, such religious tolerance within her lands has not been known since the era of Peter the Great.

GETTING THERE

Many travel organizations (both international and local) offer package tours specifically to Golden Ring destinations that also include stops in Moscow and St Petersburg. Once you are in Russia, a hotel service desk or local agency can also suggest excursions along the Golden Ring route. (See Travel Agencies and Tour Companies in Moscow Practical Information section, page 411.) Some places, like Sergiyev Posad or Alexandrov, can be visited as a day trip from Moscow.

The Golden Ring area is easily accessible to the independent traveler by car, train or bus, though planning and patience is needed. Pre-plan an itinerary by finding out the best routes to each location. Try renting a car and driver, or bargain with a taxi or owner of a private car. If not journeying by car, check train and bus schedules in advance (trains depart from different Moscow stations). The easiest and most expensive way to the nearest towns, such as Sergiyev Posad and Alexandrov, is by taking an *elektrichka* commuter train (with no reserved seats) from Moscow's Yaroslavsky Station. (Dress warmly in winter as many of these trains are not heated.) Regular train routes have daily departures to the larger regions like Vladimir and Yaroslavl. Long-distance buses to most Golden Ring areas also run from Moscow's northeast Shchyolkovsky Station. The best way is to spend several days on the road and combine a few towns during the tour. It is always better to go during weekdays, when trains and towns are less crowded, especially in summer. Today, many more restaurants and supermarkets have opened, so it is no longer as difficult to find a meal. But it is always a good idea to bring along some snacks. Even Internet cafés have popped up in many of the larger towns. A more detailed description on how to get to each Golden Ring location and where to stay is provided under each individual listing. Check out the websites www.all-hotels.ru

and www.waytorussia.net for updated hotel listings in Golden Ring areas. Prices of hotels range from inexpensive to moderate and most still do not accept credit cards. The towns of the Golden Ring are a majestic mirror of Russia's past grandeur. The churches and monasteries are beautifully preserved and their frescoes and icons have been painstakingly restored. Many of the churches hold religious services, which you are welcome to attend. (Do not wear shorts or sleeveless shirts; men should remove hats.) Other religious buildings have been converted into museums that house the art and historical artifacts of the region.

A splendid skyline of golden-domed churches, tent-shaped towers, ornamental belfries, picturesque old wooden buildings and rolling countryside dotted with birch trees greets you—as it did the visitor more than seven centuries ago.

SERGIYEV POSAD Сергиев Посад
CENTER OF RUSSIAN ORTHODOXY

A 75-kilometer (46-mile) ride northeast of Moscow leads to Sergiyev Posad, the most popular town on the Golden Ring route. As soon as the road leaves Moscow, it winds back in time through dense forests of spruce and birch, past old wooden dachas, country homes and farms, and eventually opens onto a magical view upon which fairy tales are based.

You can drive via the M8 Yaroslavskoye Highway (a continuation of Prospekt Mira) or take an inexpensive *elektrichka* train from Moscow's Yaroslavsky Railway Station (Komsomolskaya Metro station), which depart quite frequently during the day; the journey takes about 90 minutes and the stop is called Sergiyev Posad. Departure times are listed on a board in front of the station. Buy your ticket at an inside *kassa* booth; you do not need to show any ID. Usually, only same-day tickets are sold. Get on the train early to secure a window seat. The bus station is situated alongside the Yaroslavsky Train Station and frequent buses to Sergiyev Posad run daily from 8.30am to about 7.30pm. Once in Sergiyev Posad, other buses also depart for more towns along the Golden Ring route.

Upon arrival, head west a few hundred meters and then turn right onto Krasnoi Armii Prospekt, the main street. It is only about a 15-minute walk to the complex; you will spot the bell tower and main entrance up on the west side.

If you are driving, the **Russkaya Skazka** (Russian Fairytale) Restaurant is by the 43 kilometer marker on the M8 (Yaroslavskoye) Highway from Moscow. This unique wood-carved restaurant offers hearty appetizers, soups and stews. Open daily noon–10pm, tel. 584-3436/3836. Another popular restaurant, **Trapeza na Makovtse**, is located across the square from the monastery entrance. Also along

Krasnoi Armii Prospekt is **Sever**, at number 141, and **Russky Dvorik**, across from the main gate, at number 34 (tel. 9654-45114) which both serve traditional dishes such as *pelmeni* and *blini*. At the southern end of the street, at number 21, is the **Zolotoe Koltso** restaurant (tel. 9654-41517), popular with tour groups. You can also bring food with you (or buy snacks at the monastery entrance or local market) and have a picnic by the pond or river. The main **Hotel Druzhba** (formerly Zagorsk), tel. 9654-25926/42516 is located near the complex at 171 Krasnoi Armii and offers singles/doubles with private bathrooms for reasonable prices. Next door is the Café Zagorsk, and one block south is the town's first McDonalds. Other hotels in the area are the 3-star **Aristocrat**, at 1a Sergievskaya Street; the smaller **Kovcheg Hotel**, 11b Druzhba Street, and the **Russian Dvorik** at 14/2 Mitkina Street.

A small fee is charged at the front kiosk to enter the monastery grounds, camera and video permits cost extra. Tours of the complex are also available with a private guide. Shops on the premises sell souvenirs, books, art works and religious items. The grounds are open 10am–6pm daily, and museums from 10am–5pm; closed Mondays.

The 18th-century baroque bell tower in Sergiyev Posad

HISTORY

In the early 14th century two brothers, Sergius (Stefan) and Varfolomei (Bartholomew), built a small wooden church and monastic retreat in the forests of Radonezh (lands inherited from their father, a pious Rostov boyar). Varfolomei took his monastic vows as Sergius and founded his own monastery in 1345; St Sergius would one day be named the patron saint of all Russia. Sergius and his pupils went on to establish 50 other monasteries across northeastern Russia that also acted as educational centers and regional strongholds during the Mongol occupations. Seventy of St Sergius' disciples attained sainthood.

In 1380, Grand Prince Dmitri Donskoi and his armies were blessed before battle by Sergius Radonezhsky. Outnumbered four to one, they defeated Khan Mamai's hordes—the first major Mongol defeat in over a century. At the monastery, one of St Sergius' pupils, the famous iconist Andrei Rublyov (see Special Topic on page 329), painted the *Old Testament Trinity* (now in Moscow's Tretyakov Gallery) to commemorate this famous battle at Kulikovo on the Don. After the victory, Moscow princes and rich boyars contributed heavily to the establishment of the Troitse-Sergiyev Lavra (Trinity Monastery of St Sergius) until it became not only the wealthiest in all Russia, but also the most revered pilgrimage shrine in Moscovy.

The thick kremlin walls were built around the monastery in 1540 during the reign of Ivan the Terrible to protect it from attack. A half-century later, the *lavra* (monastery) withstood a 16-month siege by Polish forces; it was protected by over 3,000 monks. The monastery complex was such an important center for the Russian people that its fall would have meant the end of Rus. The monastery remained an important fortress that defended Moscow well into the 17th-century. Eleven octagonal towers

The Chapel-over-the-Well in Sergiyev Posad. It is customary for pilgrims to fill bottles with holy water to take home.

were built into the walls as key defense points. The most famous, the northeast tower, is known as the Utichya (Duck) Tower; the duck atop its spire symbolizes Peter the Great's hunting expeditions in Sergiyev Posad. (He also enjoyed taking shots at the ducks swimming in the pond below.) The place also played an important cultural role; the manuscript-writing and color miniature painting sections date back to the 15th-century.

After his death, Sergius was canonized; he is buried in the Holy Trinity Cathedral on the monastery grounds. In 1992, the Orthodox Church celebrated the 600th anniversary of St Sergius' passing. Each year special church processions are held, especially during St Sergius and Holy Trinity Days, New Year's and Easter holidays.

Today the Trinity-Sergius Monastery is the largest *lavra* run by the Orthodox Church, with over 100 monks. The monastery remains a place of devoted pilgrimage, and believers from all over the country continue to pay homage to 'the saint and guardian of the Russian land'.

In 1930, the town's name of Sergiyev Posad (Settlement of Sergius) was changed to Zagorsk, after the revolutionary Vladimir Zagorsk. The monastery was closed down and converted into a State museum by Lenin in 1920 and during the Stalinist era it lost most of its wealth and power. The town officially reverted back to its original name of Sergiyev Posad in 1990, when the monastery was also returned to the Orthodox Church. Sergiyev Posad has a population of over 100,000, but receives nearly a million visitors a year.

The art of carving wooden toys has long been a tradition here; the first toys were made and distributed by St Sergius to the children of the town. Many painters, sculptors and folk artists trace their heritage back to the 17th-century, when the first toy and craft workshops were set up in the town. The shop to the left as you pass through the main gates sells many locally made wooden toys.

SIGHTS

The parking square, near the main gates of the monastery complex, looks out over many ancient settlements that dot the landscape and the large kremlin citadel that houses priceless relics of old Russian architecture. Enter the main gates at the eastern entrance; paintings of the Holy Pilgrims depict the life of Sergius Radonezhsky, the 14th-century monk who established the Trinity Monastery of St Sergius. The small **Gate Church of St John the Baptist**, built in 1693 by the wealthy and princely Stroganov family, stands over the main or Holy Uspensky Gates. It now functions as a confessional for Orthodox pilgrims.

The first large structure that catches the eye is the monastery's main **Assumption (Uspensky) Cathedral**. This blue and gold-starred, five-domed church with elegant sloping *zakomara* archways was consecrated in 1585 to commemorate Ivan the Terrible's defeat of the Mongols in the Asian territory of Astrakhan. Yaroslavl artists, whose names are inscribed on the west wall, painted the interior frescoes in 1684. The iconostasis contains the *Last Supper*, a painting by the 17th-century master icon-artist Simon Ushakov. The burial chambers of the Godunov family (Boris Godunov was czar from 1598 to 1605) are located in the northwestern corner. Its design resembles the Kremlin's Uspensky Cathedral. By the south wall is the Sergius Church (1686–92). The first oak coffin of St Sergius is preserved here. Under the cathedral is the Orthodox church crypt where patriarchs Alexis I (1970) and Pimen (1990) are buried. Many of these churches are open for worship and conduct services throughout the day. Respectfully dressed visitors are welcome. Photography without flash is usually permitted, but you may need to buy a permit.

The brightly painted **Chapel-over-the-Well**, located outside by the cathedral's west wall, was built in Naryshkin, cube-shaped, octagonal-style at the end of the

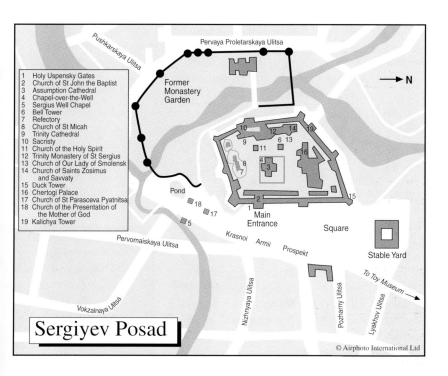

1 Holy Uspensky Gates
2 Church of St John the Baptist
3 Assumption Cathedral
4 Chapel-over-the-Well
5 Sergius Well Chapel
6 Bell Tower
7 Refectory
8 Church of St Micah
9 Trinity Cathedral
10 Sacristy
11 Church of the Holy Spirit
12 Trinity Monastery of St Sergius
13 Church of Our Lady of Smolensk
14 Church of Saints Zosimus
   and Savvaty
15 Duck Tower
16 Chertogi Palace
17 Church of St Parasceva Pyatnitsa
18 Church of the Presentation of
   the Mother of God
19 Kalichya Tower

Pushkarskaya Ulitsa

Pervaya Proletarskaya Ulitsa

Former Monastery Garden

N

Pond

Pervomaiskaya Ulitsa

Krasnoi Armii Prospekt

Main Entrance

Square

Stable Yard

Vokzalnaya Ulitsa

Nizhnyaya Ulitsa

Pozharny Ulitsa

Lyakhov Ulitsa

To Toy Museum

Sergiyev Posad

© Airphoto International Ltd

17th-century. Legend has it that when St Sergius touched a stick to the earth here, a well miraculously appeared, and a blind monk was the first to be healed by the holy water. Near the riverbank stands the **Sergius Well Chapel**. It was customary for small chapels to be built over sacred springs; today, pilgrims still bring bottles to fill with holy water.

Directly beyond the cathedral, standing in the complex center, is the five-tiered turquoise and white baroque **Bell Tower** (88 meters/288 feet high), designed by Prince Ukhtomsky (1740–70) and Rastrelli. Topped with a gilded dome in the form of a crown, it once held 40 bells; the largest weighed 65 tons. The chiming clock of the tower dates back to 1905.

Head past the cathedral to the southern end of the complex. A stroll in this direction to the Refectory may lead past long-bearded monks dressed in the traditional black robes and *klobuki* tall hats. The **Refectory**, rebuilt in 1686, is painted in colorful checkerboard patterns of red, blue, green and yellow. It has a large open gallery with 19th-century paintings and wide staircases, and is decorated with carved columns and gables.

The small chapel at the end of the hall has a carved iconostasis by the altar and a beautiful red jasper inlaid floor. Another quaint church, standing next to the Refectory, is the **Church of St Micah**. In 1379, St Sergius' cell attendant, Micah, witnessed the appearance of the Blessed Mary promising prosperity for the monastery. In 1734, this church was built to hold the relics of St Micah.

Near the Refectory, in the southwestern corner, is the oldest building in the monastery, the one-domed **Trinity Cathedral**, which the Abbot Nikon erected over the site of the original Church of St Sergius in 1422 (the year Sergius was canonized). Pilgrims still visit the remains of St Sergius of Radonezh, which lie in a silver sarcophagus donated by Ivan the Terrible. An embroidered portrait of St Sergius that covered his coffin is now preserved in the History and Art Museum, a short walk away. In 1425, Andrei Rublyov and Daniil Chorny painted the icons on the cathedral's iconostasis, which include a copy of Rublyov's *Holy Testament Trinity* (the original is now in Moscow's Tretyakov Gallery). The cathedral contains 42 works by Rublyov and is joined by the smaller **Church of St Nikon** (1548), Sergius' first successor. Behind the Cathedral is the **Sacristy**, now a small museum that exhibits early Russian applied art (14th–17th centuries), and includes collections of metalwork, jewelry, icon covers and exquisite embroideries or 'needle paintings'.

Across from the cathedral is the slender **Church of the Holy Spirit** with a tall bell tower under its dome. It was built in 1476 by Pskov stonemasons. Prominent Russian saints are buried here: St Maxim the Greek (1556), a translator of church books; St Innocenti of Moscow (1879), a missionary; and Church metropolitans Platon (1812) and Philaret (1867).

Behind this church in the northwest corner stands the **Trinity-Sergius Monastery**, one of the most important monuments of medieval Russia. The Metropolitan's House, vestry and adjoining monastery buildings now house the **Art Museum** and the **Treasury** (Museum of Ancient Russian Art). These museums, which display gifts in the order presented to the monastery, contain one of Russia's richest collections of early religious art. The exhibits include icons from the 14th to 19th centuries, and portraits, chalices, china, costumes, crowns, furniture, latticework and handicrafts from the 14th to 20th centuries. The art museum also has the original 15th-century gates from the iconostasis of the cathedral; open 10am–5pm, but closed Monday and Thursday. In front of the museum is the **Church of Our Lady of Smolensk** (1745–53) with a blue baroque-style rotunda. In 1730, a pious psalm reader who

One of the most outstanding collections of Russian church architecture is to be found in the town of Sergiyev Posad. A monk walks toward the bell tower; beyond stands the blue 18th-century Church of Our Lady of Smolensk. On the left is the Church of Saints Zosimus and Savvaty and in the background stands the Pilgrim Tower, part of the monastery walls.

suffered from paralysis was allegedly healed after praying to the Icon of the Mother of Smolenskaya. The building of the church honored this miracle.

The monastery also served as the town's hospital and school. Next to the museum is the red-brick and yellow-and-white sandstone hospital building with the adjoining all-white tent-roofed **Church of Saints Zosimus and Savvaty** (1635). Behind the church, you can climb up the **Kalichya Tower** for a splendid view of the complex and town (it is usually open in summer months).

In the northeastern corner, behind the Duck Tower, is the colorfully painted and tiled **Chertogi Palace**, built at the end of the 17th-century for Czar Alexei, who often came to Sergiyev Posad with an entourage of over 500 people. One of the ceilings in the palace is covered with paintings that honor his son's (Peter the Great) victories in battle. It now houses the Moscow Theological Academy and Seminary. The seminary, founded in 1742, and the academy, founded in 1812, now have over 1,000 students. In 1744, the monastery was awarded the title of *lavra*, the country's highest accolade given to a teaching monastery.

Exiting through the main gate, turn right and walk southwest toward the **Kelarskiye Ponds**, situated beyond the southeastern Pyatnitskaya Tower. There you may find artists sketching and people strolling among the old garden walls. Two churches built in 1547 stand outside the walls—the **Church of St Paraskeva Pyatnitsa** and the **Church of the Presentation of the Mother of God**, nearest the pond. The Zolotoye Koltso (Golden Ring) Restaurant is only a few minutes' walk away.

The craft of wood carving remains alive in Sergiyev Posad. The famous *matryoshka*, the nest of carved dolls, has its origins here. First appearing in Russia in the 1890s, the *matryona* doll was later called by its diminutive form, *matryoshka*, representing peasant girls. The dolls were carved from wood and painted in traditional Russian dress, with *sarafan* jumpers, embroidered blouses and *kokoshniki* headdresses. Up to 24 smaller dolls could be nested within the largest, including Russian lads or fairy-tale figures. The doll first attained popularity at the 1900 World Exposition in Paris.

Today, there are even Putin *matryoshki* (containing past leaders from Yeltsin down to Nicholas II) as well as dolls representing other foreign leaders. In 2000, a Matryoshka Museum (marking the centenary of the doll) opened in Moscow, in the Folk Art Museum near the Arbat. Its largest doll stands one-meter high and houses 50 smaller ones inside. Another popular Russian folk art—Zhostovo trays—celebrated its 175th anniversary in 2001. Artists paint designs on metal trays, which are then coated with several coats of lacquer.

The history of toys and folk art can be viewed in the large red-brick **Toy Museum**, at 123 Krasnoi Armii Prospekt. There are displays of over 30,000 toys dating back to the Bronze Age. A special souvenir section sells carved wooden dolls, boxes, trays and jewelry. Open 10am–5pm, closed Mondays, Tuesdays and last Friday of the month.

ALEKSANDROV Александров
RESIDENCE OF IVAN THE TERRIBLE ON THE GRAY RIVER

From Moscow, you can travel here directly (120 kilometers/74 miles north) and inexpensively by *elektrichka* train from Moscow's Yaroslavsky Railway Station (Komsomolskaya Metro station) in about two and a half hours. You can also travel by train from Sergiyev Posad in less than an hour. By car, take the M8 past Sergiyev Posad and then turn east (at Dvoriki) on the P75. (It is possible to cover both towns in one day.) The old town is about a ten-minute ride from Aleksandrov Railway Station. (Inside the station, departure times are posted for both Moscow and Sergiyev Posad.) When exiting the station, walk directly across the street to the bus stop. Take bus number 7 (facing the station, travel right) five stops to 'Museum'. The bus will pass the main square with a statue of Lenin, cross the Gray River and climb up a hill. You will see the old kremlin on your left. If you have time, it is a pleasant half-hour walk through town back to the train station. A number of cafés dot the path, along with markets selling bread, fruit and drinks.

The museum town is currently closed on Mondays and Tuesdays. A small gift shop is located inside the entrance gates on the left.

The **Aleksandrovskaya Sloboda**, packed full of grim history, was once the residence of Ivan the Terrible for 17 years (1564–1581) and headquarters to his police army of ruthless *oprichniki*. (After the suspicious deaths of his wife and first son, Ivan abandoned Moscow for Aleksandrov.) It is from here that Ivan launched his reign of terror over Russia and kept its citizens in the grip of fear. Ivan married six more times in Aleksandrov. (Of his wives, six died mysteriously and one was sent off to a nunnery.) The most unfortunate, Martha Sobakina, whose story is depicted in Rimsky-Korsakov's *The Bride of the Tsar*, lasted a mere two weeks.

The oldest buildings are the (nonfunctioning) convent and white-rectangular one-domed **Trinity Cathedral** that women helped build in the early 15th-century. The interior walls are decorated with the Icon of the Virgin Mary, said to be her real portrait from first-century Rome. After Ivan's army sacked Novgorod in 1570 (suspicious of the town's betrayal during a war with Poland, his troops slaughtered 35,000 of its citizens), he brought the golden oak doors from the Hagia Sophia Cathedral to adorn the Trinity's entrance. A covered gallery surrounds the cathedral which contains several coffins of white limestone.

Each morning Ivan climbed the nearby tent-shaped bell tower with its three-tiered layers of arched *kokoshniki*; he enjoyed ringing the bells and giving morning sermons. Adjacent to the bell tower are residential quarters which later housed Marfa, the stepsister of Peter the Great (who forced her to become a nun); she was exiled here between 1698 and 1707. (Two daughters of Czar Alexei, Peter's father, are buried in the Church of the Purification.) The future Empress Elizabeth was also banished to Aleksandrov for nine years.

Opposite the bell tower stands Ivan IV's personal church, the red-brick and green tent-roof **Church of the Intercession**. It was in the adjoining palace (later destroyed by invading Poles) that Ivan the Terrible committed his last and most atrocious crime—the murder of his own son. The son became enraged one night when finding Ivan in his bedroom with his wife whose dress was in 'slight disarray'. The ensuing fight between father and son ended in Ivan the Terrible beating his son to death with a cane. The czar was so horrified by what he had done that he left Aleksandrov and returned to govern from Moscow, where he died a few years later. (When in Moscow's Tretyakov Gallery, note the famous painting by Ilya Repin, *Ivan the Terrible and His Son—16 November 1581*, the date of the murder.)

The **Aleksandrov Hotel** is at 59 Alexandrov Revolutsii Street.

In 1885, realist artist Ilya Repin painted Ivan the Terrible and His Son—16 November 1581.
On this date Ivan the Terrible killed his son in a fit of jealous rage.
The painting now hangs in Moscow's Tretyakov Gallery.

PERESLAVL-ZALESSKY Переславль-Залесский
IMPORTANT OUTPOST OF MOSCOVY

The tranquil town of Pereslavl-Zalessky, which celebrated its 850th anniversary in 2002, is situated on a hilltop by the southeastern shores of Lake Pleshcheyevo, about 56 kilometers (35 miles) northeast of Sergiyev Posad. Approaching Pereslavl from the road, pleasantly scented by the surrounding groves of pine and birch, you have an enchanting view of the shimmering azure waters of the lake, three old monasteries on the side of the road, and golden crosses on top of painted onion domes that loom up from sprawling green fields dusted with blue and yellow wildflowers. Young boys wave at passersby as they fish in the lake with long reed poles. The River Trubezh meanders through the old earthen kremlin that winds around the center of town. These ramparts date back over eight centuries. One of Russia's most ancient towns, Pereslavl-Zalessky (today with 45,000 residents) is a charming place, scattered with well-preserved churches and monasteries that once numbered over 50. Take a pleasant walk along the dirt roads and imagine that Peter the Great may have traversed the same footpaths before you.

With no train station, the easiest way is to visit by car; it is about a two-and-a-half hour drive north on the M8 from Moscow. Inexpensive buses also run from Moscow's northeast Shchyolkovsky Station (located near the metro of the same name) with frequent departures to Pereslavl (three hours) and most other Golden Ring towns. In addition, many buses destined for Rostov Veliky or Yaroslavl also stop in Pereslavl enroute; and those marked 'SP' also stop in Sergiyev Posad. Daily buses also run between Sergiyev Posad and Pereslavl (a one-hour ride), Rostov (one-and-a-half hours) and Yaroslavl (three hours). Return buses to Moscow from these locations are also frequent.

The bus station in Pereslavl is located two kilometers southwest of the town. Once there, catch the local bus number 1, which runs up and down the main thoroughfare. To dine, try the **Skazka** (Fairytale) restaurant set in a lovely old wooden building near the town center. Inside the Kremlin, on Sovietskaya Street, the **Blini Café** also has Russian fare. The area code for Pereslavl–Zalessky is 48535.

The 3-star **Zapadnaya Hotel**, opened in 2002, has wireless internet connections. It's located on the bank of the Trubezh River in the historical center of town at 1A Pleshcheyevskaya Street (tel. 34378; www.westhotel.ru). The large old Soviet-style **Hotel Pereslavl** (tel. 32687 or 21559) has the **Bar Rita** that serves Russian food. It's centrally located north of the river at 27 Rostovskaya Street (www.hotel.pereslavl.ru).

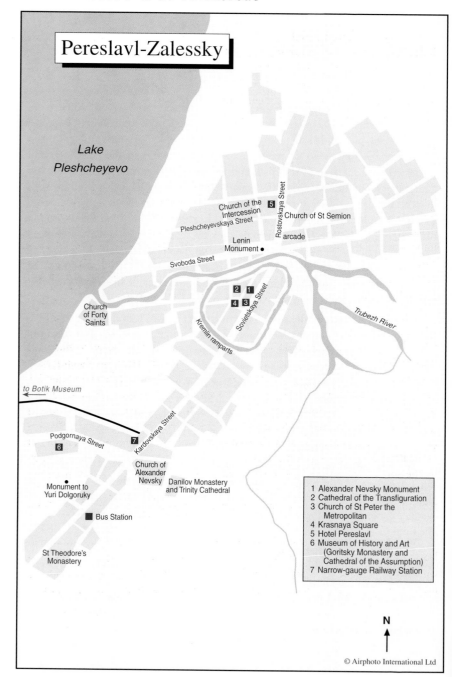

Pereslavl-Zalessky

Lake Pleshcheyevo

Church of the Intercession

Church of St Semion

Pleshcheyevskaya Street

Rostovskaya Street

Lenin Monument ●

arcade

Svoboda Street

2 1

3

4

Sovietskaya Street

Church of Forty Saints

Kremlin ramparts

Trubezh River

to Botik Museum

Kardovskaya Street

Podgornaya Street

7

6

Church of Alexander Nevsky

Danilov Monastery and Trinity Cathedral

● Monument to Yuri Dolgoruky

■ Bus Station

St Theodore's Monastery

1 Alexander Nevsky Monument
2 Cathedral of the Transfiguration
3 Church of St Peter the Metropolitan
4 Krasnaya Square
5 Hotel Pereslavl
6 Museum of History and Art (Goritsky Monastery and Cathedral of the Assumption)
7 Narrow-gauge Railway Station

N

© Airphoto International Ltd

The small **Komfort Hotel** is at 2 Severny Pereulok (tel. 32403 or 93301). The **Botik Tourist & Camping Complex** (tel. 98085) is situated down the path from the **Botik Museum** on the bank of the Lake near Veskovo Village. It offers wooden cabins, camping areas, a sauna and beach. The **Botik Café**, designed in the shape of a boat, serves traditional Russian food. Driving into Pereslavl from Moscow, in Krest Village, is the **Lesnaya Skazka Hotel** ('A Forest Tale'; tel. 30863 or 20853).

HISTORY

Pereslavl-Zalessky's long and fascinating history can be traced back to the year 1152, when Prince Yuri Dolgoruky (who founded Moscow five years earlier) fortified the small village of Kleschchin on the banks of the Trubezh and renamed it Pereslavl after an old Kievan town. Situated in an area on the *zalasye* (beyond the dense woods of Moscow), it became known as Pereslavl-Zalessky. The area was an important outpost of Moscow; Prince Alexander Nevsky set out from Pereslavl to win his decisive battle against the Swedes in 1240. Since the town also lay on important White Sea trade routes, it quickly prospered. By 1302 Pereslavl had grown large enough to be annexed to the principality of Moscovy.

SIGHTS

Ivan the Terrible later consolidated Pereslavl, along with the nearby village of Aleksandrov, into a strategic military outpost and headquarters for his *oprichniki* bodyguards. In 1688, the young Czar Peter I came here from Moscow to build his first *poteshny* (amusement) boats on Lake Pleshcheyevo. It was in a small shed near the lake that Peter discovered a wrecked English boat, which he learned to sail against the wind. In 1692, Peter paraded these boats (forerunners of the Russian fleet) before members of the Moscow court. One of them, the *Fortuna*, can be found in the **Botik Museum**, which lies about three kilometers (two miles) from Pereslavl, by the south bank of the lake near the village of Veskovo. Other relics from the Russian flotilla are also displayed here. Two large anchors mark the entrance and a monument to Peter the Great by Campioni stands nearby. Open from 10am–4.45pm; closed Mondays.

An easy way to get to the Botik Museum is by taking the narrow-gauge train that leaves three times daily from the bus station on Kardovskaya, just north of the Goritsky Monastery. It departs at 9am, 1pm and 4.30pm daily and returns from the museum at 12.30pm, 4pm and 8.30pm. The single-track train also continues all around the lake to Kupan.

Make your way to the central Krasnaya Ploshchad (Red Square). The small grassy hills around you are the remains of the town's 12th-century earthen pr otective walls. In front of the **Statue of Alexander Nevsky** (who was born in Pereslavl) is the white stone **Cathedral of the Transfiguration**, the oldest architectural monument in northeastern Russia. Yuri Dolgoruky himself laid the foundations of this church, which was completed by his son, Andrei Bogoliubsky (Lover of God), in 1157. This refined structure with its one massive fringed dome became the burial place for the local princes. Each side of the cathedral is decorated with simple friezes. The *zakomara*, the semicircular rounded shape of the upper walls, distinguish the Russian style from the original simpler cube-shaped Byzantine design. Frescoes and icons from inside the cathedral, like the 14th-century *Transfiguration* by Theophanes the Greek and Yuri Dolgoruky's silver chalice, are now in Moscow's Tretyakov Gallery and Kremlin Armory. The other frescoes were executed during the cathedral's restoration in 1894. Across from the cathedral is the **Church of St Peter the Metropolitan**. Built in 1585 (with a 19th-century bell tower), the octagonal frame is topped with a long white tent-shaped roof. This design in stone and brick was copied from the traditional Russian log-cabin churches of the north.

In the distance, north across the river, is the **Church of St Semion** (1771). Between this church and the Lenin Monument on Svoboda Ulitsa are the early 19th-century shopping arcades, Gostiny Dvor. Religious services are held at the **Church of the Intercession** on Pleshcheyevskaya Ulitsa.

Take a leisurely stroll towards the river and follow it westwards down to the lake. Scattered along the paths are brightly painted wooden dachas with carved windows covered by lace curtains. Children can be found playing outside with their kittens or a *babushka* hauling water from the well. *Dedushka* may be picking apples and wild strawberries or carving a small toy for his grandchildren

In 1147 the Prince of the Rostov-Suzdal principality, Yuri Dolgoruky, erected a wooden fortress overlooking the Moskva River, where the Kremlin stands today, to serve as a defensive outpost. This settlement later became Moscow, the capital of Russia. Five years later Prince Yuri also fortified the area along the banks of the Trubezh River and named the new town Pereslavl after an old Kievan town. As Prince of the Rostov-Suzdal principality, Yuri received the honorary name of Dolgoruky (Long Arms) for his wide-sweeping territorial conquests.

out of wood. Stop for a chat; it is amazing how far a few common words can go— an invitation for tea may soon follow. At the point where the Trubezh flows into the lake stands the **Church of the Forty Saints** (1781) on Ribnaya (Fish) Sloboda, the old fish quarter. With a little bargaining or a smile, get a rowing boat to go out on the lake or go out with the fishermen. On a warm day, it is a perfect place for a picnic; you may even want to take a dip.

In the town center, housed in an old merchant house, is the **Iron Museum**, exhibiting a large collection of old irons (the smallest weighs 10 grams) and other household items. The owner has also created the nearby **Museum of Teapots**. Situated outside of town, on the way to Uglich, is the **Steam Engine Museum**, a large depot filled with old train engines, wagons, and even an old Stalin-era limousine, the bottom reconfigured to ride the rails.

At the southern end of town, you may have glimpsed a number of monasteries and chapels if you arrived from Sergiyev Posad. The four monasteries lining the southern road into Pereslavl also acted as protective strongholds, guarding the town from invasions. The one farthest away is the **Convent of St Theodore**, six and a half kilometers (four miles) south on Kardovskaya Street. Ivan the Terrible built this convent and the **Chapel of St Theodore** to honor his wife Anastasia, who gave birth to their first son, Fedor (Theodore), in 1557. Ivan often stopped at the shrine to pray when he visited his bodyguard army residing in Pereslavl-Zalessky.

About one and a half kilometers (a mile) closer to town is the memorial **Church of Alexander Nevsky** (1778). A few minutes' walk from this church, set in a woody rustic setting, is the **Danilov Monastery**. A few buildings remain of this 16th-century structure. The **Trinity Cathedral** was commissioned by Grand Prince Vasily III in 1532. The single-domed cathedral, with 17th-century frescoes by renowned Kostroma artists Nikitin and Savin, was built by Rostov architect Grigory Borisov in honor of Vasily's son, Ivan the Terrible. The Abbot Daniel, who founded the monastery in 1508, was in charge of the cathedral's construction and present at Ivan's christening. The smaller **Church of All Saints** was built in 1687 by Prince Bariatinsky, who later became a monk (Ephriam) at the monastery and was buried near the south wall. Other surviving structures are the two-story Refectory (1695) and the large tent-roofed bell tower (1689), whose bell is now in the Moscow Kremlin's Ivan the Great Bell Tower.

On the west side of the road, behind the Monument to Yuri Dolgoruky, is the **Goritsky Monastery**, surrounded by a large red-brick kremlin. On the hilltop, a cluster of sparkling onion domes rise up from inside the fortified walls. The monastery is now the **Museum of History and Art** (open from 10am–5pm; closed

Tuesdays). The monastery, founded during the reign of Ivan I in the 14th century (rebuilt in the 18th), is a fine example of medieval architecture with its octagonal towers, large cube-shaped walls and ornamental stone entrance gates. The tiny white gate-church next to the gatekeeper's lodge was once known as the 'casket studded with precious stones', for it was richly decorated with gilded carvings and colorful tiles. The large seven-domed **Cathedral of the Assumption** was built in 1757. The exquisite golden-framed and figured iconostasis, designed by Karl Blank, was carved and painted by the same team of artists who decorated the churches in the Moscow Kremlin.

The monastery, with 47 rooms filled with local treasures, is now one of the largest regional museums in Russia. The rooms include a unique collection of ancient Russian art, sculptures and rare books. The museum also exhibits the plaster face mask of Peter the Great by Rastrelli (1719) and Falconet's original model of the Bronze Horseman. The elaborately carved wooden gates from the Church of the Presentation won the Gold Medal at the 1867 Paris World Exhibition. May 2nd is a town holiday, Museum Day, at the Goritsky Monastery.

Heading north toward Rostov and Yaroslavl, you will find the last monument structure of Pereslavl-Zalessky, the 12th-century **Monastery of St Nicetas**, encased in a long white-bricked kremlin. In 1561, Ivan the Terrible added stone buildings and the five-domed cathedral. He intended to convert the monastery into the headquarters of his *oprichniki*, but later transferred their residence to the village of Aleksandrov.

ROSTOV VELIKY Ростов Великий
THE WEALTHY ECCLESIASTICAL CENTER OF EARLY CHRISTIANITY

Approaching Rostov on the road from Moscow (54 kilometers/34 miles north of Pereslavl-Zalessky), the visitor is greeted with a breathtaking view of silvery aspen domes, white-stone churches and high kremlin towers. Rostov is one of Russia's most ancient towns and has stood along the picturesque banks of Lake Nero for more than 11 centuries. It was once called 'a reflection of heaven on earth'. Named after Prince Rosta, a powerful governing lord, the town was mentioned in chronicles as far back as AD 862. Rostov's size and splendor grew to equal the two great towns of Novgorod and Kiev. By the 12th-century Rostov was named Veliky (the Great) and became the capital of the Russian north. Rostov later came under the jurisdiction of Moscow and lost its importance as a cultural center by the end of the 18th century.

Today Rostov is the district center of the Yaroslavl region, and considered a historical preserve, heralding the glory of old Russian art and architecture. The town, with a population of about 50,000, has been restored to much of its original grandeur after a tornado destroyed many of the buildings in 1953. The oldest section of the town, set by the lake, is still surrounded by low earthen walls built around 1630.

Rostov is about an hour's drive on the M8, north of Pereslavl-Zalessky. Trains depart from Moscow's Yaroslavl Station (Metro Komsomolskaya). Many long distance trains on the way to Yaroslavl also stop in Rostov (taking between three and four hours). Or take the local *elektricka* which leave regularly, and then change trains at Aleksandrov. (*Elektricka* also run frequently between Rostov and Yaroslavl.) Various bus routes from Moscow's Shchyolkovsky station (in the northeast, by metro stop of same name) also make runs and transit stops at Rostov (about 5 hours).

The main bus station is situated right in town. Once there, the local bus number 6 runs the one and a half kilometers between the station and the town center along Lunacharskaya Street. (The area code for Rostov is 48536). In 2006, Rostov's first 3-star hotel, **Moscow Trakt**, opened with over 90 beds. Inside the Kremlin, near the east gate, is the **Hotel Dom na Pogrebakh** (tel. 31244). The former servants' quarters have been turned into a basic hotel—nice clean rooms with shared bathrooms, and a café. Also inside the Red Palace is the **Krasnaya Palata** eatery. Near the hotel is the **Restaurant Trepeznaya**, and a few blocks west of the Kremlin is the **Traktir na Pokrovskoy**, both serving traditional Russian food. The **Restauran Teremok**, at 9 Moravskaya Street, serves delicious soups and *blini* with caviar. An outdoor market is located across the street. Another quality hotel is the **Boyarsky Dvor** at 4 Kammeny Most. The smaller **Pleshanov's Manor** is located at 34 Leninskaya Street. The inexpensive **Khors Guesthouse**, on the waterfront at 30 Ul Podozerka is run by an artist and his mother in two independent parts of their house (one room with two beds, and a separate two-room apartment). Another section is also an enamel museum (tel. 62483; http//selishchev.khors.org; email:selishchev@mail.ru).

HISTORY

Rostov Veliky was one of the wealthiest towns in all Russia and the most important trade center between Kiev and the White Sea. Rostov became not only the capital of its own principality, but also the northern ecclesiastical center of early Christianity and the seat of the Orthodox Church. In the 17th-century the metropolitans Jonah and Ion Sisoyevich built a large number of magnificent cathedrals and church

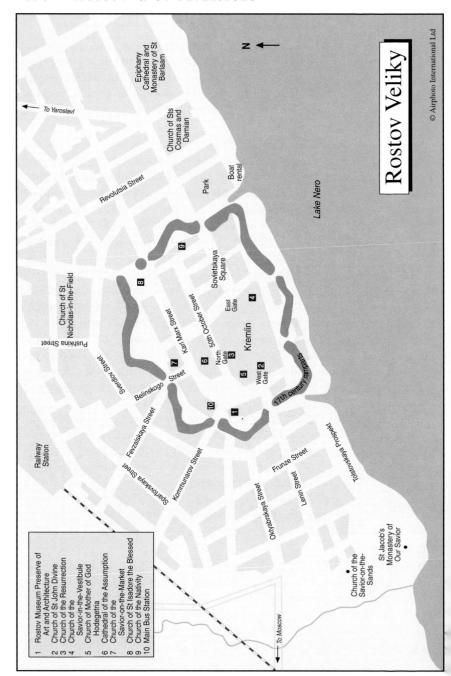

Rostov Veliky

© Airphoto International Ltd

N

To Yaroslavl

Epiphany Cathedral and Monastery of St Barlaam

Church of Sts Cosmas and Damian

Revolutsia Street

Park

Boat rental

Lake Nero

Church of St Nicholas-in-the-Field

Pushkina Street

Sverdlov Street

Belinskogo Street

Karl Marx Street

Sovietskaya Square

50th October Street

East Gate

North Gate

Kremlin

West Gate

17th century ramparts

Railway Station

Feyzalskaya Street

Spartovskaya Street

Kommunarov Street

Frunze Street

Oktyabrskaya Street

Lenin Street

Tolstokskaya Prospekt

To Moscow

Church of the Savior-on-the-Sands

St Jacob's Monastery of Our Savior

1 Rostov Museum Preserve of Art and Architecture
2 Church of St John Divine
3 Church of the Resurrection
4 Church of the Savior-in-the-Vestibule
5 Church of Mother of God Hodegetria
6 Cathedral of the Assumption
7 Church of the Savior-on-the-Market
8 Church of St Isadore the Blessed
9 Church of the Nativity
10 Main Bus Station

residences, decorated with the Byzantine influence of icons and frescoes. The many religious shrines of a Russian town symbolized its wealth and status. Unlike other Russian towns, the Rostov kremlin was not originally built as a protective fortress, but served as a decorative feature that surrounded the palace of the metropolitan. Also the main cathedral stood outside the kremlin walls and not in the town's center.

SIGHTS

The kremlin itself, built in 1670, has 11 rounded towers and encompasses an area of about five acres. At the west gate is the **Church of St John-the-Divine** (1683), whose interior paintings depict the life of this saint. The five-domed **Church of the Resurrection** (1670) at the northern gates is designed with intricate white-stone patterns and the classic Russian *zakomara*, forming the 24 slopes of the roof. The towers on either side of both churches are made from aspen, and sparkle with a silken sheen. Stone iconostasis (instead of traditional wooden ones) inside both churches are decorated with beautiful frescoes painted by the artists Nikitin and Savin from the Golden Ring town of Kostroma. The Church of the Resurrection stands over the Holy Gates, so named because the metropolitan passed through them on the way from his residence inside the kremlin to the main cathedral.

Situated between the north and west gates stands the colorful **Church of the Icon of the Mother of God Hodegetria**, built after the death of Jonah in 1690 by the new Metropolitan Josephat. Its exterior is covered by trompe l'oeil diamond rustication, imported from Italy. Inside is a small exhibition of church vestments.

The first stone of the massive **Cathedral of the Assumption** was laid by Prince Andrei Bogoliubsky (son of Yuri Dolgoruky who founded Moscow) in 1162. Bogoliubsky ruled the Russian north from Rostov. The 11th-century Vladimir Virgin hangs to the left of the Holy Doors. A few of the 12th-century frescoes have survived, along with the original lion mask handles that guard the western doors. Rostov frescoes were known for their soft color combinations of turquoise, blue, yellow and white. Five large aspen-hewn onion domes and beautiful white-stone friezes decorate the outside of the structure. The four-tiered bell tower (1687), standing alongside the Assumption Cathedral, was the most famous in all Russia. Bells played an important role in the life of Russian towns. The 13 bells (the heaviest, the *Sysoi*, weighs 32 tons) can be heard 15 miles away. They are usually rung on the half hour and full hour and can play four tunes.

Other churches include the one-domed **Church of the Savior-on-the-Marketplace** (1690) that is located a few blocks north of the cathedral; it is now the town library. In the northeast corner stands the single-domed **Church of St Isodore the Blessed** (1566), built during the reign of Ivan the Terrible. Directly behind this

*The 17th-century Church of
St John-the-Divine in Rostov Veliky
with its aspen-shingled domes*

church, on the other side of the earthen walls, stands the **Church of St Nicholas-in-the-Field** (1830) on Gogol Street. This is one of the few places in town open for religious services. At the eastern end, within the ramparts, is the **Church of the Nativity**. Gostiny Dvor (Traders' Row) marks the town's center. This long yellow arcade, with its many carved white archways, is still the shopping and market district of Rostov. The southeast part of the kremlin is made up of 17th-century civic buildings and the cube-shaped, single-domed **Church of the Savior-in-the-Vestibule** (1675), whose interior is made up of stone arcades that rest on thick gilded columns; it served as the house chapel of the metropolitan's residence. The walls and stone altar iconostasis are decorated with exquisite frescoes painted by local master artists, and the chandelier and candelabra are also from the 17th-century.

The large complex along the southwestern end is the **Metropolitan's Palace** (1680), containing the highly decorated Otdatochnaya Hall; here people gathered to pay their respects to the metropolitan. The White Chambers were built for the prince, and later, visiting czars. The Red Chambers accommodated other church and civil dignitaries. This complex of buildings now houses the **Rostov Museum Preserve of Art and Architecture**. The chambers are filled with collections of icons, wood carvings and enamels from the 14th to 20th centuries. Of particular interest is the 15th-century Icon of the Archangel Michael, the carved limestone cross (1458) of the prince's scribe, and the 15th-century wooden figure of St George the Victorious.

Rostov enamels (known as *finift*), produced here since the 12th-century, were famous throughout Russia. The art originated in Byzantium and the name stems from the Greek word meaning colorful and shiny. Craftsmen painted miniature icons, personal portraits, and other decorative enamels for church books and clergy robes. The complex process of enamel making involves oxidizing different metals to create an assortment of colors: copper produces green and blue; iron, yellow and orange; and gold mixed with tin oxidizes into a rich ruby-red. Rostov's factory has been open since the 18th-century and the local craftsmen still produce elegant enamel jewelry, ornaments and small paintings that are sold in stores throughout Russia. Museums are open 10am–5pm (closed Wednesdays) and tickets can be bought at the west gate. One can enter the kremlin grounds at any time from the east gate.

Heading west out of the kremlin brings you to the small three-domed **Church of the Savior-on-the-Sands**. This is all that has survived of a monastery built by Princess Maria, whose husband was killed by invading Mongols in the 13th-century. Princess Maria and other noblewomen of Rostov chronicled many of the events of medieval Russia. During the 17th-century the library of Countess Irina Musina-Pushkina was one of the largest in Russia.

On the banks of Lake Nero are the 17th-century remains of **St Jacob's Monastery of Our Savior** (founded in 1389); the original walls are still standing. The Immaculate Conception Cathedral (1686) and Church of St Demetrius (1800) are designed in the Russian classical style. Along the water is a park where boats can be rented. Fishing is also possible.

Along the shores of the lake at the eastern end of town is the **Church of Saints Cosmas and Damian** (1775). Next to this small church stands the larger five-domed **Epiphany Cathedral** (1553; the oldest standing building in Rostov), part of the **Monastery of St Barlaam** (Abraham); this is one of the oldest surviving monasteries in Russia, dating back to the 11th-century.

Outside Rostov, in the northwestern suburbs of the village of Bogoslov, is the lovely red **Church of St John upon Ishnya**, one of the last wooden churches left in the region. It stands on the River Ishnya and legend has it that it miraculously appeared from the lake and was washed up on the shores of its present location. It is open daily for visits and closed on Wednesdays.

The ancient walls and towers of the kremlin in the Golden Ring town of Rostov Veliky, built in the 17th-century

VICINITY OF ROSTOV VELIKY

About 20 kilometers (12 miles) northwest of Rostov Veliky (on road P153), lies the **Borisoglebsky Fortress-Monastery**. Built in the early 14th century, it was later surrounded by a kremlin during the reign of Boris Godunov to protect it from Polish invasions. Surrounded on three sides by the River Ustye, the fourth was once protected by a moat. The fortifications were as strong as those of Moscow's Kremlin; the walls were 12 meters (40 feet) high and over three meters (ten feet) thick and had 14 observation towers. (The towers were placed the distance of an arrow's flight apart.) The walls also had stone arches that held cannon and archer posts, and the two gateways were fortified with heavy oak and iron doors.

The famous Rostov architect Grigory Borisov built the single-domed **Cathedral of Saints Boris and Gleb** in 1524, and had it decorated with colorful tiles, gables and frescoes. Boris and Gleb, sons of Prince Vladimir (who introduced Christianity to Russia in AD 988), were the first saints of Russia. As political and religious turmoil swept Kiev, they passively accepted their deaths without fighting, believing in Christ's redemption.

Borisov also built the five-domed **Gate Church of St Sergius** (1545); each narrow window is topped by cylinder-shaped *kokoshniki*. Other buildings inside the monastery grounds include the **Church of the Annunciation** (1526), Refectory, Head Monk's Residence, Dormitory Quarters, Treasury and Wafer Bakery (which once contained the dungeon), all designed by Borisov. The **Church of the Purification** stands over the Water Gates on the north side. The three-tiered bell tower (1680) was the last structure built, with the **Church of St John** on the ground floor.

RUSSIAN BELLS

Bells were first introduced to Russia from Byzantium in the 10th century. By the 14th century, Russia began to cast its own bells, and they played a prominent role in Russian town life. They chimed the hours, sounded alarms, tolled for funerals, heralded special announcements and summoned parishioners to worship. Russian bells do not swing when rung; only the interior clappers hang free. This affords the bell ringers more control over the intensity and rhythmic patterns, especially when playing together with other bells. By the 17th-century, bell ringing was a profession (150 bell ringers were employed in the Moscow Kremlin alone), and 100-ton bells (as the Czar Bell, today on display in the Moscow Kremlin) could be cast.

(previous pages) The massive bell cote inside the kremlin at Rostov Veliky. Its 13 large bells can be heard 15 miles away. In ancient times bells played a significant role in village life—sounding as a fire alarm, calling the town to battle, summoning the congregation to church or celebrating a joyous occasion.

By the earth 19th century, over 200 bells hung across Moscow. But, on December 6, 1929, the new Soviet government issued Decree No. 118, which forbade bell ringing, and ordered that all bells be removed from church towers; many of these were sadly melted down to make anything from cauldrons to tractors. The Rostov Bells survived because the Rostov Museum director wrote to the Minister of Culture, Anatoly Lunacharsky (a street is named after him), asking to protect them. Even though the historical bells remained intact, they hung silent until the 1960s when the government allowed them featured in a recording. Today, bell founding and ringing is experiencing a new Renaissance in the Golden Ring area, and every year in Yaroslavl contemporary casters present their works.

NIKOLA-ULEIMA Никола-Улейма

About 60 kilometers (37 miles) west of Borisoglebsky, along the P153, lies the quaint **Monastery of St Nicholas-on-the-Uleima**. Founded in 1400 as a lookout post, it was one of the bloodiest sites of the attempted Polish invasions of Muscovy. The monks and village inhabitants fought to their deaths trying to resist the enemy; during the last battle the monastery burnt to the ground. Later, in 1675, the five-domed **Cathedral of St Nicholas** was reconstructed on the old foundation, and the helmet-domed **Church of the Presentation-in-the-Temple** restored. A refectory and bell tower were later added next to its *kokoshniki*-gabled walls. The monastery is surrounded by white birch and dark-green lime trees and its towers are covered with ornamental shapes and colorful pilaster panels.

UGLICH ON THE VOLGA Углич

Only 18 kilometers (11 miles) west of Nikola-Uleima along the P153 road lies the town of Uglich, with a population of 40,000. Trains also stop here on their way to Rybinsk; they depart from Moscow's Savelovsky Railway Station, and it is a half-day's journey. Buses also run from Rostov. Opened in 2003, the best place to stay is the **Hotel Uspenskaya**, located at 3 Uspenskaya Square (tel. 48532–51370). Also try the **Hotel Uglich** at 50 Yaroslavskoye Highway.

In the 16th century the seventh wife of Ivan the Terrible, Maria Nagaya, was banished here to live in a palace within the kremlin walls. Later, Dmitri, the youngest son of Ivan the Terrible, was found dead in the palace garden on May 15, 1591; many believed he was killed by assassins sent by Boris Godunov. Alexander Pushkin wrote of the event in his epic poem *Boris Godunov*.

The **Church of St Demetrius-on-the-Blood** (1630) was built over the spot where Dmitri was murdered. It was replaced in 1692 by a more elaborate red-and-white stone and five-domed church which now functions as a museum. All that remains of the czarina's court is the two-story stone **Palace of Czarevich Dmitri**, built in the 15th-century by Prince Andrei Bolshoi. Later, after a feud with his brother Grand Prince Ivan III, Andrei died in prison. The palace walls are decorated with bands of brick terracotta, and the tent roofs with sheets of weathered copper. It now houses a small museum; closed Mondays. Outside the kremlin stands the five-domed **Church of St John the Baptist** (1689–1700) with an adjoining octagonal bell tower, made famous by the painting by Russian artist Nikolai Roerich.

Across the street stands the **Monastery of the Resurrection**, ordered built in 1674 by Metropolitan Jonah of Rostov. The enclave is made up of a cathedral, bell tower, refectory and the **Church of Our Lady of Smolensk**. The neighboring **Monastery of St Alexis** is the oldest in Uglich and was founded in 1371 by Alexis, Metropolitan of All Russia. It was burnt to the ground during Polish and Lithuanian invasions, and rebuilt in the 1620s. Next to the two-story Refectory stands the slender triple-spired **Church of the Virgin Dormition** (1628). This church, nicknamed the Divnaya (Wondrous), has long remained dear to the people of Uglich. A few surviving secular structures are also of interest: the two-story wooden **Voronin House**, once owned by the Mekhov family, has a tile stove that is still located on the ground floor. The two-story 18th-century stone houses of the Kalashnikov family (a member of the family invented the famous rifle of the same name) and Ovsiannikov merchants are located nearby.

In 1999, Uglich opened the **Library of Russian Vodka**, where visitors can sample different brands and browse books on vodka, and in 2001, well-known sculptor Ernst Neizvestny was commissioned to create a monument to Russian vodka for the town. Folk legend has it that the town's name is derived from the phrase, *Tut zhgli ugli* (here they burned coals). Charcoal is an essential element for filtering fine vodkas. In town, one can also visit a varied collection of other museums; the **Puppet Museum**, **Museum of Prison Art**, and the **Museum of Russian Superstition**.

VICINITY OF UGLICH

A short drive to the northwest, crossing the Volga River (along the top of a hydro-electric dam), brings the visitor to the quaint town of **Myshkin**, with a population of just 6,000. Legend has it, that a prince, after a hunting expedition, fell asleep here and dreamt of a mouse—thus, the name Myshkin, derived from mysh, the Russian word for 'mouse'. Across from the **Mouse Museum**, is the **Ethnographic Museum**, which exhibits everything from ancient pagan decorations to machinery from Stalin's First Five Year Plan. Another interesting place to visit is the **Museum of Pyotr Smirnov**, born in a nearby village. The museum displays the history of Smirnov vodka production and contains other old 19th-century glass and bottles. The brothers Smirnov also built homes designed with fancy carved façades, which are still found throughout this little gem of a town.

YAROSLAVL Ярославль

JEWEL ON THE VOLGA

The English writer and adventurer Robert Byron wrote of his first visit to Yaroslavl in the early 1930s:

> *While Veliki Novgorod retains something of the character of early Russia before the Tartar invasion, the monuments of Yaroslavl commemorate the expansion of commerce that marked the 17th-century... The English built a shipyard here; Dutch, Germans, French and Spaniards followed them. Great prosperity came to the town, and found expression in a series of churches whose spacious proportions and richness of architectural decoration had no rival in the Russia of their time.*

Today Yaroslavl is still an important commercial center and regional capital with a population of almost a million. Lying 280 kilometers (174 miles) northeast of Moscow on the M8 Highway, it occupies the land on both sides of the Volga at its confluence with the River Kotorosl. Yaroslavl, the oldest city on the Volga, will celebrate its millennium in 2010. A monument commemorating its 975th anniversary was placed in the city center in 1985. The seven-ton Ice Age boulder was unearthed on the site of the *strelka* and the inscription reads: 'On this spot in 1010 Yaroslavl the Wise founded Yaroslavl.' Another statue, dedicated to Yaroslavl the Wise and unveiled by Yeltsin in 1983, has him holding a piece of the town's kremlin while gazing toward Moscow. The oldest part of town, located at the confluence of the two rivers, contains many grandiose churches and residences erected by the many prosperous merchants. Not far from the city is the estate-museum of the poet Nekrasov and the Cosmos Museum, dedicated to the first Soviet woman cosmonaut, Valentina Tereshkova.

Several trains depart daily for Yaroslavl from Moscow's Yaroslavsky Train Station (metro Komsomolskaya); the journey takes about four hours. (Departing Moscow at 8.23am and 4.20pm, and returning from Yaroslavl at 7am and 4.30pm) Buses run from Moscow's Central Shchyolkovsky Station and take five-and-a-half hours. From Yaroslavl, buses and trains also depart for other Golden Ring locations, or routes farther east into the Urals or north to St Petersburg. *Elektrichka* run regularly between Yaroslavl and Rostov Veliky and Sergiyev Posad. (Yaroslavl has two train stations. The main one being Yaroslavl Glavny, on the north side of the river, and then Yaroslavl Moskovsky on the southern side, where the bus station is located). A hydrofoil departs daily (around 6.20am) for Kostroma (two hours) and Plios (except Tuesdays and Thursdays, and when icy in winter) from the River Station at 2a Volzhskaya Embankment (tel. 485-254325).

As the largest city of the region, many hotels and eateries are scattered about the area. The area code for Yaroslavl is 485. The new 4-star business-class **Ring Premiere Hotel**, located at 55 Svoboda St (tel. 581-158), has over 100 rooms, a restaurant and pub. On the same street, at number 46, is the 7-room **Old Town (Stary Gorod) Hotel** (tel. 320-488). One block away is the **Restauran Vlasevski** with a downstairs café and upstairs restaurant. The inexpensive **Hotel Yuta** is at 79 Respublikanskaya St. A few 3-star hotels are the **Kotorosl** at 87 Bolshaya Okyabrskaya St near the main train station (tel. 211-581); the **Yubileynaya Hotel**, conveniently located near the monastery on the west bank of the river, at 11a Korotoslnaya Embankment (tel. 0852-309-259), and the **Medvezhny Ugol** at 16 Sverdlova St. Along the Volzhskaya Embankment (on the Volga) is the **Volzhskaya Zhemchuzhina Hotel**, near the Bashnya Arsenal. The 1920s-era **Hotel Volga** (formerly known as the Bristol) is centrally located at the corner of Andropov and Kirov Sts (tel. 308-131) with the **Café Rus** next door. A few blocks down on Pervomaiskaya St, Russian dishes are served at the **Golden Bear Café**, at number 3, and **Premiera** (number 5), located behind the Volkov Theater.

HISTORY

The bear was long worshipped by pagan inhabitants as a sacred animal. Another legend provides the story of Prince Yaroslavl the Wise (978–1054 AD) who wrestled a bear on the banks of the river and won. On the city's coat-of-arms a bear stands on his hind legs and holds a gold pole-ax, representing the endurance of the Yaroslavl spirit. In the ninth century a small outpost arose on the right bank of the Volga River and became known as Bear Corner, forming the northern border of the Rostov region. When Kievan Grand Prince Yaroslavl the Wise visited the settlement in 1010, its name was changed to honor him. It grew as large as Rostov; an early chronicle entry stated that in one great fire 17 churches burned to the ground. By the 13th century Yaroslavl had become the capital of its own principality along the Volga and remained politically independent for another 250 years.

The hordes of the Mongol Khan Batu invaded in 1238 and destroyed a great part of the city. In 1463, when Prince Alexander handed over his ancestral lands to Ivan III, the Grand Prince of Moscow, Yaroslavl was finally annexed to the Moscovy principality. For a short time Yaroslavl regained its political importance when it was made the temporary capital during the Time of Troubles from 1598 to 1613.

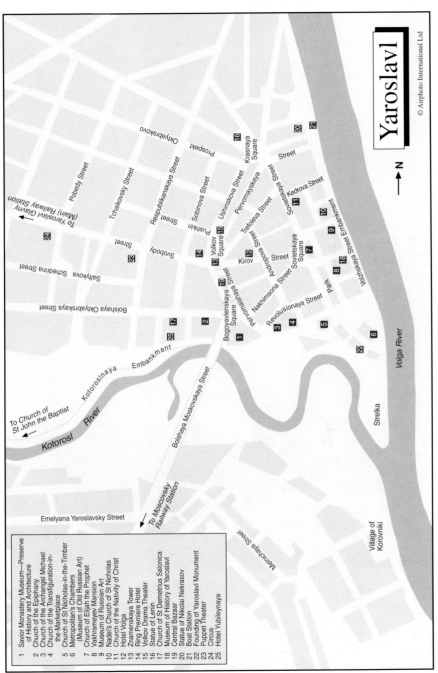

© Airphoto International Ltd

Yaroslavl

N

Okryabrskovo Prospekt

Tchaikovsky Street

Pobedy Street

To Yaroslavl Glavny (Main) Railway Station

Shchedrina Street

Salykova Street

Bolshaya Oktyabrskaya Street

Respublikanskaya Street

Svobody Street

Pushkin Street

Sobinova Street

Ushinskova Street

Krasnaya Square

Street

Pervomayskaya

Pervomaiskaya Street

Volkov Square

Kirov Street

Trefoleva Street

Nakhimsona Street

Androova Street

Sovietskaya Square

Sovietskaya Street

Kedrova Street

Bogoyavlenskaya Square

Revolusionaya Street

Park

Volzhskaya Street Embankment

Volga River

KotorosInaya Embankment

Kotorosl River

To Church of St John the Baptist

Bolshaya Moskovskaya Street

To Moscovsky Railway Station

Emelyana Yaroslavsky Street

Melnichnaya Street

Village of Korovniki

Strelka

1 Savior Monastery Museum—Preserve
   of History and Architecture
2 Church of the Epiphany
3 Church of the Archangel Michael
4 Church of the Transfiguration-in-
   the-Marketplace
5 Church of St Nicholas-in-the-Timber
6 Metropolitan's Chambers
   (Museum of Old Russian Art)
7 Church of Elijah the Prophet
8 Vakhrameyev Mansion
9 Museum of Russian Art
10 Nadel's Church of St Nicholas
11 Church of the Nativity of Christ
12 Hotel Volga
13 Znamenskaya Tower
14 Ring Premiere Hotel
15 Volkov Drama Theater
16 Statue of Lenin
17 Church of St Demetrius Salonica
18 Museum of History of Yaroslavl
19 Central Bazaar
20 Statue of Nikolai Nekrasov
21 Boat Station
22 Founding of Yaroslavl Monument
23 Puppet Theater
24 Circus
25 Hotel Yubileynaya

The city reached the height of its prosperity in the 17th-century when it became known for its handicrafts. Located along important trade routes, merchants journeyed from as far away as England and the Netherlands to purchase leather goods, silverware, wood carvings and fabrics. At one time, one-sixth of Russia's most prosperous merchant families lived in Yaroslavl, which was the second most populated city in the country. These families, in turn, put their wealth back into the city. By the middle of the 17th-century, more than 30 new churches had been built. During this time the city became an architectural chronicle etched in stone on a scale unmatched anywhere else in Russia. Yaroslavl was also Moscow's Volga port until the Moscow–Volga canal was built in 1937.

The *burlaki* (barge haulers) were a common sight, as portrayed in Repin's famous *Barge Haulers on the Volga*. Merchants would travel along the Volga and Kotorosl rivers to Rostov, and then along a system of rivers and dry land (*volokoi*), on to Vladimir. In 1795, Count Musin-Pushkin discovered in the Savior Monastery the famous 12th-century chronicle *The Lay of Igor's Host*. This text was based on the fighting campaigns of Prince Igor of Novgorod who, in the words of the chronicle, 'did not let loose ten falcons on a flock of swans, but laid down his own wizard fingers on living strings, which themselves throbbed out praises....' Later Borodin composed the opera *Prince Igor* based on this chronicle.

Barge Haulers on the Volga *was completed by Ilya Repin in 1873, shortly after he graduated from St Petersburg's Art Academy. Besides portraying the brutal reality of hard physical labor, the artist also symbolizes the spiritual strength of man which cannot be broken. The painting now hangs in St Petersburg's Russian Museum.*

Today there are over 300 historical sites listed in the city, many in need of restoration. But the cash-strapped Orthodox Church and city council have teamed up with international organizations to help revitalize the area. Joint ventures have been established, Kassel, Germany and Burlington, Vermont were even named sister cities. A local foundation has financed the re-creation of a whole pedestrian street to look like old Rus, with everything from coach inns and trading stalls to craft workshops and eating houses.

SIGHTS

A tour of Yaroslavl, known as the Florence of Russia, begins at the oldest part of town, the *strelka* (arrow or spit of land), lying along the west bank of the Volga, where the Kotorosl empties into it. The Bear Ravine, now Peace Boulevard, once separated the timber town from the *posad*, earth town.

By the Kotorosl, on Bogoyavlenskaya Ploshchad (Square), is the oldest surviving structure in Yaroslavl, the **Transfiguration of Our Savior Monastery**, founded at the end of the 12th-century. Northern Russia's first school of higher education was set up here, and the monastery library contained a huge collection of Russian and Greek literature. (Today the city remains one of the country's major learning centers.) It also grew into a large feudal power—by the end of the 16th century the monastery was one of the strongest fortresses in the northern states, with a permanent garrison of its own Streltsy, musketeer marksmen, to protect it. The white kremlin walls that dominate the town center were fortified to three meters (ten feet) thick in 1621. During an attack, the defenders would pour boiling water or hot tar on their enemies.

The Holy Gates of the monastery were built at the southern entrance in 1516. The archway frescoes include details from the Apocalypse. The 16th-century **bell tower** stands in front of the gates; climb up to the observation platform along its upper tier for a breathtaking panorama of the city.

The monastery's gold-domed **Cathedral of the Transfiguration of the Savior** (1506) was one of the wealthiest churches in Russia. The frescoes that cover the entire interior are the oldest wall paintings in Yaroslavl. The fresco of the *Last Judgment*, painted in 1564, is on the west wall; the east side contains scenes of the *Transfiguration and Adoration of the Virgin*. It served as the burial chamber for the Yaroslavl princes. The vestry exhibits icons and old vestments that were used during church rituals and services.

Behind the bell-clock tower are two buildings, the Refectory and the Chambers of the Father Superior and Monks, which now house branches of the **Yaroslavl Museums of Art, History and Architecture**. The museums are open daily 10am–5pm; closed Mondays and the first Wednesday of each month. The Refectory exhibits the history of the Yaroslavl region up to the present day. The monk cells contain collections of Old Russian art, including icons, folk art, manuscripts, costumes, armor and jewelry. Here also is the **Museum of The Lay of Igor's Host.** The story of this famous epic, along with ancient birch-bark documents and early printed books, is on display. Twelve years after Count Musin-Pushkin discovered the epic and other old rare manuscripts in the monastery library, the great fire of Moscow, during Napoleon's invasion, destroyed all the originals. **The Church of the Yaroslavl Miracle Workers** (1827), at the southern end of the cathedral, is the museum's cinema and lecture hall.

The red-brick and blue five-domed **Church of the Epiphany** (1684) stands on the square behind the monastery. The church is open from May 1 to October 1 from 10am–5pm; closed Tuesdays. It is festively decorated with *kokoshniki* and glazed colored tiles, a tradition of Yaroslavl church architecture. The interior is a rich tapestry of frescoes illustrating the life of Christ, painted by Yaroslavl artists in 1692; notice that the faces of the saints appear decidedly more human than in earlier decades. It also has an impressive gilded seven-tiered iconostasis. Across the street is the **Hotel Yubileynaya.**

Crossing the square and walking up Pervomaiskaya Ulitsa (away from the Volga) leads to the early 19th-century **Central Bazaar.** Today this area is still a busy shopping district. A short walk behind the walls of the arcade brings you to the Znamenskaya (Sign) Tower of the kremlin. Towers in Russia were usually named after the icon that was displayed over their entrance. This tower once held the icon known as Sign of the Mother of God.

On Volkov Ploshchad is the **Volkov Drama Theater,** founded by Fyodor Volkov, who opened Russia's first professional theater to the public in 1729; he formed his own drama company in 1748, and it was the first to stage *Hamlet* in Russia. Down the street at 59 Svobody is the city's first McDonalds.

At the end of Ushinskov Ulitsa is a statue of Lenin on Krasnaya Ploshchad (Red Square). Circle back toward the Volga, heading south on Sovietskaya Ulitsa until it intersects with Sovietskaya Ploshchad. Dominating the town's main square is the **Church of Elijah the Prophet,** now a Museum of Architecture (said to be built over the spot where the prince wrestled the bear). The church is open from May 1 to October 1, 10am–6pm; closed Wednesdays. Built in 1647, the white-stone church is decorated with ornamental tiles and surrounded by a gallery with chapels and a bell tower. The wooden iconostasis is carved in baroque fashion; the frescoes were painted in 1680 by the Kostroma artists Sila Savin and Gury Nikitin. These murals depict Christ's ascension, his life on earth, the lives of his Apostles, and the prophet Elijah. Prayer benches carved for Czar Alexei (father of Peter the Great) and Patriarch Nikon are also to be found inside.

Behind this church, by the Volga, at 23 Volzhskaya Avenue Embankment, is a **Branch Museum of Russian Art** from the 18th to 20th centuries, housed in the former governor's residence. Open 10am–5pm; closed Fridays. Across the street from the museum is **Nadei's Church of St Nicholas** (1620), a gift to the city from a wealthy merchant named Nadei Sveteshnikov. This church is open from May 1 to October 1, 10am–5pm; closed Thursdays. Ten churches in Yaroslavl were dedicated to St Nicholas, the patron saint of commerce. A wonderful stroll can now be taken on the pedestrian promenade that now runs along the bank of the Volga.

The impressive **Vakhrameyev Mansion** is a few blocks south near the water. The house was built in the 1780s in the baroque fashion. Members of this wealthy noble family were avid patrons of the arts in Yaroslavl. Behind the mansion (at 17 Volzhskaya Embankment) is a small Branch, the **Museum of Local Art and History**. Open 10am–5.30pm; closed Mondays.

Walking south along the Volga, on Volzhskaya Avenue Embankment, leads to the two-story building of the Metropolitan's Chambers (1690), located in the old timber town. It was originally built to accommodate the Metropolitan of Rostov Veliky when he visited. The chambers are now a **Museum of Old Russian Art**, displaying many icons, paintings and ceramic tiles. The museum is open from 10am–5pm; closed Fridays. Of interest is the icon *The Lay of the Bloody Battle with Khan Mamai*, a portrait of Count Musin-Pushkin and a bronze sculpture of Yaroslavl the Wise.

Making your way back west toward the Savior Monastery, along the Kotorosl River, leads past three distinctive churches. The first is the simple white cube-shaped **Church of St Nicholas-in-the-Timber** (1695), built by the local shipbuilders who lived in this part of the timber town. Next is the **Church of the Transfiguration-in-the-Market-Place** (1672). It was built from funds collected by the townspeople in the old marketplace of the original earth town, where the local merchants and artisans lived. In the summer of 1693, 22 Yaroslavl artists helped paint the interior frescoes. The red-brick **Church of the Archangel Michael** (1658), directly across from the monastery, stands on the site of a former palace. It once marked the boundary between the kremlin and the marketplace and is filled with brightly colored frescoes painted by local Yaroslavl artists in 1730.

In the village of Tolchkovo (in the southwestern part of the city) is the picturesque 15-domed **Church of St John the Baptist** (1671), located at 69 Kotorosl Embankment. The five central green domes with a tulip-shaped dome in the middle, gold crosses and ornamental tiles, are prime examples of the architecture of the Golden Age of Yaroslavl. The whole principality of Yaroslavl donated funds to build the church. In 1694, 15 masters from around Russia painted the frescoes and icons that adorn every part of the interior. The baroque-style iconostasis was carved in 1701. The complex also includes a seven-tiered bell tower. The church is open 10am–6pm; closed Tuesdays.

Just south of the confluence of the Kotorosl with the Volga (at 2 Port Embankment), is a delightful architectural ensemble in the **Village of Korovniki**. (From the Savior Monastery, it is a 1 kilometer walk, or ride two stops on bus number 4). The most impressive structure is the five-domed **Church of St John Chrysostom** (1649). Its tent-shaped, 100-foot-tall bell tower is known as the Candle of Yaroslavl. The **Church of Our Lady of Vladimir** (1669) was used as the winter church. Other buildings of interest are the **Church of St Nicholas-the-Wet** and its 'twin' winter **Church of Our Lady of Tikhvin**. The Korovnikova Sloboda was built in 1654, and its churches decorated with colored ceramic tiles and faceted tent-shaped roofs and bell towers.

If you have time, take a boat ride along the Volga. Summer services leave from a pier at the end of Pervomaiskaya Ulitsa. The trip to Dolmatovo takes about half an hour. For a longer excursion, try the 35-minute ride to the **Village of Tolga** (on the Konstantinovo route), where one can explore and picnic in the area.

In 1992, the **Tolga Convent** and **Tolchkovo Church** were beautifully restored with funds donated by city and local firms. The structures are highly decorated with ornamental bricks, terracotta and colorfully glazed tiles. On Tugova Hill, to the left of the village, looms the single-domed **Church of St Paraskeva**, built over the mass grave of Yaroslavl warriors who were killed in battle against the invading Mongols. To its right stands the **Church of St Theodore**, the **Church of St Nicholas Pensky**, and beyond another **Church of St Nicholas-at-Melenki**.

Long-distance cruiseships also stop in Yaroslavl on their way to Moscow or Astrakhan. These ships are rarely full, and tickets can often be bought at short notice.

For an evening's entertainment, go to the **Yaroslavl Circus** (located at 69 Svobody Ultisa across from Truda Square). The Puppet Theatre is at 25 Svobody. Each summer, beginning on August 1st, the Yaroslavl Sunsets Music Festival is held, which usually opens with the overture to Borodin's *Prince Igor*.

VICINITY OF YAROSLAVL

On the Uglich Highway, 29 kilometers (18 miles) southwest of Yaroslavl, is the **Cosmos Museum**, dedicated to Valentina Tereshkova the first female cosmonaut. In 2000, Tereshkova was honored as a 'Woman of the Century.' She was born on March 6th 1937 to a family of communal farmers. Soviet leader Nikita Khrushchev picked her (from among four final candidates) to be the first woman in space. Tereshkova's first space flight was on June 16th 1963 on the board Vostok-6. It lasted 70 hours and 41 minutes and she orbited the earth 48 times. 'It is I, Chaika [Seagull],' she radioed back after reaching orbit. From then on, she was known as 'Our Chaika' by fellow Russians. The museum, near the house where she was born in the village of Nikulskoye, displays her space capsule and the history of Soviet space travel. The museum is open 10am–5pm, closed Mondays. The service desk at your hotel may arrange excursions to these places.

About 16 kilometers (10 miles) south from Yaroslavl, along the Moscow–Yaroslavl M8 Highway, is the **Nekrasov Estate Museum** in the village of Karabikha. The famous Russian writer Nikolai Nekrasov (1821–78) stayed on the estate in the summer months; it retains much of its former appearance. Among his works is the satire *Who is Happy in Russia?* His poems and other works are on display. The museum is open 10am–5pm; closed Mondays. Each summer there is a Nekrasov Poetry Festival at Karabikha.

TUTAYEV ON THE VOLGA Тутаев

About 40 kilometers (25 miles) northwest of Yaroslavl, on the way to Rybinsk (along the P151 road) lies the village of Tutayev. *Elektrichka* trains also travel here from Yaroslavl. If you have time, and enjoy viewing historical architectural sites, it is a pleasant short trip along the Volga to this quaint town.

In the 13th century when Prince Roman (great-grandson of Grand Prince 'Big Nest' Vsevolod) was granted lands in this area, the village district became known as Romanov-Borisoglebsk. On opposite banks of the Volga, the prince constructed two fortified towns with ramparts and a moat. The prince's troops lived in Romanov, while the townspeople congregated in Borisoglebsk, on the right bank. It was not until 1921 that the town's name was changed to Tutayev, in honor of a Red Army hero.

In the 1670s the five-domed **Cathedral of the Resurrection** was built on the foundations of an older 12th-century church and embellished with a tent-shaped bell tower, elaborate porches and ornamental brickwork and tiling. Yaroslavl artists painted the 17th-century interior frescoes. *The Tower of Babel, The Last Judgment,* and *Tortures of Hell* attest to their love of biblical scenes.

Along the left bank, six other churches and their tent-shaped bell towers rise above the maple and birch sprinkled countryside. The oldest is the **Cathedral of the Exaltation of the Cross**, standing on the town's old ramparts. Further up the river is the **Spaso-Arkhangelskaya Church**, the **Church of the Virgin of Kazan** (on the hillside), and the **Church of the Intercession**, all built in the early 18th-century.

(following pages) Most all the towns in the Golden Ring contain elaborately decorated Russian-Orthodox churches with zakomara semi-circular arches and carved kokoshniki gables, topped with colorful onion domes—a magnificent sight even on a bleak winter's afternoon.

KOSTROMA Кострома

Kostroma, 76 kilometers (47 miles) northeast of Yaroslavl, can be reached by the A113 road, or taking a commuter *elektrichka* train from Yaroslavl (two-and-a-half to three hours). A six and a half-hour overnight train runs from Moscow's Yaroslavsky Station. It departs at 10.19pm and arrives in Kostroma at 5am. A return train for Moscow departs at 11pm. Buses make more frequent departures from Moscow's Shchyolkovsky Terminal (eight hours, twenty minutes). Buses also depart from here for other Golden Ring towns. From Yaroslavl, a hydrofoil departs daily (around 6.20am) for Kostroma (two hours) and Plios (except Tuesdays and Thursdays, and when the river is icy in winter); the boat makes trips in both directions.

Kostroma is the only city in Russia which has retained the original layout of its town center; it was founded by Yuri Dolgoruky in the 12th-century. Reconstructed in the early 18th-century, it is one of the country's finest examples of old Russian classic design; no two houses are alike.

Once a bustling trade center known as the Flax Capital of the North, Kostroma (pronounced with last syllable accented) supplied Russia and Europe with the finest sail cloth. The emblem of this picturesque town set along the confluence of the Kostroma and Volga Rivers depicts a small boat on silvery waters with sails billowing in the wind. The central mercantile square was situated on the north banks of the Volga. The Krasniye (Beautiful) and Bolshiye (Large) stalls were connected by covered galleries where fabrics and other goods were sold. Today the modernized **Arcade** still houses the town's markets and stores. In the center of these stands the **Monument to Ivan Susanin** on the town's central square of the same name. Susanin was a local peasant hero who saved the first Romanov czar from a Polish assassination attempt. A popular patriotic opera, *Ivan Susanin*, was later written in his honor by Mikhail Glinka. After a 1773 fire, Catherine the Great had the Susaninskaya Square rebuilt and today it still appears as if it were the original, complete with fire tower, former military jail, and town hall (now a UNESCO protected area). The **Borschchov Mansion** (home of the general who fought in the War of 1812), the largest of the older residential buildings, is now a courthouse.

North from the square, at 5–7 Pavlovskaya Ulitsa, is the **Art Museum**, originally built in 1913 to honor 300 years of Romanov rule. Today, it has a small exhibit of 16th- to 19th-century Russian art. Open 10am–5pm, closed Mondays and Fridays. A few minutes walk west along Ulitsa Simanovskovo brings you to the recently restored **Monastery of the Epiphany**, currently undergoing restoration. The monastery's cathedral is the main functioning church in the town. Inside can be found the "Icon of the Fyodorovsky Virgin", said to have worked miracles for Alexander Nevsky.

The real gem of the area is the **Ipatyevsky Monastery**, located west of town on the opposite side of the Kostroma River. It was founded in the 14th century by the Zernov Boyars, ancestors of the Godunovs. This large structure is enclosed by a white-brick kremlin and topped by green tent-shaped domes. Later the relatives of Boris Godunov built the monastery's golden-domed **Trinity Cathedral**. While Boris Godunov was czar (1598–1605), the Ipatyevsky Monastery became the wealthiest in the country, containing over 100 icons. The Godunov family had its own mansion (the rose-colored building with the small windows) within the monastery, and most members were buried in the cathedral. The monastery was continually ravaged by internal strife, blackened by Polish invasions, and captured by the second False Dmitri in 1605, who claimed the throne of the Russian Empire. Later the Romanovs who, like the Godunovs, were powerful feudal lords in Kostroma, got the young Mikhail elected czar after the Time of Troubles. In 1613, Mikhail Romanov left the monastery to be crowned in the Moscow Kremlin. In 2006, Britain's Prince Michael of Kent (who is related to the Romanov Dynasty) presented a new eight-ton, brass bell to the cathedral. Today the famous Ipatyevsky Chronicles are displayed here; this valuable document, found in the monastery's archives, traces the fascinating history of ancient Rus. Open daily 10am–4.30pm. Right next to the monastery, at 3a Beregovaya Street, is the small wooden hotel **Ipatyevskaya Sloboda** (tel. 577-179), with seven cozy guest rooms.

The **Church of St John the Divine** (1687), which functioned as the winter church, stands nearby. From the monastery's five-tiered bell tower, there is a pleasing view of the countryside and the **Museum of Old Wooden Architecture**, open daily to the public. Intricately carved old wooden buildings gathered from nearby villages include the **Church of the Virgin** (1552), a typical peasant dwelling, a windmill and a bathhouse.

Other churches on the north bank of the Volga are the **Church of the Transfiguration** (1685), **Church of St Elijah-at-the-Gorodishche** (1683–85) and the beautiful hilltop **Church of the Prophet Elijah**.

The beautiful **Church of the Resurrection-on-the-Debre** is situated on the eastern outskirts of town. In 1652, the merchant Kiril Isakov built this elaborate red-brick and green-domed church from money found in a shipment of English dyes. When informed of the discovery of gold pieces, the London company told Isakov to keep the money for 'charitable deeds'. Some of the bas-reliefs on the outside of the church illustrate the British lion and unicorn. The towering five-domed church has a gallery running along the sides; at the northwestern end is the **Chapel of Three Bishops**, with a magnificently carved iconostasis. The gates of the church are surrounded by ornamental *kokoshniki*, and the interior is ornately decorated with frescoes and icons from the 15th-century.

The area code for Kostroma is 494. The moderately-priced **Kostroma Hotel**, at 120 Sovietskaya, (tel. 533-661 or 541-081), is on the south bank of the Volga (request a room on the river side with balcony). On the same street, at number 29, is the inexpensive, comfortable **Mush Guesthouse** (tel. 312-400 or 311-045; email: bacha@mush.ru). The **Hotel Stary Dvor** is down the street at number 6. The three-star **Shelestoff Hotel** is at 1 Kommunatov Street.

On the Yaroslavl road, about two kilometers south of town, is the moderately-priced three-star **Hotel Intourist Kostroma**, at 40 Magistralnaya Street (tel. 533-661). The **Volga Hotel** is located about two kilometers east of town at 1 Yunosheskayay Street (tel. 546-163 or 546-262). The **Berezovaya Rosha** is at 38 Malyshkovskaya (tel. 537-532).

VICINITY OF KOSTROMA

The areas in and around Kostroma were well known in Moscovy for their production of gold and silver ornaments, and the major jewelry workshops were situated in the village of **Krasnoye-on-the-Volga**. The lands of Krasnoye were once owned by the Godunov family. The oldest building in the village is the white-stone and octagon-shaped **Cathedral of the Epiphany** (1592). Its helmet drum, tented roof (the tent-shape style became popular in the early 16th century), long gallery, side chapels and decorative *kokoshniki* patterns are similar to Moscow's St Basil's Cathedral, built three decades earlier.

Situated 63 kilometers (38 miles) southeast of Kostroma is the small enchanting town of **Plios**. In summer, boats make the trip along the Volga from Yaroslavl and Kostroma. Local buses also run from Kostroma. The son of Dmitri Donskoi, Vasily I, founded the village in 1410 as a stronghold and lookout point from the area's *plios*, the straight part of a river between its bends. The fortress protected the region from the Mongols, who had already conquered the Kingdoms of Kazan and Astrakhan further down the Volga. The lovely white five-domed **Church of the Resurrection**, built in the 18th-century, stands on a bluff overlooking the water. One of Russia's finest landscape artists, Isaak Levitan, loved to spend his summers here. He painted the famous *Golden Plios in the Evening*, one of Anton Chekhov's favorites. The **Levitan House Museum** is situated in the eastern part of town, across the Shokhonka River. Here are exhibited some works by Levitan and other local artists. Open 10am–5pm, closed Mondays.

Inside Kostroma's Museum of Old Wooden Architecture stands the weathered Church of the Virgin, built in 1552.

IVANOVO Иваново

Ivanovo, an industrial and regional center 288 kilometers (180 miles) northeast of Moscow (and about 80 kilometers/50 miles south of Kostroma), began as a small village on the right bank of the River Uvod. Trains run here from Yaroslavl, as well as from Moscow's Yaroslavsky Station. One train departs Moscow at 10.09pm and arrives at 4.45am. It returns from Ivanovo at 10.40pm for Moscow. Buses also run from Moscow's Shchyolkovskoye station (six and a half hours), Vladimir (three hours), Yaroslavl and Kostroma (two hours). To drive, take the A113 south from Kostroma, or the M7 from Moscow then the A113 north from Vladimir. The River Talka also crosses the town; both rivers flow into the River Klyazma, a tributary of the Moskva. The village of Voznesensk on the left bank was annexed by Ivanovo in 1871. In 1561, a chronicle mentioned that Ivan the Terrible presented the village of Ivanovo to a powerful princely family. When two centuries later an Ivanovo princess married a Sheremetyev, the town passed over to this powerful aristocratic family. In 1710, Peter the Great ordered weaving mills and printing factories built here. Soon the town grew into a major textile and commercial center with little religious significance. Ivanovo calico was famous worldwide; by the mid-1800s, the town was known as the Russian Manchester. Today almost 20 percent of the country's cloth is produced in this city of more than half a million people. Ivanovo is nicknamed the City of Brides—since 80 percent of textile workers are women, many men come here to look for a wife.

Ivanovo participated actively in the revolutionary campaigns and was called the Third Proletarian Capital after Moscow and the former Leningrad. Major strikes were held in the city. In 1897, 14,000 workers held a strike against the appalling conditions in the factories. A 1905 strike, with over 80,000 participants, was headed by the famous Bolshevik leader Mikhail Frunze, who established the town's first Workers' Soviet, which provided assistance to the strikers and their families during the three-month protest.

Compared to other Golden Ring towns, Ivanovo is relatively new and modern, with only a few places of particular interest. On Lenin Prospekt, the **Ivanovo Museums of Art and History** portray the city's historical events and display collections of textiles, old printing blocks and other traditional folk arts. Off Kuznetsov Street is the **Museum-Study of Mikhail Frunze**. On Smirnov Street is the 17th-century **Shudrovskaya Chapel**; on nearby Sadovaya Street stands the large red-bricked **House Museum of the Ivanovo-Voznesensk City Council**. Other locations of interest in the city are the circus, puppet theater, a 17th-century wooden church and **Stepanov Park**, with an open-air theater, planetarium and boats for hire.

The **Soyuz Hotel** is at 47b Fr. Engelsa Prospekt and the inexpensive **Tsentralnaya** is down the same street at number 1 (tel. 493-328-122). The larger **Tourist Hotel** is at 9 Naberezhnaya St (tel. 493-376-436), and the centrally located **Sovietskaya Hotel** is at 64 Lenin Street (tel. 493-372-547).

PALEKH Палех

This village lies 48 kilometers (30 miles) east of Ivanovo and is famous for its colorfully painted lacquer boxes. Drive east along the P152/80, or local buses run here from Ivanovo, Vladimir or Suzdal. After the Revolution when icon production was halted, it became popular to paint small miniatures on lacquer papier-mâché boxes, which combined the art of ancient Russian painting with the local folk crafts. Ivan Golivko (1886–1937), the Master of Palekh Folk Art, created many beautiful lacquer scenes drawn from traditional Russian fairy tales, folk epics and songs; he sometimes lined the box interiors with Russian poetry. The **Museum of Palekh Art** displays a magnificent collection of painted boxes and other lacquer art by the folk artists of Palekh. These include works by the master Golivko, who established a shop of ancient folk art in 1924. This included a wide assortment of objects: wooden toys, porcelain, glass and jewelry boxes. The most popular became the lacquered papier-mâché boxes. The **Timber House of Golivko** where he lived and worked, is also open to the public. The best eatery in town is the Palekh Restaurant.

The painter, Pavel Korin (1892–1967) was born in Palekh, and his family house, a typical *izba*, hosts a museum dedicated to this gifted artist. Korin often featured Palekh in his watercolors, and later amassed one of the largest collections of icons in Soviet Russia. He also worked as the head of restoration at Moscow's Pushkin Museum of Fine Arts.

Traditionally the Palekh box was fashioned from birch wood or linden and varnished black on the outside, with a red interior and gold highlights. (This trinity of colors has a meaning: the word red, *krasny*, also signifies beauty, black symbolizes the mystery and sorrows of life, and gold represents the spirit's eternal glory.) The artists used special tempura (egg-based) paints and made fine brushes from squirrels' tails.

Today, fine layers of papier-mâché (slow-cooked for up to three months) are applied to the wood, followed by several coats of clear lacquer. Then the outline of the painting is sketched on with white paint. It can then take up to a year for an artist to paint a more complex design. Upon completion, between seven and 12 more coats of lacquer must be applied, and each one dried and polished to achieve the perfect finish. The top can be further decorated with gold, silver and mother-of-pearl. A wolf's tooth was once used to fine polish the decorative colors. Besides Palekh, three other nearby villages also developed their own schools of Russian lacquer art, including Kholui and Mstyora.

The fourth, Fedoskino, located north of Moscow, also has its own speciality school, where students train up to five years. It was first established in 1798, when the merchant Korobov began to produce snuff boxes. He was the first in Russia to produce boxes of papier-mâché, a process he discovered in Germany. The artists became known for their snow and troika scenes, and village landscapes with girls in traditional costumes. The paintings are also characterized by an underlay of gold leaf or mother of pearl, which adds to the miniature an iridescent glow.

Beware when purchasing a lacquer box. A recent survey in Moscow found that over 90 percent of the so-called lacquer miniatures were not genuine. (There are less than 2,000 qualified artists trained in this tradition, so many boxes sold are not high quality.) Stores often tout authenticity, but sell replicas at inflated prices (and count on the ignorance of the buyer). Check out the smoothness of the lacquer; if pimple dots bubble along the surface, it's not an original. Often, on cheaper boxes, the design is a decal lacquered on, not an original painting. If interested in purchasing an expensive box, buy only from a reputable dealer. Ultimately, let your eye be the best judge.

The 17th-century **Cathedral of the Exaltation of the Holy Cross**, now a museum, stands in the town center. A plaque on the outside of the west wall shows the builder to be Master Yegor Dubov. Local craftsmen carved and painted the magnificent golden baroque-style iconostasis inside the church, bedecked with nearly 50 icons from floor to ceiling. In front stands a near life-size sculpture of Christ on the cross, with a large intricate chandelier hanging above. The Czar Gates were brought from a church in the town of Uglich. For centuries before the Revolution the highly respected Palekh artists were sent all over Russia to paint beautiful icons and frescoes in the Central Russian style.

Today the artists of Palekh carry on the traditions of lacquer design and over 250 craftsmen are employed at the Palekh Art Studio. Palekh lacquerware and jewelry are widely sold throughout Russia and the world. One of the most popular motifs is the Firebird, a well-known Russian folk tale (see page 556). The writer Maxim Gorky, who often asked Golivko to illustrate his texts, wrote: 'The masters of Palekh carry on the icon painting traditions through their boxes... and with these beautiful achievements, win the admiration of all who see them.'

THE FIREBIRD

*O*nce upon a time, a very long time ago, there was a beautiful girl named Marushka, who was orphaned at an early age. This maiden was capable of embroidering the most beautiful and exquisite patterns on cloths and silks; no one, on all the earth, could match her talents.

Word of her marvelous works spread far and wide, and merchants from all over the world sought Marushka, trying to lure her off to their kingdoms. 'Come

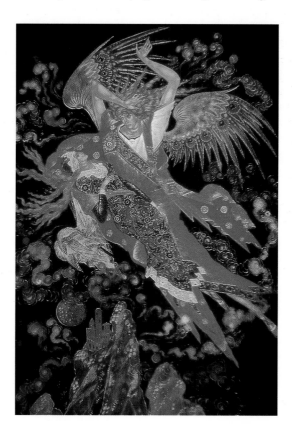

away with us,' they pleaded, 'riches and fame will surely be yours.' Marushka always replied, 'I shall never leave the village where I was born. But if you indeed find my work beautiful, then I will sell it to you. If you don't have the money, you can repay me whenever you can. I get my pleasure from the work itself; the money I distribute throughout my village.'

Even though the merchants would leave the village without Marushka, they spread their stories of her incredible talent across the world. The tales finally reached the ears of Kaschei the Immortal, the most wicked of the sorcerers. Kaschei was immediately curious and enraged to think that such beauty existed somewhere that he had never seen. He learned too that Marushka was quite beautiful herself, so he turned himself into the handsomest of princes and flew out over the mountains, oceans, and almost impassable birch forests until he found Marushka's village.

'Where is the maiden who embroiders the most exquisite of patterns?' He was led to her very door, as the villagers were used to the many visitors. When Marushka answered the door herself, the disguised sorcerer asked to see all the needlework and tapestry that she had ready to show. Marushka fetched all her shirts and sashes, towels and trousers, handkerchiefs and hats. Kaschei could hardly contain his delight.

Marushka said, 'My lord, I hope my work pleases you. Anything that meets your fancy is yours to keep. If you don't have the money, you needn't pay me. My happiness comes from your delight.'

Although the great Kaschei could not believe that this girl could fashion things even better than he, he was also taken by her beauty and kindness. He decided that if he could not make such things himself, then he most possess her and take her home to his kingdom.

'Come away with me, and I will make you my queen. You shall live in my palace, all the fruits of my kingdom shall be yours, your clothes shall be covered with jewels, and birds of paradise will sing you to sleep every night. You shall even have your own chamber, containing the most exotic of threads and materials, where you will embroider for me and my kingdom.'

Marushka listened quietly to all this, then she softly replied, 'I couldn't ever leave this village where my parents are buried, where I was born. Here my heart shall always be. There is nothing sweeter than the fields and woods and neighbors of my own village. I must give my embroidery to anyone who receives joy from my work. I could never embroider for you alone.'

The Great Kaschei had never been refused, nor had he ever failed to bewitch a mere girl. Furious, his face suddenly changed from that of the handsome prince to his very own, dark and raging. At this sight, Marushka gasped and tried to flee the room. But it was too late.

'Because you will not leave your village and come to be my queen, because you dared to refuse the Great Kaschei, from this moment on I cast a spell on you. You shall be a bird! I shall make sure that you fly far, far away and never see your village again!'

As he spoke these terrible words, the beautiful Marushka turned into a magnificent, flaming red firebird. In the same moment, the Great Kaschei turned himself into a great black falcon, who swooped down on the firebird, grasping her in his enormous claws. He carried her high into the clouds so she would never return to her birthplace.

Marushka knew that she had to leave something behind. As the great falcon carried her through the sky, the firebird began to shed her flaming plumage. Soon, feather after feather floated down, dusting her beloved homeland. A rainbow of colors dotted the meadows and forests; and by the time the falcon had reached its own kingdom, all her feathers had fallen, leaving a shimmering trail right back to her cottage.

Even though the firebird died, all her magical feathers continued to live forever. The firebird's feathers carried their own spell: All those who loved and honored beauty in themselves and others, as Marushka, and who sought to create beauty for others, without expecting anything in return, would always be able to see the firebird's feathers.

VLADIMIR Владимир
THE CENTER OF THE GOLDEN AGE OF RUS

Vladimir lies 190 kilometers (118 miles) northeast of Moscow along the M7 Highway. It is recommended to spend at least a few days in the Vladimir region. Suburban and long-distance trains run to Vladimir and the surrounding region, departing daily from Moscow's Kursk (Metro Kurskaya) or Yaroslavl stations and take nearly four hours to reach Vladimir, passing through the hundred miles of cultivated countryside dotted with farms that raise corn and livestock. The same rural scenes of farmers, dressed in embroidered peasant shirts with wide leather belts and *valenki* (black felt boots), plowing the fertile land were painted by Russian artists such as Kramskoi, Vrubel and Repin over a century ago.

By car, take the M7 Highway. An expensive express train to Vladimir now departs Moscow's Kursky Station at 6.04pm and arrives at 8.30pm. The return train leaves at 7.25am and arrives at 9.55am. Cheaper long-distance trains also depart from Moscow's Kursky station and stop in Vladimir (taking about three hours); these depart at 2pm and 6.20pm. (A return train is at 8.59am). Direct and transit buses also run to Vladimir from Moscow's Shchyolkovsky central terminal and take between three and four hours. From Vladimir, buses also depart for other Golden Ring towns as Suzdal, Ivanovo and Yaroslavl. Both train and bus stations are located in the southeast section of Vladimir, and trolley buses cover all the main routes about town.

The area code for Vladimir is 492. Two inexpensive three-star hotels are located on the town's main street of Bolshaya Moskovskaya—the **Hotel Vladimir** at number 74 (tel. 327-239 or 324-447,) and the **U Zolotykh Vorot** at number 15. At number 88 is the **Tri Peskarya** (Three Minnows) Restaurant serving Russian-style food. Another three-star hotel is the **Orion** at 3 Nikolskaya Street. At the west end, is the largest hotel in town, the two-star Soviet-style **Zolotoye Koltso** (Golden Ring) at 27 Chaikovskaya Street (tel. 248-807 or 247-208), and the similar-styled **Zarya Hotel** is at 36a Studionaya Gora (tel. 327-960). Other hotels include the **Klyazma**, set 2 kilometers from the center, at 15 Sudogorskoye Hwy. (tel. 324-483 or 324-237), and the two-star **Hotel Dobroye**, about 5 kilometers from the railway station, at 217 Dobroselskaya Street (tel. 213-760 or 213-564). Cafés are plentiful along the main steet, a supermarket is at 10 Moskovskaya, and an Internet Café is near the main shopping arcade.

After visiting Vladimir, spend the next day in the ancient town of Suzdal, only 16 miles (26 kilometers) to the north. Between these two cities is the historic village of Bogoliubovo and the Church-of-the-Intercession on the River Nerl.

Children swim and fish in the Klyazma River in Vladimir. The old Refectory buildings and bell tower of the town stand over the residents' wooden dacha-style homes.

HISTORY

Even though Vladimir is now a bustling city of nearly 350,000 and the administrative head of the region, it is still one of the best preserved centers of 12th- and 13th-century Old Russian architecture. Eight centuries ago Vladimir was the most powerful town of ancient Rus. Located on the banks of the Klyazma River, a small tributary of the Volga, Vladimir was an important stop on the trade routes between Europe and Asia. Greeks from Constantinople, Vikings from the north, Bulgars from the Volga and Central Asian merchants all journeyed through the Vladimir-Suzdal principality.

Vsevolod, the son of Kievan Grand Prince Yaroslavl the Wise, first began to settle the area of Vladimir in northeastern Rus while Kiev was being attacked by numerous hostile tribes in the late 11th-century. At this time many Russians began to migrate northward; this exodus is described in one of Russia's earliest epic chronicles, *The Lay of Igor's Host*. With the death of his father, Vsevolod became the most powerful prince in the land. Prince Vsevolod built a small fortress near the village of Suzdal on the road from Kiev. Later a trading settlement was established around the fort by Vsevolod's son, who also built the first stone church. The town was named after Vladimir Monomakh in 1108. After Monomakh's death in 1125, the Kievan states in the south began to lose their political and economic importance; under Monomakh's son Yuri Dolgoruky, the northern territories began to flourish. Vladimir grew so large and prosperous that it became the capital of northern Rus by the middle of the 12th-century.

Dolgoruky's heir Andrei Bogoliubsky decided to rule Russia from a more centralized and peaceful area, and transferred the throne of the grand prince from Kiev to Vladimir in 1157, after a vision of the Blessed Virgin directed him to do so. Bogoliubsky (Lover of God) left Kiev under the protection of a holy icon, said to have been painted by St Luke from Constantinople, known as Our Lady of Vladimir. This revered icon became the sacred palladium of the Vladimir region; the prince even took it on his military campaigns. As the protectorate of the city, it became the symbol of divine intervention and power of the grand princes, and now hangs in Moscow's Tretyakov Gallery.

Andrei brought in master artists and craftsmen to recreate the splendors of Kiev in the new town of Vladimir. A crowned lion carrying a cross was the town's coat-of-arms. Under his brother Vsevolod III (who ruled from 1174 to 1212) the Vladimir-Suzdal principality, with Vladimir as its capital, reached the zenith of its political power.

When the Mongol Tartars invaded in 1238, Vladimir, like many other towns in Russia, suffered extensive damage. A Novgorod chronicle described the Mongol invasion: 'The Tartars struck the town with their wall-battering weapons; they

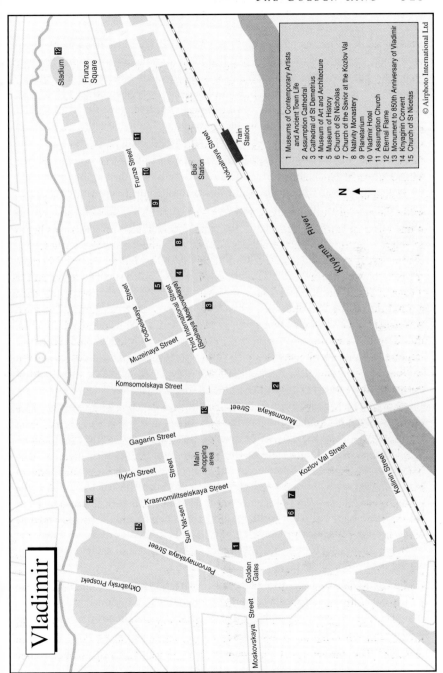

Vladimir

1 Museums of Contemporary Artists
   and Ancient Town Life
2 Assumption Cathedral
3 Cathedral of St Demetrius
4 Museum of Art and Architecture
5 Museum of History
6 Church of St Nicholas
7 Church of the Savior at the Kozlov Val
8 Nativity Monastery
9 Planetarium
10 Vladimir Hotel
11 Assumption Church
12 Eternal Flame
13 Monument to 850th Anniversary of Vladimir
14 Knyaginin Convent
15 Church of St Nicetas

© Airphoto International Ltd

Stadium

Frunze
Square

Frunze Street

Bus
Station

Vokzalnaya Street

Train
Station

Klyazma River

N

Podbelskaya Street

Muzeinaya Street

Third International Street
(Bolshaya Moskovskaya)

Komsomolskaya Street

Muromskaya Street

Gagarin Street

Main
shopping
area

Ilyich Street

Street

Krasnomilitseiskaya Street

Sun Yat-sen

Kozlov Val Street

Kalinin Street

Pervomayskaya Street

Golden
Gates

Oktyabrsky Prospekt

Moskovskaya Street

released endless streams of arrows. Prince Vsevolod saw their fierce battle axes, took fright (because of his youth), and fled forth from the town with his group of men, carrying many gifts and hoping to save his life. Batu Khan [son of Genghis], like a wild beast, did not spare him, but ordered that he be slaughtered before him, and then he slew the rest of the town. When the bishop, with the princess and her children, fled into the church (the Assumption Cathedral), the godless one commanded it to be set on fire. Thus, they surrendered their souls to God.'

For a brief time, Vladimir retained the seat of the Church Metropolitan, and the grand princes were still crowned in the town's Uspensky Cathedral. But eventually the princes of Moscovy began governing Russia through the Khans (until the Tartar yoke was broken in 1480). In 1328, Grand Prince Ivan I transferrd his residence from Vladimir to Moscow and shortly thereafter Vladimir was annexed to the principality of Moscovy. When Moscow became the capital of the country in the 16th century, Vladimir's importance slowly declined; by 1668, the population numbered only 990. After the Revolution the city grew with industrialization and today it is a large producer of electrical machinery. The Vladimiret tractor, sold around the world, once won a Gold Medal at a Brussels Machinery Exhibition.

SIGHTS

To enter the old part of town along the river, pass through the **Golden Gates** (the only surviving gates of the city), built in 1158 by Prince Bogoliubsky, who modeled them after the Golden Gates of Kiev. The oak doors of the now white gates were once covered with gilded copper; the golden-domed structure on top of the gates was the Church of the Deposition of the Robe. These gates were used as a defense fortification for the western part of town and also served as a triumphal arch— Alexander Nevsky, Dmitri Donskoi in 1380 and troops on their way to fight Napoleon in the Battle of Borodino in 1812 all passed through the arch. The gates were damaged many times through the years, and were reconstructed in the 18th-century. Today the Golden Gates house the local **Military Historical Museum**. Next to the Gates, in the red-brick building (formerly a church) and the fire observation tower, are the **Museums of Contemporary Artists and Ancient Town Life**. The latter has many interesting old illustrations and black and white photographs tracing the history of the region.

During and after the reigns of Catherine the Great, Vladimir became best known for the 'Road of Tears,' called Vladimirka, along which an innumerable stream of prisoners were marched into exile from Moscow to Siberia. The town was also used as a transit prison during the Stalin era.

One block south of the Golden Gates are the simple white **Church of St Nicholas** and the **Church of the Savior at the Kozlov Val**, both built in the late 17th-century. Climb the Kozlov Tower for a great view of the city. Nearer the water is the **Church of St Nicholas-at-Galeya**, with its tent-shaped bell tower. The church was built by a wealthy citizen of Vladimir in the early 18th-century.

The oldest buildings of the city were constructed on the hills by the water, which served as a defense. As you walk through the gates, a cluster of golden-domed white churches come into view. In 1158, Andrei Bogoliubsky brought in master craftsmen from all over Russia and Europe to build the triple-domed Uspensky Sobor, the **Assumption Cathedral**. Built to rival Kiev's St Sophia, the cathedral was decorated with gold, silver and precious stones. It was the tallest building in all of Rus. Filled with frescoes and icons, the iconostasis was also the largest of its kind in Russia. A tenth of the grand prince's revenue was contributed to the upkeep of the cathedral. After much of it was destroyed by fire in 1185 (along with 33 other churches), Prince Vsevolod III had it rebuilt with five domes. Since the original walls were encased within a larger structure, the cathedral doubled in size, with an area for a congregation of 4,000 people. The Italian architect Fioravante used it as his model for the Moscow Kremlin's own Assumption Cathedral. After more fires blackened the walls, the famous iconists Andrei Rublyov and Daniil Chorny were sent to restore the interior in 1408 and painted over 300 square meters (3,200 square feet) of wall space; frescoes from the 12th and 13th centuries are still evident on the western and northern walls. Rublyov's and Chorny's frescoes, including scenes from the Last Judgment, decorate two vaults beneath the choir gallery and the altar pillars. Rublyov's famed icon of the Virgin of Vladimir that once hung by the altar was transferred to Moscow's Assumption Cathedral in 1380; it is now in the Vladimir-Suzdal Museum of History and Art (see picture on page 331). A replica now hangs here.

This cathedral was one of the most revered churches in Russia; all the Vladimir and Moscow grand princes were crowned inside it, from the son of Yuri Dolgoruky to Ivan III, in the early 15th-century. It was the main center of the Church Metropolitan in the 14th-century. The Assumption Cathedral was also the burial place of the princes of Vladimir, including Andrei Bogoliubsky and Vsevolod III. The three-story belfry was built in 1810. The cathedral has been under continuous restoration during the last century. It is usually open between 1.30–4.30pm. Mass is celebrated on Saturday evenings, Sundays and Orthodox feast days. Visitors are welcome in respectful attire. Flash photography is not permitted.

A short walk away, northwest of the cathedral, is one of the most splendid examples of Old Russian architecture, the **Cathedral of St Demetrius** (1193–97). It was built by Vsevolod III as his court church; his palace once stood nearby. The cathedral, with its one large helmet drum, was named after 'Big Nest' Vsevolod's patron saint (St Demetrius of Thessaloniki) and newborn son Dmitri. (Vsevolod was nicknamed 'Big Nest' because of his large family of 12 children.) It is built from blocks of white limestone and decorated with intricate *kokoshniki* along the doorways and arches. Over 1,300 bas-reliefs cover the outer walls: decorative beasts, birds, griffins, saints, prophets, the labors of Hercules and many elaborate floral patterns all glorify the might of Vladimir. The friezes of King David and Alexander the Great symbolize Vsevolod's cunning military exploits. At the top of the left section of the northern façade is Prince Vsevolod seated on the throne with his young son; the other sons are bowing to their father. The interior frescoes date back to the 12th-century. In 1834, Nicholas I ordered the cathedral restored; it is now part of the local museum complex. Preservation experts still battle the ongoing effects of town pollution on the limestone.

Across from this cathedral at number 64 is the **Vladimir Museum of Art and Architecture**, with displays of old religious paintings, manuscripts and architectural designs. Directly across the street is the **Museum of History**. A rich collection of

*The Cathedral of St Demetrius in Vladimir, built by Vsevolod III in the 12th-century.
More than 1,300 bas-reliefs decorate its outer walls.*

artifacts, archeological materials, old fabrics and weapons, princely possessions and the white-stone tomb of Alexander Nevsky are on display. Another branch of the museum with lacquered art, crystal and embroidery is located at the end of the street past the Golden Gates. The museums are open daily 10am–4pm, closed Mondays.

At the eastern end of Bolshaya Moskovskaya is the **Nativity Monastery** (1191–96), one of Russia's most important religious complexes until the end of the 16th century; it was closed in 1744. Alexander Nevsky was buried here in 1263; his remains were transferred to St Petersburg by Peter the Great in 1724. The Nikolskaya Church next door is now the Planetarium.

Next to the Vladimir Hotel (down the street from the Planetarium on Frunze Street) is the brick and five-domed **Assumption Church** (1644), built from donations given by rich local merchants. At the end of Frunze Street is the Eternal Flame, commemorating the soldiers who lost their lives during World War II.

Down the street from the Golden Gates is the city's main shopping district, the Torgoviye Ryady. Across the street is the **Monument to the 850th Anniversary of Vladimir**.

Stroll north along Gagarin Street and look out over the old section of Vladimir. In the distance are many old squat wooden houses with long sloping roofs and stone floors. Many of the town's inhabitants have lived in these homes for generations. The people enjoy a simple town life. During the day you may see residents hanging out laundry, perhaps painting the lattice work around their windows a pastel blue-green, chopping wood, or gathering fruits and mushrooms. The children enjoy having their pictures taken. Bring a few souvenirs from home to trade.

West from the end of Gagarin Street is the **Knyaginin (Princess) Convent**, founded by the wife of Vsevolod III, Maria Shvarnovna, in 1200. The grand princesses of the court were buried in the convent's **Assumption Cathedral**, rebuilt in the 16th century. The cathedral's three-tiered walls are lined with fancy *zakomara* and topped with a single helmet drum. In 1648, Moscow artists painted the colorful interior frescoes. The north and south walls depict the life of the Virgin Mary, and the west wall shows scenes from the Last Judgment. Paintings of Vladimir princesses, portrayed as saints, are on the southwest side, and the pillars recount the lives of the grand princes. The cathedral is the only remaining building of the convent complex and now houses a restoration organization. Near the convent stands the **Church of St Nicetas** (1762). This green and white, three-tiered baroque church was built by the merchant Semion Lazarev. The interior is divided into three separate churches on each floor. It was restored in 1970. In front of this church is a bust of the writer Gogol. Pervomaiskaya Street winds south back to the Golden Gates.

At the end of the day, you may stop at the rustic log-hewn **Traktir Restaurant** for an enjoyable meal of the local cuisine. For current events and festival listings in Vladimir, check www.museum.vladimir.ru.

VICINITY OF VLADIMIR

The quaint village of **Bogoliubovo** lies eight kilometers (five miles) northeast of Vladimir. Group tours sometimes stop here; if not, go by local bus (a half-hour ride), taxi or car, a short hop along the M7. One legend says that when Prince Andrei was traveling from Kiev to Vladimir, carrying the sacred icon of Our Lady of Vladimir, his horses stopped on a large hill and would move no farther. At this junction, by the confluence of the Klyazma and Nerl rivers, Andrei decided to build a fortress and royal residence. He named the town Bogoliubovo (Loved by God) and took the name of Bogoliubsky; he was canonized by the Church in 1702. Supposedly, after the Virgin appeared to him in a dream, he built the **Nativity of the Virgin Church**. This cathedral was still standing in the 18th-century, but when one father superior decided to renovate it in 1722 by adding more windows, the cathedral collapsed; it was partially rebuilt in 1751. Only a few of the 12th-century palace walls remain, of which chronicles relate: 'it was hard to look at all the gold.' On the staircase tower are pictures depicting the death of Andrei Bogoliubsky—assassinated by jealous nobles in this tower in 1174. The coffins of his assassins were said to have been buried in the surrounding marshes and their wailing cries heard at night. The buildings in Bogoliubovo are now museums, which are closed on Mondays.

About one and a half kilometers (one mile) southeast of Bogoliubovo on the River Nerl (to walk, head west of the complex, down Frunze Street, and under a railway bridge, and then follow the path through a field to the church) is the graceful **Church of the Intercession-on-the-Nerl**, built during the Golden Age of Vladimir architecture. Standing alone in the green summer meadows or snowy winter landscape, it is reflected in the quiet waters of the river that is filled with delicate lilies. It has come down from legend that Andrei built this church in 1164 to celebrate his victory over the Volga Bulgars. The Virgin of the Intercession was thought to have protected the rulers of Vladimir. With the building of this church, Andrei proclaimed a new Church holiday, the Feast of the Intercession. Taxi vans run back to Vladimir.

THE RUSSIAN ICON

The ancient art of icon painting has been a part of Russian life for over 11 centuries and is still being passed on to future generations. The core of this art portrays spiritual and aesthetic ideals, as well as historical events and lifestyles of Old Russia. Soon after Prince Vladimir introduced Christianity in AD 988, Byzantium's art and religious customs were quickly absorbed into Russian culture. The word *icona*, in Russian, stems from the Greek *eikon*, meaning holy image; icons portrayed the likenesses of Christ, the Virgin, saints and martyrs.

Byzantine art dissipated greatly during the Mongol invasions in the mid-13th-century, when artistic styles transcended their Byzantine heritage. During Russia's long period of isolation (two and a half centuries of Mongol occupation), several unique types of icon painting were established. The main schools were the Novgorod, Pskov, Moscow and Central Russian. Each retained some of the original elements of color and design from early Byzantium, while adding their own distinctive flair.

The purpose of the icon was to bring spiritual power to light. The icon's own light and color mirrored the sacred qualities of the celestial world. In addition, the icon's impersonation of the divine and earthly planes was based on a hierarchy of colors: the tops were white, purple and gold, which symbolized divine light, purity, salvation and love. Blue and green, the earthy colors, represented heaven, joy and hope; and red portrayed the Holy Spirit's flame, the passions of Christ, and the burning fire of faith and martyrdom. The treachery of Judas was symbolized in yellow. Black was derived from Russia's old folk beliefs: the gloom of the underworld and the emptiness of the nonbeliever; the icon educated the viewer how to overcome this chaos and darkness. Many monks fasted for several days before starting work on an icon, chanted prayers, and wholeheartedly believed in the moral and educational powers of their creations.

The Novgorod school mainly used a symmetrical design and painted in bold and simple outlines using red, white, and black—with a style similar to folklore traditions. The iconographers of Pskov, one of the last remaining regions to be annexed to Moscovy, developed a more dynamic style, using dramatic color schemes of gold, green, red and yellow. The Central Russian school was greatly affected by Moscow and Novgorod, but used blue as its dominant color combined with yellow and white. This style was centered in the Golden Ring towns of Rostov, Pereslavl-Zalessky, Palekh, Yaroslavl, Vladimir and Suzdal.

Icons were painted on panels of wood with tempera paints. Designs were initially sketched with chalk or charcoal and then filled in with colors. First glazes, then a varnish of linseed oil were applied to the completed work. But, after about 80 years, the linseed oil darkened the icon, at which time another artist usually painted over the original design. With some icons, this process was repeated many times. Today, restorers can remove paint layer by layer to recreate many of the original portraits. These efforts have been especially concentrated in churches in Moscow and the Golden Ring area.

Icons were at the center of Old Russian art and kept in churches, chapels and homes. Later the iconostasis, a number of icons layered together on wooden or stone tiers, were painted as well. This allowed Christ, the Virgin and numerous saints to be brought together as one entity. Icons played an essential role in people's lives; they were given a place of honor in the homes and thought to possess healing powers. The 16th-century icon of the Kazan Virgin was believed to have saved Moscow residents from the plague. Icons were also placed along roads, at the entrances to gates and towers and were even carried on poles high above troops as they entered military campaigns.

By the beginning of the 15th-century, Andrei Rublyov was recognized as the Church's foremost artist. The master lived in Moscow, establishing it as the new center of icon painting. No one is quite sure of the year of Rublyov's birth, but his name became a symbol for the highest values in Old Russian art; he eventually painted for all the grand princes of Moscovy. His innovative style, luminous colors, symbolic images, and rhythmical lines had a profound effect on the other schools. In his later life Rublyov became a monk, lived at the Spaso-Andronikov Monastery in Moscow, and painted frescoes in the Cathedral of Our Savior. He died in 1430.

Rublyov's technique was asymmetrical in form, and his colorful images possessed a narrative and harmonious tone. He meticulously

The Virgin of Vladimir is one of Andrei Rublyov's most beautiful icons. Painted in the early 15th-century for the Assumption Cathedral in Vladimir and based on the Byzantine Virgin of Eleousa, it can be seen today in the Vladimir-Suzdal Museum of History and Art.

individualized his portraits and gave each figure a life of its own. Instead of the simple Novgorod outline, Rublyov's personages were enveloped with character and movement. Rublyov also used the circle as a symbol for the unity of life, and angels and saints were portrayed in real-life scenes on earth, surrounded by rocks, trees and animals. Allegorical symbols were introduced: Christ wore purple robes; the golden chalice contained a calf's head; and angels held trumpets or swords. Dark and somber colors gave way to vibrant greens, blues and yellows. Attention was paid to background; gems and metal were even added to create a more multidimensional setting.

Both Theophanes, Greek leader of the Novgorod school during the late 14th-century, and Rublyov painted frescoes and the iconostasis in the Moscow Kremlin's Annunciation Cathedral. Rublyov and Daniil Chorny painted in Vladimir's Assumption Cathedral, where many of the icons and frescoes are still visible today. In the Trinity-Sergius Monastery, Rublyov portrayed the famous religious figure of Old Russia—St Sergius who blessed Dmitry Donskoi before the decisive Battle of Kulikova, where Donskoi destroyed the Mongol-Tatar yoke in 1380. For once, icons not only symbolized God, but also the awesome events of human life. The saint's blessing (as portrayed in the Old Testament Trinity) symbolized Russian's desire for freedom and unity; the Eucharist served as a metaphor to sacrifice in battle and the chalice hope, faith and the common bond of the Russian people.

Many of Rublyov's works were lost through the centuries, destroyed in fires or painted over. But, some of his works, such as the Virgin of Vladimir, can still be found in the Vladimir-Suzdal Museum; the Archangel Michael, the Savior, Apostle Paul and the Old Testament Trinity can be viewed in the Tretyakov Gallery in Moscow. Other copies are exhibited at the Rublyov Museum in the Spaso-Andronikov Monastery. When British travel author, Robert Byron, made his first visit to Moscow and viewed Rublyov's icons, he professed: in Rublyov's masterpieces 'live the eternal sorrows, joys, and the whole destiny of man. Such pictures bring tears to the eye and peace to the soul'.

The genius of Andrei Rublyov can be compared to that of other major artists of Renaissance Europe, such as Giotto and Raphael. He was so revered that a century after his death, the Church Council decreed that Rublyov's icons were merited as the true standard of artistic Orthodoxy. It was Rublyov's desire in life to help lead the world out of medieval darkness and despair and back into realms of beauty, harmony and love. By capturing infinite goodness on a simple and timeless icon, Andrei Rublyov achieved his own immortality and will always live in the hearts of those who view his work. The renowned Soviet film director, Andrei Tarkovsky, made a classic film on the life of Andrei Rublyov.

By the 17th-century, Western European art had greatly influenced Russian religious painting. The icons became smaller and more intricate, decorated with jewels and cloisonné enamels and mosaics. With the reforms of Peter the Great (in the early 18th-century) and the subsequent Westernization of Russian society, the popularity of icon painting made a sharp decline. It took several centuries before an interest returned to the old icon masterpieces; the first to be restored was Rublyov's Old Testament Trinity. A leading exhibition of restored medieval icons took place in Russia in 1913; many artists, such as Henri Matisse and Kazimir Malevich were greatly influenced by their beauty. Sadly, during the Communist era, icon painting was banned altogether, and the art of painting lacquered wooden boxes and dolls replaced religious art. Thousands of icons were burnt and destroyed, and many more stolen, smuggled or sold to the West.

Today restoration and icon painting schools are being revived in Russia, and the art of *spiski*, making copies of old icons, is flourishing. Most major monasteries (particularly in Sergiyev Posad) now have their own icon workshops. Many of these incorporate old-style techniques: the icons are painted atop wooden boards which are covered with *levki*, a mixture of linen oil, chalk, glue, bones and sturgeon skin. The color blue, for example, is made by crushing lapis lazuli, and the pigments are then mixed with eggs and water. It usually takes up to three months to create an average icon; generally students paint the nature scenes, architecture and clothing, while the most experienced artists design the faces, hands and feet. The Moscow Icons Workshop is considered one of the best in Russia; one of their most recent creations was the iconostasis for St Nicholas Church on Bersenevskaya Embankment. One private Russian company even presented Boris Yeltsin with the icon Boris and Gleb (based on the original). Boris and Gleb are patron saints of Russia as well as being the names of Yeltsin's grandsons.

The 15th-century icon by Andrei Rublyov known as the Old Testament Trinity is one of the greatest masterpieces of Old Russian art. Painted for his teacher St Sergius, it once hung as the central icon in Sergiyev Posad's Trinity Cathedral. The three angels represent the harmony of the Father, Son and Holy Spirit. It now hangs in Moscow's Tretyakov Gallery.

YURYEV-POLSKY Юрьев-Польский

About 65 kilometers (40 miles) northwest of Vladimir (situated halfway to Pereslavl-Zalessky along the P74 road) lies the old town of Yuryev-Polsky. Trains also stop here on the way from Ivanovo. Prince Yuri Dolgoruky founded Yuryev-Polsky in 1152, and named it after himself. Since two other Russian towns were already named Yuryev, Dolgoruky added Polsky, meaning 'Yury's town among the fields'. At the confluence of the Koloksha and Gza rivers, Dolgoruky had a fortress built, complete with moat and rampart walls that stood over six meters (20 feet) high; for a short period the town became the capital of Dolgoruky's principality. During the next several centuries Yuryev-Polsky was taken over by invading Lithuanians and Mongols, and never again regained its status and power. The original Holy Gates had four separate entrances, two for pedestrians and two for carriages. The **Monastery of the Archangel Michael** (1250) was reconstructed at the end of the 17th-century. The **Cathedral of the Archangel Michael** and tent-shaped bell tower are decorated with green-glazed tiles. The town's greatest treasure is the limestone **Cathedral of St George** (1234), modeled after Vladimir's Cathedral of St Demetrius. The elegant helmet-shaped dome survived a partial collapse of the walls in the 15th-century. Today carved scenes and floral designs are still visible on some of the greenish-yellow walls. Figures include St George, patron saint of Dolgoruky; lions with tails in shapes of trees, masks and emblems; and the fairy-tale bird, Sirin. Burial vaults and the tomb of Grand Prince Svyatoslav (13th-century) are situated in the northwest corner.

SUZDAL Суздаль

Suzdal is a pleasant half-hour journey from Vladimir (26 kilometers/16 miles north along the A113 road) through open fields dotted with hay stacks and mounds of dark rich soil. There are no trains to Suzdal. It's easiest to take a train or bus to Vladimir and then a local bus on to Suzdal. (The more frequent running Moscow-Ivanovo buses also stop in Suzdal.) Buses run from Suzdal to other Golden Ring towns as well. Take one of the frequent buses leaving Vladimir, or take a train or bus to Vladimir, and then take a local bus to Suzdal. Buses leave from Moscow's Shchyolkovsky Station, and from Ivanovo, Kostroma and Yaroslavl. Suzdal's bus station is located about one and a half kilometers east of the town center on Vasilevskaya Street. Vladimir was the younger rival of Suzdal which, along with Rostov Veliky, was founded a full century earlier. The town was settled along the banks of the Kamenka River, which empties into the Nerl a few miles downstream. Over 100 examples of Old Russian architecture (in a space of only nine square kilometers/three and a half square miles) attract a half million visitors each year to this remarkable medieval museum. For event listings in the Vladimir-Suzdal area, check www.musuem.vladimir.ru. Suzdal is not only famous for its churches, but also for its cucumbers. The annual Cucumber Festival occurs here every summer, along with the Festival of Crafts.

Just east of Suzdal is Kideksha, a small preserved village that dates back to the beginning of the 12th-century. On the west bank of the river is the delightful **Suzdal Museum of Wooden Architecture**, portraying the typical Russian life-style of centuries ago (see picture page 339). In 1983, the town received the Golden Apple. Awarded by an international jury, the prize symbolizes excellence in historical preservation and local color.

The first view of Suzdal from the road encompasses towering silhouettes of gleaming domes and pinkish walls atop Poklonnaya Hill, rising up amidst green patches of woods and gardens. It is as though time has stopped in this enchanting place—a perfection of spatial harmony. Today Suzdal is a quiet town with no industrial enterprises. Crop and orchard farming are the main occupations of the residents who still live in the predominant *izba* (wooden houses). The scenic town is a popular site for film-making. The American production of *Peter the Great* used Suzdal as one of its locations.

Traveling along the Golden Ring route, you may have noticed that the distances between towns are similar. When these towns were settled, one unit of length was measured by how much ground a team of horses could cover in 24 hours. Most towns were laid out about one post-unit apart. So the distance between Moscow and Pereslavl-Zalessky, Pereslavl and Rostov, or Rostov and Yaroslavl could easily be covered in one day. Distances in medieval Russia were measured by these units; thus the traveler knew how many days it took to arrive at his destination—from Moscow to Suzdal took about three days.

Suzdal offers many unique places in which to stay overnight and all are comfortable and reasonably priced. (The area code of Suzdal is (4-9231) The **Convent of the Intercession (Pokrovskaya) Hotel** offers moderately-priced 19th-century log cabins on the grounds of the Pokrovsky Monastery (tel. 20-889). Their **Trapeznaya Restaurant** serves delicious old-style Russian fare. Across the street, at 35a Pokrovskaya St, the more expensive **Traktir Kuchkova Hotel** offers 17 double rooms (tel. 20-252 or 21-507). Centrally located at 34 Slobodskaya Street, is the stylish **Dom Kuptsa Likhonina**, a cozy bed-and-breakfast with 7 rooms in a 17th-century merchant house (tel. 21-901). Within the complex of the Convent of the Deposition of the Robe, at 9 Kommunalny Gorodok, is the inexpensive **Hotel Rizopolozhenskaya** (tel. 20-706 or 20-553). The three-star **Hotel Pushkarskaya Sloboda**, with 90 rooms, is at 43 Lenin St, and the mini-hotel **Cherry Garden** is at number 10. Down the street, at number 73, is the **Kharchevnya Café** which offers tasty Russian food at reasonable prices. On Torgovaya Square is the 35-room **Sokol Hotel**.

Three hotels are situated on Korovniki Street, (at the north end of the river); the large Soviet-style **GTK Tourist Complex** (430 rooms), at number 7, offers both simple and upgraded rooms (tel. 21-530 or 20-908), the **Suzdal Tour Center**, at number 45, is newly renovated with 205 rooms, and the **Goryachie Klyuhi**, with 29 rooms is down the street at 14b.

For more luxurious accommodations, Jeff Wilgus (an American) and his wife Nastya own three houses in Suzdal and rent them out. Two of the homes are classic village houses that have been modernized, and the third is a large two-story log house complete with sauna and jacuzzi. For reservations, call Moscow at 928-5246 or Jeff's mobile 920-1755; email wilgus@online.ru.

Within the Suzdal Kremlin, the more formal **Trapeznaya Kremlya Restaurant** (tel. 21-763 or 20-937) (with a 300-year-old menu) serves both meals, tea and pastries. Situated in the town center, along Kremlyovskaya Street, are numerous eateries such as the **Pogrebok** (Cellar) Café, **Gostiny Dvor** and the **Slavyansky Bar**. By the river, at the western end of the trading stalls is the **Yakor** (Anchor) Bay with exquisite sunset vistas.

HISTORY

The area of Suzdalia was first mentioned in chronicles in 1024, when Kievan Grand Prince Yaroslavl the Wise came to suppress the rebellions. By 1096 a small kremlin had been built around the settlement, which one chronicle already described as a town. As Suzdal grew, princes and rich nobles from Kiev settled here, bringing with them spiritual representatives from the Church, who introduced Christianity to the region. The town slowly gained in prominence; Grand Prince Yuri Dolgoruky named it the capital of the northern provinces in 1125. From Suzdal, the seat of his royal residence, he went on to establish the small settlement of Moscow in 1147. His son Andrei Bogoliubsky transferred the capital to Vladimir in 1157.

After the Kievan states crumbled in the 12th-century Suzdal, along with Rostov Veliky, became the religious center of medieval Rus. The princes and boyars donated vast sums of money to build splendid churches and monasteries; by the 14th century Suzdal had over 70 churches, 15 monasteries, 400 dwellings and a famous school of icon painting. No other place in all of Russia had such a high proportion of religious buildings. The crest of Suzdal was a white falcon wearing a prince's crown.

Since the town itself was not situated along important trade routes, the monks (and not the merchants) grew in wealth from large donations to the monasteries. The Church eventually took over the fertile lands and controlled the serf-peasants.

Suzdal was invaded many times, first by the Mongols in 1238, then by Lithuanians and Poles. After the Mongol occupation no new stone buildings were erected until well into the 16th century. Suzdal was annexed to Moscovy in the late 14th-century and as a result lost its political importance, but remained a religious center.

In the early 17th-century, the Russian state collapsed and Polish troops occupied Moscow. One of Suzdal's most famous residents, Prince Dmitri Pozharsky (a Suzdal street is named after him), organized an army to beat back the foreign invaders. Today a monument to Pozharsky (along with merchant Kuzma Minin) stands on Red Square in front of St Basil's Cathedral.

During the 1700s Peter the Great's reforms undermined ecclesiastical power and the Church in Suzdal lost much of its land and wealth. Churches and

monasteries were mainly used to house religious fanatics and political prisoners. Many barren or unpopular wives were forced to take the veil and exiled to Suzdal's convents. By the end of the 19th century only 6,000 residents remained, and one account described Suzdal as 'a town of churches, bell towers, old folk legends and tombstones'. On a bright note, because Suzdal had become so insignificant, a railroad was never built through it; the result was that no industrialization ever came to Suzdal, and thus the town's rural character and historic architecture was preserved. The local historian Voronin wrote: "The future of Suzdal lies in its past...in carefully preserving itself for future generations." Today with a population of well over 12,000, this enthralling poetic spot has been restored to the majesty of its former days. As one 13th-century chronicler observed: "Oh, most radiant and bountiful, how wondrous art thou with thy beauty vast."

Residents of Suzdal sell their homegrown vegetables at the local market. Most people living outside the bigger cities grow their own potatoes, cabbage, tomatoes and other vegetables in small garden plots by their homes out of economic necessity.

SIGHTS

Approaching Suzdal from Vladimir, as horse coaches once did, two churches are passed on the right before crossing the Kamenka River. These are the summer **Church of Our Lady of the Sign** (1749) and the winter **Church of the Deposition of the Robe** (1777). The former houses the Suzdal Excursion Bureau.

As you cross the river, down along the northeastern embankment stands the charming **Church of Saints Kosma and Damian** (1725), built by the local black-smiths to honor their patron saints. Many of the local artisans built their own churches. Across the river are several other churches, constructed between the 16th and 18th centuries, with money raised by local tanners.

Further along Lenin Street, stands the simple red and white **Church of St Lazarus**. Built in 1667 by the townspeople, it is the oldest of the posad churches. The slender helmet-domed winter **Church of St Antipus** stands next to it. According to local lore, a toothache can be healed here. Just walk around the church, and chew on each of the four corners!

The old kremlin can be sighted along the southwestern side of Lenin Street. The present-day 1.4 kilometer long kreml was once protected on three sides by the river; along the eastern wall ran a large moat, now the main street. Remnants of the 11th-century earthen walls are still evident today. These ramparts are topped with wooden walls and towers.

Suzdal's open-air Museum of Wooden Architecture exhibits old wooden buildings based on architecture dating back to 1238. Using the simplest of tools—chisel, plane and axe—early Russian architects created structures without the use of nails. This log-built church is covered with hand-hewn aspen shingles, an early trademark of the region.

A tour of Suzdal begins on the east bank of the river, where much of the old architecture is clustered. Take a moment to gaze out over the fertile plains and meandering waters of the river. The rich arable land in this area first attracted settlers seeking greater freedoms from Novgorod, where pagan priests were still leading uprisings against Kievan attempts to Christianize and feudalize the northern lands. In Old Russian, *suzdal* meant to give judgment or justice. Today several streets still carry the names of Slavic pagan gods, such as Kupala, Netyoka and Yarunova.

The 13th-century **Korsunsky Gates** lead to the main cathedral and are covered with Byzantine patterns; religious scenes from the New Testament were engraved and etched with acid on copper sheets and then gilded.

Prince Vladimir Monomakh laid the first stone of the town's main **Cathedral of the Virgin Nativity** at the beginning of the 12th-century. This structure was rebuilt many times. In 1528, Grand Prince Vasily III of Moscow reconstructed it from brick and white stone and surmounted it with five helmet-shaped domes. In 1748, the domes were altered to the present dark-green onion and gold-star pattern.

The southern doors, surrounded by elaborate stone decorations, were the official entrance of the princes. Lions, carved along the portals, were the emblems of the princes of Vladimir. The carved female faces symbolize the Virgin Mary, whose nativity is celebrated. The southern and western doors (1230–33) are made of gilded copper and depict scenes from the life of St George, the patron saint of both Prince Georgi and his grandfather Yuri Dolgoruky.

Early 13th-century frescoes of saints and other ornamental floral patterns are still visible in the vestry. Most of the other murals and frescoes are from the 17th-century. Tombs of early bishops and princes from as far back as 1023 are also found inside. The burial vaults of the early princesses are near the west wall. The octagonal bell tower was built in 1635 by order of Czar Mikhail Romanov and repaired in 1967. Old Slavonic letters correspond to numbers on the face of the clock.

The impressive whitewashed Archbishop's Palace, now the **Suzdal Museum**, was built next to the cathedral on the bank of the Kamenka between the 15th and 18th centuries. The main chamber of the palace, a large pillarless hall, held important meetings and banquets. In the 17th-century this *krestovaya* (cross-vaulted) chamber was considered one of the most elegant rooms in Russia. The museum contains collections of ancient art and traces the evolution of architecture in the Suzdal region.

Enter the palace chamber through the western entrance. In the center stands a long wooden table, covered with a rich red cloth, once used by the archbishop and his clergy. An 18th-century tiled stove stands in one corner. The walls are decorated with many 15th–16th-century icons. Suzdal developed its own school of icon painting in the early 13th-century. Its use of lyrical flowing outlines, detailed facial qualities and soft designs in red and gold, were later adopted by the Moscow school, headed by Andrei Rublyov. Both the Moscow Tretyakov Gallery and the St Petersburg Russian Museum include Suzdal icons among their exhibits.

Pass through the gateway to the left of the palace to reach another art section of the museum. Here are more displays of icons, paintings, sculptures, ivory carvings, embroideries and other crafts. Buildings in this complex are open 10am–5pm, closed Tuesdays. and the last Friday of the month.

For a lunch break, try dining at the **Trapeznaya Restaurant**, located in the Refectory of the Archbishop's Palace. Sample the splendors of ancient Suzdalian monastic cooking—the local fish soup and home-brewed mead are especially tasty. Also try the *medovukha*, an alcoholic beverage combined with honey that is made only in Suzdal. According to local legend, the recipe was developed by Suzdal's St. Euphemius in the 14th-century. For centuries, it was the most popular drink in Russia, but during the reign of Peter the Great, vodka finally eclipsed it as the beverage of choice. A visitor can sample up to 10 varieties of *medovukha* in the Suzdal Honey Plant at the end of the Trading Rows off Kremlyyovskaya Street, open until 5pm on weekdays and 8pm weekends.

In front of the palace is the wooden **Church of St Nicholas** (1766). It represents one of the oldest types of Old Russian wooden architecture and is built from logs into a square frame with a long sloping roof. The early architects used only an ax, chisel and plane to build these designs. No nails were needed; the logs were held together by wooden pegs and filled with moss. The church was transferred from the village of Glotovo in 1960. Beside it, in lovely contrast, stands the red-and-white-trimmed **Church of the Assumption** (1732), with its green rounded roof and horseshoe *kokoshniki*.

The long trading stalls near Torgovaya Square, built in 1806, mark the center of town. During holidays the grounds were opened to fairs and exhibitions and were filled with jolly jesters, merry-go-rounds and craft booths. Horses were tied up along the arcade. Today, the colonnade has numerous stores and outdoor markets where the townspeople congregate, especially around midday. Pick up a charming picnic basket made from native willow branches. They are sold at the entrance of the Museum of Wooden Architecture.

Along the northwestern side of the arcade, by the riverbank, is the lovely white-washed summer **Church of the Entry into Jerusalem** (1707). The winter **Church of Paraskeva Pyatnitsa** (1772), surmounted by a half-dome drum and gilded cross, stands next to it.

Near the southwestern corner of the Torgoviye Ryady stands the **Church of the Resurrection-on-the-Marketplace** (1720), a large white-brick cube crowned with an onion dome on a tall drum. It is now a branch of the Suzdal Museum, with exhibits of architectural decorations, wooden carvings, and colorful tiles used to adorn buildings in the 17th and 18th centuries. Behind it stands the more modest winter **Church of Our Lady of Kazan**.

Across the street on the northeastern side of Torgovaya Square are two other sets of church complexes. Not only did the number of churches in a town symbolize its wealth, but it was also customary in medieval Russia to build twin churches. This added even more to the cluster of religious structures. These twin churches usually stood in close proximity to each other—one cool, high-vaulted and richly decorated was used only in summer, the other, simpler and smaller, held the congregation in winter.

The white summer **Church of the Emperor Constantine** (1707), with elaborate *kokoshniki* designs and bell tower, is located nearest the square (still a functioning church today). Its five, slender drum domes are a unique feature of Suzdalian architecture. The neo-classical rotunda was later added to the western façade. The plainer white-bricked **Church of Our Lady of Sorrows** (1787), with green-glazed tent roof, was used in winter.

Suzdal had the largest monasteries and convents in the region, which served as protective citadels for the citizens during times of war. These institutions, besides being religious, became the educational centers of the town. Husbands could also force their wives to take the veil as a quick way to divorce. Fathers would also place daughters in a convent until they were married.

North along Lenin Street, across from Krasnaya Ploshchad, is the **Convent of the Deposition of the Robe**, founded by Bishop John of Rostov Veliky in 1207. The convent's Deposition Cathedral was built in 1560 by Ivan Shigonia-Podzhogin, a rich boyar who had served Vasily III. The real gems of the ensemble are the white Holy Gates (1688), flanked by two red and white octagonal tent-roofed towers that are decorated with colored glazed tiles. The citizens of Suzdal erected the 72-meter (236-foot) neo-classical bell tower in 1813 to commemorate Napoleon's defeat; it remains the largest structure in the town. Open 9.30am–4pm; closed Tuesdays and last Friday of the month. An art restoration school is located nearby at number 106 Lenin Street. Over 100 university-age students from across the country come here to learn how to restore historical works of art. A visitor can drop by to observe the teachers and pupils restoring icons, frescoes and paintings. The school celebrated its 25th anniversary in 2006.

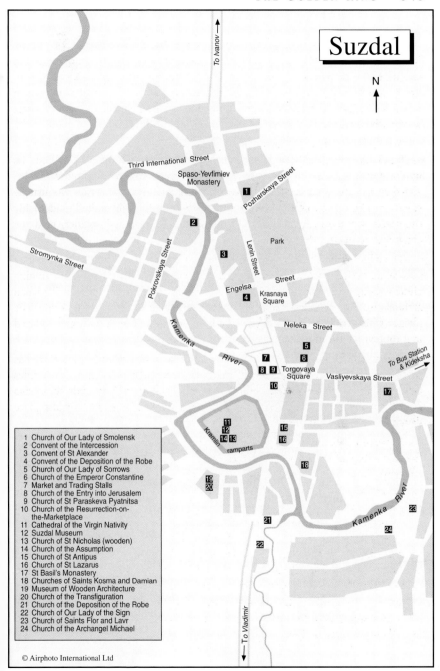

Suzdal

N

To Ivanov →

Third International Street

Spaso-Yevfimiev Monastery

Pozharskaya Street

1

2

Stromynka Street

Pokrovskaya Street

Lenin Street

3

Park

Engelsa Street

4

Krasnaya Square

Kamenka River

Neleka Street

5

7

6

8 **9**   Torgovaya Square

10

To Bus Station & Kideksha →

Vasliyevskaya Street

17

11
12
14 **13**

Kremlin ramparts

15

16

18

Kamenka River

19
20

23

21

24

22

To Vladimir →

1 Church of Our Lady of Smolensk
2 Convent of the Intercession
3 Convent of St Alexander
4 Convent of the Deposition of the Robe
5 Church of Our Lady of Sorrows
6 Church of the Emperor Constantine
7 Market and Trading Stalls
8 Church of the Entry into Jerusalem
9 Church of St Paraskeva Pyatnitsa
10 Church of the Resurrection-on-
   the-Marketplace
11 Cathedral of the Virgin Nativity
12 Suzdal Museum
13 Church of St Nicholas (wooden)
14 Church of the Assumption
15 Church of St Antipus
16 Church of St Lazarus
17 St Basil's Monastery
18 Churches of Saints Kosma and Damian
19 Museum of Wooden Architecture
20 Church of the Transfiguration
21 Church of the Deposition of the Robe
22 Church of Our Lady of the Sign
23 Church of Saints Flor and Lavr
24 Church of the Archangel Michael

Walking a few blocks northwest brings you to the red-brick **Convent of St Alexander**, originally founded in 1240 in honor of Prince Alexander Nevsky, who defeated the Swedes on the Neva River that same year. It was later burned down by invading Poles. In 1682, the Ascension Cathedral, with its five small onion domes, was constructed from funds donated by Peter the Great's mother, Natalya Naryshkina. The convent closed in 1764, but the ensemble remains open to the public.

Nestled by the park, a few blocks north, is the elegant **Church of Our Lady of Smolensk** (1696). Directly across the street, in the area of the former *posad*, is the 18th-century, gabled-roof, tailor's **House of Nikita Pustosviat**. It is now a domestic museum with displays of furniture and utensils from the 17th to 19th centuries. The rooms represent a typical peasant hut. Across from the *pechka* (stove), over which the eldest member of the family slept, was the *krasnaya ugol* (beautiful corner) where the family icons were kept. Usually the *gornitsa* (living area) comprised one or two rooms. Here were found a few beds, chairs, tables and a clothes chest. The kitchen was situated in the corner nearest to the *kamin* (fireplace or stove). A small storage house was also built into the hut. It is open 10am –4pm, closed Mondays.

Dominating the northeast bank of the river is Suzdal's largest architectural complex, the **Spaso-Yevfimievsky Monastery** (Savior Monastery of St Euthymius). It was founded in 1350 by a Suzdal prince to protect the town's northern entrance. Over the next few centuries, the monastery continued to receive funding from czars and noble families until it grew into a massive fortress enclosed by a one-and-a-half-kilometer-long kremlin. Of the 12 towers, the southern 23-meter-high decorative Vkhodnaya was used as a watchtower; it is used as the entrance today. In front of this tower is the 17th-century Church of the Annunciation-over-the-Gates. The monks eventually owned vast amounts of land and their monastery became the wealthiest in the region. By the 17th-century it controlled over 10,000 serfs. Today, film companies often use the high red brick walls to double as Moscow's Kremlin. In 2006, the Golden Treasury exhibit was opened in the complex.

The centerpiece of the complex is the **Cathedral of the Transfiguration**, built in 1594. Both exterior and interior 17th-century frescoes, painted by masters from Kostroma, depict the history of the monastery. Prince Dmitri Pozharsky, hero of the 1612 Polish war and Governor of Suzdal, is buried beside the altar; a monument to him, standing outside the cathedral, is inscribed: 'To Dmitri Mikhailovsky 1578–1642.' Adjoining the cathedral is a small chapel that stands over the grave of the Abbot Yevfim. A particular treat is to listen to the ringing of the bells in the adjacent bell tower. On the hour, the bell-ringer ascends the tower and performs a ten-minute concert. It sounds like an entire bell choir, but it is just one man tugging on the multitude of ropes that hold the clappers.

The **Assumption Church** (1526) on the west side was added to the chambers of the Archimandrite for his private use. It was decorated with *kokoshniki* and a large tent-shaped dome. The Kostroma artists Nikitin and Savin painted the frescoes on the outside southern and western walls. On the other side of the bell tower, the monk cells on the first floor now contain an exhibit of contemporary Russian folk art, including works by local painters, potters, sculptors and glass blowers. The prison at the northern end was built by Catherine the Great in 1766. Many revolting Decembrists were later interned here as political prisoners. The writer Lev Tolstoy was almost imprisoned here, after he was excommunicated by the church. Next door is the old hospital and **St Nicholas Church** (1669), now a museum of Russian applied art. The complex and museums are open 10am–5pm, closed Mondays, and the last Thurday of the month.

The large complex across the river is the **Convent of the Intercession**, built by Prince Andrei in 1364. Prince Vasily (Basil) III commissioned the convent's churches in 1510 as supplication for the birth of a male heir. The polygonal bell tower, rebuilt in the 17th-century, is one of the earliest examples of a brick tower and conical roof design. The white three-domed Cathedral of the Intercession served as the burial place for Suzdal noblewomen. Eventually, in 1525, Vasily exiled his wife Solomonia Saburova to the convent. He wanted to divorce her on the grounds that she was barren; Solomonia accused Vasily of sterility. The metropolitan granted Vasily his divorce and sent Solomonia to the Pokrovsky (Intercession) Convent to live out her life as a nun. Vasily remarried a Polish girl named Elena Glinskaya. Some time later news reached Moscow that Solomonia had given birth to a son. Fearing for her son's life, Solomonia hid him with friends and then staged a fake burial. For centuries this tale was regarded only as legend, but in 1934 a small casket was unearthed beside Solomonia's tomb (she died in 1594). There was no skeleton, only a stuffed silk shirt embroidered with pearls. The small white tomb and pieces of clothing are on display in the Suzdal Museum. Ivan the Terrible (son of Elena Glinskaya) also sent his wife Anna to this convent in 1575. Peter the Great even exiled his first wife Evdokia Lopukhina here in 1698. The convent buildings have been returned to the Orthodox Church; there is also a hotel residence and restaurant in the complex. A museum of the convent's history is open 9.30am–4pm, closed Tuesdays. For a splendid panoramic view of Suzdal, climb the bank of the river in front of the convent.

At the southern end of town, on the west bank of the Kamenka on Pushkarskaya Street (a 10-minute walk from the Kremlin), is the **Suzdal Museum of Wooden Architecture**. Old wooden village structures have been brought in from all around the Vladimir-Suzdal region and reassembled at this location on Dmitriyevskaya Hill to give an idea of old peasant life in a typical Russian village. For nearly 250 years,

Besides churches, Suzdal is full of historic residential architecture.
Children play after school by the elaborately decorated 18th-century
wooden house that once belonged to an influential merchant named Bibanov.

beginning in 1238, not a single stone building was erected. Using the simplest of tools, structures were created without the use of iron or nails. Unfortunately, none of these survive today. The outstanding wooden **Church of the Transfiguration** (1756), was assembled by old methods, and brought in from the neighboring village of Kozlyatyevo. This open-air museum consists of other log-built churches covered with aspen-shingled roofs, residential houses, windmills, barns and bathhouses. Open May–October, 9.30am–4pm, closed Tuesdays and the last Friday of the month.

At the end of the day take a walk along the river as the sun sets over the town. Young boys can be seen swimming and fishing in the warmer months or skating in winter. Many small side streets are filled with the local wooden dachas, covered with elaborate wood carvings and latticework. Ask your driver to stop by the **House of Merchant Bibanov**, the most lavishly decorated house in town. If you are lucky, a pink full moon will rise above the magical display of gabled roofs and towers, to signal an end to the delightful Suzdalian day.

VICINITY OF SUZDAL

Four kilometers east of Suzdal is the small **Village of Kideksha**. In 1015, according to chronicles, the brothers Boris and Gleb, sons of the Kievan Prince Vladimir who brought Christianity to Russia, had a meeting here where the Kamenka River empties into the Nerl. They were later assassinated by their elder brother Svyatopolk (who was later murdered by a fourth brother, Yaroslav). Boris and Gleb, who died defending the Christian faith, became Russia's first saints. In 1152, Prince Yuri Dolgoruky (who founded Moscow in 1147) chose to build his country estate on this spot. Dolgoruky also erected the simple white-stone **Church of Saints Boris and Gleb**, where his son Boris and daughter-in-law Maria are buried. The winter Church of St Stephan was erected in the 18th-century.

On the road to Kideksha are the remains of the **St Basil Monastery**, the fifth monastery complex of Suzdal. Only a small cathedral and church remain standing. Near the village, situated in a pine forest, is the **Hunting Lodge Hotel** with six rooms that have carved wooden furniture.

One entrepreneurial Suzdalite company, Yamskoi Dvor, offers horseback and carriage rides (fits up to 7 people) about town and also an idyllic ride through the woods to **Kideksha**. To reserve a day in advance, call 23-099 or mobile 8-903-647-4116. The barn is at the east end of town at 34a Vasilyevskaya St, but the horses can meet up with you at your hotel.

THE TRANS-SIBERIAN RAILWAY

Although today Russia has one of the world's largest rail networks and arguably the most famous of train journeys—the Trans-Siberian—for years it actually lagged behind the railway systems of other European powers. Fourteen years after George Stephenson began building his railway in England from Stockton to Darlington, and eight years after the engineer's locomotive *Rocket*, was built, Czar Nicholas I opened Russia's first railroad. The Tsarskoye Selo to St Petersburg line was inaugurated on October 30th 1837, and was 30.5 kilometers (18 miles) long. It was succeeded by additional tracks including a St Petersburg to Moscow service in 1851. It took over a year and a half to build the 647-kilometer- (388-mile-) long route between the two cities, one of the straightest railway lines in the world. It took the first train more than 20 hours to cover the distance, where today the new high-speed train takes less than five hours.

Russia's transport and military supply service was shown to be woefully inadequate in 1854 when British, French and Turkish armies inflicted a humiliating defeat on the country in the Crimean War. More Russian troops died on the freezing march to the Crimea and from disease than perished in battle.

The first proposal of a steam railway through Siberia by the American Perry McDonough Collins in 1857 was rejected. But soon after, the reform-minded Czar Alexander II instituted programs of modernization, often inspired by military campaigns, which included railway building. The St Petersburg to Warsaw line was initiated in 1861; a decade later the rails reached the Volga. At the time of his death in 1881, Russia had 22,500 kilometers (14,000 miles) of track.

Construction of the Trans-Siberian Railroad was ordered by Alexander III and on May 31, 1891, his son Nicholas laid the foundation stone. By 1898 it linked Chelyabinsk in the Ural Mountains to Irkutsk. The last leg to the Pacific port of Vladivostok was finally completed in 1916. At Lake Baikal (until track was laid around the south of it) a ferry carried passengers across in summer, and in winter they were pulled across the frozen lake on horse sleighs to the next depot or track was laid across the ice; it would take over five hours to cross the 48-kilometer (30-mile) wide lake.

The railroads held enormous economic and strategic importance for the country. The Trans-Caspian line to Central Asia was part of a military campaign to conquer the territory. As the rails snaked their way from the Baltic Sea through the rolling heartland of Russia and on across the Siberian wilderness and the deserts of Uzbekistan and Kazakhstan, markets and trade opened up almost overnight. The railways were responsible for Russia's first speculative boom. In the 1890s the population of Siberia was just 5 million, today it is over 32 million.

Today the Commonwealth of Independent State's network carries some 11 million travelers every day on some 233,300 kilometers (145,000 miles) of rails. Thanks to Lenin's prognosis that Communism was Soviet power plus the electrification of the whole country, nearly half the rail network is now electrified while the rest runs on diesel. (Steam engine production ceased in 1956.) The most heavily used route is between Moscow and St Petersburg.

In 2005, the Ministry of Transportation completed the 10,000 (6,250-mile) Trans-Siberian Highway, the first road to completely stretch across all of Russia. To commemorate the event, the Expedition Trophy Car Rally was held in a race across Siberia, from Murmansk to Vladivosotok, and the grand prize was 10 kilos of gold. The race is planned annually in February/March. **www.expedition-trophy.com.**

And, now over 100 years after the first tracks were laid, the Trans-Siberian, one of the greatest travel adventures, is still one of the cheapest ways of traveling from Europe to Asia. The main section of the railroad stretches approximately 8,000 kilometers (5,000 miles) from Moscow to Beijing, or 9,342 kilometers (5,805 miles) to Vladivostok.

The Trans-Mongolian train number 4, via Ulan Bataar, Mongolia to Beijing, departs Moscow from Yaroslavsky Station on Tuesdays at 9.30pm and arrives in Beijing five-and-a-half days later at 2.31pm. Train number 3 returns from Beijing, via Mongolia, to Moscow on Wednesdays at 7.40am and arrives at 2.28pm.

Train number 6, which only goes as far as Ulan-Bataar, departs Moscow on Wednesdays at 9.30pm (4 days and 5 hours), and arrives at 7.35am; and train number 5 departs from UB on Fridays at 1.50pm and arrives in Moscow at 2.28pm.

The Trans-Manchurian train number 20 leaves Moscow, via Harbin, on Fridays at 11.53pm and arrives in Beijing six days and 22 minutes later at 5.20am. The return train number 19 from Beijing, via Manchuria, departs on Saturdays at 10.56pm and arrives back in Moscow at 5.57pm.

Two trains depart Moscow's Yaroslavsky Station for Vladivostok on odd-numbered dates at 9.20pm and 12.35am, arriving at 2.07am (148.5 hours later) and 8.09am (175.3 hours later). The quickest return train from Vladivostok to Moscow departs on even dates at 1.11pm and arrives 148 hours later at 5.42pm. A second train leaves on odd dates at 6.55am, and takes an extra day, arriving in Moscow at 11.03am.

Train number 44 leaves Moscow for as far as Khabarovsk on odd dates at 12:43am.

Number 43 returns on even dates at 9.14am; the distance takes two and a half days. There are many trains running to/from Novosibirsk, and take over two days. Several daily trains also run to/from Irkutsk on Lake Baikal which cover the distance in three days. With trains covering such large distances, schedules are often delayed.

Depending on the route and type of class, fares can run between US$225 and $750. For example, currently on the Trans-Mongolian train to Beijing, a first-class compartment costs $500, and second-class $289. For updated schedules check **www .waytorussia.com**.

One can now fly directly to Vladivostok or Khabarovsk from the West Coast of the United States via Alaska and from there, journey westwards on the train to Moscow. On Russian trains the timetable runs according to Moscow time (across 11 time zones), but local time often applies to stations and dining-car hours! Beijing time is the same as Ulan Bator, Mongolia, but is four hours ahead of Moscow summer time or five ahead of Moscow winter time.

A separate branch of the Trans-Siberian is known as the BAM (Baikal Amur Main Line). This railway, running through northeastern Siberia, was completed (for about 60 billion dollars) in 1990 as part of Brezhnev's Fifteen-Year Plan. The task was monumental—seven large tunnels and 2,400 bridges were built across 3,200 kilometers (2,000 miles) of permafrost (the ten-mile-long Severomuisk tunnel was not completed until 2001). Earthquakes, mud flows and avalanches continue to pose additional hazards. There is nothing much but endless *taiga* to see on the journey; the route was mainly built to stimulate timber, coal and oil production and increase industrial transport. The line begins at Tayshet (slightly west of Irkutsk), continues north to Bratsk (along the Angara River), across the northern end of Lake Baikal (at Severobaikalsk), on to Tynda and Komsolmolsk-na-Amure (north of Khabarovsk), and terminates at Imperatorskaya (formerly Sovyetskaya) Gavan on the Pacific.

Reservations are essential, especially during summer, and should be made at least two months in advance. Many travel agencies,

The Cyrillic on this Trans-Siberian dining car reads RESTORAN and illustrates how a little time spent learning the Cyrillic alphabet can help visitors understand and pronounce many simple words and street names.

including places in Moscow and Beijing, can book space on the Trans-Siberian. Tourists have the option of reserving a berth in a two- (first-class cabin with a shower), four- or six-berth compartment (the last is not recommended). Compartments are often set aside just for foreigners. If traveling alone, you may be booked into a compartment with local travelers. Avoid buying open tickets, as they are virtually impossible to book and expire after several months. Russian and/or Chinese visas are required for both trains, and an additional Mongolian visa is needed for the Trans-Mongolian, even if only transiting.

From Vladivostok on the Pacific Ocean, a ferry service operates to Niigata, Japan from May to September. Air connections also run between Khabarovsk and Vladivostok throughout the year. There is a ferry between Sakhalin Island and Hokkaido. You can also stop overnight or spend a few days in Siberian cities, such as Novosibirsk or Irkutsk on Lake Baikal. (If you do get off along the way, make sure you have already prebooked the continuation of your journey.)

Popular connection destinations to the West include: Berlin, which can be reached from Moscow in 24 hours; Budapest (34 hours) and Helsinki (15 hours). If you are a real train fanatic, you can extend the journey all the way to Paris, London or beyond on the East-West Express via Berlin.

Travelers on the Trans-Siberian should always pack basic foods, snacks and drinks, including bottled water and alcohol if so desired. Items such as bread and sweets can be bought at stations along the way. The Russian restaurant car has a tasty enough menu but a limited supply as time goes by. Other handy items to have are earplugs, a Swiss army knife, instant soup, coffee, tea and milk creamer, a large mug, bowl and utensils, Thermos flask, toilet paper, tissues and a Russian phrase book. Hot water is available from each wagon's titan-samovar usually located at the end of the hallway. Dress appropriately for the season and pack lounging clothes. Bring along plenty of reading material; a Walkman, MP3 OR Ipod with music can also help pass the time.

(Ticket prices may vary, depending on whether bought in Moscow, Beijing or from a Western ticket agency, and on the time of year. Trans-Siberian packages can also include a night or two in Moscow with hotel accommodation, and additional stops in Novosibirsk and Irkutsk. Various travel companies even offer private rail car tours along Trans-Siberian routes. These include the US-based MIR Corporation (www.mircorp.com) and the UK's GW Travel (www.gwtravel.co.uk). Russia's Intourist (www.intourist-usa.com) also lists special train trips.)

See Recommended Reading (page 704) for details of specific books on the Trans-Siberian Railway.

HISTORY OF THE RAILWAY GAUGE

The United States has the same track gauge (distance between the rails) as England, as British expatriates built the first American railroads. The first rail lines were actually designed by the same people who built the earlier tramways; they incorporated the same gauge on the rail roads. And the tramways were built as the same width between two covered-wagons wheels. The wagon wheel standard dates all the way back to the chariots of Imperial Rome, which were designed wide enough to fit two horses. Thus, the U.S. standard railroad gauge of 4 feet 8.5 inches (1435mm) is derived from the original specifications of a Roman chariot.

In the 19th-century, Russia chose a broader gauge (1520mm) than what the European or American railways were using. It is widely believed that the choice was made for military reasons, and to prevent foreign invaders from using the Russian railway system.

MOSCOW PRACTICAL INFORMATION

TELEPHONE NUMBERS
Country Code for Russia (7)

Moscow Tourist Information Center
4 Ilyinka Street; tel. 232-5657 ; www.moscow-city.ru

CITY CODES (Many city codes were changed in 2006)

Moscow	(495)	Klin	(9624)	Suzdal	(49231)
St Petersburg	(812)	Kostroma	(494)	Tula	(487)
Aleksandrov	(49244)	Novgorod	(8162)	Tver	(482)
Gatchina	(8127)	Pereslavl Zalessky	(48535)	Uglich	(48532)
Istra	(49631)	Pskov	(8112)	Vladimir	(492)
Ivanovo	(493)	Rostov Veliky	(48536)	Yaroslavl	(485)
Kaluga	(484)	Sergiyev Posad	(49654)	Zvenigorod	(49632)

(Note that some Golden Ring towns are Moscow time plus one hour.)

EMERGENCY SERVICES
Moscow Rescue Service   937-9911
Fire   01   **Police**   02   **Ambulance**   03
(Note: it has been said that these three numbers are to be combined into one emergency number '112' in 2008.)

TELEPHONE INFORMATION
Time   100   **Intercity Information**   07
Directory Enquiries   09   **Lost Property (Metro)**   222-2085
Moscow City Information 285-4718; www.Gorodmoskva.ru; www.Moscow-guide.ru
International Calls To order an int'l call through the operator, dial 8-194.

The following are charged calls:

Moscow Addresses/		Weather: Moscow and	
Telephone	943-5001	Vicinity	975-9133
Museum Information	975-9144	Weather: International	975-9111
Theater Information	975-9122		

TAXIS
Central Taxi Bureau	927-0000 (info 923-8052)
Moscow taxi	238-1001
Capital Cabman	225-9225/743-5300/740-3777 www.citytaxi.ru
Red Hill (Krasnaya Gorka)	381-2746
Taxi Blues	105-5115 www.taxi-blues.com

Transport to Sheremetyevo Airport from city center is about $30.

ON-LINE SERVICES

Traveller's Yellow Pages for Moscow: www.infoservices.com
See Recommended Reading for more Russia information and on-line services.

EXPRESS MAIL/POST

DHL, (Main) 11 3rd Samotechny Pereulok, Metro Novoslobodskaya. tel. 956-1000; www.dhl.ru. (DHL has over 20 locations in Moscow.)

Federal Express, (Main) 17 Gogolevsky Blvd.; other locations are in the hotels Metropole, National and Kosmos. Metro Kropotkinskaya. tel. 787-5555; www.fedex.com.

City Express, 27 Petrovka Ulitsa, Metro Tverskaya. tel. 792-3232. www.cityexpress.ru

United Parcel Service, International Trade Center in Mezh Hotel, Metro Ulisa 1905 Goda. tel. 253-1937; www.ups.com.

TNT Express, 31 Svobody. tel. 797-2700/2777

For Moscow Post Office addresses, see Post and Mail, page 80.

USEFUL PUBLICATIONS IN ENGLISH

The best place to find newspapers and magazines from home is to check in the city's main hotel newsstands, or at central kiosks around town. *The Travellers' Yellow Pages of Moscow* contains over 30,000 useful addresses (in English and Russian); on sale in stores throughout the city. tel. 229-7914; fax 209-5465; e-mail: Moscow@infoservices.com; www.infoservices.com. To order books in the US, see Recommended Reading. *Moscow News* is published daily in Russian and English.

The *Moscow Times* (www.themoscowtimes.com) is distributed daily and together with the *Moscow Times Weekly*, provide current local and international news, along with listings of events in theaters, concerts, movies, and reviews of restaurants and other shows. Their monthly "60 Magazine" is Moscow's most complete guide to restaurants and nightlife. Look for both distributed in hotels, restaurants and selected shops. *Pravda* newspaper is at english.pravda.ru/. The *Moscow Tribune* and *The Russia Journal* and *Lifestyle* magazine (www.lifestyle.ru) also offer news and entertainment guides, published daily. *Moscow Magazine* (monthly) is in English and Russian, reports on the city; city guide and information on restaurants, shops, museums. *Where in Moscow* (monthly) and *Pulse* (weekly) provides information for consumers and details of cultural events.

MEDICAL

Most top-end hotels have a resident nurse or doctor. In case of major medical emergencies, contact a clinic below or an embassy; you may need to arrange for evacuation to a foreign hospital. If you have a preexisting condition, consider purchasing travel medical insurance before departing; a medical evacuation can be very costly.

American Medical Center, 31 Grokholsky Pereulok, . Metro Prospekt Mira. Can be contacted 24 hours a day. It also has a pharmacy, ambulance service, and medical evacuations can be arranged; tel. 937-5757/5774; www.americanclinic.ru, www.amcenters.com.

European Medical Center, 5 Spiridonevsky Per. Metro Pushkinskaya. Open 24 hours; whole range of medical services; tel. 956-7999, 933-6655, www.emcmos.ru.

International SOS Clinic & American Clinic, 31 Grokholsky Per. 10th floor. Metro Prospekt Mira. Open 24 hours a day, emergency and primary care. Can arrange evacuations; tel 937-5760; www.internationalsos.com. The SOS 24-hour Alarm Center is at 16 Dokukina St, Bldg 1, tel. 937-6477. www.internationalsos.com or www.klinik.ru.

DENTAL

American Russian Dental Center, 21a Sadovaya-Kudrinskaya. Metro Barrikadnaya. Also provides emergency care; tel. 797-9759; www.ardc.ru.

American Dental Clinic, 5 1st Tverskaya-Yamskaya Ul. Full dental services; tel. 730-4334; www .americandental.ru.

European Dental Care, 6 1st Nikoloschepovsky Per. Metro Smolenskaya. Full dental services and 24 hour dental emergencies, including night and weekend; tel. 933-0002.

MedStar (British-Russian), 43 Lomonovsky Prospekt, 2nd floor. tel. 143-6076/6377. Metro Universitet. Open Mon–Fri 9am–9pm, Sat 9am–3pm.

US Dental Care, 7/5 Bolshaya Dmitrovka. tel. 933-8686. www.usdentalcare.com

The **American Medical Center** and **European Medical Center** also have dental clinics (the latter at 34 Konushkovskaya Ulitsa, tel. 797-6767).

OPTICAL

For emergencies (including trauma, infection, etc), see European Medical Center above.

Interoptika, 16a Krasikova. Metro Profsoyuznaya. Daily 10am-8pm; tel 128-5717. **Medstar-Optics**, 43 Lomonosovsky Prospekt. Metro Universitet. Mon–Fri 10am–6.30pm; tel. 143-6354.

Paris Optique, 4 Malaya Bronnaya. Metro Pushkinskaya. Mon–Sat 10am–8pm; tel. 290-5496.

EMBASSIES

This is a partial listing of foreign embassies in Moscow which are open Monday through Friday and closed on weekends. For a visa, call first to find out department hours and locations—the visa department may be in a separate location.

Australia, 13 Kropotkinsky Per. tel. 956-6070. Metro Park Kultury. Open 9am–5pm; closed 12.30–1.15pm.

Austria, 1 Starokonyushenny Per. tel. 201-2166/7379. Metro Kropotkinskaya. Open 9am–5pm.

Belgium, 7 Malaya Molchanovka Ul. tel. 937-8040. Metro Arbatskaya. Open 9.30am–5.30pm; closed 1–2.30pm.

Bulgaria, 66 Mosfilmovksya Ul. tel. 143-6045. Metro Universitet. Open 9am–5.30pm; closed 1–2pm.

Canada, 23 Starokonyushenny Per. tel. 105-6000, 956-6666. Metro Kropotkinskaya. Open 8.30am–5pm; closed 1–2pm. (Consular department open Mon, Tues, Thurs, Fri, 8.30–11am to receive documents; 2–2.30pm to issue visas.)

China, 6 Druzhbi Ul. tel. 143-1951/1543. Metro Universitet. Open 8.30am–6pm; closed 12–3pm.

Cuba, 9 Leontevsky Per. tel. 290-2882. Metro Arbatskaya. Open 9am–5pm.

Czech Republic, 12/14 Yuliusa Fuchika Ul. tel. 250-5491/0545. Metro Mayakovskaya. Open 9am–5.30pm.

Denmark, 9 Prechistensky Per. tel. 201-7860/7868. Metro Kropotkinskaya. Open 9am–5pm; closed 1–2pm.

Estonia, 5 Malaya Kislovsky Per. tel. 290-5013. Metro Arbatskaya. Open 9am–6pm; closed 1–2pm.

Finland, 15/17 Kropotkinskaya Ul. tel. 246-4027 (Consular dept. 247-3125). Metro Park Kultury. Open 9am–5pm; closed 1–2pm.

France, 45 Bolshaya Yakimanka Ul. tel. 937-1500 (Consular dept. 937-1599). Metro Okyabrskaya. Open 9am–6pm; closed 1–3pm.

Germany, 56 Mosfilmovskaya Ul. tel. 937-9500 (Consular dept. 933-4312). Metro Universitet. Open 8am–5pm; closed 1–2pm.

Greece, 4 Leontevsky Per. tel. 290-4558 (Consular dept. 290-1446). Metro Arbatskaya. Open 9am–4pm.

India, 6–9 Ulitsa Vorontsovo Polye. tel. 917-1841/0820. Metro Kitai-Gorod. Open 9.30am–6pm; closed 1–2pm.

Israel, 56 Bolshaya Ordynka Ul. tel. 230-6700 (Consular dept. 230-6072). Metro Tretyakovskaya. Open Mon–Thurs. 9am–5pm; Fri 9am–3pm.

Italy, 5 Denezhny Per. tel. 241-1536 or 796-9691 (Consular dept. 253-9287). Metro Smolenskaya. Open 9am–6pm; closed 1–3pm.

Japan, 12 Kalashny Per. tel. 291-8500. (Consular dept. 5a Mal. Kislovsky. 202--3248) Metro Arbatskaya. Open 9am–6pm; closed 1–2.30pm.

Latvia, 3 Chapligina Ul. tel. 925-2707. Metro Turgenskaya. Open 9am–6pm.

Lithuania, 10 Borisoglebsky Per. tel. 291-6109. Metro Arbatskaya.
Open 9am–6pm; closed 1–2pm.

Mexico, 4 Bol. Levshinsky Per. tel. 201-5631 (Consular dept. 201-4848).
Metro Kropotkinskaya. Open 9am–5pm.

Mongolia, 11 Borisoglebsky Per. tel. 290-6792. Metro Arbatskaya.
Open 8am–6pm; closed 1–2pm.

Netherlands, 6 Kalashny Per. tel. 797-2900 (Consular dept. 797-2979).
Metro Arbatskaya. Open 9am–6pm; closed 1–2.30pm.

New Zealand, 44 Povarskaya Ul. tel. 956-3579 (Consular dept. 956-2642).
Metro Barrikadnaya. Open 9am–5.30pm.

Norway, 7 Povarskaya Ul. tel. 203-2270. Metro Arbatskaya.
Open 9am–5pm; closed 1–2pm.

Poland, 4 Klimashkina Ul. tel. 255-0017 (Consular dept. 254-3612).
Metro Belorusskaya. Open 9am–5pm.

Slovakia, 17/19 Yuliusa Fuchika Ul. tel. 250-1071. Metro Belorusskaya.
Open 9am–5.30pm; closed 12–1pm.

Spain, 50/8 Bol. Nikitskaya Ul. tel. 202-2180/2161 (Consular dept. 937-5627).
21 Mal. Nikitskaya St. Metro Arbatskaya. Open 8am–3pm.

Sweden, 60 Mosfilmovskaya Ul. tel. 937-9200 (Consular dept. 937-9201).
Metro Universitet. Open 9am–5pm; closed 1–2.30pm.

Switzerland, 2/5 Ogorodnoi Slobody. tel. 258-3830 (Consular dept. 258-3838).
Metro Turgenevskaya. Open 8.30am–4.30pm; closed 12.30–1.30pm.

Thailand, 9 Bol. Spasskaya Ul. tel. 208-0856. Metro Sukharevskaya.
Open 9.30am–4pm.

United Kingdom, 10 Smolenskaya Nab. tel. 956-7200/7429. Metro Smolenskaya.
Open 9am–5pm; closed 1–2pm. www.britemb.msk.ru.

United States, 19–23 Novinsky Bul. tel. 255-9555, 728-5000.
Metro Barrikadnaya. Open 9am–6pm.

CIS EMBASSIES

A foreign visitor may now need a visa to the following areas:

Armenia, 2 Armyansky Per. tel. 924-6110. Metro Kitai-Gorod.
Open 9am–6pm; closed 1–2pm.

Azerbaijan, 16 Leontevsky Per. tel. 229-2687/4262. Metro Pushkinskaya.
Open 9am–6pm; closed 1–2pm.

Belarus, 17/6 Maroseika Ul. tel. 777-6644. (Consular dept. 924-7095)
Metro Kitai-Gorod. Open 9am–6pm; closed 1–2pm.

Georgia, 6 Maly Rizhsky Per./Khlebny Per. tel. 201-5993.
(Consular dept. 203-1662) Metro Arbatskaya. Open 9am–6pm; closed 1–2pm.

Kazakhstan, 3a Chistoprudny Bul. tel. 927-1873. (Consular dept. 927-1836)
Metro Chistiye Prudy. Open 9am–6pm; closed 1–2pm.

Kyrgyzstan, 64 Bolshaya Ordynka Ul. tel. 237-4601. (Consular dept. 237-3364)
Metro Dobrinskaya. Open 9am–6pm; closed 1–2pm.

Moldova, 18 Kuznetsky Most. tel. 928-1050. Metro Kuznetsky Most.
Open 9am–6pm; closed 1–2pm.

Tajikistan, 13 Granatny Per. tel. 290-0270. Metro Barrikadnaya.
Open 9am–6pm; closed 1–2pm.

Turkmenistan, 22 Filippovsky Per. tel. 202-0278. (Consular dept. 291-6593)
Metro Arbatskaya. Open 9am–6pm; closed 1–2pm.

Ukraine, 18 Leontevsky Per. tel. 229-1079. (Consular dept. 229-6922)
Metro Pushkinskaya. Open 9am–6pm; closed 1–2pm.

Uzbekistan, 12 Pogorelsky Per. tel. 230-0802. Metro Polyanka.
Open 9am–6pm; closed 1–2pm.

AIRPORTS

There are five airports around Moscow. Express buses run to each airport from the
Aerovokzal Terminal at 37a Leningradsky Prospekt. Metro Aeroport/Dynamo.

Sheremetyevo-II International Airport is 32 kilometers (20 miles) northwest of the
city on Leningradskoye Highway. tel. 578-7518 (arrivals); 578-7816 (departures),
tickets: 578-1396. Take an express bus or go to Metro Rechoi Vokzal, then take bus
551, or to Metro Planernaya and take bus 517. Rides take 30–45 minutes. Taxis from
the city cost $25–30. Sheremetyevo III Terminal is due to be completed by 2008. (See
also page 66.)

Sheremetyevo-I, flights within CIS, Russia and Baltic states. tel. 578-2372/3510.

Vnukovo (flights within CIS and Russia) is 20 kilometers (12 miles) southwest of
the city on Vorovskoye Highway. tel. 436-2281. Take an express bus (30 minutes)
or go to Metro Yugo-Zapadnaya, then take bus 511, or a minibus.

Domodedovo (flights within Russia and the CIS and a few international flights) is
52 kilometers (32 miles) southeast of Moscow on the Kashirskoye Highway. tel.
323-8160/8565. The first airport to offer services for the handicapped. Take the
Metro to Domodedovskaya or new high-speed trains also run from Paveletsky
Station in about 45 minutes. Express bus takes 1 hour 20 minutes, 30 minutes by car.

Vykovo (flights within the CIS, Russia and some charters) is located 75 kilometers (45 miles) southeast of the city on Ryazanskoe Highway. tel. 558-4738. Metro Vykhino.

AIRLINES

This is a partial listing of major airlines. If an airline is not listed below, check at your hotel service desk for telephone number and location.

Central Information Bureau, 37a Leningradsky Prospekt. tel. 155-0922.

International Information on Arrivals/Departures, daily 9am–8pm. tel. 156-8019.

Aeroflot, tel. 753-5555; www.aeroflot.org. There are 20 city branch offices with central offices at 20 Petrovka Ul, tel. 921-7164, and 3 Kuznetsky Most, tel. 923-0488. Open 9am–8pm, Sun until 4pm.

Air France, 7 Kirovy Val. tel. 234-3377, 937-3839; www.airfrance.com. Mon–Fri 9am–6pm. Metro Oktybrskaya. Sheremetyevo Airport, tel. 578-5237.

Air India, 7 Kirovy Val. tel. 237-7494. Mon–Fri 9.30am–5pm; closed 1–2pm. Metro Dobrininskaya.

Alitalia, 18 Olimpisky Dr., M. Prospekt Mira. Sheremetyevo Airport, tel. 578-8246, 258-3601.

All Nippon Airways, Sheremetyevo Airport, tel. 578-2921; www.ana.co.jp.

American Airlines, 20 Sadovaya Kudrinskaya, Metro Mayakovskaya. tel. 234-4074.

Austrian Airlines, 5 Smolnskaya Ul. Golden Ring Hotel. tel. 955-0995; www.aua.com.

Balkan Bulgarian Airlines, 3 Kuznetsky Most. tel. 921-0267, 928-9866. Mon–Fri 9am–6pm; Sat 10am–3pm. Metro Kuznetsky Most.

British Airways, 23 Tverskaya–Yamskaya 1st. tel. 363-2525, 258-1866/2492; Sheremetyevo tel. 956-4676; www.britishairways.com. Mon–Fri 9am–5.30pm. Metro Belorusskaya.

Cathay Pacific, 20 Sadovaya Kudrinskaya. tel. 234-4076. Metro Mayakouskaya.

Continental Airlines, 15 Neglinnaya Ul. tel. 921-1674, 925-1291. Mon–Fri 9am–5pm. Metro Kuznetsky Most.

Delta Airlines, 11 Gogolevsky Bulvar. tel. 937-9096/9090; www.delta-air.com. Metro Kropotkinskaya.

Finnair, 7 Kropotkinsky Per. tel. 933-0056; www.finnair.com. Metro Park Kultury.

JAL Japan Airlines, 3 Kuznetsky Most. tel. 921-6448/6648. Mon–Fri 9am–6pm. Metro Kuznetsky Most.

KLM Royal Dutch Airlines, 33 Usacheva Ul, Bldg 1/3rd Fl. tel. 258-3600. Mon–Fri 9.30am–4.30pm. Metro Sportivnaya. www.klm.com.

Korean Air, 1 Bol. Gnezdnikovsky. tel. 725-2727. Rechnoi Vokzal. www.koreanair.com. Metro Belorusskaya.

LOT Polish Airlines, Sheremetyevo Airport, tel. 956-4658.

Lufthansa, 18/1 Olympisky Pr./Hotel Renaissance. tel. 737-6400; www.lufthansa.com. Mon–Fri 9.30am–6pm. Metro Prospekt Mira.

Malev Hungarian Airlines, 21 Povarskaya Ul. tel. 202-8416. Mon–Fri 9am–4pm. Metro Arbatskaya.

SAS, 3 Kuznetsky Most. tel. 291-6200, 231-4747; www.sas.se. Mon–Fri 9am–5.30pm. Metro Okhotny Ryad.

Swissair, 2 Paveletskaya. tel. 937-7767; www.swisair.com. Mon–Fri 9.30am–5.30pm, closed 12–1pm; Sat 9am–1pm. Metro Paveletskaya.

Transaero, 3/4 2nd Smolensky Per. tel. 241-7676; www.transaero.com. Daily 9am–8pm. Metro Smolenskaya.

RAILWAYS

See Getting Around section for more details on train travel and buying tickets. To book tickets for home or office delivery (see page 57/XX), or to obtain information on railway routes, tel. 266-9333; for international routes, tel. 262-0604; to order tickets through Russia, CIS and Baltics, tel. 266-8333, and other international routes, tel. 262-9605 (open 8am–7.30pm); takes 2–3 days; pay upon delivery. The Central Railway Ticket offices are at 5 Komsomolskaya, 15 Petrovka, and 6 Malaya Kharitonevsky. For rail information concerning all stations, tel. 266-9000/9333.

Byelorussky, 7 Tverskaya Zastava Pl. tel. 973-8191/8557. Trains to western Europe eg. Berlin, Geneva, Madrid, Vilnius, Smolensk, Brest, Minsk, Prague and Warsaw. *Elektrichka* run to suburbs of Borodino and Zvenigorod. Metro Byelorusskaya.

Kazansky, 2 Komsomolskaya Pl. tel. 264-6556, 266-3181. Trains to Siberia and Central Asian States. Metro Komsomolskaya.

Kievsky, 2 Kievsky Vokzal Pl. tel. 240-1115/0415. Trains to the Ukraine and Eastern Europe. *Elektrichka* run to Vnukovo Aeroport and Vladimir. Metro Kievskaya.

Kursky, 29 Zemlyanoi Val Ul. tel. 917-3152, 266-5846. Trains to south and southwest, Azerbaijan, Crimea and Caucasus. Metro Kurskaya.

Leningradsky, 3 Komsomolskaya Pl. tel. 262-9143. Trains to St Petersburg, Murmansk, Finland, Novgorod, Pskov and Estonia. Metro Komsomolskaya.

Paveletsky, 1 Paveletskaya Pl. tel. 235-0522/6807. Trains to east and southeast, Volgograd region. Metro Paveletskaya.

Rizhsky, 2 Rizhsky Vokzal Pl. tel. 631-1588. Trains to Baltic areas. *Elektrichka* trains to Istra and New Jerusalem. Metro Rizhskaya.

Savelovsky, Savelosky Vokzal Pl. tel. 285-9005/9000. Trains to Uglich and Rybinsk areas. Metro Savelovskaya.

Yaroslavsky, 5 Komsomolskaya Pl. tel. 921-5914/0817. Trains to the Far East. The Trans-Siberian departs daily. *Elektrichka* also run to Sergiyev Posad and Aleksandrov in the Golden Ring area. Trains also stop at Vladimir and Yaroslavl. Metro Komsomolskaya.

ACCOMMODATION

In the 1990s, a lot of new accommodation, from foreign-owned five-star luxury to bargain rooms in homestays, opened up throughout the city. One can now select a hotel based on location, cost, service and style. (For more information see Being There/Hotels section, page 72.) Before booking, find out what extras and amenities are included, such as breakfast, private bath, visa support, and airport/town center transportation. Ask if the 20 percent VAT and city tax are already included in the price. What is the closest Metro station? Cheaper hotels can be situated far from the city center; you may consider booking a slightly more expensive yet more centrally located hotel to save time and money on travel within the city. Think to ask for a room without street noise or the best view available. Depending on the type of visa, you may have to pre-pay the hotel before departure. Most higher-end and mid-range hotels now take credit cards. Especially in winter months, when occupancy is lower, you may try and negotiate the price. Upon check-in you will be asked for your visa and passport for registration. (Always keep a copy of both.) Some hotels may still charge a separate tariff for Russian citizens and international guests. Often you can get a better hotel rate by booking through a travel company or agent. (see www.allrussianhotels.com; www.moscow-hotels.net).

DELUXE—FIVE STAR

Most luxury hotels provide visa invitation services and airport transportation. The complex contains restaurants, bars, fitness, business and bank-exchange centers, and all the other amenities usually associated with luxury hotels. The following average from $300 a night (single/double) up to more expensive suites. Many of these have special weekend rates.

Ararat Park Hyatt, opened in 2003 in the center near the Bolshoi Theatre, at 4 Neglinnaya St. It has 219 spacious rooms (including 16 suites), fitness center and indoor pool, the Gallery Restaurant and Enoki Sushi Bar, and Café Ararat open 24 hours a day. Metro Lubyanka. tel. 783-1234. www.moscow.park.hyatt.com.

Baltschug Kempinski, 1 Balchug Ul. by the Moskva River, only a short walk south of the Kremlin (across the Moskva River) and Tretyakov Gallery. (The hotel dates back to 1898—the area was once known as the *balchug*, a Tartar word meaning muddy. In 1552, Ivan the Terrible had the first *tabak* or tavern built in this area.) Completely reconstructed in 1992, it has over 230 rooms (and even accepts pets), great views, indoor pool and sauna, and a nightclub (member of *Leading Hotels of* *the World*), Metro Tretyakovskaya. tel. 230-6500; fax 230-6502. In the US and Canada, toll-free at 800-426-3135. www.kempinski.com or www.kempinskimoscow.com.

Marriott Grand Hotel, in the center of town at 26 Tverskaya Ul. It has over 350 rooms, indoor pool and sauna and a rooftop patio. Metro Mayakovskaya. tel. 937-0000; fax 937-0001. For all Moscow Marriotts, in the US and Canada, call toll-free at 800-228-9290. www.marriotthotels.com.

Marriott Royal Aurora Hotel, 11/20 Petrovka Ul is located a block from the Bolshoi Theater in Moscow's historical district. It has 230 rooms, a basement pool, and even offers butler service. Metro Teatralnaya. tel. 937-1000; fax 937-1001. www.marriotthotels.com.

Marriott Courtyard Hotel, 7 Voznesensky Per. tel. 981-3300; fax. 981-3301.

Metropol Hotel, originally built in 1901 by a British architect in style-moderne and decorated with ceramic friezes by Vrubel (Rasputin even had gatherings here); it was completely restored in 1990. At 1/4 Teatralny Proezd (near the Bolshoi Theater), it is decorated with antiques and paintings and has over 350 rooms, three restaurants (one with a famous stained-glass ceiling), two bars, and an indoor swimming pool. In 2006 it celebrated its 105th anniversary. Metro Teatralnaya. tel. 927-6000; tel/fax 927-6010. www.metropol-moscow.ru.

Le Royal Meridien National, built in 1903 in art-nouveau style, right across from Red Square (at 15/1 Mokhovaya Ul), and reopened (after four years of reconstruction) in 1995 after an $80 million transformation (a member of *Leading Hotels of the World* and winner of the prestigious *Diamond Star 2002* award). Check out the historic exterior mosaic-façade. (Lenin lived in Room 107 after moving the capital back to Moscow in 1918.) It has 221 rooms (some museums in themselves), an indoor heated rooftop pool, and the famous Restaurant Moskovsky. Another of Moscow's most historic and elegant hotels. Metro Okhotny Ryad. tel. 258-7000; fax 258-7100. In North America, call toll-free at 800-543-4300, in the UK 08000-282840, and Australia 800-622240. www.national.ru.

Ritz-Carlton Hotel, 3–5 Tverskaya, opened in 2007 (on site of former Intourist Hotel), right off Red Square. This 11-storey hotel has 334 large guest rooms with bathrooms finished with Siberian marble from the Altai. The restaurant 'Cuisine Vitale' is run by a 3-star Michelin chef. Also has Café Vintage, 2 bars, Spa and indoor pool; tel. 225-8888; fax 225-8400; www.ritzcarlton.com.

Sheraton Palace Hotel, 19 1st Tverskaya-Yamskaya Ul. (a five-minute drive from the Kremlin), has over 200 rooms and a marble mosaic of Moscow in the lobby; Metro Belorusskaya.tel. 931-9700; fax 931-9708. In US, toll-free (800) 325-3535. www.sheraton.com.

Swissôtel Krasnye Holmy, 52 Kosmodamlanskaya Emb. Part of the Riverside Towers office complex, it's situated 3 kilometers from the Kremlin, off the Garden Ring between the Obvodny Canal and the Moscow River. Metro Paveletskaya; tel. 787-9800; fax. 787-9898; www.swissotel.com.

TOP END FOUR AND FIVE STAR

These hotels offer all the amenities of high-end hotels. They start at around $200 (single/double) per night.

Art Hotel, 2 3rd Peshchnaya Ul. The Berlin art-gallery owner has covered the hotel walls in contemporary Russian art. A quiet hotel on the edge of a park, and a 20-minute car ride north of the Kremlin. A 15-minute walk from Metro Oktyabrskoye Pole/Sokol; tel. 725-0905.

Golden Ring Swiss Diamond, is at 5 Smolenskaya Ul near the White House and river. It reopened in 1998 as a five-star hotel with over 240 rooms and a panorama restaurant with great views of the city. Metro Smolenskaya. tel. 725-0119/0100; fax 725-0101. www.hotel-goldenring.ru.

Hotel Savoy, formerly known as the Hotel Berlin, built in 1912 and fully restored in 1989 as a four-star hotel. It has 85 rooms and centrally located near the Bolshoi Theater at 3 Rozhdestvenka Ul. Metro Kuznetsky Most; tel. 620-8500; www.savoy.ru.

Katerina Hotel, is a four-star hotel with Scandinavian management. Located at 6/1 Shluzovaya Nab, it has a cosy European atmosphere. Metro Paveletskaya. tel. 933-0400; fax 795-2443; www.Katerina.msk.ru.

Le Meridien Hotel, situated inside the Moscow Country Club, is a five-star complex located 30 kms (18 miles) northwest of town in the forested village of Nahabino at 30 Volokolamskoye Highway. It has 130 rooms, restaurants, Russia's only 18-hole, par 72-championship golf course (designed by Robert Trent Jones, II), a huge sports and fitness center, and hosts various summer and winter sports activities. tel. 926-5911; fax 926-5921. www.starwoodhotels.com.

Marco Polo Presnya Hotel, is a four-star hotel (61 rooms) at 9 Spiridonevsky Per (remodeled in 1991) in the quiet Patriarch's Pond area. Metro Pushkinskaya.tel. 926-5402/244-3631.

Marriott Tverskaya, 34 1st Tverskaya-Yamskaya Ul, this four-star hotel is situated in an elegant art-nouveau style building about 3 kms northwest of Red Square. Metro Belorusskaya. tel. 258-3000; fax 258-3099. In US, toll-free (800) 228-9290. www.marriotthotels.com.

Mezhdunarodnaya Hotel Complex, The 'Mezh' (meaning International) is a five-star business hotel (I & II), part of the World Trade Center complex, and situated across the Moskva River from the White House. Over 550 rooms, indoor pool, and casino. Located at 12 Krasnopresnenskaya Nab. (provides free shuttle service to city center, but a long walk from the metro stop), Metro 1905 Goda. tel. 258-2287/2222; www.hotel.wtcmoscow.ru.

Novotel, is ten minutes from the center at 23 Novoslobodskaya St. It has 255 rooms, fitness center and restaurant and bar. Metro Mendeleevskaya. tel. 780-4000 (in US and Canada, 1–800–Novotel); www.novotel.com or www.accorhotels.com.

President Hotel, at 14 Yakimanka Bol. Ul, was the hotel for former world Communist Party leaders. Renovated, it has five-stars and over 200 rooms and an indoor pool and sauna. Metro Polyanka/Oktyabrskaya, south of the Kremlin. tel. 239-3800; fax 230-2318.

Radisson Slavyanskaya, 2 Europe Square, this four-star hotel is centrally located on the banks of the Moskva River across from Kiev Metro Station. Has over 400 rooms, indoor pool and the American House of Cinema (information hotline 941-8895/8747). tel. 941-8020; fax. 941-8000. (note: The Radisson SAS Belorusskaya is located further out of town at 26 3rd Yamskaya–Polya St.) In US, toll-free (800) 333-3333 www.radisson.com.

Renaissance Moscow Hotel, a five-star complex located by the northern ring at 18 Olympisky Prospekt, has over 475 rooms and an Olympic-size pool (the hotel was originally built for the 1980 Olympics, and it formerly opened in 1991 as the Olympic Penta.) Metro Prospekt Mira near the Olympisky Sport Complex.; tel/fax 931-9000; tel/fax 931-9076. www.renaissancehotels.com.

MID-RANGE

These hotels average around $100 (single-double) per night.

Arbat Hotel, is in one of Stalin's 'Seven Sisters' buildings (107 rooms), at 12 Plotnikov Per, near the Old Arbat. Metro Smolenskaya. tel. 244-7635/31; fax 244-0093.

Budapest Hotel, 2/18 Petrovskiye Linii. A 19th-century building transformed into an elegant and quiet three-star hotel. With a central location, behind the Bolshoi Theater, it has over 100 rooms and a popular tavern. Metro Teatralnaya. tel. 923-2356; fax 921-1266.

Club 27, 27 Malaya Nikitskaya, by the northwest ring. Exclusive four-star club-hotel (over 45 rooms) with Victorian atmosphere, indoor swimming pool and sauna. Metro Pushkinskaya. tel. 202-5611/5650.

Cosmos Hotel, 150 Prospekt Mira, French-built in 1977, at the northern end of town by Metro VDNKh and the All Russia Exhibition Center. Over 1,700 rooms, pool, sauna, casino and even a bowling alley. tel. 234-1000/1206; fax 234-8880. (See also Globus and Zolotoi Kolos under budget hotels in same area.) www.hotel-cosmos.ru.

Danilovskaya Hotel, 5 Bol Starodanilovsky Per. (situated at the Danilovsky Monastery complex), run by the Orthodox Church. The modern four-star hotel has over 100 rooms, a pool and two Finnish saunas. Metro Tulskaya. tel. 954-0503/0308; fax 954-0750.

East–West Hotel, 14 Tverskoi Bulvar. Set in a charming 19th-century mansion, the small 26-room hotel sits in a quiet garden behind the boulevard. It's a 15-minute stroll to downtown and the Kremlin. Metro Tverskaya; tel. 290-0404; fax 956-3027.

Holiday Inn-Lesnaya, 15 Lesnaya, 3 kilometers west from city center; tel. 783-6500.

Holiday Inn-Suschevsky, 74 Suschevsky Val, 5.7 kilometers north of the Kremlin; tel. 225-8282

Holiday Inn-Sokolniki, at 24 Rusakovskaya, is 7.37 kilometers northeast of the center; tel. 786-7373. In US/Canada 888-465-4329; www.ichotelsgroup.com.

The site of the **Moskva Hotel** (at 2 Okhotny Ryad) was demolished in 2003, and a new fivestar hotel, keeping the design of the original facade, is scheduled to open in 2007/2008.

Pallada, 14 Ostrovityanova Ul, in the southwest part of town near Metro Konkovo. This small three-star hotel (27 rooms) also has a pool, sauna and disco. tel. 336-0545.

Pekin, recently privatized by the city, this three-star hotel within the Gothic-style building built in the 1950s, has over 240 rooms, a pool, sauna, and the first Chinese restaurant in town. 5/1 Bol Sadovaya Ul. near Metro Mayakovskaya. tel. 209-2135/0935; fax 200-1420.

Royal Zenith Hotel, First Liniya Tamanskaya (Serebryany Bor.). near Metro Polezhaevskaya. Provides free schuttle to/from downtown. tel. 721-9000; fax. 199-1436.

The site of the former **Rossiya Hotel** (at 6 Varvarka Ul, behind St Basil's Cathedral) was demolished in 2006. (When it was built in 1969, it was one of the world's largest hotels.) A large retail and entertainment complex is now planned for the 30-acre site.

Sovietsky Hotel, this three-star hotel (100 rooms, restaurant) is home to the Gypsy Theater, Roman. 32/2 Leningradsky Prospekt. Near Metro Belorusskaya; tel. 250-7253, 960-2000; fax 250-8003, 960-2006.

Ukrainia Hotel, facing the White House by Kalininsky Bridge, it is one of Moscow's seven skyscrapers, with terrific views of the Moskva River. Built in 1957 (before the Rossiya Hotel, it was Russia's largest hotel), this four-star complex has over 1,000 rooms, located at 2/1 Kutuzovsky Prospekt. Metro Kievskaya; tel. 933-6801; www.ukraina-hotel.ru.

BUDGET HOTELS

Be aware that many of these hotels were built in the old Soviet style and have not yet been completely rennovated. But, they are certainly more of a bargain at average prices of $30–$80 for single/double, and offer comfortable accommodation (if a little more spartan). Check to find out what amenities are included, such as television or air conditioning. Some offer cheaper room rates for shared hallway bathroom, and there may be different classes of rooms, such as standard, upgraded or even semi-lux. Some may not take credit cards. Note the location, for it can be situated far from the center and not close to a Metro station. Checkout www.cheap-moscow.com.

Belgrade Hotel, at 8 Smolenskaya Ul, this three-star hotel is centrally located opposite Arbat St and the (MID) Foreign Ministry Building and has 434 rooms, five restaurants, and a business center. Metro Smolenskaya; tel. 248-2841/1676; fax 248-1852.

Berlin Hotel, 1/2 Mal. Yushnunskaya Ul, south of the city center. Metro Kashovskaya; tel. 319-8121.

Brighton, 29 Petrovsko-Razumovsky Lane, a three-star quiet hotel with ten comfortable rooms, located in the northern part of town. Includes a pool, sauna, health club and restaurant. Metro Dynamo; tel. 214-9511; tel/fax 214-9332.

Globus, 17 Yaroslavskaya Ul, is a three-star hotel (over 350 rooms) with a fitness center. Located behind the Cosmos Hotel. A 15-minute ride to town from Metro VDNKh. No credit cards; tel. 286-2244/4189; fax 286-4616.

Izmailovo Complex, 71 Izmailovo Shosse, matching drab high-rise blocks built as accommodation for the 1980 Moscow Olympics, with over 2,000 beds; known as Gamma and Delta, having three standards of rooms: average, business and first-class, and accepts credit cards. The complex offers three-star modern rooms with bath; restaurants, business center, spa, bowling. (Weekend Izmailovo flea market is nearby). A 20-minute Metro ride to town center. Metro Izmailovo Park; tel. 737-7070/7000; www.izmailovo.ru.

Leningradskaya, 21/40 Kalanchyovskaya Ul, this three-star hotel is located within the shortest of Stalin's 'Seven-Sister' buildings. Its once grand rooms have dulled over the years, but offers suitable rooms, restaurant/bar and business center. Located by three of the city's main train stations: Leningradsky, Kazansky and Yaroslavsky (which means a lot of local travelers congregate in the area). Metro Komsomolskaya; tel. 975-3032/1815; fax 975-1802.

Minsk, 22 Tverskaya, very centrally located this three-star hotel offers plain, yet adequate rooms, café/bar and sauna. Plans are in the works to close the hotel and redevleop the area into a business and shopping complex. Metro Pushkinskaya; tel. 299-1213/1349; fax 299-0362.

Orlyonok (Eagle), 15 Kosygina Ul, is located about six kms southwest of town. Offers over 280 three-star rooms, restaurants, business center, sauna and casino. Transportation is inconvenient—near the Leninsky Prospekt Metro, plus a 20-minute walk or continuing trolleybus ride. tel. 939-888/8000; www.orlenok.ru.

Salyut, 158 Leninsky Pr, low priced with over 1,000 beds, several cafés and a sauna. Located in the southwest part of town; from Metro Yugo-Zapadnaya, continue with a bus ride about two stops. tel. 234-9292/9325; fax 234-9363.

Sevastopol, a two-star complex at the southern end of town at 1a Bol Yushunskaya Ul. (Restaurant, pool, sauna). Metro Sevastopolskaya/Kakhovskaya; tel. 318-4981/ 0381; fax 318-7766. www.Tours.ru/sevast.

Seventh Floor, 88 Vernadskovo, bldg 1, is a small, cozy, bed & breakfast hotel in the southwest part of town. Metro Yugo-Zapadnay; tel/fax 437-9997, 956-6038.

Sputnik, 38 Leninsky Prospekt, this basic three-star hotel is about four kms southwest from the center of town. Metro Leninsky Gory, and a 15-minute walk; tel. 961-2115; fax 930-6383. www.hotelsputnik.ru.

Tourist Hotel, 17/2 Selskokhozyaystvennaya Ul, located near the Yauza River inside a drab-looking building, the adequate rooms are on the cheaper side, inquire about the upgraded rooms. Friendly service and tasty café. Metro Botanichesky Sad; tel 187-7045.

Tsentralny Dom Turista, located 13 kilometers southwest of the center at 146 Leninsky Prospekt. This three-star 'Central Tourist House' has 700 rooms, each with TV, refrigerator and private bath. It also has ethnic restaurants, pool, sauna, super-market, bowling and a nightclub. Inexpensive prices for a comfortable room. Metro Yugo-Zapadnaya and then two stops by bus; tel. 434-9467/2782; www.cdt-hotel.ru.

Varshava Hotel, at 2 Leninsky Prospket. Opened in 1960, and has 122 adequate, inexpensive rooms, and a restaurant. Located by the Okyabrskaya Metro on the southern ring. No credit cards; tel. 238-1970; fax 238-9639.

Yunost, at 34 Khamovnichesky Val (near Novodevichy Convent), this three-star hotel has 200 rooms, singles, doubles and 'Euro-class' doubles, and a restaurant. Metro Sportivnaya; tel. 242-4860/242-8922; fax 242-4861.

Zolotoi Kolos, 3 Yaroslavsky Ul. Bldg.15. With 390 rooms, it's located near VDNKh metro. tel. 217-6666.

AIRPORT HOTELS

Aerostar, located on the way to the airport at 37 Leningradsky Prospekt, Complex 9, with over 200 rooms. tel. 213-9000; fax 213-9001. www.aerostar.ru. Between Metro stations Dynamo and Aeroport. A cheaper hotel is the three-star Hotel Aeropolis, at same address, Complex 5. tel. 151-0442; fax 151-7543.

Holiday Inn Vinogradovo, 171 Dmitrovskoye Highway. This four-star hotel, built in 1998, has over 150 rooms and transfer service to the airport and downtown. Metro Altufevo, located far north of the city enter; but only a 20-minute drive to Sheremetyevo airport; tel. 937-0670; fax 937-0671. In US, toll-free (888) 465-4329. www.Ichotelsgroup.com.

Novotel, built in 1992, located 200 meters from Sheremetyevo II airport, this four-star airport hotel has over 400 rooms. tel. 926-5900/5907; fax 926-5903. In US, toll-free 800-221-4542. www.accorhotels.com.

The **Sheremetyevo-2 Hotel** is also at the airport. tel. 753-8094/578-3464; tel/fax 578-9470.

Sofitel Iris Hotel, a four-star hotel (195 rooms, pool) is located at 10 Korovinskoye Highway, north of the city. Metro Petrovsko-Razumovskaya; tel. 933-0533, 488-8000. In US, toll-free (800) 221-4542. www.accorhotels.com.

Domodedovo-Aerohotel, at the Domodedovo airport with 400 rooms. tel. 795-3867; fax 795-3573.

Vnukovo Hotel, at the Vnukovo Airport has 370 rooms. tel. 436-2972/2462. A second three-star hotel is planned to open in front of Terminal I in 2007.

GUESTHOUSES

For each hostel, advance bookings are recommended—prepayment is required, and credit cards are accepted as a guarantee. In case of cancellation a charge of one night will be made. All provide visa support and other travel agency services.

Travellers Guest House, formerly at 50 Bol Pereyaslavskaya Ul, 10th floor. After 14 years of operation, it closed its doors in 2006. Metro Prospekt Mira (ten-minute walk north). Check www.tgh.ru for potential re-opening/relocation information.

Hostel Sherstone, 8 Gostinichny Proezd, Building 1. It has 100+ beds and high season costs are 25 Euros for Dorm, 33E (per person) for double and 60E for a single. A 15-minute Metro ride to northern part of city. A five-minute walk from Vladykino Metro stop; tel. 783-3438, www.sherstone.ru.

Godzillas Hostel, 6 Bolshoi Karetny. Metro Tsvetnoi Bulvar. One of the most centrally located hostels in Moscow, set up in a pre-revolutionary building near Pushkin Square. Has both female and mixed dorms and singles/doubles. Also provides airport/train transfers. Two other hostels are: **Moscow Home Hostel** at 2 Neopalimovsky Pereulok and **Sweet Moscow** at 51 Stary Arbat; metro Smolenskaya. All start at around $25. For more information and direct bookings, try www.bootsnalltravel.com

Prakash Guest House, 83/1 Profsoyuznaya St (entrance-2 on south side of bldg). Also has a four-bed dormitory room. No credit cards. Metro Belyayevo in the southern part of town; tel./fax. 334-2598.

International Hostel Holiday, currently offers hostel budget accommodation in St Petersburg (see hotel listings for the city). Also provides transportation/travel help and guided city excursions. www.hostel.ru.

HOMESTAYS AND BED & BREAKFASTS

Several international organizations can now book homestays in Russian apartments that average between $15-60 per night, depending on whether single or double room. (A two-night minimum stay may be required, and there can be discounts for longer stays.) This usually includes a private room within the family apartment, breakfast (sometimes other meals), use of a shared bathroom, and kitchen. The host family is normally English-speaking and the apartment and family pre-approved by a Russian host organization. Plus, the added advantage is that you are able to experience the life of a typical Russian family and have conversations about their opinions and lifestyles. Check to find out what the price includes: how many meals/day, city walking tours guided by host, city transfers, etc. Many of these homestays can now be pre-booked through an overseas travel agency (working with a corresponding Russian agency) who can also provide visa and other travel support. (Extra fees may be charged for these services.) Never wait till the last minute to book these homestays.

HOFA (Host Families Association), established in 1991, HOFA offers a full choice of budget accommodation: homestays, apartment rentals and hotel reservations for guests in more than 60 cities of the former USSR. They also can provide visa sponsorship and assistance, transportation transfers, travel information and bookings, and city guided tours (walking or with car/driver), even Russian language lessons. see www.hofa.ru.

International Bed & Breakfast, comfortable and moderately-priced accommodation provided for Russia. Also offers group tours and other independent travel to Moscow and St Petersburg. PO Box 823, Hungtindon Valley, Pennsylvania, 19006. In US, toll-free 800-422-5283, (215) 663-1438; fax (215) 379-3363.

Moscow Bed & Breakfast has daily and weekly rentals in private apartments. Located near Belorussky Station. In Moscow, tel. (095) 147-0021.

In the UK, Interchange Travel offers rooms in apartments in both the Moscow and St. Petersburg areas. tel. (020) 8681-3612; e-mail interchange@interchange.uk.com.

In Australia, the Russia Travel Centre in Sydney (tel. 02-9262-1144) and Passport Travel in Melbourne can book homestays in Russia (tel. 03-9867-3888)

APARTMENTS AND LONG TERM RENTALS

For a visitor, it is also worth considering renting an apartment while in town. They can be cheaper than a hotel stay, and offer more space and amenities. Many hotels, such as the Mezhdunarodny and President hotels, offer rooms with kitchens for long-term rent. Park Place, located nine miles southwest of the center, at 113 Leninsky Prospekt, also offers over 300 high-end apartments for rent. Check www.hofa.ru and www.bootsnalltravel.com that also include cheaper short-term apartment listings. See also HOFA in Homestay listings.

There are now numerous real-estate agencies in Moscow. The best bet is to peruse the English language publications, such as the Moscow Times (www.themoscowtimes.com) listings of apartments. Other popular websites are: Moscow Rick at www.enjoymoscow.com and www.moscow-star.com; Penny Lane www.realtor.ru; www.apartmentres.com; Aventec at www.aventec.ru; FlatLink at www.flatlink.ru; Kalitagrad at www.kalitagrad.ru; Like Home at www.likehome.ru and Moscow Apartments 4U at www.moscowapartments4U.com. Many of these also offer transportation to and from airports and railroad stations.

CAMPING

There are no real camping grounds in or near the city. Unfortunately, because of safety reasons, it is no longer recommended. One place that does offer camping is the **Rus-Hotel** on the Varshovskoye Highway, 20 kilometers (13 miles) from the city center.

DINING

If you have not visited Russia since the Socialist era, it is time to be flabbergasted at the sight of over 1,000 eating establishments in Moscow alone—from cafés and fast-food outlets to the most elegant restaurants in old palaces and new hotels. (Before the problem was finding a place to eat, now it is choosing one!) If not in the mood for the classic Russian fare (see the Menu vocabulary on page 620), hundreds of ethnic restaurants serving cuisines from Italian to Mongolian have sprung up throughout the city; many are usually open from noon or 6pm to well past midnight and even offer live music or variety shows, and serve wine, beer and other alcoholic beverages. (In Moscow, many settings mix and match, so be prepared: one evening a restaurant may stage chamber music, the next a striptease show.) Every type of dish imaginable is offered, as well as matching prices, which vary from the very cheap to amazingly expensive. The larger hotels all have their own restaurants, bars and cafés. For many of these establishments, reservations are recommended. Besides Russian rubles, most now accept credit cards (check before you go). Decide what cuisine you are game for, then locate the closest restaurant by finding its Metro stop on the map. (If it is on the other side of town, plan for travel time, or reconsider.) If the menu prices are marked 'Y.E.' this means 'conventional units' or US dollars/Euros, but payment is in rubles or by credit card. Many offer reasonably-priced set business luncheons. For more restaurant selections, check www.whererussia.com or www.themoscowtimes.com.

So many food stores, supermarkets and mini-malls have opened, just ask the hotel staff to direct you to the nearest one. (The chain Global USA is at 6 Tverskaya and 35 Usachyova.) Fast food is also found everywhere, with scores of McDonalds, Russkoye Bistros, and Yolki-Palki Cafés scattered about the city. A Westerner can now find practically everything in Moscow that is available at home.

AFRICAN

Bungalo Bar, 6 Zemlyanoi Val. Dishes can be exotic (eg. alligator, ostrich or kangeroo). Thatched roof bar. Daily 11am–midnight. Metro Kurskaya; tel. 916-2432.

Limpopo, 1 Varsonofievsky Per. African-style food and live music in African hut atmosphere. Daily noon–midnight. Metro Kuznetsky Most; tel. 925-6990.

AMERICAN

American Bar and Grill, 2/1 1st Tverskaya-Yamskaya. American burgers, chicken rings, pork ribs; country and blues music at night. Daily 24 hours. Metro Mayakovskaya; tel. 250-9525.

American Steakhouse, 18/1 Olimpiisky Pr, in Renaissance Hotel. Juicy steaks and unlimited salad bar. Blues music at night. Daily 6pm–10.30pm. Metro Prospekt Mira; tel. 931-9000.

Hard Rock Café, 44 Stary Arbat, Open 8am–11pm. Metro Smolenskaya; tel. 205-8335.

City Grill, 2/30 Sadovaya Triumfalnaya. New York and Philadelphia fare, such as sandwiches and fries. Metro Mayakovskaya; tel. 299-4189.

Exchange, 2 Berezhkovskaya, in Radisson Slavyanskaya Hotel. American steak house. Daily 6pm–11pm. Metro Kievskaya; tel. 941-8020.

Louisiana Steakhouse, 30 Pyatniskaya. Setting is a 19th-century saloon, serving generous portions of a variety of steak from Black Angus to filet mignon. Daily 11am–12.30am. Metro Tretyakovskaya; tel. 951-4244.

Planet Hollywood, 23b Krasnaya Presnya. American chain serving American food and drink; overly expensive. Open 11am–6am; Mon/Tues till 1am. Metro Krasnopresnenskaya; tel. 255-9191.

Starlight Diner, 16 Bol Sadovaya. American diner with everything from milkshakes to grilled cheese sandwiches, and breakfasts all day. Open 24 hours. Metro Mayakovskaya. A second diner is at 9 Korovy Val near Metro Oktyabrskaya; tel. 290-9638.

T.G.I. Friday's, 18/2 Tverskaya (Also at three other locations). Delicious steaks, burgers, sandwiches. Daily noon–midnight. Metro Pushkinskaya.. tel. 200-3921.

Uncle Guilly's, 6 Stoleshnikov Per. More steaks, burgers and sandwiches. Different daily specials. Daily noon–midnight. Metro Pushkinskaya; tel. 229-4750, 933-5521.

ARMENIAN

Café Ararat, 4 Neglinnaya in Ararat Park Hotel. Also has a summer dining terrace. Noon to midnight. Metro Kuznetsky Most; tel. 783-1234.

Moosh, 2/4 Okyabrskaya. Traditional Armenian dishes and wine at reasonable prices (try the sturgeon shashlik). Daily 10am–11pm. Metro Novoslobodskaya; tel. 284-3670.

Noah's Ark, 9 Mal Ivanovsky. Live music 8–10pm. Daily noon–midnight. Metro Kitai-Gorod; tel. 917-0717.

Noyev Kovcheg, 9 Maly Ivanovsky Per. A bit pricier than Moosh, with good eggplant appetizers and shashlik dishes. Live music begins at 7pm. Daily noon to midnight. Metro Kitai-Gorod; tel. 917-0717.

At Tigranych's, 13 Lesnaya. Good food, ethnic interior and live music. Daily 1pm–11pm. Metro Belorusskaya; tel. 251-0257.

AUSTRALIAN

Hunter's Sketches, 53 Bol Nikitskaya. Kangaroo shashlik. Metro Barrikadnaya; tel. 202-7986.

AZERBAIJANI

Agdam, 4 Khlebnikov Per. Azerbaijiani cuisine and live music after 7pm. Daily noon–2am. Metro Ploshchad Ilicha; tel. 278-7149.

Farkhad, 4 Bolshaya Marfinskaya, oriental decor and live music. Daily 11am–11pm. Metro Vladykino; tel. 218-4136.

BAKERIES

Moscow has bread and bakery stores on practically every street corner—freshly baked goods abound. A must is trying the traditional Russian brown or black bread. To order in Russian: *khleb* is bread; *baton* (oval white loaf); *bely kirpich* (white brick loaf); *chorny kirpich* (dark brick loaf); *tort* (sweet cake); *bulochki* (sweet rolls). The French bakery is at 3 Boyarsky Per. Mon–Sat 8am–8pm. Metro Krasniye Vorota. Speciality confectionary shops are: Krasny Oktybr, 12 lst Tverskaya-Yamskaya (Metro Myakovskaya); Slastena-M, 21 Petrovka; and Stoleshniki-632, 11 Stoleshnikov (both Metro Pushkinskaya).

SUNDAY BRUNCH

The following hotel.s offer superb Sunday brunches with live music; cost ranges from US$20–35 for all-you-can-eat-and-drink. The Baltchug in the Baltchug Hotel. serves its special Sunday 'Linner' from 12.30pm–7pm. Café Taiga, is in the Aerostar Hotel. Four Seasons in the Le Meridien Hotel. and Moscow Country Club, serves from 1–5pm. Gratzi in the Marriott Grand Hotel. has live jazz, too, and serves from noon to 4pm. Lomonosov in the Sheraton Palace Hotel. is open from noon–5pm.

The main dining hall in the **Metropolel Hotel** has a great spread and live jazz ensemble, open noon–4pm. The **Radisson Slavyanskaya Restaurant** in the hotel of the same name has everything from smoked salmon to French pastries, serves noon–5pm. **Samobranka** in the Marriott Grand Hotel offers delicious theme country brunches.

BULGARIAN

Mekhana Bansko, 9/1 Smolenskaya Sq. Delicious Bulgarian cuisine, wine and nightly ethnic music. Daily noon to 11pm; weekends till 2am; Thurs–Sun disco 10pm–6am. Metro Smolenskaya; tel. 241-3132, 244-7387, www.mekhanabansko.ru.

Sofia, 7/1 Ul Krasnaya. Small and cozy. Metro Mayakovskaya; tel. 254-4641.

CAFÉS & COFFEE SHOPS
(Good news: coffee abounds in a city that once only knew Nescafé!)

Caffeine/Klon, 16 Bol Dmitrovka. (**Kofe-In** is at number 18.) Has over 20 varieties of coffee, food and pastries. Daily 10am–11pm. Metro Teatralnaya.

Coffee Bean, 18 Ul Petrovka. Also at 10 Tverskaya. The Seattle-style coffee shop whips up lattés and cappacinos. Daily 8am–10pm. Metro Chistiye Prudy.

Coffee House, 16 Tverskaya (also at 10 Tverskaya, 18/7 Kuznersky Most). Coffees, cakes and Belgian chocolates. Daily 9am–9pm. Metro Pushkinskaya. Next door is **Coffeetune** at No. 18. This is one of Moscow's biggest coffee chains; branches are everywhere.

Coffee Republic, 21 Novy Arbat. Over 30 kinds of coffee. Daily 24 hrs. Metro Arbatskaya.

Deli France, 4 Triumfalnaya Sq in Tchaikovsky Concert Hall (the **Coffee Club** is also here). Daily 9am–10.30pm. Metro Mayakovskaya.

Donna Clara, 21/13 Ul Malaya Bronnaya. Café serves good breakfasts. Daily 10am–midnight. Metro Mayakovskaya.

Gostinaya, 3 Shmitovsky. This café is named after 19th-century *gostinaya*, or sitting rooms. Has cozy atmosphere, soft couches and fireplaces. Daily 1pm–2am. Metro Ulitsa 1905 Goda.

Great Canadian Bagel, 27 Tverskaya. Serves up bagels with cream cheese, soups, sandwiches, salads and desserts. Daily 10am–midnight. Metro Mayakovskaya.

Krem, 3 Solyansky Proezd. Café and cinema room. Metro Kitai-Gorod.

Moskva-Roma, 12 Stoleshnikov Lane. Café with music or DJs. Metro Teatralnaya.

Schizlong (Chaise Lounge), 5/8 Maly Vlasyevsky. Café and Moscow's first oxygen bar. Open 10am–late, DJ Thurs–Sat 8–11pm. Metro Kropotkinskaya.

Shokoladnitsa (Chocolate's), 58/2 Bol Yakimanka. Coffee, tea and all things chocolate, including desserts, *blini* and hot chocolate. Daily 11am–11pm. Metro Oktyabrskaya.

Soleil Express, 24 Sadovaya-Samotyochnaya. Relaxing atmosphere with business lunch noon–3pm. Daily 9am–11pm. Metro Paveletskaya.

Zen Café, 5/6 Bol Dmitrovka. Great coffee and food. Daily 8am–11pm. Metro Belorusskaya.

INTERNET CAFÉS (usually open daily 9am–11pm)
Internet Café, 15 Tshayanova. Metro Novoslobodskaya; tel. 250-6169.

Internet Club, 12 Kuznetsky Most. Metro Kuznetsky Most; tel. 924-2140.

Netcity Internet Café, 2 Paveletskaya Square. Coffee, web access and DJ music. Metro Paveletskaya; tel. 969-2125; also at and 6 Kamergersky Per. Open 10am–11pm. Metro Okhotny Ryad; www.netcity.ru.

Newmail.ru, 3 Ul Zabelina/Novaya Pochta. Metro Kitai-Gorod; tel. 923-0863.

Timeonline, 1 Manezhanaya Sq in Okhotny Ryad Trade Complex, lower level. Open 24 hrs. Becomes cheaper when you purchase 5/10 hour cards. Metro Okhotny Ryad; tel. 363-0600. www.timeonline.ru.

CHINESE
Ancient China, 5/6 Kamergersky Per. Over 100 Chinese dishes available, and tea ceremonies. Open daily till 11pm. Metro Okhotny Ryad; tel. 292-2900.

China Club, 21 Ul. Krasina. Open noon to midnight. Metro Mayakovskaya; tel. 232-2778.

China Garden, 12 Krasnopresnenskaya, in Mezhdunarodnaya Hotel. Offers over 100 national dishes. Metro Ul 1905 Goda; tel. 967-0586.

Dim Sum, 3 Smolenskaya. Shanghai cooks, offering over 40 dishes. Metro Smolenskaya; tel. 937-8425.

Five Spice, 3/18 Sivtsev Vrazhek Per. Serves Chinese as well as Tandoori dishes. Open noon to midnight. Metro Kropotkinskaya; tel. 203-1283.

Formosa, 23 Leonyevsky Per, superb Taiwanese food and Japanese beer. Business lunch noon–5pm weekdays. Daily noon–11pm. Metro Pushkinskaya; tel. 299-7216.

Hong Kong, 7 1st Tverskaya-Yamskaya. Fusion Asian-European. Open 11am to midnight. Metro Mayakovskya; tel. 200-5763.

Imbir, 16 1st Tverskaya-Yamskaya. Delicious Pan-Asian food. Open noon to midnight. Metro Prospekt Mira; tel. 775-2601.

Ki Ka Ku, 28/30 Begovaya. Expensive Chinese food and buffet, sushi. Karaoke bar. Metro Begovaya; tel. 945-3031.

Lili Wong, 3/5 Tverskaya. Pleasant dining room with cuisine prepared by native chef. Business lunch noon–3pm. Daily Noon–6am. Metro Okhotny Ryad; tel. 956-8301.

Mao, 2 Ul 1905 Goda. Nouvelle-chinese cuisine, speciality kitchen where dishes are prepared in front of customer. Daily noon–midnight; weekends till 2am. Metro Ulitsa 1905 Goda; tel. 255-5955.

Peking Duck, 24 Tverskaya, 10am-midnight. Metro Pushkinskaya; tel. 755-8401.

Silk, 29/1 Tverskaya-Yamskaya. Traditional Chinese food by Beijing chef, and choice of teas. Open 11am–5am. Metro Belorusskaya; tel. 251-4134.

Taipei, 13 Volkov Per. First Taiwanese restaurant in Moscow. Karoke. Business lunch noon–5pm. Daily 11am–midnight. Metro Krasnopresnenskaya; tel. 255-0176.

Temple of the Moon (Khram Luny), 1/12 Bolshoi Kislovsky Per. One of Moscow's first Chinese restaurants; tasty dishes, include seafood prepared by Chinese chef in cozy ethnic setting. Daily 1.30pm–11pm. Metro Biblioteki im Lenina; tel. 291-0401.

Zen, 3 Bol Putinkovsky Per, just off Pushkin Square. Interior setting with waterfall, red lanterns and limestone cliffs. Dishes prepared by Chinese chef. Daily noon–11pm. Metro Pushskinskaya; tel. 299-5444.

CUBAN
Aruba, 4 Narodnaya. Delicious Cuban food. Daily 11.30am–5am. Metro Taganskaya; tel. 912-1836.

Trinidad, 9/10 Pr Vernadskovo. Cuban and Caribbean fare with Cuban rum and cigars. Live Cuban music. Open noon to 11pm. Metro Universitet; tel. 938-2765.

EUROPEAN
011, 10/12 Sad-Triumfalnaya. European cuisine, live music. Daily 1pm–1am; closed Sunday. Metro Mayakovskaya; tel. 299-3964.

Bulvar, 30/7 Ul Petrovka, Deliciious fusion cuisine by French chef Thomas Chiarelli. Metro Kuznetsky Most; tel. 209-6798.

Crab House, 6 Tverskaya. Fancy seafood restaurant with salad bar; pricey. Metro Tverskaya; tel. 292-5359.

Discreet Charm of the Bourgeoisie (named after the Bunuel film), 24 Bol. Lubyanka. Has a casual atmosphere and music. Open 24 hours. Metro Lubyanka; tel. 923-0848.

Golden Fish, 4 Nashchokinsky Per. Fish flown in from Dubai, with aquariums on each table; expensive. Daily 10am–11pm. Metro Kropotkinskaya; tel. 202-0778.

Le Gastronome, 1 Kudrinskaya Sq. Gourmet European-style cuisine. Daily noon–midnight. Metro Barrikadnaya; tel. 255-4433.

Loft, 25 Nikolskaya, Great view of Moscow out the windows. tel. 933-7713.

Mesto Vstrechi (Place to Meet) 9/8 Maly Gnednikovsky Per. Restaurant and bar with a back-room disco. Daily noon–5am. Metro Pushkinskaya.

Metropole, in Metropole Hotel., offers superb European dishes in a beautiful setting; expensive. Also a buffet from 7pm–10.30pm. Daily noon to midnight. Metro Pl. Revolyutsii; tel. 927-6061.

Old Square Piano Bar, 8 Bol Cherkassky Per. European cuisine, piano music, near the Kremlin. Disco opens at 11pm. Daily 11am–6am. Metro Kitai-Gorod; tel. 298-4688.

Pyramida, 18a Tverskaya. Currently one of trendiest restaurants in town, serving fusion-style selections. Metro Pushkinskaya; tel. 200-3600.

Scandinavia, 7 Maly Palashevsky Per. Superb Scandinavian food and smorgasbord; expensive. Daily noon–midnight. Metro Pushkinskaya; tel. 200-4986.

Schwein, 50/12 Baumanskaya. In summer, offers spit-roast pig. Daily 7pm–5am. Metro Baumanskaya; tel. 267-4504.

Shokolad (Chocolate), 5 Strasntoi Bulvar. Cozy café atmosphere with a great selection of European food. Live music or DJ's at night. Open 2 hours. Metro Pushkinskaya; tel. 787-8666.

Sirena, 15 Bol Spasskaya. Expensive excellent European cuisine and seafood; there is a glass floor with sturgeon swimming under your feet. Daily noon–midnight. Metro Sukharevskaya; tel. 208-0200.

Stanislavsky, 23 Tverskaya in theater. European-style fare and disco at night. Daily 5pm–1am; weekends till 4am. Metro Teatralnaya; tel. 209-5020.

Strastnoi 7, 7 Strastnoi Bul. European/Russian-style food, wines, folk music. Daily noon–11pm. Metro Chekhovskaya; tel. 299-1751.

Tri Peskarya, 4 Zubovsky Bulvar. European seafood, live chamber music. Daily noon–midnight. Metro Park Kultury; tel. 201-8738.

U Dyadi Gilyaya, 7 Mal Palashevsky Lane. European fare. Metro Pushkinskaya; tel. 200-4986.

Ulei, 7 Gasheka, Cucat Plaza II. American chef with own version of d'fusion cuisine; credo is "food is art". Metro Mayakovskaya; tel. 797-4333.

Vkus Blyuza (Taste of Blues), 5 Teatralnaya Square. European cuisine. Live jazz and blues on Tues–Sat from 7–11pm. Daily noon–midnight. Metro Teatralnaya.

White Swan (Bely Lebyed), 12 Chistoprudny Bul. Pricey gourmet European cuisine and caviar. Metro Chistiye Prudy; tel. 924-8636, 928-6000.

EASTERN EUROPEAN

Belgrade, 8 Smolenskaya. Yugoslavian specialities. Daily 1pm–2am. Metro Smolenskaya; tel. 248-2696.

Bo Emi, 1 Abrikovsovsky Per. Serbian dishes. Daily 11am–11pm. Metro Sportivnaya near Novodevichy Monastery; tel. 248-5317.

Drago, 32 Bol Dmitrovka. Traditional Serbian food. Daily noon–midnight. Metro Pushkinskaya; tel. 209-3971.

Morova, 3 Sad-Kudrinskaya. Yugoslavian cuisine, wine. Daily noon–11pm. Metro Barrikadnaya.

Praga, 2 Arbat. The building now houses seven different restaurants, including Czech, Italian and Brazilian. Praga restaurant pastry chef, Vladimir Guralnik, invented the now-famous dessert, *Ptichye Moloko* or Bird's Milk Tort (a biscuit-type chocolate soufflé cake). Daily noon–5am. Metro Arbatskaya; tel. 290-6171.

At Schweik's, 1 Manezhnaya Sq. Czech food. Daily 10am–10pm. Metro Okhotny Ryad.

FRENCH
(Open noon to midnight unless stated otherwise.)

Balaganchik, 10/2 Trekhprudny Per. Named after a traveling theater, it has a cabaret stage and French menu. Daily noon–3am. Metro Pushkinskaya; tel. 209-5444.

Brasserie du Soleil, 21 Taganskaya. Reasonably-priced good food and bar. Metro Taganskaya; tel. 258-5900.

Café Absinthe, 11/16 Bol. Karetny Per. Dishes to order and take-out, over 100 wine brands. Metro Tsvetnoi Bulvar; tel. 209-9908.

Carré Blanc, 19/2 Seleznyovsky. Created by Expats, the French cuisine is delicious. A bar and bistro are also here. Metro Novoslobodskaya; tel. 258-4403.

Café des Artistes, 5/6 Kamergersky Per. Swiss chef prepares French bistro-style food. Metro Okhotny Ryad; tel. 292-0673/4042.

Count Orlov, 2 2nd Verkny Mikhailovsky Lane. Located in the former home of Catherine the Great's lover, Count Orlov, it serves up scrumptuous (pricey) French cuisine. Good business lunch. Metro Shabolovskaya; tel. 954-0583.

Grand Alexander, 26 Tverskaya in Marriott Grand Hotel. Food is exquisite and expensive. Mon–Sat 6pm–midnight. Metro Mayakovskaya; tel. 937-0028.

La Part Des Anges, 8/2 Kursovoi Per. Restaurant and cognac club, with over 700 cognac brands. Metro Kropotkinskaya; tel. 502-9071.

La Premiere, 2 Nikitsky Per, 2nd floor. French food and wines. Metro Okhotny Ryad; tel. 292-0676.

Le Cardinal Richellieu, 5/1 Teatralnaya. French gourmet Provençal cuisine and wines. Closed 3pm–6.30pm; weekends open 6.30pm–3am. Metro Teatralnaya; tel. 298-1475.

Le Chalet, 1/2 Korobeinikov Per. French specialities, Cuban cigars, live music. Metro Kropotkinskaya; tel. 202-0106.

Le Duc, 2 Ul 1905 Goda. Superb food, extremely formal (waiters in tails and white gloves) and expensive. Metro Ulitsa 1905 Goda; tel. 255-0390.

Le Gastronome, 1 Kudrinskaya Square. Metro Smolenskaya; tel. 255-4433.

Na Monmartre, 9 Vetoshny, in French Galleries Passage behind GUM. Great French food and wines, surrounded by Picasso prints. Metro Teatralnaya; tel. 725-4797.

Nostalgie Art-Club, 12a Chistoprudny Bul. Good French food and live music. Metro Chistiye Prudy; tel. 916-9478, 925-7625.

Parisienne, 31 Leningradsky Pr. Decorated to look like a French street, with a model of Eiffel Tower. Expensive, but delicious food in secluded setting. Daily 1pm–2am. Metro Dynamo; tel. 213-0784.

Reporter, 8 Gogolevsky Bul. French food, large wine cellar and live music. Metro Kropotkinskaya; tel. 956-9997.

St Michel, 23 Tverskaya. Trendy and expensive French food with wine and cigar selection. Metro Pushkinskaya; tel. 937-5679.

Versai, 9/2 Spiridonovka. Pricey French cuisine, wines, cigars and offers oysters all year round. Metro Mayakovskaya; tel. 202-4540.

GEORGIAN

Georgian specialities include: *shashlik* (shish kebab), *lavash* (bread), *khachapuri* (bread and melted cheese), *chebureki* (thin fried bread with a meat filling), *khinkali* (large steamed dumplings), *tsatsivi* (cold chicken in walnut sauce), *piti* (lamb and potato soup), *kharcho* (spicy meat soup), *lobio* (spicy beans), *baklazhany* (eggplant stuffed with nuts), and *gutap* (stuffed crepes). All are open daily from noon to midnight unless stated otherwise.

Aragvi, 6 Tverskaya. Georgian ensemble after 7pm. Metro Okhotny Ryad; tel. 928-4572.

At Nikitsky Gate, 23/9 Bol Nikitskaya. Tasty Georgian fare with bar. Metro Okhoyny Ryad; tel. 290-4883.

Dolche Vita, 88 Taganskaya Sq. Metro Taganskaya; tel. 915-1130.

Dioscarius, 2 Merzlyankovsky Per. Superb Georgian food and wine; live music every evening. Metro Arbatskaya; tel. 290-6908.

Genatsvale, 12/1 Ul Ostozhenka. Delectable Georgian food and live folk music most evenings. Metro Park Kultury; tel. 202-0445.

Guriya, 7/3 Komsomolsky Pr. A favorite among the locals. Daily noon–11pm. Metro Park Kultury; tel. 246-0378.

Kabanchik, 27/1 Ul Krasina. Traditional fare, especially meat dishes. Metro Belorusskaya; tel. 254-9664.

Kavkazskaya Plennitsa, 36 Prospekt Mira. Named after a popular Yuri Nikulin (famous Russian clown) movie, entitled *Prisoner of the Caucasus* (also a novel by Lermontov). Delicious appetizers, main courses, buffet, Georgian wines, and music most nights; expensive. Metro Prospekt Mira; tel. 280-5111.

Mama Zoya, 16 Fruzenskaya Emb. On a boat across from Gorky Park. Delicious cheap Georgian food and music. Metro Park Kultury; Tel 202-0445, 242-8550.

Mimino, 46 Novoslobodskaya. Upscale Georgian restaurant with gourmet-style food, live music and a dance floor. Metro Novoslobodskaya; tel. 972-4412.

New Astoria, 57 Trifonovskaya, Georgian chef, Metro Prospekt Mira; tel. 288-8744.

At Pirosmani's, 4 Novodevichy Pro. Traditional Georgian fare in cozy Tbilisi setting with pictures by the Georgian artist, Pirosmani. Lovely view of Novodevichy Monastery. Daily 1pm–11pm. Metro Sportivnaya; tel. 247-1926, 246-1638.

Rytzarsky Klub (Knight's Club), 28 Kosygina. Located on Sparrow Hills under the ski jump; it has one of the best views of Moscow. Medieval displays. Open 1pm to midnight. Metro Universitet; tel. 930-0726.

Suliko, 42/2 Bol Polyanka. Tasty Georgian food, buffet, business lunches and live music. Daily noon–2am. Metro Polyanka; tel. 238-1027/2586.

Tiflis, 32 Ostozhenka. Good food and wines set in a traditional Georgian house. Metro Park Kultury; tel. 290-2897.

GREEK

Fermida, 20 Sadovaya-Kudrinskaya. Named after the Greek Goddess of Justice, offers Greek fare with names like Trojan Horse Salad. Daily noon–1am. Metro Barrikadnaya; tel. 737-3264.

Greek Quarter, 11/3 Chasovaya. Great Greek cuisine and wines. Business lunch from 1–5pm. Daily noon–midnight. Metro Aeroport; tel. 151-2600.

Santorini, 15 Bol Nikitskaya. Speciality is Greek-style seafood. Daily noon–midnight. Metro Pushkinskaya; tel. 291-4588.

INDIAN

Bombay Nights, 19 Starovagankovsky Per. Club and restaurant. Metro Bib. Imena Lenina; tel. 202-2643, 203-1353.

Darbar, 38 Leninsky Pr (Hotel Sputnik). One of Moscow's best Indian restaurants with Indian chef. Daily noon–midnight. Metro Leninsky Prospekt; tel. 930-2925.

Devi Café, 21 Ul Mikhlukho-Maklaya. Inexpensive Indian food in cafeteria-like setting. Daily noon–midnight. Metro Yugo-Zapadnaya; tel. 424-6360.

Maharaja, 2/1 Ul Pokrovka. Another of Moscow's best Indian restaurants, serving up many traditional dishes. Daily noon–10.30pm. Metro Kitai-Gorod; tel. 921-9844.

Moscow Bombay, 3 Glinishchevsky Per. Indian food prepared by New Delhi chef. Live music in the evenings. Daily noon–midnight. Metro Pushkinskaya; tel. 292-9731/9375.

Tandoor, 30/2 Tverskaya. Moscow's very first Indian eatery. Tasty kebab, curries and tandoori. Daily 11am–11pm. Metro Mayakovskaya; tel. 299-4593. www.tandoor.narod.ru.

ITALIAN AND MEDITERRANEAN
(Open daily noon to midnight unless stated otherwise.)

Adriatico, 3 Blagoveshchensky Per. Offers over 190 dishes. Metro Mayakovskaya; tel. 209-7914.

Angelicos, 3 Bol Karetny Per. Mediterranean cuisine and wines. Metro Tsvetnoi Bulvar; tel. 299-4503.

Café na Lestnitse, 1/4 2nd Smolensky Per. Sicilian specialities and music; can get pricey. Metro Smolenskaya; tel. 244-0655.

Cappaccio, & The Corner, 42 Ostozhenka, Expensive restaurant has creative Mediterranean cuisine. The Corner serves less expensive, international fare with wi-fi access inside. Open noon-11pm. Metro Park Kultury; tel. 246-0433.

Capri, 7 Ak Sakharova Pr. Homemade Italian food and 18 kinds of pizzas. Metro Turgenevskaya; tel. 207-5253.

Cheese, 16 Sad Samotechnaya. Mediterranean selections and delicious cheese boards. Daily 11am–midnight. Metro Tsvetnoi Bulvar; tel. 209-7770.

Da Cicco Trattoria, 13/12 Profsoyuznaya. Family-style tavern with tasty Italian fare, pizzas and desserts. Metro Profsoyuznaya; tel. 125-1196.

Dorian Gray, 6/1 Kadashevskaya Emb. Homemade pasta and good seafood dishes and tiramisu. Open noon–1am. Metro Tretyakovskaya; tel. 238-6401, 237-6342.

Gamibrinus, 3/5 Tverskoi Bul. Italian, Spanish cuisine, wines. Metro Tverskaya; tel. 203-0149.

Gratzi, 34 1st Tverskaya-Yamskaya in Marriot Grand Hotel. Formal Italian dining, and brunch on Sundays. Daily 7am–10.30pm (closed 10.30am–noon and 2–6pm). Metro Mayakovskaya; tel. 258-3036. Down the street, at no. 22, is **My Friends** with over 30 varieties of pasta; also has fish dishes and great desserts. tel. 917-9353.

Il Pomodoro, 5/2 Bol Golovin Per. Tasty spaghettis and live music. Metro Tsvetnoi Bulvar; tel. 924-2931.

In Town, 12 Bol Nikitskaya. Superb Italian cuisine; expensive. Metro Tverskaya; tel. 229-5325.

La Cipolla d'Oro, 39 Ul Gilyarovskovo, previously named the city's best Italian restaurant, has delicious but expensive food. Daily 10am–11pm. Metro Prospekt Mira; tel. 281-9498.

La Vera Italia, 4 Arbat. Great place to relax after walking the Arbat. Good food and pizza selection. Metro Arbatskaya; tel. 291-7074.

Leonardo, 23 Petrovka. Decor is influenced by Leonardo Da Vinci. Italian food and live music; expensive. Metro Chekhovskaya; tel. 200-5626. Down the street, at no. 6, is the more reasonably-priced Amarcord.

Mario's, 17 Klimashkina, one of city's top Italian restaurants, food flown in from Italy twice weekly. Beautiful summer dining garden. Expensive. Metro Ul. 1905 Goda; tel. 253-6505.

Moi Dryzhya (My Friends), 22 1st Tverskaya-Yamskaya, close to Belorusskaya Station. Cheap, good-quality Italian fare. Metro Belorusskaya; tel. 251-1116.

Palazzo, 19 Kuznetsky Most. Italian food, business lunches. Metro Kuznetsky Most; tel. 925-1729.

Patio Pizza, 13a Ul Volkhonka. Hand-tossed wood-oven pizzas, with plenty of pasta and seafood dishes. Metro Kropotkinskaya; tel. 298-2530.

Portofino, 16/4 Mal. Lubyanka. Excellent Italian food; pricey. Metro Lubyanka; tel. 923-0286.

Salon De Gusto, 6 Pevchesky Per (same building as Expeditsiya Resturant). Wine restaurant offering over 350 brands. Live Jazz after 7pm. Metro Kitai-Gorod; tel. 917-9510.

Settebello, 3 Sadovaya-Samotechnaya (in Puppet Theatre), Mediterranean specialities from imported Italian ingredients. DJ's Friday/Saturday. Metro Tsvetnoi Bulvar; tel. 299-3039.

Spago, 1 Bol Zlatoustinsky Per. Wide-range of exotic Italian fare. Metro Lubyanka; tel. 921-3797.

Venezia, 4/3 Strasnoi Bul. Metro Pushkinskaya; tel. 209-6009.

JAPANESE
(Open daily noon to midnight unless stated otherwise.)

Fiji, 32 Ul Bol Dmitrovka. Expensive Japanese cuisine and sushi bar. Metro Pushkinskaya; tel. 209-3240.

It's Sushi, 4/31 Triumfalnaya Sq, in the foyer of the Concert Hall. Best bargain sushi in the city. Metro Mayakovskaya; tel. 299-4236.

Izumi, 9/2 Ul Spiridonovka. Japanese food and sushi dishes. Metro Pushkinskaya; tel. 202-4540.

Justo, 9 Bol Tolmachevsky Perulok. Technically a Japanese restaurant, but opens as nightclub after 11pm, with famous DJs at weekends. (Check out the submarine bathrooms.) Open 4pm–6am. Metro Tretyakovskaya; tel. 937 -3750, 953-6595. www.justo.ru.

Laluna, 69 Sadonicheskaya Emb. Delicious Japanese food with European & Indian choices. Selection of exotic wines, champagnes and liquors. Open noon–1am (business lunch until 5pm). Metro Paveletskaya; tel. 725-4425.

Old Tokyo, 30/7 Petrovka. Japanese and Chinese fare. Metro Chekhovskaya; tel. 209-3786.

Planeta Sushi, a chain of sushi restaurants, located at 2 lst Tverskaya-Yamskaya (Metro Mayakovskaya); 40 Ul Udaltsova (Metro Vernadskovo); 3 Ul Smolenskaya (Metro Smolenskaya); and another near Taganskaya Metro.

Samurai, 21/13 Mal Bronnaya. Small Japanese restaurant with huge sushi selection. Metro Mayakovskaya; tel. 202-8694.

Yakitoria, popular and inexpensive Japanese restaurant chain. A few of the branches are located at: 29 lst Tverskaya-Yamskaya (Metro Belorusskaya); 10 Novy Arbat (Metro Arbatskaya); 16 Ul Petrovka (Metro Okhotny Ryad). Daily 11am–6am.

Yapona Mama, 11 Tsvetnoi Bulvar. Chefs prepare the food right in the dining room. Open daily noon–5am. Metro Tsvetnoi Bulvar; tel. 921-6098.

JEWISH

At Josef's, 11/17 Dubininskaya. Russia's first Jewish restaurant, serving old-style Jewish fare and live music on weekends. Daily noon–11pm. Metro Paveletskaya; tel. 238-4646.

Tsimmis, 3 Novoslobodskaya. 19th-century interior, live music and theater Friday and Saturday nights. Open noon–midnight. Metro Novoslobodskaya; tel. 973-0873.

Karmel, 7 lst Tverskaya-Yamskaya. Jewish cuisine. Daily noon–midnight. Metro Mayakovskaya; tel. 200-5763.

On Monmartre, 9 Vetoshny, 5th floor. Offers kosher dishes. Metro Pl. Revolyutsii.

KOREAN

Arirang Seoul, 5 Strelbishchensk Per. South Korean cooking. Daily noon–11pm. Metro Ulitsa 1905 Goda; tel. 256-0897/0892.

Manna, 48 Prospekt Andropova. Serves Korean-style food and other Asian fare. tel. 112-7247. Daily noon–midnight. Metro Kolomenskoye.

Ureok (Korean House), 26 Volgogradsky Pr. Korean food and beer; live music and karaoke. Daily 11am–11pm. Metro Volgogradsky Prospekt; tel. 270-1300.

LEBANESE

Shafran, 12/9 Spiridonyevsky Per. Including falafel, hummus, Lebanese wines. Open noon to midnight. Metro Pushkinskaya; tel. 737-9500.

Sultan, 3 Ordzhonikidze. Cushioned booths with belly dancers on Friday and Saturday nights. Open noon–5am. Metro Leninsky Prospekt; tel. 958-2921.

MEXICAN

Azteca, 11 Novoslobodskaya. Traditional Mexican with Latin music and dancing in the evenings. Metro Novoslobodskaya; tel. 972-0511.

Cactus Jacks, 13 Ordzhonikidze. Music club with Mexican fare. Daily noon–2am; weekends noon–6am. Country, blues, rock, and disco Thurs–Sat midnight–6am. Metro Leninsky Pr.; tel. 958-0866.

Ola Mexico, 7/5 Pushechnaya. Great Mexican food, margaritas and Mexican music. Daily noon–5am. Metro Kuznetsky Most; tel. 925-8251.

La Cantina, 5 Tverskaya. Serves up a Tex-Mex menu, with bar. Live music in the evenings. Daily 8am–midnight. Metro Okhotny Ryad; tel. 292-5388.

Pancho Villa, 44/1 Arbat. Filling burritos and margaritas. Daily 24 hours. Metro Smolenskaya; tel. 241-9853.

San Diego, 11/3 Shkolnaya. Texan-Mexican fare in old-time Americana setting. Daily noon–midnight. Metro Ploshchad Ilyicha; tel. 271-0111.

Sante Fe, 5/1 Mantulinskaya. Tasty Mexican selections and margaritas. Daily noon–2am. Metro Ulitsa 1905 Goda; tel. 256-2126/1487.

MOROCCAN

Marrakesh, 4/3 Strasnoit Bulvar. Arabian and Eastern favorites. Belly-dancing Friday–Sunday 10pm. Metro Pushkinskaya; tel. 200-3956.

MONGOLIAN

Tamerlaine, 30 Prechistenka. Diner chooses the ingredients and the chef stir-fries to perfection. Daily noon–11pm. Metro Kropotkinskaya; tel. 202-5649.

Yolki Palki Po, 18 Tverskaya. Cheap, hearty Mongolian and Russian fare. choose your own ingredients and then the chef prepares your dish. Daily 11am–5am. Metro Pushkinskaya; tel. 200-3920, 287-8127.

PUBS AND BARS

Angara, 19 Novy Arbat. Enormous bar (with food) that sells its own in-house brews. Metro Smolenskaya. **Molly Gwynn's** is at No.24 and **Zhiguli** at No.11.

Chesterfield Café, 26 Zemlyanoi Val. One of Moscow's premier bars, featuring the second longest bar in Russia. DJ music and swinging nights. Daily noon–6am. Metro Kurskaya.

Churchill's, 66 Leningradsky Pr. British-style pub with Sunday evening concerts. Daily 11am–11pm. Metro Aeroport.

CULT, 5 Yauzskaya. Popular basement lounge with DJ music on weekends. Open noon–midnight, weekends till 6am. Metro Kitai-Gorod.

Durdin, 80 Leningradsky Pr. 19th-century interior. Offers five kinds of beer brewed to an old family recipe. Live music at weekends. Metro Sokol.

Embassy Club, 8/10 Bryusov Per. Moscow's premiere cigar/bar (including cognacs and single-malt scotches) lounge. Smart dress code. Also has an excellent restaurant. Metro Pushkinskaya.

John Bull Pub, 2/9 Smolenskaya Pl. (Metro Smolenskaya) and 25/1 Krasnaya Presnya (Metro 1905 Goda). Cozy British-style pub with good music.

Monks & Nuns, 3/18 Sivtsev Vrazhek, daily 1pm to midnight. A great Belgian beer cellar with fine Belgian and Russian food. Metro Kropotkinskaya.

Museum, 11 1st Tverskaya-Yamskaya. Hip lounge for gallery crowd. Metro Mayakovskaya. www.museum-cafe.ru.

News Pub, 18 Petrovka, restaurant/club with 22 beers on tap, nightly entertainment. Metro Teatralnaya.

O.G.I. Club, 55 Leninsky Pr, cheap drink and food, poetry and literary readings. Metro Leninsky.

Rosie O'Grady's, 9/12 Znamenka. Authentic Irish pub, Guinness and Irish food. Metro Borovitskaya. www.rosie.ru.

Tinkoff, 11 Protochny Per. Oleg Tinkoff started Moscow's first microbrewery. Ten different beers are brewed on site according to old family recipes. Restaurant. Metro Smolenskaya; tel. 777-3300.

Yorkshire, 28 Trubnaya. English pub, draft beer and food. Metro Tsvetnoi Bulvar.

RUSSIAN

Hundreds of Russian-style restaurants have opened throughout the city and can be found on practically every corner. Open daily noon–midnight unless stated otherwise.

Bochka, 2 Ul 1905 Goda. Good Russian fare served in cozy wood and brick interior. Metro Ul 1905 Goda; tel. 252-3041.

Babochka & U Babushki (Butterfly & At Grandma's) are two separate rooms at the same address: 42 Bol Ordynka. Serve up hearty home-style Russian cooking, and live piano music after 7pm. Metro Tretyakovskaya; tel. 230-2797.

Cafe Ogonyok, 36 Krasnaya Presnya. Inexpensive cafe with tasty Russian fare. Metro Ulitsa 1905 Goda; tel. 252-2927.

Central House of Writers, 50 Povarskaya. Excellent Russo-French food (Austrian chef) and elegant dining in the former 100-year-old mansion of Countess Olsufieva. Some recipes are over 200 years old, and specialities include Czar Nicholas Salmon, Quail Golitsyn and Veal Orlov. Metro Barrikadnaya; tel. 291-1515, 290-1589.

Expeditsiya, 6 Pevchesky Per. Exotic Siberian cuisine such as wild polar partridge and wild reindeer. Metro Kitai-Gorod; tel. 917-9510, 775-6075; www.expedicia.ru.

Godunov, 5/1 Teatralnaya Sq. Setting inside the Zaikonospassky Monastery that dates back to the reign of Boris Godunov. Has three halls of different sizes and decor. A Russian gourmet feast, flavored vodkas, gypsy music every night; expensive. Metro Teatralnaya; tel. 298-5609; www.godunov.menu.ru.

Grand Opera, 2/18 Petrovskiye Linii. Elegant dinner theatre. Interior designed to look like Odessa in the 1920s. Russian/Ukrainian dishes; expensive. Variety show at 9pm. Metro Kuznetsky Most; tel. 923-9966.

Grand Imperial, 9/5 Gagarinsky Per. Located in the old mansion of Prince Kurakin. Open noon to late. Metro Kropotkinskaya; tel. 291-6063.

Fyodor's, 19 Lyubyansky Lane. Old aristocratic hunting lodge with antique decor. Metro Kitai-Gorod; tel. 923-2578.

Karetny Ryad, 2 Karetny Ryad. Three rooms serving Russian/European cuisine. Metro Chekhovskaya.

Kitezh, 23/10 Petrovka. Setting is very traditional, part barn; serves generous inexpensive portions of traditional Russian food. Metro Pushkinskaya; tel. 209-6685.

Kot Begemot, 10 Spiridonyevsky Lane. Reasonably-priced, decent food in stylish setting. Metro Mayakovskaya; tel. 209-6463.

Kropotkinskaya 36, 36 Prechistenka St. The city's first cooperative restaurant located in an elegant building near Pushkin Art Museum. Delicious food and live music daily. Metro Kropotkinskaya; tel. 201-7500.

Margarita's, 28 Malaya Bronnaya across the street from Patriarch's Pond. Good simple food with live music in the evenings. Metro Pushkinskaya; tel. 299-6534, 783-1234.

Mesto Vstrechi, (Meeting Place—named after a famous Russian war film), 9/8 Maly Gnezdnikovsky Per. Quiet cellar setting. Metro Pushkinskaya; tel. 229-2372.

Metropole, Teatralnaya in hotel. Situated in stunning 3-story high art-nouveau decorated hall with stained glass roof. Russian-French food. Expensive, jacket and tie. Metro Teatralnaya; tel. 927-6061.

Moskovsky, in National Hotel., has often received the annual award of Moscow's Best Hotel. Restaurant. Russian gourmet dishes prepared from traditional recipes; live folk music at weekends; expensive. Metro Okhotny Ryad; tel. 258-7000.

Oblomov, 1st 5 Monetchikovsky Per. Named after the aristocratic hero of the 19th-century novel by Ivan Goncharov, it offers set-priced meals of seven different courses and flavored vodkas; pricey. Metro Paveletskaya; tel. 953-6828/6620.

Oblomov in Presnya, 1905 Goda St, Bldg 2. Interior in the style of a 19th-century country estate. Traditional Russian food. Metro 1905 Goda; tel. 255-9290.

One Red Square (Krasnaya Ploshchad) in History Museum on Red Square. Offers delectable dishes based on original 19th-century recipes; expensive. Each year a number of extraordinary historical and literary banquets are held, including the December 9th dinner to honor the Cavaliers of St George. Metro Okhotny Ryad; tel. 925-3600/292-1196; www.redsquare.ru.

Petrovich, 24 Myasnitskaya. Bar-club restaurant, nouvelle-Russian fare. Daily 2pm–5am. Metro Chistiye Prudy; tel. 923-0082.

Petrov Vodkin, 3/7 Pokrovka. Moscow's first real vodka restaurant with more than 400 varieties; traditional Russian food, live piano and gypsy music in the evenings; expensive. Metro Kitai-Gorod; tel. 923-5350.

Pushkin, 26 Tverskoi Bul. Set in 18th-century elegance, the cuisine is absolutely scrumptuous; expensive (open 24 hours). Metro Tverskaya; tel. 229-5590.

Raisky Dvor, 25 Spiridonovsky Per. Cozy restaurant, walls covered with sayings from George Orwell's *Animal Farm*. Open noon to late. Metro Barrikadskaya; tel. 290-1341.

Razgulyay (Merrymaking), 11 Spartakovskaya. Traditional Russian food, wine cellar and gypsy music. Metro Baumanskaya; tel. 267-7613.

Samovar, 13 Myasnitskaya. Includes ten different *blinis* and 20 different types of *pelmeni*. Evening music. Metro Turgenevskaya; tel. 921-4688.

Seven Fridays, 6 Vorontsovskaya Ul. Traditional Russian cuisine in traditional setting (even includes beds). Metro Taganskaya; tel. 912-1218; www.fhouse.ru.

Sudar, 36/2 Kutuzovsky Pr. Traditional Russian cuisine in elegant setting. Open noon–5am (disco). Metro Kutuzovskaya; tel. 249-6529.

Uncle Vanya, 17 Bol Dmitrovka. Delicious inexpensive traditional food in dark-wood interior. Live jazz and blues on weekend. Metro Chekovskaya; tel. 232-1448.

SOUTH AMERICAN

El Gaucho, 3/2 Bol Kozlovsky Per. Argentinian cuisine cooked on open fire. Daily noon–midnight. Metro Krasniye Vorota. Another restaurant is located at 6 Zatsepsky Val. Metro Paveletskaya; tel. 923-1098, 953-2826; www.elgaucho.ru.

Rio Rio, 16 Krasnopresnenskaya Emb. Moscow's best Brazilian restaurant and churrasceria. Open 11am to midnight. Metro Ul 1905 Goda; tel. 255-8144.

THAI

Baan Thai, 11 B. Dorogomilovskaya. Metro Kievskaya; tel. 240-0597.

Bangkok, 10 Bol Strochnyonovsky Per. One of the city's best Thai restaurants with two Thai chefs. Daily 1–11pm. Metro Serpukhovskaya; tel. 237-3074.

Izumrudny Buddha, 1 Ul Sretenka. Selection of Thai cooking and French wines. Daily noon–midnight. Metro Chistiye Prudy; tel. 925-9482.

Pattaya, 14 Bol. Sukharevskaya. Good inexpensive Thai selections. Open 11am–11:30pm. Metro Sukarevskaya; tel. 207-7725.

TIBETAN

Tibet Himalaya, 19 Ul Pokrovka. Moscow's first Tibetan restaurant. Serves spicy Tibetan fare and Tibetan tea with butter and salt. Daily noon–midnight. Metro Chistiye Prudy; tel. 917-3985.

Tibet Kitchen, 5/6 Kamergersky Per. Tibetan-Chinese fare. Daily noon–midnight. Metro Okhotny Ryad; tel. 923-2422.

UKRAINIAN

Getman, 9 Arbat. Traditional Ukrainian fare in three halls; expensive. Daily noon–midnight. Metro Arbatskaya; tel. 737-0447.

Shinok, 2 Ulitsa 1905 Goda. Expensive Ukrainian theme restaurant with a staged farmyard in the center. Daily 24 hours. Metro Ulitsa 1905 Goda; tel. 255-0888.

Taras Bulba, 30/7 Ul Petrovka. Decor designed to resemble a traditional *hata* or single-room country home. Good food and flavored vodkas. (There are three other branches about town). Daily noon–midnight. Metro Pushkinskaya; tel. 200-6082.

UZBEK

(Open daily noon to midnight.)

Bakhor, 12 Tovarishchesky Lane. Live music after 6pm. Metro Taganskaya; tel. 911-7192/0116.

Beloye Solntse Pustiny (named after the Soviet film, *White Sun of the Desert*), 29 Neglinnaya. Uzbek cuisine and wines; pricey. Evening gypsy entertainment. Metro Tsvetnoi Bulvar; tel. 209-7525, 200-3620. www.uzbek-rest.ru.

Khodzha Nasreddin v Kivye (named after a Bukhara folk tale), 10 Pokrovka. Central Asian fare with nightly belly dancing. Metro Kitai-Gorod; tel. 917-0444.

Kishmish, 28 Novy Arbat. Central Asian with kebabs and *plov*. Open 11am–midnight. Metro Arbatskaya; tel. 290-0703. Also at 8/9 Barrikadnaya. Metro Barrikadnaya; tel. 202-1083.

Utskuduk (Under an Open Sky), 6 Vorontsovskaya. Cozy, airy restaurant where diners can sit on pillows. Open May–September. Metro Taganskaya; tel. 911-7704.

Uzbekistan, 29/14 Neglinnaya. Exotic interior with cushions, Belly dancing and hookahs. Open noon–midnight. Metro Teatralnaya; tel. 923-0585.

VEGETARIAN

Avocado, 12/2 Kuznetsky Most. Salads, dried nut and fruit bar, other vegie dishes. Open 11am–11pm. Metro Kuznetsky Most; tel. 921-7719.

Dzhagannat Express, 11 Kuznetsky Most. All vegetarian dishes and big salad bar. tel. 928-3580. Daily 11am–11pm. Metro Kuznetsky Most.

VIETNAMESE

Shanti, 2/1 Myasnitsky. Also has a tearoom and gallery. Open noon–midnight. Metro Krasniye Vorota; tel. 783-6868.

Saigon, 6 1st Ul Mashinostroyeniya. Inexpensive, delicious Vietnamese selections. Open 12.30pm–10.30pm. Metro Dubrovka; tel. 275-0427.

SHOPPING

Since most places do not provide bags (or a few rubles are charged for a *paket*), always take some type of carrying bag along for purchases. Bring small bills, for often the seller will not have change. Some stores require you to check in large bags at the front with a security guard. Before purchasing an antique made prior to World War II, always check to see if you need special permission to take it out of the country —particularly icons, artwork and samovars; otherwise it could be confiscated at customs upon departure. Beware of fake icons, artwork and lacquer boxes.

ANTIQUES

Arbat Antiques, there are many antique stores located along the Arbat pedestrian shopping street; Metro Arbatskaya. These include: Antikvariat-Kartiny-Mebel, at no. 23; Arbatskaya Nakhodka, no. 11; Iskusstvo, no. 4; Kartiny-Baget-Antikvariat, no. 6; Kupina, no 18; Raritet, no. 31; Russkaya Usadba, no. 23; and Traditsiya i Lichnost at no. 2.

Antikvariat na Bronnoy, 27/4 Bol Bronnaya. Open Mon–Sat noon–7pm. Metro Pushkinskaya.

Antikvar na Myasnitskoi, 13 Myasnitskaya. Open Mon–Fri 10am–7pm; Sat 10am–6pm (closed 2–3pm). Metro Turgenevskaya.

Antikvar-Metropol, 2 Teatralnaya alongside Metropole Hotel. Mon–Fri 11am–8pm; weekends 11am–5pm. Metro Teatralnaya.

Izmailovsky Market on weekends has a large selection of old items from icons to coins. Metro Izmailovsky Park. (See page 188.)

Russkaya Antikvarnaya Galereya, 5/25 Vozdvizhenka. Mon–Sat noon–7pm; Metro Bib. im. Lenina.

Starina, 24/1 Petrovka. Mon–Sat 11am–8pm; Metro Pushkinskaya.

ART GALLERIES

Official permission for export of all antiques and expensive art works can be obtained at the Ministry of Culture, open noon–3pm, and closed Wednesday, Saturday and Sunday, at 7 Kitaigorodsky Lane, 1st floor/office 103. tel. 928-5089. OR at the Committee of Contemporary Art Expertise at 8 Neglinnaya, third floor, office 29, tel. 921-3258. Open 10am–5.30pm (break 2–3pm), Saturday until 2pm, closed Sunday. Usually the store where a purchase is made can help with the proper permits. If you do not have proper permission, customs may not let you take an old or expensive object out of the country. The Friday edition of the Moscow Times (www.themoscowtimes.com) carries a listing of current exhibits.

A-3, 39 Starokonyushenni. Open 11am–7pm; closed Sundays. Metro Kropotkinskaya.

Aidan Gallery, 22 1st Tverskaya-Yamskaya, 3rd floor. Metro Mayakovskaya; tel. 251-3734. The Gallery of Contemporary Artists is at number 20.

Art Studio-Rebrov, 19/1 Nikolskaya. Paintings, icons and sculptures. Metro Lubyanka; tel. 928-1522.

Central House of Artists (Tsentralny Dom Khudozhnikov—TsDKh), 10 Krymsky Val. Filled with different galleries selling everything from traditional landscapes to contemporary works. Outside, a huge painting market winds its way along the river; bargaining is a must! Metro Park Kultury; tel. 238-9843.

Dom Naschokina Gallery, 12 Vorotnikovsky Lane. Metro Mayakovskaya; tel. 299-1178.

Gallery of Contemporary Artists, 20 1st Tverskaya-Yamskaya. Monday–Friday 10am–7pm; Saturday till 5pm; Metro Belorusskaya.

Galereya-salon na Varvarke, 14 Varvarka. Metro Kitai-Gorod.

Gertsev Gallery 5/10 Karetny Ryad. Contemporary Russian and Baltic art; tel. 209-6665/7014; www.gertsevgallery.ru.

Glaz, 18 Ostozhenka St. The Moscow House of Photography, with photographic selections. Metro Kropotkinskaya; tel. 202-0610.

Guelman Gallery, 7/7 Mal. Polyanka St/bldg 5. One of the Moscow's first galleries, and very avant-garde. Metro Polyanka; tel 238-2783/8492; www.guelman.ru

James, 28 Tverskaya, Art and photographic exhibitions and upstairs boutique. Metro Mayakovskaya; tel. 937-9447. At number 5/6 is the **Asti Gallery**.

Karina Shanshieya's Gallery, 10/14 Krymsky Val. One of Moscow's best galleries with works of contemporary painters; tel. 238-8392.

M'ARS Contemporary Art Center, 5 Pushkarev Per. Ten exhibition halls of paintings, graphics, sculptures and photographs. tel. 923-5610.

Moscow Fine Arts Gallery, 3/10 Bol. Sadovaya. Displays of contemporary artists. Metro Mayakovskaya; tel. 251-7649. Down the street, at number 16, is the New Collection Gallery with modern and graphic art.

Russkaya Ikona, 6/2 Arbat. Mon–Sun 11am–7pm; Metro Arbatskaya.

S'ART Art Gallery, 14/16 Zemyyanoi Val. Metro Kurskaya.

Universal Art, 29/14 Neglinnaya. Metro Tsvetnoi Bulvar. (The Moscow Arts Center is at number 14.)

Zverev's Modern Art Center, 29 Novoyazanskaya, Building 2. Houses over 50 exhibits. Metro Baumanskaya; tel. 261-6196; www.zverevcenter.ru.

ARTS AND HANDICRAFTS
Shops along the Arbat and in Izmailovsky Park have a large selection of handicrafts and other souvenirs.

Arbatskaya Lavitsa, 27 Arbat. Russkaya Vyshivka (Embroidery) is at number 31. Daily 10am–8pm; Other shops are at numers 12, 23 and 28. Metro Arbatskaya.

Arts & Handicrafts of Russia, 31/1 Povarskaya. Mon–Fri 11am–6pm; Metro Barrikadnaya.

Gallery Kitai-Gorod, 14 Varvarka St. Metro Kitai-Gorod.

Gift Shop at Museum of Contemporary History, 21 Tverskaya. Full of eclectic choices. Metro Tverskaya.

Khudozhestvenny Salon, 12 Petrovka. Mon–Sat 9am–8pm; Metro Kuznetsky Most.

Roza Azora in Museum of Oriental Art, 12a Nikitsky Bulvar. Interesting mixture of antiquities and modern art. Metro Arbatskaya.

Rostovskaya Finift (Rostav Enamel), 5 Vozdvizhenka. Daily 10am–7pm. Metro Arbatskaya.

Rukotvorets and Azhur are at 5 Zabelina; open Mon–Sat; Metro Kitai-Gorod.

Salon na Prospekta Mira, 41 Pr Mira. Mon–Sat 11am–7pm; Metro Prospekt Mira.

Salon na Pyatnitskoi, 16 Pyatnitskaya. Mon–Sat 10am–7pm; Metro Novokuznetskaya.

BOOKSTORES
Open Monday to Friday 10am–7pm; Saturdays 11am–6 pm.

Angliya (Books in English), 23 Khlebny Per. Metro Arbatskaya; tel. 203-5802. www.anglophile.ru.

Art & Literary (Russian and foreign books in English), 1 and 18 Kuznetsky Most; Metro Kuznetsky Most.

BiblioGlobe, 6 Myasnitskaya Street. Metro Lubyanka; tel. 924-4680.

Dom Knigi (House of Books), 8 Novy Arbat; Metro Arbatskaya.

Moskva, 8 Tverskaya; Metro Pushkinskaya.

Inostrannaya Kniga (Foreign Books), 8 Novy Arbat. Metro Arbatskaya.

IPS (American Bookstore), 43 2nd Brestskaya, Metro Belorusskaya.

Progress (Russian literature in foreign languages), 17 Zubovsky Bulvar; Metro Park Kultury.

Shakspeare & Co (bestsellers from New York Time's List), 5/7 lst Novokuznetsky; Metro Paveletskaya.

Universum (foreign languages), 16 Mal Nikitskaya; Metro Barrikadnaya.

DEPARTMENT STORES

Over 100 department stores are scattered throughout the city. The Russian equivalent of a department store is called an *Univermag*. The following are the largest and most popular, and centrally located. Most are open daily from 10am to 9/10pm. Western stores include: IKEA (which gets over 10,000 daily shoppers and amounts to tenth in sales volume of all its 160+ stores worldwide) and Benetton's, which recently opened a new 21,500 square foot megastore in downtown Moscow; this Italian clothing giant now has 40 stores thoughout Russia. Some stores accept credit cards.

Berlin House, 5 Petrovka. Metro Teatralnaya.

Detski Mir (Children's World), 2 Teatralny Square. Metro Lubyanka.

French Galleries, 9 Vetoshny Lane. Metro Teatralnaya.

Galereya Akter, 16 Tverskaya. Metro Pushkinskaya.

GUM (Two-story State department store), 3 Red Square. Metro Okhotny Ryad.

Kursk Shopping Complex, Zemlyanoi Val; Metro Kursk, next to Kursk railway station. (Six floors, ten-screen cinema complex, 20-lane bowling alley, and food court.)

Okhotny Ryad (three-level underground shopping center) on 1 Manezh Square in front of Red Square. Metro Okhotny Ryad.

Petrovsky Passazh, 10 Petrovka; Metro Kuznetsky Most. Berlin Haus is across the street.

Trading House Gallery, 162 Tverskaya. Metro Pushkinskaya.

Trading House Moscow, 31 Kutuzvosky Pr. Metro Kutuzvosky.

Tretakovsky Passazh, located next to Metropol Hotel. on Teatralny Proyezd. Moscow's Park Avenue Shopping District (Armani, Gucci, Brioni). Metro Tretyakovskaya.

TsUM (Central Department Store), 2 Petrovka, Metro Teatralnaya.

FOOD STORE

See Special Topic on Yeliseyev's on page 486.

Yeliseyev's, 14 Tverskaya. Open 8am–10pm, Sun 10am–8pm. Metro Pushkinskaya.

GIFTS AND SOUVENIRS

Many souvenir shops and kiosks are located throughout the city. Stroll down the Arbat, Izmailovsky market, or the underground mall by Red Square. Tverskaya Street and the lanes around Kuznetsky Most are also good for souvenir browsing where you can find *matryoshka* dolls, handpainted boxes, lacquerware and pottery, samovars and other handicraft items. Besides the handicraft, book and department stores listed above, here are some other suggestions.

Mir Samotsvetov, 11 Mokhovaya; Metro Okhotny Ryad.

Podarki (Gifts), 4 Tverskaya (Okhotny Ryad), and 7 1st Tverskaya-Yamskaya; Metro Belorusskaya.

Russian Souvenirs, 3 Nametkina; Metro Cheremushki

Russky Uzory (Ornaments), 16 Petrovka; Metro Kuznetsky Most.

Skazki Starovo Arbata (Fairy Tales of Old Arbat), 29 Arbat; Metro Arbatskaya.

JEWELRY

Many department stores, markets and higher-end hotel.s have jewelry for sale. In addition, check gift and souvenir shops which may carry items made from amber, malachite, lacquerware, etc.

Stores on the Arbat include Consul at no. 49; Sady Seramidy at 36/2; and Samotsvety at no. 35. Stores along Tverskaya include Kosmos-Zoloto (Gold) at no. 4, and Yuveliya at no. 17.

Alexandrite, 6 Starosadsky Lane; Metro Kitai-Gorod.

'Diamonds of Yakutia', 9 Kolpachny. Metro Kitai-Gorod.

Karl Fabergé, 20 Kuznetsky Most. Open Mon–Fri 11am–8pm; Sat till 7pm; Metro Kuznetsky Most.

Galereya, 4/5 Nikolskaya; Metro Pl. Revolyutsii.

Grimtavs-Medikor (jewelry with Yakut diamonds), 1 Bol Dorogomilovskaya; Metro Kievskaya.

Tsentr Yuvelir (Jewelery Center) has over 12 branches in the city, including 6 Novy Arbat (Metro Arbatskaya), 14 Gruzinsky Val (Belorusskaya), 10 Nikolskaya (Lubyanka), 24 Petrovka (Kuznetsky Most), and 13 Stoleshnikov and 12 Tverskaya (Okhotny Ryad).

MUSIC

Melodiya, 22 Novy Arbat. Mon–Sat 9am–8pm; Metro Arbatskaya.

Rapsodiya, 17 Myasnitskaya. Mon–Fri 10am–7pm; Sat till 6pm. Metro Turgenevskaya.

Soyuz, 6 Atbat; Metro Arbatskaya, and **Transilvania** at 25 Tverskaya; Metro Pushkinskaya.

FARMERS' MARKETS OR *RINOK*

The markets are usually open Mon–Sat 8am–7pm; Sun 8am–4pm. A better selection is usually found in the mornings. Here people sell market items, fresh fruit and vegetables, flowers and other wares. Bring a few empty bags to carry your purchases in.

Arbat Market runs along Stary Arbat, a pedestrian street.

Cheryomushkinsky Rinok, 1 Lomonovsky Prospekt. Along with food and plants, this market also sells homemade crafts. Metro Universitet.

Danilovsky Rinok, 74 Mytnaya; Metro Tulskaya. Produce and flea market.

Dorogomilovsky Rinok, 10 Mozhaisky Val; Metro Kievskaya.

Izmailvosky Rinok, Metro Izmailovsky Park.

Palashevsky (Fish Market), 3a Sytinsky. Metro Puskinskaya.

Tishinsky Rinok, Tishinskaya Square at 50 Bol. Gruzinskaya Street; Metro Belorusskaya. This is one of Moscow's oldest markets; rebuilt in 1996.

Tsentralny Rinok, 15 Tsvetnoi Bulvar; Metro Tsvetnoi Bulvar. One of Moscow's largest markets with the best selections.

Rizhsky Rinok, 94 Prospekt Mira; Metro Rizhskya.

MUSEUMS

There are over 100 museums in Moscow; this is a partial listing. Many ticket *kassa* close one hour before closing time. Beware of duel pricing: a foreigner in Russia can still pay from double to ten times more than locals at cultural sites such as museums and theaters. A photography/video permit is usually an extra fee. Showing some type of international Student ID can receive up to a 50 percent discount on the ticket price. www.museums.ru.

Information on museums and exhibition halls, tel. 975-9144.

Aircraft Exhibition, Khodynskoe Field, 24a Leningradsky Pr. History of Russian aircraft industry. Daily 10am–6pm. Metro Aeroport; tel. 155-6619.**Andrei Bely Apartment Museum**, 55 Arbat. Open 11am–5pm; closed Mondays and Tuesdays. Metro Smolenskaya; tel. 241-7702.

Andrei Rublyov Museum of Old Russian Art, Spaso-Andronikov Monastery, 10 Andronevskaya Pl. Open 11am–6pm; closed Wednesdays and last Friday of month. Metro Ploshchad Ilicha; tel. 278-1467/1489.

Archaeological Museum, Manege Pl. 10am–6pm (Wednesday/Friday 11am–7pm) Closed Mondays and last Friday of month. Metro Okhotny Ryad; tel. 292-4171.

Armed Forces Central Museum, 2 Ul. Sovyetskoi Armii. Open 10am–5.30pm; closed Mondays/Tuesdays. Metro Novoslobodskaya; tel. 281-4877, 681-5367.

Bakhrushin Theater Museum, 31/12 Bakhrushina Ul. Open 12–7pm; closed Mondays and last Friday of month. Metro Paveletskaya; tel. 953-4470/4848.

Battle of 1812 Borodino Museum, 38 Kutuzovsky Pr. Open 10am–5pm; closed Fridays and last Thursday of month. Metro Kutuzovskaya; tel. 148-1967.

Book Museum, 3/3 Ul. Vozdvizhenka. Open 10am–6pm, Sunday 11am–5pm; closed Tuesdays and first Monday of the month. Metro Borovitskaya; tel. 222-8672.

Boyar Romanov House Museum, 10 Varvarka Ul. tel. 298-3706/3235. Open 10am–5pm, Wed 11am–6pm; closed Tues. Metro Kitai-Gorod.

Church of the Virgin Intercession in Fili (branch of Andrei Rublyov Museum), 6 Novozavodskaya Ul. Open 11am–5.30pm; closed Tuesday/Wednesday. Metro Fili; tel. 148-4552.

Chambers of Old English Yard, 4a Varvarka Ul. Concerts held last Saturday of month. Open 10am–6pm, Wednesday/Friday 11am–7pm; closed Monday and last Friday of the month. Metro Kitai-Gorod; tel. 298-3961.

Chekhov House Museum, 6 Sadovaya-Kudrinskaya Ul. Open 11am–5pm; Wednesday/Friday 2–6pm; closed Sunday/Monday. Metro Barrikadnaya; tel. 291-3837.

Contemporary History of Russia Museum, 21 Tverskaya Ul. Open 10am–6pm, Sunday until 5pm; closed Monday and last Friday of month. Soviet-era museum shop. Metro Tverskaya; tel. 229-5217; www.sovr.ru.

Cosmonauts Memorial Museum, 111 Prospekt Mira. Open 10am–6pm; closed Monday and last Friday of month. Metro VDNKh; tel. 283-7914/8197; www.museum.ru/kosmanov.

Decorative and Folk Art Museum, 3 Delegatskaya Ul. Open 10am–6pm; closed Friday and last Thursday of month. Metro Mayakovskaya; tel. 923-7725/921-0139.

Defense of Moscow Museum, 3 Olimpiiskaya Derevnya Ul. Open 10am–6pm; closed Sun/Mon. Metro Yugo-Zapadnaya; tel. 430-0549.

Dostoevsky Memorial-Apartment, 2 Ul. Dostoevskovo. Open 11am–6pm, Wednesday/Friday 2–8pm; closed Monday/Tuesdays. Metro Novoslobodskaya. tel. 281-1085.

Folk Art and Matryoshka Museum, 7 Leontevsky Per. Open 11am–6pm; closed Sunday/Monday. Metro Arbatskaya; tel. 290-5222.

Folk Graphics Museum, 10 Maly Golovin Per. Open 10am–5pm; closed Sunday/Monday. Metro Sukharevskaya; tel. 208-5182.

Glinka Music Culture Museum, 4 Ul. Fadeeva. Open 11am–7pm; closed Monday and last day of month. Metro Mayakovskaya/Novoslobodskaya; tel. 972-3237, 970-7401.

Gorky Literary Museum, 25a Povarskaya Ul. Open 10am–4.30pm, Wed/Fri 12–6.30pm; closed Saturday/Sunday and first Thursday of month. Metro Arbatskaya; tel. 290-5130.

Gorky Memorial Apartment, 6 Malaya Nikitskaya Ul. Open 10am–4.30pm, Wednesday/Friday 12–6pm; closed Monday/Tuesday. Metro Arbatskaya; tel. 290-5130.

Great Patriotic War Museum (WWII), 10 Ul. Fonchenko Bratev (Park Pobedy). Open 10am–5pm; closed Monday. Metro Kutuzovskaya; tel. 148-5550.

Herzen Memorial House, 27 Sivtsev Vrazhek Per. Open 11am–6pm, Wednesday/Friday 1–6pm; closed Monday and last day of month. Metro Kropotkinskaya; tel. 241-5859.

Historical State Museum, 1/2 Krasnaya Pl. Open 11am–6pm; closed Tues/1st Mon of month. Metro Okhotny Ryad. www.shm.ru; tel. 924-4529; tours 292-3731.

History of Moscow Museum, 12 Novaya Pl. Open 10am–6pm, Wednesday/Fri day11am–7pm; closed Monday. Metro Kitai-Gorod/Lubyanka; tel. 924-8490.

Krasnya Presnya Museum, 4 Bolshoi Predtechensky Per. Open 10am–6pm, Wednesday 11am–7pm; Sunday 11am–5pm; closed Monday and last Friday of month. Metro Krasnopresnenskaya; tel. 252-3035.

Kremlin Museums Red Square, open 10am–5pm (ticket office 10am–4.30pm); closed Thursday. www.kremlin.museum.ru; tel. 928-5232. (**Armory Museum** tel. 921-4720)

Excursion Bureau of Moscow Kremlin, 3 Lebyazhy Lane. Closed weekends. Metro Aleksandrovsky Sad; tel. 202-4256/3776, 203-0349; www.kremlin.museum.ru.

Diamond Fund, Open 10am–4.30pm. Metro Aleksandrovsky Sad; tel. 229-2036.

Kutuzov Hut, 38 Kutuzovsky Pr. Open 10am–5pm; closed Monday/Wednesday/ Friday. Metro Kutuzovskaya; tel. 148-1875.

Lermontov Memorial House (Poet), 2 Malaya Molchanovka Ul. Open 11am–4pm, Wednesday/Friday 2–5pm; closed Sunday/Monday. Metro Arbatskaya; tel. 291-5298.

Lights of Moscow Museum, 3 Armyansky Per. Open 10am–5pm; closed Saturday/Sunday. Metro Kitai-Gorod/Lubyanka; tel. 924-7374.

Literary Museum, 28 Petrovka Ul. Open 11am–5.30pm, Wednesday/Friday 2–6pm; closed Monday/Tuesday. Metro Pushkinskaya; tel. 921-7395.

Mayakovsky Museum, 3 Lubyansky Proyezd. Open 10am–5pm, Thursday 1–8pm; closed Wednesday. Metro Lubyanka; tel. 928-2569, 921-9560.

Moscow Metro Museum, 36 Khamovnichesky Val (in Metro Sportivnaya). Open Thursdays only 9am–4pm. Metro Sportivnaya; tel. 222-7309. (See page 106.)

Museum of Military Regiments, 1/1st Krasnokursantsky Proyezd. Open 10am–5pm; closed Sunday/Monday. Metro Baumanskaya; tel. 261-5576.

Museum of Modern Art, 25 Petrovka Ul. Open 12–7pm; closed Tuesday. Metro Kuznetsky Most.

Museum of Private Collections (branch of Pushkin Museum), 14 Volkhonka Ul. Open 12–6pm; closed Monday/Tuesday. Metro Kropotkinskaya; tel. 203-1546.

Nemirovich-Danchenko Memorial Apartment, 5 Glinishchevsky Per./5th floor. Open 11am–4pm; closed Saturday/Sunday/Monday. Metro Okhotny Ryad/Pushkinskaya; tel. 209-5391.

Novodevichy Convent, 1 Novodevichy Per. Open 10am–5.30pm. Closed Tuesday and first Monday of month. Cemetery open daily 9am–6pm. Metro Sportivnaya; tel. 246-8526/2201.

Operetta Theater Museum, 6 Bolshaya Dmitrovka Ul. (inside Operetta Theater) Metro Okhotny Ryad; tel. 292-6377.

Oriental Museum, 12a Nikitsky Bul. Open 11am–7pm; closed Monday. Metro Arbatskaya; tel. 291-9614/0212.

Ostankino Museums, see page 208.

Ostrovsky Museum Center (author N A), 14 Tverskaya Ul. Open 11am–6.30pm; closed Monday/Tuesday. Metro Pushkinskaya; tel. 229-8552.

Ostrovsky Memorial House (playwright A N), 9 Malaya Ordynka Ul. Open noon–7pm; closed Tuesday and last Monday of month. Metro Novokuznetskaya/Tretyakovskaya; tel. 951-1140.

Paleontology Museum, 123 Profsoyuznaya Ul. Open 11am–6pm; closed Monday/Tuesday. Metro Tyoply Stan; tel. 339-4544.

Politechnical Museum, 3 Novaya Pl. Open 10am–6pm (*kassa* closed at 5pm); closed Monday and last Thursday of month. Metro Lubyanka; tel. 923-0756.

Pushkin Memorial Apartment, 53 Arbat. Open 11am–6pm; closed Mondays/Tuesdays. Metro Smolenskaya. Another is at 12 Prechistenka Ul; tel. 241-2246.

Pushkin Museum of Fine Arts, 12 Volkhonka Ul. Open 10am–7pm; closed Monday. Metro Kropotkinskaya; tel. 203-7412/9578.

Roerich Museum, 3/5 Maly Znamensky Lane. Open 11am–6pm. Closed Monday. Metro Kropotkinskaya; tel. 203-6419; www.roerich-museum.ru.

Sakharov Human Rights Museum, 57 Zemlyanoi Val. Open 11am–7pm; closed Mon/Tues. Metro Kurskaya; tel. 923-4401/7998.

Shalyapin Memorial House, 25 Novinsky Bul. Open 11am–6pm; closed Monday/Friday amd last day of month. Metro Barrikadnaya; tel. 252-2530.

Skryabin Memorial Museum, 11 Bolshoi Nikolopeskovsky Per. Open 10am–4.30pm, Wed/Fri 12–6.30pm; closed Mon/Tues. Metro Arbatskaya/Smolenskaya; tel. 241-1901.

St Basil's Cathedral, 2 Red Square. Nov–April: open 11am–4pm; May–Oct: open 10am–5pm; closed Tuesday. Metro Kitai-Gorod/Okhotny Ryad; tel. 298-3304.

Stanislavsky Memorial Museum, 6 Leontevsky Per. Open 11am–5pm, Wednesday/Friday 2–8pm; weekends 11am–3pm; closed Monday/Tuesday and last Thursday of month. Metro Pushkinskaya; tel. 229-2855.

Tetris Wax Museum, 14 Tverskaya Ul. Open 11am–7pm; closed Mon. Metro Pushkinskaya; tel. 229-8552.

Tolstoy Country Estate Museum, 12 Pyatniktskaya Ul. Open 11am–5pm; closed Mon. Metro Novokuznetskaya; tel. 951-7402.

Tolstoy Museum, 11 Ul. Prechistenka. Open 11am–5pm; closed Monday and last Friday of month. Metro Kropotkinskaya; tel. 202-9338, 201-3811.

Tolstoy Museum, 21 Ul. Lva Tolstovo. Open 10am–5pm, winter 10am–4pm; closed Monday and last Friday of month. Metro Park Kultury; tel. 202-2190.

Tolstoy Museum (this is not Leo Tolstoy, but another writer Alexei who lived here 1942–1945), 2/6 Spiridonovka Ul. Open Wednesday/Friday 1–6.30pm; Thursday/Saturday/Sunday 11am–5pm; closed Monday/Tuesday. Metro Pushkinskaya; tel. 290-0956.

Tropinin Museum, 10 Shchetininsky Per. Open 12–7pm Saturday/Sunday 10am–5pm; closed Tuesday/Wednesday. Metro Polyanka/Tretyakovskaya; tel. 951-1799/953-9750.

Tretyakov Gallery, 10 Lavrushinsky Per. (also at 10 Krymsky Val) Open 10am–7pm; closed Monday. Metro Tretyakovskaya. tel. 951-1362/230-7788; www.tretyakov.ru.

Tsvetaeva House Museum, 6 Borisoglebski. Open 12–5pm. Closed Saturday and last Friday of month. Metro Arbatskaya; Tel 202-3543.

Vasnetsov (Appolinary) Memorial Apartment (brother of artist), 6 Furmanny Per. Open 11am–5pm, Wednesday/Friday 2–8pm; closed Monday/Tuesday and last Thursday of month. Metro Chistiye Prudy; tel. 208-9045.

Vasnetsov (Vasily) Memorial House (artist) (branch of Tretyakov), 13 Pereulok Vasnetsova. Open 11am–5pm; closed Monday/Tuesday and last Thursday of month. Metro Sukharevskaya; tel. 281-1329.

Vysotsky Cultural Museum, 3 Nizh. Tagansky. Open 11am–5.30pm. Closed Sunday/Monday. Metro Taganskaya; tel. 915-7578.

Yermolova Memorial House, 11 Tverskoi Bul. Open noon–7pm, Saturday/Sunday noon–7pm; closed Tuesday. Metro Tverskaya/Pushkinskaya; tel. 290-0215/5416.

Zoological Museum of Moscow University, 6 Bolshaya Nikitskaya Ul. Open 10am–5pm; closed Mondays and last Tuesday of month. Metro Aleksandrovsky Sad/Okhotny Ryad; tel. 203-8923.

Zoo, 1 Bolshaya Gruzinskaya Ul. Renovated in 1996. Open 10am–8pm, in winter 10am–4pm; closed Mon. Metro Barrikadnaya; tel. 255-5375.

LIBRARIES

There are 15 major libraries in Moscow where one can browse through books in reading rooms, but not take books out.

Library of Foreign Literature, 1 Nikoloyamskaya Ul. Monday–Friday 9am–7.45pm; Saturday/Sunday 9am–6pm. Metro Kitai-Gorod; tel. 915-3528.

Russian State Library (formerly Lenin Library), 3 Vozdvizhenka Ul. Open 9am–9pm; closed Sunday. Metro Biblioteka Imeni Lenina; tel. 202-7371/5790.

Russian Art Library, 8/1 Bolshaya Dmitrovka. Monday–Friday 11am–6.45pm; Saturday 11am–5.45pm. Metro Teatralnaya; tel. 292-0653.

Russian Historical Library, 9 Starosadsky Per. Monday–Friday 9am–8pm; Saturday/Sunday 10am–6pm. Metro Kitai-Gorod; tel. 928-0522.

PLACES OF WORSHIP

After the fall of Communism every type of religious denomination has taken root in Russia.

RUSSIAN ORTHODOX

There are over 100 Orthodox places of worship in Moscow. These are a few that hold regular religious services. Usual time of services: Monday–Saturday 8am and 6pm. Sundays and holidays: 7am, 10am and 6pm. Women should dress modestly and men not wear hats.

CATHEDRALS

Cathedral of Christ the Redeemer, 37 Prechistenskaya Emb. Moscow's largest cathedral. Open daily 6.30am–10pm, closed Mon. (Museum, tel. 202-8024; open 10am–5.30pm, closed last Monday of month) Metro Kropotkinskaya; tel. 203-3823.

Cathedral of the Epiphany in Elokhovo, 15 Spartakovskaya Ul. Metro Baumanskaya; tel. 267-7591.

Holy Trinity Cathedral, on Borisovskye Ponds, southern Moscow. Consecrated in 2004, the cathedral is Moscow's second largest.

Kazansky Cathedral, 8 Nikolskaya Ul. Red Square. Metro Okhotny Ryad; tel. 298-0131.

St Basil's Cathedral, 2 Red Square. Metro Kitai-Gorod; tel. for excursions 298-3304.

CHURCHES

Assumption Church in Novodevichy Convent, 1 Novodevichy Per. Daily 7am–7pm. Metro Sportivnaya; tel. 245-3168.

Church of All Saints in Sokol, 73a Leningradsky Pr. Metro Sokol; tel. 158-2952.

Church of All Sorrows, 20 Bolshaya Ordynka. Daily 7am–8pm; services held at 8am. Metro Tretyakovskaya; tel. 951-1300.

Church of the Deposition of the Robes, Donskoi Monastery. tel. 954-1531.

Church of the Epiphany, 15 Spartakovskaya Ul. Seat of Russian Patriarch from 1943–1988. Daily 8am–8pm. Metro Baumskaya; tel. 267-7591.

Church of the Nativity of Christ, 28 Izmailovsky Passage. Daily 9am–9pm. Metro Izmailovskaya; tel. 164-2877.

Church of Prelate Philip, Patriarch of Moscow, 35 Gilyarovskovo Ul. Metro Prospekt Mira; tel. 281-0539.

Church of St Ilya the Prophet, 6/2nd Obydensky Per. Open 8–11am; closed Tuesday/Thursday. Metro Kropotkinskaya; tel. 203-1951.

Church of St John the Warrior, 46 Yakimanka Ul. Metro Okyabrskaya; tel. 238-2056.

Church of St Nicholas, 2 Ul. Lva Tolstovo. Daily 7.30am–8pm. Metro Park Kultury; tel. 246-6952.

Church of Saints Peter and Paul in Kulishki, 4 Petropavlosky Per. Metro Kitai-Gorod; tel. 917-2975.

Church of the Trinity on Sparrow Hills, 30 Ul. Kosygina. Daily 8am–5pm. Metro Oktyabrskaya; tel. 939-0046.

MONASTERIES AND CONVENTS
Convent of the Conception, 2 2nd Zachatevsky Lane. Metro Kropotskinskaya; tel. 203-1512.

Convent of the Nativity of the Virgin, 20 Rozhdestvenka Ul. Metro Kuznetsky Most; tel. 921-3986.

Danilovsky Monastery, 22 Danilovsky Val. Metro Tulskaya; tel. 952-9059.

Donskoi Monastery, 1 Donskoi Sq. Metro Shabolovskaya; tel. 232-0221.

New Monastery of the Savior, 10 Krestyanskaya Sq. Metro Proletarskaya; tel. 276-9570.

Novodevichy Convent, 1 Novodevichy Lane. tel. 246-2201.

OTHER ORTHODOX DENOMINATIONS
Armenian Apostolic Church of the Resurrection, 10 Ul. Sergeya Makeeva. Services Sundays at noon; open daily 10am–7pm. Metro Ulitsa 1905 Goda; tel. 255-5019.

Greek Orthodox Church of Archangel Gabriel/Church of Martyz Fedor, 15a Arkhangelsky Per. Daily 8am–7.30pm. Metro Turgenevskaya.

Metropolitan Old Believers Church/Cathedral of the Intercession, 29 Rogozhsky Poselok. Monday–Friday 10am–5pm; services at 7.30am and 4pm. Metro Taganskaya; tel. 361-0920.

Ostozhenskaya Old Believers Commune, 4 Turchaninov Per. Services Saturdays, Sundays and holidays at 8am and 3pm. Metro Park Kultury; tel. 245-3029.

ROMAN CATHOLIC

Church of St Louis, 12 Malaya Lubyanka. Daily 7.30am–8pm. Masses in Latin, English, French, Polish and Russian. Metro Lubyanka; tel. 925-2034.

Church of Our Lady of Hope and Catholic Chaplaincy, 7 Kutuzovsky Pr. Masses in English on Saturday and Sunday at 6pm. Metro Kutuovskaya; tel. 243-9621.

Christian Science Group, 14 Sushchevsky Val. Services Sundays at 11am. Metro Novoslobodskaya; tel. 158-6096.

OTHER CHRISTIAN CHURCHES

Baptists of Russia, Kamerny Hall, Olympic Village. 11 Michurinsky Prospekt. Sunday services.

Bible Society of Russia, 51/14 Pyatnitskaya Ul. Mon–Fri 10.30am–4pm. Metro Novokunetskaya.

Church of Evangelical Christian-Baptists, 3 Maly Trekhsvyatitel.sky Per. Daily 10am–6pm; services Tuesday/Thursday/Saturday/Sunday. Metro Chistiye Prudy; tel. 917-5167.

International Christian Assembly, in concert hall of Central House of Artists. 2 Ul. Akademinka Vargi. English services Sundays at 10.30am. Metro Tyoply Stan; tel. 338-1150.

PROTESTANT DENOMINATIONS

The Anglican Church of St Andrews, 9 Voznesensky Per. Metro Okhotny Ryad.

Calvary Church, 31 Ul. Usievicha. 3rd floor. tel. 156-5679. Metro Sokol; tel. 229-0990.

Lutheran Worship in Church of St Peter and Paul, 7 Starosadsky Per. Metro Kitai-Gorod; tel. 928-3262.

Mormons/Church of Jesus Christ of Latter Day Saints, 2 Chistoprudny Bul. (also at 37 Donskaya Ul. Metro Shabolovskaya). Services Sundays at 10am. Metro Chistiye Prudy; tel. 925-0398.

Seventh-Day Adventists, 3 Maly Trekhsvyatitel.sky Per. Services on Wednesday and Saturday at 10am and 6pm. Metro Chistiye Prud; tel. 917-0568.

United Methodist Church, 50/7 Fruzenskaya Nab.

OTHER DENOMINATIONS

Religious Adminstration of Buddhists in Russia, 49 Ostozhenka Ul. Metro Park Kultury; tel. 245-2289.

Temple for the Realization of Krishna, 8 Khoroshchevskoye Shosse. Services at 7am, 1.30pm and 7pm. Metro Begovaya; tel. 945-4858/4755.

JEWISH
Chabab Lubavitch Polyakova Synagogue, 6 Bolshaya Bronnaya. Services on Fridays after sunset and Saturdays at 10am; open 8am–9pm. Metro Pushkinskaya; tel. 202-4530.

Choral Synagogue, 8 Bolshoi Spasoglinishchevsky Per. Services Monday–Friday at 8.30am, Saturday and holidays at 9am, and evenings after sunset. Metro Kitai-Gorod; tel. 923-9697.

Marina Rostcha Moscow Jewish Commune, 5a 2nd Vysheslavtsev Lane. Services Wednesday–Friday at 9am. Metro Rizhskaya; tel. 289-2325.

Representatives of World Council of Progressive Judaism, 14/2 Solyanka.

MOSLEM
Grand Mosque, 7 Vypolzov Lane. Main service Friday at 1pm. Metro Prospekt Mira; tel. 281-3866.

Bayt-Allah Religious Society, 28 Bolshaya Tatarskaya Ul. Daily 9am–6pm. Metro Novokuznetskaya; tel. 231-1781.

Islamic Cultural Center, 5 Maly Tatarsky Per. Monday–Friday 10am–6pm. (Moslem Mission, tel. 247-15080. Metro Novokuznetskaya; tel. 231-8856.

ENTERTAINMENT
THEATERS
There are over 100 theaters and concert halls in Moscow. A partial listing of main theaters and halls is included here. Theater, concert and circus performances begin on weekdays between 6pm and 8pm with matinée performances on weekends, with an earlier evening show. Each theater usually has its own box office; in addition, tickets can often be reserved through a travel/service bureau in your hotel., or purchased from street/Metro theater kiosks. Some main ticket/concert ticket offices are at 2, 15, 19, 29 Tverskaya Ul; open 9am–8pm. And Arba is at 22 Tverskoi Bulvar; open 10am–7pm. For information on theater repertoires, call 975-9122 or look for the free addition of the *Moscow Times* in English which has listings of theater, concert, circus and cinematic events. You can also find out event scedules and order tickets by calling 258-0000 or go online at www.parter.ru.

Bat Cabaret, (Letuchnaya Mysh), 33 Povarskaya Ul. Metro Barrikadnaya; tel. 290-2811/5524.

Bolshoi Opera and Ballet Theater, 1 Teatralnaya Pl. (closed until March 2008) Metro Teatralnaya; tel. 292-0050/9986; www.bolshoi.ru.

Buff Theater, 59 Lesnaya Ul. Metro Mendeleyevskaya; tel. 251-3257.

Chekhov Academic Art Theater, 3 Kamergersky Per. Metro Teatralnaya; tel. 229-5370/8760; www.mxat.ru.

Chekhov Theater, 5 Novozykovsky Proyezd. Metro Dynamo; tel. 214-6669/212-8211.

Children's Fairy Tale Theater, 15 Taganskaya. Metro Marksistskaya; tel. 912-5206.

Chamber Musical Theater, 17 Nikolskaya Ul. Metro Lubyanka; tel. 929-1320/1326.

Children's Puppet Theater, 9 Ul. Bazhova. Metro VDNKh; tel. 181-0193/2044.

Children's Variety Theater, 6 Bolshaya Sadovaya. Metro Mayakovskaya; tel. 299-5941/8137.

Classical Ballet Theater, 3 Skakovaya Ul. Metro Dynamo; tel. 251-3221.

Gogol Drama Theater, 8a Ul. Kazakova. Metro Kurskaya; tel. 261-5528/262-9214.

Gorky Academic Art Theater, 22 Tverskoi Bul. Metro Tverskaya; tel. 203-6222/8773.

Gypsy Theater Roman, 32 Leningradsky Pr. Metro Dynamo; tel. 250-9980, 214-5628.

Jewish Chamber Music Theater, 12/4 Taganskaya. Metro Taganskaya; tel. 912-5651.

Jewish Drama Theater Shalom, 71 Varshovsky Shosse. Metro Varshavskaya; tel. 110-3758/113-2753.

Helikon Opera Theater, 19 Bolshaya Nikitskaya. Metro Pushkinskaya.; tel. 290-6592/291-1323; www.helikon.ru.

Lencom Theater, 6 Malaya Dmitrovka Ul. Metro Tverskaya; tel. 299-9668/0708; www.lencom.ru.

Maly Theater, 1/6 Teatralnaya Pl. Metro Teatralnaya; tel. 924-4083/923-2621.

Maly Theater Branch is at 69 Bolshaya Ordynka. Metro Dobryninskaya; tel. 237-3181.

Marrionette Theater, 7 Maly Kharitonevsky Per. Metro Chistiye Prudy; tel. 924-3651.

Mayakovsky Theater, 19 Bolshaya Nikitskaya. Metro Pushkinskaya.; tel. 290-4232/4658; www.mayakovsky.ru.

Mayakovsky Theater Branch is at 21 Pushkarev Ul. Metro Sukharevskaya; tel. 208-3312.

Moscow Drama Theater, 4 Malaya Bronnaya. Metro Tverskaya; tel. 290-6731/4093.

Moscow Operetta Theater, 6 Bolshaya Dmitrovka. Metro Okhotny Ryad.; tel. 292-1237/6377; www.operetta.msc.ru.

Moscow Theater School of Dramatic Arts, 20 Povarskaya Ul. Metro Arbatskaya; tel. 291-4533/4796.

Moscow Theater of Mimicry and Gesture, 39/41 Izmailovsky Bul. Metro Pervomaiskaya; tel. 465-5859.

Mosoviet Theater, 16 Bolshaya Sadovaya. Metro Mayakovskaya; tel. 299-2035/200-5943; www.mossovet.ru.

Novaya Opera, 3 Karatny Ryad. Metro Mayakovskaya; tel. 200-0868; www.novaya-opera.ru.

Obraztsov Puppet Theater, 3 Sadovaya Samotechnaya Ul. Metro Mayakovskaya; tel. 299-3310/5373.

Old Arbat Theater, 11 Filippovsky Per. Metro Arbatskaya; tel. 291-1546.

Puppet Theater, 26 Spartakovskaya Ul. Metro Baumanskaya; tel. 261-2197.

Pushkin Drama Theater, 23 Tverskoi Bul. Metro Pushkinskaya; tel. 203-8587/8582.

Russian Army Academic Theater, 2 Suvorovskaya Pl. Metro Novoslobodskaya; tel. 281-2110/5120.

Satircon Theater, 8 Sheremetyevskaya Ul. Metro Rizhskaya; tel. 289-7844.

Satire Theater, 2 Triumphfalnaya Pl. Metro Mayakovskaya; tel. 299-6305/3642.

Sovremennik Theater, 19 Chistoprudny Bul. Metro Chistiye Prudy; tel. 921-6473/1790.

Stanislavsky Drama and Arts Theater, 23 Tverskaya Ul. Metro Tverskaya; tel. 299-7621/7224.

Stanislavsky and Nemirovich-Danchenko Musical Theater, 17 Bolshaya Dmitrovka Ul. Metro Pushskinskaya; tel. 229-2835/8388; www.stanislavskymusic.ru.

Taganka Drama and Comedy Theater, 76 Zemlyonoi Val. Metro Taganskaya; tel. 915-1217/1155; www.taganka.org.

Vakhtangov Academic Theater, 26 Arbat. Metro Arbatskaya; tel. 241-0728/1679.

Variety Theater, 20/2 Bersenevskaya Nab. Metro Polyanka; tel. 959-0593.

Yermolova Drama Theater, 5 Tverskaya Ul. Metro Okhotny Ryad; tel. 203-7952/9063.

CONCERT HALLS
Central House of Tourists Concert Hall, 149 Leninsky Pr. Metro Yugo-Zapadnaya; tel. 438-9531, 434-9492.

Gnesin Institute Concert Hall, 30 Povarskaya Ul. Metro Arbatskaya; tel. 291-1581/1554.

House of Unions Concert Hall, 1 Bolshaya Dmitrovka. Metro Okhotny Ryad; tel. 292-0956/0736.

Izmailovo Concert Hall, 71 Izmailovo Hgwy. Metro Izmailovsky Park; tel. 166-7880.

Kremlin Palace of Congresses, the Kremlin (entrance through Borovitsky Gate). Metro Borovitskaya; tel. 928-5232, 917-2336; www.kremlin-gkd.ru.

Moscow Philharmonia, 31 Tverskaya Ul. Metro Mayakovskaya; tel. 299-3957.

Novaya Opera, 3 Karetny Ryad. Metro Mayakovskaya; tel. 200-0868; www. novayaopera.ru.

Pushkin's Concert Hall, 2 Pushkinskaya Square. Metro Pushkinskaya; tel. 299-0141.

Sadko, 3a Litovsky Bulvar. Metro Yasyenevo; tel. 427-6100.

Tchaikovsky Concert Hall, 4/31 Triumphfalnaya Pl. Metro Mayakovskaya.; tel. 299-5362/0378; www.philharmonia.ru.

Tchaikovsky Conservatory Complex, 13 Bol. Nikitskaya Ul. The complex is composed of three major concert halls and several lecture buildings. The Bolshoi Hall seats over 1,600 (but restoration work is ongoing). (The Rachmaninov Hall is next door at number 11; tel. 229-9401/8183). Metro Pushkinskaya; tel. 229-3957.

CIRCUSES
Bolshoi New Circus, 7 Vernadsky Pr. Metro Universitet; tel. 930-2815/0272.

Clown Theater of Teresa Durova, 6 Pavlovskaya Ul. Metro Tulskaya.

Durov Animal Theater, 4 Durov Ul. Metro Prospekt Mira; tel. 971-3047/281-9812.

Kuklachyov's House of Cats, 25 Kutuzovsky Pr. Metro Kievskaya; tel. 249-2907.

Moscow Delfinary, 27 Mironovskaya Ul. Metro Semyonovskaya; tel. 369-7966.

Moscow Ice Ballet, 24 Luzhnetskaya Nab. Metro Sportivnaya; tel. 201-1679.

Nikulin's Old Circus, 13 Tsvetnoi Bul. Metro Tsvetnoi Bulvar; tel. 200-1820/0668; www.circusnikulin.ru.

Summer Circus, Nyeskuchny Gardens. Metro Oktybrskaya; tel. 236-1462.

Tent Circus Raduga (Rainbow), Druzhba Park. (May–Sept) Metro Vodnyy Stadion.

Tent Circus Rus, 31 Ul. Novinki. (May–Sept) Metro Kolomenskaya; tel. 116-5676.

Tent Circus, 9 Paromnaya Ul. (spring/summer) Metro Kashirskaya; tel. 342-5928.

CINEMAS
Moscow has more than 100 cinemas. Most show movies in Russian; some screen foreign films in original language with subtitles, or with simultaneous translation.
35mm, 47/24 Pokrovka. Russian subtitles. Metro Krasniye Vorota; tel. 917-5492, 244-0553.

American House of Cinema, 2 Berezhkovskaya Nab., Radison-Slavyanskaya Hotel. American films with Russian simultaneous translations via headset. (Daily show listings in Moscow Times.) Metro Kievskaya; tel. 941-8747/8895.

Dome Theater, in Renaissance Hotel, 18 Olympisky Pr. Foreign language films. Metro Prospekt Mira; tel. 931-9873.

Kino Center at Krasny Presnye, 15 Druzhinnikovskaya Ul. tel. 255-9292/9057.

Kodak Cinema World, 2 Nastasinsky Per. Metro Pushkinskaya; tel. 209-6526/4359.

MDM Multiplex, 28 Komsomolsky Pr. Metro Frunzenskaya; tel. 961-0056.

Oktyabr, 24 Novy Arbat. Metro Arbatskaya; tel. 291-2263.

Pushkin Theater, 2 Pushkin Square. Metro Pushkinskaya; tel. 299-7300, 795-3795.

BLUES AND JAZZ
More than ten clubs in Moscow now feature regular jazz concerts and events. The most popular are Le Club, Forte, Blues BB King, Cool Train and Sinyaya Ptitsa (Blue Bird).

Alabama, 7 Stoleshnikov Lane. Live jazz and blues concerts at 8pm. Metro Pushkinskaya; tel. 229-2412.

Arbat Blues Club, 11 Filippovsky Per, features blues-rock bands. Open Friday/ Saturday nights from 8.30pm–5.30am. Metro Arbatskaya; tel. 291-1546.

Birdland, at 16 Shchipok, a jazz club café with jazz performances on Tuesday/Friday nights from 7–11pm. Daily noon to 2am. Metro Serpukhovskaya; tel. 236-3363.

Blues Club B B King (Moscow House of Blues), 4/2 Sadovaya-Samotechnaya. Open noon–2am; Friday/Saturday noon–5am. Usually live jazz on Thursday–Saturday 8.30-10pm, and blues jam sessions, Wednesday 8.15pm. Metro Tsvetnoi Bulvar; tel. 299-8206; www.blues.ru/bbking.

Club Forte, 18 Bolshaya Bronnaya, a restaurant with live jazz and blues concerts; heart of club is jazz rock, with added fusion and funk. Daily 2pm–midnight. Metro Pushkinskaya; tel. 202-8833.

Club na Brestskoi, 6 2nd Brestskaya. Cool, minimalist interior with jazz-influenced music. Open noon to midnight. Metro Mayakovskaya; tel. 200-0936.

Club Kurs, 8/2 Kursovoi Lane. Café with jazz concerts six nights a week. Open noon to midnight. Metro Kropotkinskaya; tel. 290-5750.

Cool Train is the B2 (see Nightclubs).   All kinds of jazz; on Sundays children can get introduced to jazz from 2–6pm during brunch. Jazz club on third floor.

Cream, 3 Solyansk Per. a cosy Jazz/Blues coffeehouse. Open Sunday–Wednesday 10am–1am; Thursday–Saturday 10am–6am. Metro Kitai-Gorod; tel. 923-4902.

Jazz Art Club, 20 Leningradsky Pr (in Bulgarian Cultural Center), has popular jazz and jam sessions surrounded by exhibition of paintings by Moscow artists. Open Fridays from 7.30pm–11pm. Metro Belorusskaya; tel. 191-8320; www.jazz.ru.

JVL Art Club, 14/19 Novoslobodskaya. Live jazz/blues. tel. 978-1030.

Kafe Jazz, 27 Bol Ordynka, cozy brick-cellar interior with music and good food. Daily noon–1am; weekends noon–5am. Metro Tretyakovskaya; tel. 231-9777.

Le Club, 21 Verkhnyaya Radishchevskaya Ul (in Taganka Theater Bldg) Considered one of the world's top 100 jazz clubs with concerts daily at 8pm (Wednesday/ Thursday piano jazz during lunch). Bar and restaurant, jazz and DJ rock music, Club's patron saint is legendary Russian saxophonist, Igor Butman, whose big band plays every Monday night. Open noon–2am. Metro Taganskaya; Tel 915-1042; www.le-club.ru for programs.

Red Square, top jazz bar beneath the restaurant at 1 Red Square (in basement of Historical State Museum). Open nightly. Metro Okhotny Ryad.

Rhythm & Blues, 19a Starovagankovsky Per, Bldg 2, Restaurant and jazz/rock club. Open 5pm until midnight. Metro Arbatskaya; tel. 203-6556.

Sinaya Ptitsa (Bluebird), 23/15 Malaya Dmitrovka, (enter from Staropimenovsky) the city's oldest jazz club which celerbrated its 40th anniversary in 2004. Newly restored, the underground space is bathed in a soft blue light and offers plenty of jazz diversity. Open Noon to midnight. Metro Mayakovskaya; Tel 299-2225; www.bluebirdjazz.ru.

CASINOS

Moscow is now said to have more casinos than Las Vegas. (If you win money, never leave unescorted.) These are open 24 hours daily; all offer food and alcoholic beverages. Many have entrance fees.

Barkhat (Velvet), 3 Varvarka Ul (in Gostiny Dvor Trade Center). full-service casino with two levels, restaurant and live-salon music. tel. 298-1515; www.barxat.ru.

Chekhov, 3 Mal. Dmitrovka. Casino with blackjack, poker, roulette and guarded escort home. Metro Pushkinskaya.

Golden Palace, 15 3rd Yamskaya Polya, large casino and entertainment complex with restaurant/bar. Metro Belorusskaya; tel. 232-1515; www.goldenpalace.ru.

Kosmos, 150 Pr. Mira in Kosmos Hotel, large casino. Metro VDNKh.

Kristall, 38 Marksistkaya. Casino with 100 tables, poker, roulette, blackjack, etc. Metro Proletarskaya; tel. 911-7711.

Luxe, 4/1 Michurinsky Pr. Casino with Thurs/Sat musical nights. Metro Yugo-Zapadnaya; tel. 430-3763.

Metelitsa, 21a Novy Arbat, entertainment complex and casino, roulette, poker, slot machines. Metro Arbatskaya; tel. 291-1170.

Metropole, 1 Teatralny Lane in hotel., casino (starting fee is $200). Dress code. Metro Teatralnaya; tel. 927-6950.

Moskva, 21 Kalanchevskaya, first casino in Moscow, with roulette, poker, blackjack, two bars and live music. Metro Komsomolskaya; tel. 975-1967.

Royale, 22 Begovaya. Club-casino with restaurant/bar and disco. Dress code. Metro Begovaya; tel. 945-1410.

Shangri-La, 2 Pushkinskaya Square, Gaudy, city-center casino. Metro Pushkinskaya; tel. 209-6400.

Sol, 2 Nikoloyamsy Per, 30+ tables and slot hall; live music on weekends. Metro Taganskaya; tel. 911-2737.

NIGHTCLUBS AND MUSIC
In the last decade, Moscow has finally generated nightlife! There are now hundreds of places offering nightly entertainment, and many of these have cover charges, and dress codes (and often expensive drinks). All serve food and alcohol. (Most take credit cards.) Be prepared to walk through a metal detector upon entering, and pass the *feis kontrol* (face control) scutiny of big bodyguard doormen. These are some of the most popular. Find one nearest to your location (you do not what to travel far to get home at 3am!).

B-2, 8 Bol. Sadovaya. An enormous, 4-story, entertainment complex with live rock performances and several bars. Cool Train jazz club performs on 3rd floor. Metro Makayakovskaya; Tel. 209-9909; www.b2club.ru.

Boogie-Woogie, 11 Delegatskaya. Dance club and sushi bar. Open Thursday through Saturday 8pm–6am. Metro Tsvetnoi Bulvar; tel. 972-1132.

Bunker, 12 Tverskaya. Popular, multi-room hangout with dancing in the evenings. Open 24 hours. Metro Pushkinskaya; tel. 200-1506.

Cabana, 4 Raushskaya Emb. Club and restaurant. Open Monday–Friday noon–6am, Saturday/Sunday 6pm–6am. Metro Tretyakovskaya; tel. 238-5006.

Club Che, 10/2 Nikolskaya Ul. Popular Latin American dance club and cuisine (rum & cigars), live music. Metro Lubyanka; tel. 621-7477, 924-7477; www.clubche.ru.

Chinese Pilot Dzhau Da (Kitaisky Letchik Jao Da), 25 Lubyansky Pr, bldg 1, Trendy club with great bands and restaurant. Daily 24 hours. Metro Kitai-Gorod; tel. 924-5611.

Club XIII, 13 Myasnitskaya, located in a 19th-century mansion, attracts super suave of Moscow nightlife scene. Expensive. Dress well to get in. Open all night. Metro Turgenevskaya; tel. 927-2391.

Expat Club, 4 Pevchesky bldg 1, Disco club and restaurant. Open noon–6am. Metro Kitai-Gorod; tel. 298-5414.

Fabrique, 33 Sadovnicheskaya (entrance from side-street) A huge, well-designed club with food. Open 11pm–7am. Metro Novokuznetskaya; tel. 109-0219.

Garage, 16 Tverskaya. Very funky dance club with underground New York-style bar and garage-themed decor; dress way hiply to get in. Open into wee morning hours. (**The Last Drop** cellar pub is nearby at 4 Strasnoi Bulvar) Metro Pushkinskaya; tel. 209-1848.

Gvozdy Radio Club, 19 Bol Nikitskaya. Disco with live music, restaurant and bar. Daily noon–5am. Metro Pushkinskaya; tel. 290-2254.

Karma Bar, 3 Pushechnaya St. Popular dance club of Latin music and Europop & restaurant. DJ's playing top 40 hits; dance floor packed on weekends. Open Wednesday–Sunday 7pm–6am. The Buddha Bar with Tibetan cuisine and caviar & noodle selections is on the premises. (The Hungry Duck is down the street at number 9/6.) Metro Kuznetsky Most; tel. 924-5633; www.karma-bar.ru.

Ministerstvo (Ministry), 24 Malaya Nikitskaya, located on the grounds of the former Soviet Ministry. Dance club with DJ's. Open Friday/Saturday 11pm–6am. Metro Barrikadnaya; tel. 222-0158; www.ministryclub.ru.

Mirage (Mirazh), 21 Novy Arbat. Nightclub with large dance floor and pop music, and separate quieter restaurant/bar areas. Daily 6pm–6am. Metro Arbatskaya; tel. 291-6723.

Most (Bridge), 6/3 Kuznetsky Most, is another popular club. Open 6pm–6am. (Nearby, at No. 3, is **Shambala DJ** with more trendy dancing). Metro Kuznetsky Most; tel. 928-1707.

News Pub, 18 Petrovka Ul, bldg 1. Club restaurant. DJ and disco music; varied music from jazz & rock to string quartets; Open noon–6am. Metro Okhotny Ryad.; tel. 928-8343.

Night Flight (Nochnoi Polet), 17 Tverskaya. Nightclub, with restaurant, disco and DJ music; party atmosphere. Restaurant opens at 6pm. Disco 11pm–5am. (Territoriya, at number 5, plays DJ, pop & Techno music; and Lili Wong, at number 3/5, is another club/restaurant) Metro Tverskaya; tel. 229-4165; www.nightflight.ru.

Papa John's, 22 Myasnitskaya, dancing with Latin and funk DJ music, back restaurant. Daily 6pm till dawn. Metro Turgenevskaya; tel. 755-9554.

Paris Life (Parizhskaya Zhizn), 3 Karetny Ryad (Hermitage Gardens). After a French meal, head upstairs to the crowd dancing under the replica of the Eiffel Tower. Open 11am–7am. Metro Tsvetnoi Bulvar; tel. 209-4524.

Park, Gorky Park theater area, two dance floors, techno music, outdoor terrace in summer with live music. Open into wee morning hours. Metro Park Kultury.

Project O.G.I., There are 5 OGI establishments throughout the city. In addition to music, dancing and a large cocktail menu, bookshops here are also open all night. 8/12 Potapovsky (enter through courtyard). Music and dancing. Metro Chistiye Prudy; tel. 927-5366. www.ogi.ru/proekt.

Propaganda, 7 Bol. Zlatoustinsky Per (entrance thru Polytechnical Museum), top disco joint and all night hip dance club, featuring British DJ's. (The place to be on Thursday nights; on Sunday nights turns into a popular gay club) Daily noon till 6am. Metro Kitai Gorod; tel. 924-5732.

Respublika, 17 Nikolskaya. Trendy nightclub with way cool people; has quieter interior bar rooms. Daily 6pm–6am. Metro Lubyanka; tel. 928-4692.

Tabula Rasa, 28 Berezhkovskaya Emb. Low-key club with live musical bands. Daily 7pm–6am. Metro Kievskaya; tel. 240-9289.

Voodoo Lounge, 5 Sred Tishinsky Per. Restaurant and nightclub dancing lounge with outdoor seating, live music and special Cuban Room; free salsa dance lessons on Tuesday/Wednesday nights. Daily noon–midnight; Thursday/Friday/Saturday to 6am. Metro Belorusskaya; tel. 253-2323.

GAY AND LESBIAN VENUES

Chameleon, 14 Prenensky Val, has two large dance floors, restaurant, five bars, beer garden, and friendly-mixed crowd. Restaurant open daily 24 hrs; bopping from 6pm–8am; disco Thursday through Sunday nights. **Kazarma**, the men-only dance club, is located downstairs. Metro Ulitsa 1905 Goda; tel. 253-6343.

Central Station, 16/2 Bol Tatarskaya, Bldg 2. Moscow's most popular gay club with two dance floors and disco/bar inside post-industrial brick, metal and glass interior. Friday nights is Gay Broadway. Open 7pm–7am (closed Tuesday/Wednesday); Metro Novokuznetskaya; tel. 959-4643.

Chance, 11/15 Volocharskovo (inside Dom Kultury Serp i Molot), mixed crowds, dancing, and mermaid act (men swimming in large aquariums). Daily 11pm–6am. Metro Ploshchad Ilyicha; tel. 298-6247.

Dietrich Bar, 8 Mokhovaya. Decorated with Dietrich photos, also puts on occasional drag shows. Open Thursday–Sunday 10pm–6am. Metro Bib. Imena Lenina; tel. 506-0348.

Imperial Kino, 33 Povarskaya, relaxed student-aged gay (and straight) hang-out. Pop music and disco; Chinese restaurant. Open Thursday through Sunday, 11pm–6am. Metro Barrikadnaya; tel. 290-4489.

Pride, 7 Sovetskoi Armii St, Open 9pm–6am, Strict face control and no women allowed. Metro Rizhskaya; tel. 786-0959.

See **Propaganda Night Club**, turns into a popular gay atmosphere on Sunday nights (10pm–6am)

SED, 9 Maly Gnezdnikovsky Per, Bldg 6, small intimate basement setting. Open noon to midnight. Metro Chekhovskaya; tel. 229-8984.

Three Monkeys (Tri Obezyany), 71 Sadovnicheskaya Ul, Bldg 2. DJ's pop music, dancing and Lesbian nights. Open daily 6pm–9am. Metro Paveletskaya; tel. 951-1563; www.Gay.ru/3monkeys.

Twelve Volt, 12 Tverskaya. Has comfy sofas with a kissing room. Open noon to 6am. Metro Pushkinskaya; tel. 209-3172.

MISCELLANEOUS
TRAVEL AGENCIES AND TOUR COMPANIES
Hundreds of travel companies have opened throughout the city. If you have a touring question, inquire at a hotel service desk, they can also direct you to a speciality agency.

Academservice Company, 49 Arkhitektora Vlasova. tel. 789-9090/9080; www.acase.ru.

Aero (Air) Tour, 80 Leningradskoye Hwy, Bldg 1. tel. 105-3030/451-8300 (Four city locations and at Sheremetyevo II). Offers air tickets, travel services and hotel reservations. www.aerotour.ru.

Andrew's Travel House, 2 Volkhonka, Bldg 18; tel. 916-9898. (St petersburg tel. 325-9400; London 44(0) 7727-2838) Offers travel and visa services. www.ath.ru.

American Express, 17 Gazetny Per. tel. 755-9000/9018. Can help with air tickets, hotels, transfers and visas. Metro Okhotny Ryad.

Capital Tours, 4 Ilyinka, Ent 6. tel. 232-2442. Specializes in Moscow city and Kremlin Armory tour. www.capitaltours.ru.

Diner's Club Travel, tel. 912-0009/745-8407. Offers tickets, hotel.s, car rentals, sightseeing. www.diners.ru.

Eyevista Travel, tel. 737-7150/7950 (24h). St Petersburg tel. 578-1254/1095. Offers visas and other travel. www.eyevista.ru.

Freestyle XXI, 20/1 Petrovka. tel. 621-2151; Travel services for Moscow, St Petersburg and The Golden Ring. www.free-style.ru.

GOTO RUSSIA Travel, 24/6 Bolshoi Sergievsky Lane. tel.225-5012/623-5902/6922. Provides extensive travel services: visas, hotels, apartments. www.gotorussia.com.

Infinity Travel, 13 Komsomolsky Pr. tel. 234-6555. (St Petersburg tel 494-5085 in Hotel Astoria) Affiliated with the Travellers Guest House, offers air and train tickets, visa support, and tour packages. www.infinity.ru (See **Travellers Guest House and Intl Hostel Holiday** in Accommodation section under Guesthouses www.hostel.ru)

Intourist Travel, 13/1 Milyutinsky Per. tel. 924-9860/956-8844. Offers air tickets, packaged tours, hotel and transportation services. Metro Chistiye Prudy.

Marlis Travel, 43-A Kronshtadtsky Bul. tel. 453-4368 (St Petersburg tel 492-9360). Travel agency of the Academy for Tour & Hotel Management. www.marlis.ru.

Moscow Travel, 14 Pushkinskaya St, tel. 956-5445/292-9065. Comprehensive travel agent. Daily 9am–7pm.

Moscow City Tourist Bureau, 5 Rozhdestvenka St. tel. 924-9446. Has walking and bus tours around the city and environs. Monday–Friday 10.30am–6.30pm; Metro Kuznetsky Most.

Norvista (Finnair), 35 Myasnitskaya St. tel. 204-1630. Offers tours in Moscow and St Petersburg and travel services to/from Scandinavia. Open Monday–Friday 10am–6pm; Metro Kuznetsky Most.

Patriarchsky Dom Tours, 6 Vspolny Per. tel./fax 795-0927. (In US tel./fax 650-678-7076) Offers great excursions through Moscow, the Golden Ring and other vicinities (in four languages). Monday–Friday 9am–6pm; Saturday 11am–5pm. Metro Barrikadnaya. www.russiatravel-pdtours.netfirms.com, pdtours@co.ru (US: pdtours@yahoo.com).

BOAT EXCURSIONS AND RIVER CRUISES
See Down The Moskva River section, page 209, for available river cruises.

Capital River Cruises (and River Ticket Office) offers cruises along Volga River and Moscow River canal (from April–October). 1 Leningradsky Pr. Metro Belorusskaya; tel. 458-9624.

River Terminals:
Northern Terminal 1 is at 51 Leningradskoye Hwy. Boats travel north through the Moskva and Oka Rivers to Golden Ring towns and other points. Moscow to St Petersburg takes about 14 days. Metro Rechnoi Vokzal; tel. 457-4050.

Southern Terminal is at 11 Andropova Pr. From 11am–8pm, the riverboat Moskva departs about every half hour for sightseeing cruises along the Moskva River. For longer cruises, the Passenger Port boards at 6 Proektiruemy Proezd. Tours to Golden Ring towns and southern points. Moscow to Astrakhan along the Volga takes about 20 days. Metro Kolomenskoye; tel. 118-0811.

BUS EXCURSIONS—LOCAL AND INTERNATIONAL
Central Bus Station, 75 Shchyolkovskoye Shosse. Buses to Vladimir, Ivanovo, Kostroma, Rybinsk, Suzdal, Tula, Yaroslavl, Nizny Novgorod and other towns. Metro Shchyolkovskoye; tel. 468-0400.

Avtotur-Satellite, 125b Varshavskoye Sh. Long-distance bus travel through Russia and abroad; tel. 381-7325. Metro Yuzhnaya.

Baltic Express (tel. 938-2998); **Evropa-Soyuz** (tel. 187-6763)

Marvel-Tour, 95 Leninsky Pr. tel. 131-5501. Offers bus service to numerous European countries. Metro Prospekt Vernadskovo.

Priltravel, 9 Smolenskaya Sq. tel. 241-5640. Has bus service to Finland. Metro Smolenskaya.

CAR RENTALS

Moscow has nearly 50 car rental agencies scattered around the city offering everything from compact cars to minibuses. Inquire if rental car comes with or without a driver. Check your insurance coverage; most policies do not cover Russia. (Make sure rental coverage includes theft and break-ins.) Since most Moscovites drive without insurance, and driving in Moscow can be a nightmare, it is recommended not to rent a car unless excursions into the countryside are planned. (Gas stations can be hard to find). Always inquire at the hotel. service desk for recommendations. If you do not know the city, it really is easier, safer (and cheaper) to get around with public transportation.

Europcar, locations include Sheremetyevo II International Airport and Domodedovo Airport, and Hotel Courtyard and Hotel Novotel. www.europcar.com.

Hertz, locations include Sheremetyevo II International Airport and Domodedovo Airport, and a main office in town is at 2 Tverskaya Zastava Square. www.hertz.ru.

HEALTH CLUBS/FITNESS CENTERS AND SAUNAS (*BANYAS*)

Most high-end hotel.s offer fitness club facilities, some with pools. For non-guests, some offer a daily entrance fee into the facilities. Some of these hotel.s include: Grand Hotel. Mariott, Metropole (pool), Mezhdunarodnaya (pool), Radisson-Slavyanskaya (pool), Sheraton Palace, and Renaissance (pool). Scores of other health clubs have opened throughout the city, and Moscovites are taking up everything from aerobics to yoga, and paying to be pampered. Always check at your hotel. service desk for recommendations.

Atlantis Fitness Club, 12 Krasnopresenskaya Emb. tel. 967-0373.

Fit & Fun, 12 Chistoprudny Bul. Equipped gym, sauna and steam. Open Monday –Saturday 7am–11pm; Sunday 9am–10pm. Metro Chistiya Pridy; tel. 924-4315.

Gold's Gym, 31 Leningradsky Pr. Monday–Friday 7am–11pm; Saturday/Sunday 9am–10pm. Metro Dynamo; tel. 931-9616; www.goldsgym.com.

Moscow Beach Club, 6 Malaya Dmitrovka. Open 24 hours. Metro Pushkinskaya; tel. 299-5732.

Planet Fitness, 8 Korolenko Ul (and 3 other locations). Open 7am–10.30pm; Saturday/Sunday 9am–9pm. Metro Sokolniki; tel. 964-2405.

World Class Fitness Centers, 3/6-months & one-year memberships also available. Call 234-4590, 239-1994 for locations (six clubs in the city). www.worldclass.ru.

Saunas/Banyas: (see also Special Topic on page 418) Many hotel.s offer sauna facilities. Bring towels and flip-flops. Some favorite Russian *banyas* or bathhouses are:

Bani na Presnye, 7 Stolyarny Per. Cost approx. R400. Open 8am–10pm; Tues 2pm–10pm. Metro Ulitsa 1905 Goda; tel. 253-8690 (women), 255-0115 (men).

Sandunovskiye Bani, 14 Neglinnaya Ul (behind 'Note' Store). Open daily 8am–10pm. Two classes of group saunas from R600-800 per session, together with private ones. Metro Ulitsa Teatralnaya; tel. 925-4631.

Luxe, 19 Starovagankovsky. Open daily 24 hours. Metro Biblioteka Imeni Lenina; tel. 203-0232.

Seleznyovskiye Bani, 15 Seleznyovskaya St. Open 8am–10pm; closed Mondays. Cost R400. Metro Novoslobodkaya; tel. 978-8491/7521.

Astrakhanskiye Bani, 5/9 Astrakhansky Per. tel. 280-4329. Open 8am–11pm; closed Mon. Plainer and less expensive at R170. Metro Prospekt Mira.

Russkaya Banya Istobka (private), 6 Pevchesky Per (inside Expeditsiya restaurant, see p.349). Traditional *banya* with two-hour sessions, including massage; expensive. Metro Kitai-Gorod; tel. 917-9269, 775-6075; www. expedicia.ru.

SPORTS
The Federations of: **Archery** (tel. 201-1991); **Arm Wrestling** (tel. 201-1214); **Badminton** (tel. 201-1435); **Baseball** (tel. 201-1589); **Basketball** (tel. 201-1349); **Boxing** (tel. 201-1122); **Figure Skating** (tel. 201-1356); **Gymnastics** (tel. 201-1342); **Ice Hockey** (tel. 201-0288) (matches are held year-round at Dynamo and Central stadiums); **Orienteering** (tel. 201-1701); **Rugby** (tel. 201-0822); **Russian Track and Field** (tel. 201-0150); and **Weightlifting** (tel. 201-0152) are all found at 8 Luzhnetskaya Emb. Metro Sportivnaya.

Bowling: The popularity of bowling soared in Russia after the 1998 movie of the Coen Brothers, *The Big Lebowski*. **Bi-Ba-Bo**, 9 Karmanitsky, at end of Stary Arbat. tel. 937-4337; **Cosmic Bowling & Entertainment Center**, 18 Lva Tolstovo Ul, open noon–5am. Metro Park Kultury; **Crazy Ball** has a great view of the Moskva River, 16 Krasnopresnenskaya Emb (inside pedestrian bridge). Metro 1905 Goda; **Krali Marco**, 24 3rd Yamskovo Polya Ul. Bowling & Balkan restaurant. Metro Belorusskaya; **Megasfera–Ostankino**, 8a Akademika-Kuroleva Street, 16 lanes, open 24 hours, Metro VDNKh; **Samolyot** (Airplane), 14/1 Presnensky Val, one of biggest bowling centers in town—their 'Island of Entertainment' even has an indoor ferris wheel. Metro 1905 Goda; **V-69**, 69 Vavilova, bowling and a great Mediterranean cuisine restaurant, Metro Profsoyuznaya.

Bicycling: Caravan (tel. 390-4915) and the Russian Bicycle Club (tel. 916-8894, which also has a recording of upcoming bike events) or Moscow Bike Touring Club (267-4468) offer bike tours around the area. If you have access to a bike, touring in the city parks are your best bet. (Moscow has no special bike paths, as in Europe, and it is too dangerous to bike on Russian main roads.) Some good biking locations are: Bitsevsky and Sokolniki Parks, the Botanical Gardens, and Krylatskoye Hills, which was built for the 1980 Olympics and has the only track venue for bike racing.

Checkers and **Chess** can be played at Izmailovsky Park. The Central Chess Club is at 14 Gogolevsky Bulvar, Metro Kropotkinskaya. tel. 291-0641.

Golf: Moscow Country Club has Russia's first pro-18 hole/par-72 course, designed by American Robert Trent Jones, II (see Vicinity section). Located 30 kilometers (18 miles) northwest of the city at 31km Volokolamskoye Hwy. Also has driving range and pro shop; open year round. The Country Club also has a hotel., fitness center and tennis club. tel. 926-5911/5928. The **Moscow City Golf Club** is at 1 Dovzhensko Ul. tel. 143-7210. It has a 9-hole golf course and tennis courts. Metro Kievskaya.

Hiking: The Moscow Central Tourist Club offers weekend hikes, and canoe and bicycle trips. 4 Sadovaya-Kudrinskaya Ul. tel. 203-1094. Metro Barrikadnaya.

Horseback Riding: Horses can be rented in Tsaritsyno Park by the Zoo; and at the **Bitsa Equestrian Sports Center** at 33 Balaklavsky Pr, which has show jumping and an indoor riding school. tel. 318-5744/2277. Metro Kaluzhskaya. The **Hippodrome** also has horse rentals and riding lessons (tel. 945-3224).

Horse Racing takes place at the Hippodrome at 22 Begovaya, usually on Saturday, Sunday and Wednesday. tel. 945-4516/0437. Metro Begovaya. Includes mainly harness and thoroughbred horse racing (small-stake betting), with flat racing, *kachalki*-in lightweight carriages and occasional troika events in winter.

Society of Hunting and Fishing is at 6 Stroitel.ey Ul. tel. 930-4978. Offers a choice of over 100 sport lodges. Metro Universitet. The resort of Zavidovo on the Volga River (see Vicinity Section) also offers hunting and fishing excurions. tel. 539-2044.

Karate Club: 9 Spiridonovka Ul. tel. 291-0825. Metro Arbatskaya.

Karate, Judo and Tensin Club, tel. 499-9010.

Painball Club at Luzhniki. tel. 201-1504/782-7887/423-7822. Metro Sportivnaya.

Ice Skating: Gorky Park in winter months has skate rentals and troika rides. You can also skate at Chistoprudny Blvd (Metro Chistiye Prudy) and Patriarch's Pond (Metro Mayakovskaya). Sokolniki and Tagansky Parks also have skating and rental facilities. Indoor rinks are at Dynamo, 39 Leningradsky Pr. (Metro Aeroport); Kristall at 24 Luzhnetskaya (Metro Sportivnaya); and Sokolniki at 16 Sokolnichesky Val (Metro Sokolniki).

Moscow Marathon Information: tel. 924-0824. Held annually.

Running: The best spots for jogging are within parks, or along the path from Gorky Park to Sparrow Hills. Most of Moscow streets are polluted by heavy traffic. The local Hash House Harriers, a social running club, meets once a week in front of the Ukrainia Hotel; schedules are often listed in the *Moscow Times* bulletin board.

Skiing: Parks Sokolniki, Bittsa and Luzhniki offer cross-country skiing rentals and trails. Cross-country is also popular in nearby Peredelkino. If you have your own gear, practically any park allows skiing in winter. The Alpine Skiing International Club offers ski tours (tel. 276-1565). Four downhill ski facilities are located outside town. About an hour's drive south of the city is **Kant** (7 Elektrolitny Pr, Metro Nagornaya, tel. 939-0037), with several runs and a snowboard half-pipe. The **Krylatskoye Ski Center** (tel. 140-4308) offers mountain (3100-foot slope), cross country, skiing and ice skating. **Ski Park Volen** (1 Troitskaya Ul. tel. 993-9502; www.volen.ru) is an hour's drive north of the city along the Dmitrovskoye Hwy . It has seven ski lifts, over 13 snowboard and ski trails, ice skating, cafes and restaurants, and wooden cottages for rent. **Sorochani**, in Kurovo Village (tel. 363-8961; www .sorochany.ru), has ten runs. For the Federation of **Alpine Skiing**, tel. 201-1771.

Soccer: The teams Asmaral, Dynamo, Lokomotiv Spartak and Torpedo all have their own stadiums. The season is from March to November.

Swimming Pools: **Dom Plavaniya** (Swimming Dome), 32 Ibragimova. One of the biggest swimming complexes in Moscow with two 50-meter and three 25-meter heated indoor pools. About $3/hr. Open daily 6.30am–10.30pm. tel. 369-0649. Metro Izmailovsky Park. **Atlant**, 28 Talalikhina Ul. Moscow's only salt-water pool. $4 for 45 minutes from 8am–4pm and $7 from 4pm–9.30pm. tel. 277-0513. Metro Proletarskaya. **Chaika Sports Complex** (two open-air heated pools, gym, tennis courts, sauna), 1/3 Turchaninov Per. One of most popular of Moscow's pools. Daily 7am–9.30pm, Sun 8.30am–7pm. tel. 246-1344. Metro Park Kultury. **Greenway Pool and Central Army Sports Club**, 39a Leningradsky Pr. tel. 213-2288. Metro Aeroport. **Luzhniki Sport Complex**, 24 Luzhnetskaya Emb. Indoor and outdoor heated pools, $2 for one hour daily from 9am–4pm. tel. 201-1164. Metro Sportivnaya. **Olympic Sports Complex**, 18 Olimpiisky Pr. 25-meter pool and gym/solarium. Costs $3 before 4pm and $4 thereafter and on weekends. Call for times. tel. 288-1333, 786-3216. Metro Prospekt Mira.

The **Olympic Nautical Sports Center** is at 30 Ibragimovia; Metro Semenovskaya. tel. 369-0649. It has eight swimming pools, gym, sauna, massage, aerobics. Daily 7am–10pm.

Tennis: Moscow has numerous tennis facilities. A few of the main centers are at: Tennis Courts in Gorky Park, 9 Krymsky Val, Metro Park Kultury; Luzhniki Druzhba, 10a Luzhnetskaya Emb, Metro Sportivnaya; Moscow Sports Complex, 14 Krasnopresnenskaya Street, Metro Ulitsa 1905 Goda; Russian Tennis Club, 13 Uglichskaya Street, Metro Altufevo; Tennis Center, 19 Kasatkina Street, Metro VDNKh; Tennis Palace, 38 Leningradsky Pr, Metro Aeroport, and Dynamo Tennis Courts at 26 Petrovka, Bldg 9, Metro Chekhovskaya.

View of the Kremlin from the Moskva River. In the center stands the Bell Tower of Ivan the Great and the golden-domed Assumption Cathedral.The eleven small golden turrets on the left belong to the Terem Palace, and the polished silver domes on the right grace the Church of the Twelve Apostles, now housing an art museum.

BANYAS

Nothing gives a better glimpse into the Russian character than a few hours spent in a Russian bathhouse or *banya*. This enjoyable sauna tradition has been a part of Russian culture for centuries. Traditionally each village had its own communal bathhouse where, at different times, males or females would stoke wood-burning stoves and spend hours sitting, sweating and scrubbing. The Greek historian Herodotus reported from Russia in the fifth century BC: 'They make a booth by fixing in the ground three sticks inclined toward one another, and stretching around them wooden felts, which they arrange so as to fit as close as possible; inside the booth a dish is placed upon the ground, into which they put a number of red hot stones; then they take some hemp seed and throw it upon the stones; immediately it smokes, and gives out such a vapor that no Grecian hot mist can exceed; they are immediately delighted and shout for joy, and this hot steam serves them instead of a water bath.' Later, many homes even had their own private *banyas* and during winter naked bodies could be seen rolling in the snow after a well-heated sweat. Today the *banya* ritual is still a much favored pastime; this invigorating washing process has proudly been passed down from generation to generation.

Banya complexes are located throughout Russian cities and towns. Some of the most popular in Moscow are the Sandunovskiye and Bani na Presnye, and in St Petersburg the Nevskiye Bani. Here the bather can spend many a pleasurable hour in the company of fellow hedonists. No *banya* is complete without a bundle of dried birch branches with leaves, called *veniki*, usually sold outside the complex. *Berioza* (birch) has always been a popular symbol of Russia, which claims more birch than any other country in the world. Buy a switch of birch and enter to pay the *banya* fee; the cashier can then point you in the right direction—*muzhchina* (men) or *zhenshchina* (women). Once inside, an attendant is there to assist you.

Many older *banyas* are housed in splendid prerevolutionary buildings; marble staircases, mirrored walls and gilded rooms, though somewhat faded, are filled with steam and cold pools. The best *banyas* even offer massage, facials, and a café. Bring along a towel, shampoo, head-cap and flip-flops; otherwise you can often rent them there. It is recommended to leave valuables behind, or give them to the attendant for safe-keeping if there is no place to lock them up.

There are three main parts of the *banya*: the sitting and changing room, the bathing area and the sauna itself. The bathing area is usually one immense room filled with large benches. Soak your *veniki* in one bucket filled with warm water (it prevents the leaves from falling off), while using another to rinse yourself. Then carry the wet branches into the hot *banya* (start out on the bottom level then slowly work your way up). The custom is to lightly swat the body with the birch branch; this is believed to draw out toxins and circulate the blood. It is also traditional to whack each other, and since you will easily blend in like a native, you may find your *banya* buddy asking if you would like your own back gently swatted!

An old Russian folk-saying claims that 'the birch tree can give life, muffle groans, cure the sick and keep the body clean'. Cries of *oy oy, tak khorosho* (how wonderful) and *s lyokim parom* (have an enjoyable sweat) emanate from every corner. When someone, usually one of the *babushki* (grandmothers) or *dyedushki* (elderly men), get carried away with flinging water on the heated stones, moans of *khavatit* (enough) resound from the scorching upper balconies, when lobster-red bodies come racing out of the hot steamy interior. (Even though temperatures are lower than in Finnish or Turkish saunas, the humidity makes it feel hotter.) Back in the washroom, the bather rinses alternately in warm and cold water or plunges in the cold pool and then uses a loofah for a vigorous rubdown. Go in and out of the steam as often as you like. Afterwards, wrapped in a crisp sheet or towel, your refreshed body returns to the sitting room to relax and sip tea, cold juices, or even beer or vodka. With skin glowing and soul rejuvenated, it is time to take an invigorating walk about the city!

ST PETERSBURG

St Petersburg

The Neva is clad in granite
Bridges stand poised over her waters
Her islands are covered with dark green gardens
And before the younger capital, ancient Moscow
Has paled, like a purple clad widow
Before a new Empress...

Alexander Pushkin

Illuminated by the opalescent White Nights of summer, when the sun hardly sets, then sunk into gloomy darkness in winter, St Petersburg's history is equally juxtaposed with great artistic achievement and violent political upheaval. This p aradoxical place has long inspired a flood of poetry, arts and revolutions, and combines the personality of three unique cities into one. It was Petersburg for the czars, Petrograd for a nation at war, and Leningrad for the followers of the Bolshevik Revolution. A visitor today cannot help but get swept into the remarkable vortex of all three distinctly different atmospheres.

St Petersburg initially sprang from a collision of two very different cultures and adapted the tastes of both East and West to the far northern latitudes. Situated only 800 kilometers (500 miles) south of the Arctic Circle, the population grew up along the shores of the Neva River that winds around the 44 islands which comprise the city, and flows 74 kilometers (46 miles) from Lake Ladoga into the Gulf of Finland. The swift-flowing Neva, contrasted with the wide prospekts and unique architecture, all add to the city's mystery, character and charm.

Strolling along the enchanted embankments at any time of year, the first thing one notices is the incredible light that washes over the city. Joseph Brodsky, the Nobel prize-winning poet who was born in St Petersburg, wrote: 'It's the northern light, pale and diffused, one in which memory and eye operate with unusual sharpness. In this light... a walker's thoughts travel farther than his destination.'

It was Peter the Great who brought the majesty of the West to this isolated northern region. He called his new creation Sankt Pieterburkh, from the Dutch, and named it after Christ's first apostle, his patron saint. The city was one of the first in the world built according to preconceived plans, drawn up by the most famous Russian and European architects of the day. Only nine years after its inception in 1703, Peter the Great moved out of Moscow and proclaimed his beloved city the capital of the Russian Empire; it remained so for 206 years.

Over the next 150 years, sparked by the reigns of two great women—Peter's daughter, Elizabeth I, and then Catherine the Great—St Petersburg became the host to Russia's Golden Age and a Mecca to some of the world's greatest composers, writers, artists and dancers. As the catalyst for Russia's Renaissance, St Petersburg flowered in the music of Tchaikovsky, Glinka and Rimsky-Korsakov; the Ballets Russes of Diaghilev, Pavlova and Nijinsky; in the arts and crafts of Repin, Benois and Fabergé; and in the literature and poetry of Gogol, Dostoevsky and Akhmatova. St Petersburg's first two centuries were forged on beauty, innovation and progress.

But the city, born of a forceful will and determined vision, was also destined to become the cradle of turbulent revolutions. Around the time its name was Russianized to Petrograd during World War I, political and philosophical ideas flourished. By February 1917 the monarchy of Nicholas II had been toppled, and on October 24, 1917, Lenin gave the command for the start of the great October Revolution. The battleship *Aurora* fired a blank shot at the Hermitage—the signal for the beginning of what American writer John Reed termed 'the ten days that shook the world'. Red Army troops stormed the Winter Palace and the Bolsheviks seized control of the new Soviet State.

Practically overnight, Leninist and Communist ideals took the place of czars and the aristocracy. Czar Nicholas II and his family were executed in 1918 to thwart the hopes of a return to Romanov rule. Amidst all this turmoil, Lenin transferred the capital of the new Soviet Union back to Moscow. When Lenin died in 1924, ironically (he had hated the place) the city of Petrograd was renamed Leningrad in his honor.

But an even greater tragedy lurked in the shadows. Hitler invaded the USSR in 1941 and laid siege to the city for 900 days. In three years alone, more than half a million residents died from starvation or in the defense of their city. Then, during the subsequent years of Stalin's Great Terror, many of the city's finest were executed or sentenced to gulags and never heard from again. St Petersburg's monuments not only immortalize its crowning achievements, but also serve as testaments to thousands of persecuted souls.

Much has happened to St Petersburg over the past three centuries. She has lived through revolutions and repression, sieges and purges, isolation and humiliations. But through all of this, the city has retained its propensity for courage and change. The White Nights of her spirit have always shown through the darkness as on a midsummer's night. Subdued for many years by tragedy and war, the fairy-tale Sleeping Beauty has reawoken to find her glorious past, prolific poetry and dedicated subjects intact.

(above) *The front façade of the Pavlovsk Palace (built 1782–86) is graced with a statue of Paul I, a copy of the statue at Gatchina, Paul's other summer residence.*

(opposite) *Russian folk singers perform in front of Catherine's Palace at Tsarskoye Selo.*

Today there is much to behold. One day of sightseeing brings you to the former palaces of Peter the Great, from his first modest cottage on the banks of the Neva River, to his stunning summer palace at Peterhof, modeled on Versailles. The fabulous Hermitage, created by Catherine the Great as her own personal museum, now contains one of the largest and most valuable art collections in the world. The center of Senate Square is marked by the celebrated statue of Peter the Great, known as the Bronze Horseman.

Another day of touring re-creates past splendors and revolutions as you stand in the Winter Palace or onboard the battleship *Aurora*. Nevsky Prospekt, the city's most popular thoroughfare, stretches five kilometers (three miles) from the golden-spired Admiralty to Alexander Nevsky Monastery, one of the largest Russian Orthodox centers in the country. A stroll along the Nevsky and adjoining side streets (many now being converted into pedestrian walkways, brimming with outdoor cafés in summer), or a boat trip through the numerous canals leads you past former palaces of aristocrats and on to the Mariinsky (Kirov) Ballet, where Balanchine and Baryshnikov once danced, or the Maly Theater to hear opera and music written by Stravinsky, Tchaikovsky and Shostakovich.

In 1991, as a grand gesture to honor its historic foundation, the country's second largest city of 4.6 million people won the battle to change its name from Leningrad back to St Petersburg. The new 'Pieter', as residents lovingly call their city, is rising forth to embrace its past and reclaim its heritage. In 1998, the remains of the executed family of Nicholas II were ceremoniously reburied in the Peter and Paul Cathedral. Even though Moscow is still the capital, St Petersburg residents resoundingly prefer their own city. At the Baby Palace, each newborn is honored with a ceremony and medal that reads, Born in St Petersburg. And Russia's current president, Vladimir Putin, who was born in St Petersburg, has one.

Putin's influence has raised the fortunes of the city as it continues to strive for a wider renaissance. For the 2003 tercentenary, the President earmarked $1.5 billion for refurbishments and celebrations, and everyone from world leaders to foreign tourists marveled at the beauty of the newly restored city. Few cities in the world can compare with St Petersburg—in its vast beauty, turbulent history and remarkable endurance of the human spirit. Now the 300-year-old city pushes forward into the 21st century with renewed faith and optimistic vigor. As we embark on our timeless journey through this extraordinary place, let us recall the words of Alexander Pushkin, a long-time resident of the city:

> *Be beautiful, city of Peter*
> *Stay as unshakable as Russia*
> *And let no vain wrath*
> *Ever trouble the eternal dream of Peter.*

HISTORY

The delta at the mouth of the Neva River was settled long before the founding of St Petersburg. The Neva was an important trading route between Northern Europe and Asia. Finns, Swedes and Russians established settlements there at one time or another and frequently fought over the land. In the early 17th century, Russia's Time of Troubles, the nation's military power was so debilitated that Mikhail, the first of the Romanov czars, was forced to sign a treaty ceding the land to Sweden in 1617.

After Peter the Great returned from his tour of Holland, England and Germany, one of his first actions was to oust the Swedes from the Neva delta. In the winter of 1702–3, Russian forces attacked and captured Swedish forts at Nyenshatz, a few miles upstream from the river's mouth, and Noteborg on Lake Ladoga. Peter ordered that the keys to these forts be nailed to their gates. Two keys hanging from a sailing ship became the symbol representing the future of St Petersburg. On May 16, 1703, seven weeks after ousting the Swedes, Peter the Great lay the foundation stone of the Peter and Paul Fortress on an island near where the Neva divides into its two main branches. The primary role of the new settlement was as a military outpost, but right from the beginning Peter had greater designs.

While the construction of the fortress was under way, Peter lived in a rough log cabin nearby and from it planned his future capital. He decided that the hub of the new city was to be on the opposite bank of the Neva, at the present site of the Admiralty. Here he founded Russia's first great shipyard, where he built his navy. But Peter's project was hampered from the start by the occasional flooding of the Neva and by the lack of workers willing to move to the cold and isolated swamp. With typical ruthlessness, he ordered the conscription of 40,000 laborers to lay the foundations and dig the canals. It is estimated that approximately 100,000 people died from disease, exhaustion and floods during the first few years. 'The town is built on human bones,' the saying goes. The construction of the city began along the banks of the river and radiated inland along broad avenues from the shipyards.

In 1712, three years after the Swedes were finally and decisively defeated, Peter the Great decreed that St Petersburg was now the capital of the Russian Empire. Unfortunately, the aristocracy and merchants did not share his enthusiasm. Peter did not have the patience to persuade them, so he simply commanded the 1,000 leading families and 500 of the most prominent merchants to build houses in the new capital. Aside from the Peter and Paul Fortress and Peter's cabin, the notable buildings of this era still standing are the Menschikov and Kikin palaces, the Alexander Nevsky Monastery and the Monplaisir Palace at Petrodvorets. The construction of St Petersburg was the first time—but certainly not the last—that the hand of the State intervened on a national scale in the lives of the Russian masses.

St Petersburg in the early 1800s. A view of the Strelka and lighthouse with the Peter and Paul Fortress in the distance. The city was a busy port even then. In one summer month alone, contrary to the impression given by this painting, over 19,000 ships anchored here from all over the world.

By 1725, the year of Peter's death, St Petersburg had a population of 75,000 unwilling subjects. For the next few years the future of the new capital was shaky due to the lack of Peter's strong hand. The council which then ruled Russia under the 12-year-old Peter II moved the imperial court back to Moscow and thousands of people thankfully left the half-built city. They stayed away until Peter II's early death, after which Empress Anna took the reins and in 1732 decreed that the capital would return to St Petersburg. Under Anna, the second great phase of the construction of St Petersburg began. She hired Bartolomeo Rastrelli, the son of an Italian sculptor hired by Peter the Great, to build her a Winter Palace (no longer standing), the first permanent imperial residence in the city. She also ordered the construction of a 24-meters-long (80-feet) and 10-meters-high (33-feet) ice palace complete with rooms and ice furniture on the frozen Neva. This was built for a courtier who had been unfaithful to her and was forced to marry an ugly Kalmyk tribeswoman from Central Asia in a mock ceremony. They were stripped naked and had to spend the night in the ice palace with only each other for warmth.

Anna died the same winter, and after the brief rule of another child czar, Ivan VI, the extravagant Empress Elizabeth, daughter of Peter the Great, took the throne and built many of the most important buildings in St Petersburg. At this time (1741–61), Rastrelli and other imported European architects had developed a style that later became known as Elizabethan rococo. Like a wedding cake, the basic structures disappeared underneath an ornate icing of pilasters, statuary and reliefs. The other recurrent theme was size. These buildings did not reach for the heavens like the churches of the Moscow Kremlin; they sprawled across acres of flat, empty countryside. Huge architectural clusters like the Winter Palace and the Hermitage and the palaces at Peterhof and Pushkin, all painted an ethereal turquoise, were testament mostly to Elizabeth's power to do as she pleased. By the end of her rule, St Petersburg looked more like a stage set than a working city, with broad avenues built for parades and palaces like props for some grandiose drama.

After Elizabeth's death another weak czar, Peter III, took the throne and soon died after forging an unpopular alliance with Prussia. The scepter was handed to his wife, Catherine II, an independently-minded German princess who ruled the empire for 34 years. Under Catherine, later dubbed 'the Great', St Petersburg solidified its position as the artistic and political center of the empire, as intellectuals flocked to the now-thriving academies of arts and sciences. The latest political ideas from Western Europe were hotly debated among the aristocracy, and the streets and squares of the city were dotted with sculptures crafted by the finest European artists, including the enormous Bronze Horseman sculptural portrait of Peter the Great cast by the Frenchman Falconet. At the end of Catherine's reign in 1796, there was a profound sense of achievement in St Petersburg; in less than a century it had become one of the leading cities in the world. But there was also unease: the winds of change were blowing, and no one knew how to reconcile the new political ideas of St Petersburg with the profoundly conservative and deeply religious Russian countryside.

Catherine's son, the mentally unstable Paul I, built a fortress variously known as the Mikhailovsky or Engineer's Palace to protect himself from conspirators against the throne (see page 518). His paranoia proved justified, because in 1801, just 41 days after he moved in, his own courtiers strangled him to death. His successor was Alexander I, whose liberal reforms during the first half of his reign were wildly popular among the aristocracy and intelligentsia. In 1861, when he emancipated the serfs, thousands of freed families flocked into the capital to try and earn a living. By 1862 St Petersburg had a population of 532,000 and was the fourth largest city in Europe after Paris, London and Constantinople. The latter half of

Alexander's rule was less successful, and a number of revolutionary cells were formed within the aristocracy to overthrow the imperial system. When Alexander died in December 1825, these cells were violently opposed to the accession of his anointed successor, his younger brother Nicholas, who was known to be a conservative and sympathetic to the Prussians. A group of guard officers, later known as Decembrists, took over the Senate Square and demanded a constitutional government. Nicholas ordered the army's cannons to fire on them, and the Decembrists fled in confusion. The main plotters were arrested and interned in the Peter and Paul Fortress (see page 473), where five of them were executed and 115 were sent to Siberia. Later, in 1849, this fortress was also the prison for the writer Fyodor Dostoevsky and the rest of the Petrashevsky Circle of socialist revolutionaries. Under Nicholas' orders they were sentenced to death, led before a firing squad and then reprieved at the last minute and exiled to Siberia. Dostoevsky fashioned his book *Notes from the Underground* after this experience.

The period from Nicholas I through the Russian Revolution in 1917 was an era of more or less constant political repression of the aristocracy and intelligentsia. Paradoxically, in St Petersburg it was the time of a great flowering of creativity that gave us some of the masterpieces of world literature, music and ballet, with writers like Pushkin, Gogol and Dostoevsky; the Mighty Band of the composers Rimsky-Korsakov, Mussorgsky and Borodin; and the choreographers of the Mariinsky Ballet, whose dances are still performed today.

Political turmoil proceeded apace with the artistic ferment during the latter half of the 19th-century. St Petersburg was at the center, and a number of prominent revolutionary theorists, including the anarchist Mikhail Bakunin, and the writer Nikolai Chernyshevsky, spent time in the Peter and Paul Fortress. In March 1881, these activities finally bore fruit when a terrorist cell called the People's Freedom Group succeeded in mortally wounding Czar Alexander II with a bomb on the banks of the Ekaterininsky Canal. This led to more decades of oppression under Alexander III and Nicholas II, which only served to heighten the political unrest. By this time the imperial system was not only unpopular among the St Petersburg elite but throughout Russian society. (See Genealogy on page 706.)

In 1905, Russia was given a portent of its future when a series of strikes by soldiers and workers led to a huge demonstration in St Petersburg. A radical priest named Father Gapon led thousands of workers in a march to the Winter Palace to present a petition to Nicholas II (see page 454). As they entered Palace Square, soldiers opened fire and hundreds of unarmed protesters were killed. 'Bloody Sunday' shocked the nation and galvanized the revolutionary movement. Socialist intellectuals and workers formed mass parties for the first time and demanded a share of the power. Nicholas gave them a weak advisory body named the Duma, which was accepted by the moderates but not by the extreme left, and arrested as many revolutionary rabble-rousers as he could. Trotsky went to jail and Lenin escaped to Switzerland. (See page 551.)

When Russia went to war against Germany in 1914, St Petersburg's name was changed to Petrograd to avoid the Germanic implications of having a 'burg' at the end of its name. World War I was disastrous for the Russian Empire. The long and bloody war in the trenches sapped the economically and politically weak nation. Back in St Petersburg, the czar and the Duma fought for power, while the charismatic priest Rasputin played mind games with the czarina and her circle, and the people starved. On March 12, 1917, the people of the capital rioted. They killed policemen, broke open the jail and set the courthouse on fire. The soldiers stationed in the city refused to quell the rioters; instead they joined them. Three days later the czar abdicated, and Russia was ruled by the Provisional Government led by the socialist leader Alexander Kerensky.

In April 1917, Vladimir Lenin arrived in Petrograd's Finland Station (see page 485) after a decade of exile and plotting and was met by a cheering mass of thousands. From the top of an armored car in front of the station Lenin gave a speech rallying his Bolshevik Party and their allies, the Soviets of Workers and Soldiers, against Kerensky's government. There followed months of agitation and attempted revolution which culminated in the events of the night of November 7, 1917.* The battleship *Aurora*, under the control of the Bolsheviks, fired one blank shell at the Winter Palace giving the signal for the Bolshevik troops to storm the palace and the other principal government buildings. The party of Lenin, Trotsky and Stalin was in command of the Russian Empire. A month later Lenin ordered the formation of the Extraordinary Commission for the Suppression of Counter revolution, the Cheka—later known as the KGB.

For the next three years civil war raged through the nation. The Soviets were attacked first by the Germans, then the White Russian army and the British Royal Navy. During that time Petrograd's population dropped from 2,500,000 to 720,000, due to hardship. In March 1918, Lenin moved the Soviet Government to Moscow because Petrograd was vulnerable to German attack—and perhaps also because of his distaste for the artificial imperial city.

On July 17, 1918, under Lenin's orders, the former Czar Nicholas II, his family and four servants were secretly executed by a Bolshevik firing squad in the town of Yekaterinburg where they had been held in exile after Nicholas' abdication. Their unmarked graves were not discovered until 1991; the remains were reburied in

---

* In 45 BC Julius Caesar introduced the Julian calendar to the Western world. A new reformed calendar was introduced by Pope Gregory XIII in 1582 which calculated time more accurately. By the 20th-century the difference between the Julian and Gregorian calendars was 13 days. Russia continued to use the old Julian calendar until February 1, 1918. This is why the October Revolution came to be celebrated at the beginning of November.

1998 in the Peter and Paul
Cathedral (see page 474).

On Lenin's death in
1924, Petrograd was
renamed Leningrad
after a man who publicly
despised the city and
spent less than a year of his
life there. Ominously, that
same year, there was a great
flood in his namesake city.
During the next two decades
Moscow became the center of
cultural and political life, while
Leningrad became identified as a
center of shipbuilding and
industry. Its tradition
of political

assassination nevertheless continued with the 1934 shooting of Leningrad Party leader Sergei Kirov at the Smolny Institute. Some say that Stalin was behind the, shooting, and he certainly used it as the excuse to start the purges of 1934–6 in which thousands of Communist Party members were killed.

Leningrad received its next great blow during World War II. For 900 days, from September 1941 to January 1944, the German army laid siege to the city and hundreds of thousands of inhabitants died, adding more bones to the foundations. By 1944 there were fewer than 600,000 people left, compared to a 1939 population of 3,100,000. The poet Mandalstam wrote, 'living in St Petersburg is like sleeping in a coffin.' (See pages 449 and 451.)

Adding further to the city's misery, Stalin instigated another purge in 1948–9, known as the Leningrad Affair, in which many of the city's artists and top Party members vanished forever or were sent to Siberia. In this purge it was apparent that the Moscow leadership remained suspicious of the Leningrad Party hierarchy because they retained some of the idealism of the original revolutionaries.

The years following the war were devoted to reconstruction of the city center and the development of huge satellite suburbs to the south. Thankfully, the government banned high-rises in the center, sustaining Catherine the Great's edict that no building should be higher than the Winter Palace.

Under Khrushchev and Brezhnev, Leningrad became even more of a second-rate provincial city. It was forced to concentrate on military matters and industrial accomplishments. By the mid-1970s the population had increased significantly to 4,500,000 people. In the stagnant atmosphere of these ensuing decades the city still nurtured a reactionary climate; this time it was between the suppressed artistic community and the brainwashed bureaucrats. It was no accident that the first major post-Stalinist trial of an artist (the Jewish writer Joseph Brodsky) took place in Leningrad. In 1964, Brodsky was sentenced to Siberian exile (and later expelled from the country); his crime—not having official permission to write poetry. Brodsky wrote about his beloved city: '...during the White Night, let your immovable earthly glory dawn on me, a fugitive.'

Members of the intellectual community were forced to reject professions not officially recognized. Thus to earn a living they had to take on such menial jobs as night-watchmen, janitors, furnace stokers and dock workers, while secretly pursuing their passions. Despite this ironclad curtain, forbidden works were secretly circulated in underground *samizdat* publications. The up-and-coming rock pioneers began *magnitizdat* where homemade music tapes were circulated like manuscripts. The poet Gorgovsky recalled the 1970s in Leningrad as 'dead, inert times, and fatal for art's breathing'.

The stifling censorship and cruel punishment drove many Leningrad artists to alcoholism, madness and even suicide. On top of all this, the unchecked industrial pollution of the city added further to the suffocation of the population.

(previous pages) On May 9 Russia marks Victory Day with a holiday, commemorating the end of World War II which Russians call the Great Patriotic War. Many veterans dress in uniform and wear their medals while marching in parades and visiting war memorials.

THE OLD GUARD

*A*n old man of eighty-four attracted my attention in the Mikhailovsky gardens. He brandished a sabre-shaped walking-stick as he strode down the paths, his war medals dangled in ranks at his chest, and his features showed bellicose above a mist of white beard. He looked like God the Father peering over a cloud.

'I'm an Old Bolshevik,' he announced to me. 'One of the original Revolutionaries!'

A ghost from the twenties, he still exulted in the people's common ownership. He patted the tree trunks possessively as he marched by and frequently said 'This is my tree, and this is my tree.'

In 1907 he had become a revolutionary, and had been sent in chains to Siberia. But a fellow-prisoner, he said, had concealed a file in the lapel of his coat, and together they had cut through the manacles and fled back to Leningrad. Those were the days when Siberian exiles and prisoners— Trotsky, Stalin and Bakunin among them—escaped from Siberia with laughable ease and slipped over frontiers with the freedom of stray cats.

Then the old man had joined the Revolution and fought for the three years against the Whites. He settled into a military stride as he spoke of it, and thrust out his beard like a torpedo, while all the time his gaze flashed and fulminated over the gardens. 'Get off the grass, comrade!' he bellowed. A young mother, seated on the sward beside her pram, looked up in bewilderment. 'Get off our motherland's grass!'

He embodied the intrusive precepts of early Communism, whose zealots were encouraged to scrutinize, shrivel and denounce each other. He was the self-proclaimed guardian and persecutor of all about him, and he entered the 1980s with the anachronism of a mastodon. Farther on a girl was leaning in the fork of one of his precious trees. 'Keep away from there!' he roared. 'Can't you see you're stopping it grow? Get off!' She gaped at him, said nothing, did not move. He marched on unperturbed. He even anathematized a mousing cat. 'What are you looking for, comrade? Leave nature alone!' He did not seem to mind or notice that nobody obeyed him.

We rested under a clump of acacias. 'When I was a boy,' he said, 'I saw these trees planted.' He pointed to the largest of them, which bifurcated into a gnarled arm. 'That tree was no taller than a little lamp-post then. The garden was private, of course, but as a boy I often squeezed in over the railings. The tsar and tsaritsa used to walk here in the summer.' His voice dwindled from an alsatian growl to purring reminiscence. 'Once, while I was hiding in the shrubs, I saw them myself... What were they like? It's hard to recall exactly. But she was a beautiful woman, I remember. She had her hand on his arm. And he seemed very large and handsome, and...' But he never finished. The lurking commissar in him erupted again. 'What are you doing, comrade?' Beneath us, a man was raking weeds out of an ornamental pond. 'How can you weed a lake?'

The gardener looked up stoically. 'I'm at work.'

Work. The magic syllable.

Immediately, as if some benedictory hand had passed its grace across the old man's brow, his expression changed to a look of benign redress. 'Fine,' he murmured, 'work.' For him the word had the potency of 'revolution' or 'collective.' The mousing cat, too, had been at work, I thought, but had been unable to voice this watchword.

Before we parted he said: 'I'll give you my address, not the real one. That's secret. You see,' he repeated, 'I'm one of the Old Bolsheviks.'

I wondered then if he were not deranged. He scribbled out his address on the back of a newspaper, in enormous handwriting. It was only as he was leaving me that I realized from his age that the history he had given me was nonsense. The tsars did not send lone boys of eleven to Siberia.

'How old did you say you were?' I asked. For he looked timeless.

'I know what you're thinking,' he answered. His eyes twinkled at me collusively. 'You Estonians, you're a clever lot. You're thinking that I can't have been sent to Siberia aged eleven. But actually I'm ninety-four...'— and he strode away through the trees.

Colin Thubron, Among the Russians, 1983

Period Of Perestroika

With the advent of Gorbachev and his new policy of perestroika (restructuring), the harsh totalitarian regime that had ruled Leningrad for more than seven decades began to crack. In the 1980s the most popular and controversial TV program in the country, *600 Seconds*, was broadcast from Leningrad. Its brazen reporter Alexander Nevzorov exposed the corruption and misery of the old socialist system; he was hailed as the Russian 'Robin Hood'. The State also allowed long-banned and shelved works to officially appear—everything from film, prose and poetry to music, art and ballet. In the spring of 1987, almost half a century after their completion, Anna Akhmatova's poems *Requiem* and *Poem Without a Hero* were published. Other Leningrad authors such as Mandalstam, Zoshchenko and Nabokov were widely read for the first time. The two émigrés, composer Stravinsky and choreographer Balanchine, were allowed to return and visit the city of their birth, and their creations were played and staged in the Kirov Theater's repertoire.

In 1990, the economic law professor Anatoly Sobchak was elected Leningrad city council chairman. Later, as mayor, he brought about sweeping changes to crumbling Soviet dogma. During the August attempt to overthrow Gorbachev, Mayor Sobchak lead the city back into the political arena, and personally stopped putsch plotters from a planned military takeover of the city. Sobchak had allied himself with Captain Melnikov, the commander of the nearby Kronstadt naval base, and Melnikov had offered to protect Sobchak and the city council within the fortress. Instead of hiding, Sobchak rallied 250,000 residents into Palace Square (the site of past revolutions) in support of Yeltsin. When the coup failed, Sobchak became a national hero, second only to Yeltsin.

In the early years of glasnost (openness), a democratic movement pushed to change the city's name back to St Petersburg. On October 31, 1991 (two months after the attempted coup), Leningrad was officially renamed Sankt Pieterburg. The Nobel prize-winning writer Joseph Brodsky was pleased: 'It is much better for them to live in a city that bears the name of a saint than that of a devil!' By December 1991, the Soviet Union had collapsed.

St Petersburg Today

After the Baltic States broke away from the Soviet Union in May 1991, St Petersburg's presence as a major port increased sharply. The city was once again becoming the country's 'window to the West.' But, hard-liners (calling themselves everything from pro-communists to imperialists and ultra-nationalists) continued to protest the difficult transitions. For example, in 1992, a coupon system for buying rationed food products was being used—forty percent of the city's budget

Nicknamed the "Venice of the North, St Petersburg is intersected by three main canal systems, known as the Moika, Griboyedov and Fontanka.

went just to subsidizing meat. But, the city forged ahead with democratic reforms. St Petersburg was the first city in the new Russia to sell government-owned shops to private enterprises, open joint-ventures, and create a private banking sector. A stock and commodities market opened in the original 18th-century Stock Exchange. 'I believe the worst is over,' Mayor Sobchak announced a few years later from his Smolny Institute office. 'Privatization is moving along fast and we are slowly converting factories, which used to serve the defense industry, to making essential products for the city.' The mayor also returned many of the churches and religious buildings to the Orthodox Church, and innovative new theaters and artistic endeavors were opened throughout the city. St Petersburg began to re-evolve into the cultural and spiritual capital of her former years.

By 1996, the mayor was replaced by his deputy, Vladimir Yakovlev. Within the next several years, Yakovlev managed to balance the budget (even though he was accused of corruption) and garner a European bond backing—allowing for some major repairs of the city's wealth of architectural monuments. (Over 15,000 historic palaces, mansions, museums and theaters have deteriorated over time, and the city still depends on the West for further funding to help preserve these landmarks and solve its ecological woes.) In March 1997, two centuries after the original patrols were created, the new *gorodovoy* ceremoniously marched down Nevsky Prospekt. These patrolmen, whose sole duty it is to make foreigners welcome, have extensive knowledge of the city and environs.

PETER THE GREAT (1672–1725)

Peter the Great, one of Russia's most enlightened and driven rulers, pulled his country out of her dark feudal past into a status equal with her European neighbors. Possessing an intense curiosity toward foreign lands, he opened Russia's window to the West and became the first ruler to journey extensively outside Russia. Standing at six feet seven inches, with a passionate will and temper to match his great size, Peter I, against all odds, also built a city that became one of the most magnificent capitals in all of Europe.

Peter's father, Czar Alexei, ruled the Empire from 1645 to 1676. Alexei's first wife had 13 children; but only two, Fyodor and Ivan, were destined to inherit the throne. Natalya Naryshkin became Alexei's second wife and gave birth to a son named Peter in 1672.

When Alexei died, his son, Fyodor III, succeeded to the throne and reigned from 1676 to 1682. During this time, his half-brother, Peter, along with ill-favored Natalya, were sent away from Moscow to live in the country. Instead of the usual staunch upbringing within the Kremlin walls, Peter had the freedom to roam the countryside and make friends with peasant children. When Fyodor died, a rivalry broke out between the two families as to which son would gain the throne. Peter won the first battle and was proclaimed czar at the age of ten. But soon Ivan's side of the family spread rumors to the Streltsy, or Musketeers (the military protectors of Moscow), that the Naryshkins were plotting to kill Ivan. The Streltsy demanded that Peter's half-brother be crowned, too. So, for a time, the throne of Moscovy was shared by the two boys, the feeble-minded Ivan V and the robust Peter I. In actuality, however, it was Sophia, Peter's older half-sister, who ruled as Regent for seven years with the help of her lover, Prince Golitsyn.

Peter spent most of this time back in the country, mainly engaged in studies that had a practical use. One fateful day, on his father's estate in Izmailovo, the young boy discovered a wrecked English boat that could sail against the wind. He had the boat repaired and learned how to sail it. In 1688, Peter built a flotilla on Plescheyevo Lake at Pereslavl-Zalessky to practice his ideas for a future navy. Infatuated now with sailing, he also immersed himself in the study of mathematics and navigation and tried to instill a maritime spirit into the whole of society. Naval training courses and marine sports clubs were offered to nobles, and jobs as seamen opened to the lower classes. Later, St Petersburg became one of the most important trading ports on the Baltic.

In addition, the young czar worked well with his hands and became an accomplished carpenter, blacksmith and printer; he even mended his own clothes. As a child, he loved to play soldiers, and drilled his companions in military maneuvers, eventually staging mock battles with weapons and in uniforms supplied by the Royal Arsenal. Peter was also fascinated with the techniques of torture. Later in his reign, fearing an assassination attempt, he would torture his first son, Alexei, to death.

Sophia was eventually removed from court affairs and sent off to live in Novodevichy Convent outside Moscow. When Ivan died, Peter I, at the age of 22, assumed the throne as the sole czar and took up his imperial duties with earnest. On the throne, his first real battle was against the Turks. His plan was to take the Sea of Azov at the mouth of the Don in order to gain access to the Black Sea. Peter built a fleet of ships, and for the first time in her history, Russia led a surprise attack from the water. The Turks were defeated in 1696 and Russia had her first southern outlet to the sea.

After this successful campaign, Peter set off on a long journey to the West. He traveled to England, France, and Germany, and worked as a shipbuilder in Holland. Back home, the Streltsy, with the help of Sophia, began to organize a secret revolt to overthrow the czar. Peter caught wind of their plans; upon his return, he captured and tortured almost 2,000 men and dissolved the corps. By this time, the now cultured ruler had lost interest in his first wife and sent her off to a convent in Sergiyev Posad, the equivalent of divorce.

Peter was greatly impressed by Western ways and, to him, change symbolized Russia's path to modernization. Knee-length coats became the new fashion. One of the new State laws prohibited the growing of beards. Since the Church taught that man was created in God's image (ie with a beard), many believed Peter I to be the Antichrist. In addition, in the same year (1700), after centuries of celebrating the Russian New Year on September 1 (after crop harvests were completed), Peter I changed New Year's day to fall on January 1, to coincide with the West.

Peter the Great in England, painted by Sir Godfrey Kneller in 1698

But Peter was as determined as ever to pull Russia out of her isolation. He tolerated new religions, allowing the practices of Catholics, Lutherans and Protestants, and even approving of the sacrilegious scientific stance taken by Galileo. He exercised State control over the Russian Orthodox Church by establishing the Holy Synod. This supremacy of the czar over the Russian Church lasted from 1721 until 1917. In 1721, Peter also declared himself Emperor of All Russia.

During the Great Northern Wars, while trying to chase the Swedes out of the Baltic, Peter organized the building of the first Russian fleet on the Gulf of Finland. After conquering the Swedes in 1709, the Russian navy returned to the city where thousands of citizens lined the Neva River embankments to cheer the victorious ships. (To this day, St Petersburg celebrates Navy Day, the last Sunday in July, when the naval fleet is paraded down the Neva.) Engravings of the city filled with ships decorated the proud czar's palaces. It was during this time that Peter met and fell in love with a good-natured peasant girl named Catherine, whom he later married; Empress Catherine ruled for two years after his death.

In 1703, Peter began the fanatic building of a new city in the north at a point where the Neva River drained into Lake Ladoga. The city was constructed on a myriad of islands, canals and swamps. The conditions were brutal and nearly 100,000 perished the first year alone. But within a decade, St Petersburg was a city of 35,000 stone buildings and the capital of the Russian Empire. Peter commissioned many well-known foreign architects: the Italian Rastrelli, the German Schlüter, the Swiss Trezzini and the Frenchman Leblond, who created Peter's Summer Palace of Petrodvorets. Montferrand later designed St Isaac's Cathedral, which took over 100 kilos of gold and 40 years to build. Peter brought the majesty of the West to his own doorstep. It was no small wonder that St Petersburg was nicknamed the Venice of the North.

Peter died looking out from his window to the West. Today in St Petersburg stands a monument to the city's founder, a statue of Peter the Great as the Bronze Horseman. The statue, made by the French sculptor, Falconet, shows Peter rearing up on a horse that symbolizes Russia, while trampling a serpent that opposes his reforms. Pushkin wrote that Peter 'with iron bridle reared up Russia to her fate'. By a great and forceful will, Peter the Great had successfully led Russia out of her darkness into the light of a Golden Age.

To usher in St Petersburg's 300th anniversary in 2003, the city selected an anthem, composed from a movement in the ballet, *The Bronze Horseman*, written in 1949 by Belgian-born Russian composer Reinhold Gliere. In 2001, the St Petersburg Union of Composers chose the opening stanzas from Alexander Pushkin's famous poem, after which the ballet is named, and set them to Gliere's music. However, they realized that in order to fit the meter of the music, Pushkin's famous words would have to be edited; but no one dared edit Pushkin, the national poet. So St Petersburg mayor Yakovlev staged a contest stating, "The lyrics have to be ceremonial, patriotic and fit well with the music." In all, 341 different texts were submitted from poets and teachers to pensioners and homemakers. The chosen winner was local poet, Oleg Chuprov, who worked for three months on ten versions. He said, "For me, an anthem is something that should unite people. It is like a confession of love." He received a prize of "30 minimum wages", or about R13,500 ($425). A special choir sang the city's praises during the 300th anniversary celebrations.

This magnificent and soulful city seems to have always been trying to find a balance between order and chaos. With newfound freedoms, the artistic and business communities (where many *biznesmeni* have become multi-millionaires overnight) are thriving. But a grimmer reality, formed by the many changes and market reforms, also exists. With escalating inflation many residents, especially the elderly, struggle daily just to survive (they receive a pension of less than $100 per month). But despite the difficulties, the city's inhabitants remain hopeful. 'Of course it's still a crazy time, but a new nation is being born,' observed the mayor. 'Considering the conditions that were overcome to even build this city, the St Petersburg tradition will surely guide us.'

After 300 years St Petersburg still exultantly stands at the forefront of determination and progress. Legend has it that as long as the statue of the Bronze Horseman remains in its place overlooking the Neva River, St Petersburg will never falter.

And high above him all undaunted
Deaf to the storm's rebellious roars
With hand outstretched, the Idol mounted
On steed of bronze, majestic soars.

Alexander Pushkin (see page 625)

CULTURE

A political and social history tells only half the story of St Petersburg. Of equal consequence are the literary and artistic creations set in St Petersburg, because in them writers and artists have created a parallel city that lives just as much in the minds of the inhabitants as today's crowded, slightly faded metropolis. Since the reign of Elizabeth, the realms of fiction, poetry, symphony, opera and ballet have all collaborated to produce an intellectual St Petersburg that is one of the great artistic creations of humankind.

LITERATURE

In the earliest years of St Petersburg, Peter the Great emphasized the practical sciences, particularly engineering, and his image of the city as a glorified barracks left little room for the arts. St Petersburg's first great contributor to Russian culture, Mikhail Lomonosov, arrived in the city in 1736 and went on to become the director of the Academy of Sciences.

Lomonosov was a kind of Russian Benjamin Franklin—a chemist, physicist, geologist, educator, historian and poet. He had also studied in the West and was a friend of the French philosopher Voltaire. Lomonosov devoted his life to bringing the ideas of the European Enlightenment to Russia and at the same time tried to advance Russia's cultural thought in distinctly Russian ways. His greatest achievement in the cultural sphere was his Russian grammar, which codified and encouraged the use of the language of the common people in Russian literature.

If Lomonosov was the genius of the 18th century, then Alexander Pushkin was the soul of the 19th-century. Pushkin was born into an aristocratic family; his mother was the granddaughter of Peter the Great's Abyssinian general, Hannibal, and the poet was proud of his nobility and African blood. In 1811, Pushkin was sent to the school at Tsarskoye Selo (also called Pushkin, see page 588) where he began to write light romantic poetry. In his 20s he led a life of aristocratic dissoluteness in the salons and bordellos of the imperial capital. Many of his friends were politically active young officers associated with the Decembrist group, which Pushkin was never asked to join because they considered him too frivolous for their revolutionary mission. Nevertheless, he wrote some mildly seditious poems; one of them, *Ruslan and Ludmilla*, caused such a stir with the younger generation that it was censored by Alexander I, who also exiled the poet to the Caucasus in 1820.

During his exile from St Petersburg he wrote some of his most famous works, including his epic *Boris Godunov*, the story of the pretender to the Russian throne

The popular Propaganda Restaurant is housed in a renovated 19th-century building, situated along the Fontanka Canal off of Nevsky Prospekt.

at the start of the Time of Troubles in the early 17th century. At the end of his exile Pushkin began his masterpiece *Eugene Onegin*, a novel in verse about two star-crossed lovers, Onegin and Tatyana. His famous novel *Queen of Spades* came out in 1833; the gambler Ghermann symbolized the secret craving of the people to take a hand in the gamble of winning freedom during an opportunistic age. That same year Pushkin completed his last narrative poem *The Bronze Horseman*, revered as one of the greatest works about St Petersburg (see page 625). In it a young government clerk watches a huge storm cause a flood in St Petersburg which destroys most of the city and kills thousands, including his fiancée. Driven mad by grief, he comes upon Falconet's statue of Peter the Great, the Bronze Horseman, and he associates Peter's terrible imperial power with the destructive force of the flood. The mad clerk shakes his fist at the statue, and the horseman comes to life in a rage and chases him out of the square with a great clattering of bronze hoofs. In 1836, Pushkin was mortally wounded in a pistol duel over his wife's honor and died on January 29 1837 (old-style calendar) at the age of 37. Immediately upon his death he was lionized as the greatest Russian writer and that acclaim continues to this day. He was buried in Pskov near the family's Mikhailovskoye Estate in the Svyatogorsky Monastery. In 1999, Russia celebrated the 200th anniversary of their beloved poet's birth. Pushkin in his own words had predicted:

> *News of me then will cross the whole of Russia*
> *And every tribe there will have heard my name...*
> *And they will all love me, because my songs.*
> *Evoked some kindness in a cruel age.*

Pushkin's mantle was inherited by Nikolai Gogol, a Ukrainian-born writer. Upon Pushkin's death, Gogol declared, 'In him, as in a dictionary, is contained all the riches, the strength and flexibility of our tongue. Pushkin is a rare and perhaps unique phenomenon of the Russian spirit... I did not write a single line without imagining him standing before me.' In his play *The Inspector General*, Gogol satirized the vast bureaucratic state that had taken over the Russian Empire. His famous short story *The Overcoat* is more enigmatic. A petty government clerk in St Petersburg invests all his savings in a new overcoat, but as he is returning home late at night he loses it to a band of robbers. After he discovers that none of his superiors will help him find his coat he dies of grief, only to reappear on the streets of St Petersburg as an avenging ghost. Gogol followed *The Overcoat* with *Dead Souls* (see Excerpt on page 208), which was to be the first volume of a projected trilogy envisioned as a sort of Russian divine comedy about sin, atonement and salvation. As Gogol wrote the second volume he began to go mad, thinking that the flames of hell were licking at his heels, and eventually threw the pages into the fire. He died in 1852, at the age of 43, after doctors applied leeches and bled him to death. Gogol was regarded as the greatest satirist of the regime of Nicholas I, thus, the government allowed no obituary or public tribute to be printed.

'Just imagine: the censorship here already forbids all mention of his [Gogol's] name!' wrote Ivan Turgenev, one of Russia's finest prose writers. In protest, he wrote the eulogy, *In Memory of Gogol*, in which he also symbolized the plight of the oppressed Russian peasant and his opposition to serfdom. After it was circulated in 1852, Czar Nicholas I exiled Turgenev from St Petersburg to his country estate.

Born in the Ukraine in 1818 to a rich aristocratic family, Turgenev graduated from Moscow University and later St Petersburg University's Philosophy Department. By the time of his graduation, he had already authored numerous plays, poems and novels (including *A Month in the Country*, *The Boarder*, *Mumu* and *First Love*), but it was his collection of short stories, *Notes of a Hunter* (*Zapiski Okhotnika*), which brought him national acclaim. A great critic of the socio-political and revolutionary climate of his time (serfs were finally emancipated in 1861), his other popular writings include, *Diary of a Superfluous Man* (1850), *Rudin* (1856), *Nakanune* (On the Eve, 1860), *Dym* (Smoke, 1867), and his last novel, *Virgin Soil* (1877).

With over 100 works, Turgenev is probably best remembered for his novel, *Father and Sons* (1862),

Statue of Alexander Pushkin in St Petersburg's Arts Square.

which incorporated his three favorite themes: the tumultuous political protests and changes within Russia; the blind, impersonal force of nature; and the overriding importance of love in human relations. Before his death in 1883, Turgenev wrote of his deep love for his country, 'Russia can go without each of us, but none of us can go without her.' He is buried in the Volkov cemetery.

The next great St Petersburg writer was Fyodor Dostoevsky, who although anguished and epileptic managed to live a full lifespan. Dostoevsky studied to be a military engineer and fell in with the Petrashevsky Circle of socialist revolutionaries in St Petersburg. After being condemned to death and reprieved at the last minute, Dostoevsky was exiled to Omsk in Siberia for four years. When he returned he wrote *Memories from the House of the Dead* about his Siberian experiences, and the acclaim at its publication in 1860

A bronze bust of Fyodor Dostoevsky (1821–81) graces his tomb in the cemetery of St Petersburg's Alexander Nevsky Monastery.

launched his career as a writer. Most of Dostoevsky's novels were written in serial form for magazines so he could stay one step ahead of his many creditors. He took his subject matter from popular melodramas and sensational newspaper stories and wrote about them with the methods of psychological realism, a form that he pioneered. His greatest novel, *Crime and Punishment*, tells the story of Raskolnikov, an impoverished former student who murders an old woman—a pawnbroker, and feels such guilt that by the time he is finally brought to justice he welcomes it.

Late in life Dostoevsky became a devout believer in Orthodox Christianity. Luckily for world literature he never lost his commitment to artistic realism, so his novels show the passionate struggle of trying to reach, but never attain, an ideal goal. When Dostoevsky died in 1881, thousands of Russians, ordinary citizens and fellow writers alike, accompanied his coffin to the Alexander Nevsky Monastery for a hero's burial.

Anton Chekhov (1860–1904), famous for such plays as *The Cherry Orchard* and *The Seagull*, had his first stories published in St Petersburg magazines. As a realist, he expressed human drama in plain and simple words. He also loved contributing

A CULTURAL EXTRAVAGANZA

*I*n *the season of 1903–4 Petersburg witnessed concerts in the grand manner. I am speaking of the strange, never-to-be surpassed madness of the concerts of Hoffmann and Kubelik in the Nobility Hall during Lent. I can recall no other musical experiences, not even the premiere of Scriabin's* Prometheus, *that might be compared with these Lenten orgies in the white-columned hall. The concerts would reach a kind of rage, a fury. This was no musical dilettantism: there was something threatening and even dangerous that rose up out of enormous depths, a kind of craving for movement; a mute prehistorical malaise was exuded by the peculiar, the almost flagellant zeal of the halberdiers in Mikhaylovsky Square, and it whetted the Petersburg of that day like a knife. In the dim light of the gas lamps the many entrances of the Nobility Hall were beset by a veritable siege. Gendarmes on prancing horses, lending to the atmosphere of the square the mood of a civil disturbance, made clicking noises with their tongues and shouted as they closed ranks to guard the main entry. The sprung carriages with dim lanterns slipped into the glistening circle and arranged themselves in an impressive black gypsy camp. The cabbies dared not deliver their fares right to the door; one paid them while approaching, and then they made off rapidly to escape the wrath of the police. Through the triple chains the Petersburger made his way like a feverish little trout to the marble ice-hole of the vestibule, whence he disappeared into the luminous frosty building, draped with silk and velvet.*

The orchestra seats and the places behind them were filled in the customary order, but the spacious balconies to which the side entrances gave access were filled in bunches, like baskets, with clusters of humanity. The Nobility Hall inside is wide, stocky, and almost square. The stage itself takes up nearly half the area. The gallery swelters in a July heat. The air is filled with a ceaseless humming like that of cicadas over the steppe.

Osip Mandelstam, The Noise of Time, *1922*

to the city's monarchist daily newspaper *Novoye Vremya* (*New Times*), which even the czar read. From 1885 to 1888, Chekhov wrote more than 300 stories for the St Petersburg weekly magazine *Fragments*.

In 1906, the twenty-six-year-old writer and poet Alexander Blok was published in the St Petersburg weekly periodical *Niva*. He soon ignited the new Symbolist movement that heralded Russia's Silver Age of Literature. After many years of classical and realist prose, readers regained an interest in poetry, not popular since the era of Pushkin. Many of the symbolists looked upon the Revolution as an event that would purge Russia of its sins and bring on a new era of wholesome equality. Poets readily participated in political and spiritual themes that thrived in the dissident and decadent atmosphere of the times.

Blok's poems were also filled with erotic and romantic motifs, and the handsome blonde poet soon had a massive cult following among the female population. (His first book of poetry was *Verses on the Beautiful Lady* in 1904.) But soon frustrated with the new Soviet regime, Blok wrote the narrative epic poem *The Twelve* in 1918, about an army patrol who transform into the twelve apostles while walking through ruined Petrograd after the Revolution; led by Christ, they hope for redemption. A year later, Blok was arrested by the Cheka police for participating in anti-Soviet conspiracies. He was eventually released, but as he later wrote to a friend: 'I'm suffocating... and the old music is gone.' Broken, Blok never again picked up his pen. When he died in Leningrad on August 7 1921, at the age of 40, his friends knew that the lack of creative freedom had stifled his spirit. The obituary in *Pravda* for one of the greatest poets of the 20th century was composed of one sentence: 'Last night the poet Alexander Blok passed away.' His poem *The Artist* ends with:

> The wings have been clipped and the song sung—so often
> Does it please you to stand by the sill in the sun?
> The song gives you pleasure? But, I, in exhaustion,
> Wait, bored as before, for a new one to come.

Two weeks after Blok's funeral Nikolai Gumilyov, the ex-husband of the poet Anna Akhmatova, was arrested on false charges by Bolshevik police for participating in anti-Soviet propaganda. Before his arrest Gumilyov had written a poem called *The Streetcar Gone Astray*, about the outcome of the Revolution. He was executed by firing squad without a trial. Prior to the Revolution he had founded a new poetry movement in St Petersburg known as Acmeism. Their idea was to reject the ethereal aspects of symbolism and write about the direct and tangible 'salty skin of the earth'.

The cofounder of the Acmeist movement, Osip Mandalstam, possessed a prophetic understanding of the country's suffering and fate as expressed in his three collections of poetry: *Stone*, *Tristia* and *Poems*. Mandalstam also did not escape persecution under Stalin, and was eventually sentenced to five years hard labor for counterrevolutionary activities. He died in 1938 from heart failure in a freezing transit camp in Vladivostok, Siberia. His widow Nadezhda Mandalstam wrote an incredibly moving memoir about her life with Osip. It was published in two large volumes entitled *Hope Against Hope* and *Hope Abandoned*.

With these quintessential St Petersburg poets dead, the new regime severely underscored the fact that the cultural elite would be under their control. Not able to live with his own disillusionment, the futurist poet Vladimir Mayakovsky shot himself while playing Russian roulette at the age of 36. His suicide stunned an already desolate nation. It was Anna Akhmatova who took up the poetic reins during these times of terror. (See Special Topic on page 620)

Her contemporary, Vladimir Nabokov, made his debut as a poet in St Petersburg, though he emigrated to Europe in 1919 and then in 1940 to America. Born in the city in 1899, Nabokov frequently used St Petersburg as a theme for his stories. Some of his classic works include *Pale Fire*, *Pnin*, *Laughter in the Dark* and *Lolita*—later made into a film by Stanley Kubrick. Nabokov's brilliant autobiography *Speak, Memory* was one of the first contemporary books to introduce the city of St Petersburg to an international audience.

In 1903, Ivan Bunin won the Pushkin Prize for Literature, and in 1909, was elected to the Academy of Sciences in St Petersburg. Like Turgenev and Chekhov, Bunin portrayed the reality of Russian life while encompassing the themes of universal human passions and struggles. Some of his works include, *The Village* (1910), *Dry Valley* (1911), *The Brothers* (1914) and *Nooselike Ears* (1916). In the wake of the Russian revolution, Ivan Bunin (then aged 48) and his wife fled to the Black Sea port of Odessa. Living here during the years of 1918 and 1919 (before they emigrated to France), Bunin kept a diary of his observations on revolutionary events entitled *Cursed Days*, in which he reflected, 'I will never accept that Russia has been destroyed... Socialism contradicts and is completely unsuited to the human soul.' He predicted, only wrong in his timing, that 'in twenty five years, the passion for individualism would rise from the ashes of communism.' In 1933, Bunin received the Nobel Prize for Literature, the first Russian writer to ever be awarded this honor.

With Akhmatova's death in 1966, the one heroic figure that had connected the three eras of St Petersburg, Petrograd and Leningrad was gone. Joseph Brodsky, born on Vasilyevsky Island in 1940, was considered the heir apparent to both Nabokov and Akhmatova. But, in 1964, the writer and poet was sentenced to five years hard labor in the Arctic Circle for writing poetry without official permission.

Interrogated at the trial about where his poetry came from, he replied: 'I thought that it came from God.' After being imprisoned three times and twice thrown into a madhouse for his writings, Brodsky was finally expelled from the Soviet Union in 1972. He wrote:

> I let the burnished gaze of the warden into my dreams.
> Gnawed the bread of exile, leaving no crusts.
> I allowed my chords to voice every sound, but for howls:
> I switched to a whisper. Now I am forty.
>
> May, 24, 1980.

The old regime tried to erase his existence from history, but Brodsky received international acclaim when he won the Nobel Prize for Literature in 1987. He became an American citizen in 1980 and died in New York in 1995. In Brodsky, Leningraders felt that the Nobel prize also honored the other literary geniuses who were never recognized by their own country.

In 1964, shocked by Brodsky's trial, the writer Andrei Bitov began work on his novel *Pushkin House*, a requiem for the disillusioned St Petersburg intelligentsia. The novel's hero works at Leningrad's Pushkin House, the research academy of Russian literature. Bitov uses this theme to interweave writings by many of the city's past respected authors—from Pushkin to Akhmatova. It was published in 1978 by an American publishing house, but was not allowed past Soviet censors until 1987, when it immediately became a sensation during Gorbachev's glasnost era.

Another work that had laid in a desk drawer for 20 years, and also finally was published in 1987, was *Children of the Arbat* by Anatoly Rybakov, one of the milestones of perestroika. The novel was fairly autobiographical—in 1933 Rybakov was arrested and sentenced to three years in exile for obscure counter-revolutionary activities. He eventually joined the army during WWII and participated in the storming of Berlin. The book was the first literary description of Stalin's regime and the era of Soviet stagnation. It was ardently read and passed from hand-to-hand in underground xeroxed *samizdat* fashion. In 1999, Rybakov died in his sleep, at the age of 87.

By 1990 many long-banned works by authors such as Nabokov, Pasternak, Akhmatova and even Solzhenitsyn were allowed to be published and distributed among a new generation of Russian readers. Many foreign authors were also translated into Russian for the first time. But ironically, with the demise of socialism, the Writers' Union and most State-subsidized publishing also collapsed. Post-perestroika Russia appeared just as devastated as its corrupt Communist shadow; this time however, instead of for political reasons, contemporary writers were stifled out of economic needs.

In the early 1990s, the International Booker Prize Committee instituted a special Smirnov-Booker Russian novel prize to annually recognize the new generation of Russian writers. In 1999, Mikhail Butov (a former TV antenna repairman) won the $12,500 prize for his novel *Svoboda* (Liberty). The novel tells the story of the country's first liberated generation (born in the 1960s) who grew up in the final era of Soviet stagnation and passed into adulthood during the reform years of the late 1980s. Butov's protagonist blindly follows his friend Andrukha on wild adventures around the newly liberated country, yet remains apprehensive about the looming capitalist reality. He wants out of the old way of life, but does not yet know how to fit into the new climate the tumultuous changes have created. 'Unfortunately,' Butov explained, 'winners of the Russian Booker don't automatically see their books printed in huge print runs... *Svoboda* was first printed in 2,500 copies. It was only in the Soviet past that books were printed in the millions!' In 2005, a new literary contest was unveiled, entitled the Bunin Prize, which emphasizes the revival of the best traditions of Russian literature. Offering 20,000 Euros for the winner, it's become the heftiest of Russia's literary awards.

In Soviet times, there were some 230 publishing houses (every book had to pass through the censors); presently, there are well over 10,000 registered publishing agencies. But, today, even with all the current literary freedoms and publications, an ordinary reader cannot even afford to buy books. A monthly subscription to the popular literary journal, *Novy Mir* or 'New World' (for which Butov is managing editor), now costs more than the average Russian pension. In the early 1990s, it had a circulation of 2.75 million readers, today it is down to 25,000. (Even the readership of *Pravda* has dropped from nine million to 100,000.) The middle class buy on average five books a year, while no one knows how many books the richer *Noviye Russkiye* (New Russians) care to read.

With the advent of a new century, however, Russian literature has slowly begun to recover with a revitalized exuberance and freshness of vision. Aside from the classics and innovative contemporary novels (such as Victor Pelevin's *Buddha's Little Finger*, *Omon Ra*, and *Generation P* (Babylon)), even pulp fiction, romance (nicknamed 'love-burgers' for the way they are mass produced—like fast-food) and detective novels (the latter claims a whopping 38 percent of the Russian fiction market; science fiction and mysticism, a 26 percent share) have become more popular than ever. Among Russia's best-selling authors is Grigory Chkhartashvili, whose pen name, Boris Akunin, is a play on words for the 19th-century Russian anarchist Mikhail Bakunin. Akunin's first detective novel, *The Winter Queen*, is set in both Moscow and St Petersburg. The central charismatic character, Erast Petrovich Fandorin, begins his adventures in 1876, the day of Bakunin's death. Many of Akunin's novels have now been translated into English.

THE PETITION OF JANUARY 9, 1905

A Most Humble and Loyal Address of the Workers of St Petersburg Intended for Presentation to HIS MAJESTY on Sunday at two o'clock on the Winter Palace Square.

SIRE:

We, the workers and inhabitants of St Petersburg, of various estates, our wives, our children, and our aged, helpless parents, come to Thee, O SIRE, to seek justice and protection. We are impoverished; we are oppressed, overburdened with excessive toil, contemptuously treated. We are not even recognized as human beings, but are treated like slaves who must suffer their bitter fate in silence and without complaint. And we have suffered, but even so we are being further pushed into the slough of poverty, arbitrariness, and ignorance. We are suffocating in despotism and lawlessness. O SIRE, we have reached that frightful moment when death is better than the prolongation of our unbearable sufferings.

Hence, we stopped work and told employers that we will not resume work until our demands are fulfilled. We did not ask much; we sought only that without which there is no life for us but hard labor and eternal suffering. Our first request was that our employers agree to discuss our needs with us. But even this we were refused. We were prohibited even from speaking of our needs, since no such right is given us by law. The following requests were also deemed to be outside of the law: the reduction of the work day to eight hours; our manual participation in determining the rates for our work and in the settlement of grievances that might arise between us and the lower managerial staff; to raise the minimum daily wages for unskilled workers, and for women as well, to one ruble; to abolish overtime work; to give our sick better medical attention without insults; and to arrange our workshops so that we might work there without encountering death from murderous drafts, rain, and snow.

According to our employers and managers, our demands turned out to be illegal, our every request a crime, and our desire to improve our conditions an insolence, insulting to them. O SIRE, there are more than 300,000 of us but we are human beings in appearance only, for we, with the rest of the Russian people, do not possess a single human right, not even the right to speak, think, gather, discuss our needs, and take steps to improve our conditions. We are enslaved, enslaved under the patronage and with the aid of Thy officials. Anyone of us who dares to raise his voice in defense of the working class and the people is thrown into jail or exiled. Kindheartedness is punished as a crime. To feel sorry for a worker as a downtrodden, maltreated human being bereft of his rights is to commit a heinous crime! The workers and the peasants are delivered into the hands of the bureaucratic administration, comprised of embezzlers of public funds and robbers, who not only care nothing for the needs of the people, but flagrantly abuse them. The bureaucratic administration brought the country to the brink of ruin, involved her in a humiliating war, and is leading Russia closer and closer to disaster. We, the workers and people, have no voice whatsoever in the spending of huge sums collected from us in taxes. We do not even know how the money, collected from the impoverished people, is spent. The people are deprived of the opportunity to express their wishes and demands, to participate in the establishment of taxes and public spending. The workers are deprived of the opportunity to organize their unions in order to defend their interests.

O SIRE, is this in accordance with God's laws, by the grace of which Thou reignest? Is it possible to live under such laws? Would it not be preferable for all of us, the toiling people of Russia, to die? Let the capitalists—exploiters of the working class and officials, the embezzlers and plunderers of the Russian people, live and enjoy their lives.

Translated by Walter Sablinsky

Translated foreign works by leading authors, such Tom Clancy and Barbara Cartland (nicknamed 'Baba Katya'), and works on new technologies (such as the 'for Dummies' series—*dlya Chainikov*) are also widely read. As one noted Russian writer observed, 'Dissidence via literature has evaporated. Back then our most widely read literature, the *samizdat* 'underground' books served a different function. Today literature has simply become a pastime.'

BALLET

The first *balli*, or *balletti*, originated in Italy during the Renaissance, when dance became an important social function in court life. Men would entertain at court festivities in routines combining music, dancing, singing and acting; women, on the other hand, were forbidden to dance openly in public. By the late 15th century, it was the vogue for court entertainment to be combined with banquets—each course was accompanied by a new scene in the story. Menus still list the entrées as they did five centuries ago. The French soon copied the Italians by staging their own *ballets de cour*. Their courts brought in Italian dancing masters, and many outstanding French painters and poets collaborated in the elaborate displays. These staged spectacles were set up to glorify the power and the wealth of the monarchy.

King Louis XIV of France was an avid dancer himself and took the part of the sun in the *Ballet de la Nuit*. Later in life, when Louis could no longer dance, he established the first *Académie Royale de Musique* (now the Paris Opera) where a dancing school was added that set the foundation of classical ballet.

As the Italians invented the idea of the *balli* as a combination of all the arts, the French developed this new vision of dance into a professional school, the *danse d'école*. A style of classical dancing was born with its own vocabulary of individual steps, the five positions of the feet (fashioned from court ballroom dance moves) and synchronized group movements. French terminology is still used today.

This form of ballet-dance was first staged in Moscow in 1672 by a German ensemble for Czar Alexei I. The theatrical performance, lasting ten hours, was based on the Bible's Book of Esther. Alexei's daughter, Sophia (the future regent), was very fond of dancing herself and composed comedy ballets, such as *Russalki* (the Mermaids). Sophia's half-brother, Peter the Great, encouraged Western dance and later, as czar, brought in many French, English and Polish companies for lavish productions in his new city of Sankt Pieterburkh. Later the St Petersburg Imperial Ballet was founded in 1738.

During the reigns of Elizabeth (1741–61) and Catherine the Great (1762–96), many French and Italian masters took up residence in St Petersburg and Moscow. By the turn of the century St Petersburg was approaching the peak of its cosmopolitan fame. It had four separate opera houses with permanent companies, all fully supported by the czarinas and czars. While ballet grew in popularity and artistic importance in Russia, it declined throughout the rest of Europe.

One of the most influential characters of the early Russian ballet scene was the Frenchman Charles Didelot, who arrived in Russia in 1801. He taught at the St Petersburg Imperial Ballet School for more than 25 years and wove French classical and Russian folk themes through the new romantic style of the times. He was the first to translate Pushkin's poems, *The Prisoner of the Caucasus* and *Ruslan and Ludmilla*, into the physical world of ballet. Under his direction, the ballet was made into a grand spectacle, incorporating the entire *corps de ballet*, costumes, scenery, and even special effects—dancers were fitted with wings and live pigeons flew across the stage.

Another of St Petersburg's well-known dancers was the Frenchman Marius Petipa, who came to Russia in 1847. Petipa was the master of the grand spectacle and produced an original ballet for the opening of each new season. During his 56-year career on the Russian stage, Petipa choreographed over 60 ballets for the Imperial Ballet, highlighting solos within each performance. In the early 1890s this grand master worked almost exclusively with Tchaikovsky, choreographing *Sleeping Beauty*, *The Nutcracker*, and *Swan Lake*. It was Petipa who brought the Imperial Ballet to the pinnacle of the ballet world.

All the St Petersburg ballets premièred at the Mariinsky Theater. Built by Albert Kavos in 1860, it was named after Maria, wife of Czar Alexander II. (In 1935, it was renamed the Kirov, after the prominent Communist leader under Stalin; but in 1992, the original name was restored.) The Mariinsky remains one of the most respected names in the ballet world. It is situated in St Petersburg on Ploshchad Teatralnaya (Theater Square; see page 548). This section of land was once the location for St Petersburg carnivals and fairs. (In the 18th-century, it was known as Ploshchad Karusel, Merry-Go-Round Square.) This gorgeous 1,700 seater, five-tiered theater is decorated with blue velvet, gilded stucco, ceiling paintings and chandeliers.

By the end of the 19th-century the Mariinsky Theater had almost 200 permanently employed dancers, graded in rank. Each graduate of the Imperial Ballet School was placed into the *corps de ballet*; only a few rose to coryphée, *sujet*, prima ballerina and lastly *prima absoluta* (or, for a man, soloist to the czar). They were employed by the czar for 20 years and retired with full pensions. Ballet dancers were often invited to court banquets, and favorites received many luxurious presents from admirers and the royal family themselves. Nicholas II bestowed large gifts of diamonds and emeralds upon his jewel *danseuse* Kchessinskaya, which she often wore during performances.

(following pages) Dancers of the Mariinsky (Kirov) Theater. (bottom right) Ballet slippers of the famous ballerina Anna Pavlova in the Vagonova Ballet School Museum.

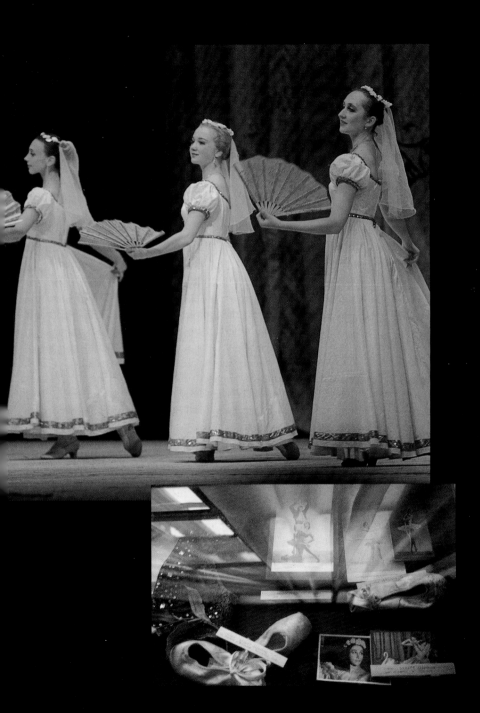

As the spirit of revolution hung in the air, the Imperial Ballet's conventional classical style plunged into decline. It was the St Petersburg artistic entrepreneur Sergei Diaghilev (1872–1929), who revived the stagnating Imperial Ballet with the individual and innovative style of the Ballets Russes. Diaghilev brought Russia's best dancers, choreographers, musicians and artists together to create some of the most stunning spectacles that the world had ever known. His dancers were Pavlova, Karsavina and Nijinsky; his choreographers Fokine, Massine, Nijinskaya (Nijinsky's sister) and later Balanchine; musicians Tchaikovsky, Chopin, Stravinsky and Rimsky-Korsakov; and artists Benois, Bakst, Goncharova and even Picasso. During the first season abroad in Paris in 1909, the repertoire of the Ballets Russes consisted of Borodin's *Polovtsian Dances* from *Prince Igor*, Chopin's *Les Sylphides* and *The Banquet*, with music by Tchaikovsky, Mussorgsky and Rimsky-Korsakov. The programs were designed by the French writer Jean Cocteau and posters painted by Moscow artist Valentin Serov. Even Erik Satie joined the group of musicians. In the center of all this furor were two of the most magnificent dancers of the 20th-century, Anna Pavlova and Vaslav Nijinsky.

Born the illegitimate daughter of a poor laundress, Pavlova did not seem destined for the stage. But in 1891, at the age of ten, this petite dark-eyed beauty was accepted into the St Petersburg Imperial Ballet School. When she graduated in 1899, the stunning performer leaped right into solo roles in the Mariinsky Theater. Anna then left to dance with the Ballets Russes; after her first performance in Paris, a French critic exuberantly claimed: 'She is to dance what Racine is to poetry, Poussin to painting, Gluck to music.' Pavlova was known for her dynamic short solos, filled with an endless cascade of jumps and pirouettes as in *The Dying Swan* and *The Dragonfly*.

Nijinsky was heralded as the greatest male dancer of his day—dancing was in his blood. For generations his family worked as dancers, acrobats, and circus performers. Vaslav was born in Kiev, Russia, in 1888, where his Polish parents were performing. When he was 11, his mother enrolled him in the St Petersburg Imperial Ballet School, where he studied for eight years. His graduation performance so impressed the *prima absoluta* ballerina Matilda Kchessinskaya that he immediately began his career at the Mariinsky Theater as a principal soloist.

His full genius emerged at the Ballets Russes' 1909 Paris debut. One spectator felt that 'his was the victory of breath over weight, the possession of body by the soul.' In 1911, Nijinsky was fired from the Imperial Ballet for not wearing the required little pair of trunks over his tights when he danced *Giselle*; this did not go down well with the dowager empress, who witnessed with crimson face the entire performance. His range in roles was astonishing. Everywhere he went, Nijinsky captured the hearts and adoration of the critics and audiences. One American critic noted, 'few of us can view the art of Nijinsky without emotion... he completely erased the memory of all male dancers that I had previously seen.' Nijinsky danced with Pavlova in *Cleopatra* and as the ethereal spirit in *Le Spectre de la Rose*. Jean Cocteau, who saw his first performance in Paris, exclaimed that Nijinsky's jumps 'were so poignant, so contrary to all the laws of flight and balance, following so high and curved a trajectory, that I shall never again smell a rose without this unerasable phantom appearing before me.' Fokine choreographed up a storm of innovative and dynamic ballets and stressed strong male dancing; Nijinsky danced in almost all his creations, including *Le Pavillon d'Armide*, *Sheherazade*, *The Firebird*, *Narcisse*, *Daphnis and Chloe*, and *Le Dieu Bleu* (The Blue Clown). In his diary, Nijinsky wrote 'I am beginning to understand God. Art, love, nature are only an infinitesimal part of God's spirit. I wanted to recapture it and give it to the public... If they felt it, then I am reflecting Him. The world, in turn, would regard him as *Le Dieu de la Danse*.

His first choreographic work, *L'Après-Midi d'un Faune*, was performed in 1912. Even though only eight minutes long, it managed to cause a scandal that rocked even Paris. With his natural faun-like eyes, waxed pointed ears and horns, and dressed only in tights with a curly golden wig, Nijinsky danced around seven lively nymphs. At the end of the ballet, each nymph fled as she dropped her veil. During this flight of passage, he caught up with each nymph and swept down under her in one convulsive, erotic movement. The audience gasped audibly.

Nijinsky's *Le Sacre du Printemps*, performed a year later on May 29, 1913, stopped just short of causing a riot in Paris; even the composer, Igor Stravinsky, had to flee the theater. The story of the ballet weaves around the ritual of the pagan rites of spring. The dancers' movements were not traditional gentle swayings and graceful turns, but asymmetrical rhythms and gestures, twists and jerks. By the time the first act was completed, many spectators were already hissing and screaming; the music was barely audible over the cries of emotional insults.

Nijinsky gave his last dance in Switzerland in 1919, at the age of 31, ten years after his first performance. By then he had already embarked on his voyage into madness; his memory became a blank. Prophesying in his diary, he had written, 'people will leave me alone, calling me a mad clown.' Nijinsky lived out the rest of his days in an asylum; his body died in 1950.

On the night of March 15, 1917, the day Nicholas II abdicated the throne to the Provisional Government, *Sleeping Beauty* was performed at the Mariinsky Theater in Petrograd. This parable, about a kingdom plunged into a century-long sleep on the whim of an evil witch, prophetically foretold the fate of an entire nation.

During the Soviet era, one of the most famous ballerinas was Galina Ulanova, whose father was the director of the Imperial Marinsky and mother a dancer and teacher at the Imperial school. In 1944, on Stalin's personal order, she left the Kirov Ballet for Moscow's Bolshoi to become the Prima Ballerina, where she danced all the greatest roles in classical ballet.

"Galina was an angel, and danced like one," stated another extraordinary dancer of the time, Maya Plisetskaya, who rose to fame in 1945 when she premiered in Prokofiev's ballet, *Cinderella*. Rodion Schedrin, her husband, composed a special ballet for her based on Bizet's opera *Carmen*. But it was her portrayal of the dying swan in Tchaikovsky's *Swan Lake* that became her signature role. Each year in St Petersburgh there is an annual ballet contest bearing her name, 'Maya.'

As Ulanova and Plisetskaya, the troika of today's reigning ballerinas, Lopatkina, Vishneva and Zakharova are also products of the famed Vagonova Ballet School on Rossi Street. Dating back over two centuries to the Imperial Ballet academy, the famous St Petersburg academy was renamed after Agrippina Vagonova who taught here between 1921 and 1951, and exemplified the Russian dance style in her book, *Basic Principles of Classical Ballet*. Each year over 2,000 hopefuls apply for the eight-year study program, and only about 100 are chosen. The Vagonova remains one of the world's premiere ballet institutions; and over former years, it has produced numerous other ballet icons, such as Karsavina, Semenova, Kolpakova, Makarova, Nureyev, Balanchivadze (Balanchine) and Baryshnikov.

From the 1930's to the 1960's, the Ballets Russes (which eventually dissolved into two different troupes, the Original Ballet Russes, and the Ballet Russes of Monte Carlo), continued to revolutionize ballet with groundbreaking productions around the world. In 2005, American filmmakers, Dayna Goldfine and Dan Geller, created a fabulous documentary, entitled *Ballet-Russes*, for which they interviewed the surviving dancers during their first-ever reunion in 2000. These included: Dame Alicia Markova who, until her death in 2004, continued to coach dancers in London; George Zoritch; Frederic Franklin, who traveled the world in his nineties to teach Ballet-Russes choreographies; and the famed teenage "Baby Ballerinas" Irina Baranova, Tamara Toumanova and Tatiana Riabouchinska. The film creatively intertwines the interviews with fascinating archival footage and old photographs of the talented dancers. This brilliant film, celebrates the remarkable legacy of the Russian dance world and the Ballets Russes.

MUSIC

The development of Russian music in St Petersburg followed the same patterns as literature, only later. In the 1830s and 40s Mikhail Glinka, a close friend of Pushkin, composed many symphonies and two operas based on Russian folk songs from his childhood. Glinka put these folk themes together with many of Pushkin's poems and produced some of the first distinctly Russian musical works. One of his most famous pieces is *Ruslan and Ludmilla*, an opera based on Pushkin's mock-romantic epic about the court of Kievan Russia.

Glinka's patriotic opera *A Life for the Czar* (later renamed *Ivan Susanin*) is about a peasant who saved the first Romanov czar from a Polish invasion. Another of his popular works, *Farewell to Petersburg*, is composed of a kaleidoscope of sounds that mixes Spanish boleros, Jewish songs and Italian barcaroles. *Travel Song* depicts images in sound of the first Russian railway, built between St Petersburg and the czar's palace in Tsarskoye Selo. Russians consider Glinka to be the father of their national music.

By the mid-19th-century St Petersburg had become a major musical center and Berlioz, Verdi, Strauss and Wagner conducted their works there. In response to this invasion of Western talent, particularly Wagner, whom they believed had imperial aspirations, a group of Russian composers banded together to promote their own 'Russian' music. Known as the Mighty Band or the Mighty 'Handful', they included Nikolai Rimsky-Korsakov, Alexander Borodin and Modest Mussorgsky. The Band followed Glinka's example and composed music based on folk songs and themes from Russian literature. Borodin's most famous work was the opera *Prince Igor*, which was based on an old Russian heroic song and included the famous Eastern dance number *The Polovtsian Dances*. Rimsky-Korsakov also wrote a number of operas based on mythic-historical themes from early Russian history and folklore. Mussorgsky, an epileptic like Dostoevsky, was the most artistically ambitious of the Band. He began by writing works based on Gogol's stories, which he considered were the closest to the Russian soul. Another piece tried to reproduce musically the babble in the marketplace at Nizhny Novgorod. Mussorgsky's two greatest works are the opera *Boris Godunov*, based on Pushkin's poem, and *Pictures from an Exhibition*, inspired by the drawings of his friend Viktor Hartman. *Khovanshchina*, the first part of an unfinished trilogy, is a kind of tone poem rendition of Russian-style chaos and social anarchy set at the end of the Time of Troubles just before Peter took the throne. While Mussorgsky was finishing this piece he went mad, and died a few weeks after Dostoevsky in 1881. He was buried near the writer in the Alexander Nevsky Monastery (see page 534).

As the Mighty Band was striving to lead Russia back to her roots, another faction, led by Anton Rubenstein, preferred the influence of European-oriented music. Rubenstein, a piano prodigy, organized state sponsorship for musical training; the St Petersburg Conservatory became the first of its kind in Russia. The talented performer and composer charmed audiences with his piano pieces that included *Kamenny Island* and *Soirées à St Petersburg*.

In 1862, Peter Tchaikovsky, then aged 22, was accepted as part of the first group of students into the St Petersburg Conservatory, having earlier received a degree in law. During his time, St Petersburg was a melting pot of sounds—everything from French waltzes and Italian arias to military marches and Gypsy songs. Their effect can be recognized in his first three symphonies, and in the *Slavonic March* and *1812 Overture*. In his popular opera *Queen of Spades*, based on Pushkin's novella, Tchaikovsky rekindled a patriotic theme. The talented musician also composed for the Mariinsky Ballet; some of his most evocative works include *The Nutcracker*, *Sleeping Beauty* and *Swan Lake*.

Alexander III was enraptured with the composer's genius and in 1888 granted him a lifetime annual pension of 3,000 rubles. In 1891, Tchaikovsky was even invited to conduct at the grand opening of New York's Carnegie Hall. Tchaikovsky's most popular symphony is considered to be the Sixth (*Pathétique*), written shortly before his death. Peter Tchaikovsky became one of the world's most popular composers.

Sergei Prokofiev (1891–1953) studied piano, and composition at the St Petersburg Conservatory under Rimsky-Korsakov. He wrote numerous sonatas, concertos and symphonies, composed for the ballets *Romeo and Juliet* and *Cinderella*, and collaborated with the filmmaker Sergei Eistenstein on his screen epics *Alexander Nevsky* and *Ivan the Terrible*. In Prokofiev's well-known *Album for Children*, he created the classic 'Peter and the Wolf.'

The Bolshevik Revolution would put a serious damper on experimentation in Russian music. Many composers such as Stravinsky, Rachmaninov and Prokofiev later fled Russia for the West. (Prokofiev eventually returned to Russia in the mid 1930's, where he remained until his death.) Igor Stravinsky, who had composed the music for some of the finest Mariinsky ballets, eventually settled in America where he helped score Walt Disney's animated film *Fantasia* in 1940. Abroad, Stravinsky also began a close collaboration with Diaghilev and the Ballet Russes, where *The Firebird*, *Petrouchka* and *Le Sacre du Printemps* became phenomenal successes. In 1937, the New York Metropolitan opera staged *Apollon Musagète* and *Le Baiser de la Fée*—the composer's special tribute to Tchaikovsky.

Leningrad's greatest musical resident after the Revolution was Dmitri Shostakovich, born in the city on September 25 1906. (The 100th Anniversary of his birth was celebrated in 2006.) He studied at the St Petersburg Conservatory, both as a composer and pianist. His graduation thesis was the First Symphony, which was played at the Leningrad Philharmonic in 1926, when the composer was just 19 years old. His Second Symphony was named *Dedication to the October Revolution*, and his Third honored May Day, the official holiday of the proletariat. Boxed in by the demands of socialist realism, Shostakovich soon found an outlet by experimenting with constructionist principles and the avant-garde.

In 1930, tiring of this nonsensical propaganda, Shostakovich followed with an experimental opera entitled *The Nose*, based on Gogol's unsettling 1836 novel about a St Petersburg aristocrat. Even though Shostakovich called it 'a satire on the era of Nicholas I', the innate message of the story was not lost on Soviet censors. It was removed from the repertoire and not restaged again for more than 40 years. Following this Shostakovich feared for his life living under Stalin, and he kept a toothbrush and towel permanently packed in a bag, expecting an arrest to come at any moment. He later credited his survival to his movie scores, used for propaganda purposes by the Soviet Union (he frequently composed scores for Eisenstein's films, see Special Topic on page 202).

On the eve of the purges in 1937, Shostakovich wrote his tragic Fourth Symphony, which was withdrawn from its premiere and not heard in public again until 1961. During the midst of the purges he premiered his Fifth Symphony in Leningrad; with its slow requiem-like movements, it clearly represented the tragedies of the times.

Saved by the patriotic events of World War II, Shostakovich fervently began to compose his famous Seventh Symphony, dedicated to the fate of Leningrad. It was broadcast throughout the country on March 5, 1942 during the German blockade. Ironically, on April 11, Shostakovich was bestowed with the country's highest cultural award, the Stalin Prize. (The composer later declared that the symphony was written as a protest against both Hitler and Stalin.) The score was flown on a bomber to the United States and leading conductors vied for the honor of its American premiere—Toscanini won. His Eighth Symphony was strongly denounced by the authorities. It was only in 1949 that Shostakovich produced Stalin's desired masterpiece, *Song of the Forests*. Shostakovich was eventually internationally honored with the Sibelius Prize and, in 1958, with an honorary doctorate from Oxford University.

All told, Shostakovich wrote fifteen symphonies and works in every major genre, including concertos, sonatas, quartets, and the operatic masterpiece, *Lady Macbeth of the Mtsensk District*.

(following pages) The Hermitage on the Neva River. On the right the golden dome of St Isaac's Cathedral stands behind the spire of the Admiralty.

Today both Russians and foreign visitors alike enjoy performances by these and other contemporary composers in the theaters and philharmonic halls of Moscow and St Petersburg. UNESCO named 1989 as the year of the composer Modest Mussorgsky. In the spring of 1990, the renowned cellist and conductor Mstislav Rostropovich and his opera singer wife were allowed to return and visit Russia after 16 years of exile.

During the reform years of the 1980s, Leningrad's most popular musician was Boris Grebenshchikov, considered the country's equivalent of Bob Dylan or John Lennon. He founded his band, Aquarium, in 1972, but they toiled for many years in the 'unofficial' underground (the government did not recognize rock n' roll—in an early popular song, Grebenshchikov sang, 'I'm tired of being the ambassador of rock n' roll/In a country that can't feel the beat'). In 1980, after the band performed at a national music festival, Grebenshchikov was labeled an anti-Soviet agitator, fired from his job as a computer programer, and forced to work as a janitor.

But eventually, during glasnost, the singer/songwriter had his band's illicit homemade recordings officially released, which immediately sold millions of copies. (This also meant that the government made a hefty profit. The irony was not lost on Grebenshchikov. A song on the *Equinox* album: 'We were silent like dogs/As they sold off all they could sell/Including our children...')

By 1989, when the walls between East and West were crumbling, the Russian rock superstar had an American record contract, a US Tour, a documentary film, videos for MTV, and interviews with *Rolling Stone* magazine. Today, he performs around the world, and is still going strong (see www.planetaquarium.com for tour schedules). Grebenshchikov continues to sing the final lines from his now famous song, *Railroad Water*: 'I wrote these songs at December's end/Naked, in the snow, by the light of the moon/But if you can hear me/Maybe it wasn't in vain.' He speaks for all his country's artists who were suppressed during the Soviet regime.

In 1987, Igor Matvienko created another popular St Petersburg group, Lyube, devoted to working class Russians. Their first album, *Atas* ("Be Alert!" in Russian slang) came out in 1991; and their subsequent album, *Who Said We Were Living Poorly?*, was marked by nostalgia for socialism's lost way of life. The 1996 album *Battalion Commander* was dedicated to those who fought in Chechnya; and, in 2000, *Polustanochki* (a small station on a railway where a train does not even stop) was for all those persecuted Russians who had been forgotten along the way. The meaning of their next record, *Davai Za* (Here's to) was a hymn to Russia's past and its people who managed to survive the horrors and dangers of the 20th-century. Today, new Russian music ensembles abound, from rock groups, such as 'Uma Thurman,' (a band from Nizhny Novgorod whose favorite actress is!) to the popular world-touring 'Bering Strait,' that blends country, rock and bluegrass sounds. And many famed western groups have now come to perform in Russia. In 2003, former Beatle Paul McCartney played in a packed Red Square in Moscow. The songs included classics 'Let It Be' and 'Back in the USSR'. President Vladimir Putin, who was also in the audience, confessed that he had been an avid Beatle's fan during his childhood; Sir Paul then performed one year later in St Petersburg's Palace Square for his 62nd birthday, He also received an honorary doctorate from the St Petersburg Conservatoire. The year 2006, marked Madonna and Eric Clapton taking their concert tours to Moscow.

ART

During Russia's Golden Age in the 19th-century, the arts strove to portray the realistic aspects of Russian life. Russian art grew beyond the depiction of spiritual realms, as symbolized by frescoes and icons, to encompass the whole contemporary world of the common man with his hopes, sufferings and desire for change. In 1827, Karl Bryullov's masterpiece *The Last Days of Pompeii* was exhibited in St Petersburg. The public compared the Italian romantic upheaval to their own city's tendency to natural disaster. Another meaning—of citizens forced to flee their burning city— symbolized the Decembrist uprising that had taken place only two years before.

The painter Ilya Repin greatly influenced the artistic developments of the late 19th-century. Repin's arrival at the St Petersburg Academy of Arts in 1863 coincided with one of the most significant events of the city's artistic life: a small group of art students led by Ivan Kramskoi rebelled against the strict academic standards and were soon forced to resign. In 1870, this group formed their own artistic movement known as the Peredvizhniki or the Wanderers. In his last year at the academy, Repin painted *The Barge Haulers*, symbolizing the heavy burdens borne by the Russian people (see page 273); after graduation he joined the Wanderers. In 1887, while living in Moscow, Repin also frequented the art salons of Pavel Tretyakov and Savva Mamontov. These circles included other well-known painters as Serov, Korovin and Vrubel.

When Repin witnessed the public execution of five people who had taken part in the assassination of Alexander II, it had a great impact on his artistic life. Soon after, he moved back to St Petersburg and explored revolutionary ideas. Like his l iterary contemporaries, Repin strove to capture the moral and philosophical issues of the time. His paintings *Arrest of a Propagandist, They Did Not Expect Him* (concerning the unexpected return of a political exile to his home) and *Ivan the Terrible and his Son—16 November 1581* (the date Ivan IV killed his son in a fit of rage; see picture on page 282) can now be seen along with many of his other works in Moscow's Tretyakov Gallery.

In 1899, Repin bought an estate (now a museum, see page 585) outside St Petersburg that he named the Penates, after the Roman gods who protected home and family, and continued to live and paint there until his death in 1930, aged 86. St Petersburg's Repin Institute of Painting, Sculpture and Architecture is one of the largest art schools in the world (see page 489).

In 1898, Diaghilev, Bakst and Benois created Russia's first art magazine *Mir Iskusstva* (World of Art), which caused an immediate sensation throughout St Petersburg. The innovative journal introduced art concepts from around the world: Postimpressionism, pointillism, cubism and art nouveau. These artists wanted to free Russia from the old artistic standards established by such groups as the Wanderers. By 1910, the avant-garde maximalists and futurists were at the center of design and art. They welcomed the Revolution—believing it would serve as a hotbed for their own radical ideas.

In 1903, Boris Kustodiev graduated from the St Petersburg Academy of the Arts with a gold medal for his colorful painting "Village Bazaar". His other realistic paintings (based on scenes from ordinary Russian life) include "A Merchant's Wife" (1915) "The Blue House" (1920), "A Sailor and His Mistress" (1920), and "Portrait of Fyodor Shalyapin" (1922). (He eventually became so famous that the Uffizi Gallery in Italy ordered a self-portrait.) Kustodiev's paintings and drawings contain nearly all the remarkable Petersburg people of the 1917 era. The 'World of Art' members would frequently gather at his apartment for concerts, literary readings and art exhibitions. Alexander Benois wrote of his works: "It seems to me that the real Kustodiev is the Russian fair, multicolored, with large print fabrics, barbarous battles between colors, the Russian land and the Russian village, with its harmonics, gingerbread, boldly dressed girls and jaunty young fellows." Today, some of his paintings are mounted in St Petersburg's Russian Museum, and Moscow's Tretyakov Gallery exhibits the famous "Moscow Traktir."

The abstract painter Kazimir Malevich was renowned in St Petersburg for his theatrical costumes and scenery, along with his innovative paintings that included *Victory Over the Sun*. His *Black Square*, which Malevich thought to represent the universality of existence, became the icon of Russian abstract art. The painter believed that this pure simple style of color and shape would act as a catalyst to the unconscious and open a way to spiritual transcendence.

In 1988, Sotheby's held the first auction of Russian art, with one painting selling for over $400,000. Today the art scene is booming and scores of exhibition halls and galleries, displaying and selling the works of contemporary artists, grace the streets of Moscow and St Petersburg.

GETTING AROUND

ORIENTATION

St Petersburg is 660 kilometers (410 miles) north of Moscow on the same latitude as Helsinki and Anchorage. The city lies at the mouth of the Neva River as it flows into the Gulf of Finland. The city is divided into several districts and islands, and a few moments with a map familiarizing oneself with these will make a visit to St Petersburg more enjoyable.

The eastern bank of the Neva is known as the Vyborg Side (see Finland Station on page 539). At the tip of Vasilyevsky Island the river splits into two main branches; the Bolshaya and Malaya Neva. Here the northern bank is known as Petrogradskaya or the Petrograd Side (see Across the Kronverk Strait on page 477), and includes the islands of Zayachy, Petrogradsky, Aptekarsky and Petrovsky. To the northwest are the Kirov Islands (see page 479). Many of the city's sights are to be found on the south bank of the Neva, known as the mainland.

St Petersburg was originally spread over 101 islands. Today, because of redevelopment, there are 44 islands that make up one-sixth of the area of the city. These are connected by 620 bridges which span 100 waterways and canals. St Petersburg is a cultural treasure-house with over 125 museums and galleries, 50 theaters and concert halls, 2,500 libraries and hundreds of well-preserved palaces and monuments.

ARRIVAL

See Getting There section (page 61) for details of international arrivals. Passengers arriving at the international Pulkovo II or domestic Pulkovo I airports (these share a common area and are located 17 kilometers south of the city), can choose between a taxi or an express or local bus into town. Both airports are 30 minutes by taxi from the center of St Petersburg. From Pulkovo II, a monopolized taxi can cost up to $30 for a ride into town; but from town it is much cheaper, costing half the price. From Pulkovo II, the airport's city bus No. 13 runs to Moskovskaya Metro station (take the Metro or taxi from here); it picks up every 20 minutes for the return 15-minute run to the airport. Minibus Taxi No. 213 also leaves to the airport from Sennaya Square, and returns. From Pulkovo I airport via Moskovskaya Metro, take bus no. 39, about a 25-minute ride.

Those arriving in St Petersburg by train or bus will find the main stations located around the city center, each with it own Metro station. You can either jump on the Metro (if you have little luggage) or take a taxi from here to your destination.

Sights

Peter and Paul Fortress

The origins of the city can be traced back to the Peter and Paul Fortress, known as Petropavlovskaya Krepost in Russian. Peter the Great was attracted to Zayachy Ostrov (Hare Island), situated between the Neva and the Kronverk Strait, because of its small size and strategic position in the area. On May 16, 1703, the first foundation stone of the fortress, named after the apostles Peter and Paul, was laid by Peter himself. The fortress was designed to protect the city from the invading Swedes, and was built as an elongated hexagon with six bastions that traced the contours of the island. Over 20,000 workers were commissioned and within only six months the earthen ramparts were set in place. Work continued on the fortress, replacing the wooden buildings with brick and stone until its completion in 1725. The new walls were over 12 meters (39 feet) thick and 300 guns were installed. Soon after its completion the fortress lost its military significance and over the next 200 years it served instead as a political prison. In 1922, the fortress was opened as a museum. The museum is open 11am–5pm, Tuesdays 11am–4pm; closed Wednesdays and the last Tuesday of the month. Metro Gorkovskaya.

Ironically, the first prisoner was Peter's son, Alexei, who was suspected of plotting against the czar. Peter supervised his son's torture and Alexei died here in 1718. (Peter had Alexei buried beneath the staircase of the cathedral, so he would always be 'trampled upon'.) An outer fortification built to cover an entrance into the fort is known as the **Alexeyevsky Ravelin** (Bastion), after Peter's son. The history of the fortress is also closely connected with revolutionary movements. Catherine the Great locked up Alexander Radishchev, who criticized the autocracy and feudal system in his book *Voyages from St Petersburg to Moscow*. In 1825, the Decembrists were placed in the Alexeyevsky Bastion, a special block for important prisoners. Five were executed on July 13, 1826, and hundreds of others were sentenced to hard labor in Siberia. Members of the Petrashevsky political movement, including Dostoevsky, were sent here in 1849 and sentenced to death. Only at the last minute did Nicholas I revoke the sentence. Nikolai Chernyshevsky wrote his influential novel *What Is To Be Done?* while imprisoned here for two years in 1862. In the 1880s many members of the Narodnaya Volya (Peoples' Freedom Group) were placed in solitary-confinement cells in the Trubetskoi Bastion. In 1887, five

The St Peter and Paul Cathedral inside the Peter and Paul Fortress. When it was constructed in 1732 the spire, topped with an angel holding a cross, was the highest structure in Russia. Peter the Great purposely made it taller than the Bell Tower in Moscow's Kremlin (see picture on page 119). Its gilded spire was scaled and camouflaged by mountain climbers during the Siege of Leningrad to protect it from German bombing raids.

prisoners were executed for the attempt on the life of Alexander III, including Lenin's brother, Alexander Ulyanov. The writer Maxim Gorky was incarcerated for writing revolutionary leaflets.

During the October 1917 Revolution, when the fortress' last stronghold was captured by the Bolsheviks and the political prisoners set free, a red lantern was hung in the Naryshkin Bastion signaling the battleship *Aurora* to fire the first shot of the Revolution. Every day at noon a blank cannon shot is fired from the Naryshkin Bastion (be prepared!). It has been sounded every day (except during the Siege of Leningrad) since a similar salute in 1721 proclaimed the end to the Great Northern War. Locals also call it the Admiral's Hour; according to tradition the cannon was fired daily after an admiral drank his glass of noon-day vodka. The shot also let the townspeople know the time.

The visitor's entrance to the fortress is at **St John's Gate**, on the east side of the island not far from Kamennoostrovsky (formerly Kirov) Prospekt. While crossing St John's (Ioannovsky) Bridge, the city's oldest, note the bronze hare installed atop one of the pylons. Legend has it that, in 1703, while Peter the Great was investigating the area, he got some water in his boot; so he took it off and set it on the grass to dry. Later, as the story goes, when Peter went to put his boot back on, he discovered a hare inside it. Peter reportedly laughed and named the area "Hare's Island. At the end of the bridge is **St Peter's Gate** (1718), the main entrance and oldest unchanged structure of the fort. Hanging over the archway is a double-headed eagle, the emblem of the Russian Empire, along with bas-reliefs of the apostle Peter. The carver Konrad Osner gave the apostle the features of the czar. Beyond the gate is His Majesty's Bastion, used as a dungeon for Peter's prisoners.

A straight path leads to **St Peter and Paul Cathedral**, built between 1712 and 1732 in the Dutch style by the architect Trezzini. Peter the Great laid the cornerstone. The cathedral, with its long slender golden spire topped with an angel holding a cross, is the focal point of the square. The belfry, 122.5 meters (402 feet) high, used to be the highest structure in the whole country; Peter purposely had the spire built higher than the Ivan the Great Bell Tower in Moscow's Kremlin. (During the Siege mountain climbers courageously scaled the spire in order to camouflage and protect it from German bombing raids.)

Inside, the gilded wooden iconostasis was carved between 1722 and 1726, and holds 43 icons. The cathedral is the burial place for over 30 czars and princes, including every czar from Peter I to Alexander III. There are no tombs for Ivan VI or Peter III, both of whom were murdered. The last czar, Nicholas II, along with his murdered family and friends were finally given an official burial in the cathedral on July 17, 1998 (80 years to the day after they were shot by a 12-man Bolshevik firing squad). They were buried in the Chapel of St Catherine the Martyr in the cathedral's

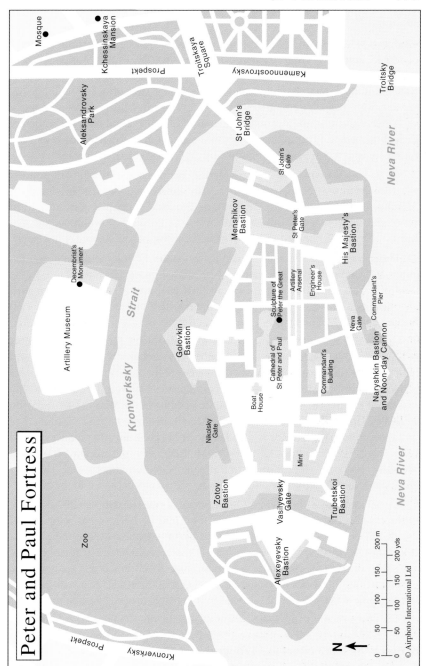

Peter and Paul Fortress

Mosque

Kchessinskaya Mansion

Prospekt

Aleksandrovsky Park

Troitskaya Square

Kamennoostrovsky

Troitsky Bridge

Neva River

St John's Bridge

St John's Gate

Menshikov Bastion

St Peter's Gate

His Majesty's Bastion

Decembrist's Monument

Artillery Museum

Strait

Kronverksky

Golovkin Bastion

Sculpture of Peter the Great

Artillery Arsenal

Engineer's House

Cathedral of St Peter and Paul

Commandant's Building

Neva Gate

Commandant's Pier

Boat House

Naryshkin Bastion and Noon-day Cannon

Nikolsky Gate

Zoo

Zotov Bastion

Vasilyevsky Gate

Mint

Trubetskoi Bastion

Neva River

Alexeyevsky Bastion

Kronverksky Prospekt

N

200 m
150
100
50
0

200 yds
150
100
50
0

© Airphoto International Ltd

southwest side. Positive DNA identifications had been made on the nine skeletons exhumed in 1991 from unmarked graves in the Ural Mountains, near Yekaterinburg, 1,450 kilometers (900 miles) east of Moscow. They belonged to Nicholas II, his wife, three children and four servants. (In a breach of tradition, the servants were also allowed burial in the lower vault.) In January 1998, after much controversy, the Russian Government announced an official and final verification of each of the bodies. (The missing bodies of the czar's fourth daughter Maria and son Alexei are believed to have been burned by the Bolshevik executioners.)

A year later the remains of Czarina Maria Fyodorovna, the Danish-born princess who was the mother of Nicholas II, were also allowed burial next to her husband, Alexander III, who had died in 1894. Maria Fyodorovna married Alexander III in 1866, and the couple had six children. After the Bolshevik Revolution, she fled Russia to Denmark. She died in 1928 with no knowledge about the fate of her family.

The sarcophagi of Alexander II and his wife took 17 years to carve from Altai jasper and Ural red quartz. Peter the Great himself chose his resting place to the right of the altar. In 1994, Queen Elizabeth II paid a visit here to her Romanov ancestors' tombs. This was the first visit by a British monarch to Peter and Paul Fortress in over 75 years.

Outside the cathedral entrance is a small pavilion with a statue of the Goddess of Navigation. The **Boat House** was erected in 1761 to house a small boat that was built by Peter the Great. Today, this Grandfather of the Russian Fleet is on display at the Central Naval Museum at 4 Birzhevaya Square on Vasilyevsky Island. Directly in front of the cathedral is the yellow-white building of the **Mint** (1800–1806). In 1724, Peter the Great transferred the Royal Mint from Moscow to St Petersburg. The first lever press in the world was used here in 1811. The Mint still produces special coins, medals and badges. Beyond the Mint are the Alexeyevsky, Zotov and Trubetskoi Bastions, where many of the revolutionaries were imprisoned. The latter houses an exhibit which traces the history of prisoners who stayed in the cells.

As you leave the Cathedral look for the **Statue of Peter the Great**, a life-size figure of the czar seated in an armchair. Unveiled on June 7, 1991, it was sculpted and donated by St Petersburg artist Mikhail Chemiakin (who now lives in the US), just before the city regained its historical name. The statue is an interpretation of Peter I's wax effigy (now in the Hermitage collection) made by Carlo Rastrelli (father of the famous architect) in 1725, right after the czar's death. The head is an actual cast from the life mask of Peter the Great (also in the Hermitage) made by Rastrelli in 1719.

The next structure is the stone Commandant's Building, built as the commander's headquarters and the interrogation center for prisoners. It now houses the **Museum of History of St Petersburg and Petrograd from 1703 to 1917**. Next door, the old

Engineer's House is now the **Architectural Museum of St Petersburg**, displaying many original drawings and drafts of the city. Both are closed on Wednesdays. Behind these stands the **Neva Gate**, once known as the Gate of Death, because prisoners were led through it to the execution site. Now it leads to the beach area (with a spectacular view of the city) that is quite crowded in summer with sunbathers. The Walrus Club gathers here in winter to swim between the ice floes of the Neva. As you pass through the gate notice the plaques that record the city's many floods. In the disastrous flood of 1824, the entire Vasilyevsky Island across to both the Petrograd Side and the mainland were underwater. Nikolai Gogol wrote, 'Now the belfry spire is alone visible from the sea.'

ACROSS THE KRONVERK STRAIT

Exiting the fortress by way of St John's Bridge takes you back to Kamennoostrovsky Prospekt. To the right is the **Troitsky Most** (formerly Kirov Bridge), with a splendid view of the fortress. This is the city's longest bridge, built between 1897 and 1903 from French designs, to commemorate the silver wedding anniversary of Alexander III. Gorkovskaya Metro station is a short walk north along the prospekt. The small path to the left of St John's Bridge circles around the Kronverk Strait. This path leads to a small obelisk, a monument to the Decembrist revolutionaries, erected on the spot where Nicholas I executed the five leaders of the 1825 uprising. A witness described the execution: 'The hangmen made them stand on a bench and put white canvas hoods over their heads. Then the bench was knocked from under their feet. Three men whose ropes had broken fell on the rough boards of the scaffold bruising themselves. One broke his leg. According to custom, in such circumstances the execution had to be canceled. But in an hour, new ropes were brought and the execution carried through.'

Past the obelisk is a large building that was once the artillery arsenal. Today it is the **Kronverk Artillery, Engineers and Signals Museum**, established by Peter the Great to display the history of Russian weaponry. Today it houses more than 50,000 exhibits of artillery, firearms, engineering equipment and military paintings; there is also an outdoor display of tanks. Open 11am–5pm; closed Mondays and Tuesdays and last Thursday of the month. Behind the museum is **Aleksandrovsky** (formerly Lenin) **Park**, stretching from the Strait to Kronverksky (formerly Maxim Gorky) Prospekt, where the writer lived at number 23 from 1914 to 1921. Inside the park is the **St Petersburg Zoo** and gardens, with over 1,000 animals (10am–6pm in summer, and 10am–4pm in winter; closed Mondays). Nearby, at 4 Aleksandrovsky Park, is the **Planetarium**, open 10.30am–6pm; closed Mondays. The **Amusement Park** just north of the zoo has roller coasters, bumper cars and other rides. Nearby is the

Baltiisky Dom Theater which in summer months throws wild all-night parties for ex-Communist youthful party animals. At 7 Kronverksky Prospekt is a working **mosque**, modeled on Samarkand's magnificent Gur Emir Mausoleum where Tamerlaine is buried.

Sergei Kirov (1886–1934), regional head of the Leningrad Party before he was murdered, lived not far from Leo Tolstoy Square at 26–28 Kamennoostrovsky Prospekt. The **Kirov Museum** on the fourth floor (open 11am–6pm; closed Wednesdays) displays his possessions including many great examples from Soviet 1920s technology (including a hotline to the Kremlin). At number 10 is Lenfilm Studios, founded in 1918.

Opposite St John's Bridge on Kamennoostrovsky Prospekt is **Troitskaya Ploshchad** (Troitsky Square, formerly Revolution Square) where many of the first buildings of the city once stood. These included the Senate, Custom House and Troitsky Cathedral, where Peter was crowned emperor in 1721. Today the square is a large garden. At the northern end of the square, at 4 Ulitsa Kuybysheva, is the art-nouveau style mansion (built between 1902 and 1906 by the architect Gogen) formerly belonging to Matilda Kchessinskaya, a famous ballerina and mistress of Nicholas II before he married (she died in Paris in 1971, aged 99). It now houses the **Museum of Political History** (open 10am–5.30pm; closed Thursdays) with exhibits of Russian political parties from 1905 to the 1990s. There is also a waxworks museum and other displays on Kchessinskaya. Frequent concerts are held in the chamber music hall.

The **Lidval Building** (1–3 Kamennoostrovsky Prospekt), an apartment block built in 1902, is named after the city's favorite architect of the moderne, Fyodor Lidval; look closely and you will see a menagerie of figures that jump out of the stone: fish, owls, spiders and webs.

Continuing along Petrovsky Embankment (Naberezhnaya Petrovskaya), you pass the two-ton granite figures of Shih-Tze, brought from Manchuria in 1907, poised on the steps by the Neva. In China these sculptures guarded the entrances to palaces (see picture on pages 14–15). Behind them is the **Cottage of Peter the Great**, one of the oldest surviving buildings of the city. It was constructed, in a mere three days in May 1703, out of pine logs painted to look like bricks. One room was a study and reception area and the other was used as a dining room and bedroom. The largest door was 1.75 meters (five feet, nine inches) high—Peter stood at 2 meters (six feet seven)! From here Peter directed the building of his fortress, which was in view across the river. Once his summer palace was completed, Peter stopped living here altogether. In 1784, Catherine the Great encased the tiny house in stone to protect it. The cottage is now a museum, displaying his furniture, household utensils, a cast of his hand and a small boat with which Peter is supposed to have saved a group of fishermen on Lake Ladoga in 1690. A bronze bust of Peter can be found in the garden. The cottage, at 6 Petrovsky Embankment, is open 10am–5pm; closed Tuesdays and the last Monday of the month.

The beautiful blue building of the **Nakhimov Naval School**, at number 4, is a short walk farther east, where young boys learn to carry on the traditions of the Russian fleet. The battleship *Aurora* is anchored in front of it. The cruiser originally fought during the Russo-Japanese War (1904–05). In October 1917, the sailors mutinied and joined in the Bolshevik Revolution. On the evening of October 24, following the orders of Lenin and the Military Revolutionary Committee, the *Aurora* sailed up the Neva and at 9.45pm fired a blank shot to signal the storming of the Winter Palace. In 1948, it was moored by the Naval School and later opened as a museum in 1956. Displays include many revolutionary photographs, documents, the gun that fired the legendary shot, and the radio room where Lenin announced the overthrow of the Provisional Government to the citizens of Russia. The battleship is open 10.30am–4pm; closed Mondays and Fridays.

The **St Petersburg Hotel** can be reached by crossing the Sampsonievsky Bridge over the Bolshaya Neva. Here you can have a quick coffee, buffet lunch or dinner at the cafeteria-type restaurant on the ground floor.

To the northeast, across the Karpovka River, special gardens once grew medicinal plants and herbs for the city's apothecaries. This is how the island got its nickname of Aptekarsky (Apothecary). The **Botanical Gardens** are now located here (not far from the TV Tower), along with the **Botanical Museum**, at 2 Ulitsa Professora Popova, filled with over 80,000 plants and seeds. The museum is open 10am–5pm Wednesday, Saturday and Sunday. The nearest Metro station is Petrogradskaya.

Today the 50,000-watt **TV Tower**, standing at 321 meters (1,053 feet), is the tallest structure in St Petersburg. It is located in the northeast corner of the Petrograd Side and is open for tours offering great views of the city; a café is on the second deck.

On the other side of the TV Tower, at 26 Graftio Ulitsa, is the **Shalyapin House Museum** with exhibits on the life of the famous Russian opera singer who lived here from 1915 to 1922. Open 11am–6pm; closed Mondays and Tuesdays and the last Friday of the month. It also has occasional chamber music performances.

KIROV ISLANDS

The northernmost islands are collectively called the Kirov Islands, the largest of which are known as Krestovsky, Yelagin and Kamenny (Stone). They lie between the Malaya, Srednaya and Bolshaya (Small, Middle and Large) Nevka, which are tributaries of the Neva.

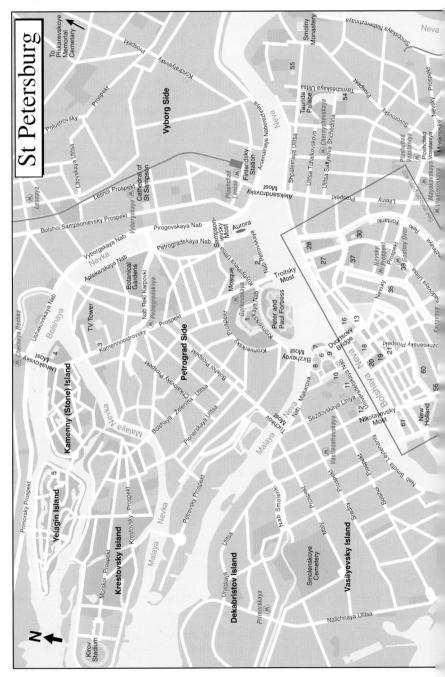

St Petersburg

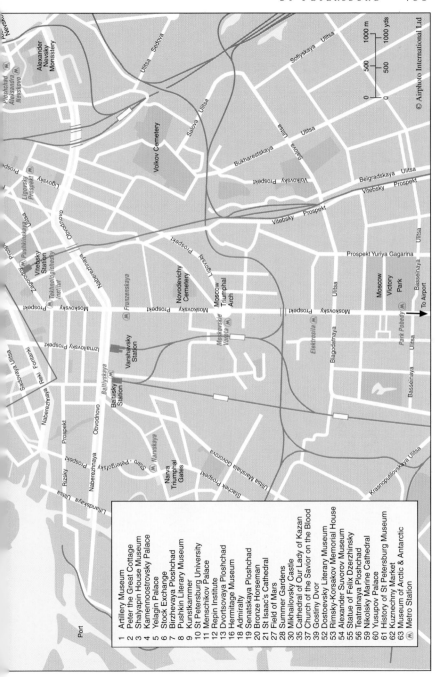

© Airphoto International Ltd

1000 m
1000 yds
500
0

Proshchad Aleksandra Nevskovo Ⓜ
Alexander Nevsky Monastery
Ulitsa Sedova
Sofiyskaya Ulitsa
Volkov Cemetery
Salova Ulitsa
Bukharestskaya
Ulitsa
Belgradskaya Ulitsa
Vitebsky Prospekt
Ligovsky Prospekt Ⓜ
Okhovo
Vitebsky Prospekt
Pushkinskaya Ulitsa Ⓜ
Vitebsky Station Ⓜ
Tekhnologichesky Institut Ⓜ
Naberezhnaya
Ligovsky Prospekt
Prospekt Yuriya Gagarina
Ulitsa
Moscow Victory Park
Basseinaya Ulitsa
To Airport →
Frunzenskaya Ⓜ
Novodevichy Cemetery
Moscow Triumphal Arch
Prospekt
Prospekt
Moskovsky Prospekt Ⓜ
Moskovskie Vorota Ⓜ
Moskovsky Prospekt Ⓜ
Elektrosila Ⓜ
Prospekt
Park Pobedy Ⓜ
Moskovsky Prospekt Ⓜ
Ulitsa
Blagodatnaya
Basseinaya
Ulitsa
Izmailovsky Prospekt
Sadovaya Ulitsa
Naberezhnaya Reki Fontanki
Varshavsky Station
Baltiyskaya Ⓜ
Baltiisky Station
Krasnoputilovskaya Ulitsa
Obvodnovo
Prospekt
Naberezhnaya
Rizsky Prospekt
Liliandskaya Ulitsa
Staro-Peterhofsky Prospekt
Narvskaya Ⓜ
Nanva Triumphal Gates
Stachek Prospekt
Ulitsa Marshala Govorova
Port

1 Artillery Museum
2 Peter the Great Cottage
3 Shalyapin House Museum
4 Kamennoostrovsky Palace
5 Yelagin Palace
6 Stock Exchange
7 Birzhevaya Ploshchad
8 Pushkin Literary Museum
9 Kunstkammer
10 St Petersburg University
11 Menschikov Palace
12 Repin Institute
13 Dvortsovaya Ploshchad
16 Hermitage Museum
18 Admiralty
19 Senatskaya Ploshchad
20 Bronze Horseman
21 St Isaac's Cathedral
27 Field of Mars
28 Summer Gardens
30 Mikhailovsky Castle
35 Cathedral of Our Lady of Kazan
37 Church of the Savior on the Blood
39 Gostiny Dvor
52 Dostoevsky Literary Museum
53 Rimsky-Korsakov Memorial House
54 Alexander Suvorov Museum
55 Statue of Felix Dzerzhinsky
56 Teatralnaya Ploshchad
59 Nikolsky Marine Cathedral
60 Yusupov Palace
61 History of St Petersburg Museum
62 Kuznechny Market
63 Museum of Arctic & Antarctic
Ⓜ Metro Station

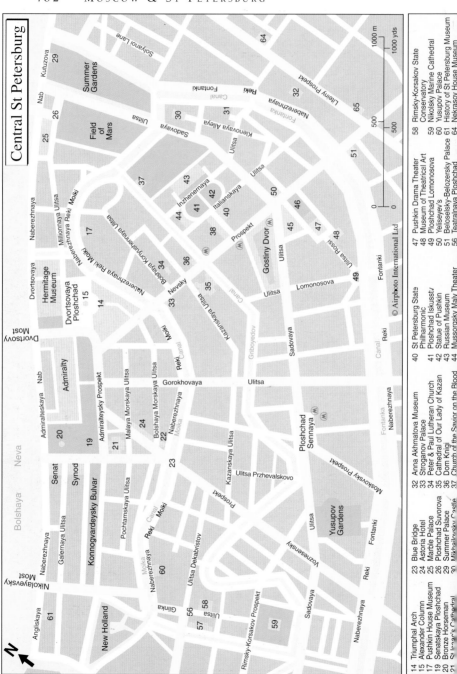

Central St Petersburg

14 Triumphal Arch
15 Alexander Column
17 Pushkin House Museum
19 Senatskaya Ploshchad
20 Bronze Horseman
21 St Isaac's Cathedral

23 Blue Bridge
24 Astoria Hotel
25 Marble Palace
26 Ploshchad Suvorova
29 Summer Palace
30 Mikhailovsky Castle

32 Anna Akhmatova Museum
33 Stroganov Palace
34 Peter & Paul Lutheran Church
35 Cathedral of Our Lady of Kazan
36 Dom Knigi
37 Church of the Savior on the Blood

40 St Petersburg State Philharmonic
41 Ploshchad Iskusstv
42 Statue of Pushkin
43 Russian Museum
44 Mussorgsky Maly Theater

47 Pushkin Drama Theater
48 Museum of Theatrical Art
49 Ploshchad Lomonosova
50 Yeliseyev's
51 Beloselsky-Belozersky Palace
56 Teatralnaya Ploshchad

58 Rimsky-Korsakov State Conservatory
59 Nikolsky Marine Cathedral
60 Yusupov Palace
61 History of St Petersburg Museum
64 Nekrasov House Museum

© Airphoto International Ltd

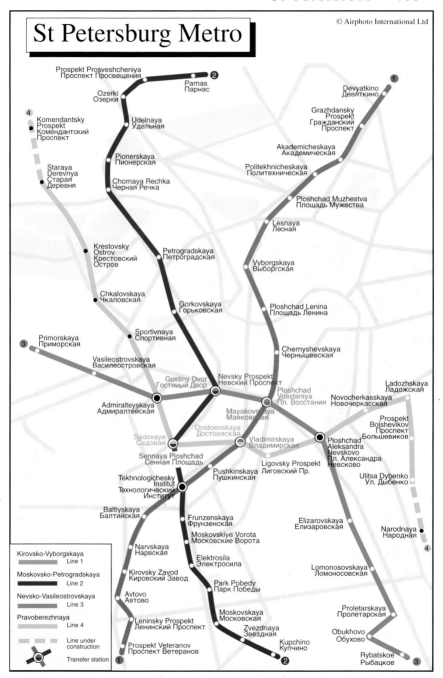

St Petersburg Metro

© Airphoto International Ltd

Prospekt Prosveshcheniya
Проспект Просвещения

Parnas
Парнас

Ozerki
Озерки

Devyatkino
Девяткино

Komendantsky
Prospekt
Комендантский
Проспект

Udelnaya
Удельная

Grazhdansky
Prospekt
Гражданский
Проспект

Akademicheskaya
Академическая

Pionerskaya
Пионерская

Staraya
Derevnya
Старая
Деревня

Politekhnicheskaya
Политехническая

Chornaya Rechka
Черная Речка

Ploshchad Muzhestva
Площадь Мужества

Lesnaya
Лесная

Krestovsky
Ostrov
Крестовский
Остров

Petrogradskaya
Петроградская

Vyborgskaya
Выборгская

Chkalovskaya
Чкаловская

Gorkovskaya
Горьковская

Ploshchad Lenina
Площадь Ленина

Primorskaya
Приморская

Sportivnaya
Спортивная

Chernyshevskaya
Чернышевская

Vasileostrovskaya
Василеостровская

Gostiny Dvor
Гостиный Двор

Nevsky Prospekt
Невский Проспект

Ladozhskaya
Ладожская

Admiralteyskaya
Адмиралтейская

Ploshchad
Vosstaniya
Пл. Восстания

Novocherkasskaya
Новочеркасская

Mayakovskaya
Маяковская

Prospekt
Bolshevikov
Проспект
Большевиков

Dostoevskaya
Достоевская

Sadovaya
Садовая

Vladimirskaya
Владимирская

Ploshchad
Aleksandra
Nevskovo
Пл. Александра
Невсково

Sennaya Ploshchad
Сенная Площадь

Ligovsky Prospekt
Лиговский Пр.

Ulitsa Dybenko
Ул. Дыбенко

Tekhnologichesky
Institut
Технологический
Институт

Pushkinskaya
Пушкинская

Baltiyskaya
Балтийская

Frunzenskaya
Фрунзенская

Elizarovskaya
Елизаровская

Narodnaya
Народная

Narvskaya
Нарвская

Moskovskiye Vorota
Московские Ворота

Elektrosila
Электросила

Kirovsky Zavod
Кировский Завод

Lomonosovskaya
Ломоносовская

Avtovo
Автово

Park Pobedy
Парк Победы

Proletarskaya
Пролетарская

Leninsky Prospekt
Ленинский Проспект

Moskovskaya
Московская

Obukhovo
Обухово

Prospekt Veteranov
Проспект Ветеранов

Zvezdnaya
Звездная

Kupchino
Купчино

Rybatskoe
Рыбацкое

Kirovsko-Vyborgskaya
Line 1

Moskovsko-Petrogradskaya
Line 2

Nevsko-Vasileostrovskaya
Line 3

Pravoberezhnaya
Line 4

Line under
construction

Transfer station

Stone Island Bridge leads from the end of Kamennoostrovsky Prospekt on the Petrograd Side (about a 15-minute walk north of Petrogradskaya Metro station) to **Stone Island**, a popular summer resort area in the days of Peter the Great. (Peter is said to have planted the large oak tree found on Krestovky River Embankment (Naberezhnaya Reki Krestovki) in 1718. It is just west of the intersection with 2-ya Berezovaya Alleya.) In 1765, Catherine the Great bought the lands for her son, and the following year erected the classically designed **Kamennoostrovsky (Stone Island) Palace** on the eastern tip of the island; it is now an off-limits military sanitarium (though one can visit the small Gothic chapel on the grounds).

Today the 107-hectare (265-acre) island is filled with holiday centers and beautiful old dachas—some of the finest wooden buildings in Russia originally constructed by wealthy aristocratic families at the turn of the century. (Many have guarded gates and are now owned by 'New Russian' businessmen.) A wonderful example on the northwest shore is the lavish mansion of Senator Polovtsev who barely escaped when the Bolsheviks took possession of it. Another is the Dolgoruky Mansion, which stands on the southern embankment near Kamennoostrovsky Prospekt. The Danish Consulate, at 13 Bolshaya Alleya, is a fairy-tale castle built in art nouveau style. On the other side of the island is the wooden **Kamenny Island Theater**, a classical giant with an eight-column portico, erected in just 40 days in the early 1820s, and now used as a TV studio.

Another interesting site is the equine cemetery for the steeds of Mad Czar Paul I. A large park fills the southwest corner and the western footbridge leads to Yelagin Island. For a bite to eat stop at the Askur Hotel (once a dacha compound for high-ranking Party officials) at 7/1-ya Berezovaya Alleya. You can also reach Kamenny Island from Chornaya Rechka Metro station, head west down Primorsky Prospekt and then walk south across the Ushakovsky Bridge.

Yelagin Island is connected by three bridges: from Kamenny Island to the west, Krestovsky Island to the south and Primorsky Prospekt to the north. It was once owned in the late-18th century by the wealthy aristocrat Ivan Yelagin. After his death it became the summer residence of the czars. In 1817, Alexander I bought the island for the summer residence of his mother Maria Fedorovna; he then had Carlo Rossi build the elegant **Yelagin Palace** (completed in 1822) near the northeastern shore, Rossi's first commission in the city. Today, along with beautifully restored furnishings, it houses an exhibit of decorative and applied arts. Open 10.30am–5pm, Wednesday to Sunday. Besides the main palace, there are also three outdoor pavilions and the kitchen and stable buildings. Rossi went on to replan the entire island, adding parks, ponds and shady tree-lined pathways. Today the **Kirov Central Park of Culture and Rest** takes up most of the western half of the island; carnivals are held here, especially during the White Nights in June. (In winter a 25-acre skating rink is opened.) It has also long been a tradition to watch the sunset over the Gulf of Finland from the western tip of the island. Row boats can be rented at the north end by the bridge.

Just across the northern bridge, at 91 Primorsky Prospekt, is the **Buddhist Datsun** or Temple. Open daily 9am–7pm with services at 9am; Metro Staraya Derevnya. It was built between 1909 and 1915 by Pyotr Badmaev, Buddhist physician to Nicholas II, combining Tibetan and art-nouveau styles. The monastery's abbot was Lama Aguan Dordjiev, a legendary Buddhist teacher and scholar from Buryatia. Donations were given by the Dalai Lama and Nikolai Roerich, a leading figure of the spiritual and occult in the city. Having been shut down after the Revolution, the buildings were returned to the Buddhist community in 1990. (The 14th Dalai Lama, Tenzin Gyatso, visited the city and temple in 1987.) In 2003, the kingdom of Thailand restored the large golden Buddha that was damaged during the revolution. Today, the temple and monastery are run by monks from the Buryatia Republic, Russia's largest Buddhist area, situated along Lake Baikal in southern Siberia. Services are held daily at 10am and 3pm.

Krestovsky, the largest island in the group, houses the 65,000-seat **Kirov Stadium** on its western side. Nearby is the place where Alexander Pushkin fought his duel; a small obelisk marks the spot where he was mortally wounded. The main attraction is **Seaside Victory Park** (built after the war in 1945), with artificial lakes and swimming pools. Leningrad poet Anna Akhmatova wrote: 'Early in the morning, the people of Leningrad went out. In huge crowds to the seashore, and each of them planted a tree up on that strip of land, marshy, deserted. In memory of that Great Victory Day.' Within two weeks, 45,000 oaks, birch, maples and other trees, and 50,000 shrubs were planted over 450 acres. The easiest way here is to get off at Petrogradskaya Metro station, and then board bus 71 or 71a to Krestovsky Island; the latter runs the whole four-kilometer (2.5-mile) length of the island to the stadium.

THE STRELKA OF VASILYEVSKY ISLAND

Vasilyevsky is the largest island in the Neva Delta, encompassing over 4,000 acres. At the island's eastern tip, known as the Strelka (arrow or spit of land), the Neva is at its widest and branches into the Bolshaya and Malaya Neva. The Dvortsovy Most (Palace Bridge) spans the Bolshaya Neva to the west bank and the Birzhevoy Most (Commerce Bridge) crosses the Malaya Neva to the Petrograd Side.

At first Peter chose to build his city, modeled after Venice, on Vasilyevsky Island. But when the Neva froze over in winter, the island was cut off from the rest of Russia. By the mid-18th century it was decided instead to develop the administrative and cultural centers on the south bank of the Neva. However, many of the original canals are still present on the island, whose streets are laid out as numbered lines (where canals were planned) and crossed by three major avenues.

After the Peter and Paul Fortress was completed, vessels docked along the Strelka. The first wooden Exchange Building was built near the fortress by Peter I for foreign merchants only. According to tradition Russian traders made their deals at the local fairs, until the end of the 18th century when they, too, were participating in stock exchange deals. Between 1805 and 1816 the present **Stock Exchange** was erected according to the designs of Thomas de Thomon. Thousands of piles were driven into the riverbed to serve as the foundation for a granite embankment with steps leading to the Neva, flanked on each side by two large stone globes. The Exchange has 44 white Doric columns, and the sea-god Neptune in a chariot harnessed to sea horses stands over the main entrance. This building, at 5 Birzhevaya Ploshchad, still serves as the city's stock exchange. At number 4 is the **Central Naval Museum**, the largest naval museum in the world. Peter the Great originally opened this museum in the Admiralty in 1709 to store models and blueprints of Russian ships. His collection of models numbered over 1,500, and today the museum contains a half million items on the history of the Russian fleet. Included is the *Botik*, Peter's first boat. Open 11am–5pm; closed Mondays and Tuesdays and last Thursday of the month. www. museum.navy.ru.

Birzhevaya Ploshchad (Commerce Square) lies in front of the Exchange. The dark red **Rostral Columns**, 32 meters (105 feet) high, stand on either side. These were also built by de Thomon from 1805 to 1810. The Romans erected columns adorned with the prows of enemy ships, or rostrals, after naval victories. These rostral columns are decorated with figures symbolizing the victories of the Russian fleet. Around the base of the columns are four allegorical figures, representing the Neva, Volga, Dnieper and Volkhov rivers. The columns also acted as a lighthouse; at dusk hemp oil was lit in the bronze bowls at the top. Nowadays gas torches are used, but only during festivals. This area is one of the most beautiful spots in all St Petersburg, offering a large panoramic view of the city. Imagine the days when the whole area was filled with ships and sailboats. The Frenchman Alexandre Dumas was obviously captivated with the area on his first visit over a century ago: 'I really don't know whether there is any view in the whole world which can be compared with the panorama which unfolded before my eyes.'

Two gray-green warehouses, built between 1826 and 1832, stand on either side of the Exchange. The northern warehouse is now the **Museum of Soil Science**. Opened in 1904, it displays soil collections and exhibits (open 10am–5pm; closed weekends). The southern building is the **Zoological Museum** which has a collection of over 40,000 animal species, including a 44,000-year-old stuffed baby mammoth nicknamed Dima, discovered in the Siberian permafrost in 1902. Open 11am–5pm; closed Fridays.

The eight-columned **Customs House** (1829–32) at 4 Makarova Embankment (Naberezhnaya Makarova) is topped with mounted copper statues of Mercury (Commerce), Neptune (Navigation) and Ceres (Fertility). The cupola was used as an observation point to signal arriving trade ships. It is now the **Pushkin House Literary Museum**, open daily 10am–4pm, the nearest Metro is Vasileostrovskaya. In 1905, the museum purchased Pushkin's library. (See also Pushkin House Museum on page 444.) Other rooms contain exhibits devoted to many famous Russian writers.

The baroque-style green and white **Kunstkammer** (1718–34), nicknamed the Palace of Curiosities, is located at the beginning of the University Embankment (Universitetskaya Naberezhnaya at number 3) which extends west along the Bolshaya Neva. Nearly every building in this district is a monument of 18th-century architecture. Kunstkammer, stemming from the German words *kunst* (art) and *kammer* (chamber), was the first Russian museum open to the public (see picture on pages 14–15). Legend has it that Peter the Great, while walking along the embankment, noticed two pine trees entwined around each other's trunks. The czar decided to cut down the trees and build a museum on the spot to house 'rarities, curiosities and monsters'. The tree was also in the museum. In order to attract visitors, admission was free and a glass of vodka was offered at the entrance. The building became known as the 'cradle of Russian science' and was the seat of the Academy of Sciences, founded by Peter in 1724. The famed scientist and writer Mikhail Lomonosov worked here from 1741 to 1765. Today the Kunstkammer is made up of the **Museum of Anthropology and Ethnography** and the **Lomonosov Museum** (both open 11am–5pm; closed Mondays). The first Russian astronomical observatory was installed in the museum's tower. The large globe had a model of the heavens in its interior where a mechanism was regulated to create the motion of the night sky, a forerunner of the planetarium. It is three meters (nine feet) in diameter —large enough for 12 people to fit inside. The Kunstkammer soon became too small and a new building was constructed next to it for the Academy of Sciences. Completed in 1788, it was designed by Giacomo Quarenghi. A statue of Mikhail Lomonosov stands outside the Academy.

Peter commissioned the architect Trezzini to build the Twelve Collegiums (1722–42) next to the Kunstkammer (along Mendeleyevskaya Liniya) for his Senate and colleges, which replaced more than 40 governmental departments. By the beginning of the 19th-century the colleges had been replaced by ministries. After governmental orders were announced, they were posted outside the colleges for the public to read. The St Petersburg University, founded in 1819, moved into the buildings of the Twelve Collegiums in 1838, where it continues to operate today. Many prominent writers and scholars studied here; Lenin passed his bar examinations and received a degree in law. Some of the teachers were the renowned scientists, Popov and Pavlov, and Dmitri Mendeleyev (periodic law and tables) worked here for 25 years; the apartment where he lived at 7/9 Mendeleyevskaya Liniya is now a museum, open 10am–5pm, closed weekends. The red and white buildings are now part of St Petersburg University, which has more than 20,000 students.

Not far from the university at 15 University Embankment is the yellow baroque-style **Menschikov Palace**. Prince Alexander Menschikov was the first governor of St Petersburg and did much for its development. Peter the Great presented his close friend with the whole of Vasilyevsky Island in 1707 (but later took it back). The palace, built between 1710 and 1714, was the first stone residential structure on the island. It was the most luxurious building in St Petersburg and known as the Ambassadorial Palace. After the death of Peter the Great in 1725, Menschikov virtually ruled the country until he lost a power struggle and was exiled to Siberia

in 1727, where he died two years later. The First Cadet Corps took over the palace as their Military College in 1831. This palace is one of the few private houses preserved from the first quarter of the 18th century. Today the restored palace is part of the Hermitage Museum and exhibits collections of 18th-century Russian culture in over 20 rooms. Open 10.30am–4.45pm; closed Mondays. Chamber music concerts are frequently held in the evenings.

Peter the Great had the idea to create a Russian artistic school. A year before his death an engraving school was opened in the Academy of Sciences. It was Count Ivan Shuvalov who created the idea for an Academy of Fine Arts in 1757; the construction of the building, the first in the city with classical designs, took

An artist paints Peter the Great's first residence in St Petersburg, built in 1711 by Domenico Trezzini. The simple two-story stone building and steep Dutch-tiled roof is now a museum.

place between 1765 and 1788. Over the entrance is a bronze inscription: 'To Free Arts. The year—1765.' Many of Russia's most renowned artists and architects graduated from here. Today it is the largest art school in the world, and known as the **Repin Institute of Painting, Sculpture and Architecture** (named after the renowned Russian painter). Part is also a museum that depicts the educational history of Russian art and architecture; open 11am–5pm, Wednesday to Sunday.

When the Academy was built, the city's seaport was still situated here along the Neva. The river was only navigable 200 days a year (the rest of the time it was frozen). In one month alone, in May 1815, this port area received 19,327 ships— among them, 182 English, seven American, 36 Scandinavian and 69 German. In 1885, the port was transferred to Kronstadt, and later moved to Gutuevsky Island (southwest of the city) where it remains today.

In front of the Academy two pink-granite **Egyptian Sphinxes**, over 3,500 years old, flank the staircase leading down to the water; they were brought to the city in 1832, and each weighs 23 tons. They were discovered in the early 1800s during an excavation of ancient Thebes and personify the Pharaoh Amenkhotep III, who once ruled Egypt.

The **Nikolayevsky Bridge** crosses the Bolshaya Neva from University Embankment. Constructed between 1843 and 50, it was originally called Annunciation after the neighboring Cathedral, and was the first permanent bridge

During the cold winter months members of the Walrus Club chop through the ice to swim in the freezing waters. They believe that this activity promotes health and a hardy disposition.

across the Neva. Later the bridge was renamed Nikolayevsky after Nicholas I; in the middle of the bridge was a chapel with the mosaic image of St Nicholas, the patron saint of navigators. Today it is also the last bridge before the river flows into the Gulf of Finland. During the White Nights, at around 2am, it is quite lovely to watch the numerous bridges of the city open from this vantage point. (They open and shut at different times throughout the night.) The rest of Vasilyevsky Island is largely residential and industrial. Vasileostrovskaya is the closest Metro station to the Strelka.

The **Pribaltiiskaya Hotel** is at the western end of the island, not far from Primorskaya (Maritime) Metro station. After shopping in the large Admiral Gallery, watch a sunset over the Gulf from the embankment behind the hotel. A few minutes walk down the road from the hotel is the International Seaman's Club, near the Morskoi Vokzal (Marine Terminal), where most cruiseboats dock. Marine Glory Square is in front with permanent glass pavilions that house international exhibitions. The Dekabristov (Decembrist) Island lies farther to the north.

For the next 320 kilometers (200 miles), the Gulf of Finland off Vasilyevsky Island is known as Cyclone Road. Cyclones traveling west to east create what is known as the long wave. It originates in the Gulf during severe storms and then rolls toward St Petersburg. Propelled by high winds, it enters between the narrow banks of the Neva with great speed. The city has experienced over 300 floods in its 300-year history. A 29-kilometer (18-mile) barrier has been built across a section of the Gulf to control the flooding. Much controversy surrounds the barrier, since many scientists believe that it is changing the ecological balance of the area.

PALACE SQUARE (DVORTSOVAYA PLOSHCHAD)

Palace Square was the heart of Russia for over two centuries and is one of the most striking architectural ensembles in the world. Carlo Rossi was commissioned to design the square in 1819. The government bought up all the residential houses and reconstructed the area into the Ministries of Foreign Affairs and Finance, and the General Staff Headquarters of the Russian Army. These two large yellow buildings curve around the southern end of the Square and are linked by the **Triumphal Arch** (actually two arches), whose themes of soldiers and armor commemorate the victories of the War of 1812. It is crowned by the 16-ton Winged Glory in a chariot led by six horses, which everyone believed would collapse the arch. On opening day Rossi declared: 'If it should fall, I will fall with it.' He climbed to the top of the arch as the scaffolding was removed.

The Square was not only the parade ground for the czar's Winter Palace, but a symbol of the revolutionary struggle as well, and was in fact the site of three revolutions: the Decembrists first held an uprising near here in 1825. On Sunday

January 9, 1905, over 100,000 people marched to Palace Square to protest intolerable working conditions. The demonstration began peacefully as the families carried icons and pictures of the czar. But Nicholas II's troops opened fire on the crowd and thousands were killed in the event known as Bloody Sunday. After the massacre, massive strikes ensued. In October of the same year, the St Petersburg Soviet of Workers' Deputies was formed. Twelve years later, in February 1917, the Kerensky Government overthrew the autocracy. At 1.50am on October 26, 1917, the Bolshevik Red Guards stormed through Palace Square to capture the Winter Palace from the Provisional Government. John Reed, the famous American journalist, wrote of the Revolution that on that night 'on Palace Square I watched the birth of a new world.'

In 1920, the anniversary of the Revolution was celebrated by thousands of people rushing through the square to dramatically reconstruct the storming of the Winter Palace. (Eisenstein's famous film *October* immortalized this embellished image.) In actuality, only one blank shot was fired by the *Aurora*, and one soldier killed—the Provisional Government surrendered virtually without a fight. For decades thereafter, parades and celebrations were held on May Day and Revolution Day. Palace Square remains the heart of the city. But today you will see anything but Socialist parades—just some die-hard nationalists. There is now everything from heavy-metal pop concerts to Hare Krishnas dancing around the square.

As you enter Palace Square from Bolshaya Morskaya Ulitsa, an unforgettable panorama unfolds. The **Alexander Column** stands in the middle of the square, symbolizing the defeat of Napoleon in 1812. Nicholas I had it erected in memory of Alexander I. The 700-ton piece of granite took three years to be extracted from the Karelian Isthmus and brought down by barges to the city. Architect Auguste Montferrand supervised the polishing in 1830, and by 1834 the 14.5 meter-high (47.5-feet) column was erected by 2,500 men using an elaborate system of pulleys. The figure of the angel (whose face resembles Alexander I) holding a cross was carved by sculptor Boris Orlovsky. The Guard's Headquarters (to the right of the column facing the Palace) was built by Bryullov (1837–43) and now serves as an administrative building.

The main architectural wonder of the Square is the **Winter Palace**, standing along the bank of the Neva. This masterpiece by Rastrelli was commissioned by Czarina Elizabeth, daughter of Peter, who was fond of the baroque style and desired a lavish palace decorated with columns, stucco and sculptures. It was built between 1754 and 1762, as Rastrelli remarked, 'solely for the glory of all Russia'. At this time, the Winter Palace cost two and a half million rubles, equal to the value of 45 tons of silver. The Palace remained the czars' official residence until the February 1917 Revolution. The magnificent Palace extends over eight hectares (20 acres) and the total perimeter

The view from the Winter Palace across Palace Square. In the center stands the Alexander Column commemorating the defeat of Napoleon in 1812. The General Staff Building and the Guard's Headquarters curve around the far side of the square and are linked by the Triumphal Arch, which is crowned by Carlo Rossi's 16-ton sculpture of the Winged Glory.

measures two kilometers (over a mile). There are 1,057 rooms (not one identical), 1,945 windows, 1,886 doors and 117 staircases. The royal family's staff consisted of over 1,000 servants. At 200 meters (656 feet) long and 22 meters (72 feet) high, it was the largest building in St Petersburg. After the 1837 fire destroyed a major portion of the Palace, architects Bryullov and Stasov restored the interior along the lines of Russian classicism, but preserved Rastrelli's light and graceful baroque exterior. The blue-green walls are adorned with 176 sculpted figures. The interior was finished with marble, malachite, jasper, semiprecious stones, polished woods,

gilded moldings and crystal chandeliers. In 1844, Nicholas I passed a decree (in force until 1905) stating that all buildings in the city (except churches) had to be at least two meters (six feet) lower than the Winter Palace. During World War II the Winter Palace was marked on German maps as Bombing Objective number 9. (See Special Topic on pages 507.) Today the Winter Palace houses the **Hermitage Museum**—the largest museum in the country, exhibiting close to 3 million items and visited by several million people annually. It contains one of the largest and most valuable collections of art in the world, dating from antiquity to the present.

Peter the Great began the city's first art collection after visiting Europe. In 1719, he purchased Rembrandt's *David's Farewell to Jonathan*, a statue of Aphrodite (*Venus of Taurida*), and started a museum of Russian antiquities (now on display in the Hermitage's Siberian collection).

In 1764, Catherine the Great created the Hermitage (*Ermitazh*—a French word meaning secluded spot) in the Winter Palace for a place to display 225 Dutch and Flemish paintings she had purchased in Berlin. Her ambassadors, who included Prince Dmitry Golitsyn and Denis Diderot, were often sent to European countries in search of art. In 1766, Golitsyn secured the purchase of Rembrandt's *Return of the Prodigal Son* from a private collector, regarded by many as one of the greatest works of art in the Hermitage. In 1769, she purchased the entire collection of Count von Brühl of Dresden, which included over 600 paintings and 1,000 drawings. The Hermitage held almost 4,000 paintings at the time of her death. Subsequent czars continued to expand the collection: Alexander I bought the entire picture gallery of Josephine, wife of Napoleon, and Nicholas I even purchased pictures from Napoleon's stepdaughter. Until 1852, the Hermitage was only open to members of the royal family and aristocratic friends. Catherine the Great wrote in a letter to one of her close friends that 'all this is admired by mice and myself'. A small list of rules, written by Catherine, hung by the Hermitage's entrance (see page 504). In 1852, Nicholas I opened the Hermitage on certain days as a public museum (but still closed to common people), and put it under the administrative direction of curators. After the 1917 Revolution, the Hermitage was opened full-time to the whole public.

The Hermitage occupies several other buildings in addition to the Winter Palace. The **Little Hermitage** housed Catherine's original collection in a small building next to the Palace; it was constructed by Vallin de la Mothe between 1764 and 1767. Stackenschneider's Pavilion Hall is decked with white marble columns, 28 chandeliers, the four Fountains of Tears and the Peacock Clock. The royal family would stroll in the Hanging Gardens in the summer, along with pheasants and peacocks. In winter, snow mounds were built for sledding. The **Old Hermitage** (or Large Hermitage) was built right next to it to provide space for Catherine's growing collection. The **Hermitage Theater**, Catherine's private theater, is linked to the Old Hermitage by a small bridge that crosses the Winter Ditch canal. The theater was built by Quarenghi in 1787, designed by the German Leo von Klenze, and modeled after the amphitheaters of Pompeii. Today concerts and ballets are staged here. The **New Hermitage** (1839–52), located behind the Old Hermitage, houses additional works of art. Its main entrance off Millionnaya Ulitsa is composed of the ten large and powerful **Statues of Atlas**. They were designed by the sculptor A Terebenyev who personally participated in the carvings of these huge blocks of polished gray marble. The first figure took a year and a half to complete. Three more years were spent cutting the other nine. The figures of Atlas became the official emblem of the Hermitage.

The Hermitage collection spans a millennium of art and culture. Mikhail Piotrovsky, the director of the museum stated, 'The Hermitage is a symbol of not only Russian but human civilization.' It is said that if a visitor spent only half a minute at each piece, it still would take nine years to view them all! A map of the layout and audio-cassette tours can be purchased inside. Plan to spend at least three hours, probably more, here and this will only cover the initial highlights of the museum's collection. The following outlines a basic tour. (See page 500 for details on how to gain admission.)

Upon entering, pass through the Classical Antiquities, and then walk left through the **Rastrelli Gallery** and up the white marble steps of the **Jordan Staircase** (after Jesus' baptism in the River Jordan) to the first floor. Both clergy and court descended the staircase each year on 6 January to celebrate the 'Blessing of the Waters.' The procession then continued outside to the Neva River where a hole was cut through the ice, and water blessed and bottled for later use in baptisms in the city's churches.

On the first floor are the State Rooms of the Winter Palace. The top of the Staircase opens onto the **Field Marshals' Hall**, and the **Throne Room of Peter the Great**. The **Armorial Hall** leads to the magnificent **1812 Gallery**, designed to commemorate the Napoleonic Wars. Portraits of over 300 generals who fought against Napoleon cover the walls from floor to ceiling. The Italian architect, Carlo Rossi, modeled the gallery after the Waterloo Chamber at Windsor Castle. In front of the gallery is the great **Hall of St George** where Czars held elaborate receptions. The ceiling is a mirrored pattern of the inlaid floors. Where the Imperial Throne once stood now hangs an enormous mosaic map of the former Soviet Union, covered with 45,000 semiprecious stones. Moscow is marked by a ruby star, and St Petersburg is written in letters of alexandrite. Above it hangs a bas-relief of St George, protector of Russia.

Continue on around to the southwest corner. Here, other rooms of interest are the **White Hall**, **Gold Room**, **Raspberry Drawing Room** and **Blue Bedroom**. Walking along the **Dark Corridor** leads to the **Rotunda** and the **Moorish Dining Hall** which opens onto the resplendent **Malachite Room**, designed by Bryullov as the Royal Drawing Room. Everything in this space, from pillars to vases, is carved from bright green malachite extracted from the Ural mountains. When the Bolsheviks raided the Winter Palace in October 1917, it was in the next door **White Dining Room** where Kerensky's Provisional Government members were captured. The clock on the mantelpiece is set to the time of their arrest at 2.10am. Circling back towards the Jordan Staircase, you will pass through **Nicholas Hall**, once used to stage balls of over 5,000 people. A portrait of Nicholas I gave the ballroom its name.

Inside the Hermitage Museum. (opposite page) The Jordan Staircase (named after Jesus' baptism in the River Jordan) leads the visitor up marble steps from the Rastrelli Gallery, entrance to the museum's many halls including the Throne Room of Peter the Great (see picture on page 445); (left) The ceiling of the Gallery is decorated with a painting of the gods of Mt Olympus; (below) the Siberian green jasper Kolyvan Vase. Visit www.hermitagemuseum.org.

Exhibits on the ground floor delineate the history of Russian culture. One of the most famous of the items that Nicholas I had placed in the New Hermitage was the **Kolyvan Vase**; standing six-feet tall, its elliptical bowl is five yards long and three yards wide. The vast piece of jasper from which it was cut was unearthed in the Siberian Altai mountains in 1819. The rough cut was not completed until 1831. The stone was then moved over the mountains to the town of Kolyvan, were it took another 12 years to cut and polish the 19-ton giant urn at a cost of over 30,000 silver rubles. Then, in 1843, it took over 150 horses to haul the vase across the wintry ice to the docks of Barnaul where it was put on a ship bound for St Petersburg. Eventually, it was moved to the New Hermitage where the walls were literally built around it. The vase still stands in its own gallery surrounded by Greek and Roman antiquities.

Primeval art (over 400,000 objects), and ancient and oriental art and culture (a quarter of a million pieces) from Egypt, Babylon, Byzantium, the Middle East, Japan, China and India occupy both the ground and second floors. (In the 1920s, academician Josif Orbelli wrote to Stalin advocating that no eastern art from the Oriental Department be sold abroad. Stalin agreed. Thus, in future years, the museum staff began to assign all treasures of uncertain origin to the Oriental Department to cunningly prevent their sale out of the country.)

Other departments include Italian, Spanish, Dutch, German, French, English and Russian art. Over 650,000 items in the collection of Western Europe art are found on the first and second floors. This includes paintings by da Vinci, Raphael, Titian, Botticelli, El Greco, Rubens, Rembrandt, and one of the world's finest impressionist collections that includes works by Monet, Matisse, Lautrec, Cézanne, Van Gogh and Picasso. In addition there are numerous displays of sculpture, tapestries, china, jewelry, furniture, rare coins and handicrafts. The museum has room to display only 20 percent of its incredible treasures.

In 1995, the Hermitage ran a highly controversial exhibition entitled Hidden Treasures Revealed, composed entirely of art confiscated by the Red Army from private German collections when it swept across Eastern Europe into Berlin at the end of World War II. The paintings, estimated to be worth several million dollars, are by impressionist and Postimpressionist artists. The centerpiece was Degas' 1875 painting *Place de la Concorde*, believed to have been destroyed during the war. Stored secretly for over half a century in a small room on the museum's second floor, the unveiled collection included many other paintings by Monet, Renoire, Gauguin, Cézanne, Matisse and Picasso. In all, during the war, the two countries pilfered from each other an estimated five million artworks. The dispute over who is the rightful owner of these paintings continues.

Inside the Hermitage Museum. (bottom) The Throne Room of Peter the Great was built to honor the czar in the early 1800s. The throne was crafted by a Huguenot silversmith and embroidered with a double-headed eagle. The czar's portrait with a woman (representing Minerva or the Spirit of Russia) was painted in 1730 for the Russian Ambasssador to London (see also pictures on pages 496–7).

IBM has installed computerized touch-screen information terminals to help visitors find their way around. A recommended book to buy at the Hermitage store is *Saved for Humanity*, tracing the history of the museum; available in several languages. A catalog of the Hidden Treasures is also on sale (and also available through the publisher Harry Abrahms in New York). A fabulous film to rent is Alexander Sokurov's *Russian Ark*, (now with English subtitles), a docu-drama on the history of Russia which takes place entirely throughout the Hermitage and Winter Palace. The museum is open 10.30am–6pm, Sundays until 5pm; closed Mondays.

The easiest way into the museum is to get a ticket through your hotel or a travel agency. The Hermitage also offers specialized tours to other museum collections, including Scythian art, Siberian goldwork and church ornaments. One can now buy entrance tickets to the Hermitage on-line with a credit card at www.hermitagemuseum.org. This can avoid the long queues at the ticket offices. Tickets are also sold at kiosks by the main southwest entrance of the palace near the gardens off Victory Square. There are often separate foreign *kassas*, since non-Russians must pay more for tickets. (Photo/video permits are extra.) For groups of four or more, tickets can be purchased inside the front entrance on the Neva river side. (Try making up a group of foreigners—this can save time standing in the longer individual queues. Once inside, you can then split up. Once inside, tourists must check coats and large bags at the designated sites.

Leaving the Hermitage through Palace Square and left past the Guard's Head-quarters takes you through the Choristers' Passage and across a wide bridge known as Pevchesky Most (Singers' Bridge). This bridge crosses the lovely **Moika Canal** and leads to the former Imperial Choristers' Capella (1831), now the Glinka Academy Capella. At 12 Moika Embankment, to the left of the Capella, is the **Pushkin House Museum** where the poet, considered the fountainhead of Russian literature, lived from October 1836 until his death in January 1837. Alexander Pushkin died following a duel on Krestovsky Island with a French soldier of fortune named George D'Anthès, who had been publicly flirting with Pushkin's beautiful wife Natalia. The affair was said to have been instigated by Nicholas I, who was tired of the famous poet's radical politics; the czar was Pushkin's personal censor. A statue of Pushkin stands in the courtyard. The rooms have all been preserved and contain his personal belongings and manuscripts. The study is arranged exactly as it was when Pushkin died on the divan from a wound he received in the duel. The clock is even set to 2.45am, the moment of his death. The next room displays the clothes worn during the duel and his death mask. Since Pushkin is still one of the most popular figures in Russia, museum tickets are often sold out; it may be necessary to buy them in advance. Audiophones can also be rented. The museum is open 10.30am–5pm; closed Tuesdays and last Friday of the month. Metro Nevsky Prospekt. www.museumpushkin.ru.

The Area of Senate Square (Senatskaya Ploshchad)

Walking west of the Winter Palace along the Neva, you come to another chief architectural monument of the city, the **Admiralty**, recognizable by its tall golden spire topped by a golden frigate, the symbol of St Petersburg after Peter the Great. The best views of the building are from its southern end. A beautiful fountain stands in the middle of Alexandrovsky Garden surrounded by busts of Glinka, Gogol and Lermontov. In 1704, Peter the Great ordered a second small outpost constructed on the left bank of the Neva, opposite the main town. This shipyard was later referred to as the Admiralty. Over 10,000 peasants and engineers were employed to work on the Russian naval fleet. By the end of the 18th century the Navy had its headquarters here. Whenever the Neva waters rose during a severe storm, a lantern was lit in the spire to warn of coming floods. In 1738, the main building was rebuilt by the architect Ivan Korobov, who replaced the wooden tower with a golden spire. From 1806 to 1823, the building was again redesigned by Andreyan Zakharov, an architectural professor at the St Petersburg Academy. The height of the spire was increased to 72.5 meters (238 feet) and decorated with 56 mythological figures and 350 ornamentations based on the glory of the Russian fleet. The scene over the main-entrance archway depicts Neptune handing over his trident to Peter the Great, a symbol of Peter's mastery of the sea. In 1860, many of the statues were taken down when the Orthodox Church demanded the 'pagan' statues removed. Today the Admiralty houses the Higher Naval School.

Across the street from the Admiralty, at 6 Admiralty Prospekt, is the building known as the All Russia Extraordinary Commission for Combating Counter-revolution, Sabotage and Speculation—the Cheka. Felix Dzerzhinsky, the first chairman of the Cheka Police Force (forerunner of the KGB), had his office here. His best-remembered words were that a member of the Cheka 'must have clean hands, a warm heart and a cold head'. A memorial museum dedicated to Dzerzhinsky has been here since 1974.

Beside the Admiralty is the infamous **Senate Square**, formerly known as Decembrists' and Peter Square. In 1925, to mark the 100-year anniversary of the Decembrist uprising, the area was renamed Decembrists' Square. (In 1992, its name reverted to Senate.) After the Russian victory in the Patriotic War of 1812 and the introduction of principles from the French Enlightenment, both the nobility and peasants wanted an end to the monarchy and serfdom. An opportune moment for insurrection came on November 19, 1825, when Czar Alexander I died suddenly. A secret revolutionary society, consisting mainly of noblemen, gathered over 3,000 soldiers and sailors who refused to swear allegiance to the new czar, Nicholas I. The members compiled the Manifesto to the Russian People, which they hoped the Senate would approve. (They did not know that the Senate had already proclaimed their loyalty to Nicholas.) They decided to lead an uprising of the people in Senate Square on December 14, 1825, and from there to capture the Winter Palace and Peter and Paul Fortress. But Nicholas I discovered the plan and surrounded the square with armed guards. The Decembrists marched to an empty Senate, and moreover, Prince Trubetskoi, who was elected to lead the insurrection, never showed up! Tens of thousands of people joined the march and prevented the guards from advancing on the main parties. But Nicholas I then ordered his guards to open fire on the crowd. Hundreds were killed and mass arrests followed. Over 100 people were sentenced to serve 30 years in penal servitude. Five leaders of the rebellion were hanged in Peter and Paul Fortress. Others received such ludicrous sentences as having to run a gauntlet of a thousand soldiers 12 times, amounting to 12,000 blows by rod; if they survived, they would be set free! Even though the 1825 uprising was unsuccessful, 'the roar of cannon on Senate Square awakened a whole generation', observed the revolutionary writer Alexander Herzen.

In 1768, Catherine wanted to commission a magnificent monument to her predecessor, Peter the Great. She considered herself Peter's political heir; he had begun to open Russia to the modern world, and Catherine had brought Europe into her country's domain. It was her close friend in France, Denis Diderot, who invited Etienne Falconet (who had written an article for Diderot's *Encyclopédie*) to Russia. The French sculptor said he was prepared to devote eight years of his life to it. In

The statue of Peter the Great known as the Bronze Horseman (Myedny Vsadnik)

ПЕТРУ ПЕРВОМУ
ЕКАТЕРИНА ВТОРАЯ
ЛѢТА 1782

Pushkin House Museum (see page 500). (top) Sketch of Alexander Pushkin. (bottom left) The writer's study and library of over 4,000 books. It is arranged exactly as it was when Pushkin died on the divan from a wound received in a duel. The clock is set to the moment of his death, 2.45am, on January 29, 1837. (bottom right) The inkstand on Pushkin's desk is decorated with an Ethiopian figure which reminded him of his great-grandfather, Abram Hannibal, an African officer who became Peter the Great's chief military engineer in St Petersburg.

CODE OF THE EMPRESS CATHERINE

*A*t the entrance of one hall, I found behind a green curtain the social rules of the Hermitage, for the use of those intimate friends admitted by the Czarina into the asylum of Imperial Liberty.

I will transcribe, verbatim, this charter, granted to social intimacy by the caprice of the sovereign of the once enchanted place: it was copied for me in my presence:-

RULES TO BE OBSERVED ON ENTERING

ARTICLE I
On entering, the title and rank must be put off,
as well as the hat and sword.

ARTICLE II
Pretensions founded on the prerogatives of birth, pride,
or other sentiments of a like nature must also be left at the door.

ARTICLE III
Be merry; nevertheless, break nothing and spoil nothing.

ARTICLE IV
Sit, stand, walk, do whatever you please, without caring for anyone.

ARTICLE V
Speak with moderation, and not too often,
in order to avoid being troublesome to others.

ARTICLE VI
Argue without anger and without warmth.

ARTICLE VII
*Banish sighs and yawns, that you may not communicate ennui,
or be a nuisance to anyone.*

ARTICLE VIII
*Innocent games, proposed by any members of the society,
must be accepted by the others.*

ARTICLE IX
*Eat slowly and with appetite; drink with moderation,
that each may walk steadily as he goes out.*

ARTICLE X
*Leave all quarrels at the door; what enters at one ear must go out at the
other before passing the threshold of the Hermitage.*

*If any member violates the above rules, for each fault witnessed by two
persons, he must drink a glass of fresh water (ladies not excepted);
furthermore, he must read aloud a page of the* Telemachiad *(a poem by
Trediakofsky). Whoever fails during one evening in three of these articles,
must learn by heart six lines of the* Telemachiad. *He who fails in the tenth
article must never more re-enter the Hermitage.*

Marquis Astolphe Louis Leonard de Custine, Russia, *1854–5* fact, Falconet toiled for 12 years to create, in his words, 'an alive, vibrant and passionate spirit.' He successfully designed the symbolic rider (Peter is depicted three times life size) on a rearing horse, crushing a serpent underfoot. Marie Collot, Falconet's pupil and future wife, sculpted the head (based on a bronze bust of Peter fashioned during his lifetime by Carlo Rastrelli), and the Russian sculptor, Gordeyev, the snake.

In addition, Falconet wanted to place his monument atop natural stone. And it was Catherine the Great who went to great lengths to transfer an enormous granite stone, shaped like a wave about to break, over ten kilometers (six miles) to the city. It had been split by lightening and was known as Thunder Rock. Peter the Great was said to have often climbed this very rock to view his emerging city. Weighing 1,600 tons, it was eight meters (22 feet) high, 13.5 meters (42 feet) long and ten meters (34 feet) wide. Catherine offered 7,000 roubles as a reward to the person who invented a way to quickly transport it to the city. A Russian blacksmith came up with a plan. First, an entire road was cut through the forest to the gulf. With the help of levers, the boulder was lifted atop a log platform. Then two large, parallel grooves were carved out along the path (rather like a railroad track). Thirty copper balls, acting like ballbearings, were placed along the grooves. Over 100 horses took five months to pull the 'moving mountain' nine kilometers to the sea. The boulder was then placed upon a raft and towed to Senate Square.

After three attempts to cast the huge statue, Falconet finally succeeded in 1782. It was in this year that the masterpiece was unveiled, the 100th anniversary of Peter's ascension to the throne. In a play of words, Catherine had inscribed: *Petro Primo Catharina Secunda*—'To Peter I from Catherine II, 1782.' This monument became known as the **Bronze Horseman**, after the popular poem by Pushkin. (See page 625). Today the statue is looked on as the symbol of St Petersburg, a sign of its splendor and endurance. It has remained a constant through nearly three tumultuous centuries. Legend has it that as long as the Bronze Horseman remains, St Petersburg will never perish.

The first governing Senate was established by Peter the Great in 1711 and ruled the country while the czar was away. Peter put the Church and ecclesiastical members under State control in 1721 by founding the Holy Synod. Carlo Rossi supervised the construction of the yellow-white Senate, Synod and Supreme Court buildings between 1829 and 1836. They are joined by an arch, symbolizing Faith and Law. Today they house the Historical Archives. Take a stroll down the small Galernaya Ulitsa that lies beyond the arch; this was the area of the galley shipyards. The two Ionic columns standing at the start of the next boulevard bear the Goddesses of Glory. These monuments commemorate the valor of Russia's Horse Guards during the war against Napoleon. The building that looks like an ancient Roman temple is the Horse Guard Manège, where the czar's horse guards were trained. It was built between 1804 and 1807 from designs by Quarenghi. In front of the portico are marble statues of the mythological heroes Castor and Pollux. Today the building is used as an exhibition hall for the Union of Artists.

St Isaac's Square (Isaakiyevskaya Ploshchad)

The whole southern end of Senate Square is framed by the grand silhouette of **St Isaac's Cathedral**. In 1710, the first wooden church of St Isaac was built by Peter, who was born on the day which celebrated the sainthood of Isaac of Dalmatia; it was replaced in 1729 by one of stone. At that time the church was situated nearer to the banks of the Neva and it eventually began to crack and sink. In 1768, it was decided to build another church farther away from the riverbank. But, on its completion in 1802, the church was not deemed grand enough for the growing magnificence of the capital. After the War of 1812, Czar Alexander I announced a

A view looking east over St Petersburg from the top of St Isaac's Cathedral.
The blue-domed cathedral in the distance is that of St Nicholas, known as
the Sailor's Church (St Nicholas is the patron saint of sailors), built in 1762.

competition for the best design of a new St Isaac's. The young architect Montferrand presented an elaborate album filled with 24 different variations, from Chinese to Gothic, for the czar to choose from. Montferrand was selected for the monumental task in 1818, and the czar also assigned the architects Stasov, Rossi and the Mikhailov brothers to help with the engineering.

The cathedral took 40 years to build. In the first year alone, 11,000 serfs drove 25,000 wooden planks into the soft soil to set a foundation. Each of the 112 polished granite columns, weighing 130 tons, had to be raised by a system of pulleys. The system was so efficient that the monolithic columns were each installed in a mere 45 minutes. The domed cathedral has a total height of 101.5 meters (333 feet). An observation deck along the upper colonnade (562 steps to climb) provides a magnificent view of the city. The State spared no expense—the cathedral cost ten times more than the Winter Palace. Nearly 100 kilograms of pure gold were used to gild the dome, which in good weather is visible 40 kilometers (25 miles) away. The interior is faced with 14 different kinds of marble, and 43 other types of stone and minerals. Inside the western portico is a bust of Montferrand, made from each type of marble. (Montferrand died one month after the completion of the cathedral. He had asked to be buried within its walls, but Czar Alexander II refused. Instead, Montferrand was buried in Paris.) The cathedral can hold 14,000 people and is filled with over 400 sculptures, paintings and mosaics by the best Russian and European masters of the 19th-century. Twenty-two artists decorated the iconostasis, ceilings and walls. The altar's huge stained-glass window is surrounded by frescoes by Bryullov, who also painted the frescoes in the ceiling of the main dome. A St Petersburg newspaper wrote that the cathedral was 'a pantheon of Russian art, as artists have left monuments to their genius in it'. On May 29, 1858, St Isaac's was inaugurated with much pomp and celebration as the main cathedral of St Petersburg. In 1931, it was opened by the government as a museum. Open 11am–6pm; closed Wednesdays. Services are sometimes held during special religious holidays.

St Isaac's Square, in front of the cathedral, was originally a marketplace in the 1830s. At its center stands the bronze **Statue of Nicholas I** constructed by Montferrand and Klodt between 1856 and 1859. The czar, who loved horses and military exploits (nicknamed Nicholas the Stick), is portrayed in a cavalry uniform wearing a helmet with an eagle. His horse rests only on two points. The bas-reliefs around the pedestal depict the events of Nicholas' turbulent rule. One of them shows Nicholas I addressing his staff after the Decembrist uprising. The four figures at each corner represent Faith, Wisdom, Justice and Might, and depict the faces of Nicholas' wife and three daughters, who commissioned the statue.

St Isaac's Cathedral on St Isaac's Square was designed by Auguste Montferrand in 1818 and took 40 years to build. Over 100 kilograms of gold were used to gild the dome, which is visible over 40 kilometers (25 miles) away.

The two buildings on each side of the monument were built between 1844 and 1853 and now house the Academy of Agricultural Sciences. Behind the monument is the **Blue Bridge** (1818), which is painted accordingly. It is the broadest bridge in the city and even though it appears to be a continuation of the square, it is actually a bridge over the Moika River. There was a slave market here before the abolition of serfdom in 1861. Many of St Petersburg's bridges were named after the color they were painted; up river are the Green and Red bridges. On one side of the bridge is an obelisk crowned by a trident, known as the Neptune Scale. Five bronze bands indicate the level of the water during the city's worst floods. The Leningrad poet Vera Inber wrote of this place:

> *Here in the city, on Rastrelli's marble*
> *Or on plain brick, we see from time to time*
> *A mark: 'The water-level reached this line'*
> *And we can only look at it and marvel.*

Beyond the bridge stands the former Mariinsky Palace. It was built between 1839 and 1844 for Maria, the daughter of Nicholas I. In 1894, it was turned into the State Council of the Russian Empire. The artist Repin painted the centennial gala of the council in 1901, entitled *The Solemn Meeting of the State Council*; it can be viewed at the Russian Museum. In 1917, the Palace was the residence of the Provisional Government. It now houses the St Petersburg City Assembly (the city parliament).

The seven-story **Hotel Astoria**, on the northeast side of the square, was built in 1912 by architect Fyodor Lidval in a Russian interpretation of art nouveau called northern moderne. It became the grandest hotel in the city. During the early 1900s, St Petersburg was alive with the innovative creations of the Ballet Russes, Diaghilev and Stravinsky. In turn, Lidval designed the hotel with rounded corners, swirling mirrors and artistic plasterwork. During the 1917 revolution, demonstrators stormed the hotel, but it remained open. The hotel became a field hospital during WW II. And, during the 900-day Siege of Leningrad, Hitler even planned to hold his victory party here; he sent out engraved invitations for a banquet to be held at the Astoria on November 7 1942, as soon as he had captured the city. Of course, this never took place. The hotel has been completely renovated, and today stands as a proud symbol of the new spirit of St Petersburg. The other side of the building is now the Angleterre Hotel.

In front of the Astoria is the Lobanov-Rostovsky Mansion. Montferrand built this for the Russian diplomat between 1817 and 1820. Pushkin mentioned the marble lions in front of the house in the *Bronze Horseman*, when the hero climbed one of them to escape the flood. The mansion is referred to as the House with Lions.

The **Museum of Musical Instruments**, at 5 St Isaac's Square, has one of the largest collections (3,000) in the world. Some of the items on display are the grand pianos of Rimsky-Korsakov, Glinka and Rubenstein. Open only Wednesdays, Thursdays and Saturdays, 12–6pm. In front of the museum stands Myatlev's House. Built for the poet by Rinaldi in 1760, it is one of the oldest structures on the square.

On the west side of the square is the Intourist Building, originally built in 1910 to accommodate the new German Embassy. It was designed by German architect Berens, who became one of the founders of the new *jugendstil* style. Behind this building, at 47 Bolshaya Morskaya (first floor), is the **Nabokov House Museum**. The famous writer was born here over a century ago on April 24 1899. This house and St Petersburg are lovingly described in his autobiography, *Speak Memory*. Other works include *Pale Fire, Laughter in the Dark* and *Lolita*—the immensely controversial novel written in 1955 (and later made into a classic movie by Stanley Kubrick). On view in the museum are original *samizdat*—secretly circulated hand-copied Nabokov works officially banned for print in Soviet times. His family, liberal aristocrats, fled to Berlin in 1917, and Vladimir later resided in the US, where he died in 1977. Open daily 11am–6pm, Fridays 11am–5pm, weekends 12–5pm; closed Mondays and Tuesdays.

At 4 Pochtamskaya Ulitsa is the **Popov Central Communication Museum**. On May 7, Russia celebrates Radio Day. On this day, in 1895, Alexander Popov demonstrated his invention of the radio receiver, with a range of 600 meters. Two years later, its range had increased to five kilometers, and by 1901, to 150. In 1900, Popov won a gold medal at the Paris World's Fair. (In 1897, it was the Italian Guillermo Marconi who received the first radio receiver patent.) The museum is open 12–6pm; closed Mondays.

At 9 Pochtamskaya Ulitsa is the General Post Office (1782–89), with the Clock of the World mounted on its archway. Dostoevsky lived at 23 Malaya Morskaya Ulitsa before his imprisonment at Peter and Paul Fortress. Here he wrote *Netochka Nezvanova* and *The White Nights*. Dostoevsky's main museum is located at 5/2 Kuznechny Pereulok, near Vladimirskaya Metro station (closed Mondays).

FIELD OF MARS (POLYE MARSOVO)

A short walk east from the Hermitage, to number 5 Millionnaya brings you to the **Marble Palace**, a masterpiece of neoclassicism. In 1768, Catherine the Great commissioned Antonio Rinaldi to build a palace for her favorite, Count Grigory Orlov. (He had helped Catherine ascend to the throne in 1762.) His response was to present the Empress with one of the world's largest cut diamonds, weighing 189.6 carats. (The 'Orlov' diamond was later mounted in the royal scepter.) Upon his retirement in 1783, Catherine wrote in a letter to him: "I shall never forget how much I owe to your family, nor the qualities with which you are endowed and how useful they can be to our Motherland." This was the only building in St Petersburg

*The young German Princess Catherine II arrived in St Petersburg to marry Peter III.
She went on to become the first foreign woman to rule Russia, and later received the title
of Catherine the Great for her many accomplishments during her 34-year reign.*

CATHERINE THE GREAT (1729–1796)

Peter the Great propelled Russia into the 18th-century; Catherine II completed it by decorating his creation in European pomp and principle. Born Sophie Frederika Augusta in 1729 to the German prince of Anhalt-Zerbst, she was chosen as the future bride, at the age of 14, to Peter III, the half-wit grandson of Peter the Great. When Peter III ascended the throne in 1762, he threatened to get rid of Catherine by imprisoning her in a nunnery (and marrying his pockmarked mistress). This only fueled Catherine's ambitions; she said, 'either I die or I begin to rule'. That same year a secret coup, headed by her lover Grigory Orlov and his brothers, overthrew the unpopular Peter. When he was killed by drunken guards a week later, Catherine became the first foreigner ever to sit upon the Russian throne; she would rule for 34 years. Catherine was clever and adventurous and had fallen deeply in love with her new homeland (instead of with her husband). She immersed herself in the problems of politics and agriculture and worked toward basing the government on philosophic principles rather than on religious doctrines or hereditary rights. Because of her European roots, Catherine held a fascination for France and avidly worked to link French culture with that of her adopted nation. She read Voltaire, Montesquieu and Rousseau and sent emissaries to study in foreign lands; she also began the education of noblewomen. The Russian aristocracy soon incorporated French culture into their daily lives, giving the noblemen a common identity. The French language also set them apart from the Russian peasantry. In 1780, she further initiated the Declaration of Armed Neutrality, helping the American colonies in their struggle for independence.

Catherine described her reign as the 'thornless rose that never stings'. Along with autocratic power, she ruled with virtue, justice and reason. By the publication of books and newspapers, and instruction by Western-trained tutors, education spread throughout the provinces, where before much of the learning originated from the Church. This allowed Russian culture to cut loose from its religious roots. Paper money was introduced, along with vaccinations; the day of Catherine's smallpox vaccination became a national feast day.

Scientific expeditions were sent to Far Eastern lands and hundreds of new cities were built in Russia's newly conquered territories. Along the coast of the Black Sea, the cities of Odessa, Azov and Sevastopol were constructed on the sites of old Greek settlements. With the formation of the Academy of Sciences, Russia now contributed to the Renaissance Age and would never again stand in the shadows. One of the most important figures of the time, Mikhail Lomonosov, scientist, poet and historian, later helped to establish Moscow University.

Catherine spared no expense to redecorate St Petersburg in the classical designs of the time. Wanting a home for the art that she began collecting from abroad, Catherine built the Hermitage. It was connected to her private apartments and also served as a conference chamber and theater. Besides the exquisite treasures kept within, the Hermitage itself was constructed of jasper, malachite, marble and gold. The Empress' extravagant reputation filtered into her love life as well. She had 21 known favorites, and loved being exceedingly generous to them—during her rule she spent nearly 100 million rubles on them. (Russia's annual budget, at the time, was 40 million rubles.) Among Catherine's ladies-in-waiting was a *probolshchitsa*, whose sole task was to test the virility of the Czarina's potential admirers. Platon Zubov, at age 22, was the Empress' lover when she was well into her sixties.

Unfortunately it became increasingly difficult for Catherine to maintain her autocratic rule while at the same time implement large-scale reform. Her sweeping plans for change planted the seeds for much more of a blossoming than she bargained for. The education of the aristocracy created a greater schism between them and the working class and her reforms further worsened the conditions of the peasantry. As the city took the center of culture away from the Church, more and more Old Believers were left disillusioned with her rule. Catherine tore down monasteries and torched the old symbols of Muscovy. In an Age of Reason, she had a deep suspicion of anything mystical.

Huge sums of money were also spent on constructing elaborate palaces for her favorite relations and advisors. One of these was Prince Grigory Potemkin, her foreign minister, commander-in-chief and greatest love for almost two decades. It was he who organized a trip for Catherine down the Dnieper River to view the newly accessed Crimean territories. The prince had painted façades constructed along the route to camouflage the degree of poverty of the peasants. These 'Potemkin villages' were also to give the appearance of real towns in the otherwise uninhabited areas. Finally in 1773, Pugachev, a Don cossack, led a rebellion of impoverished cossacks, peasants and Old Believers against the throne and serfdom. Pugachev was captured and sentenced to decapitation, but ended up exiled in Siberia.

It was not only the peasantry and the Church that felt alienated. The aristocracy too grew dissatisfied with the new European truths and philosophies. Those who yearned for more considered themselves a new class, the intelligentsia. Searching for their own identity amidst a surge of French principles, the intelligentsia proceeded not only to understand Voltaire's logic but to incorporate its heart and spirit as well.

By grasping the ideals of a foreign Enlightenment, Catherine II unknowingly gave birth to Russia's own. The catalyst of change, along with teaching people to think for themselves, brought despotism into deeper disfavor and paved the road to revolution. After the fall of the Bastille, Catherine turned her back on France. In a panic, she tried to dispose of all that she had helped create. Censorship was imposed throughout Russia, and Catherine attempted to slam shut the window to the West less than a century after Peter had opened it. But from this period of discontent and new search for meaning, Russia would give birth to some of the greatest writers and thinkers of all time. The West would be captivated by the works of Pushkin, Dostoevsky and Tolstoy, and Lenin would later lead Russia out of five centuries of autocratic rule. Peter the Great had built the wheels and Catherine set them in motion; there was to be no turning back.

In the year 2000, 25 percent of Russians polled named Catherine the Great as "the cleverest Russian woman of all time" (even though she came from Germany).

faced both inside and outside with colored marble, 32 different kinds. Marble came from Karelia the Baltic regions, and the islands of Lake Ladoga; further expeditions were carried out all the way to the Urals. Over 100 stonemasons worked daily for years to polish and fit the granite and marble pieces throughout the palace.

Since Orlov died before the palace's completion in 1785, Catherine the Great gifted it to her grandson, Grand Prince Konstantin Pavlovich. In 1832, Nicolas I gave the palace to his second son, Konstantin Nikolayevich; and one of last owners of the palace was the brother of Alexander II. From 1844–51, the architect Alexander Bryullov was commissioned to redo parts of the interiors. The palace was closed after the 1917 revolution when many of the rooms acted as offices for various Socialist organizations.

Upon entering the palace, the **Grand Marble Staircase** contains bas-relief and allegorical sculptures, one a portrait of the architect Rinaldi himself. One of the palace's highlights is the **Marble Hall**, whose ceiling depicts "The Wedding of Cupid and Psyche," painted in 1775. In 1937, the Marble Palace opened as the Leningrad branch of the Central Lenin Museum, with over 10,000 exhibits in 34 rooms relating to Lenin's life and work. In the former Leningrad alone, over 250 places were associated with Lenin. (In a small garden at the main entrance stood an armored car with the inscription, 'Enemy of Capital'. It was removed to the Artillery Museum in 1992.) After the February 1917 Revolution, Lenin returned to St Petersburg from exile in Europe in this armored car, and upon his arrival at Finland Station on April 3 delivered a speech from the turret proclaiming: 'Long live the Socialist Revolution!' After the 1991 failed coup, the Lenin Museum was removed from the Marble Palace which now, as a branch of the Russian Museum, displays a permanent exhibit entitled Foreign Painters in Russia, as well as a few other displays of Modern and Pop Art. The outdoor **Clock Tower** was restored in 1999, when three large bells were hung and connected by ropes to the clock's mechanism. Today, their chimes ring out every 15 minutes across the Neva and Summer Gardens. During the 1990's, Lenin's armored car was removed from the courtyard and replaced by the equestrian **Statue of Alexander III**. The palace is open 10am–6pm, on Mondays 10am-5pm (ticket *kassa* closes one hour earlier); closed Tuesdays. The nearest Metro is Nevsky Prospekt.

Right in front of the Troitsky Bridge is **Suvorov Square** (Ploshchad Suvorova), with the statue of the Russian generalissimo Alexander Suvorov depicted as Mars, the God of War. The square opens on to one of the most beautiful places in St Petersburg, the **Field of Mars**. Around 1710, Peter the Great drained the marshy field and held parades after military victories. The festivities ended in fireworks (known as amusement lights), so the square was called Poteshnoye Polye (Amusement Field). By the end of the 18th century the area was used as a routine drill field, which destroyed the grass; for a while the field was nicknamed the St

Petersburg Sahara. When in 1801 the monument to Field Marshal Suvorov was placed here, the area became known as Marsovo Polye (Field of Mars). It was moved to its present location, Suvorov Square, in 1818. The 12-hectare (30-acre) field is bordered on the west by the **Barracks of the Pavlovsky Regiment**. Because of their heroic deeds this regiment was rewarded with a magnificent barracks, built between 1817 and 1820. The Pavlovsky Grenadier Regiment was the first among the czar's armies to take the side of the people during the February 1917 Revolution. It is now the St Petersburg Energy Commission. The southern side is bordered by the Moika River and Griboyedov Canal, and the eastern side by the Swan Canal (Lebyazhya Kanavka).

The **Memorial to the Fighters of the Revolution** stands in the center of the field. On March 23, 1917, 180 heroes of the February uprising were buried here in mass graves. The next day the first granite stone was laid in the monument foundation, which was unveiled in 1920. On each of the eight stone blocks are words by the writer Anatoly Lunacharsky. One reads: 'Not victims, but heroes, lie beneath these stones. Not grief, but envy, is aroused by your fate in the hearts of all your grateful descendants.' During the 40th anniversary of the Revolution in 1957, the eternal flame was lit in memory of those killed.

The eastern side of the field opens up on the lovely Letny Sad or **Summer Garden** with over 250 sculptures made by 17th and 18th century Italian masters. The main entrance to the garden is from the Kutuzova Embankment. A beautiful black and golden grille (1770–84 by Yuri Felten) fences it. The open railing, decorated with 36 granite columns and pinkish urns, is one of the finest examples of wrought-iron work in the world. The Summer Garden, the city's oldest, was designed by Leblond in Franco-Dutch style in 1704. Peter the Great desired to create a garden more exquisite than Versailles. On 25 acres of land he planted trees and had hothouses, aviaries, grottos and sculptures placed within. Some of the original statues remain, such as *Peace and Abundance*, the busts of John Sobiesky (a Polish king), Christina (a Swedish queen), the Roman empress Agrippina, and Cupid and Psyche. The Swan Canal dug on the western side was filled with swans and had a tiny boat for Peter's favorite dwarf jester. The garden also had many fountains depicting characters from Aesop's *Fables*.

The water for the fountains was drained from a river on its east side; the river was named **Fontanka**, from the Russian *fontan* (fountain). Pipes made from hollowed logs ran from the Fontanka to a city pool, from which a 1.6-kilometers (one-mile) pipeline brought water to the gardens. The Fontanka formed the southern border of the city in the mid-18th century. At this time the first stone bridge was built where the Fontanka flows into the Neva. It is still known as **Prachechny Most** (Laundry Bridge) because it was located near the Royal Laundry.

The gardens received their name from the many festivals that Peter the Great loved to hold in summer; the area became the center of social life in St Petersburg.

Many of the fountains, pavilions and statues were destroyed during the 1777 and 1824 floods. The Summer Garden was open only to nobility until, in the mid-19th-century, Nicholas I issued a decree stating that it would be 'open for promenading to all military men and decently dressed people. Ordinary people, such as *muzhiks* (peasants) shall not be allowed to walk through the garden.' After the Revolution the garden was opened fully to the public.

After the garden was designed, Peter had his Letny Dvorets or **Summer Palace** built at the northeastern end by the Neva. Following its completion in 1714 by Trezzini, Peter moved from his cottage into the palace. The modest stone building was decorated with 29 terracotta figures and a weather vane of St George slaying the dragon. There are 20 rooms, ten on each floor. Peter lived on the ground floor, and his wife Catherine on the second. The czar received visitors in the reception room, and the empress enjoyed baking Peter's favorite pies in the kitchen. Nearby stood one of Peter's favorite statues, the *Venus of Taurida* (now in the Hermitage); the czar purchased it from the Pope. The House is open 10.30am–5.30pm; closed Tuesdays.

Behind the Summer Palace is an interesting bronze **Monument to Ivan Krylov** by the sculptor Klodt, dedicated to the popular Russian fabulist. There is also a playground for children with subjects from Krylov's fables. Nearer to the fountain are the Chainy Domik or **Tea House**, built in 1827 by Ludwig Charlemagne, and the **Coffee House** built by Rossi in 1826 (it is also known as Rossi's Pavilion). Recitals are now held here. The outside sculpture of *Peace and Abundance* symbolizes the peace treaty made with Sweden in 1721. It was a gift to Nicholas I from the Swedish king, Karl Johann. Nearby, across the Fontanka at 9 Solyanoi Pereulok, is the **Defense and Siege of Leningrad Museum** with exhibits concerning the 900-day blockade of the city. Open 10am–5pm; closed Wednesdays and the last Thursday of the month. Nearest Metro is Chernyshevskaya.

MIKHAILOVSKY (ENGINEER'S) CASTLE

Crossing the Moika and continuing along the banks of the Fontanka leads to the Mikhailovsky Castle, built between 1797 and 1800 (after his mother, Catherine the Great's death) by the architects Bazhenov and Brenna for Czar Paul I (1754–1801). Paul did not like his mother Catherine the Great's residence in the Winter Palace, and fearing attempts on his life, he ordered the castle constructed as an impregnable fortress. The Mikhailovsky Castle (the archangel Michael was Paul's patron saint) was bordered in the north by the Moika Canal and the east by the Fontanka Canal.

Two artificial canals, the Resurrection and Church, were dug on the other sides creating a small island (they have since been filled in). Drawbridges, protected by cannons, were raised at 9pm when the czar went to bed. In spite of all this, 40 days after he moved in Paul was strangled in his sleep by one of his guards on March 12, 1801. (In all, Paul was heir to the throne for 40 years, and was czar for exactly four years, four months and four days.) Today the Mikhailovsky Castle is part of the Russian Museum, and houses walk-through exhibits of Russian history and art. Open 10am–5pm, Mondays until 4pm; closed Tuesdays.

In February 1823, after a military engineering school was opened in the building, it became known as Engineer's Castle. Dostoevsky went to school here from the age of 16, from 1837 to 1843. It also contains a scientific and naval library. In front of the castle's main entrance is a **Statue of Peter the Great**, commissioned by Carlo Rastrelli while Peter was still alive. It was supposed to be erected near the Twelve Collegiums on Vasilyevsky Island. However, it was not completed until 1746, during the reign of Elizabeth I. And since the empress did not particularly like the statue it ended up in storage. In 1800, the monument was placed in its current location. Paul I ordered the inscription placed upon its base: 'To Great-Grandfather—From Great-Grandson. The Year 1800.' On the sides of the pedestal are bronze reliefs depicting major victories of Peter the Great.

Not far from the Mikhailovsky Castle at 3 Fontanka Embankment (Naberezhnaya Reki Fontanki) is the **St Petersburg Circus**, which celebrated its 130th anniversary in 2007. The circular building of the circus was constructed in 1877 by Kenel, making it one of the oldest permanent circus buildings in the world. During the intense revolutionary years, some of Russia's finest artists, such as Chekhov, Gorky, Eisenstein and Stanislavsky, focused their attention on the circus, so much so that the Soviet Government decided not to abolish it. Inside there is also the **Museum of Circus History and Variety Art** (established in 1928), with over 100,000 circus-related items (open 12–5pm, closed on Saturdays and Sundays). The circus has daily performances, except on Mondays, Wednesdays and Thursdays.

Further down the canal at 34 Fontanka Embankment, in the garden wing of the former **Sheremetyev Palace**, is the **Anna Akhmatova Museum**. (The entrance is from Liteiny Prospekt.) The famous St Petersburg poet (see Special Topic on page 620) lived in the "Fountain House" from 1924 to 1941 and 1944 to 1954 in a small apartment on the third floor of the south wing. She first lived here with her second husband, Vladimir Shileiko, and then later moved back with her third common-law husband, Nikolai Punin, an art historian. (By this time her first husband, Nikolai Gumilyov, had been arrested and shot, and son imprisoned. Punin was later twice arrested, and died in a Siberian labor camp in 1953). The modest spare rooms contain the original furniture, with other exhibits of photographs, publications and films. In the cramped kitchen, a recording, read in Akhmatova's own voice, plays her famous poem 'Requiem.' The motto on the Sheremetyev's coat-of-arms, *Deus Conservat Omnia* (God Preserves All) became the symbol for one of Akhmatova's most masterful works, "Poem Without a Hero", written during the Seige of Leningrad—"He will visit me at the Fountain Palace...But death he shall bring." The museum is open 10.30am–6.30pm; closed Mondays and the last Wednesday of the month; www.akhmatova.spb.ru.

The Sheremetyev Palace was constructed between 1720 and 1740, and also houses exhibits dedicated to the Sheremetyev Family. The gates are decorated with the family's gilded coat-of-arms. Concerts are often held in the White House. Open 12–5pm; closed Monday/Tuesday. The nearest Metro is Mayakovskaya.

Akhmatova wrote of St Petersburg:

> But not for anything would we exchange this splendid
> Granite city of fame and calamity,
> The wide rivers of glistening ice,
> The sunless, gloomy gardens,
> And, barely audible, the Muse's voice.

NEVSKY PROSPEKT

In the words of Nikolai Gogol: 'There is nothing finer than the Nevsky Prospekt.... In what does it not shine, this street that is the beauty of the capital.' Nevsky Prospekt, which locals refer to as Nevsky (it derives from the River Neva), is the main thoroughfare of the city and the center of business and commercial life. A stroll down part of it during any time of day is a must, for no other street like it exists anywhere in the world. It is a busy, bustling area, filled with department stores, shops, cinemas, restaurants, museums, art studios, cathedrals, mansions, theaters, libraries and cafés. The Nevsky is made even more interesting and beautiful by the stunning architectural ensembles that line the 4.8-kilometer- (three-mile-)long route that stretches from the Admiralty to Alexander Nevsky Monastery. It also brims with history; you can find the spot where Pushkin met his second on the day of his fatal duel, where Dostoevsky gave readings of his works, and where Liszt and Wagner premiered their music.

Shortly after the Admiralty was completed, a track was cut through the thick forest, linking it with the road to Novgorod and Moscow. This main stretch of the city was known as the Great Perspective Road. The road took on the name of Neva

Perspectiva in 1738, when it was linked to another small road that ran to Alexander Nevsky Monastery. In 1783, the route was renamed Nevsky Prospekt. Peter the Great had elegant stone houses built along the Nevsky and ordered food sold in the streets by vendors dressed in white aprons. The first buildings went up between the Admiralty and the Fontanka Canal. The area, nicknamed St Petersburg City, was a fashionable place to live, and it became the center for banks, stores and insurance offices. The architects desired to create a strong and imposing central district and constructed the buildings out of granite and stone brought in from Sweden.

Beginning at the Admiralty, where the street is at its narrowest—25 meters (82 feet), walk along to 9 Nevsky. On the corner you will find Vavelberg's House, which was originally a bank but is now the Aeroflot ticket office. The large stone house was built in 1912 by the architect, Peretyatkovich, to resemble the Doge's Palace in Venice and the Medici in Florence. Here the Nevsky is intersected by Malaya Morskaya Ulitsa (formerly Gogol Street), where the writer Nikolai Gogol lived at number 17 from 1833 to 1836. Here he wrote *Taras Bulba*, *The Inspector General* and the first chapters of *Dead Souls*. At 10 Malaya Morskaya is the Queen of Spades residence, the house of the old countess on whom Pushkin based his story of the same name. Tchaikovsky lived at 13 Malaya Morskaya for many years up until his death in 1893 (see Klin, page 245).

The next intersection on the Nevsky is Bolshaya Morskaya Ulitsa (formerly Herzen Street); Herzen lived at number 25 for a year in 1840. The main telephone and telegraph center is on the left by the Triumphal Arch of the General Staff. Fabergé had its main studios at number 24 (see Special Topic page 145). The architect Carlo Rossi laid out the street along the Pulkovo Meridian (which was the meridian on old Russian maps) so that at noon the buildings cast no shadows on the street.

The oldest buildings are at 8 and 10 Nevsky. Built between 1760 and 1780, they are now exhibition halls for work by St Petersburg artists. The house at number 14 (built in 1939) is a school. A pale blue rectangular plaque on its wall still reads: 'Citizens! In the event of artillery fire, this side of the street is the most dangerous!' The house with columns at number 15 was built in 1768 as a stage site for one of Russia's first professional theaters. Later a small studio was connected to the theater where Falconet modeled the Bronze Horseman. It is now the **Barrikada Movie Cinema** with cafés and shops. The building at number 18 was known as Kotomin's House (1812–16), after the original owner. Pushkin often frequented the confectioner's shop, Wolf and Beranger, that used to be on the ground floor (he lived nearby at 12 Moika Embankment). It was here on January 27, 1837, that

(following pages) Bank Bridge spans the Griboyedov Canal near Nevsky Prospekt. This lovely footbridge is adorned with lion-griffins; in ancient Greece griffins were said to stand guard over gold. At the time this bridge was built, around 1800, it led to the National Bank.

Pushkin met up with his second on the way to his fatal duel with George D'Anthés. The shop is now the **Literaturnoye Café**, a popular spot to eat that offers piano and violin music. Outside the café, you can have your portrait drawn by one of the numerous artists.

The section on the north side of the Nevsky beyond the Moika Canal was once reserved for churches of non-Orthodox faiths. The Dutch church at number 20 was built between 1834 and 1836 by Jacquot and is now a library. The central part functioned as a church and the wings housed the Dutch Mission. Opposite at number 17 is the baroque **Stroganov Palace**, built by Rastrelli in 1754 after the two-story house of Baron Sergei Stroganov burnt down. The Baron was the son of Grigory Stroganov, a wealthy industrialist and mine owner and patron of the arts. The Stroganov family owned and developed vast amounts of land in Siberia (yes, one member of the family invented the well-known beef dish), and their coat-of-arms, depicting two sables and a bear, lies over the gateway arch. Seven generations of Stroganovs succeeded one another from the mid 18th century right up until 1918. Alexander Stroganov was the president of the Academy of Fine Arts at the end of the 18th century. The exquisite décor of all the rooms were set off with sumptuous fittings of period furniture, sceltpures and paintings. The palace, now a branch of the Russian Museum, displays items from the Stroganov collection. The Palace Art Salon Shop is on the first floor. The Palace is open daily 10am–5pm; closed Tuesdays. The nearest Metro is Nevsky Prospekt.

At 22–24 Nevsky is the Romanesque-style **Peter and Paul Lutheran Church** (1833–38). In the yard behind the church was the Peterschule, one of the oldest schools in the city (1710). The architect Rossi and musician Mussorgsky graduated from here. After the Revolution it housed a swimming pool.

Across the street from the church is the large, majestic, semicircular colonnade of the **Cathedral of Our Lady of Kazan**. The Kazansky Sobor was named after the famous icon of Our Lady of Kazan that used to be here. It is now on view at the Russian Museum. The architect Voronikhin faced two challenges in 1801. First, Czar Paul I wished the cathedral modeled after St Peter's in Rome, and second, the Orthodox Church required that the altar must face eastwards, which would have had one side of the cathedral facing the Nevsky. Voronikhin devised 96 Corinthian columns to fan out toward the Nevsky. The bronze Doors of Paradise, which were replicas of the 15th-century Baptistery doors in Florence, opened on the Nevsky side. The structure took ten years to build and at that time was the third largest cathedral in the world. The brick walls are faced with statues and biblical reliefs made from Pudostsky stone, named after the village where it was quarried. The stone was so soft when dug out that it was cut with a saw. It later hardened like rock when exposed to air. In niches around the columns are statues of Alexander Nevsky, Prince Vladimir, St John the Baptist and the Apostle Andrew. The interior was decorated by the outstanding painters Bryullov, Borovikovsky and Kiprensky. There are 56 pink granite columns and polished marble and red-stone mosaic floors. On June 13, 1813, Field Marshal Mikhail Kutuzov was buried in the northern chapel. The general stopped to pray at the spot where he is now buried before going off to the War of 1812. Many trophies from this war, like banners and keys to captured fortresses, hang around his crypt. In 1837, the two statues of Kutuzov and Barclay de Tolly were put up in the front garden.

To the right of the main entrance is a small square surrounded by a beautiful wrought-iron grille called Voronikhin's Railing. In 1876, the first workers' demonstration took place in front, with speeches by the Marxist, Georgi Plekhanov. A square and fountain were later added to prevent further demonstrations. But the area remains to this day a popular spot for gatherings and, since perestroika, political and religious demonstrations as well. Today the cathedral holds daily religious services at 10am and 6pm. The old Museum of Atheism has been converted into the **History of Religion Museum** which includes exhibits on Siberian shamanism and Buryat Buddhism. Open 11am–5pm; closed Wednesdays. The nearest Metro to the cathedral is Nevsky Prospekt.

Walking behind the cathedral and south along the **Griboyedov Canal** leads to the lovely footbridge of **Bankovski Most** (Bank Bridge), adorned with winged lion-griffins (see picture on pages 522–3). At the time it was built in 1800, the bridge led to the National Bank; according to Greek mythology, griffins stood guard over gold. On the other side of Nevsky, also on the canal, is **Dom Knigi** (House of Books). This polished granite building topped by its distinguishing glass sphere and globe, was originally built in art-nouveau style between 1902 and 1907 by the architect Suzor for the American Singer Company. The first two floors now make up one of the largest bookstores in the country. Posters, calendars and postcards are sold on the second floor.

The Kazansky Bridge crosses the canal and was built by Ilarion Kutuzov, the father of the military leader. A few minutes' walk along the canal to the north stands the 17th-century Russian-style building known as the **Church of the Savior on the Blood** (Spasa Na Krovi). It was modeled on St Basil's in Moscow and erected on the spot where Czar Alexander II was assassinated by a member of Peoples' Will, a group of revolutionaries pushing for more liberal reforms. On March 1, 1881, the czar was returning from a military parade to the Winter Palace in a special armored coach built in Paris. (There had been six previous attempts on his life.) When it reached the embankment of the Griboyedov Canal, a terrorist jumped out and tossed a bomb

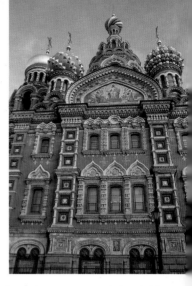

beneath the hooves of the galloping horses. The emperor leapt out of the burning carriage unharmed. But another man then threw a second bomb. This time the czar was mortally wounded, both legs torn off. Ironically, the czar had planned to sign the draft of long-awaited constitutional reforms on that very day. His successor, Alexander III, ordered architect Alfred Parland to build the altar where the former czar's blood fell on the cobblestones. After many years of restoration, the cathedral is now open to visitors. The walls inside are decorated with mosaics in the style of both Byzantine and modern icon painting. Four jasper columns still stand on the spot where the czar was murdered. The height from floor to cupola is 81 meters, corresponding to the assassination date. Outside, the narrow **Bridge of Kisses** (Most Polseluyev) crosses the Moika Canal. Behind the Church is a lively daily market full of souvenirs for sale.

The building at 30 Nevsky Prospekt was that of the Philharmonic Society, where Wagner, Liszt and Strauss performed. Today it is the **Hall of the Glinka Maly Philharmonic**. The **Church of St Catherine**, built between 1763 and 1783 in

baroque-classical design by Vallin de la Mothe, is at 32–34 Nevsky. It is the oldest Catholic Church in St Petersburg. Stanislas Ponyalovsky, the last king of Poland and one of the many lovers of Catherine the Great, is buried inside. Religious services are also held here. In front of the church is a vibrant art market, filled with paintings and portrait artists. The **Armenian Church**, at 40–42 Nevsky, was built by Felten between 1771 and 1779. It was returned to followers for worship in 1990. So many churches were opened on Nevsky Prospekt in the 18th century that it was nicknamed the Street of Tolerance.

The elaborately decorated Church of the Savior on the Blood was erected near the Griboyedov Canal off of Nevsky Prospekt, on the spot where Alexander II was assassinated by a revolutionary group in 1881.

The Kamenny or Stone Bridge,
one of the oldest bridges in St Petersburg, crosses the Griboyedov Canal.

The corner building at 31–33 was known as Silver Row. Built between 1784 and 1787 by Quarenghi, it was used as an open shopping arcade, where silver merchants would set up their display booths. In 1799, the structure was made into the Town Hall or **City Duma**, and in 1802, a European Rathaus tower was installed. This served as a fire watchtower (various colored balls raised indicated where in the capital a fire had broken out), and part of a 'mirror telegraph' that linked the residences of the czar in the city to Tsarskoye Selo. A beam of light was flashed along other aligned towers to announce the ruler's arrival or departure.

The art-nouveau **Grand Hotel Europe** is on the corner of Nevsky and Mikhailovskaya Ulitsa. Built in the 1870s, it was completely renovated between 1989 and 1991 by a Russian-Swedish joint venture. It has many antiques including one of Catherine the Great's carriages (available for guests). The hotel has a number of elegant restaurants, bars, and cafés. Across the street at number 35 is the **Bolshoi Gostiny Dvor** (Big Guest Yard) department store. Visiting merchants used to put up guest houses, *gostiniye dvori*, which served as their resident places of business. From 1761 to 1785 the architect Vallin de la Mothe built a long series of open two-tiered arcades, where merchants had their booths. It was not only a commercial center; representatives of all the estates of the capital were also found here. The Duke of Wellington, invited to Russia by Alexander I, loved to stroll past the many galleries. Pushkin and Dostoevsky shopped here as well and mentioned the Dvor in their works. In 1917, the Bolsheviks threw out the merchants and made the space into a State-run store. But some merchants, not believing the Revolution would actually last, stashed 128 kilograms of gold inside the walls of the store. It was found by workers in 1965. Today the newly renovated two-story building is the largest department store in the city and a popular place for shopping (open daily 9am–9pm). Opposite Gostiny Dvor is the **Passazh** arcade, opened in 1848, another shopper's delight. The Passazh became the first area in the city where trade, amusements and shops flourished under one roof. The small building that stands between the hall and Gostiny Dvor was built as the portico, and now holds the **Central City Theater** Booking Office, where tickets for drama, music and ballet are sold.

Just off Nevsky, at 2 Mikhailovskaya Ulitsa, is the **St Petersburg State Philharmonic** (Shostakovich Grand Hall), built in 1839 by Jacquot for the Club of the Nobility. The St Petersburg Philharmonic Society was founded in 1802. At the turn of the century, American dancer, Isadora Duncan, made her Russian debut on its stage. The works of many Russian composers, such as Glinka, Rachmaninov, Rimsky-Korsakov and Tchaikovsky, were first heard at the Society. Wagner was the official conductor during the 1863 season. The Philharmonic was named after Dmitri Shostakovich in 1976. Today the Philharmonic Symphony Orchestra performs worldwide.

Shostakovich lived in Leningrad during the 900-day siege. In July 1941, he began to write his Seventh Symphony, while a member of an air-defense unit. Hitler boasted that Leningrad would fall by August 9, 1942. On this day, the Seventh (or Leningrad) Symphony, conducted by Karl Eliasberg, was played in the Philharmonic and broadcast throughout the world. 'I dedicate my Seventh Symphony to our struggle with fascism, to our forthcoming victory over the enemy, and to my native city, Leningrad.'

The square in front of the Philharmonic is called **Arts Square** or Ploshchad Iskusstva. In the mid-18th century Carlo Rossi designed the square and the areas in between the Griboyedov Canal, the Moika Canal and Sadovaya Ulitsa. The center of the square is dominated by the **Statue of Alexander Pushkin**, sculpted by Mikhail Anikushin in 1957. Along Italianskaya Ulitsa, not far from the Philharmonic, is the Theater of Musical Comedy, the only theater in the city that stayed open during the siege. Next to it, at number 19, is the Komissarzhevskaya Drama Theater. Headed by Russian actress Vera Komissarzhevskaya from 1904 to 1906, the company staged plays (including Gorky's) around the political mood of the times.

Behind the square on Inzhenernaya Ulitsa (Engineer's Street) stands the majestic eight-columned building of the **Russian Museum**, second largest museum of art in the city. Alexander I had architect Carlo Rossi build this palace (1819–27) for his fourth son, Mikhail; it was called the Mikhailovsky Palace. In 1898, Alexander III bought the palace and decided to convert it into a public museum after having visited Moscow's Tretyakov Gallery. After the czar's death, his son Nicholas II opened the gallery, calling it the Russian Museum of Alexander III. A splendid wrought-iron fence (embossed with the double-headed eagle) separates the palace from the square. The courtyard allowed carriages to drive up to the front portico, where a granite staircase lined with two bronze lions still leads to the front door. The Hall of White Columns was so admired by the czar that he ordered a wooden model made for King George IV of England. Rubenstein opened the city's first music school in the hall in 1862. March 19, 1998 marked the museum's centenary. The 1,000-year history of Russian art is represented by over 300,000 works of art in the museum's 130 halls, the most complete gathering of Russian art anywhere in the world. Open 10am–5pm, Mondays until 4pm; closed Tuesdays. Besides a vast collection of icon paintings, romantic classicists and impressionistic landscape artists, the museum also has a large exhibition of Russian avant-garde (Kazimir Malevich, Vasily Kandinsky, Alexander Rodchenko) and contemporary art. Over the past decade, the government has signed over the Stroganov and Marble Palaces, and Engineer's Castle to the museum which has doubled its display space. The Mikhailovsky Gardens are situated behind the museum. To the right of the museum is the **Museum of Ethnography** (open 10am–5pm; closed Mondays and last Friday of the month). The nearest Metro is Gostiny Dvor.

In Arts Square, the statue of Pushkin gestures to the building known as the **Mussorgsky Maly Theater of Opera and Ballet**. Built in 1833 by Bryullov, it was known as the Mikhailovsky Theater, and housed a permanent French troupe. Today it is 'the laboratory of opera and ballet', presenting 360 performances a year in a daily alternating repertory of opera and ballet. Subsidized by the government, it employs 800 people, including an orchestra of 100 and a chorus of 65. It is the second most popular theater (next to the Mariinsky) in St Petersburg.

The building next door, at number 5, was the site of the Stray Dog, a favorite cellar hangout for the artistic elite of St Petersburg where they gathered around midnight and did not leave until dawn. Opened on New Year's Eve 1912, the club was the country's greatest bohemian meeting spot until it was closed down in the spring of 1915. After the Revolution and Stalinist terrors, Russia would never again know such a free and vibrant artistic period. The ballerina Tamara Karsavina danced works by Michel Fokine; Mayakovsky, Blok and Mandalstam read their poetry; and Anna Akhmatova and her husband Nikolai Gumilyov formed a new movement of poetry known as Acmeism. Later, after Stalin took control of the country, many of these artists, writers and musicians died in Siberian gulags or ended their lives abroad.

The **Brodsky House Museum** at 3 Arts Square exhibits many items on the life of Joseph Brodsky, who won the Nobel Prize for Literature in 1987—the second youngest writer in history to do so (see page 451). The museum is open 11am–7pm; closed Mondays.

Continuing down the Nevsky, the **Russian National Library** stands on the corner of Nevsky and Sadovaya Ulitsa. Built in 1801 by Yegor Sokolov, it opened in 1814 as the Imperial Public Library. In 1832, Carlo Rossi built further additions. The statue of Minerva, Goddess of Wisdom, stands atop the building. It is one of the largest libraries in the world with over 25 million books! A reading room is inside, but no books can be taken out.

The library faces **Aleksandriiskaya Ploshchad** (Aleksandriisky Square). Up until 1992 it was known as Ostrovsky Square, after the playwright Alexander Ostrovsky. A **Statue of Catherine the Great** graces the center; Catherine, dressed in a long flowing robe, stands on a high rounded pedestal that portrays the prominent personalities of the time: Potemkin, Suvorov, Rumyantsev and Derzhavin, to name a few. To the left are two classical pavilions, designed by Rossi, in the Garden of Rest.

Behind the square is the **Pushkin Drama Theater**, also known as the Alexandrinsky Theater, a veritable temple to the arts. Flanked by Corinthian columns, the niches are adorned with the Muses of Dance, Tragedy, History and Music. The chariot of Apollo, patron of the arts, stands atop the front facade. The yellow building, erected by Rossi in 1828, was first known as the Aleksandrinsky Theater (after Alexandra, the wife of Nicholas I), and housed Russia's first permanent theater group. Today, as the oldest drama theater in Russia, it has a varied repertoire of classical and modern plays. Behind the theater is the **Museum of Theatrical Art**, exhibiting the history of Russian drama and musical theater. It is open 11am–6pm, Wednesdays 1–7pm; closed Tuesdays. Also here is the Lunacharsky National Library with more than 350,000 volumes.

The famous **Ulitsa Rossi** (named after the architect) stretches from Aleksandriisky Square to Lomonosov Square (Ploshchad Lomonosova). The street has perfect proportions: 22 meters wide, the buildings are 22 meters high and the length is ten times the width. The world-renowned **Vagonova Academy of Ballet** is the first building on the left. Twelve boys and 12 girls (children of court servants) were the city's first ballet students, attending a school started by Empress Anna in 1738, the same year that she founded the St Petersburg Imperial Ballet. The choreography school now bears the name of Agrippina Vagonova, who taught here between 1921 and 1951. Some famous pupils of the Imperial Ballet and Vagonova have been Pavlova, Ulanova, Petipa, Nijinsky, Fokine and Balanchine. Over 2,000 hopefuls apply to the school each year; about 100 are chosen. The school's 500 pupils hope to go on to a professional ballet company such as the Mariinsky. A

*Vaganova Ballet School Museum on Ulitsa Rossi. Portraits of former students
such as Rudolph Nureyev, Natalia Makarova and Mikhail Baryshnikov grace the walls.*

museum inside the school on the first floor contains many magical displays, for example Pavlova's ballet shoes and Nijinsky's costumes. Posters and pictures trace the history of ballet from Diaghilev to Baryshnikov who, along with Natalia Makarova, attended the Vagonova School. (The museum is closed to the general public—but if you express an interest in ballet, you may get in.)

Back on Nevsky Prospekt in the corner building across the street is the impressive **Yeliseyev's**, once one of the most luxurious food stores in St Petersburg. The well-known Russian merchant Yeliseyev had this imposing art-nouveau structure built in 1903. Today the store is once again stocked with a wide assortment of goods and it is well worth seeing the interior of the (see Special Topic on page 540). The **Marionettes Theater**, started in 1918, is at 52 Nevsky, and the **Comedy Theater**, founded in 1929, is at number 56. In between is the popular Petersburg Antique Store. At the corner of Nevsky and the Fontanka Canal is the **House of Friendship and Peace**. A former residence built in the 1790s, it is now a society that promotes friendship and cultural relations with over 500 organizations in 30 countries.

The area around the Fontanka Canal (the old southern border of the city) was first developed by an engineering team headed by Mikhail Anichkov. He built the first bridge across the Fontanka here in 1715 and it is still named after him. In 1841, a stone bridge with four towers replaced the wooden structure. Peter Klodt cast the tamed-horse sculptures a century ago and today they give the bridge its distinguishing mark. During World War II the sculptures were buried in the Palace of Young Pioneers across the street. The **Anichkov Most** (Bridge) is a popular hangout, and boats leave frequently for a city tour of the canals and waterways. A kiosk by the dock provides times of departure and tickets.

The first palace built on the Nevsky was named after Anichkov. Empress Elizabeth (Peter's daughter) commissioned the architects Dmitriyev and Zemtsov to build a palace on the spot where she stayed on the eve of her coronation in 1741. In 1751, Elizabeth gave the Anichkov Palace to her favorite, Count Alexei Razumovsky. Later, Catherine the Great gave it to her own favorite, Count Grigory Potemkin, who frequently held elaborate balls here. After that, in 1794, it became part of His Majesty's Cabinet. The **Anichkov Palace** houses several concert halls. The **Beloselsky-Belozersky Palace**, at 41 Nevsk, was designed in 1846 by Andrei Stakenschneider in the baroque style of the Winter Palace. In 1884, the building was occupied by Grand Duke Sergei Alexandrovich, the brother of Alexander III. (Alexandrovich was later killed by a bomb in the Kremlin.) The Palace is now a concert hall and special guided tours are given on the history of the palace. It is also home to the **Wax Museum** with a lifelike collection of figures; open daily 11am–6.30pm. The Gostiny Dvor/Nevsky Prospekt Metro station brings you right out on Nevsky Prospekt by the department store and Dom Knigi.

Following the Nevsky a bit farther you come to **Znamenskaya Square** (Ploshchad Znamenskovo; named after the Church of the Sign Eznameniye), formerly Vosstaniya (Uprising) Square. It was so named when troops of the czar refused to shoot a group of unarmed demonstrators during the February 1917 uprising. One of the interesting buildings on the Square is **Moskovsky Vokzal** (Moscow Railway Station). It was built by the architect Thon in 1847. The St Petersburg–Moscow railway line opened on November 1, 1851. The word *vokzal* (derived from the English Vauxhall Station) is used for a station and now St Petersburg has five major *vokzals* in the city: Moskovsky, Finlandsky, Ladozhsky, Baltiisky (Baltic) and Vitebsky. The last was known as Tsarskoye Selo, the station connecting Russia's first railroad line to the czar's summer residence in Pavlovsk. Overlooking the Square, the Hotel Oktyabrskaya dates from the 1890s. The Ploshchad Vosstaniya/Mayakovskaya Metro station is near the Square; the Mayakovskaya exit is close to the junction of Nevsky Prospekt and Marata Ulitsa.

A few blocks down Marata Ulitsa from Nevsky is the **Nevsky Banya Complex,** open 8am–10pm, Wednesday–Sunday, where one can experience Russian baths. (See Special Topic on page 418.) At 24 Marata is the **Museum of the Arctic and Antarctic** (in the Church of St Nicholas); open 10am–5pm, Wednesday–Sunday.

A few minutes walk away, at 5/2 Kuznechny Pereulok, is the **Dostoevsky Literary Museum**, open 11am–5.30pm; closed Mondays (Vladimirskaya Metro Station). Dostoevsky lived here from 1878 until his death. His novel *The Brothers Karamazov* was written in this apartment. In his novel *The Adolescent*, Dostoevsky wrote of his own vision of St Petersburg and the Bronze Horseman: 'A hundred times amid the fog I had a strange but persistent dream: "What if, when this fog scatters and flies upward, the whole rotten, slimy city goes with it, rises with the fog and vanishes like smoke, leaving behind the old Finnish swamp, and in the middle of it, I suppose, for beauty's sake, the bronze horseman on the panting, whipped horse?"' Dostoevsky lived in this house with his wife Anna (who daily wrote down his dictations usually composed the night before) and children. On the evening of February 7, 1881, while writing in his spare and orderly study, the author dropped his pen, and it rolled under a heavy bookcase. When Dostovesky tried to move it, his fragile lungs began to hemorrhage (he had emphysema), and he died two days later. At number 3 is the Kuznechny Market (a lively blue-collar market in Dostoevsky's time), still one of the most colorful in the city; it has a wide variety of produce and household goods at bargain prices. The nearest Metro is Vladimirskaya.

A short walk away, at 28 Zagorodny Prospekt, is the **Rimsky-Korsakov Memorial House**, home of the great 19th-century Russian composer, who lived here until his death in 1908. Open 11am–6pm, Wednesday–Sunday. Chamber music concerts are also held on Wednesdays at 7pm, and weekends at 4pm. A few blocks south stands a statue of the writer Alexander Griboedov in Pionerskaya Ploshchad (Square). Here on December 22, 1949, members of the Petrashevsky political movement, including the writer Dostoevsky, were lined up to be shot for revolutionary activities. After spending eight months in the Peter and Paul Fortress, they were led out to the square and dressed in white canvas robes and hoods. The squad aimed their rifles at the men. 'I was in the second row, and had less than a minute to live,' Dostoevsky recalled in horror. But instead of hearing gunshots, a drum roll sounded. Nicholas I had decided to commute the death sentences to exile in Siberia. Dostoevsky was sent to Omsk Prison, where he spent four years shackled day and night; he would not write again for over ten years.

Walking north and crossing the Nevsky will bring you to the **Nekrasov House Museum**, at 36 Liteiny Prospekt, displaying the writer's works. Nikolai Nekrasov (1821–77) was a popular poet and also editor of the literary magazine *The Sovremennik* (Contemporary). Open 11am– 5pm; closed Tuesdays.

The modern **Moskva Hotel** (with restaurants and a *Beriozka*—a variety store selling souvenirs, food and liquor) stands at the end of Nevsky Prospekt on Alexander Nevsky Square (Ploshchad Aleksandra Nevskovo). Across the street is the **Alexander Nevsky Monastery** (Lavra), a complex of 16 religious buildings. This is the oldest monastery, or *lavra*, in St Petersburg. Peter the Great founded the monastery in 1710 and dedicated it to the Holy Trinity and military leader Alexander Nevsky, Prince of Novgorod, who won a major victory near this spot on the Neva against the Swedes in 1240. In Russia the name *lavra* was applied to a large monastery. Another *lavra* is the Trinity-Sergius Monastery in the Golden Ring town of Sergiyev Posad (see page 273).

The red Beloselsky-Belozersky Palace, rebuilt in 1846 in rococo-style by Andrei Stacken-schneider, stands beside the Fontanka Canal. Atlantes support the columns of the façade. In the foreground, stallions sculpted by Peter Klodt over a century ago adorn the Anichkov Bridge.

The **Holy Trinity Cathedral** or Troitsky Sobor is the main church of the complex, built for Catherine the Great by Ivan Starov between 1776–90. Inside, to the right of the iconostasis, stands the Chapel of Alexander Nevsky, where the remains of the saint (transferred to the monastery from the Golden Ring town of Vladimir in 1724) are buried. (This silver casket is a smaller variation of the original.) In 1746, the Empress Elizabeth commissioned a rococo-style Nevsky sarcophagus and donated over one and a half tons of silver to create the largest silver monument in the world. Designed by court portrait painter Georg Christoph Groot, it stands five meters (16 feet) high, topped on both sides by angels holding inscribed shields. During the Stalin years, the government wanted to melt it down to earn badly needed hard currency. Fortunately, protests by members of the art community saved it. (But sadly, the solid silver iconostasis in the Kazan Cathedral

HOLIDAY SEASON

*F*orgive the triviality of the expression, but I am in no mood for fine language... for everything that had been in Petersburg had gone or was going away for the holidays; for every respectable gentleman of dignified appearance who took a cab was at once transformed, in my eyes, into a respectable head of a household who after his daily duties were over, was making his way to the bosom of his family, to the summer villa; for all the passersby had now quite a peculiar air which seemed to say to every one they met: 'We are only here for the moment, gentlemen, and in another two hours we shall be going off to the summer villa.' If a window opened after delicate fingers, white as snow, had tapped upon the pane, and the head of a pretty girl was thrust out, calling to a street-seller with pots of flowers—at once on the spot I fancied that those flowers were being bought not simply in order to enjoy the flowers and the spring in stuffy town lodgings, but because they would all be very soon moving into the country and could take the flowers with them. What is more, I made such progress in my new peculiar sort of investigation that I could distinguish correctly from the mere air of each in what summer villa he was living. The inhabitants of Kamenny and Aptekarsky Islands or of the Peterhof Road were marked by the studied elegance of their manner, their fashionable summer suits, and the fine carriages in which they drove to town. Visitors to Pargolovo and places further away impressed one at first sight by their reasonable and dignified air; the tripper to Krestovsky Island could be recognized by his look of irrepressible gaiety. If I chanced to meet a long procession of wagoners walking lazily with the reins in their hands beside wagons loaded with regular mountains of furniture, tables, chairs, ottomans and sofas and domestic utensils of all sorts, frequently with a decrepit cook sitting on the top of it all, guarding her master's property as though it were the apple of her eye; or if I saw boats heavily loaded with household goods crawling along the Neva or Fontanka to the Black River or the Islands—the wagons and the boats were multiplied tenfold, a hundredfold, in my eyes. I fancied that everything was astir and moving, everything was going in regular *caravans to the summer villas. It seemed as though Petersburg threatened to become a wilderness, so that at last I felt ashamed, mortified and sad that I had nowhere to go for the holidays and no reason to go away. I was ready to go away with every wagon, to drive off with every gentleman of respectable appearance who took a cab; but no one—absolutely no one— invited me; it seemed they had forgotten me, as though really I were a stranger to them!*

I took long walks, succeeding, as I usually did, in quite forgetting where I was, when I suddenly found myself at the city gates. Instantly I felt lighthearted, and I passed the barrier and walked between cultivated fields and meadows, unconscious of fatigue, and feeling only all over as though a burden were falling off my soul. All the passersby gave me such friendly looks that they seemed almost greeting me, they all seemed so pleased at something. They were all smoking cigars, every one of them. And I felt pleased as I never had before. It was as though I had suddenly found myself in Italy—so strong was the effect of nature upon a half-sick townsman like me, almost stifling between city walls.

There is something inexpressibly touching in nature round Petersburg, when at the approach of spring she puts forth all her might, all the powers bestowed on her by Heaven, when she breaks into leaf, decks herself out and spangles herself with flowers ...

Fyodor Dostoevsky, White Nights, *1918*

was melted down.) Today, the Alexander Nevsky sarcophagus is on exhibit in the Hermitage Museum.

The Blagoveshchensky Sobor (Annunciation Church) is the oldest church in the complex, and was built by Trezzini in 1720. It now houses the **Museum of Urban Sculpture**, at 179 Nevsky, open 10am–5pm, closed Thursdays. In 1716, Peter the Great buried his sister Natalie in the **Lazarevskoye Cemetery** (to the left of the main entrance), St Petersburg's oldest cemetery. Other graves include those of

Lomonosov, Quarenghi and Carlo Rossi. To the right of the main entrance is the **Tikhvinskoye Cemetery**. Both open 11am–7pm (4pm in winter); closedThursdays. Here are the carved gravestones of many of Russia's greatest figures such as Tchaikovsky, Glinka, Rimsky-Korsakov, Mussorgsky, and Dostoevsky. Another entrance is across the street from the Moskva Hotel. The cathedral holds services, and on Alexander Nevsky Day, September 11–12, huge processions take place. Near the monastery is the Theological Seminary, reestablished in 1946, which trains 440 students for the clergy. About 100 women are taught to be teachers or choir conductors. Seven cathedrals, over 20 Russian Orthodox churches, and 15 other religious denomination's currently hold services in St Petersburg. (See church listings in Practical Information section.)

The Alexander Nevsky Bridge (Most Aleksandra Nevskovo), largest bridge in the city, crosses the Neva from the monastery. Ploshchad Aleksandra Nevskovo Metro station brings you right to the Moscow Hotel and the Monastery complex.

The tomb of composer Alexander Borodin (1833–87) in Tikhvinskoye Cemetery at the Alexander Nevsky Monastery. Borodin is best known for his patriotic opera Prince Igor, *based on an epic Slavic text of the 12th-century.*

Finland Station (Finlandsky Vokzal)

The Finland Railway Station is located on the right bank of the Neva (the Vyborg Side), a little east of where the cruiser *Aurora* is docked. It is a short walk from the Petrograd Side across the **Sampsonievsky Most** (Sampson Bridge), over the Bolshaya Nevka, to the Finland Station. The station dates back to 1870. It was from here that Lenin secretly left for Finland in August 1917, after he was forced into hiding by the Provisional Government. A few months later he returned on the same locomotive to direct the October uprising. This locomotive, engine number 293, is on display behind a glass pavilion in the back of the station by the platform area. A brass plate on the locomotive bears the inscription: 'The Government of Finland presented this locomotive to the Government of the USSR in commemoration of journeys over Finnish territory made by Lenin in troubled times. June 13, 1957.'

A towering **Monument to Lenin** stands in Lenin Square (Ploshchad Lenina) opposite the station. After the February 1917 Revolution overthrew the czarist monarchy, Lenin returned to Petrograd from his place of exile in Switzerland on April 3, 1917. He gave a speech to the masses from the turret of an armored car. Originally the Lenin monument was erected on the spot where he gave the speech.

Cadets from St Petersburg's Nakhimov Naval School on the battleship Aurora *which fired the blank shot to signal the storming of the Winter Palace during Lenin's 1917 October Revolution.*

YELISEYEV'S

This store, whose nickname was the Temple of Gluttons, has a long and fascinating history. In Moscow the building was originally the personal mansion of Catherine the Great's State Secretary, Prince Kozitsky, whose wife was the heiress of a Siberian goldmine. The mansion was the largest and grandest in the city.

In the 1820s, their granddaughter Princess Volkonskaya turned the drawing room into one of Russia's most prestigious salons. All the great literary figures gathered here, including Pushkin, who presented his latest poems. But in 1829, when the princess left for Italy, the mansion fell into other hands.

By the mid-1850s, the dreaded Princess Beloselskaya-Belozerskaya, a relative of Volkanskaya, was living in the mansion; she was a total recluse and only left it to attend church on Sundays. She was not popular at home since she had her servants beaten every Saturday (it was a common practice in that era to single out a few for reprimand). Not surprisingly, some of these servants ran away, and eventually banded together in the house across the street. Many Muscovites believed the dark house to be haunted, claiming to see devils and ghosts, and would not even walk by, especially at night. The bandit-servants decided to lend credence to this belief. One night they dressed up like ghosts and spooked the old princess right out of her house. Some time afterwards, an animal trainer took up residence in the mansion with his black panther.

A number of years later, Grigory Grigoryevich Yeliseyev bought the vacant building. Grigory's grandfather Pyotr had won his freedom in 1813, when his master rewarded him for discovering how to produce strawberries in winter. Pyotr went off to open a wine store in St Petersburg where he soon became a member of the merchant class. His sons in turn founded the Yeliseyev Brothers Trading House, which specialized in foreign wines and other goods from tea and spices to rum and tobacco. The firm established links with the largest trading houses across Europe from Britain to Spain, and to ship the many foreign wares, several Dutch steamships were purchased.

The Yeliseyev business reached its heyday with the third generation. It was Grigory who opened the popular chain of food emporiums from St Petersburg to Kiev. The firm also built spacious warehouses, butcheries, fish canneries and chocolate factories. The shops were filled with mouth-watering delicacies, such as Belgian Oostende oysters, smoked sturgeon, stuffed turkeys, beluga caviar, exotic fruits and Swiss and French cheeses. Its wine cellars were scattered around the world; at one point the Yeliseyevs purchased entire grape harvests in some French provinces. For promoting Russia's national trade industry, Grigory Yeliseyev was ennobled. He was also honored with France's highest award, the Legion of Honor.

Throngs of people turned out for the Moscow Yeliseyev's grand opening in 1899. There was one unexpected hitch—the liquor department turned out to be less than 50 yards from the neighboring church, which contravened the sacred law. So builders had to do a quick restructuring and move it one yard further away. The popular writer Vladimir Gilyarovsky, who lived in the area, wrote in *Moscow and Muscovites*: 'Passers-by stared at the mountains of imported fruits which looked like cannon balls, a pyramid of coconuts each the size of a child's head, bunches of tropical bananas so large you could not get your arms around them and unknown inhabitants of the ocean depths. Overhead, electric stars on tips of wine bottles flashed in enormous mirrors, the tops of which were lost somewhere up in the heights....' The store was a huge success. The Yeliseyevs even dreamed of cornering the American market and opened a chain of shops in the United States.

In his fifties, Grigory fell in love with the wife of a prominent St Petersburg jeweler. The millionaire's children and grandchildren opposed a divorce and his broken-hearted wife succeeded with suicide on her third attempt. When World War I broke out, Grigory married his lover and fled to France where he died in Paris in 1942. After this scandal, Yeliseyev's sons renounced their heritage, which included the store. This was probably just as well since the family would have lost everything anyway during the Bolshevik Revolution which broke out soon after.

The saga does not end there. Under Brezhnev, the director of Gastronom #1 (as the store was now called) was Yuri Konstantinovich Sokolov. As a friend of Brezhnev's daughter Galya, Sokolov was quite well-connected. At the store, Sokolov made up quotas and took many choice picks for himself; he also wrote a lot of food off as spoiled or sold it even more profitably on the black market. Of course, Sokolov became popular and wealthy, and was known for throwing great parties. But when Brezhnev died in 1982 and Andropov took over, the glorious days of corruption and stagnation were numbered. The head of Moscow Trade received a 15-year prison sentence, the director of another Gastronom six years, and Sokolov found himself sentenced to death—he was executed by firing squad in 1984. The police found gold, jewelry and huge bundles of rotting rubles buried in his backyard.

Today the new owners of the shops have renamed them Yeliseyev's, hoping to capitalize on their intriguing past. In the Moscow shop, a bust of Grigory Yeliseyev stands in the entrance hall, put up in 1989 to celebrate the store's 90th anniversary—the store marked its centennial jubilee with further celebrations in 1999. The Moscow store is located at 14 Tverskaya, and in St Petersburg the lavish art-nouveau building is at 58 Nevsky Prospekt.

A trolleybus on Nevsky Prospekt near Aleksandriisky Square passes Yeliseyev's Food Emporium, which celebrated its centenary in 1999.

But during the construction of the square the statue, portraying Lenin standing on the car's turret addressing the crowd with an outstretched hand, was moved closer to the Neva embankment, where it stands today. It was unveiled on November 7, 1926. Ploshchad Lenina Metro station is also at the Finland Station.

Farther north, near Vyborgskaya Metro station, at 41 Bolshoi Sampsonievsky Prospekt, stands the **Cathedral of St Sampson—Host of Wanderers**. Peter the Great defeated the Swedes in the Battle of Poltava (1709) on the feast day of St Sampson. To commemorate the victory a wooden church was built. Later, between 1728 and 1733, this five-domed stone church replaced it. A lovely gilded iconostasis crowns the altar; the church is currently under restoration. Many of the city's pre-eminent architects such as Rastrelli, Leblond and Trezzini are buried in the neighboring cemetery.

In Vyborg's northeast region lies **Piskarevskoye Memorial Cemetery**. Here are the common graves of nearly half a million Leningraders who died during the 900-day siege, marked only by somber mounds of dirt and their year of burial (see pages 559 and 562). The central path of the cemetery leads to the **Statue of the Mother Country**, holding a wreath of oak leaves, the symbol of eternal glory. Two museum pavilions are on either side of the entrance, where one realizes the horrors that faced the citizens of this city. The cemetery register is open at a page with the entries: 'February, 1942: 18th—3,241 bodies; 19th—5,569; 20th—10,043.' Another display shows a picture of 11-year-old Tanya Savicheva and pages from her diary: 'Granny died 25 January, 1942 at 3pm. Lyoka died 17 March at 5am. Uncle Vasya died 13 April at 2am. Uncle Lyosha 10 May at 4pm. Mama died 13 May at 7.30am. The Savichevs are dead. Everyone is dead. Only Tanya remains.' Sadly, Tanya later died after she was evacuated from the city. The cemetery is located at 74 Nepokorennikh Prospekt, and open daily 10am–6pm. The nearest Metro station is Ploshchad Muzhestva. (It takes about 40 minutes to get here from the center of town.) A memorial day to the Siege of Leningrad is held here every year on September 8.

Crossing the Neva in front of the Finland Station, over the **Aleksandrovsky Most**, with its beautiful railings decorated with mermaids and anchors, to the south bank leads to Shpalernaya Ulitsa and the **Taurida Palace** at number 47. The neoclassical-style palace was built by Ivan Starov between 1783 and 1789 for Prince Grigory Potemkin-Tavrichesky as a gift from Catherine the Great. Potemkin was commander-in-chief of the Russian Army in the Crimea during the Turkish Wars. The Crimean peninsula was called Taurida, and Potemkin was given the title of Prince of Taurida. One party Potemkin held in the palace used 140,000 lamps and 20,000 candles. After both he and Catherine the Great died, the new czar, Paul I (who disliked his mother Catherine and her favorites), converted the palace into a riding house and stables. It was later renovated and became the seat of the State Duma in 1906. On February 27, 1917, the left wing of the palace held the first session of the Petrograd Soviet of Workers. Today the mansion is known as the Taurida or Tavrichesky Palace, and houses the Interparliamentary Assembly of CIS countries. It is closed to tourists, but one can still stroll in the Tavrichesky Gardens or Children's Park; in the 18th century they were considered the best in St Petersburg. Intricate pavilions, small bridges and carved statues dotted the landscape, and Venetian gondolas and boats sailed on the enormous pond.

Behind the gardens, at 43 Kirochnaya Ul., is the **Museum to Alexander Suvorov**, the great 18th-century Russian military leader under Catherine the Great and Paul I; open 10am–5pm; closed Tuesdays, Wednesdays and the first Monday of the month. Across the street from the front of the palace is the **Kikin Palace**. Built in 1714 and one of the oldest buildings in the city, it belonged to the Boyar Kikin, who plotted, along with Peter's son Alexei, to assassinate Peter the Great. After Kikin was put to death, Peter turned the palace into Russia's first natural science museum. The collections were later moved to the Kunstkammer on Vasilyevsky Island. Today the yellow-white palace is a children's music school. The closest Metro station is Chernyshevskaya.

On Tavricheskaya Ulitsa stands one of the last remaining statues of Felix Dzerzhinsky, founder of the infamous Cheka that later became the KGB. The **Bolshoi Dom** (Big House), at 4 Liteiny Prospekt, used to be KGB headquarters; today it is part of the Interior Ministry. While you are in the neighborhood, on the corner of Potemkinskaya and Shpalernaya is the **Indoor Flower Market**. Throw a coin in the wishing well! Open 11am–7pm; closed Mondays and Thursdays.

THE SMOLNY

Several years after the Peter and Paul Fortress was founded, the tar yards, *smolyanoi dvori*, were set up at the Neva's last bend before the gulf to process tar for the shipyards. Empress Elizabeth I founded the monastery and convent in 1748; she had intended to take the veil at the end of her rule. The baroque (combined with Russian traditional), five-domed, turquoise and white Smolny complex is truly one of Bartolomeo Rastrelli's greatest works. After Elizabeth died the complex was still not fully complete. (The empress lavishly spent State funds—she had over 15,000 gowns, and at her death only six rubles remained in the Treasury.) Vassily Stasov later completed the structure, adhering to Rastrelli's original design. (When the new classicism vogue in architecture replaced baroque, Rastrelli fell into disfavor under Catherine II and was asked to leave the country.) Today the Smolny Cathedral is used as a musical concert hall.

In 1766, Catherine the Great set up the Institute for Young Noble Ladies in the **Smolny Convent**, Russia's first school for the daughters of nobility; they were educated here from the age of six to 18. Afterwards many of the women became maids-of-honor in the court. A series of portraits of the first graduates can be found in the Russian Museum. Between 1806 and 1808, the architect Quarenghi erected additional buildings, known as the **Smolny Institute**, to educate girls of lower estates. Today the Church of the Resurrection and the former convent is a small museum and additional parts of the complex serve as concert halls.

In August, 1917, the girls were dismissed and the institute closed. The building became the headquarters for the Petrograd Bolshevik Party and the Military Revolutionary Committee. On October 25, 1917, Lenin arrived at the Smolny and gave the command for the storming of the Winter Palace. On October 26, the Second All-Russia Congress of Soviets gathered in the Smolny's Assembly Hall to elect Lenin the leader of the world's first Socialist Government of Workers and Peasants, and to adopt Lenin's Decrees on Peace and Land. John Reed wrote in his book *Ten Days That Shook the World* that Lenin was 'unimpressive, to be the idol for a mob, loved and revered as perhaps few leaders in history have been. A leader purely by virtue of intellect; colorless, humorless, uncompromising and detached, without picturesque idiosyncrasies—but with the power of explaining profound ideas in simple terms...he combined shrewdness with the greatest intellectual audacity.' (See page 126 for a further extract.) Lenin lived at the Smolny for 124 days before transferring the capital to Moscow. In 1925, two porticoes were built at the main entrance with the inscriptions: 'The first Soviet of the Proletarian Dictatorship and Workers of the World, Unite!' A bronze monument of Lenin was set up on the tenth anniversary of the Revolution. And it was here, on December 1 1934, that Leningrad Communist Party head, Sergei Kirov, was assassinated on probable orders of Stalin, which led to other purges which became known as the Great Terror. Today some of the rooms where Lenin lived are part of the Lenin Museum. The rest of the buildings house the Mayor's offices. The nearest Metro is Chernyshevskaya. In 2006, the country's fourth largest company, Gazprom, began its fight to erect Gazprom City across from the Smolny. The proposed ultra-modern complex, designed by the British international architects RMJM, will have five sides and twist as it rises, evoking images of a gas-fueled flame, a strand of DNA, and a lady's high-heeled shoe! The city has protested the site which is set to soar four times higher than the surrounding famous, old landmarks.

A ten-minute walk along the Neva brings you to a reconstruction project of Peter the Great's flagship, the Shtandart.

(following pages) The funeral of St Petersburg's famous poet Anna Akhmatova was held at St Nicholas Marine Cathedral in 1966. The cathedral's four-tiered baroque bell tower stands beside the Kryukov Canal.

THEATER SQUARE (TEATRALNAYA PLOSHCHAD)

In the southwest part of the city along Glinka and Decembrists streets lies Theater Square or Teatralnaya Ploshchad. This section of land was once the location for St Petersburg carnivals and fairs. In the 18th century it was known as Ploshchad Karusel (Merry-Go-Round) Square. Czar Nicholas ordered the building of an Imperial Circus (modeled on the Circus Olympique in Paris) on this square, which opened on January 29, 1849. When this building caught fire on January 22 1859, Alexander II invited Alberto Kavos to rebuild it. The following year, the structure reopened as the **Mariinsky Theater**, named after Empress Maria Alexandrovna. (It was renamed the Kirov Theater from 1935 to 1992, after a prominent Communist leader.) The five-tiered theater, the city's center of opera and ballet, seats 1800 and is decorated with blue velvet chairs, gilded stucco, ceiling paintings and chandeliers. The golden eagles and royal insignia, removed after the revolution, have been reinstated on the Royal and Grand Ducal boxes.

In the 19th-century St Petersburg was the musical capital of Russia. At the Mariinsky Theater premiers of opera and ballet were staged by Russia's most famous composers, dancers and singers. Under Petipa, Ivanov and Fokine, Russian ballet took on worldwide recognition (see page 456). The Fyodor Shalyapin Memorial Room, named after the great opera singer, is open during performances. (The Shalyapin House Museum is located at 26 Graftio Ulitsa on the northern Petrograd Side near the TV Tower; see page 479.) In 2000, the US Library of Congress announced a program to help the Mariinsky preserve its unique collection of musical scores collected by the theater since czarist times. The Mariinsky Theater of Opera and Ballet continues to stage some of the world's finest ballets and operas; its companies tour many countries throughout the world. The city has proclaimed Boris Eifman 'choreographer of the 21st century.' Eifman has his own troupe known as St Petersburg's Ballet Company. In June 2003, a French architect was chosen as the winner of a competition to design an additional building for the renowned theater. One can check performance listings, and buy tickets on the website www.mariinsky.ru.

Opposite the Mariinsky stands the **Rimsky-Korsakov Conservatory**, Russia's first advanced school of music. The first wooden building on this site was used as a theater, and in 1783 was replaced by the Bolshoi Kammeny (Stone) Theater. In 1803, the drama troupe moved to the Aleksandrinsky Theater, and the opera and ballet remained at the Stone. After a fire in 1818, the Kammeny fell into such a state of disrepair that it had to close its doors on February 24 1886, after a last performance of Bizet's *Carmen*. Its Opera and Ballet companies were then transferred to the Mariinsky. In 1889, the building began extensive restoration work, and in 1896 its doors opened as the Music Conversatory. Its founder was the noted composer Anton Rubinstein. Some of the graduates include Tchaikovsky, Prokofiev and Shostakovich. On either side of the conservatory stand the monuments to Mikhail Glinka and Rimsky-Korsakov (whose museum is not far from the Vladimirskaya Metro station, at 28 Zagorodny Prospekt, open 11am–6pm, Wednesday–Sunday).

At the west end of Ulitsa Dekabristov at number 57, by the Pryazhka Canal, is the **Blok Museum** and former home of the great Russian poet during the last eight years of his life. Open 11am–5pm; closed Wednesdays.

A short walk south down Glinka Ulitsa leads to the **St Nicholas Marine Cathedral**, built between 1753 and 1762 by Chevakinsky in honor of St Nicholas, the protector of seamen. Naval officers once lived in the area, thus the full name of Nikolsky Morskoi (Marine) Sabor. Standing at the intersection of the Griboyedov and Kryukov canals, the blue and white church combines the old Russian five-dome tradition with the baroque. A lovely carved wooden iconostasis is inside and a four-tiered bell tower stands by itself in the gardens. It has church services three times a day. Thousands came here to attend the funeral of the famous poetess Anna Akhmatova on March 10, 1966. (She is buried in the village of Komarovo northwest of the city, near Repino. See page 585.)

The beautiful ensemble of St Nicholas Marine Cathedral (Nikolsky Morskoi Sabor) was built in honor of St Nicholas, the protector of seamen; the area was once inhabited by naval officers. Built in 1762, it combines old Russian traditions of a five-domed church with baroque decorations.

At the opposite end of Glinka Ulitsa, at 94 Moika Embankment (Naberezhnaya Reki Moiki), is the **Yusupov Palace** (open daily 11–4.30pm; to get around waiting for a group tour, rent an audiophone.) The last owner of the palace was the wealthy Prince Yusupov (whose family was the richest in Russia), who was responsible for the assassination of Grigory Rasputin (the *starets* who exerted much influence in the court of Nicholas II) in December 1916.

The lavish Yusupov Palace, situated along the Moika Canal near the Mariinsky Theater, was the home of the wealthy Prince Felix Yusupov. best known for participating in the murder of Rasputin in 1916. Today, his palace is a museum that contains the family's personal opulent theater (shown here), and other ornate rooms, including the basement where Rasputin was murdered.

Rasputin was first lured to the palace by an opportunity to socialize with the prince's wife Irina (the czar's niece). While music played upstairs to give the impression the couple were entertaining, Rasputin was asked to wait in a drawing room below where he was given cakes laced with cyanide. Nothing happened—the sugar in the cakes is thought to have neutralized the poison. In desperation Yusupov shot the monk. Later, however, Rasputin revived and managed to walk into the courtyard, where the conspirators shot him three times more. Finally, they tied up

LENIN AND THE RUSSIAN REVOLUTION

Lenin, founder of the first Soviet State, was born Vladimir Ilyich Ulyanov, on April 22, 1870. Vladimir, along with his five brothers and sisters, had a strict but pleasant childhood in the small town of Simbirsk (now Ulyanovsk) on the Volga River. On March 1, 1887, when Vladimir was 17, a group of students attempted to assassinate Czar Alexander III in St Petersburg. Vladimir's older brother, Alexander, was one of five students arrested. They were imprisoned in Peter and Paul Fortress in St Petersburg, and on May 8 were hung in the Fortress of Schlüsselburg (Kronstadt).

As a marked family of a revolutionary, the Ulyanovs left Simbirsk for Kazan, where Vladimir attended Kazan University. In December 1887, after the local papers reported the news of student riots in Moscow, 99 Kazan students protested against the strict rules of their university. Ulyanov, one of them, was immediately expelled, exiled to the town of Kokushkino and kept under police surveillance. Here Vladimir began to study the works of Karl Marx (*Das Kapital*, and the *Communist Manifesto*) and Chernyshevsky (*What Is To Be Done?*). Thereupon, he decided to devote his life to the revolutionary struggle. Lenin wrote that 'my way in life was marked out for me by my brother'.

Since he was refused permission to enter another university, the young Ulyanov covered the four-year law course independently, in a little over a year. He then journeyed to St Petersburg and passed the bar exam with honors. With his law degree, Ulyanov moved to the Asian town of Samara, where he defended the local peasants and secretly taught Marxist philosophy.

In 1893, he left again for St Petersburg, where he formed the revolutionary organization, the League of Struggle for the Emancipation of the Working Class. At 24, in 1894, Vladimir Ulyanov published his first book, *What Are the Friends of the People?* During a secret meeting of the League of Struggle, Ulyanov decided to publish an underground newspaper called the *Workers' Cause*. That same day he was arrested by the police, along with hundreds of other people from the League. Ulyanov was exiled to Siberia, as was Nadezhda Konstantinovna Krupskaya. They were married in the small village of Shushenskoye on July 22, 1898.

While in exile, the League planned the first party newspaper, called *Iskra* (*Spark*), inspired by words from a Decembrist poem, 'A spark will kindle a flame'. After the Ulyanovs' release, they settled in the town of Pskov outside St Petersburg (see page 611). Since it was illegal to disseminate any print media criticizing the government, they eventually moved abroad. The first issues of *Iskra* were published in Leipzig, Germany. During these years abroad, Ulyanov wrote books on politics, economics and the revolutionary struggle. In December 1901, Vladimir Ulyanov began signing his writings with the name of Lenin.

In 1903, the Russian Party Congress secretly gathered in London. During this meeting, the Social Democratic Workers Party split into two factions: the Bolsheviks (Majority) and the Mensheviks (Minority). After the session, Lenin led the Bolsheviks to the grave of Karl Marx and said, 'Let us pledge to be faithful to his teachings. We shall never give up the struggle. Forward, comrades, only forward.'

By 1905, widespread unrest was sweeping across Russia. A popular May Day song was often sung: 'Be it the merry month of May. Grief be banished from our way. Freedom songs our joy convey. We shall go on strike today.' Workers at the Putilov factory in St Petersburg began a strike that triggered work stoppages at over 350 factories throughout the city. On Sunday, January 9, 1905, thousands of workers lined the streets of St Petersburg. In a peaceful protest, the crowd carried icons and portraits of the czar. The procession walked toward the Winter Palace and congregated in Decembrists' Square (now known as Senate Square; see page 501). The palace guards opened fire. More than 1,000 demonstrators were massacred in what is known today as Bloody Sunday. Not long afterward, sailors manning the Potemkin, largest battleship in the Russian Navy, also protested against their miserable working conditions. In a mutiny headed by Afanasy Matyushenko, the sailors raised their own revolutionary red flag on June 14, 1905.

The Geneva newspapers carried the news of Bloody Sunday and Lenin decided to return to St Petersburg. He wrote in his newspaper *Vperyod* (*Forward*): 'The uprising has begun force against force. The Civil War is blazing up. Long live the Revolution. Long live the Proletariat.' But it was still too dangerous for Lenin to remain in Russia. Two years later he left again for the West, and over the next ten years, lived in Finland, Sweden, France and Switzerland.

Accounts of a new Russian Revolution were published throughout the West in February, 1917. Lenin immediately took a train to Finland and on April 3 proceeded in an armored car to Petrograd (the city had been renamed in 1914). Today the train's engine is displayed at St Petersburg's Finland Station, where Lenin first arrived (see page 539).

In Petrograd, Lenin lived on the banks of the Moika River and started up the newspaper *Pravda* (*Truth*), which was outlawed by the new Kerensky Provisional Government. Lenin was later forced into hiding outside the city on Lake Razliv (see page 583). The hut and area where he hid out has been made into a museum. With his beard shaved off and wearing a wig, Lenin was known as Konstantin Ivanov.

On the grounds of the Smolny Cathedral (see page 491), a finishing school served as headquarters for the Petrograd Workers Soviet, which organized the Red Guards. During the summer of 1917, more than 20,000 workers in Petrograd were armed and readied for a Bolshevik uprising. Lenin gave the command for attack from the Smolny on October 24, 1917. To signal the

beginning of the Great October Socialist Revolution, the battleship *Aurora* fired a blank shot near the Hermitage. The Red Guards stormed the Winter Palace and almost immediately defeated the White Guards of the Provisional Government; the Moscow Kremlin was taken two days later.

Vladimir Ilyich Lenin, father of the 1917 October Socialist Revolution and leader of the Bolshevik Party. This statue used to stand on one of the highest spots in the Kremlin gardens in Moscow, known as Kremlin Hill, but was removed in 1997.

On October 25, the Second Congress of Soviets opened in the Smolny and Lenin was elected chairman of the first Soviet State; Trotsky was his Foreign Minister. Sverdlov, Stalin, Bobnov and Dzerzhinsky (later to head the Cheka, which authorized police to 'arrest and shoot immediately all members of counterrevolutionary organizations') were elected to the Revolutionary Military Committee. Lenin introduced a Decree on Land, proclaiming that all lands become State property. At the end of the Congress, all members stood and sang the Internationale, the proletarian anthem: 'Arise ye prisoners of starvation. Arise ye wretched of the earth. For Justice thunders condemnation. A better world's in birth.' On March 11, 1918, Lenin moved the capital from Petrograd to Moscow. He lived in a room at the National Hotel across from Red Square. The Bolsheviks, known as the Communist Party, had their offices in the Kremlin.

During the last years of Lenin's life, the country was wracked by war and widespread famine. He implemented the NEP (New Economic Policy) that allowed foreign trade and investment, but he did not live long enough to bear witness to its effects. Lenin died at the age of 54 on January 21, 1924. The cause of death was listed as cerebral sclerosis, triggered, as stated in the official medical report, by 'excessive intellectual activity'. (It's suspected he really died of syphilis.) In three days a wooden structure to house his body was built on Red Square. Later, it was replaced by a mausoleum of red granite and marble. For decades, thousands lined up daily to view his embalmed body and witness the changing of the guards. A "Commission for the Immortalization of Lenin's Memory" was founded; and the Commission even approved selected Lenin designs and statues to be cloned throughout Russian towns and villages. Alexander Sokurov's 2001 film *Telets* (Taurus) is a neo-realistic story that attaches human features to the Communist idol; Lenin is shown simply as a miserable, sick, and dying old man.

Soon after his death, Petrograd's name was changed to Leningrad in his honor; it bore this epithet until 1991, when the city's name reverted back to St Petersburg (in Soviet times the city had 103 monuments to Lenin). Today, even though the Red Square mausoleum is still opened to visitors, the changing of the guards has stopped. The current government is reviewing proposals to close the mausoleum and give Lenin's body a burial elsewhere, either on Kremlin grounds or, ironically, back in St Petersburg.

Rasputin's body and threw it through a hole in the ice of the river. Three days later, his body was found floating under the ice downstream. An autopsy showed that Rasputin had water in his lungs and rope burns on his wrists, proving he had still been alive after all the attempts to kill him. Yusupov later fled Russia. Aside from the ornate rooms and famous theater, the palace also houses the **Rasputin Museum** and you can actually stand in the small basement room where Rasputin was poisoned. The Yusupov Restaurant and Rasputin Bar are located in the basement of the palace (open 12–midnight). A tour of the palace may not include the Rasputin museum.

Rasputin's daughter, Maria Grigorievna Rasputina, emigrated to the United States in 1937, where she died in Los Angeles in 1977, having just published her book, *Rasputin: The Man Behind the Myth*.

Crossing the Moika and continuing towards the Neva, you will see a number of brick buildings on a small triangular island. These were the storehouses for ship timber during the time of Peter the Great. Manmade canals created the small island known as **New Holland** or Novaya Gollandiya. The New Admiralty Canal, dug in 1717, once connected the island with the Admiralty. Konnogvardeysky (formerly Trade Union) Boulevard was laid partly along the route of the canal.

Pass through Annunciation Square (Blagoveshchenskaya Ploshchad) and turn left at the Neva. At number 44 Angliskaya Embankment (Angliskaya Naberezhnaya) is the branch **Museum of the History of St Petersburg** (in the Soviet era). It is located in the former Rumyantsev Palace, built in Empire style in 1827 and named after the son of a famous Field Marshal, who bought it from a British merchant. Open 11am–5pm, Tuesdays until 4pm; closed Wednesdays and the last Tuesday of the month.

MOSCOW AVENUE (MOSKOVSKY PROSPEKT)

Moskovsky Prospekt runs for nearly 16 kilometers (10 miles) in a straight line from **Sennaya Square** (and Sennaya Ploshchad Metro station) to the airport. The avenue follows the line known as the Pulkovo Meridian (zero on old Russian maps) that led to the Pulkovo Astronomical Observatory. The square was known even in czarist times as Sennaya Ploshchad or Haymarket, the underbelly of St Petersburg and a place used for public punishment of serfs. The area was the residence of many of Dostoevsky's characters—including *Crime and Punishment's* Sophia Marmeladova. Today the neighborhood remains a bit seedy, and it is still easy to imagine how the place fueled Dostoevsky's creative imagination. In Dostoevsky's time Stolyarny Alley was filled with drunkards and prostitutes, and brazen crowds bustled through the night in the Haymarket district. At 9 Przhevalskovo Ulitsa is the **Rodion Raskolnikov House**, where Dostoevsky's character from *Crime and*

Punishment lived. (On the fifth floor is Russian graffiti that reads, 'Don't Kill, Rodya!') Dostoevsky described this house and yard in detail—Rodion stole the murder ax from the basement, and it was 730 paces between the murderer's house and his victim's. Even the stone under which Raskolnikov hid the stolen goods was real. Raskolnikov later knelt on Sennaya Square repenting his crime.

Off Przhevalskovo is Kaznachevskaya Ulitsa. Dostoevsky lived at number 1 from 1861 to 1863 and at number 7 he wrote his famous novel *Crime and Punishment*. Imagine Dostoevsky as Raskolnikov, leaving his house and walking south down toward the Griboyedov Canal. Crossing the Kokushkin Bridge, he turns right onto Sadovaya Ulitsa and continues past the Yusupov Gardens. He then turns right into Rimsky-Korsakov Prospekt, walking several blocks until arriving at Srednaya Podyacheskaya. The entrance to the old-lady moneylender's house (approximately 730 paces from Dostoevsky's doorstep) is at 104 Canal Embankment. Head through the tunnel to block 5 (apartments 22–81). Look for the brass balls placed at the corners of the banisters by the residents; they lead to the pawnbroker's apartment, number 74, just after the third floor. (Dostoevsky's museum is actually located at 5/2 Kuznechny Pereulok, close to Vladimirskaya Metro station; see page 533.)

Walking a few blocks west along Sadovaya Ulitsa brings you to the **Railway Museum**, at number 50, with more than 6,000 exhibits on Russian railway history. One of the oldest engines dates back to 1897—a 47-ton steam engine that could travel at 32 kilometers (19 miles) an hour. Another engine carries the initials FD, those of Felix Dzerzhinsky, who became the first Soviet head of the railroads and secret police. In 1918, the S-68 steam engine transported the first Soviet government from St Petersburg to Moscow. Other items include the world's first diesel locomotive, designed in 1924, and the very last passenger steam engine built in 1956. Open 11am–5.30pm; closed Fridays and Saturdays and last Thursday of the month.

Back on Moskovsky Prospekt, continue south past the Obvodnovo Canal and Novodevichy Cemetery to the **Moscow Triumphal Arch**. It was built between 1834 and 1838 by Vassily Stasov to commemorate the Russian victories during the Russo-Turkish War (1828–9), and was the largest cast-iron structure in the world in the mid-19th-century. Modeled on the Brandenburg Gate in Berlin, the arch was decorated with figures representing Winged Victory, Glory and Plenty. It once marked the end of the city where a road toll was collected. In 1936, Stalin had it taken down; but the Arch was put back up during the Siege of Leningrad when it was hoped that it would serve as a barricade. The closest Metro station is Moskovskiye Vorota (Moscow Gates).

South of the Arch, past the Elektrosila Factory, is the 70-hectare (170-acre) **Moscow Victory Park**, through which runs the Alley of Heroes. The park was laid out by tens of thousands of Leningraders after World War II. The 20,000-seat Sports and Concert Complex is located in the park at 8 Prospekt Yuriya Gagarina, near Park Pobedy Metro Station.

Farther down Moskovsky Prospekt is the stone Gothic-style **Chesme Church and Palace**, (near Moskovskaya Metro station at 12 Lensoveta Ulitsa). Catherine the Great commissioned Yuri Velten to build the palace in 1774. It was named after the Russian victory over the Turkish fleet in Chesme Bay. It became a rest stop for the empress between the city and Tsarskoye Selo. It was here too that Rasputin's body lay in state after his murder in 1916. Today part of the palace serves as a hospital. The church, built between 1777 and 1780, appears as a red and white fairy-tale concoction with fancy Russian-style *kokoshniki* (named after a Russian woman's head-dress) decorating the archways that outline the five-domed roof. It is also known as the Church of Nativity of John the Baptist. Daily services are held at 10am.

The **Monument to the Heroes of the Defense of Leningrad** (unveiled 30 years after the Siege on May 9, 1975) is the focal point of **Victory Square**. The heroic black sculpted figures, called *The Victors*, look out on where the front once ran. (Notice how close the Germans came to capturing the city.) Pink granite steps lead down to an obelisk (dated 1941–45) that stands inside a circle symbolizing the breaking of the blockade ring. (On January 27, 1944, Leningrad was declared liberated from the Nazi blockade, which had lasted 882 days from when the final rail line into the city was cut on August 28, 1941.) An eternal flame burns at the base. Here you will find the **Siege of Leningrad Museum**, open 10am–6pm; Tuesdays and Fridays 10am–5pm; closed Wednesdays and the last Tuesday of the month. Moskovskaya Metro station.

> And on this starless January night,
> Amazed at its fantastic fate,
> Returned from the bottomles depths of death,
> Leningrad salutes itself.

Anna Akhmatova

The **Green Belt of Glory** is a memorial complex that stretches 230 kilometers (143 miles) along the front line of 1941–44. At **Moscow Square** (Moskovskaya Ploshchad), Stalin tried to transplant the heart of the old city to beat anew in these concrete suburbs; he built up the entire eastern side with gloomy apartment blocks and the House of Soviets with a Statue of Lenin at its center.

Moskovsky Prospekt was built in the early 18th-century to connect the royal residences in St Petersburg to Tsarskoye Selo. Later the road was continued all the way to Moscow. Today, on the way to Tsarskoye Selo, the prospekt passes the famed **Pulkovo Astronomical Observatory**, which once served as part of a 'mirror telegraph' that linked the residences of the czar. After crossing the Kuzminka River, you come to the **Egyptian Entrance Gates** of the city. The gates were built in 1830 and designed by the British architect Adam Menelaws, who incorporated motifs from the Egyptian temples at Karnak. A **Statue of Alexander Pushkin** stands to the left of the gates marking the beginning of the town of Tsarskoye Selo (see page 588).

To the northwest, not far from the Baltic (Baltiisky) Railway Station at Narvskaya Metro station, are the **Narva Triumphal Gates** which mark the successful outcome of the War of 1812. In 1814, the first gates were erected at the Narva outpost to meet the Russian Guards returning from France. Two decades later, the present gates were designed by Stasov and built of bricks covered with copper sheets, and placed (farther south) at the city's then boundary. The Chariot of the Goddess of Victory crowns the arch; the palm and laurel branches symbolize peace and glory. Four Russian armored warriors decorate the bottom; gold letters describe the regiments and places of battle. Words inscribed on the arch in both Latin and Russian read: 'To the victorious Russian Emperor Guard. Grateful Motherland. On 17 August, 1834.'

Near Ekateringof Park, at 1/29 Narvsky Prospekt, is the Russian Orthodox **Church of the Kazansky Icon of the Holy Mother** (1905–10), built on the grounds of the Old Ladoga Assumption nunnery, and presently under care of the Valaam Monastery (see Vicinity section). Daily services at 5am and 5pm.

> *A different time is drawing near...*
> *But the holy city of Peter*
> *Will be our unintended monument.*
>   Anna Akhmatova

THE SIEGE OF LENINGRAD

It's now the fifth month since the enemy has tried to kill our will to live, break our spirit and destroy our faith in victory.... But we know that victory will come. We will achieve it and Leningrad will once again be warm and light and even gay.

Olga Bergholts, Leningrad Poet

For 900 days between 1941 and 1944, Leningrad was cut off from the rest of the Soviet Union and the world by German forces. During this harsh period of World War II, the whole city was linked to the outside world only by air drops and one dangerous ice road, The Road of Life (opened only in winter), that was laid across the frozen waters of Lake Ladoga.

The invading Nazis were determined to completely destroy Leningrad, and Hitler's goal was to starve and bombard the city until it surrendered. The directive issued to German command on September 29, 1941 stated: 'The Führer has ordered the city of St Petersburg to be wiped off the face of the earth.... It is proposed to establish a tight blockade of the city and, by shelling it with artillery of all calibers and incessant bombing, level it to the ground.' Hitler was so certain of immediate victory that he even printed up invitations to a celebration party to be held in the center of the city at the Hotel Astoria.

But the Germans did not plan on the strong resistance and incredible resilience of the Leningrad people. For almost three years, the Nazis tried to penetrate the city. All totaled, over 100,000 high-explosive bombs and 150,000 shells were dropped on the city. The suffering was immense: almost one million people starved to death. At one point, only 125 grams (four ounces) of bread were allocated to each inhabitant per day. The winters were severe with no heat or electricity. There are many stories, for example, of mothers collecting the crumbs off streets or scraping the paste off wallpaper and boiling it to feed their hungry children. Tanya Savicheva, an 11-year-old girl who lived on Vasilyevsky Island, kept a diary that chronicled the deaths of her entire family. It ended with the words: 'The Savichevs died. They all died. I remained alone.' Tanya was later evacuated from Leningrad, but died on July 1, 1944 (see Piskarevskoye Memorial Cemetery, page 543).

Damage to the city was extensive. More than half of the 18th- and 19th-century buildings classified as historical monuments were destroyed; over 30 bombs struck the Hermitage alone. Within one month of the German invasion in June 1941, over one million works of art were packed up by the Hermitage staff and sent by train to Sverdlovsk in the Urals for safekeeping. Other works of art and architecture that could not be evacuated were buried or secretly stored elsewhere within the city. Over 2,000 staff members and art scholars lived in 12 underground air-raid shelters beneath the Hermitage in order to protect the museum and its treasures. Boris Piotrovsky, the Hermitage's former director, lived in one of these shelters and headed the fire brigade. He noted that 'in the life of besieged Leningrad a notable peculiarity manifested itself—an uncommon spiritual strength and power of endurance... to battle and save the art treasures created over the millennia by the genius of humanity.' Architect Alexander Nikolsky, who also lived in an air-raid shelter, sketched the city during the entire blockade. His pencil and charcoal drawings can be seen today in the Hermitage Department of Prints and Drawings.

The city's outskirts were the worst hit. The palaces of Peter the Great, Catherine II, and Elizabeth I were almost completely demolished. Peter's Palace of Petrodvorets was put to use as a Nazi stable. The Germans sawed up the famous Sampson Fountain for wood and took rugs and tapestries into the trenches.

The Soviet author, Vera Inber, was in Leningrad during the Siege. She wrote the narrative poem *Pulkovo Meridian* about the Pulkovo Astronomical Observatory outside Leningrad, where many scientists were killed when it was struck by an enemy bomb.

Dmitri Shostakovich's Seventh Symphony was composed in Leningrad during the siege and broadcast from the city around the world on August 9, 1942. Shostakovich was a member of the fire-defense unit housed in the Leningrad Conservatory. During bomb attacks, Shostakovich would hurriedly write the Russian letters BT, which stood for air raid, on his score before running to his post on the roof of the conservatory.

On January 27, 1944, Leningraders heard the salute of 324 guns to celebrate the complete victory over German troops. Even though most of the buildings, museums, and palaces have now been restored, the citizens of St Petersburg will never forget the siege, during which every fourth person in the city was killed. May 9, a city holiday, is celebrated as Liberation Day. Schoolchildren take turns standing guard at cemeteries.

Over half a million of the people who died between 1941 and 1943 are buried in mass graves at Piskarevskoye Cemetery outside St Petersburg. Inside the pavilion is a museum dedicated to the Siege of Leningrad. Outside, the Statue of the Motherland stands over an eternal flame. At the base of the monument are inscribed words by Olga Berggolts. The end of the inscription reads: 'Let no one forget. Let nothing be forgotten.'

The Tomb of the Unknown Soldier outside the Kremlin walls in Moscow.
An eternal flame honors the memory of the 20 million Russians who died during World War II.
It was moved to this site from the Field of Mars in St Petersburg in 1967.

STATE OF SIEGE

W*hat an incredible thing is this feeling of hunger. One can get used to it as to a chronic headache. For two successive days I have been waiting with blind resignation for one glutinous piece of bread, without experiencing acute hunger. That means the disease (ie hunger) has gone over from the acute stage to the chronic.*

It's dark. I couldn't stop myself getting out that precious candle-end, hidden away in case of dire emergency. The darkness is terribly oppressive. Mila's dozing on the sofa. She is smiling in her sleep, she must be dreaming of a sandwich with smoked sausage or of thick barley soup. Every night she has appetizing dreams, which is why waking up is particularly tormenting for her.

The entire flat is appallingly cold, everywhere is frozen, stepping out into the corridor involves putting on one's coat, galoshes and hat. The bleakness of desolation everywhere. The water supply is non-existent, we have to fetch water from more than three kilometres away. The sewage system is a thing of the distant past—the yard is full of muck. This is like some other city, not Leningrad, always so proud of its European, dandyish appearance. To see it now is like meeting a man you have become accustomed to seeing dressed in a magnificent, thick woollen overcoat, sporting clean gloves, a fresh collar, and good American boots. And here you suddenly meet that same man completely transformed—clothed in tatters, filthy, unshaven, with foul-smelling breath and a dirty neck, with rags on his feet instead of boots.

Yesterday's Leningradskaya Pravda *published an article by the chairman of the Leningrad Soviet, comrade Popov, entitled 'On the Leningrad Food Situation'. After calling on all citizens to summon their courage and patience, comrade Popov goes on to speak of the very real problems of theft and abuse in Leningrad's food distribution network.*

My candle-end has almost burnt down. Soon darkness will descend upon me—until morning...

17th January. Old age. Old age is the fatigue of the well-worn components that are involved in the working of a human body, an exhaustion of man's inner resources. Your blood no longer keeps you warm, your legs refuse to obey you, your back grows stiff, your brain grows feeble, your memory fades. The pace of old age is as unhurried as the slow combustion of the almost burnt-out logs in a stove: the flames die away, lose their colour, one log disintegrates into burning embers, then another—and now the last flickering blue flames are fading—it will soon be time to shut off the flue.

We are, all of us, old people now. Regardless of age. The pace of old age now governs our bodies and our feelings.... Yesterday at the market I saw a little girl of about nine, wearing enormous felt boots which were full of holes. She was bartering a chunk of dubious-looking brawn—probably made from dog meat—for 100 grammes of bread. Her eyes, hardly visible beneath a pair of heavy lids, looked terribly tired, her back was bent, her gait slow and shuffling, her face puckered and the corners of her mouth turned down. It was the face of an old woman. Can this ever be forgotten or forgiven?

23rd January, 11a.m. Slowly, laboriously, like emaciated people toiling up a hill, the days drag by. Monotonous, unhealthy, withdrawn days in a now silent city. Leningrad's nerve centres, which have until recently kept the life of the city going, fed it vital impulses—the power-stations—have ceased to function. And all the nerve fibres extending over the city lie dormant, inactive. There is no light, no trams or trolley-buses are running, the factories, cinemas, theatres have all stopped working. It is pitch black in the empty shops, chemists', canteens—their windows having been boarded up since autumn (as protection from shell fragments). Only the feeble, consumptive flame of a wick-lamp flickers on every counter.... Thickly coated in snow, the tram, trolley-bus and radio cables hang listlessly above the streets. They stretch overhead like an endless white net, and there is nothing to make them shed their thick snow cover.

The great city's nervous system has ceased its function. But we know that this is not death, but only a lethargic sleep. The time will come when the sleeping giant will stir, and then rouse himself...

Alexander Dymov, Winter of 1942, *translated by Hilda Perham*

VICINITY OF ST PETERSBURG

If you have time, go on a few excursions outside of St Petersburg. Day trips to Peter the Great's Summer Palace on the Gulf of Finland, or to the towns of Tsarskoye Selo and Pavlovsk are highly recommended. Here are 13 areas from which to choose.

PETERHOF OR PETRODVORETS (Петродворец)

Peterhof is located 30 kilometers (20 miles) west of the city, on the shores of the Gulf of Finland. Peter the Great named his imperial residence Peterhof; but during World War II its name was dutifully Russianized to Petrodvorets (Peter's Palace). Even though the name reverted back to Peterhof in 1992, many still refer to the area as Petrodvorets.

While Peter the Great was supervising the building of the Kronstadt fortress, he stayed in a small lodge on the southern shore of the Gulf of Finland. After Russia defeated the Swedes in the Battle of Poltava in 1709, Peter decided to build his summer residence, Peterhof, so that it not only commemorated the victory over Sweden (and of gaining access to the Baltic), but also the might of the Russian Empire. Peterhof was designed to resemble Versailles in France.

The Palace Grounds are open daily 9am–9pm, most exhibits from 10.30am–5pm, and the fountains and some of the smaller palaces are closed between October and May. (Also note that the Grand Palace is closed on Mondays and the last Tuesday of the month, and it gets quite crowded on weekends. Other complex buildings may be closed on other days.)

GETTING THERE

The most enjoyable and convenient way to Peterhof is by hydrofoil. From May to September (from about 9am–4pm daily), the *Rocket* jets across the Gulf of Finland to the Marine Canal in less than 30 minutes. Catch one at the pier right in front of the Hermitage Museum, or across the river by the Tuchkov Bridge. Hydrofoils depart about every half hour and drop you off right by the palace grounds. A round-trip ticket can be bought; foreigners may be charged double. (For a few extra dollars a VIP ticket is available, which allows a tourist to board first and get a seat at the front of the boat.) Upon arrival, you must then purchase a ticket to enter the palace grounds. A separate ticket must be purchased for entrance to each palace tour (photo/video permits are extra). For the return, line up on the dock by the sign that indicates your destination. (These lines are often long, so get there early.) A *kassa* near the pier also sells return tickets.

In front of the Peterhof Palace the five-ton Sampson Fountain wrestles open the jaws of a lion from which a jet of water shoots over 20 meters (65 feet) into the air.

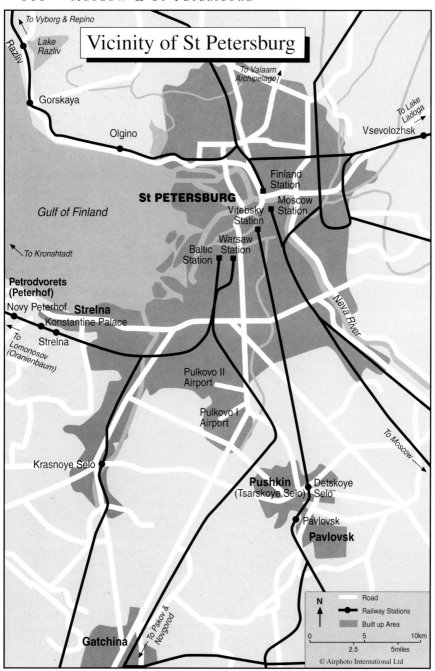

To Vyborg & Repino

Lake Razliv

Razliv

Vicinity of St Petersburg

Gorskaya

Olgino

To Valaam Archipelago

To Lake Ladoga

Vsevolozhsk

Finland Station

St PETERSBURG

Moscow Station

Gulf of Finland

Vitebsky Station

To Kronshtadt

Warsaw Station

Baltic Station

Petrodvorets (Peterhof)

Novy Peterhof   **Strelna**

Konstantine Palace

To Lomonosov (Oranienbaum)

Strelna

Neva River

Pulkovo II Airport

Pulkovo I Airport

To Moscow

Krasnoye Selo

Pushkin (Tsarskoye Selo)

Detskoye Selo

Pavlovsk

Pavlovsk

To Pskov & Novgorod

Gatchina

N

	Road
●	Railway Stations
	Built up Area

0   5   10km

2.5   5miles

© Airphoto International Ltd

The Rocket hydrofoil takes tourists on trips along the Neva River and out to Peterhof Palace on the Gulf of Finland.

You can also travel on commuter trains from Baltic (Baltiisky) Railway Station (Metro Baltiiskaya) to Novy Peterhof (not Stary Peterhof); they depart every half hour or so, and the trip takes 40 minutes. From Peterhof station take any bus numbered 349–352/356; it is then a ten-minute ride to the palace grounds (get off at Fontana, the fifth stop). Tickets for a bus tour can be booked at the excursion booth in front of Gostiny Dvor on Dumskaya Ulitsa. Coaches also leave from in front of the Cathedral of Our Lady of Kazan on Nevsky Prospekt; usually a person with a megaphone is selling tickets. You can also ask at your hotel about other travel companies that provide tours to Peterhof.

If taking a car, bus or train, on the way to Peterhof from St Petersburg, a visitor can first make a stop at the Baroque **Konstantine Palace at Strelna**, commissioned by Peter the Great as a maritime country residence in 1720; at this time, it was known as the Big Strelna Palace. The Italian architect, Nicolo Micketti, also designed the canals and fountains. Later, when Nicholas I presented the estate to his son, Konstantine, did the palace become known as the Konstantinovsky Dvorets. In turn, Alexander II then gifted it to his younger brother, Konstantine Nikolayevich. Today, this Russian Versailles has been turned into the Palace of Congresses, used to host myriad government functions. When no state affairs are taking place, several of the palace's 50 rooms are open to the public. The central **Marble Hall** is decorated with yellow marble pilasters set amongst blue marble walls. Opposite is the **Blue Hall** with blue and mirrored ornamentations, and next door, the pink **Oval Hall** is used for official meetings. Other permanent collections, as naval memorabilia from the Naval Museum, are exhibited throughout the adjoining rooms. On the third floor, a spiral staircase leads to an observation deck with breathtaking views of the grounds and Gulf of Finland. During WW II the palace was practically destroyed, and its condition greatly deteriorated over time. But, in recent years, over $200 million was collected from charitable contributions, and a medley of architects, restorers and water engineers worked together (from old photographs and plans) to restore the palace and grounds, which were reopened in 2003. Twenty bridges were built, including three drawbridges connecting the park with Peter Island where the Pavilion of Negotiations stands on the original location of Leblon's Temple of Water. The Romanov coat-of-arms is on the palace's restored front façade, and a Monument to Peter the Great stands out in front. It's a lovely stroll about the grounds and along the Upper English Park, ponds and numerous canals. **Peter the Great's Wooden Palace**, at 2 Bolnichnaya Gorka, was built in 1716 as his temporary residence. Today, it houses a small museum on the history of Strelna. Open 10.30am-4pm; closed Monday. New luxurious condos built on the property, named after different Russian cities, can be rented, albeit for a hefty fee. The 4-star Baltic Hotel is also on the grounds. Before visiting, call to make sure the palace is opened. Open 10am–6pm; closed Wednesdays and during official events. tel. 438-5360; www.strelna.ru.

Nearby is the **Trinity-Sergius Monastery**, also known as the Czar's Monastery. The recently restored interior is modeled after St Catherine's at Sinai. It also contains many aristocratic graves including that of Zinaida Yusupova, the mother of Count Yusupov who participated in the murder of Rasputin.

To build Peterhof, Peter the Great summoned architects from around the world: Rastrelli, Leblond, Braunstein, Michetti and the Russian, Zemtsov. Over 4,000 peasants and soldiers were brought in to dig the canals, gardens and parks in the marshy area. Soil, building materials and tens of thousands of trees were brought in by barge. Peter helped to draft the layout of all the gardens and fountains—built by Vasily Tuvolkov, Russia's first hydraulics engineer. Over 20 kilometers (12 miles) of canals were constructed in such a way that 30,000 liters (7,926 US gallons) of water flowed under its own pressure to 144 fountains.

The great **Cascade Fountain** in front of the palace has 17 waterfalls, 142 water jets, 66 fountains (including the two cup fountains on either side), 29 bas-reliefs and 39 gilded statues. All the statues of the Great Cascade have allegorical significance. The Russians won the Battle of Poltava on June 27, 1710—St Sampson's Day. The five-ton **Sampson** wrestles open the jaws of a lion (a symbol for conquering Sweden for a lion was featured on the country's coat of arms) with his bare hands. This was built in 1735 by Bartolomeo Rastrelli. From the lion's

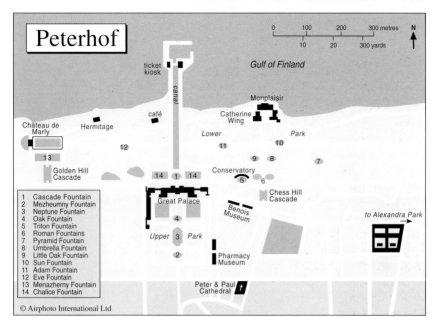

gaping jaws a jet of water shoots over 21 meters (65 feet) into the air to commemorate the 25th Anniversary of russian victory over Sweden. The eight dolphins around the feet of Sampson represent the peace of the sea. Around the rock pedestal stand the heads of four lions (the four points of the compass) which symbolize the universal glory of Russia's might.

On the upper grotto, the Tritons, gods of the sea, blow trumpet-fountains heralding the victory. And on the central terrace flows the Basket fountain, signifying wealth and abundance. Around the lower terrace stands the mythological hero Perseus, representing the great Czar Peter himself, who had conquered the Medusa-like enemy. At the reservoir that surrounds the Great Cascade, look for the **Favoritny Fountain** (1725), slightly hidden by the western colonnade. Four brightly painted ducks chase the dog, named Favoritka. If you listen closely you can hear the quacking of the ducks and the dog barking.

Fountains also grace the back of the palace. The first, in the Lower Park, is known as the **Mezheumny**. A dragon with spread wings stands in the center pool surrounded by four dolphins. Since this fountain has often changed its appearance, its name actually means 'vague.' The center fountain is that of **Neptune** (set up in 1799), who holds a trident, signifying his dominion over the seas. Four water-breathing sea monsters stand along his pedestal and other riders on winged

(following pages) The great Cascade Fountain stands in front of Peterhof, Peter the Great's Summer Palace. Its 66 fountains, 17 waterfalls and 142 water jets all flow without the aid of a single pump.

sea-horses also direct eight dolphins who swim along the walls of the fountain. These fountains were brought to Russia from Nuremberg, Germany.

The next fountain in the Upper Park is that of the **Oak Fountain**. Originally appearing as an Oak Tree, it now contains a marble statue of Cupid. Right by the walls of the Palace are the **Square Ponds**, flanked by statues of Apollo and Venus.

As you arrive and walk towards the Palace beside the central Marine Canal, make a left along the first path by the water which leads to **Monplaisir**, built between 1710 and 1723. While the Grand Palace was under construction, Peter designed and lived in this seven-room Dutch-style villa that he called Monplasisir (My Pleasure), situated beside the waters of the Gulf of Finland. Even after the larger palace was completed, Peter preferred to stay in this smaller brick abode while he visited Peterhof.

At the entrance, in the garden, stands the Wheatsheaf fountain and the four gilded statues of Psyche, Apollo, Faun and Bacchus—all basically designed (including Monplaisir) by Peter himself. Today, Monplasir mainly houses a small collection of 17th- and 18th-century European paintings. Rooms include the Lacquered Study, the Ceremonial Hall, Peter the Great's Naval Study, his Bedroom (the patch-work quilt on the bed, and the Chinese-dressing gown and nightcap are said to have belonged to the czar) and the Dutch-tiled kitchen. The complex is open daily 10.30am–5pm (closed Wednesdays), and is closed between October and May. The ticket *kassa* is along the western side of the palace.

In 1762, when Catherine the Great's husband, Czar Peter III, threatened divorce (his mistress was the pock-marked Elizaveta Vorontsova), the empress came here to live in the adjoining Tea House. A few days later, on July 28 1762, the day of their planned coup, Catherine's lover, Count Grigori Orlov, picked her up from Peterhof. Soon after, Czar Peter was mysteriously strangled in his sleep (probably instigated by the Orlov brothers). The whole army came out to pledge its allegiance to Catherine when she returned to the Winter Palace. The Tea House was eventually demolished and Empress Elizabeth had it rebuilt in the 1740s by Bartolomeo Rastrelli to stage large balls and receptions. Today, it is known as **Catherine's Wing** which exhibits historical items within its large rooms. This building is open 10.30am–5pm, closed Thursdays, the last Friday of the month, and from October to May. The **Bath Wing** stands at the opposite eastern end of Monplaisir, built in 1865, for the wife of Alexander II. The adjacent **Assembly Hall**, built by Zemtsov in 1726, has exhibits of 18th-century Russian tapestries.

Exiting the Catherine's Wing, walk along the southwest path to the **Adam Fountain**. This statue was brought to Russia from Venice by Peter the Great in 1718. (On the other side of the Marine Canal stands the **Eve Fountain**, also fashioned from marble by the Venetian sculptor, Giovanni Bonazza.)

Heading east from the Adam Fountain, you will pass the **Monument to Peter the Great**, crafted by a Russian sculptor in 1884. The next pond contains the **Sun Fountain** with 16 golden dolphins. The interior golden disks slowly rotate with 72 jets of water, creating the effect of golden rays streaming from the sun. The **Pyramid Fountain** is down the southeast path. Peter the Great designed this water pyramid, consisting of seven tiers and 505 jets. The center of the area consists of many trick fountains. A circular seat is positioned under the **Little Umbrella Fountain**. If you are tempted to have a short rest on the bench under the umbrella, be ready to scramble—as 164 jets spray out water as soon as anyone sits down! As you scamper away, you will approach the **Little Oak Fountain**, which has dozens of hidden jets (as do the artificial tulips) that spray as any weight approaches the oak tree. When you run off to the nearby bench to catch your breath, you will now get drenched by 41 more jets! And beware, too, of the **Three Fir Trees**!

Walking south towards the palace will bring you to the two **Roman Fountains**, built by Karl Blank and Ivan Davydov in 1739. They were modeled after those at the Cathedral of St Peter in Rome. In front of these, the **Chess Hill**, with a checkerboard design, contains some of the best waterfalls, cascading over bronze dragons, and flanked by marble figures of mythological heroes. The **Triton Fountain** (Neptune's son) presides over the semi-circular **Conservatory**, once used as a greenhouse. Today, it houses the Museum of Wax Figures.

At the opposite western end of the Lower Park, two other historical buildings are worth a visit. Down by the water is the two-story red-baroque structure known as the **Hermitage Pavilion**. It was built by Johann Friedrich Braunstein from the designs of Peter the Great. The retreat was surrounded by a moat and had a drawbridge that could be raised to further isolate the guests. The first floor consisted of one room with a large dining table that could be lifted from or lowered to servants on the ground floor. The guests placed a note on the table, rang a bell, and the table would shortly reappear with their orders. In 1797, when Paul I got stuck on the lift ascending to the first floor, he ordered an oak staircase built. Today, the building houses over 100 paintings by 18th-century European artists. It is open daily 10:30am–5pm, closed Tuesdays and between October and May, and during inclement weather. The **Lion Cascade Fountain** stands near the front of the Hermitage.

The western path leads to the two-storey **Château de Marly**, built between 1719 and 1723 by Braunstein in the style of Louis XIV. (Peter I had visited the hunting-lodge palace of the French Kings in Marly-le-Roi.) The balconies' wrought-iron railings are emblazoned with the monogram of Peter the Great. This house is also open daily 10:30am–5pm, closed Tuesdays and between October and May. In front of it flows the **Golden Hill Cascade**, commissioned in 1721 by Peter the Great and built by Italian architect Niccolo Michetti. All the mythological gods and

Peter the Great's Palace, Peterhof, was designed to resemble the French palace of Versailles. The rooms have magnificent parquet floors, painted ceilings and even Chippendale furniture.

goddesses that adorn the walls glorify the bounty of Russia's achievements. The front fountain, with its two huge jets, is known as the **Menazherny**, from the French *ménager*, to economize.

After a stroll around the grounds, it is time to visit its centerpiece. The **Great Palace** was built between 1714 and 1724, designed by Friedrich, Michetti and Le Blond in classical and baroque styles. It stands on a hill in the center of the Peterhof complex and overlooks the parks and gardens. Later, Rastrelli made changes and added larger wings (1747–54) for Empress Elizabeth. After Peter's death, the palace passed to subsequent czars and was declared a museum after the revolution.

The palace is three stories high with wings that contain the galleries. The central exhibition rooms lead to **Peter the Great's Oak Study** and on to the **Royal Bedchamber**. The rooms have magnificent parquet floors, gilded ceilings and crystal chandeliers, and are filled with exquisite objets d'art from around the world. The Cavalier or **Crimson Room** has furniture by Chippendale. The walls of the **Oak Study** are adorned with portraits of Empress Elizabeth, Catherine the Great and Alexander I. From the Dressing Rooms and Lounge, you enter the **Partridge Chamber**, so named for the silk ornamental partridges that covered the walls. It is decorated with 18th-century style French silk-upholstered furniture, porcelain and clocks.

The **Portrait Gallery**, in the central hall of the palace, is filled with portraits by such painters as Pietro Rotari (the whole collection was acquired by Catherine the Great) and serves as an interesting catalog of period costumes. The **White Dining Hall**, once used for State dinners, is decorated in classical style with white molded figures on the walls and a crystal and amethyst chandelier. The table is ceremoniously laid out for 30 people with 196 pieces of cream-colored English porcelain, commissioned by Catherine the Great. In the 1750s, Rastrelli built the adjacent **Throne Room** for official receptions. A portrait of Catherine the Great on horseback hangs over Peter the Great's first throne.

The **Chesme Room** commemorated the war victory of Russia over Turkey, fought between 1768–1774. In 1770, Russia finally defeated the Turkish fleet in the Aegean Sea during the battle of Chesme Bay. The German artist, Philippe Hackert, was commissioned to paint the victory scenes for the hall. Count Alexei Orlov (the commander of the famous battle and brother of Catherine's lover, Grigori) checked the artist's sketches and was dissatisfied with one that depicted an exploding ship. Hackert mentioned that he had never seen such a thing. So Orlov ordered a 60-cannon Russian frigate, anchored off the coast of Italy, to be packed with gunpowder. Hackert had to journey to Italy to witness the exploding ship. The rest of the palace is joined by numerous galleries and studies. At the east end is a Rastrelli rococo chapel with a single gilded cupola.

When visiting the palace it is mandatory to join a group tour. They are held in different languages. If you cannot find one in English, join any tour and once inside, you can slip off on your own (do not let the feisty guards at the door deter you). Tickets are sold in the lobby where you pick up your *ta'pochki* (slippers) to put over your shoes. (Photography is strictly forbidden unless you have purchased a permit.) The Grand Palace is open 10.30am–5pm, closed on Mondays and the last Tuesday of the month. tel. 420-0073; www.peterhof.org.

Exiting the palace, walk right (east) down the main walkway to the **Benois Museum**, designed by Nikolai Benois. This building includes works by the architect Benois (1813–90) and other generations of the Benois family. Nikolai became the godson of Empress Maria Fedorovna, and was educated at her expense (his father was Paul I's French chef). His son, Alexander, became a famous stage designer and artist who worked with Serge Diaghilev in the Mariinsky (Alexander's maternal grandfather, Albert Kavos, built the theater) and on the art magazine, *Mir Iskusstva*. In 1914, the Benois family sold to the Hermitage Museum the famous *Benois Madonna*, painted by Leonardo da Vinci. It had been in the family for four generations, and is said originally to have been purchased in Astrakhan. (The British actor, Peter Ustinov, was related to the Benois family.) The museum is open 10.30am–5pm, closed Mondays, and between October and May.

The **Apothecary Museum and Herbarium** was once the center for growing medicinal herbs for the royal family. Today, it still serves as a functioning pharmacy and a staff member can prepare herbal teas and tonics. Open 11am–6pm, closed Saturdays. The five-domed **Peter and Paul Cathedral**, at number 32 St Petersburg Prospekt, was built in the 1890s, and is slowly being restored (it was used as a Soviet-era movie cinema).

At the end of this path lies **Alexandria Park**, developed by Nicholas I and his wife, after whom the park is named. At the park entrance stands the Gothic-style **Court Chapel** (with 43 saints along the outer walls), built in 1831. The **Cottage Palace** was built in 1829 by Adam Menelaws who designed it to resemble an aristocratic Englishman's cottage. During WWII, the museum staff saved 1,981 of the 2,500 pieces in the cottage and these are on exhibit today. Some of the rooms to be visited are the Studies of Empress Alexandra Fyodorovna and Nicholas I, the Library, Dining Hall, Reception Halls, and the Class Room of their son, the future Alexander II (full of interesting daguerreotypes). The last building in this area is the **Farm Pavilion**, originally used as a storage house, but later converted into a summer palace by Alexander II.

Hitler invaded Russia on June 22, 1941. When the Nazis reached Peterhof on September 23, many of the art pieces and statues had still not been evacuated. The German army spent 900 days here and destroyed the complex. Monplaisir was an artillery site, used to shell Leningrad. The Germans cut down 15,000 trees for firewood, used tapestries in the trenches, plundered over 34,000 works of art and made off with priceless objects, including the Sampson statue, which were never recovered. After the war massive restoration work began, and on June 17, 1946, the fountains flowed once again. The Sampson statue was restored, according to surviving pre-war photos, and was returned to its former site the following year. The head of the Hermitage, Joseph Orbelli, who lived in the Hermitage during the siege, remarked: 'Even during our worst suffering, we knew that the day would come when once again the beautiful fountains of Petrodvorets would begin to spray and the statues of the park flash their golden gleam in the sunlight.' There are black-and-white photographs on display in the Exhibition Room that show the extensive damage to the palace. Every year, at the end of August, Sampson Holiday is marked on the day when the statue was returned to Peterhof.

Leningrad poet Olga Bergholts visited Peterhof after the siege and wrote:

Again from the black dust, from the place
of death and ashes, will arise the garden as before.
So it will be. I firmly believe in miracles.
You gave me that belief, my Leningrad.

The upper and lower parks and gardens cover about 121 hectares (300 acres), stretching around the palace to the Gulf of Finland. When warm, it is wonderful to have a picnic on the grounds or beach, stroll in the gardens, and spend the entire day here. In June during the White Nights, a variety of festivals and musical concerts are held on the palace grounds. (During the time of the czars, the city's inhabitants were invited here for one day a year to celebrate the festival of the summer solstice. Fireworks were set off from pontoons along the lake.)

One can grab a bite to eat at numerous cafés on the grounds. Off the main Marine Canal, located down the western path towards the Hermitage, is a self-service café. The Gallery Eatery is by the western end of the Grand Palace, and the Benois Museum also has a café. Or try one of the following restaurants. The best is the Trapeza (Refectory), near the Herbarium, at 9 Kalininskaya St, tel. 427-9393; open daily 1pm–10pm. The Imperatorsky Stol (Emperor's Table) is at 2 Razvodnaya St in the old *oranzhereya* or garden house, tel. 427-9106; open daily 10.30am–6pm. And Peterhof at 3 Morskovo Desanta, tel. 427-9884, serves both Russian and German cuisine; open daily 10am–8pm (and takes credit cards).

LOMONOSOV OR ORANIENBAUM (Ломоносов)

Lomonosov, also known as Oranienbaum, is situated only 10 kilometers (six miles) west of Peterhof on the Gulf of Finland, at 48 Yunovo Lenintsa. In 1707, while Peter the Great was building Monplaisir, he gave these lands to his close friend Prince Alexander Menschikov to develop. Menschikov was the first governor-general of St Petersburg and supervised the building of the nearby Kronstadt Fortress. (For his palace in the city see page 487.) He wanted to turn the estate into his summer residence. Since the prince planted orange trees in the lower parks (first grown in hothouses), he named his residence Oranienbaum, German for wild orange trees. The first palace here was built in 1710, and designed by Giovanni Fontana. Several years later Peter the Great came to visit Menschikov by ship, but because of the swampy shoreline, he was unable to land. Thus, in three days, Menshikov had a sea canal dug, over a mile long, from the palace to the sea, so that Peter could sail up to the palace.

Unfortunately Menschikov never fully enjoyed his product—he ended up in exile three years after Peter I's death. The property was briefly made into a hospital before Peter III preferred living here to the Winter Palace. After his death his wife, Sophia Augusta Fredericka of Anhalt-Zerbst (now Catherine the Great) expanded the buildings and grounds around Rococo architecture and made it her private pleasure abode. Until the 1917 Revolution it was used by members of the Romanov family. In 1948, the name was changed to Lomonosov after the great Russian scientist who had a glassworks and mosaic factory nearby. (For Lomonosov Museum see page 487.) The estate escaped major shelling during the war and is beautifully preserved.

The park is open daily 9am–9pm (the whole complex is closed on Tuesdays). The estate buildings are open 11am–5pm, Mondays until 4pm, and are also closed on Tuesdays and the last Monday of each month (be aware that some may also be closed in winter). Tel. 422-4796; for excursions 422-3753.

From the railway station, the path into the park leads to a lake where visitors can sunbathe and rent boats in summer. The two-story **Grand Palace**, built in 1725 by architects Fontana and Schädel, stands atop the hill overlooking the parks and formal gardens that were originally designed by Antonio Rinaldi. Three rooms house the exhibit, 'Oranienbaum and its Owners in 1720–1917.' The copper-roofed Japanese Pavilion also exhibits paintings and other works of art.

West of the palace, walking past the small **Stone Room** structure, leads up to the **Katalnaya Gorka** (Sliding Hill) **Pavilion**. This brilliant blue pyramid, the forerunner of a modern amusement ride, is the only structure of its kind in the world.

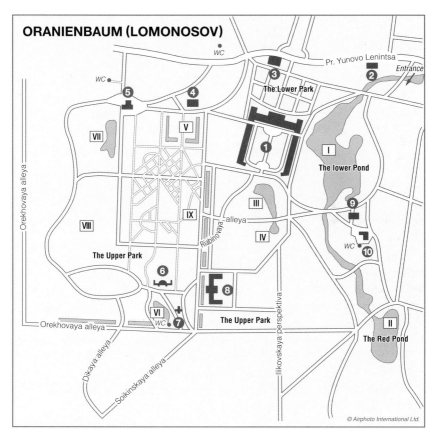

ORANIENBAUM (LOMONOSOV)

1 The Great Menshikov Palace	I The Lower Pond
2 The Lower Houses	II The Red Pond
3 The Picture House	III The Carp's Pond
4 The Stone Hall	IV The Houseshoe-shaped Pond
5 The Coasting Hill Pavilon	V The Pond near the Stone Hall
6 The Chinese Palace	VI The Pond near the Chinese Palace
7 The Chinese Kitchen Pavilon	VII The Pond near the Sliding Hill Pavilion
8 The Countiers-in-Attendance Pavilon	VIII The Figured Pondies
9 The Honorary Gate	IX The Crescent-shaped Pond
10 The palace of Peter III	

Catherine the Great wanted to toboggan in summer, so she asked Rinaldi to construct a ride so that she and her guests could roller coaster along a long wooden tract, with hills and dips, from the pavilion's third floor balcony down through the lower gardens. Oranienbaum became the center of masked balls and parties that entertained Russian royalty and foreign diplomats. The ground floor of the pavilion has a model of the original sliding Hill, and the rococo-style Round Hall has a porcelain exhibit. The 1760s faux marble floors are the last example of its kind, since the process of how to produce this gypsum-based material has been lost.

A five-minute walk down the southern path leads to the **Chinese Palace** (Kitaiskydvorets), also built by Rinaldi from 1762–68. The palace gets its name from the sumptuous decorations of the rooms and halls. Hand-carved furniture, parquet floors, porcelain, portraits and paintings detail every room. Each painted ceiling was the work of masters from the Venetian Academy of the Arts. The designer Alexander Benois commented: "The Chinese Palace is a pearl, the only one of its kind, a work of art ... with a purely musical effect of its own that has something in common with the sonatas of Haydn and Mozart." The tour through the palace runs wing-to-wing from the rooms of Catherine the Great's then seven-year-old son, the future Paul I, across to Catherine's private suites. The central State Rooms include the Blue and Pink Drawing Rooms, Billiard Room, Hall of Muses and Damask Bedchamber. Nine seamstresses spent a year and a half embroidering twelve panels with different colored silk and chenille for the Glass Bugle Study, with bases made from mother-of-pearl bugles. The mosaic furniture, decorated with opaque glass, was created by Mikhail Lomonosov. The **Large Chinese Hall** pays homage to the fascination with the Orient and what was imagined at the time to be the style of the art of China. It is decorated with Chinese furniture and beautiful inlaid wooden chinoiserie-style walls. The exterior **Chinese Kitchens** stand adjacent to the old Cavalry Barracks, where there is a small café.

Head northeast through the Upper Park to the **Palace of Peter III**, another Rinaldi creation built in 1752, and dubbed Peterstadt. Before Catherine's husband, Peter III, was assassinated in 1762, he had constructed here a model fort filled with thousands of toy soldiers. He also loved to drill and parade thousands of real soldiers about the grounds in strict Prussian disciplinary fashion. His love of the military rubbed off on his son Paul, as well. Today, the second floor contains a Picture Hall and exquisitely lacquered panels and doors.

The **Wax Museum Workshop**, at 37a Krasny Partizan (9am–6pm, Monday–Friday), manufactures figures for the wax museum in the Beloselsky-Belozersky Palace in the city (see page 532). On Komsomolskaya Ulitsa is the **Lomonosov History Museum**.

The **Lomonosov Porcelain Factory** was founded in 1744 by Elizabeth I, Peter the Great's daughter, as Russia's first porcelain enterprise. The factory was named after the influential Russian writer and scientist Mikhail Lomonosov, and run by another scientist, Dmitry Vinogradov, who had invented a mass means of porcelain production. Eventually renamed the Imperial Porcelain Factory by Catherine the Great, the facility went on to produce most of the imperial porcelain, including table settings and miniature items; and it went on to become one of the leading porcelain enterprises in all of Europe. Alexander I (1801–1825) ordered the famous Gurievsky dinner setting, celebrating Russia's 1812 victory over Napoleon; it included 4500 pieces which were gilded with several kilos of gold. The Lomonosov Porcelain Factory survived the Soviet period, and it still creates over 500 different items. On the factory site is a Museum, exhibiting objects produced from the mid 18th-century through today; other famous porcelain settings are also on display in the Hermitage Museum.

The easiest way to get to Lomonosov is by *elektrichka* train from the city's Baltic (Baltiisky) Station to the Oranienbaum stop (four stops after Novy Peterhof). This takes one hour. From the station it is about a ten-minute walk southwest (head toward the green-domed Cathedral of the Archangel Michael) to the park. There is also a ferry from Kronstadt, or a local bus from Peterhof (the bus stop is next to the railway station). Another easy way is to take a Russian excursion bus from the corner of Dumskaya (Gostiny Dvor) and Nevsky Prospekt. Check out ticket *kassas* for times and prices. If you do not speak Russian, take a guidebook; you can walk around the grounds and museums and meet up at the bus at the designated departure time. Other cafés are located in the railway station (open daily 7.30am–9pm): Lana 2nd floor, 5 Manezhnaya Ulitsa (open daily 8am–8pm); Baltika Restaurant near the post office and bank on Ulitsa Pobedy; and a cafeteria at 1 Privokzalnaya Ulitsa (open daily 7.30am–9pm).

KRONSTADT (Кронштадт)

When Peter the Great founded St Petersburg in 1703, the Great Northern War (1700–21) with the Swedes was in its early stages. To protect the gulf approach to his city, Peter began building the Kronstadt (German for "city of the crown") Fortress in 1704, located 29 km (18 miles) west of the city; it soon became one of the mightiest fortresses along the Baltic coast. Its construction, in the narrowest part of the Finnish Gulf, was overseen by Prince Menschikov (see Lomonosov, page 578). The fortress, on the island of Kotlin, also contained the shipyards. Monuments on the island are linked to the to the history of Russian fleet. On July 26, 1803, Ivan Kruzenshtern set off from Kronstadt to command Russia's first round-the-world expedition. He returned here on August 19, 1806, having sailed over 45,000 nautical miles. These Baltic sailors were always at the forefront of rebellion. During the 1917 revolution, the Kronstadt ships, which patrolled the Neva River, played a vital role in the October takeover. Later, in 1921, during the difficult Civil War and famine, the workers of Petrograd were on the brink of revolt. On March 1, 1921, masses gathered in Kronstadt's Anchor Square to form their own revolutionary committee against the Bolsheviks. The rebellion lasted for 18 days, when Red Army troops, led by General Tukhachevsky, crossed the ice to capture Kronstadt. About 600 sailors were killed in the bloody assault, 900 were executed and thousands imprisoned. Tukhachevsky wrote in his memoirs: "It was not a battle, it was an inferno.... The sailors fought like wild beasts, I cannot understand where they found the might for such rage." During WWII, and siege of Leningrad, the garrison, ships and submarines helped fend off violent enemy attacks. Over 6,000 residents were killed by bombings and starvation. Later, in 1990, during the attempted overthrow of Gorbachev, the Kronstadt naval base commander offered to safely house the St Petersburg mayor and the city cabinet. The city's centerpiece, the **Seaman's Cathedral**, built between 1902–13 in neo-Byzantine style by Vasily Kosyako, honors all those sailors who perished at sea and during the Kronstadt rebellion. Today, it also houses a museum, dedicated to the history of the fortress, which celebrated its 300th anniversary in 2004. Only after 1997 were foreign visitors allowed into this closed military city of 45,000 residents, where some of the

country's military and scientific vessels are still docked today. The former Menshikov Palace now hosts a club for island sailors, some of whom also attend the naval academy. Offshore are several forts that were constructed during the Crimean War (1853–56). The most interesting is the **Alexander Fort**, whose foundations were first laid in 1839; it was later used as an anti-plague laboratory. Today, it hosts evening dances during the summer White Nights, and yachts from the city also enjoy docking here in warmer months.

From April 25 through November 10, the daily hydrofoils leave hourly from near the Tuchkov Bridge from 9am–6pm; the trip takes 30–40 minutes. Or try taking a local *elektrichka* train from Finland Station to Gorskaya, on the north shore of the Gulf of Finland, and the ferry across to Kronstadt. An *elektrichka* also leaves from the Baltic (Baltiisky) Train Station to Oranienbaum in Lomonosov, where ferries (or a bus over the dam) depart for the island. From Peterhof, there is a local bus or train to Oranienbaum. An easy way to travel here is to take a Russian Excursion bus from Dumskaya Ul. (Gostiny Dvor) and Nevsky Pr. Check the ticket *kassas* for times and prices.

On the way, notice the 29-kilometer (18-mile) barrier built across a section of the Gulf of Finland (this was the area of the older Finnish border until 1939) to control the floods (over 300 in St Petersburg's history). Tidal waves sweep inland during severe storms. In 1824, the water level rose over four meters (13 feet), killing 569 people.

WEST OF THE CITY (NORTHERN GULF)
RAZLIV (Разлив)

The village of Razliv lies 35 kilometers (22 miles) northwest of St Petersburg on the Karelian Isthmus, near the former Finnish border. Lenin fled here in 1917 to hide from the Provisional Government.

Agents were searching everywhere for him and advertised a reward of 200,000 rubles in gold. Shaving off his trademark beard and wearing a wig, he ventured out at night from the Finland Railway Station to the village, and stayed in a barn owned by the Yemelyanov family. The glass-covered barn is now the **Sarai Museum**, housing some of the things Lenin used. On the outside wall, a plaque reads, 'Here in this barn for a period of several days from July 10 (23), 1917, Vladimir Ilyich Lenin lived and worked while in hiding from the agents of the Provisional Government.'

The centerpiece of Kronstadt is the Seaman's Cathedral, built in Neo-Byzantine style, which honors all those who perished at sea, and killed during the famous 1921 Kronstadt rebellion against the Bolsheviks.

*Russian folk singer wears a traditional peasant costume
—*sarafan *jumper, embroidered blouse and tall* kokoshniki *headdress.*

After a few days of hiding here, Nikolai Yemelyanov rowed Lenin across Lake Razliv and built a hut out of hay for a more secretive shelter. Lenin lived and wrote articles in this *shalash*, or thatched hut, by the lake. The **Shalash Museum**, near the hut, exhibits some of Lenin's personal documents and belongings. Another inscription reads, 'Here in July and August 1917 in a hut made of branches the leader of the October Revolution went into hiding from the sleuths of the bourgeois government.' A tourist boat takes visitors across the lake. The museum grounds are open 11am–5pm, closed Wednesdays. In August, Lenin left the hut and traveled ten kilometers to Dibuny Station, from where he left for Finland, only to return in October to lead the final stages of the Bolshevik revolution.

The easiest way to get to here is by *elektrickha* train from Finland Station (about an hour) along the northern shore of the Gulf of Finland toward Sestroretsk; the stop is Razliv. Enroute, it is interesting to note the town of Lakta (before Olgino). Peter the Great built a country residence here called Blizniye Dubki (Nearby Oaks). In November 1724, as he was riding along the coast, Peter noticed a ship that was sinking in a storm, and he dove into the icy waters to help rescue the drowning people. As a result the czar became gravely ill and died on January 27 1725.

It was also in Lakta where the enormous boulder was found for the pedestal for the monument of The Bronze Horseman which stands on Senate Square (see page 501).

REPINO (Репино)

The road from Razliv along the Karelian Isthmus leads to Repino about 45 kilometers (30 miles) northwest of St Petersburg. Repino is a small town in the Solnechnoye resort area once known as Kurnosovo. It bears the name of the celebrated painter Ilya Repin (1844–1930), who bought a cottage in the settlement in 1899 and made it his permanent residence. All his friends and students gathered here every Wednesday and Repin painted the rest of the week. Repin named his estate the Penates, after the Roman gods of home and well-being. Painted here were: *Bloody Sunday*, *Meeting of the State Council* and *Pushkin's Examination at the Lyceum*, as well as portraits of Gorky, Chaliapin and Tolstoy. (Many of Repin's works are on display at the Russian Museum and the Tretyakov Gallery in Moscow. One of his most famous pictures is *The Volga Boatmen*, see page 302.)

Birch trees line the path up a small hill to his grave, above it stands a bust of Repin himself. The Penates burned down during World War II, but was totally reconstructed and is now a museum, displaying Repin's art and personal belongings. The house containing his studio is at 411 Primorskoye Highway (open 10.30am–4pm, closed Tuesdays, tel 231-6828/6834).

Take an *elektrichka* train from Finland Station (or if already in Razliv, it is only about 15 minutes further west) in the direction of Zelenogorsk/Vyborg to Repino. From the station head towards the water. Make a left on Repin Street and walk about 400 meters to the estate.

One train stop west of Repino brings you to the village of **Komarovo** (once a part of Finnish territory) where the famous poet Anna Akhmatova is buried near the dacha where she lived for many years. Her funeral was held in the city's Nikolsky Marine Cathedral on March 10, 1966. In 1963, at the age of 74, Akhmatova wrote of Komarovo:

> This land, although not my native land,
> Will be remembered forever,
> And the sea's lightly iced,
> Unsalty water.

> The sand on the bottom is whiter than chalk
> The air is heady, like wine,
> And the rosy body of the pines
> Is naked in the sunset hour;

> And the sunset itself on such waves of ether
> That I just can't comprehend
> Whether it is the end of the day, the end of the world,
> Or the mystery of mysteries in me again.

NORTH OF THE CITY

VYBORG (Выборг)

When in St Petersburg, and if you are up for an excursion of something other than palaces and parks, Vyborg is an easy day trip from the city. Lying 160 kilometers (100 miles) north of St Petersburg and 300 kilometers (180 miles) south of Helsinki, Vyborg, one of the oldest cities in Europe, is a lovely 13th century town, with the Finnish influences of winding cobblestone streets, picturesque old buildings, and a 13th century medieval castle, which was built in 1293 when the Swedes captured the region of Karelia from Novgorod. Peter the Great annexed the area back in 1710; but, a century later, the city fell within autonomous Finland. After the 1917 Revolution, the area remained part of independent Finland, when it became known as Viipuri. Stalin's troops took back control in 1939, but, during WW II, Russia lost it again, this time to the Germans and Finns. After the war, when Stalin got the region back, he deported all the Finns north across the border. Shipbuilding and fishing remain important industries, and the bustling harbor is full of ships loading up timber.

Starting west of the castle, you'll come upon **Anna's Fortress** (Anninskaya Krepost), named after Empress Anna Ivanovna, and built as protection against the Swedes. Here, charming narrow streets meander through picturesque old neighborhoods. Returning east across Krepostnoy Bridge leads to the imposing medieval **Castle** (Viipuri Linna in Finnish), built upon a small rock island in Vyborg Bay. It is the city's oldest structure, and now contains a small museum (closed Monday). After visiting the castle, continue back across the bridge to the land spit. The main thoroughfare of Krepostnaya Ulitsa leads to the **Belfry Watch Tower** of the Old Cathedral. A few blocks directly north, off Prospekt Lenina, stands the 16th century **Round Tower** (Kruglaya Bashnya). Across from the tower, standing in the central square, is the **Cathedral of Sts Peter and Paul** (Sobor Petra I Pavla), built in 1799. Back on Krepostnaya is the **Cathedral of the Transfiguration** (Spaso-Preobrazhensky Sobor), constructed in 1787. The **City Hall Tower** is a short walk southwest to Vyborgskaya Ulitsa. Many of the other buildings are architecturally interesting, as is the town library; designed by the renowned Finnish architect, Alvar Aalto. All in all, Vyborg is home to a variety of architectural styles from medieval forts to pre-war functionalist masterpieces.

Elektrichka trains leave from St Petersburg's Finlandsky Station about every hour and take about three hours. In the station, departure times are posted on the board as Vyborgskoye. Fast trains and other buses enroute to Helsinki usually make stops in Vyborg as well. The bus station is situated just across the street from the old

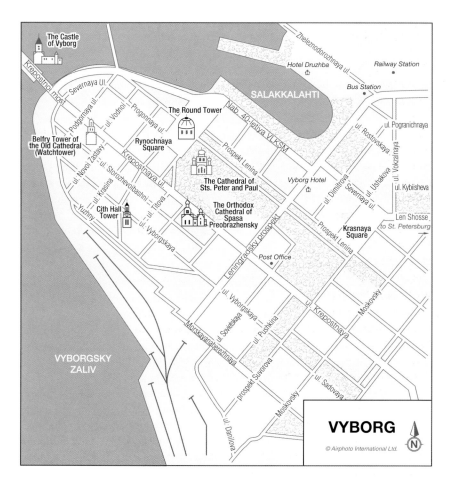

The Castle of Vyborg

Hotel Druzhba

Railway Station

Bus Station

SALAKKALAHTI

The Round Tower

Severnaya Ul.

Kreposinoi most

Podgornaya ul.

ul. Vodnoi

Progonnaya ul.

Nab. 40-letiya VLKSM

Prospekt Lenina

ul. Pogranichnaya

ul. Rostovskaya

Belfry Tower of the Old Cathedral (Watchtower)

Rynochnaya Square

Kreposinaya ul.

ul. Novoi Zastavy

ul. Krasina

ul. Storozhevoibashni

ul. Titova

The Cathedral of Sts. Peter and Paul

Vyborg Hotel

ul. Dimitrova

Severnaya ul.

ul. Ushakova

ul. Vokzalnaya

ul. Kybiisheva

Yuzhny

Cith Hall Tower

ul. Vyborgskaya

The Orthodox Cathedral of Spasa Preobrazhensky

Krasnaya Square

Prospekt Lenina

Len Shosse to St. Petersburg

Leningradsky prospekt

Post Office

ul. Vyborgskaya

ul. Sovietskaya

ul. Pushkina

Kreposinaya

Moskovsky

Morskaya naberezhnaya

prospekt Suvorova

Moskovsky

ul. Sadovaya

VYBORGSKY ZALIV

ul. Danilova

VYBORG

© Airphoto International Ltd.

N

impressive façade of the Vyborg train station, both centrally located. Leningradsky Prospekt runs southwest from the stations towards town. If staying overnight, try the moderately-priced **Druzhba (Friendship) Hotel**, with 100 rooms, at 5 Zheleznodorozhnaya St. near the Railway Station, tel. (81278) 25744/24942, or the 50-room **Vyborg Hotel** at 18 Leningradsky Prospekt, a few minutes walk from the main cathedral, tel. (81278) 22383/22143. Numerous restaurants and bars (these are usually filled with drinking Finns who come here on vacations and weekends for cheaper alcohol) dot the city. One especially popular place is the **Restaurant Pogrebok** (cellar) a few doors down from the Druzhba Hotel, at number 5. A block behind the old watchtower, near the water, is the tasty Chinese Restaurant, **Samira**.

SOUTH OF THE CITY
TSARSKOYE SELO OR PUSHKIN (Царское Село)

If you plan to visit Tsarskoye Selo and Pavlovsk in one day, come on a Monday, Wednesday, Thursday, Saturday or Sunday, when both are open. (eng.tzar.ru)

The town of Tsarskoye Selo, the Czar's Village, is located 24 kilometers (15 miles) south of St Petersburg. City residents used to flock here in summer for the beneficial effects of the climate. After the Revolution the name was changed to Detskoye Selo (Children's Village), because of the large number of orphanages in town; many of the buildings were turned into schools. Pushkin studied at the Lyceum from 1811 to 1817. In 1937, to commemorate the 100-year anniversary of the poet's death, the town was renamed Pushkin. Today the town is referred to either as Tsarskoye Selo or Pushkin, but the train station is still called Detskoye Selo.

During the Northern War, Peter the Great won back the region between the Neva and the Gulf of Finland from the Swedes. In 1724, he presented the lands to his wife, Catherine I, who commissioned Jacob Roosen to create the gardens, and the architect, Johann Friedrich Braunstein, to build a two-story stone palace. After Catherine's daughter, Elizabeth I, inherited the estate, she commissioned Bartolomeo Rastrelli to renovate the palace into her summer residence in 1752. He added three-story wings, an entrance stairway, and ornamented façades with many columns and statues. Upon completion, the beautiful baroque masterpiece, with its opulent interior, stretched 300 meters (980 feet)—the longest palace in the world. The columns of the upper story were supported by 60 large figures of Atlas. When Empress Elizabeth and her court arrived to view the glistening gold and greenish-blue painted palace for the first time, the French Ambassador heralded, 'The only thing needed is a case in which to put this jewel!' In 2002 President Putin approved the allocation of 140 kilograms of gold for the restoration of the palace.

Catherine the Great made other additions to the palace. During her reign (1762–1796) many renowned architects, such as Charles Cameron, Antonio Rinaldi and Giacomo Quarenghi, worked in the neo-classical style on the palace. In the 1800s, other buildings and gardens were also assembled. In 1887, a piped water system was installed along with a simple power station, making Tsarskoye Selo Europe's first town entirely run by electricity.

Upon entering **Catherine's Palace** (Yekaterininsky Dvorets), the visitor climbs the magnificent marble staircase, built by Ipolit Monighetti in 1860. On the interior walking tour, you first pass through the gilded black iron gates to **Rastrelli's Cavaliers' (Knights) Dining Room** and **Great Hall**, filled with gilded mirrors and ceiling painting of the Triumph of Russia. Then after passing through several exhibition halls, you arrive at one of the palace's most famous rooms, once referred to as the 'Eighth Wonder of the World'. In 1701, the eccentric Prussian King, Friederich Hohenzollern I, ordered tons of amber extracted from the Baltic Sea coast so he could create an amber room for his palace in Charlottenberg. When the King died, his heir, the militaristic Friederich Wilhelm I, ordered the amber sections packed up and stored in the Berlin Stadtschloss. In 1717, when visiting Germany, Peter the Great saw them, and convinced the King to give him the panels. In exchange, the King requested 55 six-foot-tall "giants" for his Corps of Grenadiers. Upon returning to Russia, Peter I never did anything with the panels. Later, his daughter, Elizabeth I, had her favorite architect, Bartolomeo Rastrelli, install them in a room in the Winter Palace. In

The beautiful baroque-style Catherine's Palace, built by Peter the Great for his wife and future Empress, Catherine I, in the town of Tsarskoye Selo

1755, Catherine the Great ordered them transferred and mounted in a room in Catherine's Palace in Tsarskoye Selo. The Amber Room (Yantarnaya Komnata) covered three walls and was arranged in three tiers. The Room remained intact for nearly two centuries until WW II, when the Nazis relocated them out of the country. Countless treasure hunters searched the world for decades, but no one ever discovered the room's whereabouts. Beginning in 1979, the Soviet government initiated the rebuilding of the famous site; and Russian craftsmen worked for more than 20 years to reconstruct the Amber Room (based on original surviving photographs). They used more than 500,000 amber pieces (finished as thin as a bar of chocolate) at a cost of over $11 million (some of which was donated by the German Ruhrgas company). Rebuilding the Amber Room required six tons of amber, yet only 25% of the raw material is used; the other 75% becomes dust. In other words, from a kilogram of amber (2.2 pounds), only 150 grams (five ounces) is usable. Today, covered with more than a ton of forty-million-year-old amber, the room glows with more than 10 different yellowish to red and golden-honey hues. Additionally, copies of the original 1750's Florentine mosaics (made from quartz, onyx, jasmine and jade) adorn the walls. (One original mosaic, entitled *Smell and Touch*, does exist in the room; it was discovered in 1997 in Bremen, Germany, along with an amber chest.) A nearly exact replica of the original room was re-opened to the public on March 31, 2003 for St Petersburg's 300th-anniversary.

The **Picture Hall** stretches across the entire width of the building. Of the 130 French, Flemish and Italian canvasses that were here before the war, 114 were evacuated and can be seen today. The next exhibition halls contain objets d'art presented during the reign of Catherine the Great, **Alexander I's Study**, and the photo room which displays the great destruction of the grounds and palaces caused by the war and the challenging process of the immense restorations. Next comes Cameron's **Green Dining Room** with its mythological motifs, and later, the breathtaking **Chinese Blue Room**. The walls of this room are decorated with Chinese blue silk and oriental colored landscapes, and Empress

A 19th-century ball is held annually at Catherine's Palace. Dressed in turn-of-the-century aristocratic costume, city folk gather to celebrate their historical roots.

The newly reconstructed Amber Room in Catherine's Palace, Tsarskoye Selo, which was re-opened to the public in May 2003 on the 300th anniversary of St Petersburg.

Tsarskoye Selo

Cathedral of St Fyodorov

Pushkin's Dacha

Vasenko Ulitsa

Ulitsa Kominterna

Moskovskaya Ulitsa

Ulitsa Kommunarov

Kitchen

Children's Pond

Alexander Palace

Arsenal

Chinese Theater

Catherine Palace

Hermitage

Alexander

Park

Chinese Village

Granite Terrace

Grand Pond

Admiralty

13

9

Great Caprice

Volkhonskoye Shosse

10

12

11

N

Orlov Gate

© Airphoto International Ltd

1   Lyceum
2   Carriage Museum
3   Church of the Sign
4   Upper Bath
5   Lower Bath
6   Grotto
7   Cameron Gallery
8   Agate Pavilion
9   Milkmaid Fountain
10 Marble Bridge
11 Pyramid
12 Turkish Baths
13 Chinese Creaking
    Pavilion

Elizabeth is portrayed as Flora, Goddess of Flowers. Through the Antechoir (used by the Empress during the church service), you enter the palace chapel.

The northeast section of the palace, in the chapel wing, contains the **Pushkin Museum**, made up of 27 halls displaying the beloved writer's personal belongings and manuscripts (rooms 10–13 relate to Pushkin's estate home in Mikhailovskoye, see vicinity section of Pskov).

In front of the palace's northeastern façade stands the **Statue of Alexander Pushkin**, commissioned in 1899 to mark the 100th-anniversary of his birth. The poet is wearing his Lyceum uniform and sitting on a garden seat. In his famous poem, *Evgeny Onegin*, Pushkin wrote:

> *...In the days, when in the Lyceum gardens*
> *I blossomed in untroubled ease...*
> *Close by the waters gleaming in the stillness,*

The Muse began to appear to me...
And sang of childish merriments,
And of the glory of our ancient times
And of the heart's tremulous dreams.

The four-story **Lyceum** is linked to the Palace by an archway. It was originally built by Catherine the Great as the school for her grandsons and was expanded by Alexander I in 1811 for the children of the aristocracy. The classrooms were on the second floor and the dormitory on the third (the ground floor housed the servants' and tutors' lodgings, and the first floor the mess and assembly halls). The Lyceum's first open class consisted of 30 boys between the ages of 11 and 14, and one of these students was Alexander Pushkin.

The Lyceum is now a museum and the classrooms and laboratories are kept as they were during Pushkin's time. In the dormitory is a plaque which reads, 'Door no. 14 Alexander Pushkin,' and examples of a student's narrow bed, wooden desk, chest of drawers and inkstand. In the school's assembly hall, on 8 January 1815, Pushkin read aloud his school exam poem, *Recollection of Tsarskoye Selo*, in front of the great poet Derzhavin.

Behind the Lyceum are the old royal stables, now the **Carriage Museum** with a collection of royal carriages. The neighboring **Church of the Sign** (1734) is the oldest original building in town. Continuing north down Vasenko Ulitsa (on the corner of Moskovskaya) brings you to **Pushkin's Dacha** where he lived with his wife from May to October, 1831.

Catherine's parks consisted of three types: the French was filled with statues and pavilions, the English had more trees and shrubs, and the Italian contained more sculpted gardens. The grounds stretch over 567 hectares (1400 acres).

Walking in an easterly direction into the French part of Catherine's Park leads to the **Upper Bath** (1777), modeled on Emperor Nero's Golden House of Rome, and used as baths for the Royal Family. The path, lined with mythological characters, then leads down to the **Lower Bath**, once used by the court and other visitors. The route then leads to the ornamental 64-columed **Hermitage** was built (between 1744 and 1756) to entertain the guests. No servants were allowed on the second floor. The guests wrote requests on slates and then up to five tables could be lowered and raised with the appropriate food and drink, including such delicacies as elk lips and nightingale tongues! The adjacent fish canal provided seafood for the royal banquets.

Heading south brings you out to the **Grand Pond**, and the **Grotto**, built by Rastrelli in 1753. Originally it was ornamented with over 200,000 seashells to give the illusion of a fairy-tale hideaway. During the reign of Catherine the Great the famous statue of Voltaire sitting in a chair was displayed here. Today it can be seen

The entrance gate to Catherine's Palace (Yekaterinsky Dvorets) is decorated with the Russian czarist crest of the double-headed eagle, adopted by Ivan the Great in the 15th-century.

The 18th-century Catherine's Palace in Tsarskoye Selo, designed by Rastrelli, is over 300 meters (980 feet) long. At the time it was the longest palace in the world. Two types of gardens make up Catherine Park, the naturalistic and formal. In front of the palace, beds of symmetrical red and black arabesque shapes gradually lead into a wilder area of wooded paths and fish-filled ponds.

in the Hermitage Museum. Rastrelli built the 25-meter high **Orlov Column**, sculpted from multicolored marble, on an island in the middle of the pond as a monument to the victory of the Battle of Chesme on 25 June 1770. On the eastern bank stands the old **Admiralty** which houses a collection of boats.

West of the Grotto is the **Cameron Gallery**, named after its builder, Charles Cameron. Greek and Roman bronze figures line the staircase and are placed in between the numerous Ionic columns. The gallery opens onto the **Hanging Gardens** and **Agate Pavilion** (with its semi-circular rotunda), named because of its interior which was faced with agate; it was once used as Catherine the Great's personal *banya*. From the **Granite Terrace** there is a magnificent view of the pond and English-style gardens.

Continuing south along the western bank of the pond brings you to the **Milkmaid Fountain**, sculpted in 1816 by Pavel Sokolov. At the southwest corner of the pond lies the bluish-white **Marble Bridge** (made from Siberian marble between 1770–76 and modeled on the Palladian Bridge in Wilton, England) which crosses a channel to the granite **Pyramid**, originally designed in 1781 as a summer house. On the opposite bank are the **Turkish Baths**, built in 1852 to resemble a Turkish mosque (and mark the Russian victory in the Russo-Turkish War of 1828–29).

At the northwestern end of Tsarskoye Selo stands the classical-style **Alexander Palace**, built by Catherine the Great (1792–96 by Quarenghi) for her grandson, the future Alexander I, and presented to him for his marriage. Nicholas II and his family lived here under house arrest for six months after his March 1917 abdication. The Palace is currently undergoing an extensive seven-million-dollar restoration. **Alexander Park** makes up the western side of the grounds, and many of the structures within the park, such as the **Chinese (Creaking) Pavilion** were designed in chinoiserie style. A short walk north of the Alexander Palace, at 14 Akademichesky Per, is the **Staraya Bashnya** (Old Tower) Restaurant that serves Russian and European food. Reservations recommended, tel 466-6698.

The first Russian railway was constructed between Tsarskoye Selo and Pavlovsk in 1834. By 1837 the line had been extended all the way to St Petersburg. (A model of the inaugural train which took Czar Nicholas I and his family to the summer palace in Tsarskoye Selo stands at the end of the platform in St Peterburg's Vitebsky Station; also take a look at the Royal Waiting Room.) One of the passengers who rode the first train to St Petersburg on 31 October 1837 wrote, 'The train made almost one *verst* (kilometer) a minute...60 *versts* an hour, a horrible thought! Meanwhile, as you sit calmly, you do not notice the speed, which terrifies the imagination, only the wind whistles, only the steed breathes fiery foam, leaving a white cloud of steam in its wake...' The line between St Petersburg and Moscow was built between 1843 and 1851. (See the Special Topic on the Trans-Siberian Railway on page 348.)

The interior splendors of Catherine's Palace in Tsarskoye Selo. (above) The opulent Great Hall was designed by Rastrelli for Empress Elizabeth I (daughter of Catherine I and Peter the Great). On the ceiling is the painting Triumph of Russia.

Catherine's Palace (tel 466-6669; excursions 465-5308) is open 10am–5pm, closed Tuesdays and the last Monday of each month. Russian language tours are given at set hours during the day. (In crowded months buy a ticket immediately, before they are sold out for the day!) If you cannot find a tour in English, follow a Russian group and once inside you can wander off on your own. From St Petersburg there are also foreign language excursions (for both Pushkin and Pavlovsk), each lasting about four hours (see www.eng.tzar.ru).

The Lyceum (tel 476-6411, 465-5308) is open 10am–4pm, closed Tuesdays and the last Monday of each month. Pushkin's Dacha is open 11am–6pm and closed Mondays and Tuesdays, and the Carriage Museum on Tuesdays and Wednesdays. Other museums in the area include the **Tsarskoye Selo Museum** (exhibiting 20th-century art), 40 Magazeinaya Ulitsa, open Thursday–Sunday 11am–5pm. The **Town of Pushkin Regional Museum**, at 28 Leontevskaya, features exhibits on the history of the town, open 10am–5pm and closed Thursdays. The interesting **Chistyakov Country Estate** is at 23 Moskovskoye Highway on the way into town, open on Wednesdays and weekends, 10am–5pm. In winter, cross-country skis and sledges are for rent in the semicircular wing of Catherine's Palace.

The quickest way to Tsarskoye Selo is by *elektrichka* train from Vitebsky Railway Station to Detskoye Selo; the journey takes about half an hour. Buses 371 and 382 run from the station to Ekaterininsky (Catherine's) Park in about ten minutes (or its a twenty minute walk). Tickets for the park are sold near the entrance, and for the Palace on its ground floor. To get to Pavlovsk, continue on the train one stop further to Pavlovsky Station. Bus 370 also runs from near the Orangerie (Kominterna Ulitsa) directly to Pavlovsk, only five kilometers (three miles) away. Another easy way to Tsarskoye Selo/Pavlovsk is to take a Russian Excursion bus from the corner of Dumskaya (Gostiny Dvor) and Nevsky Prospekt. Check ticket *kassas* for times and prices. (Often a tour to Pavlovsk is also combined with Tsarskoye Selo or Gatchina). Tours are in Russian, but just take along a guidebook; you are free to walk wherever you want (you may want to follow the group into museums so as not to pay), just meet the bus at the designated departure time.

Many restaurants and cafés dot the area. The Admiralteystvo is located at 7 Sadovaya, on the second floor of an old pavilion across the lake from the palace (tel 465-3549), open daily 12–11pm. D & D Beer Restaurant at 20 Moskovskaya Ul. (tel 470-7327) open 24 hours. Na Shirokoi is at 26 Shirokaya andTsarskoye Selo, at 1 Privokzalnaya Sq (near the Lyceum), both are open daily 11am–11pm. U Gusterina, 12 Oranzhereynaya, is open daily 10am–midnight. The Tsar Town Pavilion is at 1 Uritskovo Ul (tel 470-3814), open daily noon to midnight. The Russian House, 3 Malaya Ul, delicious Home-made Russian dishes (tel 466-8838).

PAVLOVSK (Павловск)

The flamboyant court life of Tsarskoye Selo scared away most of the wildlife, so the royal family went into the nearby area of **Pavlovskoye** (about four kilometers/two and a half miles away) to hunt. Two wooden hunting lodges were known as Krik and Krak. In 1777, upon hearing of the birth of her first grandson, Alexander, Catherine the Great gifted her son Pavel (Paul) and his wife, Maria Feodorovna (the former Sophie Dorothea Augusta von Wurttemberg), "one thousand acres of woodlands, ploughed fields and two villages with peasants," lying on the banks of the Slavyanka River. In 1779, Catherine invited her favorite architect, Charles Cameron, from Scotland to come and construct a palace for the couple. Cameron began his activities with the Temple of Friendship, dedicated to Catherine the Great, the Apollo Colonnade at the park's entrance, the Obelisk, laying of the Triple Lime Avenue and mapping out the areas of the Great Star and White Birch. Cameron greatly admired the 16th-century Italian architect, Andrea Palladio, whose creations interlaced modern ideas with the heritage of Ancient Rome.

In 1781, after gaining permission from Catherine the Great, the young couple, under the pseudonym of the Count and Countess Severny (du Nord), set off on a 14-month tour of Europe, where they bought up furniture, fabrics, sculptures and paintings for their new palace. They declared that Pavlovsk provided them with "more pleasure than all the beauty of Italy." Upon their arrival in Paris, King Louis XVI and Marie Antoinette gave them a ceremonial welcome, and Marie gifted them a unique toilet set decorated with her crest. Upon visiting the famed Sevres pottery, the Grand Princess purchased porcelain goods for the then astronomical sum of 300,000 livres. When Pavel and Maria returned from Europe, life in Pavlovsk transformed into a realm of amusements and gala festivities. Maria Feodorovna aspired to organize Pavlovsk after the fashion of Marie Antoinette in Trinon. The Dairy pavilion housed goats and Dutch cows, and sheep grazed on the riverbanks; she also helped design all the parks and gardens. Many of Maria's handicrafts and embroideries still adorn the walls of the palace today. A decade after the royal couple took up residence here, the palace was given a classical makeover by Vincenzo Brenna, who also worked on the park layouts and, built a popular Theater complex on the grounds. For over 40 years, the palace remained under the loving care of Maria Feodorovna, who transformed the area into an important part of Russian cultural life; one poet called it "an Abode of Muses of and Graces." During her 67 years, Maria bore and raised ten children, and continued to live here for another 27 years after her husband's tragic death; Paul I was murdered in St Petersburg's in Mikhailovsky Palace on March, 12, 1801.

The Palace of Paul I, Pavlovsk, is filled with statues, tapestries and hand-painted ceramics. (top left) The Empress' Bedroom was modeled after a state bedroom in Versailles. The bed was crafted in Paris by the Jacob studio. The floor is inlaid with arabesque designs that mirror the painted ceiling. (bottom left) The royal family's private chapel.

When Pavel ascended the throne as Paul I in 1796, Pavlovsk became the official Imperial summer residence. During this same year, the village was also officially renamed Pavlovsk. Since Czar Paul was also the Grand Master of the Maltese Order, Pavlovsk hosted grand festivities each year for the knights of the order. In all, Pavel was heir to the throne for forty years, and was Czar for exactly four years, four months and four days. Upon Maria's death, their youngest son, Grand Duke Mikhail Pavlovich inherited the estate. Pavlovsk remained in the Romanov family until after the Revolution in 1918, when the estate was confiscated by the Bolsheviks and the great-grandson of Nicholas I, Ioann Konstantinovich, his brother Igor, and the Czarina's sister were brutally murdered by the Bolsheviks in a mine-shaft in Siberia.

Pavlovsk Park was created by Pietro Gonzaga (who lived here from 1803 to 1838) and covers over 600 hectares making it (during its time) one of the largest landscaped parks in the world, with such designs as the **Valley of the Ponds** and the **White Birchtrees**. Near the palace's southern façade in the Private Garden is the **Pavilion of Three Graces**, later designed by Cameron in 1801, with 16 white Ionic columns. Around to the west, across the river over the Centaur Bridge, are the **Cold Baths** and the **Apollo Colonnade** (1783). On the northern side, descending the Great Stone Staircase, leads to the Slavyanka River and the **Temple of Friendship** (1782) with its white Doric colonnades. Further north along the riverbank lies the **Twelve Paths** with 12 bronze statues representing mythological figures. A westward path then leads to the **Monument to My Parents**, a pyramidal structure with a medallion containing the profiles of Maria Fyodorovna's parents (Maria was the wife of Paul I). A simple inscription reads, 'To my parents.' A little further north, across the river, is the **Mausoleum of Paul I** (1808); the murdered czar is actually buried in the Peter and Paul Fortress. East of the mausoleum, a very lovely part of the park is known as the Big Star where rows of white birch trees radiate from the center.

Many famous architects such as Cameron, Brenna, Quarenghi, Rossi and Voronikhin worked on the construction of the **Pavlovsk Palace**, with its 64 white columns, green dome, and classical yellow façade. The palace contains an Egyptian vestibule, Paul's Library, French, Greek and Italian Halls, orchestral chambers, billiard and ballrooms, and the dressing rooms of Empress Maria Fyodorovna and Paul I. Paul had his suites along the north side that included the **Hall of War** (he was obsessed with the military, see Mikhailovsky Castle on page 518). Maria created the **Hall of Peace**.

The royal bedchamber of Paul I and his wife Maria Feodorovna contains an elegant four-poster bed by Henri Jacob, and the famous Sèvres toilet service, gifted to them by Marie Antoinette, during their visit to Paris in 1782.

The State Bedchamber contains an elegant four-poster bed by Henri Jacob, and the famous 64-piece Sèvres toilet service, presented to Maria Fyodorovna during her visit to Paris in 1782 by Marie-Antoinette. Situated in the south block is Paul's **Throne Room**, the largest room of the palace, and the **Hall of the Maltese Knights of St John**—after the island of Malta was captured by the French in 1798, the knights chose Paul I as their Grand Master. In 1796, Paul I created the **Picture Gallery**, and some of the 200 works that were brought here from the Hermitage and purchased from other collections can still be viewed here today. Mignard's "Christ and the Woman of Samaria" and Jouvenet's "The Presentation of the Temple" come from the famous Crozat collection, purchased by Catherine the Great. After the death of her husband, the widowed Empress Maria built a ground floor study graced by her favorite works of mainly religious paintings.

On May 22, 1838, the first passenger railway line was opened in Pavlovsk, which included the construction of a Music Station (designed by Andrei Stackenschneider). The youngest son of Paul I, the Grand Duke Mikhail Pavlovich, gave his permission for the construction of a railway line that ran right into the Great Star region of the park. The Music Vauxhall attained great popularity, where grand concerts and dinner parties in the Large Room where conducted for over a century for St Petersburg society. It was here that Mikhail Glinka's Waltz Fantasia premiered; and Johann Strauss conducted and performed concerts here for over a decade to great acclaim. Even Dostoevsky described the wonderful impression that the Music Station made on him in his novel *The Idiot*. The palace and grounds, and Music Station were virtually destroyed during the war (over 70,000 trees were cut down for firewood), but were impressively restored by 1970. Luckily nearly 14,000 pieces of art and furniture were evacuated before the occupation, and later returned to their original places. The **Monument to the Defenders of Pavlovsk**, on the grounds east of the palace, is dedicated to all those who died clearing the park of mines after the war. Today, the palace, 17 pavilions, 12 bridges, parks and ponds of the estate mirror the highly poetic work of many artistic masters of the 18th and 19th centuries. The Palace (tel 470-6536) is

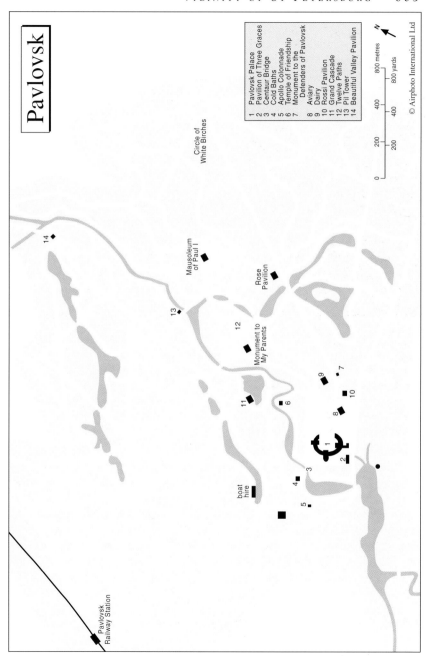

Pavlovsk

1 Pavlovsk Palace
2 Pavilion of Three Graces
3 Centaur Bridge
4 Cold Baths
5 Apollo Colonnade
6 Temple of Friendship
7 Monument to the
     Defenders of Pavlovsk
8 Aviary
9 Dairy
10 Rossi Pavilion
11 Grand Cascade
12 Twelve Paths
13 Pil Tower
14 Beautiful Valley Pavilion

© Airphoto International Ltd

0   200   400   800 metres
     200   400   800 yards

N

Circle of
White Birches

Mausoleum
of Paul I

Rose
Pavilion

Monument to
My Parents

boat
hire

Pavlovsk
Railway Station

opened 10am–5pm, closed Fridays and the first Monday of each month (www.pavlovsk.org). If you can only enter by group tour, buy a ticket for one in Russian (which operate frequently), and this will at least get you inside. There is boating in summer and cross-country skiing in winter.

Pavlovsk is located 30 kilometers (19 miles) south of St Petersburg. To get here, take an *elektrichka*, train from Vitebsky Railway Station to the Pavlovsk stop; they leave every half hour, and the trip takes about 40 minutes. It is about a fifteen-minute walk from the station southeast through the park to the palace. It is also one further train stop from Tsarskoye Selo (station name Detskoye Selo) to Pavlovsk station. Local buses also run the five-kilometer (three-mile) route from the stop by Pavlovsk palace to Tsarskoye Selo. Try booking an inexpensive Russian tour bus trip to Pavlovosk and/or Tsarskoye Selo. Buses leave daily by the kiosks on the corner of Nevsky and Dumskaya (Gostiny Dvor) (see page 670).

Cafés are located in the train station. The Pavlovsk Palace Restaurant in the Great Column Hall (tel. 470-9809) takes credit cards and is open 10am–6pm, closed Fridays. 'Near the Iron Gates' (U Chugunnikh Vorot), at 1 Krasnikh Zor (on the main road from the station to the palace), is open daily 9am–9pm. Café Slavyanka is just west of the Apollo Colonnade. On the road to Pavlovsk, at 16 Filtrovskoye Shosse (Highway), is Podvore (Town House), a lovely old wooden-style building, open daily noon–11pm (tel 470-6952 and credit cards accepted). Serves hearty Russian food, delicious Shashlik cooked in the open air. At times, a wild Cossack ensemble performs.

GATCHINA (Гатчина)

The village of Gatchina, 43 kilometers (27 miles) southwest of St Petersburg, was first mentioned in 15th-century chronicles. In the early 18th-century Peter the Great presented his sister Natalya Alekseevna with a farm in the area. In 1765, Catherine the Great acquired the land and gave the estate as a gift to her lover Count Grigory Orlov, the man who had helped her ascend the throne (and planned the murder of her husband Peter III). Between 1766 and 1781 a palace was built by Antonio Rinaldi and a park laid out. (The Eagle Pavilion, constructed in 1792, and the Chesma Column, both built to honor the Orlov brothers' military deeds, still stand in the park today.) After Orlov's death in 1783, and the birth of her first granddaughter, Alexandra, Catherine passed the estate on to her son and heir, Paul, who later redesigned the palace to look like a medieval castle. During his reign Paul I was a terribly paranoid czar (and for good reason—he was later murdered); he had the architect Vincenzo Brenna add sentry boxes, toll-gates and a military parade ground, and build a moat, fortress and drawbridges around the castle. After Paul's death the estate remained neglected until Alexander III made Gatchina his permanent residence. (Alexander was terrified of revolutionary elements and felt safe here after his own father was assassinated.) The grounds were badly damaged during World War II—the area was occupied by German forces for two years—and still have not yet been fully restored. Fortunately, a few old 1870s watercolors of some of the interiors have survived, and artists have used these to help restore the rooms to their original designs.

Several dozen of the 500 rooms within the **Gatchina Palace** are now open to the public, with magnificent collections of antique furniture and porcelain. These include Paul's Throne Room, the Dining Room, Raspberry Parlor, the White Ball Room. There is also an exhibit of old weaponry on the ground floor. A secret underground passage leads to a grotto on the edge of Silver Lake. After fleeing the Winter

Paul I (son of Catherine the Great) had the Gatchina Palace redesigned to look like a medieval castle. Later, Alexander III, after an assassination attempt, made the fortified estate into his permanent residence. Today, the complex is open as a museum.

Palace on the night of the Bolshevik Revolution, Alexander Kerensky (leader of the Provisional government) escaped to Gatchina and used the tunnel to evade revolutionary mobs. The Palace is at 1 Krasnoarmeisky Prospekt, (tel. [271] 134-92, 215-09), open 10am–5pm, closed Mondays and first Tuesday of each month.

Gatchina Park weaves around the estate's White, Black and Silver lakes. The park lands were mainly designed by a pair of Englishmen, Mr Sparrow and Mr Bush. Between the White and Silver Lakes is the largest section of the park, known as the **English Landscape Gardens**. At the end of **White Lake** there is a lovely little **Temple to Venus** on the Island of Love. Behind Long Island is **Silver Lake**, which never freezes over. The first Russian submarine was tested here in 1879. On the northeastern shore of White Lake is **Birch Cabin**, which looks just that from the outside, but inside is an unexpected suite of palatial rooms lined with mirrors. The white **Prioratsky Palace** stands in front of Black Lake, originally built for a French prior who never lived here. It was designed in the late 1700s by architect Nikolai Lyvov, who introduced 'rammed-earth' structures to Russia, a cheaper, more fire-proof method of construction. One can see examples of the rammed-earth process on the first floor. Open 10am–6pm; closed Monday and Tuesday. In warmer months, rowboats are available for rent in the lakes. Near the Pavlovsky Cathedral on Chekhov Ulitsa is the **Shcherbakov Literary Museum**, open 10am–6pm weekdays.

Gatchina is a lovely place to spend a day. Pack a picnic for there are few eateries. The Dubok Café is at 2 Oktyabr Prospekt near the Birch Cabin, open daily noon–11pm.

An easy way to get here is by *elektrichka* commuter train (about an hour's ride) from Baltiisky Railway Station to the Gatchina stop. From there it is only a leisurely ten-minute walk down the avenue behind the station building to the park grounds. Another easy way to Gatchina is to take a Russian excursion bus from the corner of Dumskaya (Gostiny Dvor) and Nevsky Prospekt. Check ticket *kassas* for times and prices. Buses leave several times a week for Gatchina and Pavlovsk. Tours are in Russian, but just take along a guidebook.

NOVGOROD (Новгород)

Novgorod is one of the oldest towns in Russia, founded almost 1,200 years ago. The first Varangian leader Rurik settled here by the shores of Ilmen Lake and named the town Novgorod, meaning 'New Town.' By 977, Novgorod had gained its independence from Kievan Rus. During the 11th and 12th centuries the town prospered when it served as a major center between the Baltic and the Black Sea trading routes. Soon the city, with its 30,000 inhabitants, one of the most educated centers in eastern Europe, became known as Novgorod the Great. A century later, while other areas of the country were sacked by the invading Tatar hordes, this region escaped severe Mongol occupation. In 1240, Prince of Novgorod, Alexander Nevsky, also battled off the attacking Swedes.

The golden age of Novgorod lay between the 12th and 15th centuries when wealthy nobles and merchants built over 200 churches. Even though the city remained a center for trade and religion well into the 16th century, it eventually lost its independence to Moscovy when Ivan the Great's troops occupied the city in 1478. Later, when Novgorod questioned Moscow's rule, it is said that Ivan the Terrible built a wall around the town, preventing anyone from leaving. Then, after the population still refused his subjugation, he had thousands of people tortured and killed in front of him. By the early 18th-century, the city had lost its strategic significance and slowly fell into a state of relative obscurity.

The old town is divided by the River Voklhov. The right bank is known as the Trading Side where the merchants lived and markets were held. The left (west) bank, the Sofia Side, is the area of the kremlin and fortress; the prince once governed from within these walls. Novgorod is an excellent example of an old Russian town and preserved medieval art with its ancient architecture (over 50 ancient churches and monasteries remain), paintings (icons, frescoes and mosaics) and history (collections of birch-bark manuscripts).

The original earthen and log ramparts of the kremlin were laid in about 1000 AD, and in 1484 Ivan the Great ordered the building of a brick wall with nine watch towers. The most famous and oldest remaining structure within the *detinets*, or citadel, is the five-domed **Cathedral of St Sophia** (1045–50). The son of Yarloslavl the Wise modeled it after the great cathedral of the same name in Kiev, which his father had built. (The town's first wooden Church of St Sophia was built at this site in 989.) The structure's enclosed galleries, chapels and iconostasis were originally decorated with icons and frescoes by artists brought in from as far away as Constantinople. Present icons date from the 16th-century on. The western portal contains the magnificent bronze Sigtuna Doors, made in Magdeburg in the early 1050s. Today, the cathedral is still used as a place of worship.

North of the cathedral is the **Palace of Facets** (built by Archbishop Yevfimy in 1433), and in the center of the kremlin stands the **The Millennium Memorial**, erected in 1862 to commemorate the 1,000th anniversary of Rurik's arrival in Novgorod. The **Museum of History, Architecture and Art** (south of the monument) is the kremlin's largest building; it was first built as administrative offices in the 1800s. The museum has 35 halls and over 8,000 exhibitions, including collections of the churches' medieval art and icons. Behind it stands the single-domed **Church of St Andrew Stratelates**, built in 1360.

Directly across the river on the Trading Side remains part of the horseshoe-shaped 17th-century arcade in Yaroslavl's Court, which boasted 1,500 stalls in its 16th-century heyday. Behind the Gostiny Dvor gate-tower stands the centerpiece of the market side, the single-domed **Cathedral of St Nicholas**, built in 1113. (Legend attributes the building to Prince Mstislav after being healed by the miraculous powers of the icon, St Nicholas the Wonder-Worker.) The interior still contains a large fragment of the famous 12th-century fresco, *Job's Wife*. Six other churches also stand in the area around the old trading complex.

East of the arcade, standing between the Cathedral of Our Lady of the Sign and the Church of St Theodore Stratelates-on-the-Stream, is the **Church of the Transfiguration of the Savior-on-Elijah-Street**, built in 1374 by the merchants on this street. The single dome and four side walls are decorated with ornamental motifs, and the interior has surviving frescoes, painted in 1378 by the great Byzantine master Theophanes the Greek. Numerous other churches also dot the landscape along the eastern bank of the river.

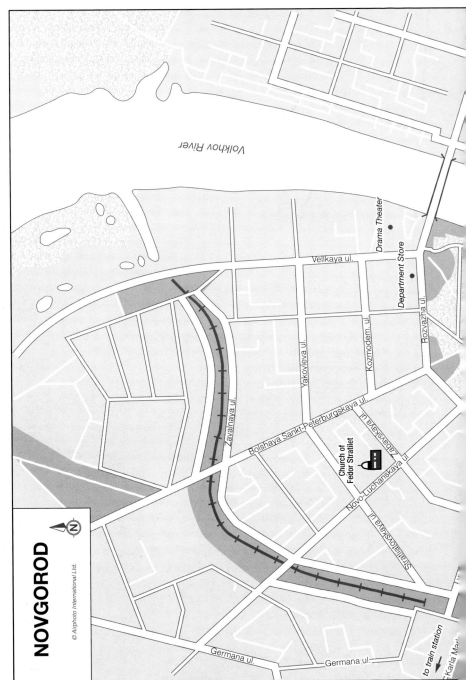

NOVGOROD

© Airphoto International Ltd.

Volkhov River

Drama Theater

Department Store

Vellkaya ul.

Rozvazha ul.

Kozmodem. ul.

Yakovleva ul.

Zavalnaya ul.

Bolshaya Sankt-Peterburgskaya ul.

Church of
Fedor Stratilet

Zabalskaya ul.

Novo-Luchanskaya

Strallalovlskaya ul.

Germana ul.

Germana ul.

to train station

Karla Mark

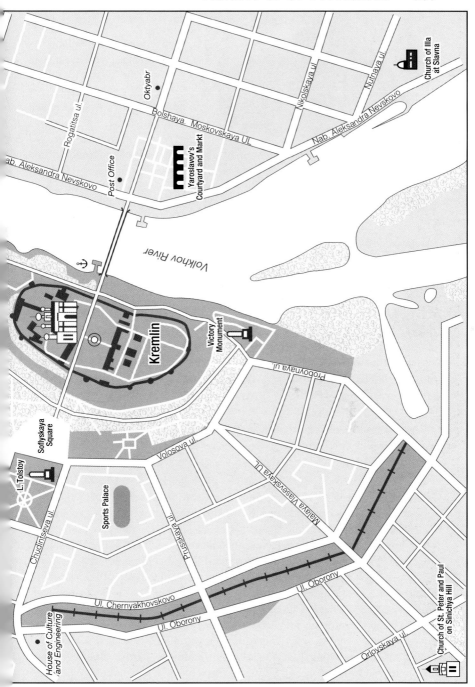

Situated outside of Novgorod is the Open Air Museum of Wooden Architecture, filled with log buildings and old izba cottages, dating back to the 16th-century.

About three kilometers (two miles) south, situated along the western bank of the river, is the **Open Air Museum Park of Wooden Architecture**, known as the Vitoslavlitsky. Here there is a remarkable collection of old wooden buildings and log architecture—churches, windmills, *izba* cottages, granaries—dating from the 16th- to 19th-centuries, and collected from outlying villages. Just a 15-minute walk further south brings you to the **Yuriev Monastery** ensemble and the magnificent asymmetric three-domed **Cathedral of St George**, commissioned in 1119 by Prince Vsevolod. One chronicle names the builder as 'Master Peter,' the earliest mention of any architect in Russian chronicles. Many believe that the oldest (1030) known surviving icon of St George (in Moscow's Tretyakov Gallery) originates from this complex, along with the many illuminated manuscripts written between 1120 and 1228, which are now in Moscow's Historical Museum. For centuries, Novgorod had his own distinctive architecture and style of icon painting (see Icon Special Topic on page 329).

In 1998, Novgorod town lawmakers voted to change the city's name back to Novgorod Veliky or Novgorod the Great, bestowed in the 12th-century to recognize the town's special status. Today the town has a population of over 230,000.

Novgorod is about a three-hour drive (190 kilometers/118 miles) south of St Petersburg on the M20 Highway. The easiest way to Novgorod is by taking an inexpensive Russian excursion bus tour. Check the ticket *kassas* on the corner of Dumskaya (Gostiny Dvor) and Nevsky; prices and departure times are posted here. There are both one- and two-day excursions. One-day excursions last about 12 hours. (If you do not speak Russian, just take along a guidebook.) The Novgorod bus and train stations are located next to each other, and a local bus takes you directly to the kremlin. Trains leave from St Petersburgh's Moskovsky Station daily around 5.20pm, and arrive in Novogorod Veliky at 8.35pm. Return trains are at 7.40am, 4.25pm (arriving to Vitebsky Station), and 5.40pm. A daily train also leaves Moscow's Leningradsky Station for Novgorod Veiliky around 9.20pm, and arrives the next morning at 5.18am. A train to Moscow departs around 9.10pm. Boat tours run from the pier at Yaroslavl's Court by the trading arcade.

There are numerous restaurants, cafés and bars scattered about town. These include, Detinets Restaurant in the Kremlin; By the Court at 3 Sovietsky Armii; Dinner Party at 40 Prospekt Mira (the Bar of Novgorod Butcher's Yard is at no. 34); Master at 14 Lomonosova (Beer Bar is at no. 20); Russia at 19 Nevskovo Embankment; and Volkhov at 24 Frolovskaya Ulitsa. The Novgorod Maly Theater is at 32 Prospekt Mira, and the Savings Bank at 17 Bol Moskovskaya.

A Novgorod wooden house-museum interior, depicting old village-style life of centuries past.

The best hotel in town is the Beresta Palace at 3 Studencheskaya Ul, with over 200 rooms, restaurant, sauna and swimming pool. Tel (816) 3-33-15 or 3-47-47; fax 3-17-07. Less expensive hotels include Sadko at 16 Fedorovsky Ruchey. Tel 7-53-66; Novgorodskaya Hotel at 6 Desyatinnaya Ul. Tel 7-22-60; fax 13-13-30; Intourist at 16 Velikaya Ul. Tel 9-42-67; fax 7-41-57; and Hotel Volkhov at 24 Frolovskaya Ul. Tel 7-59-39. Also check with HOFA in St Petersburg for an overnight stay in Novgorod or Pskov with a private host family.

PSKOV (Псков)

Pskov, a few hours drive farther southwest of Novgorod, is another of Russia's most ancient towns—it was first mentioned in a chronicle in 903 (2003 marked Pskov's 1100 Anniversary). Pskov began as a small outpost of Novgorod and later grew into a commercial center and developed its own school of icon painting. It is still filled with many beautiful churches and icons. In 1510, Vasily III, according to a chronicle "took the city without a battle." Later his son, Ivan the Terrible tried to annex Pskov, but the town resisted for many years before being subjugated. According to legend the bell on St Nicholas-on-Ushokha Church began tolling on its own as Ivan the Terrible rode by. Since the ringing startled his horse, Ivan ordered the bell's tongue cut out. Rimsky-Korsakov later wrote an opera based on the uprisings called *The Maid of Pskov*. On March 15, 1917, at a small railway station about 120 kilometers (75 miles) from Pskov ironically named Dno (Bottom), Nicholas II abdicated the Russian throne, signing the official letter of abdication while in the train enroute to Pskov.

A daily train leaves St Petersburg's Moskovsky Station around 5.38pm and arrives at 7.35am. A train departs Moscow's Leningradsky at around 7.55pm and arrives in Pskov the next morning at 8am. The return train departs around 6pm, arriving back in Moscow at 6.25am. For more information on getting to Pskov, see Novgorod (page 606).

The oldest part of town stands where the Pskova and Velikaya rivers join. Here the 17th-century white **Trinity Cathedral**, the main church, towers above the other wooden buildings of the town's kremlin, surrounded by a stone rampart. In the early 12th-century the stone Mirozhsky Monastery was constructed on the Velikaya (Great) River's left bank by by the Mirozh River and, in 1150, its **Spas-Transfiguration Cathedral** was consecrated by the Archbishop of Novgorod and Pskov; the monks of the monastery painted all the interior frescoes (it is now a UNESCO heritage site). One Pskov monk also penned the famous 12th-century epic chronicle, *The Lay of Igor's Host*, based on the fighting campaigns of Prince Igor of Novgorod. (In 1795, Prince Musin-Pushkin discovered these chronicles in Yaroslavl's Savior Monastery (see page 303).

Walking west along the left bank (at the west end of Gorky St), lies the **Ivanovsky Monastery** and the white **Predtechensky Church**. Many of the town's churches were named according to their location, such as **St Basil's-on-the-Hill**, **Assumption Church-by-the-Ferry** and **St Nicholas-at-the-Stone Wall**. Trains from St Petersburg leave daily (around 5.30pm) from Vitebsky station (with special Pskov carriages). From the Leningradsky Station in Moscow overnight trains depart around 7.30pm and arrive the next morning.

The three-star Hotel Rizhskaya, on Rizhsky Pr, is an inexpensive and comfortable place to stay; only a 15-minute walk from the kremlin. Tel. (8112) 46-22-23. The two-star Hotel Okyabrskaya at 36 Oktyabrsky Pr. has cheaper rooms and adequate service. Tel. 16-42-44. Krom, a smaller hotel, is at 5 Metallistov St. Tel. 16-15-41. The restaurant Rus, located in one of the kremlin towers with a view of the Velikaya river, is one of the most elegant places for dinner. Snezhinka is at 14 Okyabrsky Pr. Down the street, at number 8, is Cheburechnaya, offering Caucasian cuisine. The Evropeiskoye, at 1 Pobedy Sq, has tasty food and coffee; another coffee house is the Pilgrim, at 54 Rizksky Pr.

About 120 kilometers (75 miles) southeast of Pskov lies a cluster of estates known today as Pushkin Hills. (The three estates were damaged during the war, but they have been extensively recreated to their former 19th-century appearance.)

The most famous is **Mikhailovskoye**, Alexander Pushkin's family estate. The poet's great grandfather, Abraham Petrovich Hannibal (Peter the Great's Abyssinian general) received the lands from Empress Elizabeth in 1742. Pushkin stayed here after his graduation from Tsarskoye Selo's Lyceum in 1817, but then did not return again for seven years when he was exiled from the capital by Alexander I because of his slanderous writings. Pushkin's two year stay at Mikhailovskoye greatly enhanced his descriptions of country life in his novel-in-verse, *Yevgeny Onegin*, and the exile

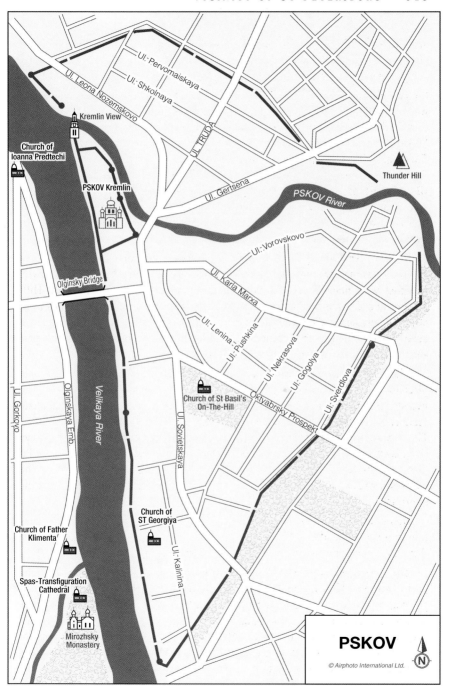

Ul. Pervomaiskaya

Ul. Leona Nozemskovo

Ul. Shkolnaya

Kremlin View

UL TRUDA

Church of
Ioanna Predtechi

PSKOV Kremlin

Ul. Gertsena

Thunder Hill

PSKOV River

Ul. Vorovskovo

Ul. Karla Marxa

Olginsky Bridge

Ul. Lenina

Ul. Pushkina

Ul. Nekrasova

Ul. Gogolya

Ul. Sverdlova

Ul. Gorkovo

Olginskaya Emb.

Velikaya River

Church of St Basil's
On-The-Hill

Oktyabrsky Prospekt

Ul. Sovietskaya

Church of Father
Klimenta

Church of
ST Georgiya

Ul. Kalinina

Spas-Transfiguration
Cathedral

Mirozhsky
Monastery

PSKOV

© Airphoto International Ltd.

N

certainly added to his tragedy, *Boris Godunov*. To break the tedium, Pushkin often visited the neighboring **Petrovskoye** estate of his great-uncle. The large white-column manor house is surrounded by a park that leads to Lake Petrovskoye.

Pushkin's favorite pastime was visiting the nearby **Trigorskoye** estate, owned by the extended Osipova family. Pushkin became quite enamored by Madame Praskovya Osipova's married niece, Anna Petrovna Kern, and was inspired to pen one of his most famous love lyrics:

> I remember the miraculous moment   And my heart beats in ecstasy,
> You appeared before me   And once again is born in it,
> Like a fleeting vision,   Divinity, and inspiration,
> Like a spirit of pure beauty...   And life, and tears, and love.

The new Czar Nicholas I allowed Pushkin to return to St Petersburg in September 1826, after deciding to take on the role of the poet's personal censor.

Nearby is the **Svyatogorsky Monastery** (founded by Ivan the Terrible in 1569) and its Assumption Church. Pushkin's mother, Nadezha, was buried here in April 1836, near the eastern wall of the church. Less than a year later, Pushkin was killed in a tragic duel. After the funeral in St Petersburg, the poet was laid to rest in a grave next to his mother. In 1840, a marble obelisk commissioned by Pushkin's widow, Natalya Nikolaevna, was placed over the grave with a simple inscription of the years of his birth and death.

EAST OF THE CITY (LAKE LADOGA AREA)
PETROKREPOST OR SCHLÜSSELBURG (Петрокрепост)

Peter's Fortress, or Petrokrepost, on a small island near the southwestern shore of Lake Ladoga, was founded by Slavs in 1323 to protect the trade waterways linking Novgorod with the Baltic. At that time, the small outpost was known as Oreshek (Nut). When Peter the Great captured the tiny fortress from the Swedes in 1702 (they took control of the lands in the 17th-century), he renamed it Schlüsselburg, the Key Fortress. The town of Schlüsselburg sprang up along the left bank of the Neva, where it flows out of the lake. After the Great Northern War ended in 1721, Peter converted the fortress into a prison. He had his sister Maria and first wife Evdokia Lopukhina imprisoned here, and many Russian revolutionaries suffered similar fates. On May 8, 1887, Lenin's brother Alexander Ulyanov, along with four others who attempted to assassinate Czar Alexander III, were hung in the prison yard. The German name of Schlüsselburg was changed to Petrokrepost in 1944 during World War II. For day trips here, check out the ticket *kassas* at the corner of Dumskaya (Gostiny Dvor) and

Nevsky Prospekt. Inexpensive Russian excursion buses make tours to the fortress several times a week. (If you do not speak Russian, just take along a guidebook.) By car, take the M18 Highway east. (See also page 617, Valaam for boat tours.)

STARAYA LADOGA (Старая Ладога)

Once the capital of ancient Rus, Staraya (Old) Ladoga celebrated its 1250th anniversary in 2003, marking it as one of the oldest towns in Russia and Northern Europe. Lying 120 kilometers (72 miles) east of St Petersburg, the enchanting town, with only 2,000 residents, is situated along the Volkhov River near Lake Ladoga. In the early 8th century, Varangians (Norsemen) established an outpost in the area where the Volkhov flows into the Ladozhka River (the earliest discovered timber structure dates back to 753). Since the town lay on important trade routes from the Baltic to the Volga and Black Seas, it quickly developed into a thriving center of culture, commerce and even decorative art; by the 9th century, the prominent 'City of Ladoga' had become the capital of the Slav-Varangian state. According to ancient chronicles, the Norseman Rurik and his army were summoned by Slavs in 862 to rule and settle the region. Ladoga thus became a capital city and the seat of the House of Rurik, the first ruling dynasty of Rus. Later Rurik's son, Prince Oleg, met his tragic end here. According to legend (and told in Alexander Pushkin's *Song of Oleg the Wise*) a fortune teller told Oleg that his death would somehow be connected to his favorite horse; thus, Oleg abandoned it for another. Later, the Prince was mortally bitten by a snake that had slithered out of the dead horse's skull. Over the next eight centuries, control of Ladoga fluctuated between Swedish, Mongol and Russian rule. In 1702, Peter the Great set out from Ladoga with over 16,000 men to assault the Swedish fortress of Noteburg (a citadel near the source of the Neva)—a campaign that eventually drove out the Swedes and led to the founding of the new capital in 1703. It was then that Peter the Great decreed that the adminstrative centers and all the citizens of Ladoga (now prefixed with Staraya) be transferred to the newly founded town of Novaya (New) Ladoga, located 12 kilometers to the north, and nearer to the southern shores of Lake Ladoga. This cruel fate ultimately helped preserve the architectural wonders of this gem of a town where over 160 historical and cultural landmarks are still evident today.

This museum-reserve includes the ancient **Burial Mounds** or *sopki* ('barrows') which are still found along the banks of the Volkhov. One of the mounds is believed to contain the grave of Prince Oleg. The town's main attraction is the pentagonal **kremlin** and its numerous gate towers, now restored to their 17th-century configuration In the mid 12th-century, the town, now annexed to the mighty Novgorod Principality, erected as many as six stone churches, two of which, still stand today (the Assumption and St George). Ladoga was the first to introduce the cross-and-dome church style architecture with four pillars and three apses, later widely adopted by other Russian towns. Behind the kremlin walls lies the **Uspensky Monastery** with its main single-domed **Church of the Assumption**. In 1718, Peter I banished his first wife, Evdokia Fedorovna Lopukhina to this monastery (she had plotted against him) where she remained for seven years before being transferred to Schlüsselberg, and finally to Moscow's Novodevichy Convent; she died in here in 1731. Overlooking the River Vokhov, outside the kremlin, is the small white **Church of St George the Victorious** (1165); frescoes still cover over 150 square meters of the interior. The medieval frescoe of St George and the Dragon is a masterpiece of Greco-Russian art. In 1445 the Monastery of St George was built around it. (In its heydey, the town contained six monasteries.) In 1695, on the grounds of St John Monastery, the five-domed masonry **Church of St John the Precursor** was built atop Malysheva Hill, where it still stands today. Another unique structure is the all wooden **Church of St Demetrius of Thessalonica**, consecrated in 1646. The **Church of Dmitry Solunsky** houses a small museum of peasant life. To the south, stands the 17th-century **Monastery of St Nicholas the Miracle Worker**, the **Nikolsky Cathedral** and the tent-roofed **Church of St John Chrysostom**. On the right bank, the **Church of St Basil the Great** is all that is left of the monastery.

Numerous limestone cliff and cave formations are found along the banks of the Volkhov river. A short ride north brings the visitor to Novaya Ladoga, whose points of interest include the **Nikolo-Medvedsky Monastery**, two 15th-century churches and an old cemetery. The helmut-domed **Klimentovskaya Church** and belfry stands on Karl Marx Prospekt. Other pre-revolutionary buildings and old merchant homes also dot the town. One kilometer north of Novaya Lagoga, is the old **Village of Krenitsy**; on the other side of the river is the ancient **Old Believer's Village of Nemyatovo**. The picturesque **Village of Sviritsa**, 30 kilometers (18 miles) to the east, is situated on islands which are surrounded by seven rivers. Resembling Venice, there are no streets here, and boats are used as the main means of transportation.

To get to Staraya Ladoga, surburban trains depart from St Petersburg's Ladozhsky or Moskovsky stations to Volkhovstroi, about a two-and-a-half hour ride. Then take a taxi or bus number 23 from the station's front square for the remaining 13-kilometer trip to the town. Group tours by bus can also be purchsed from the travel kiosks on the corner of Nevsky and Dumskaya; other travel agencies also offer other one and two-day excursions. Hotels in the area include the inexpensive 50-room Duke Rurik Hotel and the Hotel Ladya. The Duke Rurik café offers cheap tasty fare, as the Chicken Ladoga.

VALAAM ISLAND (Валаам)

The Valaam Archipelago (made up of over 50 islands) lies 170 kms (105 miles) north of St Petersburg in northwestern LakeLadoga, Europe's largest freshwater lake. ValaamIsland is the largest with 600 residents. The word *valaam* is thought to derive from the Finnish, meaning "high land." According to legend, two Greek missionaries, Sergius and Herman first visited these northern Novgorod lands in the first half of the 10th-century during the conversion of the land to Orthodox Christianity. The island's main attraction, the 14th-century **Transfiguration** (Spaso-Preobrajensky) **Monastery**, was first built as a fortress to protect the area from the Swedes. After Swedish armies destroyed the structure in 1611, Peter the Great had it rebuilt a century later, when the monastery doubled as a prison. In the 19th-century, Valaam attained its greatest prosperity under Abbot Damaskin, who was also an architect, agronomist, botanist, writer and economist. Damaskin established a regular shipping route to the island from the mainland, and a 32-kilometer railway was built to ship goods to and from the cloister. The monks also built a model farm and ponds where fish were reared for caviar. The highlight of Valaam was its orchards that contained over 60 varieties of apples, along with berries, melons and grapes. At one point, any traveler or pilgrim to the island was obliged to bring along a sack of black soil for the gardens. From 1811 to 1917, the archipelago was part of the Finnish Duchy of the Russian Empire. After the 1917 Revolution, it became part of Finland, and this lasted until the Russian-Finnish War of 1940. During WWII, the monastery was bombed several times, and its inhabitants evacuated. The island structures remained in total disrepair until 1989, when six monks arrived to restore cloistered life. Eight main *skity* (secluded monasteries-with a small collective of monks who, though living the life of a hermit, work together for common needs), are scattered about Valaam island. The closest, near the ferry dock, is the **Voskresensky (Resurrection) Monastery**, with an upper church that holds liturgical recitals. Another skete within walking distance is the **Gethsemene Monastery** with a wooden church and monastic cells. A ferry takes the visitor to the **Transfiguration of the Savior Monastery** (located 6 kilometers/4 miles from the harbor), the heart of the island's religious life. Today the complex consists of 200 residents, along with a military 12 member air-defense unit, who mostly get around by horse and boat. The cathedral's lower floor is the **Church of Sts Sergius and Herman**, completed in 1892, with an icon depicting the two saints kneeling before Christ. The upper church is still under renovation. Even though tourist souvenirs and beer are sold outside, all visitors are required to respect the environment and honor the dress code. Men must leave their heads uncovered and wear long trousers (no shorts), and women wear long skirts and cover their heads (scarves and aprons are provided at the entrance).

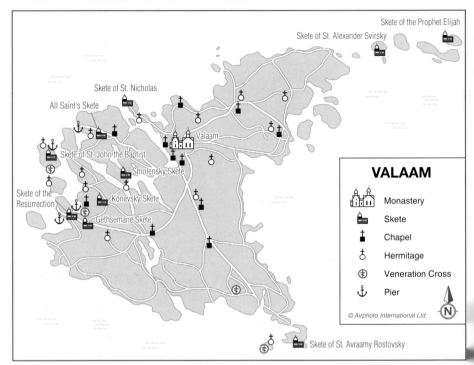

Today, Father Alexei, educated as an agronomist, is helping to restore the gardens and orchards; today the three orchards consist of over two thousand apple trees, including some that over 200 years old. One of the most beautiful roads starts from the main cloister and leads through an alley of 300-year-old Siberian fir to the Abbot's cemetery. Father Damaskin is buried near the northern altar wall of the nearby church. The island's beauty has inspired many of Russia's artists and writers, and Tchaikovsky's First Symphony is thought to portray a musical landscape poem of the island.

The most common excursion to Lake Ladoga is by boat from St Petersburg, In addition to quicker day trips, cruises also leave at night (rooms are clean, yet spartan), arrive the next morning and then tour Valaam Island (about six hours) and the lake, and return the following morning. (There is only one small hotel on Valaam, almost always full.) Although meals are provided onboard ship, it is highly recommended that you also bring along your own food. If you add Kizhi, the trip becomes four nights/five days. Boats run from mid-May to mid-September, depending when the lake is navigable. St Petersburg's main river terminal is at 195 Obvodnovo Canal Embankment; metro Ploshchad Alexandra Nevskovo. Group tour tickets can also be bought from the ticket kiosks on the corner of Nevsky and

Dumskaya Street in town. A bus takes passengers to the ferry. (For a list of boat companies that tour Lake Ladoga, see Boat Excursions and River Cruises on page 671). Also see www.valaam.ru.

KIZHI ISLAND

This island (one of almost 1,400) lies about 150 kilometers (90 miles) northwest of Lake Ladoga in Karelia's region of Lake Onega. (Lake Onega lies just south of the White Sea.) Its first settlers arrived in the sixth millennium BC, and ancient petroglyphs are still discernible on some of the rock formations. Between the tenth and 12th centuries inhabitants of Novgorod set out to colonize their own lands along the shores of the lake.

The **Church of the Resurrection of Lazarus**, on the islet of Mooch, is one of the oldest buildings in Russia. The main attraction, on the southwestern end of the six-kilometer long Kizhi island, is the 37-meter high wooden **Cathedral of the Transfiguration of the Savior**, built in 1714, to honor Peter the Great's victory over the Swedes. Pine logs form the octohedron structure, and over 30,000 curved silverish aspen shingles were handmade to cover the 22 cupolas of the three-tiered roof. The Cathedral was used in summer and during major holidays. As it was customary to build paired churches, the adjoining octagonal nine-domed winter **Church of the Intercession** was added in 1764. It has an extended wooden vestibule that was used for town meetings and on display here are icons from both churches. (Other items are exhibited in the Museum of Fine Arts in the neighboring town of Petrozavodsk.) A climb to the top of the center tent-roofed **bell tower** provides a great panoramic view of the island. The front of the old cemetery is surrounded by a low wall of wooden logs. Bells of the **Chapel of Archangel Michael** are played in summer.

A **Museum of Wooden Architecture** hosts a collection of 19th-century exhibits from northern Russia. These include the simple log-hewn late 15th-century **Resurrection of Lazarus Church, Chapel of the Icon of the Savior** from the village of Vigovo; the **Church of the Three Prelates**, with its one large wooden tower, from the village of Kavgora; the rectangular **Sergeyev House**, built in 1908, with the living space on one side and the barn on the other; and the more elaborate two-storey **Oshevnev House** (1876) from the Logmorychei village. It was customary to decorate the houses with colorfully carved window schutters and *kokoshnik* gables along the roof.

The national treasures of Kizhi Island have been established as a UNESCO site and are slowly being restored. (See Valaam for boat excursion information page 671.)

ANNA AKHMATOVA (1889–1966)

In 1889, the Gorenko family of Odessa added a new daughter, Anna. She was destined to become one of Russia's greatest 20th-century lyric poets.

When Anna was one year old, the family moved north to Tsarskoye Selo near St Petersburg, where she lived until she was 16. 'My first memories are those of Tsarskoye Selo,' she later wrote, 'the green grandeur of the parks, the groves where nanny took me, the hippodrome where small, mottled ponies jumped, and the old train station....'

She wrote her first poem at the age of 10. But poetry was a licentious pastime, according to her father, and he admonished her not to 'befoul his good and respected name.' So, Anna, while still in her teens, changed her surname to Akhmatova, honoring her maternal great-grandmother's Tartar heritage which, supposedly, was traced back to the last khan of the Golden Horde in Russia, Achmat Khan, a descendant of Genghis.

Her first book of poetry, *Evening*, appeared in 1912, and was an immediate success. 'Those pathetic verses of an empty-headed girl,' the astonished author wrote, 'have, no one knows why, been reprinted 13 times.' And yet every young person of the time could recite her *Gray-Eyed King*. Prokofiev later set the lyrics to music.

> Hail to thee, everlasting pain!
> The gray-eyed King died yesterday...
> I will wake up my daughter now.
> And look into her eyes of gray.
> And outside the window the poplars whisper.
> 'Your King is no more on this earth.'

Her second collection, *The Rosary*, was published in 1914. With the publication of Akhmatova's *White Flock* collection, Russian poetry hit the 'real' 20th-century. Her recurrent themes of romance and love and the wounded heroine of these poems speaks with intimacy and immediacy.

> There is a sacred boundary between those who are close,
> And it cannot be transcended by passion or love
> Though lips on lips fuse in dreadful silence
> And the heart shatters to pieces with love...
> Those who strive to reach it are mad, and those
> Who reach it are stricken with grief...
> Now you understand why my heart
> Does not beat faster beneath your hand.

In 1910, Anna married the talented poet Nikolai Gumilyov, who had begun to court her when she was 14. Together they traveled to Italy and then to France where Modigliani made a series of drawings using Anna as his model. Along with her talent, she had tremendous physical beauty. Anna was five-foot-eleven-inches tall, dark-haired, lithe and feline; someone once compared her light green eyes to those of a snow leopard. Positively stunning, she caught the eye of many an artist and sculptor. In addition, a whole volume could be filled with poetry and prose written just about her.

Recollections of the years with Gumilyov echoed many times throughout her poetry.

> He loved three things in the world,
> Singing at night, white peacocks
> and old maps of America.
> He hated when children cried,
> He hated tea with raspberry jam
> And women's hysterics.
> ...and I was his wife.

Gumilyov was the creator and leader of the Acmeists. After many years of romantic Symbolisism, their manifesto called for poetry of clarity and restraint. The cult lionized the city and Pushkin's Russia just as the imperial regime was about to collapse. Anna was 28 and at the center of Petersburg's artistic world of cabarets and intellectuals when the Romanov dynasty was ousted during the 1917 Revolution. She was 32 when, under Stalin, Gumilyov (by then her ex-husband) was arrested on a charge of plotting against the Soviet Government. He was executed soon afterwards. Her only son, Lev, was later twice arrested and sentenced to many years in a labor camp. (A noted scholar in later life, he died a natural death in 1994.)

Anna Akhmatova's name began to disappear from the literary scene and from 1925 until 1940 there was an unofficial ban on the publication of all her poetry. In 1935, her third husband Nikolai Punin, an art critic and historian of Western art, was arrested; he later died in a Siberian prison. The disappearance and death of friends, harassment by officials, no place to live, hours of waiting in lines for news of her arrested son, all took their voice in her prose-poem *Requiem*, dedicated to those times. Not daring to write anything down on paper, her friends memorized the verses. She wrote it between 1935 and 1940, but it wasn't allowed to be published in Russia until 1987.

In the terrible years of the Yezhov horrors, I spent 17 months standing in prison lines in Leningrad. One day somebody recognized me. There standing behind me was a woman with blue lips. She had, of course, never heard of me, but she suddenly came out of her stupor so common to us all and whispered in my ear (everybody there spoke only in whispers) 'Can you describe this'? and I said 'Yes, I can.' And then a fleeting smile passed over what had once been her face ...

Even though Akhmatova had opportunities to leave the country during Stalin's Terror, she refused to emigrate. To her, being Russian meant living in Russia, no matter what the government did to her or her loved ones. 'No! Not beneath foreign skies.... I was with my people then ... There my people, unfortunately, were...'

Pictures of Akhmatova show a beautiful woman with an aristocratic profile and a proudly raised head—a lioness with sad eyes. In the summer of 1936, a friend of hers wrote, 'She is extraordinary and quite beautiful. Those who have not seen her cannot consider their lives full.'

In November 1941, during the Siege of Leningrad, Akhmatova was evacuated to Tashkent. There she began writing her *Poem Without a Hero* set in the Fountain House (in the former Sheremeryev Palace off of the Fontanka Canal) in St Petersburg. The work consumed her for 22 years; she finished it in 1962. In 1946, after the war, Akhmatova returned to Petersburg, where her popularity was again immense. Because of her growing celebrity, and also possibly

Anna Akhmatova (1889–1966) was one of St Petersburg's legendary poets. This portrait of her was painted by Natan Altman in 1914. Earlier, during a trip to Paris in 1910, she befriended the artist Amedeo Modigliani who, enamored with her beauty, frequently sketched her portrait.

because of a meeting with Isaiah Berlin, she was expelled from the Writer's Union and denounced by Zhdanov, Stalin's cultural watchdog, who accused her of poisoning the minds of Soviets; he called her a 'half-nun, half-harlot'.

After this denunciation, Akhmatova was no longer published. She earned her money through translations and writing about accepted poets such as Pushkin. With no official residence, she lived off the help and kindness of friends. The West suspected that she was no longer writing poetry; many in Russia thought that she was no longer alive. But, somehow, she always knew that it was her fate to live through an epoch of interminable grief and upheaval.

In 1956, Akhmatova's son was released from the camps, and the last decade of her life became somewhat easier. She continued to live in the apartment on the Fontanka and was given the use of a tiny summer house in Komarovo, a writer's colony outside Petersburg. She was allowed to travel twice abroad. In 1964, Anna Akhmatova received the Etna Taormina Literary Prize in Catania, Italy; and in 1965, in England, she received an honorary doctorate from Oxford.

After her death on March 5, 1966, a memorial service was held at the Cathedral of St Nicholas the Seafarer, a 20-minute walk from her house on the Fontanka. It was said that the crowd attending her memorial looked like a human sea. The poet Joseph Brodsky, a close friend, wrote:

'At certain periods of history only poetry is capable of dealing with reality by condensing it into something graspable, something that otherwise couldn't be retained by the mind. In that sense, the whole nation took up the pen name of Akhmatova, which explains her popularity and which, more importantly, enabled her to speak for the nation as well as to tell it something it didn't know... her verses are to survive because they are charged with time....'

And timelessness. She captured the sense of the eternal in her last dated poem of February 1965, at the age of 75.

> So we lowered our eyes,
> Tossing the flowers on the bed,
> We didn't know until the end,
> What to call one another.

We didn't dare until the end
To utter first names,
As if, nearing the goal, we slowed our steps
On the enchanted way.

A literary critic who visited the house on the Fontanka described her room: 'A bed, or rather a stretcher, covered with a thin, dark blanket stands by the wall: on another wall is a mirror in an ancient gilt frame. Next to it, on a shelf, is a porcelain object, not really valuable but antique. In the corner is a folding icon. By the wall next to the door stands a small rectangular table, with a simple inkstand and a blotter—the desk. There are also one or two old chairs and a worn armchair, but neither wardrobe nor bookshelves. Books are everywhere, on the desk, the chair and on the windowsill.' The Anna Akhmatova House Museum is in St Petersburgh at 34 Fontanka and displays these rooms, where she lived and wrote, along with photos, letters and her poetry (see page 519).

Akhmatova never stopped writing about life's tumultuous truths.

These poems have such hidden meanings
It's like staring into an abyss.
And the abyss is enticing and beckoning,
But never will you discover the bottom of it,
And never will its hollow silence
Grow tired of speaking...

I know the gods transformed
Humans into objects without killing their minds.
So that my amazing sorrows will live forever...

...I am not allowed to forget
The taste of the tears of yesterday.

A monument to Akhmatova was unveiled in Moscow in 2001 in the courtyard of 17 Ordynka Street, where she once lived. Sculptor Vladimir Surovtsev modeled the elegant statue on her famous portrait painted by Amedeo Modigliani in Paris. Another stands in St Petersburg on Vosstaniya St, just off Nevsky Prospekt. In the words of Osip Mandalstam, "her poetry...will become one of the symbol's of Russia's greatness." The fascinating 60-minute documentary on *"Anna Akhmatova: Fear and the Muhse"*, is narrated by Claire Bloom; 2000.

THE BRONZE HORSEMAN

Where lonely waters, struggling, sought
To reach the sea, he (Peter the Great) paused, in thought...
The haughty Swede here we'll curb and hold at bay
And here, to gall him, found a city.
As nature bids so must we do:
A window will we cut here through
On Europe, and a foothold gaining
Upon this coast, the ships we'll hail
Of every flag, and freely sail
These seas, no more ourselves restraining.
A century passed, and there it stood,
Of Northern lands the pride and beauty,
A young, resplendent, gracious city,
Sprung out the dark of mire and wood...
Now there rise great places and towers; a maze
Of sails and mastheads crown the harbor;
Ships of all ports moor here beside
These rich and people shores; the wide,
Majestic Neva slowly labors,
In granite clad, to push its way
'Neath graceful bridges; gardens cover
The once bare isles that dot the river,
Its glassy surface still and grey.
Old Moscow fades beside her rival.
A dowager, she is outshone,
Overshadowed by the new arrival
Who, robed in purple, mounts the throne...
...the weather raged wildly
The Neva swelled and roared,
Gurgling and welling up like a cauldron
Rushed on the city. Before her, all fled...

It was then on Peter's square...
Sat motionless, terribly pale,
Eugene. He was in terror, not for himself...
The widow and her daughter, his fiancée Parasha,
Had been swept away...
Eugene shuddered...above him loomed...
A brazen head in the dusk,
Him by whose fateful will
The city by the sea was founded...
Awesome is he in the surrounding gloom!...
Where are you galloping, haughty steed,
And where will you plant your hooves?
Oh, mighty potentate of fate!
Was it not thus, aloft hard by the abyss,
That with curb of iron
You reared up Russia?...
Scowling, Eugene stood before the prideful statue...
'I'll show you!' And suddenly full tilt...
He runs down the empty square...
But, all night, wherever the wretched madman
Might turn his steps,
Behind him everywhere the Bronze Horseman
Was galloping with heavy clatter...

Alexander Pushkin (1799–1837)

Everything we have comes from Pushkin. His turning to the people so early in his career was so unheard of, so astonishing, such a new and so unexpected departure it can only have been a miracle or, failing that, the fruit of the singular grandeur of genius—one, I might add, we cannot fully appreciate even today.

Fyodor Dostoevsky, A Writer's Journal, 1876

(opposite) Alexander Pushkin

The realm of poetry is as boundless as life itself; yet every object of poetry has been set, from time out of mind, into a specific hierarchy, and to confuse the high with the low or take the one for the other is a major stumbling block. In the great poets, in Pushkin, this harmonious precision in the ranking of objects has been brought to perfection.

Leo Tolstoy, 1874

ST PETERSBURG PRACTICAL INFORMATION

TELEPHONE NUMBERS

Country code for Russia (7)   **St Petersburg** city code (812)

NOTE: TELEPHONE CHANGES: The city is currently revamping some telephone prefixes. Many prefix numbers that begin with "1" are being changed to 7. For example '117' becomes '717'. Also '177' is changing to '771', and in some town sections '313' is being reformatted to '570' and 311 to '571'. At the time of writing, all numbers have not yet changed. If you have problems dialing a number, try incorporating the new prefix number.

EMERGENCY SERVICES

It's also been stated that these three emergency numbers are to be combined into one number (112) by 2008.

Fire	01	Ambulance	03 (See also Medical)
Police	02	(First Private Ambulance Station: 327-5150/5153)	
Gas Leaks	04	Special Police Force (for foreigners) 164-9787 24hr	

TELEPHONE INFORMATION

Time	060	Intercity Information	070
Directory Enquiries	09/009	Weather	001
Addresses of St Petersburg residents	061	Info-line (Russian/English) 326-9696	
Special Police Services for foreigners	164-9787 or 278-3014		

Taxis

To order a taxi 24 hrs/day: 312-0022/3297, 294-1552, 100-000 or 068

USEFUL ON-LINE SERVICES

Traveller's Yellow Pages for St Petersburg: www.infoservices.com; www.infoservices.com St Petersburg's official website: www.spb.ru/eng or www.Saint-Petersburg.com. **About St Petersburg for Tourists**: www.travel.spb.ru (includes hotels); **Cosmos Travel Services**: www.guide.spb.ru; **The Other St Petersburg**: www.other.spb.ru; **A Guide to St Petersburg**: www.koi.travel.spb.ru/theguide; **St Petersburg at you Fingertips**: www.cityvision2000.com; Also check www.city-guide.spb.ru, which is the city's official city guide.

EXPRESS MAIL/POST

DHL International, 10 Nevsky Prospekt, Metro Gostiny Dvor, tel. 325-6161; or 4 Izmailovsky Prospekt, Metro Teknologichesky Institut, tel. 326-6400. Both open Monday–Friday 8am–9pm, Saturday 10am–4pm. Closed Sunday. www.dhl.ru.

Federal Express, 6 Grivtzova Pereulok, 9am–8pm Monday–Thursday, 9am–7pm

Friday. Metro Sennaya Ploshad, tel. 325-8825. Another location is at Nevsky 30 Business Center, 9am–6pm Monday–Thursday, 9am–5pm Friday.. Metro Kanal Griboedova, tel. 325-8825. www.fedex.com.

TNT Express Worldwide, 58a Moika Canal, Monday–Friday 9am–6pm. Metro Sennaya Ploshchad, tel. 718-3330. also 14 Sofiiskaya Ul., Monday–Friday 9am–6pm. Metro Elizaroskaya, tel. 303-9100. www.tnt.com.

United Parcel Service (UPS), 6 Voroshilova Street; (Metro Chernyshevskaya) tel. 703-3939; Monday–Friday 9am–6pm.www.ups.com.

Useful Publications in English

Many foreign newspapers and magazines can be found in hotel shops and magazine kiosks. *Neva News* was the city's first English language newspaper. *New East* is an international magazine listing the city's main current events. *Pulse St Petersburg* is published monthly with city cultural news and events. *St Petersburg Times* is published twice weekly and is the leading English-language newspaper in the city (www.sptimes.ru). *Where in St Petersburg* is published six times a year with useful information on travel and culture (www.wherespb.spn.ru). The *Moscow Times* has information on both Moscow and St Petersburg, and the world (www.themoscowtimes.com). *The Traveller's Yellow Pages of St Petersburg* contains over 7,000 useful addresses and is on sale in stores throughout the city (main office is at 64 Moika Canal) www.infoservices.com. The official city guide is www.city-guide.spb.ru.

Medical

Most top-end hotels have a resident doctor or nurse.

American Medical Center, 10 Serpukhovskaya Ul. Metro Teknologichesky Institut, tel. 326-1730. Also at 78 Moika. Metro Sennaya Ploshad, tel. 140-2090. Offers 24-hour emergency care, Western pharmacy and lab, ambulance services and medical evacuations. www.amcenters.com

British-American Family Practice, 7 Grafsky Per (off Vladimirsky Pr.). 24-hours. tel. 327-6030.

Cardiology Center, 4 Kultury Pr. Monday–Friday 9am–5pm. Provides diagnostic and treatment of cardio-related illnesses. Metro Ozerki, tel. 558-8797;

Clinic Complex, 22 Moskovsky Pr. Operates 24 hours; Metro Teknologichesky Institut, tel. 710-1102.

Coris Ambulance, tel. 327-1313

Emergency Medical Consulting, 78 Moskovsky Pr. Provides 24-hour emergency care, consultations by specialists at hotel or home, ambulance services and medical evacuations. tel. 325-0880.

EuroMed Clinic, 60 Suvorovsky Pr. Provides 24-hour emergency services, medical staff and lab, evacuation services. tel. 327-0301. www.euromed.ru

International Clinic, 19/21 Ul. Dostoevskovo. Medical services include 24-hour emergency, walk-in appointments, house calls, hospitalizations and evacuations. Metro Vladimirskaya, tel. 320-3870, 336-3333. www.icspb.ru

DENTAL

American Medical Center, (see Medical above) Mon–Fri 9am–9pm.

Dental Palace, 10 Millionnaya Ul. Monday–Friday 9.30am–9pm; Saturday 11am–6pm. tel. 314-1459. **European Dental Center**, 34 Konushkovskaya Ul. tel. 933-0002. www.emcmos.ru.

Family Dentist, 29 Marata. Metro Mayakovskaya, tel. 112-3795.

Medi, 82 Nevsky Prospekt. They also have eight other locations throughout the city. Western dental care and 24-hour emergency on-call. Metro Mayakovskaya, tel. 324-0000/0021.

CONSULATES

For consulates not listed below, see Moscow Practical Information (page 356–359).

Australia, 1 Italyanskaya. tel. 325-7333, www.australiaembassy.ru.

Austria, 43 Furshtatskaya Ul. Honorary consulate. Visa department is in Moscow. Monday–Friday 10am–1pm. Metro Chernyshevskaya, tel. 275-0502.

Belarus, 8/46 Robespera Nab. #66 Monday–Friday 9am–5pm. Metro Chernyshevskaya, tel. 273-0078/4164.

Bulgaria, 27 Ryleeva Ul. Monday–Friday 9am–5.30pm; closed 12.30–1.30pm. Metro Chernyshevskaya, tel. 273-7347/4164.

Canada, 32 Malodetskoselsky Pr. Monday–Friday 9am–5pm. tel. 325-8448.

China, 134 Griboyedov Canal Emb. Monday–Friday 9am–6pm, closed 12–3pm. tel. 114-7670.

Cuba, 7-2 Nakhimova. Monday–Friday 9am–6pm; closed 1–2pm. Metro Chernyshevskaya, tel. 356-3727.

Czech Republic, 5 Tverskaya Ul. Mon–Fri 9am–5pm. Metro Chernyshevskaya, tel. 271-0459/4612.

Denmark, 13 Bol. Alleya, Kamenny (Stone) Island. Monday–Friday 10am–4.30pm. Metro Chernaya Rechka, tel. 103-3900, 234-3755, 346-1700.

Estonia, 14 Bol. Monetnaya Ul. Tuesday–Friday 9.30am–12pm. Metro Gorkovskaya, tel. 238-1804/102-0924.

Finland, 71 Ul. Tchaikovskovo. Monday–Friday 8.30am–4.15pm. (The visa department is located nearby at 17 Chernyshevskaya Ul. Mon–Fri 9am–3.30pm; closed 11.30am–1.30pm. tel. 272-2082.) Metro Chernyshevskaya, tel. 273-7321.

France, 15 Moika River Emb. Monday–Friday 9.30am–5.30pm; closed 12.30–3.30pm. tel. 312-1130/314-1443.

Germany, 39 Furshtatskaya Ul. Monday–Friday 8am–4.30pm, closed 12.30–1pm. Metro Chernyshevskaya, tel. 320-2400.

Great Britain, 5 Proletarsky Diktatury. (Visas applications taken Monday–Friday, 9.45am–12.15pm; issued 4–5pm.) Metro Chernyshevskaya, tel. 320-3200. www.britemb.msk.ru.

Hungary, 15 Ul. Marata. (Visa applications Tuesday/Wednesday/Friday 10am–12pm.) tel. 312-6458.

India, 35 Ryleeva Ul. Monday–Friday 10.30am–5pm. Metro Chernyshevskaya, tel. 272-1731/1988.

Israel, 6 Inzhenernaya Ul. Monday–Thursday/Sunday 10am–6pm. Metro Gostiny Dvor, tel. 272-0456.

Italy, 10 Teatralnaya Pl. (Visas Monday–Friday 9.30am–12pm.) tel. 312-3217.

Japan, 29 Moika Canal. Monday–Friday 4–6pm. Metro Nevsky Prospekt, tel. 314-1418/34.

Latvia, 11 10-ya Liniya. Monday–Thursday 9.30am–12.30pm, Friday 9am–12pm. Metro Vasileostrovskaya, tel. 327-6053/54.

Lithuania, 4 Gorokhovaya Street. Monday–Friday 9am–6pm, closed 1–2pm. tel. 314-5857.

Netherlands, 11 Moika Canal. Monday–Friday 9am–5pm, closed 1-2pm. Metro Nevsky Prospekt, tel. 315-0197, 334-0200.

Norway, 25 Nevsky Prospekt. Monday–Friday 10am–4pm, closed 1–2pm. tel. 326-2650.

Poland, 12/14 5-ya Sovetskaya Ul. Monday–Friday 9am–1pm. Metro Vosstaniya, tel. 274-4170.

Sweden, 1-3 Mal. Konyushennaya Ul. Monday–Friday 9am–5pm, closed 1–2pm. Metro Nevsky Prospekt, tel. 329-1430.

Thailand, 9/6 Bolshoi Pr. Monday–Friday 11am–1pm. Metro Vasileostrovskaya, tel. 325-6271.

Ukraine, 6 Mal. Morskaya Ul. Monday/Wednesday/Friday 10am–12.30pm. Metro Nevsky Prospekt, tel. 312-1048.

United States, (main) 15 Furshtatskaya Ul. Monday–Friday 10am–5pm. (Visa by appointment at the Commercial Dept. Monday–Friday 9am–6pm. 25 Nevsky Prospekt. tel. 326-2560.) tel. 274-8689/331-2600. Off-hour emergencies 331-2852.

AIRPORTS
Flight Schedule Information

Pulkovo-II (International). Located 17 kilometres (ten miles) south of the city. tel. 104-3444.

Pulkovo-I (flights throughout Russia and CIS). Located five kilometres from Pulkovo-II. tel. 104-3822. www.pulkovo.ru.

Rzhevka (east of St Petersburg, now used only for air cargo). tel. 527-5208.

Levashovo Sports Airport is 20 kilometers (12 miles) northwest of the city. tel. 594-9519.

AIRLINES
Aeroflot, Day and night Info and Reservation Center tel. 118-5555; 1/43 Rubenstein Ul, tel. 438-5583. Open 9.30am–6pm, Friday to 5pm. Closed Saturday and Sunday. Also at 5 Kazanskaya Ul. Monday–Friday 10am–6pm; Saturday 10am–4pm. Metro Nevsky Prospekt, tel. 327-3872. (Pulkovo II, tel. 104-3433; Pulkovo I ticketing office, tel. 723-8534, open daily 9am–9pm). www.aeroflot.org.

Air France, 35 Bolshaya Morskaya. Monday–Friday 9am–5pm. tel. 325-8252. (Pulkovo-II tel. 104-3433) www.airfrance.com

Austrian Airlines, 57 Nevsky Pr. at Nevsky Palace Hotel. Monday–Friday 9am–5pm. Metro Mayakovskaya, tel. 325-3260. (Pulkovo-II tel. 324-3244) www.aua.com.

British Airways, 1/3a Mal. Konyushennaya Ul. Monday–Friday 9am–5.30pm. Metro Gostiny Dvor/Nevsky Prospekt, tel. 325-2565. (Pulkovo-II tel. 104-3749). www.british-airways.com.

CSA Czech Airlines, 36 Bolshaya Morskaya. tel. 315-5259. (Pulkovo-II tel. 324-3250) www.csa.cz.

Delta Airlines, 36 Bolshaya Morskaya. tel. 311-5819/5820. (Pulkovo-II tel. 104-3438) www.delta.com.

El-Al, 21 Baskov Pereulok. Metro Chernyshevskaya, tel. 275-1720. (Pulkovo-II tel. 104-3465) www.elal.co.il.

Finnair, 44 Kazanskaya Ul. Monday–Friday 9am–5pm. tel. 326-8170. (Pulkovo-II tel. 324-3249) www.finnair.com

KLM, 5 Zadorodny Prospekt, tel. 325-8989 and 23 Malaya Morskaya, tel. 346-6868. Monday–Friday 9am–5pm. (Pulkovo-II tel. 104-3463) www.klm.com.

LOT, 1 Karavannaya Ul. Monday–Friday 10am–6pm. Metro Gostiny Dvor/Nevsky Prospekt, tel. 273-5721. (Pulkovo-II tel. 104-3437) www.lot.com.

Lufthansa, 7 Voznesensky Prospekt, Metro Sadovaya, tel. 314-4979,314-5917 and 32 Nevsky Prospekt, tel. 320-1000. (Pulkovo-II tel. 104-3432) www.lufthansa.com.

Malev, Hungarian Airlines, 7 Voznesensky Prospekt, Monday–Friday 10am–6pm. Metro Sadovaya, tel. 315-5455, 315-6886. (Pulkovo-II tel. 104-3435).

SAS, 25 Nevsky Pr. tel. 326-2600/2601. (Pulkovo-II tel. 324-3244) www.scandinavian.net.

Swissair, 1/3a Mal. Konyushennaya Ul. tel. 329-2525. (Pulkovo-II tel. 346-8100) www.swissair.com.

Transaero, 48 Liteyny Pr. Metro Chernyshevskaya, tel. 279-1974.

Railways

See Getting Around section, page 70, for more details on train travel and buying tickets. For info about trains from all stations: tel. 168-0111. Ticket windows at each station sell same-day and advance (up to 45 days) tickets. Each station has both long distance and local electric/commuter trains. To book tickets for home delivery call 201 (takes 2–3 days; pay upon delivery), and to make reservations online go to www.express-2.ru. Also check www.tickettorussia.com for train schedules and reservations.

The **Central Railway Ticket Office**, 24 Nab. Griboyedova Kanala. Tickets for any station or destination. Monday–Saturday 8am–8pm; Sunday 8am–4pm. Metro Nevsky Prospekt. Info. tel. 162-3344, 314-3525 or 067.

Baltic Station (Baltiisky Vokzal), 120 Obvodnovo Kanala. Metro Baltiiskaya. Trains include those to Moscow, Peterhof, Gatchina and Oranienbaum and Baltic states. Tickets for the ER-200 fast train to Moscow can be bought at the ticket booth to the right of the square. tel. 168-2859, 162-3344.

Finland Station (Finlyansky Vokzal), 6 Lenina Pl. Trains include those to Helsinki, Finland, Vyborg, Lake Ladoga, Repino, Razliv and Olgino. Metro Ploshchad Lenina, tel. 168-7687/7200.

Ladozhsky Station Trains to Helsinki, Murmansk, Arkhangelsk, Ekaterinburg. Metro Ladozhsky, tel. 436-5310.

Moscow Station (Moskovsky Vokzal), 85 Nevsky Pr. Trains include those to Moscow, Novgorod, Yaroslavl, Ivanovo, Kostroma and many other points north and south. Connection to Trans-Siberian express. Ticket windows on 2nd floor near train platforms. Commuter tickets sold on right side of station. Metro Ploshchad Vosstaniya, tel. 168-4597.

Vitebsk Station (Vitebsky Vokzal), 52 Zagorodny Pr. Trains to southwest Russia, and direct trains to Brussels, Budapest, Prague and Berlin. Metro Pushkinskaya, tel. 168-5807.

Warsaw Station (Varshavsky Vokzal), 118 Obvodnovo Kanala. Closed in 2003, and turned into an art center. Metro Baltiiskaya.

ACCOMMODATION

In the 1990s a lot of new accommodation, from foreign-owned five-star luxury to bargain rooms in homestays, opened up throughout the city. One can now select a hotel based on location, cost, service and style. (For more information see Being There/Hotels section, page 72.) Before booking find out what amenities are included, such as breakfast, private bath, visa support, and airport/town center transportation. Ask if the 20 percent VAT and city tax are already included in the price. How close is it to a Metro station? (You can easily pinpoint the hotel's location in the city by its closest Metro stop.) Cheaper hotels can be situated far from the city center; you may consider booking a slightly more expensive yet more centrally located hotel to save on travel time. Ask for a room with minimum street noise or the best view available. Depending on the type of visa, you may have to pre-pay the hotel before departure. Most higher-end and mid-range hotels now take credit cards. Especially in winter months, when occupancy is lower, you may try to bargain. Upon check-in you will be asked for your visa and passport for registration. (Always keep a copy of both.) Some hotels may still charge a separate tariff for Russian citizens and international guests.

Useful websites: www.hotels.spb.ru; www.all-hotels.ru/index; www.infoservices.com; www.hotelnet.co.uk, www.moscowtimes.ru (select "travel guide"), and www.allrussianhotels.com.

DELUXE—FOUR AND FIVE STAR

Most luxury hotels provide visa invitation services and airport transportation. The complex contains restaurants, bars, fitness center, business and bank exchange centers, and all the other amenities usually associated with luxury hotels. The following average around $200 to $400 a night (single/double) up to more expensive suites.

Astoria, 39 Bolshaya Morskaya Ul., is located by St Isaac's Cathedral, Built in 1912 by architect Fyodor Lidval, it has been restored to its original five-star art-nouveau grandeur. It has 191 rooms, 41 suites, two restaurants, a bar and nightclub/casino. The Zimny Sad or Winter Garden Restaurant is decorated with the original chandeliers and statues and the tables are laid with locally made Lomonosov porcelain. (Rocco Forte Hotels). Metro Nevsky Prospekt, tel. 494-5757. www.rfhotels.com or www.astoria.spb.ru.

Next door to the Astoria is the five-star **Angleterre Hotel** which is slightly cheaper. tel. 494-5666; in US (800) 223-5652. www.angleterrehotel.com.

Corinthia Nevsky Palace Hotel, 57 Nevsky Prospekt, has 30 suites, 282 rooms, four restaurants, roof top health club (with pool and sauna), a business center and shopping arcade. The hotel was built in 1861, and restored and reopened in 1993. Metro Mayakovskaya, tel. 380-2001; www.corinthiahotels.com.

Grand Hotel Emerald, 18 Suvorovsky Pr. This luxurious hotel with marble floors and chandeliers made from Swarovski crystal, has 59 rooms, 14 suites, two restaurants, bar and Atrium café, fitness center/sauna and casino. Metro Vosstaniya, tel 740-5000. www.grandhotelsmerald.com.

Hotel Moika 22, (Yeliseyev Palace) This Kempinski Hotel, opened in 2005, is located right off Palace Square with views of the Winter Palace and Moika River. The building dates back to 1853, and first designed by Dutch architect, Basil Von Witte. 197 rooms, restaurant & bars, fitness center. tel. 335-9111. www.kempinski.com

Kempinski Grand Hotel Europe, 1/7 Mikhailovskaya Ul. (off Nevsky Pr.) After a lengthy restoration to its turn-of-the-century glory, the former Evropeiskaya Hotel was reopened in 1991. It has 301 rooms, four restaurants, two bars, shops, a health club, billiard room, business center and nightclub. Sadko, next door, is one of the city's popular hangouts. Metro Nevsky Prospekt, tel. 329-6000; in US/Canada (800) 426-3135, UK (0800) 868-588. www.grand-hotel-europe.com.

Radisson SAS Royal Hotel, 49/2 Nevsky Pr. 164 rooms, incl 17 suites, restaurants, bars, fitness center. Reservations: US (800) 333-3333; UK (800) 3333-3333; Hong Kong (800) 968356. tel. 322-5000. www.radissonsas.com.

Renaissance Baltic Hotel, 4 Pochtamtskaya St (managed by Marriott International, this complex is one of the city's newest deluxe hotels), located in a former 19th-century mansion, which served as the residence of Mikhail Yakovlev, a school friend of the poet, Alexander Pushkin. The hotel has a beautiful city view over St Issac's Cathedral, and is within walking distance of the city center, with over 100 rooms and 20 suites, fitness center/sauna and restaurant and terrace bar. tel. 380-4000, fax 380-4001. (In the US, call 800-HOTELS-1).

MODERATE
These average at around $75 to $200 (single–double) per night.

Accor Novotel Centre Hotel, 3a Mayakovsky St. Opened in 2006, with 233 rooms, it was designed with business travelers in mind. A 5-minute walk to Nevsky Prospekt. tel. 335-1188. www.novotel.com.

Alexander House, 27 Kryukov Canal Emb. A small boutique hotel with sixteen rooms, and apartments, restaurant and spa; close to the Mariinskhy Theater. Breakfast included. tel. 575-3877/3540/ fax. 575-3879. www.a-house.ru

B&B Nevsky, 11/8 Nevsky Prospekt, offers a reasonable price for such a central location. Free transportation to airport or train stations. Metro Gostiny Dvor, tel. 325-9398.

Hotel St Petersburg, at 5/2 Pirgovskaya Emb, on the Vyborg side, opposite the Aurora Battleship. This three-star hotel has restaurants and even a concert hall. Ask for a river view. Metro Ploshchad Lenina, tel. 380-1919/1909. www.hotel-spb.ru.

Moskva Hotel, 2 Alexander Nevsky Square, is just opposite the monastery at the end of Nevsky Prospekt. Offers both regular and four-star business class rooms. Has restaurants, shops and a business center. Metro Aleksandra Nevskovo, tel. 274-0022/3001. www.hotel-moscow.ru.

Petro Palace Hotel, 14 Mal. Morskaya, near Nevsky Pr and the Hermitage. The building was originally designed for the famous merchant Van Stahl in 1897. The structure was completely restored and opened as the hotel in 2005. tel. 571-2880 www.petropalacehotel.com.

Pribaltiiskaya, is located at 14 Korablestroiteley at the end of Vasilyevsky Island by the Gulf of Finland (a half-hour Metro ride from city center). This four-star hotel, built in 1978, has 1,200 rooms (ask for a water view), health club (with pool and sauna); business center; billiards and bowling; and restaurants and shops. Metro Primorskaya. tel. 356-3001, 329-2626. www.pribaltiiskaya.com.

Park Inn Pulkovskaya, 1 Pobedy Square. Situated 8 kilometers south of the city, near the Pulkovo Airport. Built in 1981 (as a Finnish-Russian joint venture), this four-star hotel has 840 rooms, two restaurants, business and fitness centers, and tennis courts. (Only a 15-minute ride to the airport.) Metro Moskovskaya, tel. 740-3900, fax. 740-3913. www.pulkovskaya.ru.

INEXPENSIVE

Average around $50–$100 for single/double. Be aware that many of these inexpensive and budget hotels were built in old Soviet-style and have not yet been completely renovated. But they are certainly more of a bargain and offer comfortable if spartan accommodation. Check to find out what amenities are included, such as television or air conditioning. Some offer cheaper room rates for shared hallway bathroom and there may be different classes of rooms, such as standard, upgraded or even semi-lux. Some may not take credit cards. Note the location, for it can be situated far from the center and not close to a Metro station.

Best Western Neptun, 93a Obvodnovo Kanala Emb. It has 70 rooms, a restaurant-bar, sauna and business center. about a ten-minute walk from Metro Baltiiskaya on the Obvodny Canal, tel. 324-4610/315-4965. www.neptun.spb.ru.

Deson-Ladoga, 26 Shaumyan Pr, is a three-star hotel with a restaurant, bar, sauna and business center. One block east of Novocherkasskaya Metro station, across the Neva from the Alexander Nevsky Monastery, tel. 528-5200/5393.

Dostoevsky Hotel, 19 Vladirmirsky Prospect. Metro Dostoevskaya, tel. 333-3200.

Hotel Sovietskaya, a three-star Russian-Finnish joint venture, is at 43/1 Lermontovsky Pr., three kilometers (two miles) southwest of the Hermitage, by the Fontanka canal. It has two restaurants, a pizzeria and business center. Metro Baltiiskaya, tel. 740-2640. www.sovetskaya.com.

Kareliya, 27/2 Ul. Tukhachevskovo, has 200 rooms, restaurant, café-bars, nightclub and business center. A long trolleybus ride from Ploshchad Lenina Metro, tel. 118-4004/226-3534. www.karelia.spb.ru.

Marshal Hotel, 41 Shpalernaya Ul., cozy three-star hotel, located in city center near the Neva. Metro Chernyshevskaya, tel. 279-9955; tel/fax 279-7500.

Matisse House (Domik Matissov), 3/1 Pryazhki River Emb, near the Mariinsky Theater. Cozy cottage atmosphere with a quiet yard. Breakfast included. Provides shuttles to airport and train stations (not close to a metro). tel. 318-5445, fax. 318-7419.

Mercury, 39 Tavricheskaya Ul., near the Smolny Cathedral, originally hosted regional Party officials. Located in a quiet residential area, it has a bar-restaurant, and winter garden. Metro Chernyshevskaya, tel. 325-6444, fax.276-1977.

Morskaya, 1 Morskoi Slavy Square, is a three-star hotel on Vasilyevsky Island. Metro Primorskaya, tel. 322-6040/6069.

Neva, 17 Chaikovskovo Ul., has a restaurant-bar. Centrally located near Metro Chernyshevskaya, tel. 278-0504.

Nevsky Prospekt Hotels, six comfortable hotels located around the central area of Nevsky Prospekt. The main inquiry number for all hotels is tel. 703-3860, fax. 703-3861. The website has descriptions and pictures posted for all six hotels. **The Astor Hotel**, at 25 Bol. Konyushennaya St, has 26 rooms. tel. 336-6583; **Delux**, at 14 Bol Konyushennaya, has 7 doubles, tel. 312-3131; **Nevsky 22**, entrance at 10 Bol Konyushennaya, has 76 rooms, tel. 312-1206; **5 Moika**, with 24 rooms, is on the canal behind the Cathedral of Spilled Blood, tel. 601-0636. (Nearest metro for all four is Nevsky Prospekt); **Nevsky 90**, with 36 rooms, is further down the Prospekt near Metro Vosstaniya, tel. 273-7314; across the street, near Moskovsky Train Station, is **Nevsky 91**, with 14 rooms, tel. 717-1888; www.hon.ru

Okhtinskaya (Victoria Hotel), a French-Russian joint venture at 4 Bolsheokhtinsky Pr. and Sverdlovsky Emb, is situated on the Vyborg side of the river across from the Smolny Cathedral. It has 300 rooms, a restaurant, bar, fitness room (with sauna), business center, and a great Italian deli. Metro Novocherkasskaya, tel. 227-4438; fax.227-2618. www.okhtinskaya.spb.ru.

Okyabrskaya Hotel, was the Grand Hotel du Nord in czarist times (1847); has a central location, located at 10 Ligovsky Pr. The old soviet complex has undergone extensive renovations. It has a restaurant and business center. Metro Ploshchad Vosstaniya off Nevsky Prospekt, tel. 118-2222/1515, fax 315-7501.

Olgino, is located 18 kilometers (11 miles) northwest of the city in pine forests at 59 Primorskoye. Very far away and inconvenient for public transport. It does have horseback riding in summer and a campground. tel. 238-3671.

Hotel Rus, 1 Artilleryskaya Ul., a three-star modern hotel with a café-bar, fitness room (with sauna) and business center. Metro Chernyshevskaya, tel. 273-4683/279-5003; fax 279-3600.

Smolenskaya, 22 Tverskaya, this three-star hotel also has a restaurant-bar. Metro Chernyshevskaya, tel. 276-1099.

BUDGET HOTELS
Less than $50 a night.

Bolshoi Teatr Kukol, or the Big Puppet Theater Hotel, is located at 12 Ul. Nekrasova (4th floor) by the theater. Metro Chernyshevskaya, tel. 272-5401.

Kievskaya, 49 Dnepropetrovskaya Ul., by the Obvodny Canal. Metro Ploshchad Vosstaniya, tel. 166-0456/5398, fax. 166-8250.

Mir, (Peace Hotel),17 Gastello Ul., is next to the Chesme Church. Metro Moskovskaya, south of Victory Park, tel. 108-5166, fax 108-5118.

Prin, 4 Vozrozhdeniya Ul., has a restaurant and business center. Metro Kirovsky Zavod in the southwest part of town, tel. 184-3550/324-4949.

Sputnik, in a quiet neighborhood at 34 Morisa Toreza. (rooms with attached or communal baths) Has a restaurant, sauna and disco. You can get a discount with a Student Identity Card. A ten-minute walk from Metro Ploshchad Muzhestva in the northeast part of town, tel. 552-5632, fax 552-8084.

Vyborkskaya Hotel, three buildings located at 3 Torzhkovskaya Ul., across the river, north of Petrovsky Island. Rooms have either attached or communal baths. It also has a restaurant with live music, and a fitness room (with sauna). Metro Chornaya Rechka in the northern part of town, tel. 246-2319/9141, fax. 246-8187.

HOSTELS
St Petersburg International Youth Hostel, is the city's first Hostelling International member. Founded in 1992, the entire 4-storey renovated building hosts the budget traveler. Rooms have two to six beds; a downstairs video café which shows movies; internet access, Continental breakfast, laundry facilities, and airport shuttle service; open 24 hours, all year round. A five-minute walk from Metro Ploschchad Vossaniya to 28 3a-Ya Sovietskaya Ul. The hostel also provides visa support, and has

the travel agency Sindbad Travel for travel, plane and train reservations, tel. 329-8018, 327-8384. Reservations can be made directly by fax on 329-8019, or by contacting any HI Hostel on the IBN international booking system. (It also takes reservations forother Russian Youth Hostels, RYHA). Price depends on the season, but average around $25/person for a double and $15–20 for a Dorm Room (less with a hostel membership). Visa support is $27. In the US (202) 783-6161; Canada (800) 663-5777; UK (171) 836-1036. email: ryh@ryh.ru, www.ryh.ru.

International Hostel Holiday became St Petersburg's second Western-style hostel in 1994. Conveniently located at 1 Mikhailova Ul. (third floor)/9 Arsenalnaya Emb on Petrograd side, overlooking Neva river, five-minutes walk from Finland Station and Metro. Has 130 beds, kitchen, laundry, breakfast and entertainment rooms, and rooftop café. High/low season: single ($37/29), double ($19/15 each), and dormitory rooms (up to six beds at $14/12 each)—all have shared bath. Ask for a river view. Discounts for IH and Student ISIC members, and longer stays. Prepayment for reservations must be by credit card. Book well in advance It also provides visa invitations and transportation to/from airport and train stations. (IHH also provides a hostel in Moscow and some other cities.) Metro Ploshchad Lenina, tel./fax. 327-1033/1070, email: info@hostel.spb.ru, www.hostel.ru.

Hostel All Seasons, 11 Yakovlevsky Lane, 4th floor. Situated south of the city center, it is a 10-minute walk from the Metro. It offers 60 beds (from 1 to 8 beds per room), visa support, self-service kitchen, internet, TV room, storage room, laundry facilities and open 24 hours year round. Price depends on season, but averages per person $24 to $40 for a single room; $12 to $20 for a double; $8 to $14 for a triple; $6 to $10 for four beds; and $5 to $9 for 5–8 bed (discounts for members). Visa support is $30. Metro station Park Pobedy through the park (a 15-minute metro ride into town). tel. 327-1070, fax. 327-1033, email: Info @hostel.spb.ru, www.hostel.ru

Petrovsky (formerly Summer) Hostel, 26 Baltiiskaya Ul., is about a ten-minute Metro ride from the city center south to Metro Narvskaya. There are two wings on the third floor. The building has a health club (with sauna) and common space with kitchen. Costs about $10 per bed in communal room, including breakfast (with single/double rooms available). You can book with them directly at tel. 252-5381/7763; fax 252-4019. Or trying reserving space through IBN or RYHA.

Student Dormitory, centrally located behind the Kazan Cathedral at 6 Plekhanova Ul. with comfortable singles and doubles. Try calling first; it is usually quite full in summer months. Tel. 314-7472. Metro Nevsky Prospekt.

BED & BREAKFASTS

Bed & Breakfasts, for room listings and furnished apartments, www.bednbreakfast.sp.ru.

International Bed & Breakfast, comfortable and inexpensive accommodation provided in St Petersburg, Moscow and other cities in Russia and Eastern Europe. English-speaking families and visa support. PO Box 823 Huntingdon Valley, Pennsylvania 19006. tel. toll-free in USA: (800) 422-5283; (215) 663-1438; fax. (215) 379-3363. email: IBB@dca.net.

St Petersburg Host Family Association (HOFA), at 5 Tavricheskaya Ul., Apt 25, places travelers with Russian families (generally professionals who speak English) in their apartments. You usually get a private room with breakfast included and a shared bathroom. Generally, the room can be rented from one day up to several weeks with a discount for longer stays. HOFA will provide a visa invitation and OVIR registration. (Also provides a network of services through more than 50 other Russian cities.) Prices range from $25 single/$40 double to $95 single and $130 double, depending on the type of services (i.e. city guides or transportation to/from airport.) Run by Professor Alexei Kostarev. tel./fax. 275-1992/cell 911-914-2762, email: info@hofa.us; www.webcenter.ru/~hofa.

Traveller's Guest House Moscow, can also book rooms in St Petersburg. Tel. (095) 971-4059; fax 280-7686; e-mail: tgh@startravel.ru; website:www.infinity.ru

For other homestay possibilities, check the website www.travel.spb.ru

APARTMENTS OR LONG TERM RENTALS

(if staying longer, an apartment may be cheaper than a hotel, and it offers more amenities such as a kitchen.)

Chaika is a hotel that can provide apartments, with kitchens, for longer stays. Located at 38 Serebristy Bulvar, Metro Pionerskaya, tel. 301-7575.

HOFA above can arrange apartment rentals from $50 to $80 per night (the latter is for two rooms and up to four guests) with kitchen. The following websites offer apartment rental selections: www.apartmentres.com; www.saint-petersburg-apartments.com; www.bednbreakfast.sp.ru; (HOFA) webcenter.ru/~hofa, and the St Petersburg Times also lists apartment rentals, www.sptimes.ru.

Russian residents may now approach travelers as they arrive in train stations offering a place to stay in their apartment. Most of these people are professionals and are just in need of some extra cash. (Many grandmothers on a pension receive less than $50 per month.) Trust your instincts, and make sure it is not too far from the city center, and do not commit yourself until you see the room. Bargain prices can be negotiated. Many train stations now have a small bureau with a dispatcher who has a list of residents with rooms to rent.

CAMPING

Because of the rising crime rates, camping is not really recommended. **Retur Motel**, is 29 kilometers (18 miles) out of town at 202 Primorskoye Highway. It offers chalets or camp sites on the Gulf of Finland. It also has a restaurant and bar, sauna, swimming pool and tennis courts. Tel/fax 437-7533. Metro Chornaya Rechka, followed by bus 411/416. You can also take the train from Finland Station to Sestroretsk and get off at Aleksandrovsky. **Olgino**, see Olgino Hotel under listings.

DINING

Surprise! St Petersburg has changed dramatically over the past decade. There are now over 1,000 eating establishments from corner take-outs to elegant dining in restored palaces; practically every street in the city center has a place that offers a bite of something (and summer outdoor sidewalk cafés are the latest trend). In addition, many now accept major credit cards. The larger hotels all have their own restaurants and cafés. And most restaurants have a bar or a selection of liquors available. The city offers a wide range of dishes that include Russian, European, Asian, Georgian, Uzbek, Arabian, Mexican and American—with or without music and entertainment. Prices vary from cheap to extremely expensive. For the more upscale or popular eateries, reservations (along with appropriate attire) are recommended. Most open from noon to midnight, unless indicated. (For more information, see Food section, page 82.)

So many food stores and supermarkets have opened up, from grocery stores and gastronomes to 24-hour mini-markets, that you just need to ask the staff of your hotel to direct you to the nearest one. A Westerner can now find practically everything that is available at home. **Yeliseyev's**, at 58 Nevsky Prospekt, is the original lavish 19th-century speciality food store. Other supermarkets are **Supermarket at Pazzazh**, at 48 Nevsky, **Kalinka Stockman**, 1 Finlandsky Prospekt (Metro Pl. Lenina) and **Super Babylon** at 54 Maly Prospekt, Petrograd Side (Metro Petrogradskaya).

BARS

City Bar, 10 Millionnaya, near the Hermitage. American-owned, this bar/restaurant is one of the city's Expat hangouts. Daily food specials under $5. Metro Nevsky Prospekt, tel. 314-1037.

Cynic, 4 Antonenko Per. (tucked in a basement by St Issac's Square). The popular hangout gets packed on weekends. www.cynic.spb.ru

Liverpool, 16 Ul. Mayakovskovo. Daily 11am–2am; Fri/Sat till 5am. Metro Mayakovskaya.

Mollie's Irish Bar, 36 Ul. Rubinshteina. Daily noon–2am; Fri/Sat till 3am. Metro Dostoevskaya.

Red Lion British Pub, 1 Pl. Dekabristov. Open 24 hours.

Telegraph Bar, 3 Rubinshtein St. English and European cuisine. Large beer, wine, whisky and cognac selections. Metro Vladimirskaya.

The Office Pub, 5 Kazanskaya, off Nevsky. Draught beers, Sport-TV channels. Open noon–2am.

Warsteiner Forum, 120 Nevsky. Beer restaurant with German and Russian selections. Metro Pl. Vosstaniya.

Whisky Bar William Grant's, 17 Chekhova St. 250 kinds of whisky.

CITY CENTER
Closest Metro is Nevsky Prospekt/Gostiny Dvor unless indicated.

Arirang, 20 8-ya Sovietskaya Ul., Korean & Japanese. Daily 11am–11pm. Metro Pl. Vosstaniya, tel. 274-0466.

Bagrationi, 5/10 Liteiny Pr., Georgian cuisine & music. Metro Chernyshevskaya, tel. 272-7448.

Barcelona, 25 Ligovsky Pr., Spanish cuisine & wine. Tel. 277-0213. Daily noon–11pm. Metro Ploshchad Vosstaniya.

Brazilia, 24 Kazanskaya Ul., Brazilian cuisine & live Latin music. tel. 320-8777. Daily noon–3am; Fri–Sat till 6am.

Cat, 24 Karavannaya, Russian & European dishes; live piano music. tel. 315-3800.

Federico Fellini, 4/2 Mal. Konyushennaya Ul., cinema-themed restaurant (film stars' favorite recipes); interior atmosphere of a film set. Tel. 311-5078. Daily noon–1am.

Hermitage, 8 Palace Square in the General Staff Bldg near the Museum. Two halls (one "Music" and the other "Cameo") both with a Russian and European menu. tel. 314-4772.

Il Grappolo, 5 Belinsky St. One of city's best Italian restaurants, with the downstairs bar, Probka (Try). tel. 273-4904.

Kalinka-Malinka, 5 Italyanskaya Ul., Russian food & Gypsy songs. tel. 314-2681.

Krasny Terem (Red House), 10 Razezzhaya Ul., Chinese food. Metro Vladimirskaya, tel. 315-9145.

La Cucina, 13 Ul. Belinskovo, Greek dishes. Daily 11am–midnight. Metro Mayakovskaya, tel. 272-7943.

La Strada, 27 Bol. Konyushennaya Ul., Italian food & pizza (kids looked after by nanny). Daily noon–11pm. tel. 312-4700.

Le Chandeleur, 1 Bol. Konyushennaya. French food in a French-style village interior; live music. Daily 11am–midnight. tel. 314-8380.

Macaroni, 23 Rubinshtein St. Italian-style trattoria with delicious, reasonably-priced food. Metro Vladimirskaya, tel. 315-6147.

Milano, 8 Karavannaya Ul., Italian cuisine & live music. tel. 314-7348.

Saigon Neva, 33 Kazanskaya Ul., Asian decor, Vietnamese & European food. Daily noon–11pm. Metro Sennaya Ploshchad, tel. 315-8872.

Shogun, 26 Ul. Vosstaniya. Japanese cuisine & chef. Daily noon–11pm. Metro Ploshchad Vosstaniya, tel. 275-3297.

Sudarnaya (Lady), 28 Rubinshteina Ul., Russian food. Daily noon–11pm. Metro Dostoevskaya, tel. 312-6380.

Troika, 27 Zagorodny Pr., Russian & European cuisine. Closed Sundays. Metro Dostoevskaya, tel. 113-5343.

GRIBOYEDOV CANAL (NABEREZHNAYA GRIBOYEDOVA KANALA)

All addresses are Griboyedov Canal unless otherwise shown. Nearest Metro for all listed is Nevsky Prospekt.

Chaika German Restaurant, 14, German cooking and draft & bottled beer. Daily 11am–3am. tel. 312-4631.

Denisov & Nikolaev Café, 77, Cosmopolitan café and dessert hall. tel. 571-9495.

Golden Ostap, 4 Italianskaya Ul. International food and wine selection & live music in the evenings. Daily 11am–1am. tel. 303-8822.

Gridnitsa, 20, Russian grill bar with live music. Daily 11am–11pm. tel. 314-8705.

Joy, 28/1, European dishes. tel. 312-1614.

Laima Bistro, 16, serves inexpensive Russian food. Near the Cathedral on Spilled Blood. Open 24 hours. tel. 318-9219

Sakura, 12, Japanese cuisine (chef from Japan). Daily noon–11pm. tel. 315-9474.

Sankt-Peterburg, 5, gourmet Russian food, live music and folk shows, interior decorated from Peter the Great times. Daily noon–2am. tel. 314-4947.

Señor Pepe's Cantina, 3 Ul. Lomonosova. Tel. 310-2230.

FONTANKA RIVER EMBANKMENT (NABEREZHNAYA REKI FONTANKI)

All addresses are Fontanka River Embankment unless otherwise shown.

Bagrationi, 5/19 Liteiny Pr. Georgian cuisine; live music. tel. 272-7448.

Bella Leone, 9 Vladimirsky Pr (Golden Country Complex), Home-made pasta, grappa selection. Business lunch noon–4pm. Metro Vladimirskaya, tel. 575-2229.

Demidov, 14, Russian cuisine prepared from old recipes, live music, views of Summer Garden. Metro Gostiny Dvor, tel. 272-9181.

Don Quixote, 21 (in House of Friendship), International cuisine & music. Tel. 313-4517. Daily 10am–6pm. Metro Gostiny Dvor.

Dostoevsky, 9 Vladimirsky Pr (Golden Country Complex), Old 18th-century Russian recipes mixed with European cuisine. Many dishes cooked right in front of you. Business lunch 12–4pm. Open 24 hours. Metro Vladimirskaya, tel. 575-2229.

Erivan, 51, Delicious Armenian cuisine. tel. 703-3820.

Pavlin, 118, Chinese cuisine. Tel. 251-1441. Metro Teknologichesky Institut.

Kavkaz-Bar, 18 Karavannya Ul. Georgian food in a Caucasian-style courtyard; live music after 8pm. Metro Gostiny Dvor, tel. 312-1665.

Kyoto, 77, Japanese cuisine. Daily 1pm–midnight. Metro Sadovaya, tel. 310-2547.

La Cucaracha, 39, Tex-Mex cuisine & live music. Daily noon–1am; Friday/Saturday till 5am. Metro Gostiny Dvor, tel. 110-4006.

Propaganda, 40, European & Russia. Daily noon–5am. Metro Gostiny Dvor, tel. 275-3559.

Shinok, 13 Zagorodny Pr., Ukrainian cuisine. Daily 24 hrs. Metro Vladimirskaya, tel. 311-8262.

Triton, 67 Fontanka, Expensive, European-Russian cuisine. tel. 310-9449.

MOIKA CANAL EMBANKMENT (NABEREZNAYA REKI MOIKI)
All addresses are Moika Canal Embankment unless otherwise shown.

Arcadia, 58a Moika, Pleasant atmosphere with Russian-Euroepean food. tel. 571-6173.

Adamant, 72, Russian & European fare, classical interior. Daily 1–11pm. Metro Nevsky Prospekt, tel. 571-5575.

Assambleya, 26, Russian & French fare & live nightly entertainment. Daily noon–11pm. Metro Nevsky Prospekt, tel. 314-7510.

Caliph, 21/6 Millionnaya. Oriental cuisine, live music (saxophone). tel. 312-2265

Feliks at the Yusupov Palace, 94, European & Russian cuisine. Daily noon–11pm. Metro Sennaya Ploshchad, tel. 314-8790.

Idiot, 82, cosy home environment, vegetarian food and all kinds of drinks. Popular hang-out. tel. 315-1675.

Pogreba Monakha (The Monk's wine cellars), 22 Millionnaya, European fare, wine and live music. tel 314-1353.

Privyet Komedianta (The Comedians' Rest Stop), 1/7a. Traditional Russian fare in a classic cabaret-style setting, featuring stage performances. tel. 314-3849.

Shury-Mury, 28 Galernaya Ul. Russian and European food; live instrumental music at night. tel. 110-6399.

The City, 20, American, Russian & European dishes; interior design is France of the 30s. Daily 11am–midnight. Metro Nevsky Prospekt, tel. 314-1037.

The Pushkin Inn, 14, traditional Russian and European, live music. tel. 314-0663.

NEVSKY PROSPEKT
All addresses are Nevsky Prospekt unless otherwise shown.

Afrodita, 86, specializes in seafood from lobsters to oysters. Daily noon–5am. Metro Pl. Vosstaniya, tel. 275-7620.

Beck's, 60, European & draft beer. Daily noon–2am. Metro Mayakovskaya, tel. 277-7855.

California Grill, 176, American-style food. Daily 11.30am–2am; Fri/Sat/Sun opened 24 hrs. Metro Aleksandra Nevskovo, tel. 274-2422.

Cinema, 151, Russian & European. Metro Aleksandra Nevskovo, tel. 277-5953.

Comme il Faut, 13 Stremyannaya Ul. Very stylish interior and French food. Metro Mayakovskaya, tel. 110-8000.

Grand Hotel Europe, 1/7 Mikhailovsky Ul. (off Nevsky), tel. 329-6630, **Rossi's** (Mediterranean-style food); **Chopsticks**, (Cantonese & Sichuan specialties); **Europe** (Russian & European); **Mezzanine Café & Caviar Bar**. **Sadko's** (tel. 329-6000) has Western-style bar food, draft beer & nightly entertainment. Daily 11am–1am. Metro Nevsky Pr.

El Toro, 1/71 Marat, Spanish food & live music. Metro Mayakovskaya, tel. 311-2602.

Forty Nevsky, German restaurant (delicious desserts) and bar; pre-revolutionary interior. tel. 312-2457.

Gambrius, 125, Czech beer-club. Daily 11am–2am. Metro Pl. Vosstaniya, tel. 320-7606.

Garçon Bistro, 95, Parisian-style café with tasty, traditional French. Open for breakfast, lunch and dinner. Metro Pl Vosstaniya, tel. 277-2467.

Gondola, 150, European seafood specialities. Daily 24 hrs. Metro Aleksandra Nevskovo.

Hannover, 142, European & Russian; beer on tap. Daily 9am–midnight. Metro Pl. Vosstanyia, tel. 271-2811.

Kalinka-Malinka, 5 Italyanskaya Ul. Russian food and gypsy music. tel 314-2681.

Kolkhida, 176, Georgian cuisine and folk singing. Daily noon–1am. Metro Aleksandra Nevskovo, tel. 272-2514.

Las Palmas, 67, Brazilian/Spanish & live music. Daily 1pm–6pm. Metro Mayakovskaya, tel. 314-6248.

Lavka Smirdina Café, 22–24, Russian café bakery. Metro Nevsky Prospekt, tel. 315-9017.

Lenin's Mating Call (Zov Ilicha), 34 Kazanskaya, Decorated with images of Lenin, Dzerzhinsky and Stalin; the menu is divided into 'Soviet' (Russian) and 'Anti-Soviet' choices (Western) choices. Selection of flavored vodkas. Business lunches. tel. 571-8641.

Literatornoye Kafe, 18, Dates back to czarist times (In 1837, Pushkin left for his duel from here); Russian cuisine, classical music & literary and poetry readings. Daily 11am–1am. Metro Nevsky Pr. tel. 312-6057.

Marrakesh, 3/5 Karavannya, Moroccan cuisine, 100 kinds of world teas. Metro Gostiny Dvor, tel. 717-8047.

Matrosskaya Tishina, 54 Ul Marata. Cosy with French gourmet chef. Metro Ploshchad Vosstaniya, tel. 164-4413.

Milano Ristorante, 8 Karavannaya Ul., Traditional Italian fare & live music. tel. 314-7348.

Nevsky Restaurant, 71, Russian & European fare. Metro Mayakovskaya, tel. 311-3093.

Palkin, 47, The original eatery was established in 1785; today it's set in an elegant and formal atmosphere with expensive and excellent Russian and French food and an extensive wine list. Reservation recommended. tel. 103-5371. www.palkin.ru

Patio Pizza, 30 & 182, Italian dishes & pizza. Daily noon–midnight. Pizza Hut is at 96.

Planet Sushi, 94, Metro Mayakovskaya, tel. 273-3558.

Rasputin, 163, Russian cuisine and variety show on weekends. tel. 277-3141.

Sheraton Nevsky Palace Hotel, 57, has the **Landskrona** (Mediteranean) Restaurant. **St Petersburg Corner Restaurant**, 79, Russian food according to old St Petersburg recipes, live music. Metro Mayakovskaya, tel. 571-8589.

Stray Dog (Jacquot's House) 5/4 Arts Square (in basement). Previous hang-out of 20th-century artists and poets (such as Akhmatova, Mandalstam), which continues to feature poetry, paintings and song. Open 11.30am–11.30pm. tel. 315-7764.

Stroganoff Yard, 17, located in court of Stroganov Palace, live music in evenings. Metro Nevsky Prospekt, tel. 315-2315.

Tebe Mirra, 10 Mal. Konushennaya, Fantastic vegetarian restaurant. tel. 314-5697.

Tinkoff, 7 Kazanskaya Ul. The city's only brewery-restaurant, which offers beer, burgers, and even a sushi bar. Metro Gostiny Dvor, tel. 314-8485.

Torres, 53, Spanish & disco. Daily noon–5am. Metro Gostiny Dvor, tel. 113-1453.

U Kazanskovo, 26, Russian-style food. Daily 11am–10pm. Metro Nevsky Prospekt, tel. 314-2745.

Zhyly-Byly, ("Once upon a time"), 52, Corner of Sadovaya. Decorated with folk-lore objects, it's open 24 hours a day, serving salads and pastries; wine list. tel. 314-6230.

COFFEE
Idealmaya Chaska (Ideal cup), 26, Ru, is St Petersburg's equivalent to Starbucks (branches all over the city).

SUNDAY BRUNCHES
Astoria Hotel, in the **Zimny Sad** (Winter Garden) has daily breakfasts from 7–10.30am.

Europe Restaurant in the Grand Hotel Europe has a daily buffet breakfast (7–10.30am), and Sunday brunch 12–3pm. The **Mezzanine Café** also has pastries and cappucino.

Taleon, 59 Moika Canal. Connected with Yeliseyev Palace Hotel, it offers Sunday brunch in an opulent restored mansion. Also offers an expensive dinner menu, and more affordable business lunches. Metro Nevsky Prospekt. tel. 312-5373.

ICE CREAM PALORS
Baskin Robbins, main locations are at 79 Nevsky, 19 Ekaterininsky Kanal and 31 Moskovsky Pr. Daily 10am–11pm.

Frogs Pool, 24 Nevsky, Ice cream, desserts & pizza. Daily 10am–10pm.

Gino Ginelli, 14 Giboyedov Canal, ice cream to salads. Daily 10am–midnight.

Vienna Café in the Nevsky Palace Hotel, 57 Nevsky Prospekt.

INTERNET CAFÉS
CafeMax, 90/92 Nevsky, open 24 hours.

Internet Café, 7 Ekaterininsky (Griboyedov) Canal. Metro Gostiny Dvor.

Internet Café Zebra, 85a Nevsky (in Moskovsky Train Station), tel. 336-3346.

Quo Vadis, 24 Nevsky Pr. Open 24-hours. (Another Internet Club is at 90 Nevsky) Metro Gostiny Dvor, tel. 311-8011.

Red Fog, 30–32 Kazanskaya (in Hotel Angleterre), open 24 hours Grivtsova. Metro Sadovaya, tel. 595-4138.

Tetris Internet Café, 33 Ul. Chernyakhovskovo. Daily noon–11pm. Metro Ligovsky Prospekt, tel. 164-8759.

SADOVAYA ULITSA
All addresses are Sadovaya Ulitsa unless otherwise shown.

Bomond, 28 Gorokhovaya Ul., European dishes & French wine. Tel. 325-9452. Daily 11am–11pm. Metro Sennaya Ploshchad.

Count Suvorov, 26, Splendid dishes from the aristocratic Russian court; musical evenings. Metro Gostiny Dvor, tel. 315-4328.

Circus, 4 Mal. Sadovaya. Small, turn-of-the-century tavern with European-Russian fare. Local avant-garde artists painted the walls. tel. 310-1077.

Diana, 56, European & Russian with French wines. Live music. Metro Sadovaya, tel. 310-9355.

Hong Kong, 42, Southern Chinese cuisine and music. tel. 310-1211.

Metropol, 22, City's oldest restaurant with Russian food. Daily noon–11pm. Metro Gostiny Dvor, tel. 310-1845.

Mu-Mu, 94, European dishes & live music. Daily 11am–11pm. Metro Sadovaya, tel. 114-5084.

Montreal-Canadians, 22 Apraksin Per, Canadian fare. Metro Sennaya Ploshchad, Tel. 310-9256.

Onegin, 11, the restaurant turns into a dance club at night. Interior feels as if you are in a 19th-century baroque aristocratic home. Tel. 311-8384.

Oriental Paris (Vostochny Paris), 12/23, Chinese-Russian selections. Tel. 314-8373.

Parnas Bistro, 8 Mal Sadovaya. Hearty Russian food. tel. 571-2526.

Pekin, 60, Chinese food and karaoke bar. Metro Sadovaya, tel. 310-1141.

Shashlychnaya, 36, Shish-kebab specialities. Daily 11am–midnight. Metro Sennaya Ploshchad, tel. 310-7946.

Tusovka, 40, Delicious Russian-style dishes. tel. 319-4426.

SENATE SQUARE (SENATSKAYA PLOSHCHAD) & ST ISAAC'S CATHE-DRAL AREA

Astoria Hotel, 39 Bol. Morskaya, **Davidov's** Russian cuisine. tel. 313-5815 and **Winter Garden** (Zimny Sad) tel. 313-5815.

Karavan, 46 Voznensky Pr. Middle-eastern restaurant decorated with Turkish carpets and even a stuffed camel. Offers more than 30 varieties of kebabs. tel. 310-5678.

Krokodil, 18 Galernaya Ul., Latin American and live music. tel. 314-9437.

Le Francais Bistro, 20 Galernaya Ul., French cuisine, wines and dancing. Daily 11am –1am. tel. 315-2465.

Prince Kochubey's Palace, 7 Konnogvardeysky Bul. European. tel. 312-8934.

Senat, 1 Galernaya Ul. in the Senate Bldg., European cuisine, wines and over 60 different beers from Holland and Belgian. Daily 11am–5am. tel. 314-9253.

Tandoor, 2 Voznesensky Pr., Indian cuisine. Daily noon–11pm. tel. 312-3886.

Tandoori Nights, 4 Voznesensky Pr. Indian cuisine. tel. 312-8772.

BOLSHAYA AND MALAYA MORSKAYA

Antalia, 14 Bol Morskaya, Turkish/ Azerbaijani cuisine. tel 315-9536.

At Gorchakov's, 19 Bol Morskaya. Four rooms with 19-century interiors. Russian-Ukrainian recipes; live music. tel. 238-0412.

Borsalino, 39 Bol. Morskaya, bar-eatery with live piano music. tel. 313-5115.

Christopher Columbus, 27 Bol Morskaya, Russian-European selections in a maritime setting. Evening live music. tel. 312-9761.

Creature, 6 Bol. Morskaya, French food and music. Daily 11am–midnight. tel. 318-6132.

Da Vinchi, 15 Mal. Morkskaya, Italian & live music. Daily noon–6am. tel. 571-0173.

House of Architects Nikolai Restaurant, 52 Bol. Morskaya (five minutes walk from St Isaac's Cathedral). European & Russian dishes. Daily noon–11pm. tel. 311-1402.

Khristofor, 27 Bol. Morskaya, seafood specialities. Daily noon till late. tel. 314-6213.

Le Paris, 63 Bol. Morskaya, French gourmet cuisine. tel. 311-9545.

Nikolai, 52 Bol Morskaya. Savory Russian fare. tel. 571-1402.

Pizzicato, 45 Bol. Morskaya, Italian. tel. 315-0319.

Seville, 7 Mal. Morskaya. Spanish cuisine and variety performances. Metro Nevsky Prospekt, tel. 315-5371.

Vienna, 13 Mal. Morskaya, Austrian, European & Russian selections with live piano music. tel. 571-3227.

THEATER SQUARE

Dvorianskoye Gnezdo (Noble Nest), 21 Ul Dekabristov, located in the former teahouse of the Yusupov Palace. One of city's top restaurants, Russian & European cuisine, live classical music. Expensive. Metro Sadovaya, tel. 312-3205.

1913, 13/2 Voznensky Pr. Serves giant portions of Russian-European-style fare, and close to the Mariinsky Theater. Reservations recommended. Metro Sennaya Ploschad, tel 315-5148.

Nairi, 6 Dekabristov, European-style café. Daily 11am–11pm. Metro Sadovaya, tel. 314-8093.

Za Stsenoi (Backstage), 18/10 Theater Squar, across from the Mariinsky Theater, it overlooks the Kryukova Canal. It's decorated with theater props and the floors are from the old Mariinsky stage. European dishes, wines. Reservations needed for post-theater dining. tel. 327-0684.

Zolotoi Drakon (Golden Dragon), 62 Dekabristov, Chinese and Southeast Asian dishes. tel. 114-8441.

EAST

Amadeus, 34 Suvorovsky Pr., Austrian-style food. Daily noon–1am. tel. 275-7172

Antalia, 19 Metallistov Pr., Azerbaijani/Turkish cuisine and folk orchestra. Daily 1pm–3am. tel. 224-0208.

Evropa, 41 Bolsheokhtinsky Pr., European cuisine. Daily noon–midnight. tel. 227-2924.

Kavkaz, 5 Ul. Stakhanovtseva, Traditional dishes & wines from the Caucasus. A summer café is open 24 hours. tel. 444-4309.

Harbin, 58 Nekrasov & 34 Ul. Zhukovskovo. Chinese cuisine. Daily 1–11pm. Metro Ploschad Vosstaniya.

Polese, 4 Sredneokhtinsky Pr., Belorussian cooking. Daily 12.30–11.30pm.

Schwabsky Domik, 28 Novocherkassky Pr. German food and beer. Daily 11am–1am. Metro Novocherkassky, tel. 528-2211.

U Petrovicha, 44 Sredneokhtinsky Pr., Russian/European; 18th-century decor. Music and dancing Thursday/Sunday nights. Daily noon–11pm. tel. 227-2135.

SOUTH

Daddy's, 73 Moskovsky Pr., a mixture of everything from European and Chinese to Mexican dishes; live music. Metro Frunzenskaya, tel. 252-7744.

Korean House, 2 Izmailovsky Pr., Korean cuisine. Folk music. Metro Teknologichesky Institut. tel. 259-9333.

Nektar, 25 Malodetskoselsky Pr., Russian food, wine tasting room and live piano/violin music. Daily 10am–11pm. Metro Teknologichesky Institut, tel. 316-6818.

Mama Roma, 192 Moskovsky Pr., Italian food and pizza. Daily 9am–2am. Metro Park Pobedy, tel. 294-0152.

Moskovsky Trakt, 125 Moskovsky Pr., Russian fare. Metro Moskovskiye Vorota, tel. 298-1327.

On Les Champs Elysees, 200 Moskovsky Pr., French & Russian; live music. Daily 24 hrs. Metro Moskovskaya, tel. 443-3047.

Okhotnichya Izba, 30 Lermontovsky Pr., hearty Russian food. Metro Teknologichesky Institut, tel. 114-6088.

Pietari, 222 Moskovsky Pr., European & Scandinavian-style cuisine. Daily 11am–midnight. Metro Moskovskaya (on way to airport), tel. 373-1809.

Rotunda, 157 Moskovsky Pr., European & Russian. Daily 10am–2am. Metro Park Pobedy, tel. 298-3584.

Seoul, 24 Narvsky Pr., Korean cuisine. Daily 11am–11pm. Metro Narvskaya, tel. 186-6720.

Shalom, 8 K. Tomchaka Ul. Traditional Jewish and live music. Daily noon–11pm (closed on shabbat). Metro Moskovskiye Vorota, tel. 327-5475.

Yantze, 208 Moskovsky Pr., Chinese cuisine. Daily noon–11pm. Metro Moskovskaya, tel. 293-3475.

Zolotoi Altai, 8 3-ya Krasnoarmeiskaya Ul., Siberian dishes. Metro Teknologichesky Institut, tel. 316-7930.

PETROGRAD SIDE (PETROGRADSKAYA STORONA), NORTH
Open noon to midnight, Metro Gorkovskaya, unless otherwise shown.

Akvarium, 10 Kamennoostrovsky Pr., (near Peter and Paul Fortress) Tasty Chinese cuisine & Singapore chef. tel. 326-8286.

Antverpen Grand Kafe, 13/2 Konversky Pr., Dutch-style café with international dishes, live music and Belgian draft beer. tel. 233-9746.

Aquarel, Restaurant/boat docked next to Birzhevoy Bridge. Fashionable with Fusion food. Panoramic views. Metro Petrogradskaya, tel. 320-8600.

At Gorchakov's, 19 Bol Monetnaya. Interior atmosphere of provincial town, traditional Ukrainian & Russian dishes. Piano music. Metro Gorkovskaya, tel. 233-9372.

Austeria at Peter and Paul Fortress, Traditional Russian dishes in quaint 18th-century setting; live music. tel. 238-4262.

Ayvengo, European fare, grilled on charcoal, medieval interior. Open 24 hrs/day. Metro Chkalovskaya, tel. 230-7212.

Demyanova Ukha, 53 Kronversky Pr., traditional Russian seafood specialties (such as fish soup). Live music. Daily 12–11pm. Metro Gorkovskaya, tel. 232-8090.

Dionis Club, 31/20 Ul. Voskova. European & Russian. Daily 11am–11pm. Metro Gorkovskaya, tel. 233-3352.

Flora, 5 Kamennoostrovsky Pr., European & Russia; live music. Daily 1pm–12.30am. tel. 232-3400

Fortetsiya (Fortress), 7 Ul. Kuibysheva, European & Russian. tel. 233-9468.

Gorny Orel (Mountain Eagle), 1a Alexandrovsky Park (near the zoo entrance). Georgian fare and shashlik. A clag jug of Georgian wine is served with meals. tel. 232-3282.

Khizhina Rybaka (Fisherman's Hut), 59 Kronversky Pr., seafood dishes. tel. 232-8040.

Koreisky Dom (Korean House), 5 Torzhkovskaya Ul., Korean & karaoke. Daily 11am–11pm. Metro Chornaya Rechka, tel. 324-4015.

Mesto (Place), 16 Lenina Ul., International food. tel. 230-5359.

Moskva (Moscow), 18 Petrograd Emb. Moderately-priced Russian food. tel. 332-0200.

Mozart, 23 Kronversky Pr., Hungarian cuisine. tel. 232-5555.

Na Zdorovye, 13 Bolshoi Pr., Russian food. tel. 232-4038.

Picasso Art Restaurant, 3 Bolshoi Pr., European and Russian.Thursday–Saturday till 6am. Metro Sportivnaya, tel. 232-3787.

Russian Fishing, 11 Yuzhnaya Doroga, Krestovsky Island. The attraction is you have to catch your own meal! tel. 323-9813.

Russian Moderne, 32 Ul. Lenina, Georgian/Russian fare & piano music. Daily noon –11.30pm. Metro Metro Petrogradskaya, tel. 232-6208.

Salhino, 25 Kronvserksy Pr. European atmosphere, artwork on walls for sale. tel. 232-7891.

Sushi Bar Fujiyama, 54 Kamennoostrovsky Pr., Japanese with tatami room. Daily noon–11pm. Metro Petrogradskaya, tel. 234-4922.

Tbilisi, 10 Sytninskaya Ul., Georgian cuisine. Daily noon–11.30pm, tel. 232-9391.

Tête-à-Tête, 65 Bolshoi Pr., European cuisine & piano music. Daily 1–11pm. Metro Petrogradskaya, tel. 232-7548.

VYBORG SIDE, NORTH
(Near Metro Chornaya Rechka (across Bolshaya Nevka River)

Nobile, 74 Bol. Sampsonievsky Pr., Italian & European cuisine. Daily noon–11pm. (Saturday from 2pm). Metro Lesnaya, tel. 245-3644.

Sem-Sorok, 108 Sampsonievsky Pr., Jewish cuisine and live music. Daily noon–11pm; Monday 5–11pm. Metro Lesnaya, tel. 246-3444.

Slavyanskoye Podvorie (Slavic Town House), 13 Lanskoye Hwy. Traditional *izba* decor; Russian food and music. Daily noon–11pm. tel. 246-2256.

Staraya Derevnya, 72 Ul. Savushkina, Russian food and theatrical performances on weekends. Daily 1–11pm. Metro Staraya Derevnya, tel. 431-000.

Uratu, 25 Runeva Ul., Armenian & Georgian cuisine. Metro Proveshcheniya, tel. 558-6919.

VASILYEVSKY ISLAND
Byblos, 5 Maly Pr, Lebanese cuisine, wines and hookahs. Oriental dancing after 8pm. tel. 325-8564.

Chardash, 22 Makarova Emb (near Tuchkov Bridge), Hungarian cuisine. Open 24 hrs. Metro Vasileostrovskaya, tel. 323-8588.

Delovoi Mir, 103 Bolshoi Pr., Russian & European. Metro Primorskaya, tel. 355-5123.

Great Wall, 11 Sredny Pr., Chinese cuisine. Daily 12.30pm–midnight. Metro Vasileostrovskaya, tel. 323-2638.

Kalinka, Sezdovskaya 9-aya Liniya, traditional Russian dishes and folk music. Daily 11am–11pm. Metro Vasileostrovskaya, tel. 323-3718.

Ketino, 23, 8th Liniya. Georgian cuisine and vegetarian dishes. tel. 326-0196.

Koloradsky Otets (Colorado Father), 72 Maly, Popular bar. tel. 355-0859.

Pirozhki Café, 50 1st Liniya. Delicious home-made pierogi, stuffed with many different fillings. Metro Vasileostrovskaya, tel. 328-7860.

Poseidon, 92 Bolshoi Pr., Seafood specialities. Metro Vasileostrovskaya, tel. 322-7237.

Restoran, 2 Tamozhenny Per. Serves virtually every traditional Russian dish imaginable. tel. 327-8979.

Swagat, 91 Bolshoi Pr., Indian cuisine. Daily noon–11pm; closed Monday. Metro Vasileostrovskaya, tel. 322-2111.

The Old Customs House, 1 Tamozhenny Per, 5-star French haute cuisine. tel. 327-8980/8982.

Zhemchuzhina, 2 Shkipersky Protok, Traditional Jewish dishes and music. Metro Vasileostrovskaya, tel. 355-2063.

(For restaurant locations for towns outside of St Petersburg, see individual listings under Vicinity of St Petersburg.)

Shopping
ANTIQUES
Most open daily 11am–7pm. Some antiques may need export certificates.

Antikvariat, 17 Kamennoostrovsky Pr., antiques and old books. Metro Gorkovskaya.

Antikvarnaya Galereya Arkhipova, (Arkhipov's Antique Gallery), 31 Griboyedov Kanal, antiques & furniture. Metro Nevsky Prospekt. At no. 19 is **Griboyedovsky** with jewelry, icons & furniture.

Antikvarny Tsenter (Antique Center), 21 Nalichnaya Ul., includes paintings, china and furniture. Metro Primorskaya.

Peterburg Salon, 54 Nevsky Pr., Everything from art, furniture and paintings to icons, jewelry and antique souvenirs. Metro Gostiny Dvor. Other antique shops on Nevsky are **Belazh**, at no. 57; **Na Staronevskom** at no. 122; **Nevsky 86** and **Antikvariat** at no. 86, **Antique Retro** at no. 48, and **Russkaya Starina** at no. 20.

City Antiques, 32 Moika Emb. (copies of items in 'History of St Petersburg' musuem).

Demak and **Garmoniya** are at 31/32 Mokhovaya Ul, with art and furniture. Metro Chernyshevskaya.

Rapsodiya, 13 Bol. Konyushennaya Ul., has a collection of everything from antiques to sheet music & musical instruments. Metro Nevsky Prospekt. At no. 19/8 is **Starinnye Chasy** (Old Watches).

Sekunda, 61 Liteiny Pr (in courtyard) has posters, postcards, books, Soviet art & old photos. Metro Mayakovskaya. The **Antique Center** is at no. 24. Metro Chernyshevskaya.

Starye Gody (Old Years) is at 23 Bol. Monetnaya Ul. Metro Gorkovskaya.

Tertsiya, 5 Italyanskaya Ul. has old books, postcards, paintings, china and icons. Metro Nevsky Prospekt.

ARTS & HANDICRAFTS, SOUVENIRS
Most open daily 11am–7pm.

Ananov, 31 Nevsky. Very expensive jewelery and crafts designed by Andrei Ananov who has taken up art in the style of Carl Fabergé.

Art City can be found at 3 Ul. Dekabristov and 16 Robespera Emb. Has souvenirs and paintings.

Babushka, 33 Lieutenant Shmidta Emb. The store is decorated in the style of a 17th-century nobleman's house, filled with souvenirs.

Dyukamen, 20 Liteiny Pr., souvenirs. Metro Chernyshevskaya.

Imperator (Emperor), 3 Dekabristov St. The spacious rooms house works by well-known Russian artists and craftsmen, and other souvenirs.

Katarina Souvenir Boutique, 46 Angliskaya Emb, a huge collection of souvenir items.

Khudozhestvenniye Promysly (Arts & Handicrafts), 51 Nevsky, has traditional wooden & ceramic crafts, and amber. Metro Mayakovskaya. Other shops on Nevsky are: **Nasledie** (Heritage) at no. 116 with a collection of boxes, jewelry, embroidery & paintings (Metro Pl. Vosstaniya); **Nevsky Buket** (Nevsky Bouquet) at no. 184 (Metro Pl. Aleksandra Nevskovo); and **Stroganovsky** at no. 17 with traditional Russian arts & handicrafts, lacquers and jewelry (Metro Nevsky Prospekt).

The city's best **Outdoor Market** is across from the Cathedral of the Savior on the Blood, selling a wide range of souvenirs and paintings.

The Hermitage e-Shop, offers high-quality relicas of masterpieces from the Hermitage Museum's collections. www.hermitagemuseum.org. From the US or Canada, call toll-free (866) 701-5653, or world-wide (818) 701-5652.

Klenovaya Alleya Art Market is an outdoor arts and handicrafts market held in the Klenovaya Alley near the St Petersburg Circus.

Melodiya, 34 Moskovsky Pr. and 47 Bolshoi Pr. Sells records, CDs and musical instruments.

Onegin, 11 Italianskaya St. The 8 rooms are chocked full of Russian gifts and souvenirs.

Ozhidaniye Prazdnika (Waiting for a Holiday) has three outlets at 6 Kamennoostrovsky Pr, 3 Ul. Mayakovskaya, and 29 Sadovaya.

Podari (Give a Gift), 13 Sadovaya, souvenirs. Metro Gostiny Dvor.

Singer's Bridge (Pevchesky Most), 20 Moika Emb. Metro Nevsky Pr.

Vasilyevsky Ostrov (Vasilyevsky Island), 31 Sredny Pr., items include wooden handicrafts, lacquer boxes, model ships. Metro Vasileostrovskaya.

Vernissage, 1 Griboyedov Canal. Open 8am–9pm. All types of Russian souvenirs.

ART GALLERIES
Display and sale of paintings and graphics. Most open daily 11am–7pm.

Art-Gorod Gallery, 47 Bolshoi Pr. Vasilyevsky Island. Metro Vasileostrovskaya.

Atlantida Art Salon, 123 Obvodnovo Kanal. Metro Frunzenskaya.

Borey Art Gallery, 58 Liteiny Pr. Exhibition & poetry readings. The **Mikhailov Gallery**, at no. 53, features the city's largest private modern art collection. Metro Mayakovskaya.

Delta, 51 Nevsky, has paintings, graphics, photos and sculptures (closed Sunday/ Monday). Other shops on the Nevsky are: **Independent Artists Society**, at no. 20; **D-137**, at no. 90/92 (closed Sunday); **Galereya 102** (Metro Mayakovskaya); **National Center**, 38/2 Bol Morskaya, exhibits and sells contemporary paintings from realism to avant-garde.

Exhibition Center of St Petersburg Artist Union (also known as the Blue Drawing Room) **Gallery** at no. 166 (Metro Pl. Aleksandra Nevskovo); **Gildiya Masterov** (Craftsmen Guild) at no. 82 (Metro Mayakovskaya).

Free Arts Foundation, 10 Pushkinskaya St. (Entrance at 53 Ligovsky Pr), Founded in 1989, during the new perestroika period, it continues to function as a 4,000 square meter arts cooperative with galleries and studios; and is still a central part of the city's progressive (often weird) arts scene. It's also connected with the **Fish Fabrique**, where well known city bands play. Generally closed Monday/Tuesday. Metro. Pl Vosstaniya. Down Ligovsky Prospekt, at no. 64, is the **Arts Collegium**, a gallery that showcases graphics and modern art.

INK Club, 79 8-aya Liniya, Vasilevsky Island. Hosts art exhibitions, concerts and other eclectic soirees. Also has a library and bookshop.

Marina Gisich Gallery, 121 Fontanka, Apt 13. One of the city's best small galleries, exhibiting both Russian and international   artists. Metro Teknologichesky Inst. www.gisich.com.

Plastika, 91 Griboyedov Canal, has paintings, sculptures and ceramics. Metro Sennaya Ploshchad.

S.P.A.S., 93 Moika Emb, collection of modern paintings; closed Sunday. The **Heritage New Arts Shop** is at no. 37. Metro Sadovaya.

BOOKSTORES
Most open daily 10am–7pm.

ABUK, 18 Nevsky Pr., antique books & other collector's items. Metro Nevsky Prospekt. **Writers' Bookstore** is at no. 66.

Bukvoed, 13 Nevsky Pr. Open 9am–10pm.

Dom Knigi (House of Books), at 28 Nevsky, the largest bookstore in the city. Great selection from books to posters and postcards.

England-British Books, 40 Fontanka, fiction & artbooks in English.

Iskusstvo (Art), at 16, 52 & 72 Nevsky, has a large collection of art books, art supplies and other souvenirs. Metro Nevsky Prospekt.

Knizhnaya Lavka Pisateley (Writer's Bookcorner), 66 Nevsky, has both Russian and foreign-language books & art albums. Metro Gostiny Dvor.

The European Book Company, 7 Saperny Per., English-language books, audio & video tapes. Metro Chernyshevskaya.

DEPARTMENT STORES
Most are open daily 9am–9pm. Department stores are known as an "Univermag." These are a few of the ones located in the city center.

Apraksin Dvor, Ul. Sadovaya, is a complex containing various shops. The Veschovoi Rinok (flea-market) takes place inside the courtyard. Metro Nevsky Prospekt.

Bolshoi Gostiny Dvor, 35 Nevsky. The old shopping & trade center of the city; entirely rennovated and now contains many Western stores. Metro Gostiny Dvor.

DLT (Leningrad House of Trade), 21 Bol. Konyushennaya Ul. Metro Nevsky Prospekt.

Kalininsky Univermag, 40 Kondratevsky Pr. Metro Ploshchad Lenina.

Maly Passazh, 44 Nevsky, has clothing, shoes & furs. **Passazh** is right next door at no. 48. **Stockmann** is down the street at no. 25.

Tatyana Parfenova's Fashion House, 51 Nevsky, exclusive collection of women's clothing. Metro Nevsky Prospekt.

FURS
Auctions are usually held in January, May/June, and October, when fur hats are the best buy. Selections can also be found at major department stores and street kiosks.

Soyuzpushnina (Auction-house), 98 Moskovsky Pr., Mon–Fri 9am–5.30 pm. Tel. 298-4636/7601. The retail store is **Elita**. Metro Frunzenskaya.

Lena, 50 Nevsky. Metro Gostiny Dvor. The **Fur Fashion House** is nearby at no. 61 Nevsky and **Salon IT** at no. 25. At no. 57 is **Vinicio Pajaro**, and no. 44, **Mala Mati**.

Mekha na Kamennoostrovskom, 13 Kamennoostrovsky Pr., has clothing made from fur and leather. **12 Mesyatsev** (12 Months) is at no. 45. Metro Gorkovskaya.

Rot Front, has three locations at 34 Bol. Morskaya, 5 Smolenki Reki Embankment (Metro Vasileostrovskaya) and 22 Zagorodny Pr. (Metro Vladimirskaya).

JEWELRY
Agat (Agate), 47 Sadovaya. Metro Sadovaya.

Cosmos Gold, 22 Nevsky, has gold and silver jewelry. Other Nevsky locations are: **Ananov** at no. 31 with Fabergé jewelery; **Babylon** at no. 69; **Belazh** at no. 57; **Biryuza** at no. 69; **Diamond Classic** at no. 86; **Maska** at no. 13; **Monomakh** at no. 90; **Polyarnaya Zveda** (Pole-Star) at no. 158; and **Russian Jewelry House** at no. 27.

Grand Collection Gallery, 40 Suvorovsky Pr. Dedicated to the creations of Carl Fabergé's daughter and grandson. tel. 279-9778.

Na Vasileostrovskoi, 27 6th Liniya, has jewelery and antiques. Metro Vasileostrovskaya on Vasilyevsky Island.

Russkiye Samotsvety, 8 Karla Fabergé Pl, has Russian gems. Metro Nevsky Prospekt. Another gem store, **Samotsvety**, is at 4 Mikhailovsky Ul.

Yuvelirny Salon (Jewelry Salon), 6 Mal. Sadovaya. Metro Gostiny Dvor.

FARMERS' MARKETS OR RINOK
Markets usually open Mon–Sat 8am–7pm; Sun 8am–4pm. (*Highly recommended)

***Kuznechny Rinok**, 3 Kuznechny Pereulok. Metro Vladimirskaya. (Opened in 1927, this was the city's first indoor market. Still the best market with a wide selection of food and produce.)

Maltsevsky Rinok, 52 Ul. Nekrasova. Metro Pl. Vosstaniya.

Moskovsky Rinok, 12 Ul. Reshetnikova. Metro Elektrosila.

Narvsky Rinok, 54 Stachek Pr. Metro Kirovsky Zavod.

Nevsky Rinok, 75a Obukhovskoi Oborony Pr. Metro Elizarovskaya.

***Polyustrovsky Rinok**, 45 Polyustrovsky Pr. Famous for its outdoor weekend pet & bird market; really busy on weekends, so best to get there early (fur, clothing & hats in back). Metro Ploshchad Lenina. (More popularly known as the Kondratevsky Market.)

Sennoy (Hay) Market, 4/6 Moskovsky Pr. Metro Sennaya Ploshchad.

Sytny Rinok (oldest market), 3/5 Sytninskaya Pl. Metro Gorkovskaya.

Torzhkovsky Rinok, 20 Torzhkovskaya Ul. Metro Chornaya Rechka.

Vasileostrovsky Rinok, 16 Bolshoi Pr, Vasilyevsky Island. Metro Vasileostrovskaya.

Velomarket, 13 Pestelya Ul, bicycle market; closed Sunday.

The City Clothing Market (Gorodskaya Veshchevaya Yarmarka) is at 8 Yuriya Gagarina Ul. Has a large election of imported goods, clothes and electronics. Open daily 10am–7pm. Metro Park Pobedy.

MUSEUMS
For information on city museums and exhibitions, call 063. (*Highly recommended)

Anichkov Palace, 39 Nevsky Pr., Houses several concert halls. Metro Gostiny Dvor, tel. 310-4395.

*Anna Akhmatova Museum, 34 Fontanka Emb. in the former Sheremetyev Palace (entrance from 53 Liteiny Pr.). Daily 10.30–6.30pm; closed Monday and last Wednesday of month. Metro Gostiny Dvor, tel. 117-0952, 272-2211. www.akhmatova.spb.ru.

Anna Akhmatova Silver Century, 14 Avtovskaya Ul., Daily 10–5.30pm; closed Sun. Metro Avtovo, tel. 185-0442.

Applied Arts Museum, 13–15 Solyanov Lane, Tuesday–Saturday 11am–5pm. Metro Chernyshevskaya, tel. 273-3258.

Blok House, 57 Dekabristov Ul., Daily 11am–5pm; Tues until 4pm; closed Wednesday and last Tuesday of month. Metro Sadovaya, tel. 113-8616/8633.

Botanical Museum, 2 Professora Popova. Open Wednesday/Saturday/Sunday 10am–5pm. Greenhouse 11am–4pm; closed Friday. Metro Petrogradskaya, tel. 234-8470/1764

Brodsky House, 3 Pl. Iskusstvo. Tuesday–Sunday 11am–7pm. Metro Gostiny Dvor, tel. 314-3658, 272-0006.

Cathedral of the Savior-on-the-Blood, see Places of Worship, page 662.

*Cemeteries (Necropolis) of Alexander Nevsky Monastery (See also Museum of Urban Sculpture), 1 Monastery River Emb. Lazarevskoe is open 11am–7pm, closed Thursday; Nikolskoe, open 9am–6pm, closed Saturday and Sunday; Tikhvinskoe, open 11am–7pm, closed Thursday. Metro Pl. Aleksandra Nevskovo. tel. 274-2952.

Communication Museum, 7 Pochtamtskaya Ul., Tuesday–Saturday 9.30am–6pm. Metro Nevsky Pr., tel. 315-4873.

*Circus Museum, 3 Nab. Fontanka, worth a visit before performance begins (enter circus building from side by canal; 2nd floor.) Monday–Friday 12–5pm. tel. 313-4413.

*Cruiser Aurora, 4 Petrogradskaya Nab., Open 10.30am–4pm; closed Mon and Fri. Metro Gorkovskaya, tel. 230-8440.

*Defense and Siege of Leningrad Museum, 9 Solyanoi Lane, tel. 275-7208. Open 10am–5pm; Tues until 4pm; closed Wed and last Thurs of month. Metro Chernyshevskaya. (Another museum is located in the Memorial to Heroes of the Defense of Leningrad on Victory Square. Metro Moskovskaya. See page 505.)

Dostoevsky Literary Memorial Museum, 5/2 Kuznechny Lane. Open 11am–6pm; closed Monday and last Wednesday of month. Metro Vladimirskaya, tel. 571-4031. www.md.spb.ru.

Fyodor Shalyapin Museum, 26 Graftio. Open noon–6pm. Closed Monday, Tuesday. Metro Petrogradskaya, tel. 234-1056.

*Hermitage, 34 Dvortsovaya Nab., Open 10.30am–5pm; Sunday until 4pm; closed Monday. Metro Nevsky Pr., tel. 110-9625, 311-3465. www.hermitagemuseum.org.

History of Religion Museum, 14/5 Pochtamtskaya Ul., Open 11am–5pm; closed Wednesday. Metro Sadovaya, tel. 314-5838/117-0495.

Icebreaker *Krasin* Museum, moored 22L Schmidta Emb, Vasilyevsky Island, Daily 10am–5pm; closed Monday. Metro Vasileostrovskaya, tel. 356-2969.

*Kazan Cathedral/Religion Museum, 2 Kazanskaya Pl., Daily 11am–5pm; Saturday –Sunday 12–5pm; closed Wednesday. Metro Nevsky Pr., tel. 311-0495.

Kirov Museum, 28 Kamennoostrovsky Pr., Open 11am–6pm; closed Wednesday. Metro Petrogradskaya, tel. 346-1481/0217.

*Kunstkammer/Museum of Anthropology and Ethnography, 3 Universitetskaya Nab., Daily 11am–6pm; closed Monday and the last Wednesday of month (museum of Ethnography closed last Friday of month). Metro Vasileostrovskaya. (also visit the nearby Zoological Museum.), tel. 328-1412. www.kunstkamera.ru.

Lomonsov Museum, Kunstkammer, 3 Universitetskaya Nab., Open 11am–5pm; closed Monday. tel. 328-1011. At 17 Universitetskaya is the Museum of the Academy of Art exhibiting works of Academy graduates. Wednesday–Sunday 11am– 6pm.

Marble Palace, 5/1 Millionnaya Ul., Displays art exhibitions. Open 10am–5pm; Monday until 4pm; closed Tuesday. Metro Nevsky Pr., tel. 312-9196.

Menschikov Palace, 15 Universitetskaya Nab., Hall of chamber music and exhibits on 18th-century Russian culture. Open 10.30am–4.30pm; closed Monday. tel 323-1112.

Mikhailovsky Castle (now a branch of the Russian Museum), 2 Sadovaya Ul., Open 10am–5pm; closed Tuesday. Metro Gostiny Dvor, tel. 313-4173, 210-4173.

Militia Museum, 12 Poltavskaya Ul., Monday–Friday 10am–5pm. Metro Pl. Vosstaniya, tel. 279-4233.

Museum of the Arctic and Antarctic, 24a Marata Ul., Wednesday–Sunday 10am– 4.15pm. Metro Vladimirskaya, tel. 113-1998. www.polarmuseum.sp.ru.

Museum of the Artillery and Military, 7 Aleksandrovsky Park, Wednesday–Sunday 11am–6pm, closed last Thursday of month. Metro Gorkovskaya, tel. 232-0296.

Museum of Bread, 73 Ligovsky Pr., Tuesday–Saturday 10am–5pm. Metro Pl. Vosstaniya, tel. 164-1110.

Museum of History of Leningrad (Rumyantsev Mansion) 44 Angliskaya Nab., (A branch of St Petersburg City Museum), open 11am–5pm; Tuesday until 4pm; closed Wednesday and last Tuesdat of month. tel. 117-7544.

Museum of Musical Instruments, 5 Isaakievskaya Pl., Wednesday/Thursday/Sat urday 12–6pm. Metro Nevsky Pr., tel. 314-5394.

Museum of Political History, in the former Kchessinskaya Mansion at 2/4 Ul. Kuybysheva, Open 10am–5pm; closed Thursday. Metro Gorkovskaya, tel. 233-7052.

Museum of Printing, 32/2 Nab. Moika, open 11am–5pm; Tuesday until 4pm; closed Wednesday and last Tuesday of month. Metro Nevsky Pr., tel. 312-0977.

Museum of Urban Sculpture, on the grounds of the Alexander Nevsky Monastery, Also an exhibit of avant-garde paintings and graphics. Open 10am–7pm; closed Thursday. Metro Ploshchad Aleksandra Nevskovo, tel. 274-2635.

Naval Central Museum, 4 Birzhevaya Pl., open 10.30am–5pm; closed Monday/ Tuesday and last Thursday of month. Metro Vasileostrovskaya, tel. 328-2701. www.museum.navy.ru.

Nabokov House, 47 Bol. Morskaya, open 11am–6pm, Friday until 5pm, weekends 12–5pm; closed Monday, Tuesday. tel. 315-4713.

Nekrasov House, 36 Liteiny Pr., open 11am–5pm; closed Tuesday. Metro Chernyshevskaya, tel. 272-0165.

October Railroad Central Museum, 62 Liteiny Pr., Open 11am–5pm; Friday until 4pm; closed Saturday/Sunday. Metro Vladimirskaya, tel. 168-6891.

Oreshek Fortress and Memorial Center of WWII, Schlüsselburg on Orekhovy Island. Open daily 10am–5pm from May 15 to October 1. tel. 238-4679.

***Peter and Paul Fortress/History of St Petersburg Museum**, 3 Petropavlovskaya Krepost, open 11am–5pm; closed Wed and last Tues of month. Metro Gorkovskaya, tel. 238-4511/0505; excursion tel. 238-4540.

***Peter the Great's Cabin**, 6 Petrovskaya Nab., open 10am–5.30pm; closed Tuesday and last Monday of month. Metro Gorkovskaya, tel. 232-4576.

***Piskarevskoye Memorial Cemetery**, 74 Nepokorennykh Pr., Metro Pl. Muzhestva, tel. 247-5716.

Planetarium, 4 Aleksandrovsky Park, open 10.30am–6pm; closed Monday. Metro Gorkovskaya, tel. 233-5312.

Popov's Memorial Museum, 5/33 Professora Popova, open 10am–5pm; closed Saturday/Sunday. Metro Petrogradskaya, tel. 234-5900.

Pushkin House Literature Museum, 4 Makarova Nab., open 11am–5pm; closed Saturday/Sunday. Metro Vasileostrovskaya, tel. 328-0502.

***Pushkin House Museum**, 12 Nab. Moika, tel. 312-1962. Open 10.30am–5pm; closed Tues and last Fri of month. Metro Nevsky Prospekt. www.museumpushkin.ru.

Railway Museum, 50 Sadovaya Ul., open 11am–5.30pm; closed Fri/Sat and last Thurs of month. Metro Sennaya Pl., tel. 315-1476. (If you're a railway buff, ask here about the National Railway Bridge Museum at Krasnoye Selo, the Shushary Museum of Railway Technology in Paravozy Museum, or the Lebyazhe Railway Museum Depot in the town of Lubyaze.)

Razliv Barn (Lenin) Museum, 3 Emelyanova in town of Sestroretsk, tel. 434-6117. Also in the same town is the Razliv Hut Museum, tel. 437-3098. Both open 10am–6pm; closed Mon.

Repin Penates Estate, 411 Primorskoye Shosse in town of Repino, (Check first, the estate is often closed for repairs) Open 10.30am–5pm; closed Tuesday. tel. 231-6828. **Rimsky-Korsakov Memorial House**, 28/3 Zagorodny Pr., Open 11am–6pm; closed Mon/Tues. Metro Vladimirskaya, tel. 113-3208.

***Russian Museum**, 4 Inzhenernaya Ul., Open 10am–5pm (10am–4pm on Mondays); closed Tuesday. tel. 314-8368/595-4248. Right next door, at 4/1, is the **Russian Museum of Ethnography**, open 10am–6pm; closed Monday. Metro Gostiny Dvor. www.rusmuseum.ru.

Russian Vodka Museum, 5 Konnogvardeisky Bul. The history of vodka, even offers vodka tastings and traditional Russian hors dóeuvres. Open daily 11am–10pm.

Sheremetyev Palace, 34 Fontanka. Open 12–6pm; closed Monday/Tuesday. tel. 272-4441.

***St Isaac's Cathedral**, Isaakievskaya Pl., Open 11am–6pm; closed Wednesday. (Great panorama of city from its roof.) Metro Nevsky Pr., tel. 315-9732.

***Stroganov Palace**, 17 Nevsky Pr., Open 10am–5pm; closed Tuesday. Metro Nevsky Pr., tel. 314-5801/311-2360.

Suvorov Museum, 43 Kirochnaya Ul. Open 10am–5pm; closed Tuesday/Wednesday. tel. 279-3914.

Submarine *Narodovolets* is moored at 10 Shkipersky Protok, Open 11am–3pm; closed Monday/Tuesday/Friday. tel. 356-5266.

***Summer Garden and Palace of Peter the Great**, Open 10.30am–5.30pm; closed Tuesday. Metro Chernyshevskaya, tel. 314-0456, 312-7715.

Theater and Musical Arts Museum, 6 Pl. Ostrovskovo., open 11am–6pm; Wednesday 1–7pm; closed Tuesday. Metro Gostiny Dvor, tel. 311-2195.

Vagonova Ballet School, 2 Rossi Ul., A small ballet museum is located within the school. Usually closed to public, but try visiting. tel. 312-1702/311-4317.

Wax Museum, 41 Nevsky Pr., located in the Beloselsky-Belozersky Palace, now also a concert hall. Special tours on the history of the palace are also given. Open daily 11am–6.30pm. Metro Gostiny Dvor, tel. 315-5636.

Yelagin Palace, 1 Yelagin Island, open 11am–5pm; closed Monday/Tuesday. Metro Staraya Derevnya, Krestovsky Ostrov, tel. 430-1131.

*****Yusupov & Rasputin Museum** and the Yusupov Palace, 94 Nab. Moika, open daily 12–4pm; tours leave every hour from noon to 4pm daily. tel. 314-9883/9892.

*****Zoological Museum**, 1 Universitetskaya Nab. Here resides the 45,000-year-old Siberian baby mammoth, Dima, the unofficial city mascot! (Also try to visit the nearby Kunstkammer.) Open 11am–5pm; closed Friday. Metro Vasileostrovskaya, tel. 328-0112.

Zoo, 1 Aleksandrovsky Park, summer hours, 10am–7pm; winter hours, 10am–4pm. Metro Gorkovskaya, tel. 232-2839.

LIBRARIES

St Petersburg has more than 3,000 libraries with over 250 million volumes. The best known libraries are the **Russian National Library** at 18 Sadovaya Ul., tel. 310-7137, and 36 Fontanka, daily 9am–9pm, Metro Nevsky Pr.; and the **Russian Academy of Sciences Library** at 1 Birzhevaya Liniya, daily 8am–8pm, closed Sunday, tel. 328-3592. **Hermitage Museum Research Library**, 34 Dvortsovaya Emb., daily 10am–5pm, closed Sunday/Monday tel. 110-9664. The **American Info. Center** is at 5/1 Millionnaya Ul., tel. 110-6416; Monday–Friday 1–5pm.

PLACES OF WORSHIP
RUSSIAN ORTHODOX
CATHEDRALS

(There are over 30 other churches located throughout the city, and over half now conduct daily religious services.) Women should dress modestly and cover heads; men remove hats.

Cathedral of the Holy Trinity, 1 Monastery River Emb. in Alexander Nevsky Monastery, Services Monday–Saturday at 7am, 10am and 5pm; Sunday and religious holidays 7am, 8am, 10am and 5pm. Metro Pl. Alek. Nevskovo, tel. 274-1702/0409. www.lavra.spb.ru.

Cathedral of Prince Vladimir, 26 Blokhina Ul., Services Monday–Saturday at 10am and 6pm; Sunday and religious holidays 7am, 10am and 6pm. Metro Sportivnaya, tel. 232-7625.

Cathedral of the Savior on the Blood, 2a Nab. Griboyedova Kanala, (now open to visitors after an extensive renovation and houses an icon collection), daily 11am–6pm; closed Wednesday. Metro Nevsky Pr., tel. 315-4053.

Cathedral of the Transfiguration, 1 Preobrazhenskaya Pl., 1-2 services Monday–Saturday at 10am and 6pm; Sunday and religious holidays at 7am, 10am and 6pm. Metro Chernyshevskaya, tel. 272-3662.

Church of the Savior, 1 Konyushennaya Sq., Services Saturday/Sunday at 10am and 5pm. Burial service for Pushkin was held here on 1st February 1837. Metro Nevsky Prospekt, tel. 311-8261.

Kazan Cathedral, 2 Kazanskaya Pl. Services daily at 10am and 6pm. (Also houses a Museum of Religion.) Metro Nevsky Pr., tel. 318-4528. www.kazansky.ru.

Smolensky Icon of the Holy Mother Church, 24 Kamskaya, Services Monday–Saturday 10am and 5pm; Sunday 7am, 10am and 5pm. tel. 321-1483.

Smolny Cathedral of the Resurrection of Christ, 3/1 Rastrelli Pl., Open 11am–6pm; closed Thursday. No services. Metro Chernyshevskaya, tel. 271-9182/7632.

St Isaac's Cathdral, 1 Isaakievskaya Pl., open 11am–6pm; closed Wednesday. Beautiful panorama of the city from the top. No services. tel. 315-9732.

St Nicholas Cathedral, 1/3 Nikolskaya Pl., services daily 7am, 10am and 6pm. Metro Sadovaya, tel. 114-6926.

St Peter and Paul Cathedral, in Peter and Paul Fortress, open 11am–5pm; closed Wednesday. No services. tel. 238-4540.

Trinity Cathedral, 7a Izmailovsky Pr., Several domes were destroyed by fire in 2006. Open Monday–Friday 9am–5pm; Saturday–Sunday 8am–5pm. Services (chapel) Wednesday–Sunday at 10am and 5pm. Metro Teknologichesky Inst, tel. 310-7402.

OTHER DENOMINATIONS

Armenian Church of Holy Resurrection, 29 Nab. Smolenki. Daily 10am–6pm. Services daily 10am and 6pm; Saturday at 5pm. Metro Vasileostrovskaya, tel. 350-5301.

Armenian Orthodox Church of St Catherine, 40/42 Nevsky Pr., open daily 9am–11pm. Services daily 9am and 11pm; Saturday at 5pm. Metro Nevsky Pr., tel. 318-4108.

Baptist Church of the Gospel, 52 Borovaya Ul., Services Wednesday at 6.30pm; Friday 6pm; Sunday 11am and 4pm. Metro Ligovsky Pr., tel. 166-4419.

Buddhist Temple Monastery, 91 Primorsky Pr., Open daily 9am–7pm. Services at 9am. Metro Staraya Derevnya, tel. 430-1341.

Cathedral of the Assumption of the Virgin, 11a 1-aya Krasnoarmeiskaya Ul., Services Monday–Saturday 8.30am and 7pm; Sunday 10am, 11am, 12pm, 1pm and 7pm. Metro Teknologichesky Institut, tel. 316-4255.

Church of Evangelical Christian Baptists, 29a Bol. Ozernaya Ul., Services Tuesday/Thursday at 7pm; Saturday 11am; Sunday 10am, 4pm. Metro Ozerki, tel. 553-4578.

Church of St Catherine, (Lutheran) 1 Bolshoi Pr., Vasilyevsky Island, services Sunday at 11am and 1pm. tel. 552-0816.

Evangelical Christian Church, 2 Pargolovo Polevaya Ul., Services Wednesday at 7pm; Saturday 6pm; Sunday 12pm. Metro Ozerki, tel. 594-8463.

Evangelical Lutheran Church of St Peter & Paul, 22/24 Nevsky Pr., Services held on Sunday at 10.30am in Spartak movie house, 8 Kirochnaya Ul., tel. 311-2423.

Hare Krishna Temple, 17 Bumainaya Street. Metro Narvskaya, tel. 186-7259.

Jewish Community Centre, 3 Rubenshteina Street (see *Synagogue*), tel. 113-3889.

Mosque of the Congregation of Moslems, 7 Kronversky Pr., Open daily 12–4pm. Services daily at 2.20pm in summer and 1.20pm in winter. Metro Gorkovskaya, tel. 233-9819.

Roman Catholic, Our Lady of Lourdes, 7 Kovensky Pereulok, services Monday–Saturday 9am, 7pm; Sunday and religious holidays at 9am, 10.30am, 12pm, 2pm, and 7pm. Metro Mayakovskaya, tel. 272-5002.

Roman Catholic Church of St Catherine, 32/34 Nevsky Pr., Services (in chapel) Monday–Saturday 8am, 6.30pm; Sunday 9.30am, 10.45am, 12pm, 1.30pm, 3pm, 7pm. Metro Nevsky Pr., tel. 350-5301.

Synagogue (Choral) and Jewish Religious Center, 2 Lermontovsky Pr., Open 10am–8pm; closed Sat. Services Mon–Fri and Sun at 9am, Sat at 10am. (Time of sunset determines evening services.) tel. 114-0078/1153.

Synagogue at Preobrazhenskoe Jewish Cemetery, 2 Aleksandrovsky Fermy Pr. The cemetery (tel. 262-0397) is at 66a. Daily 9am–4pm.

ENTERTAINMENT
THEATERS AND CONCERT HALLS

Theater, concert and circus performances usually begin on weekdays at 7pm, 7.30pm or 8pm with matinée performances on weekends, with an earlier evening show. Be on time, as ushers are strict about curtain time! The date and time of the performance, and your seat number are written on the ticket. It is usually required to leave your coat in the lobby cloakroom. Opera glasses are available for a small rental fee. Programs are also sold. During the intermission, drinks and snacks are served in the lobby. Each theater usually has its own box office, open daily 11am–7pm, closed 3–4pm. Tickets also often can be reserved through a travel/service bureau in your hotel, or purchased from street/Metro theater kiosks. Also try the Central Ticket Office at 42 Nevsky Prospekt (open 9am–8pm, closed Sunday, Metro Nevsky Pr.). The Central Aerial Communications Agency at 7/9 Nevsky (1st floor) sells all theater tickets. The Mariinsky Theater box office is at the corner of Nevsky and Perinnaya Lane (1st Floor) by Gostiny Dvor. The ticket office for the State Philharmonic is nearby at 2 Mikhailovskaya Ul., and for the St Petersburg Opera, at 4 Marata. On the night of the performance you can also bargain for tickets from touts at the door.

Aleksandrinsky or Pushkin Academic Drama Theater, the oldest drama theater in Russia, at Pl. Ostrovskovo. Box office open daily 11am–7pm; performances Tuesday–Friday at 7pm; Saturday/Sunday at 11am and 6pm. Metro Nevsky Pr./Gostiny Dvor, tel. 110-4103/312-1545.

Anichkov Palace Carnival Hall, 30 Nevsky Pr., Metro Nevsky Pr., tel. 310-9744/113-4362.

Askold Makarov Theater of Ballet, 15 Ul. Mayakovskovo, Metro Mayakovskaya, tel. 273-1997.

Ballet Theater of Konstantin Tatchkine, 20 Liteiny Pr., Metro Chernyshevskaya, tel. 273-4881.

Beloselsky-Belozersky Palace Mirror Hall, 41 Nevsky Pr., Has symphonic musical concerts and theater performances. Metro Nevsky Pr., tel. 315-4784/5236.

Bolshoi Drama Theater, 65 Nab. Fontanka, Performances Tuesday–Sunday at 7pm. Box office open daily 11am–7pm. Metro Sennaya Ploshchad, tel. 310-0401/9242.

Bolshoi Puppet Theater, 10 Nekrasov Ul., Performances Wednesday–Sunday at 11.30am, 2pm and 7pm. Metro Chernyshevskaya, tel. 272-8215.

Boris Eyfman's Contemporary Ballet, 2 Lizy Chaikinoy Ul., Metro Sportivnaya, tel. 230-7891.

Bryantsev Theater for Children, 1 Pionerskaya Pl., Metro Pushkinskaya, tel. 112-4066.

Children's Ballet Theater, 4 Stachek Pr., Metro Narvskaya, tel. 186-2426.

Children's Ice Theater, 148 Ligovsky Pr., Metro Moskovskaya, tel. 112-8625.

Circus, 3 Nab. Fontanka, tel. 314-8478, Closed Monday/Wednesday/Thursday. Metro Gostiny Dvor, ticket office 570-4411; museum tel. 570-4413.

Comedian's Refuge, 27 Sadovaya Ul., Performance at 7pm. Metro Sennaya Ploshchad, tel. 310-1074.

Comedy Academic Theater, 56 Nevsky Pr., Metro Nevsky Pr., tel. 314-2610.

Composer's House, 45 Bol. Morskaya, tel. 311-0262.

Drama Theater (Komissarzhevskaya), 19 Italyanskaya Ul., Metro Gostiny Dvor, tel. 311-3102.

Estrady Variety Theater, 27 Bol. Konyushennaya Ul., Metro Nevsky Pr., tel. 314-7060.

Etno Folklore Theater, 3 Mokhovaya Ul., Metro Chernyshevskaya, tel. 275-4226.

Glinka Kapella Concert Hall, 20 Moika River Emb., Metro Nevsky Pr., tel. 314-1058.

Glinka Maly Zal, 30 Nevsky Pr., Chamber music. tel. 311-8333, 312-4585.

Hermitage Theater of Concerts and Ballets, 34 Dvortsovaya Nab. in Hermitage complex, Metro Nevsky Pr., tel. 297-0226.

Litsedei Minus 4 Clown-Mime Theater, 14 Chernyshevskovo Pr., Metro Chernyshevskaya, tel. 272-8879.

Maly Drama Theater, 18 Rubinshteina Ul., Metro Dostoevskaya, tel. 113-2094/2078.

Maly Theater of Opera and Ballet Mussorgsky, 1 Pl. Iskusstvo. Metro Nevsky Pr., Tel. 318-1949/595-4305.

Mariinsky (Kirov) Theater of Opera and Ballet, 1 Teatralnaya Pl., Ticket office open daily 11am–7pm. tel. 326-4141, 114-1211. www.mariinsky.ru.

Marionettes Theater, 52 Nevsky Pr., Metro Gostiny Dvor, tel. 310-5879, 311-2156.

Miniature Theater, 15 Mokhovaya Ul., Metro Chernyshevskaya, tel. 272-0015.

Music Hall and Baltiisky Dom, 4 Aleksandrovsky Park, Metro Gorkovskaya, tel. 232-6244/9201.

Musical Comedy Theater, 13 Italyanskaya Ul., Metro Nevsky Pr., tel. 570-4205, 4316.

Na Neve for Children, 5 Sovyetsky Per., Metro Tekno. Inst., tel. 259-9104.

Nikolaevsky Folklore Art and Dance Center, 4 Truda Pl., tel. 311-9304.

Open Air (or Len Soviet) Theater, 12 Vladimirsky Pr., Metro Vladimirskaya, tel. 113-2191.

Oktybrsky Concert Hall, 6 Ligovsky Pr., Metro Pl. Vosstaniya, tel. 275-1273.

Petersburg Mosaic Dance Theater, 41 Nevsky Pr., Metro Mayakovskaya, tel. 274-1287.

Petersburg Opera, 33 Galernaya Ul., Performances held at Yusupov Palace and Hermitage Theater. tel. 312-3982, 314-7586. www.opera.spb.ru.

Puppet Opera for Children, 4 Tavricheskaya Ul., Metro Chernyshevskaya, tel. 275-6090.

Puppet Theater of Fairy Tales, 121 Moskovsky Pr., Metro Moskovskiye Vorota, tel. 298-0031.

Rimsky-Korsakov Opera and Ballet Theater, 3 Teatralnaya Pl., Metro Sadovaya, tel. 312-2507/2519.

Rock Opera Theater, 36 Labutina Ul. tel. 114-0547.

Shostakovich Philharmonic Hall, 2 Mikhailovskaya, tel. 311-7333.

Smolny Cathedral Concert Hall, 3/1 Rastrelli Pl., Metro Chernyshevskaya, tel. 271-9182.

St Petersburg Hotel Concert Hall, 5/2 Pirogovskaya Nab., Metro Pl. Lenina, tel. 542-9680.

Theater of Satire, 48 Sredny Pr., Metro Vasileostrovskaya, tel. 323-0012.

Vagonova School Of Ballet, 2 Zodchedgo Rossi Ul., small ballet museum located inside; performances by pupils in Mariinsky ensembles. tel 312-1702, 311-4317.

Zazerkaye Music and Drama Theater, 13 Rubinsteina Ul., Metro Dostoevskaya, tel. 164-1895.

JAZZ AND BLUES

Check *Pulse St Petersburg* and other publications for current listings. Many have a cover charge to enter.

Che Café-Club, 3 Poltavskaya Ul. One of the more popular city hang-outs, live music 10pm–2am; open 24 hrs. Metro Pl. Vosstaniya, tel. 277-7600. www.cafe-clubche.ru

Jazz Philharmonic Hall, 27 Zagorodny Pr. Concerts in Big Hall at 7pm, Ellington Hall 8pm. Metro Vladimirskaya, tel. 164-8565. www.jazz-hall.spb.ru

JFC Jazz Club, 33 Shpalernaya Ul. One of the most progressive jazz venues in town. Daily from 7pm. Metro Chernyshevskaya, tel. 272-9850.

Jazz & Phrenia, 91 Nevsky. A jazz club-cum-restaurant which features a mixture of jazz/blues and Latin music. Daily noon–5am. Concerts at 9pm. Metro Pl. Vosstaniya, tel. 277-5130.

Jazz Time Bar, 41 Mokhovaya. Located in three small rooms which feature jazz, butes and Latin music. Opens from 11am. Live concerts Wednesday-Sunday at 9pm. Metro Chernyshevskaya, tel. 273-5379.

Jimi Hendrix Blues Club, 33 Liteiny Pr. Open 11am-1am; concerts start at 8:30pm. Live jazz, rock and blues concerts. Metro Chernyshevskaya, tel.279-8813.

Kvadrat, 83 Bolshoi Pr. Mainstream jazz; Monday–Saturday 8–11pm. Metro Vasileostrovskaya, tel. 315-9046.

Palitra Art Café, 5 Mal. Morskaya Ul. Live jazz and Blues. Photo and art exhibitions. Concerts at 9pm. Open from 9am–11pm. Metro Nevsky Pr., tel. 312-3435.

Sunduk Art Café, 42 Furshtatskaya (near the US Embassy). Pleasant café that features jazz, blues and rock. Daily 10am–11.30pm. Metro Chernyshevskaya, tel. 272-3100.

GAY AND LESBIAN NIGHTCLUBS

Nonexistent during the Soviet era (homosexuality received up to three years imprisonment), gay culture has finally taken root (but take care since 'gay bashing' still exists). In Russian, the slang word for gay is *goloboy*, meaning 'blue,' and the word for lesbian is *lesbianka*, taken from the English. Many have entrance cover fees.

Cabaret, 34 Ul Dekabristov, located in former Soviet "Palace of Culture", near the Mariinsky Theater. Thurs–Sun 11pm–6am. Metro Sennaya Pl. Xs.gay.ru.

Greshniki (Sinners), 29 Griboyedov Canal, spread over four floors. Daily 6pm–6am. Metro Gostiny Dvor. tel. 318-4291. www.greshniki.gay.ru.

Mono, 4 Kolomenskaya, small and intimate club. Daily 10pm–6am. Metro Ligovsky Prospekt, tel. 164-3678.

Tri El (Lesbian Club), 45 5-aya Sovietskaya, Closed Sunday/Monday. Women only except Thursday/Friday. Tuesday 5pm–midnight; Thursday 7pm-midnight; Wednesday/Friday/Saturday 9pm–6am. Metro Pl Vosstaniya, tel. 110-2016. www.triel.spb.ru

NIGHTCLUBS
Many have a cover charge to enter.

Deep Sound, 3 Chernyshevsky St. Housed in a former bomb shelter, it features live concerts and film screenings. Metro Ligovsky Pr., tel. 572-1111.

Fish Fabrique, 10 Pushkinskaya Ul. (entrance through arch at 53 Ligovsky Prospekt) Live rock and alternative music. Open daily after 3pm. Live gigs at 10.30pm. Open 24 hours a day. Metro Pl. Vosstaniya. tel. 164-4857. www.fishfabrique.spb.ru. **GEZ-21** is in the same complex on the 3rd floor. The 'experimental sound gallery' provides music, film screenings and even philosophical readings. Concerts begin at 9pm. www.tac.spb.ru

Front, 31 Ul Chernyshevskovo, located in a bomb-shelter, features live rock bands. Daily 7pm–6am. Metro Ligovsky Pr. www.front.vov.ru.

Griboyedov, 2a Voronezhskaya Ul (at intersection Kon. Zaslonova) Considered one of the city's best clubs, it's situated in a bomb shelter, and operated by the band Dva Somalota (Two Airplanes). Live mixed music and DJs spinning records. Wednesday is disco night. Daily 5pm–6am. Concerts start at 10pm; DJ parties after midnight. Metro Ligovsky Pr., tel. 164-4355. www.griboedovclub.ru

Havanna, 21 Moskovsky Pr. Smart Cuban-themed club with live bands and three dance floors playing Latin music. Daily until 6am. Metro Tek. Institute, tel. 259-1155. www.havanaclub.ru

Metro, 174 Ligovsky Pr. Multiple bars and three dance floors, popular with a younger crowd. Daily 10pm-6am. tel. 166-0204. www.metroclub.ru

Moloko (Milk), 12 Perekupnoi Per. Another favorite underground rock club. Open 7pm–midnight; closed Monday. Metro Pl Vosstaniya. tel. 274-9467. www.molokoclub.ru

Money Honey, 28-30 Sadovaya/Apraksin Svor. The city's first rock bar, complete with Confederate flags, and Elvis and Marilyn Monroe posters. Gets rowdy crowds. Bar opens at 11am. Daily shows at 8pm and 12.30am. tel. 310-0549. www.money-honey.org.

Located above it is **City Club**, specializing in pop/rock and reggae/blues. Live shows at 8.20pm; Friday/Saturday also at 1am. tel. 310-0549. www.moneyhoney.org/cityclub

Orlandia, 36a Mira Ul. Underground rock club is owned by Caravan and Rock Podval records. Daily concerts at 8pm. Metro Petrogradskaya.

Par.spb, 5b Alexandrovsky Park. Trendy spot that attracts some of the best world's DJs. (Par is the Russian word for steam-the site used to house a laundry.) Fri-Sun 11pm-8am. Petrograd side; Metro Gorkovskaya, tel. 233-3374. www.par.spb.ru.

Platforma, 40 Nekrasov Ul. Hosts rock and jazz concerts, along with other literary events and film screenings. Open 24 hours. Metro Pl. Vosstaniya, tel. 314-1104. www.platformaclub.ru.

Red Club, 7 Poltavskaya Ul. Housed in a former horse-fodder warehouse behind Moscovsky Train Station, it hosts some of the top local bands, along with foreign acts. Daily 6pm–6am. Concerts at 8pm Thursday–Sunday. DJ music after midnight. Metro Pl Vosstaniya, tel. 277-1366. www.clubred.ru.

Revolution, 26 Sadovaya. A restaurant during the day, it becomes a multi-level dance club at night, decorated in revolutionary symbolism. Daily 7pm–6am. tel. 571-2391. www.revolutionclub.ru.

Miscellaneous
The **St Petersburg City Tourist Information Center** is at 41 Nevsky Prospekt, Metro Gostiny Dvor, tel. 311-2843/2943. The **City Excursion Bureau of St Petersburg** can help with reservations, excursions and various tours of the city, 28 Sadovaya, Monday–Friday 10am–6pm. Metro Sadovaya, tel. 311-4019.

TRAVEL AGENCIES
Most can help with accommodation, travel, excursions, river cruises, theater tickets, airport pick-ups, and visa support.

Balt Express, 6 Vosstaniya Ul., tel/fax. 355-0178. www.betours.spb.ru.

Cosmos Travel, 35 2nd Liniya, Vasilyevsky Island, tel. 327-7256. www.guide.spb.ru.

Corporate Travel Network (CTN), 36 Shpalernaya Ul., tel. 346-7575. www.ctnet.ru.

Globus, 83 Moika Emb., Also offers guided tours of the city. tel/fax. 314-3259.

GO TO RUSSIA, is based in Moscow at (495) 255-5012. Visit www.gotorussia.com and find links to hotels, apartments, visa support, tours, and train schedules, etc. Other informative websites are: www.waytorussia.net; www.expresstorussia.com; www.Russian-st-petersburg.com and www.discount-travel-petersburg.ru.

Infobusiness, Offers hotel discounts throughout St Petersburg, Moscow and other CIS cities. tel. 324-4955/56.

Intourist-St Petersburg, 8 Admiralteiskaya Emb., tel. 314-6096. Tours in St Petersburg and other Russian cities. Mon–Fri 10am–6pm. Metro Nevsky Prospekt.

Lenart, 40 Nevsky Pr., tel. 315-1336/8402. Mon–Fri 9am–6pm. Metro Nevsky Pr.

Norvista (run by Finnish Air), 44 Kazanskaya Ul, tel. 326-1850/1856. Also provides ferry tickets and cruises.

Peter's Walking Tours offers over 10 walking (lasting 3 to 5 hours) and biking tours and trips to environs, all led by experienced locals, all fluent in English. www.peterswalk.com

Reiseburo Welt, 3 Moika, 6th floor. tel. 329-2656. www.welt.ru.

Sinbad, 28 3rd Sovietskaya Ul., tel. 327-8384. (Located in the Russian Youth Hostel, see this listing under hotel section).

St Petersburg Tourism Council, 27 Konyushennaya Pl. Many travel agencies located in this building.

St Petersburg Travel Company, 60 Moika Emb., City excursions for foreigners in different languages. Daily 9am–6pm. Metro Sennaya Pl. , tel. 312-2433.

TOUR COMPANIES: Bus Travel
The main bus terminal is at 36 Kanal Obvodnovo; From here, buses depart for Novgorod and Pskov. Metro Ligovsky Prospekt.

Eurolines, 10 Shkapina Ul., Bus routes to Baltic, and points in Europe. Daily 6.30am–11.30pm. Metro Baltiiskaya, tel. 168-2740/2748. www.eurolines.ru.

Davranov Travel, 17 Italyanskaya Ul., Offers excellent bus excursions within St Petersburg and to its suburban attractions. Check their ticket *kassa* at the corner of Dumskaya (Gostiny Dvor) and Nevsky where times and prices of excursions are posted (may charge more for foreigners). Their buses also depart from here. Excursions in Russian are much cheaper, just take along a guidebook. Excursions include city tours and trips to Peterhof, Tsarskoye Selo, Pavlovsk, Gatchina, Lomonosov, Kronstadt (average about 5 hours/less than $10), and to Vyborg, Novogorod and Pskov (one and two day trips). Other company excursion ticket *kassas* are also located here. If one is fully booked check out the others. (Other ticket *kassa* locations can be found at St Issac's and Palace Squares. Monday–Friday 10am–7pm; Sat 11am–3pm. Metro Gostiny Dvor, tel. 595-9173, 314-2344. www.davranov.ru.

Finnord, 37 Italyanskaya Ul., Bus service to Helsinki; buses depart from Hotel Pulkovskaya. Monday–Fri day10am–5pm; Saturday/Sunday noon–4pm. Metro Gostiny Dvor, tel. 314-8951.

Reichert Piter, 50 Furshtatskaya Ul., Bus service to Germany. Monday–Friday 10am–6pm. Metro Chernyshevskaya, tel. 273-0158.

Saimaan Liikenne, 53 Sadovaya Ul., Bus routes to Finland and Sweden; buses depart from Hotel Pulkovskaya. Monday–Friday 10am–6pm. Metro Sadovaya. tel. 310-2920.

Scandinavia-St Petersburg, 37 Lermontovsky Pr., Metro Baltiiskaya. Buses to Scandinavia, Baltic States, Moscow, Novgorod and Tver. tel. 113-8507.

Sovato, located in Hotel Pulkovskaya, 1 Pobedy Sq., Buses to Vyborg and Finland depart daily from Hotel Pulkovskaya, Moscow Hotel and Grand Hotel Europe. Metro Moskovskaya, tel. 123-5125.

TOUR COMPANIES: Boat Excursions, River Cruises & Ferries
The main Sea Passenger Terminal is at 1 Morskoi Slavy Square, Vasilyevsky Island. Metro Primorskaya. You can also purchase tickets directly at each Passenger Boat Dock listed in the next section. Check the travel kiosks on the corner of Nevsky Prospekt and Dumskaya Ul (end of Gostiny Dvor); often they offer tours to such places as Valaam and Kizhi, Peterhof, Kronstadt and Schlusselburg.

Baltic Prima Tour, 1 Morskoi Slavy Square, Ferries to Scandinavia. Monday–Friday 10am–7pm. Metro Primorskaya, tel. 322-6063.

Baltiiskaya Liniya (Baltic Line), 1 Morkskoi Slavy. Ferries to Sweden and Germany. Metro Primorskaya, tel. 322-1616.

Mir, 29–31 Nevsky Pr., River cruises in Russia. Monday–Friday 10am–7pm. Metro Gostiny Dvor, tel. 325-7122.

Neva Travel Company, 3 Dvinskaya Ul., Riverboat excursions along the Neva and Gulf, tel. 251-6577.

Nord-Soyuz, 9a Akademika Pavlova Ul., Excursions on the Neva and canals and to Peterhof and Kronstadt. Metro Petrogradskaya, tel. 234-6722.

Russian Cruises, 42 Kazanskaya Ul., Boat excursions and river cruises. tel. 311-4022/6925. www.russian-cruises.com.

St Petersburg Sputnik, 4 Chapygina Ul., river cruises on the Volga and to Lake Ladoga (and other Golden Ring Tours). Monday–Friday 10am–6pm. Metro Petrogradskaya, tel. 234-3500.

St Petersburg Central Travel Bureau, 27 Bol. Konyushennaya Ul., Monday–Fri day 10am–8pm; Saturday 11am–5pm. Metro Nevsky Prospekt, tel. 311-5538.

Sunny Sailing, 55 Vosstaniya Ul., River cruises to Lake Ladoga, Valaam and Kizhi, and south to Moscow and Astrakhan. Yacht charters. Monday–Friday 10am–8pm; Saturday noon–6pm. Metro Chernyshevskaya, tel. 327-3525, 332-9686. www.sailing.spb.ru.

BOAT PASSENGER DOCKS

Boats are in service between May and October. During crowded summer months, try to purchase tickets in advance (which you can do directly at each pier's ticket kiosk).

Anichkov Pier is at the corner of Nevsky Prospekt and the Fontanka River. Small riverboats depart daily about every half hour from 11am to 10pm. The canal tours last about one hour.

Griboyedov Canal Pier is on the corner of Nevsky and the canal. Boats operate between noon and 7pm and tour the canals.

Moika Pier is at the corner of Nevsky and the Moika River. Riverboats tour between noon and 8pm. (During the White Nights, all night river tours are also available.)

Hermitage Pier is across from the museum on Dvortsovaya Emb. From the upper deck, hydrofoils depart for Peterhof (from 9am to 3pm every 20 minutes), taking 20 minutes. From the lower deck, double-decker river boats depart for one-hour excursions along the Neva River. Another pier is situated across from Senate Square, near the Bronze Horseman Statue. Large riverboats leave for both one-hour trips along the Neva River, and across the Gulf to Peterhof.

Main River Terminal, at 195 Canal Obvodnovo, has river cruises (which depart every few days) to points north, such as Valaam and Kizhi (that last one to five days), and south to Moscow. Metro Proletarskaya.

Tuchkov Bridge Pier has daily hydrofoils to Kronstadt that depart every hour between 9am and 6pm.

CAR RENTALS

Many of the more expensive hotels have car rentals available. You often have to rent both a car and driver. Car, minivan, and bus rentals (with and without driver) can also be found. It is recommended not to drive yourself, unless it is really necessary. Public transportation is quite adequate to use around town.

EUROPCAR-SPB, 38a Fontanka. Both rental and chauffeur-driven cars available. Open daily 9am–9pm. tel. 380-1662.

Exima, 93a Kanal Obvodnovo. Open 24 hours. Rentals and passenger transfers. tel. 340-9030.

Hertz, at Pulkovo I and II airports, and a city office is at 'White Nights House' Business Center at 23 Mal. Morskaya Ul. tel 326-4505/4506. Open daily 10am– 6pm.

Pulkowo-Rent-a-car, 5 Staravaya Ul. tel 331-7779, 332-0101. Provides rental cars and insurance. Open daily 9am–8pm. www.pulkowrent.ru

CINEMAS

Most of the main movie theaters are situated along Nevsky Prospekt. **Avrora** (occasional movies in English) is at no. 60; **Barrikada** at no. 15; **Khudozhestvenny** at no. 67; **Kristall-Palas** (with occasional movies in English; www.crystalpalace.spb.ru) is at no. 72; **Neva** at no. 108; Pariziana at no. 80, and **Stereo** at no. 88. **Spartak**, at 8 Kirochnaya Ul. (Metro Chernyshevskaya), shows old movies from the Gosfilm archives. **Dom Kino** at 12 Karavannskaya, has some English movies.

HEALTH CLUBS AND SAUNAS

Most top-end hotels have fitness centers and saunas and/or swimming pools. Usually, for a fee, non-hotel residents or members can use the facility. (See Accommodation section.)

Galaktika, 2 Petrovsky Island. Open 8am–11pm; Saturday/Sunday 10am–10pm. Metro Sportivnaya.

Planet Fitness has five locations about town: 37 Kazanskaya (Metro Sadovaya, tel. 315-6220); 1/7 Mikhailovskaya (in Grand Hotel Europe); 18 Petrogradskaya Emb (Metro Gorkovskaya); and 224b Moskovsky Pr., open 8am–10pm and Saturday/Sunday 9am–9pm. www.fitness.ru.

Sun & Step, 63 Ul. Zhukovskovo. Open 9.30am–10pm; Saturday/Sunday 11am–7pm. Metro Ploshchad Vosstaniya.

SAUNAS & *BANYAS*

Upmarket *banya* usually have saunas, pools, showers, massage, and private rooms. There are over 50 banya complexes located throughout the city. (see Special Topic on *Banya*, page 418)

Bani 82 Moika, three banyas are located here. The main one was built by architect Count Pavel Suzor and opened in 1871. It was visited regularly by the aristocracy and was furnished accordingly with 300 bronze gas lamps; and the women's section was furnished in Louis XVI style. Today, much of the former splendor has gone, although remnants, such as wall tiles with Old Church Slavonic inscriptions, can still be seen. To get to the most historic one: go through the first yard and pass under the sign "Bani No. 43"; turn to the right, and go up the metal staircase and through the door at the top. (Well equipped with steam rooms, pool, bar and attendants.)

Banya Nevsky, 5/7 Marata Ul., Thursday–Sunday 8am–10pm. Metro Mayakovskaya, tel. 311-1400.

Banya House, several locations include 12 Makarenko Per., Open 9am–10pm; closed Monday/Tuesday. Metro Teknologichesky Institut, tel. 114-3447; also at 55 Moskvosky Pr., Open 8am–9pm; closed Wednesday/Thursday. Metro Fruzenskaya.

Krugliye Bani, 29a Ul. Karbysheva. Has a large outdoor heated pool. Open 8am–9pm; closed Wednesday/Thursday. Metro Pl. Muzhestva, tel. 550-0985.

Lotmanskiye Bani, 20 Lotmanskaya Ul., Open daily 8am–midnight. Metro Sadovaya, tel. 318-5833.

Neptun, 38 17th Liniya on Vasilyevsky Island, Open 8am–10pm; closed Tuesday/Wednesday. Metro Vasileostrovskaya, tel. 321-8154.

Pushkarskiye Bani, 22 Bol. Pushkarskaya Ul., Open 8am–10pm; closed Monday/Tuesday. Metro Petrogradskaya, tel. 237-0294.

Relax-Club, 6 Proletarskoi Diktatury, Open daily 8am–10pm. Metro Ploshchad Vosstaniya, tel. 276-1899.

VIP Sauna, 5 Gavanskaya Ul. on Vasilyevsky Island, Daily 24 hours. Metro Vasileostrovskaya, tel. 325-5564.

Yamskiye Bani, 9 Ul. Dostoevskovo, Open 8am–9pm; closed Monday/Tuesday. Metro Vladimirskaya, tel. 312-5836.

SPORTS STADIUMS

Dinamo, 44 Dinamo Pr. Metro Chkalovskaya.

Kirov Stadium, 1 Morskoi Pr. (on Krestovsky Island). The city's largest stadium with over 60,000 seats. Metro Krestovsky Ostrov.

Ledovy Dvorets (Ice Palace), 1 Pyatiletok Pr., was built for the 2000 World Ice Hockey Championships. Seating 14,000, it is also a venue for rock concerts and other sporting events. Metro Prospekt Bolshevikov.

Peterburgsky Sport & Concert Complex, 8 Yuriya Gagarina Ul., indoor 20,000 seat sports arena and concert venue. Metro Park Pobedy.

Petrovsky Stadium, 2 Petrovsky Ostrov. Has over 25,000 seats. Metro Sportivnaya.

Winter Stadium (Zimny), 2 Manezhnaya Sq., (2,000 seats). Metro Nevsky Prospekt.

Yubileiny (Jubilee) Stadium & Sports Complex, 19 Dobrolyubova Ul. Metro Sportivnaya.

SPORTS

Bowling: Locations are at: On Vasilyevsky Island, try the Pribaltiiskaya Hotel's Ball Lightning club (Metro Primorskaya). In the southern part of town, 5th Avenue is at 2 Konstitutsii Square (Metro Moskovskaya); the Bowling Center is at 10 Ul. Ivana Chernikh (Metro Narvskaya). On the Petrograd side, try Space Bowling, at 16 Aptekarsky Pr. (Metro Petrogradskaya). On the Vyborg side is Akvatoriya at 61 Vyborgskaya Emb. (Metro Lesnaya).

Billiards is now experiencing a revival. In town, try the Ambassador at 33 Ul. Kuibysheva (Metro Gorkovskaya); Leon at 34 Ul. Dekabristov (Metro Sadovaya); Oniks at 2 Aleksandra Nevskovo Square; and Trick-Shot at 73 Marata Ul. (Metro Pushkinskaya).

Chess, the Castle Club is at 3 Vladimirsky Pr. Metro Vladimirskaya. Also try Chisorin Chess Club, 25 Bol. Konyushennaya.

Golf, the United Club can arrange for lessons or play on the course of the Zenit Sports Complex (clubs for rental, too). tel. 534-0426.

Horse Riding, the Equestrian Sports Center at the Kirov Stadium has an indoor ring and riding lessons. tel. 235-5448. Try also KSK Repino, tel. 432-0144.

Rowing, the Spartak Rowing Club is at 24 Bol. Nevki Emb. Offers rowing and sculling. Metro Chornaya Rechka, tel. 234-3644.

Skating, year-round ice skating is at the Yubileiny Sports Palace, where skates can be rented (see stadiums). Other ice rink locations are at: Babushkin Park (Metro Lomonovskaya); Central Park of Culture (Metro Krestovsky Ostrov, Yelagin Island); Moscow Victory Park (Metro Park Pobedy); SKA Sports Palace (Metro Sportivnaya). In winter, many pond locations are flooded for skating, as in the Tavrichesky Gardens (Metro Chernyshevskaya), and the Kronwerk Canal, behind the Peter & Paul Fortress.

Skiing, Okhta Park Downhill Ski Center has downhill trails, ski lift and rental gear. Take a commuter train from Finland Station to Kuzmolovo. The best places for cross-country skiing are in the nearby villages of Kavgolovo (also has Alpine) and Sosnovo. If you have your own gear, try the Palace Park in Pavlovsk, Primorsky Victory Park on Krestovsky Island, the Central Park of Culture on Yelagin Island, and at Tsarskoye Selo. You can rent skis/sledges in the semicircular wing of Catherine's Palace.

Swimming Pools, many high-end hotels have their own pools. The Army Sports Club pool is at 3 Litovskaya Ul. Dinamo pool is at 38 Bol. Porokhovskaya Ul; daily 8am–10pm (Metro Novocherkasskaya). The LDM Aquatic Center is at 47 Ul. Professora Popova; daily 8am–11pm (Metro Petrogradskaya).

Tennis, the best tennis courts in the city are at the Tennis Club, 23 Konstantinovsky Pr. (Metro Chkalovskaya); on Yelagin Island (indoor & outdoor courts) at 6 Yelagin (Metro Staraya Derevnya); Gloriya (indoor & outdoor courts) at Moscow Victory Park, 25 Kuznetsovskaya Ul. (Metro Park Pobedy). The Tennis Federation is at 8 Ul. Lva Tolstovo, tel. 510-8515.

USEFUL ADDRESSES

IN THE USA

Contact information for embassies and consulates of the Russian Federation around the world: www.russianembassy.net.

Russian Embassy, 2650 Wisconsin Ave NW Washing DC 20007. tel. (202) 298-5700, fax. (202) 298-5735, www.russianembassy.org.

Visa Consular Section, 2641 Tunlaw Rd NW. Washington DC 20007. Visa desk: Monday-Friday 9am-12.30pm. tel. (202) 939-8907, fax. (202) 483-7579.

RUSSIAN CONSULATES GENERAL

New York, 9 East 91st St. New York, NY 10128. tel. (212) 348-0926, fax. (212) 831-9162. (Visa Desk: Monday-Friday 9am-12.30pm), www.ruscon.org.

San Franciso, 2790 Green St. San Francisco, CA 94123. tel. (415) 202-9800, fax. (415) 929-0306 (Visa desk: 9am-noon), www.consulrussia.org

Seattle, 2323 Westin Bldg, 2001 6th Ave. Seattle, WA 98121. tel. (206) 728-1910, fax. (206) 728-1871. (Visa Desk: Mon-Fri 2pm–4.45pm.)

Houston, 1333 West Loop South, Ste 1300, Houston, TX 77027. tel (713) 337-3300, fax. (713) 337-3305.

VISAS

Andrew's Consulting provides Russian visas/sponsorship to areas within Europe, UK and USA. (See *In the UK* for contact numbers.)

GO TO RUSSIA In US toll free (888) 263-0023, (404) 827-0099, www gotorussia.com (another visa website is: www.waytorussia.net).

Red Star Travel, in the US (800) 215-4378, (206) 522-5995 (Seattle), www.travel2russia.com (see also Travel Agencies).

Russian National Group, tel. (877) 221-7120, www.russia-travel.com.

Russia Gateway, in the US toll-free (866) 821-6434, 6435, (212) 480-2233. Provides complete Russian travel visa services. www.RussiaGateway.com.

Visa Advisors: www.visaadvisors.com; part of Global Visa & Passport (CIBT) at www .cibt.com (issues Russian Tourist/Business visas).

Visa House: www.visahouse.com.

Visas Online: www.visatorussia.com.

AIRLINES

Aeroflot, tel. (888) 340-6400, www.aeroflot.org.

Air France, tel. (800) 237-2747, www.airfrance.com.

Alaska Airlines, tel. (800) 426-0333 (flights to Siberia), www.alaskaair.com.

American, tel. (800) 433-7300, www.aa.com.

British Airways, tel. (800) 247-9297, www.britishairways.com.

Delta, tel. (800) 241-4141, www.delta.com.

Finnair, tel. (800) 950-5000, www.finnair.com.

KLM, tel. (800) 447-4747, www.klm.com.

Korean Air, tel. (800) 438-5000, www.koreanair.com.

Lufthansa, tel. (800) 645-3880, www.lufthansa.com.

United, tel (800) 241-6522, www.united.com.

SAS, tel. (800) 221-2350, www.scandinavian.net.

TRAVEL AGENCIES, TOUR AND SPECIALITY GROUPS

For Hostels & Homestays and Independent Russian Travel Agencies, see Practical Information Sections for both Moscow and St Petersburg.

GO TO RUSSIA has offices in Atlanta, San Francisco and Moscow. 309 Peters St. Unit A. Atlanta, Georgia 30313. tel. (888) 263-0023, (404) 827-0099, fax. (404) 827-0435. Visit www.gotorussia.com—with links to hotels & apartments, visa support, tours, and train schedules, that includes: www.allrussianhotels.com; www.allrussiantours.com; www.TicketToRussia.com; and www.apartmentres.com. Other websites include www.waytorussia.com; www.selectrussia.com and www.visatorussia.com.

Eastern Tours, 10 East 39th St. Ste 914, NY, NY10016. tel. (800) 339-6967, (212) 683-8930, fax. (212) 481-3570, www.traveltorussia.com.

MIR, 85 South Washington St #210, Seattle, WA 98104. tel (800) 424-7289/(206) 624-7289, fax. (206) 624-7360, www.mircorp.com.

Center for Citizen Initiatives, PO Box 29912, Presidio, San Francisco, CA 94129. tel. (415) 561-7777, (888) 729-7071, fax. (415) 561-7778, www.ccisf.org.

Council on International Exchange (CIEE), www.ciee.org.

Exeter Intl, 25 Davis Blvd, Tampa, FL33606. tel. (800) 633-1008, (813) 251-5355, www.exeterinternational.com.

Intourist-USA Inc., 12 South Dixie Highway, Lake Worth, FL33460. tel (800) 556-5305/(561) 585-5305, fax (561) 582-1353, www.intourist-usa.com.

Pioneer East-West Initiative, 203 Allstone St Cambridge, MA 02139. Custom designed Russian trips, specialty tours, and homestays. Tel. (800) 369-1322, (617) 547-1127, fax. (617) 547-7304, www.pioneerrussia.com.

Rail Europe, Specializing in Russian, CIS & European train travel. Can reserve and order tickets directly through them. Tel. (800) 848-7245, www.raileurope.com.

Red Star Travel, 123 Queen Anne Ave N Ste 102, Seattle, WA 98109. tel (800) 215-4378 or (206) 522-5995, fax. (206) 522-6295, www.travel2russia.com. Full service Russian travel agency that also supplies all types of visas to Russia.

Russian National Group, 224W 30th Street #701, NY, NY 10001. tel. (877) 221-7120, (646) 473-2233, fax. (646) 473-2205, www.russia-travel.com.

T.E.I. Tours and Travel, PO Box 23784, Pleasant Hill, CA 94523. tel. (800) 435-4334, (925) 825-6104, fax. (925) 825-5106, www.teiglobal.com.

Tour Designs, 713 Sixth Street SW, Washington DC 20024. tel. (800) 432-8687, (202) 554-5820, fax. (202) 479-0472, www.tourdesignsinc.com.

Uniworld, 17323 Ventural Blvd, Uniworld Plaza, Encino, CA 91316. Cruises along waterways of Russia & Ukraine. tel. (800) 360-9550. www.traveluniworld.com.

Value World Tours, Plaza Del Lago Bldg, 17220 Newhope St #203 Fountain Valley, CA 92708. Premier River Cruise operator. tel. (800) 795-1633, (714) 556-8258, fax. (714) 556-6125, www.vwtours.com.

ADVENTURE TRAVEL

Abercrombie & Kent, tel. (800) 554-7016, fax. (630) 954-3324, www.abercrombiekent.com

Boojum Expeditions, (Horse) tel. (800) 587-0125, (406) 587-0125, fax. (406) 585 3474, www.boojum.com

Geographic Expeditions, tel. (800) 777-8183/(415) 922-0448; fax. (415) 346-5535, www.geoex.com

MIR (see travel agencies)

Mountain Travel/Sobek, tel. (888) 687-6235, 594-6000, fax. (510) 594-6001, www.MTSobek.com

Quark Expeditions, (Arctic) tel. (800) 356-5699/(203) 656-0499; fax. (203) 655-6623, www.quark-expeditions.com

REI Adventures, tel. (800) 622-2236/(253) 437-1100, fax. (253) 395-8160; www.rei.com/travel

IN THE UK

Russian Embassy, 13 Kensington Place Gardens, London W8 4QX. tel. (020) 7229-2666/7281/8027, fax. (020) 7229-3215/5804.

Russia Visa Consulate, 5 Kensington Place Gardens, London W8. (Visa Dept. Monday–Friday 9am–11.30am). tel (020) 7229-8027, fax. (020) 7229-3215.

In Scotland, 58 Melville St Edinburgh, Scotland EH3 7HF. (Visa Dept. Monday–Friday 9am–12.30pm). tel. (131) 225-7098/7121, fax. (131) 225-9587.

AIRLINES

Aeroflot, tel. (0207) 355-2233.

British Airways, tel. (08457) 799-977.

Finnair, tel. (0870) 241-4411.

KLM, tel. (08705) 074074.

Lufthansa, tel. (08457) 737747.

SAS tel. (08456) 727727

TRAVEL AGENCIES

Andrew's Travel House, 23 Pembridge Square, Notting Hill, London W2 4DR. tel/fax. (020) 7727 2838. In Moscow: 2 Volkhonka Ul. Bldg 18. (495) 916-9898.

Exodus, 9 Weir Road, London SW12 ONE. Tel. (0870) 240-5550, 8673-0859, int'l: 0(20) 8675-5550; www.exodus.co.uk.

Explore Worldwide Ltd, www.exploreworldwide.com.

Findhorn Ecotravels, The Park, Forres, Marayshire, Scotland. IV36 3TZ. tel. (01309) 690 095, fax. (01309) 691-009.

Intourist Ltd, 7 Wellington Terrace, Notting Hill, London W2 4LW. tel. 020-7727-4100; fax. 020-7727-8090, www.intouristuk.com.

Progressive Tours, 12 Porchester Place, Connaught Square, London W2 2BS. tel. (027) 262-1676, fax. (027) 724-6941.

Regent Holidays, 15 John St, Bristol BS1 2HR. tel. (0870) 499-0911, fax (117) 925-4866, www.regent-holidays.co.uk.

Russian Gateway, www.russiangateway.com.

Russia National Tourist Office, www.visitrussia.org.uk.

STA Travel, tel. (171) 361-6161/6262. www.statravel.co.uk.

Steppes East, 51 Castle St, Cirencester, Gloucestershire GL7 1QD. tel. (01285) 880-980; fax (01285) 885-888; www.steppeseast.co.uk.

The Russia Experience, Research House, Fraser Road, Perivale, Middlesex U86 7AQ. tel. (020) 8566-8846, fax. (020) 8566-8843, www.trans-siberian.co.uk.

Voyages Jules Verne, 21 Dorset Square, London NW1 6QG. tel. (0845) 166-7003; www.vjv.com.

IN CANADA

Russian Embassy, 285 Charlotte Street, Ottawa, Ontario K1N 8LS. tel. (613) 235-4341, fax. (613) 236 6342, www.rusembcanada.mid.ru.

CONSULATES

52 Range Road, Ottawa, Ontario K1N 8JS. tel. (613) 336-7220, fax. (613) 238-6158. 3685 Avenue du Musée, Montréal, Quebéc H3G 2E1. tel. (514) 843-5901; fax. (514) 842-2012.

Consulates General of the Russian Federation in Toronto, 130 Bloor St West Suite, 700 Toronto, Ontario M5S 1N5. tel. (416) 962-9911, fax. (416) 962-6611, www.toronto.mid.ru

AIRLINES

Aeroflot, tel. Montréal (514) 288-2125, Toronto (416) 642-1653.
Air France, tel. (800) 667-2747, or in Montréal (514) 847-1106.
British Airways, tel. (800) AIRWAYS, or in Montréal (514) 287-9282.
Finnair, tel. (416) 222-0740.
Northwest/KLM (Domestic) (800) 225-2525 (Intl) (800) 447-4747.
Lufthansa, tel. (800) 563-5954.

TRAVEL AGENCIES

Canadian Gateway, 4915 Bathurst #221, Toronto, Ontario M2R 1X9. tel. (800) 668-8401/(416) 223-2100, fax. (416) 223-6252.
STA Travel, 200 Bloor St West Toronto, Ontario M5S 1TB. tel. (416) 925-5800, toll free 1888 242 0121, fax. (416) 925-6300.
STA Travel, 568 Dunsmuir Street, Vancouver, BC V6B1Y4. tel. (416) 925-5800, toll free 1888 242 0121, fax. (416) 925-6300.
Exotic Destinations, 8 King St #1709, Toronto, Ontario M5C 1B5. tel. (877) 698-6588/(416) 214-2235, fax. (416) 214-2236, www.exoticdestinations.com.
Travel Cuts, 187 College St Toronto, Ontario M5T 1P7. tel. (416) 979-2406, fax. (416) 979-8167; www.travelcuts.com.

IN HONG KONG

Russian Embassy, Room 2932, Sun Hung Kai Centre, 30 Harbour Road, Wanchai. tel. 2877-7188/5024, fax. 2877-7166.

AIRLINES

Aeroflot, tel. 2537-2611.
British Airways, tel. 2868-9000.
Finnair, tel. 2117-1238.
Northwest/KLM , tel. 2810-4288.
Lufthansa, tel. 2769-6560.
United, tel. 2810-4888.

TRAVEL AGENCIES

Global Union Express HK Ltd, Rm 22 2/F New Henry House, 10 Ice House Street, Central. tel. 2868-3231, fax. 2845-5078. (For Aeroflot bookings tel. 2845-4232, fax. 2537-2605.)
Time Travel Service, 40 Nathan Road, Chungking Mansions, 16th floor Block A, Kowloon. tel. 2723-9993, fax. 2739-5413. (For Trans-Siberian, also try Moonsky Star at tel. 2723-1376, fax. 2723-6653, e-mail: 100267.2570@compuserve.com).

IN AUSTRALIA

Russian Embassy, 78 Canberra Avenue, Griffith ACT, Canberra 2603. tel. (06) 6295-9033, fax. (06) 6295-1847.

Sydney Consulate, 7-9 Fullerton Street, Woolahra, Sydney NSW 2025. tel. (02) 9326-1188/1866, fax. (02) 9327-5065.

AIRLINES IN SYDNEY

Aeroflot, tel. (02) 9262-2233.   **Qantas**, tel. 131313.

British Airways, tel. (02) 8904-8800.   **Lufthansa**, tel. (300) 685-5727.

TRAVEL AGENCIES

Gateway Travel, 48 The Boulevard, Strathfield, NSW 2135. tel. (02) 9745-3333; fax (02) 9745-3237; e-mail: agent@russian-gateway.com.au; www. russian-gateway.com.au.

Sundowners Adventure Travel, 600 Lonsdale Street, Lonsdale Court #15, Melbourne, Victoria 3000. tel (300)-133-457/(03) 9672-5300, fax. 9672-5311, www.sundowners-travel.com.

STA Travel, 855 George St. Sydney 2000. tel. (03) 9212-1255, www.statravel.co.nz (lists all Australian branch locations).

STA Canberra, tel. (02) 6248-8633, fax. (02) 6247-2214.

IN NEW ZEALAND

Russian Embassy, 57 Messines Road, Karori, Wellington. tel. (04) 476-6113, consular department (04) 476-6742, fax. (04) 476-3843.

AIRLINES

Air New Zealand, tel. (0800) 737-000.

British Airways, Auckland. tel. (09) 356-8690; outside Auckland (0800) 274-847.

TRAVEL AGENCIES

STA Travel, 267 Queen Street, tel. (09) 356-1550, fax. (09) 356-1558. Head office 229 Queen Street, tel. (09) 309-9723. To call toll-free within New Zealand, tel. (0508) 782-872. www.statravel.co.nz. (check website for listings of New Zealand offices.)

STA Wellington, 130 Cuba Street, tel. (04) 385-0561, fax. (04) 385-8170.

STA Christchurch, 90 Cashel Street, tel. (03) 379-9098, fax. (03) 365-7220.

(For listings of embassies, consulates, travel agencies and other useful addresses in Moscow and St Petersburg, see Practical Information sections.)

RUSSIAN ORTHODOX CHURCH HOLIDAYS AND FESTIVALS

There are 11 fixed Orthodox Church observances that fall on the same date each year:

Jan 6	*Sochelnik*	Christmas Eve
Jan 7	*Rozhdestvo Khristovo*	Nativity of Christ
Jan 19	*Bogoyavlenie Gospodne*	Epiphany
Feb 15	*Sretenie Gospodne*	Candlemas Day or Feast of the Purification and preparing for Lent
Apr 7	*Blagoveshchenie Bogoroditsy*	Annunciation of Our Lady
Aug 19	*Preobrazhenie Gospodne*	Transfiguration of Christ (Second Savior)
Aug 28	*Uspenie Bogoroditsy*	Assumption of the Holy Virgin
Sept 21	*Rozhdestvo Bogoroditsy*	Nativity of Our Lady
Sept 27	*Vozdvizhenie Zhivotvoryashchevo Kresta Gospodnya*	Exaltation of the Cross
Oct 14	*Pokrov Bogoroditsy*	Intercession of Our Lady
Dec 4	*Vvedenie vo Khram Bogoroditsy*	Feast of Presentation of the Blessed Virgin

The Orthodox Church celebrates numerous holidays and religious events; many of these Church holy days stem from old pagan rituals. The month of May, for example, is very significant in the Orthodox religion. The first Sunday after Easter is known as *Krasnaya Gorka* or Little Red Mountain. It originated as a pagan spring rite when newlyweds and their relatives celebrated fertility, both for the land and their future offspring. In May, some of Russia's most revered saints are also honored: Saint Georgy Pobedonosets (Victory-Bringer) is remembered on May 6 and Saint Nikolai Chudotvorets (the Miracle-Maker) on May 22. The Day of Slavic Language and Culture falls on May 24. This marks the birth of Saint Cyril (827–869) who helped create the first Slavic written language, based on Greek characters.

Fifty days after Easter the Church celebrates the holiday week of *Pyatidesyatnitsa* (50)—the feast of the descent of the Holy Spirit on the Apostles. The festival is also known as *Troitsa* (Trinity), an honoring of the Father, Son and

Holy Spirit. Centuries ago, this was merged with the old Slavonic pagan feast *Semik* (Seven Days) which heralded the beginning of summer. Villagers cut down a birch tree, decorated it with ribbons and flowers, and then held parties beneath it. Afterwards they threw the garlands into the river; how they floated predicted the village's future year.

Additionally, Slavs made sure to pay an annual visit to their ancestors' graves. They believed that the dead influenced the fate of the living. The cult of the dead is also linked with the legend of the mermaid. Spirits of young women or unbaptized children who died unnatural deaths were thought to be transformed into mermaids who, each spring, roamed the riverbanks to entice victims into the water. Anyone who had a relative die in this way paid extra attention to their gravesites. Mermaids were considered the female spirits of the water, and *Troitsa/Semik* week is also nicknamed *Rusalnaya* (Mermaid).

In August the Orthodox Church celebrates three feast days connected with the life of Christ. Since both Russian farmers and Christians were concerned with their summer harvests and sowing seeds for the following year, they developed protective religious rites. Spas the First (Festival of the Savior's Cross or First Savior) falls on August 14; it is also known as 'Honey Day'. The holiday let people know it was time to gather honey from the beehives. A large festival was held on Moscow's Trubnaya Square where peasants sold crimson honey from large vats along with *barankas* (ring-shaped rolls). On this day peasants also brought their seeds to church and the priest sprinkled the fields with holy water. In old Rus, the cleansing of the water also took place; everyone down to livestock would be baptized in the rivers and blessed by the priests. This was thought to ward off evils and cure all ills.

August 19, Transfiguration Day of Christ (or Spas the Second/Second Savior), is also known as 'Apple Day'. On the morning of Apple Day, everyone would take their apples to local churches. They couldn't be eaten until blessed—people believed that worms would appear in their stomachs if they broke this rule. It was customary for thousands of vendors to pour into Moscow's Zamoskvorechye district across the river from the Kremlin to sell many varieties of this fruit.

Spas the Third or Third Savior-on-the-Veil falls on August 29; this is also known as 'Nut Day'. Nuts in the woods were gathered in sacks for the winter. Everywhere throughout Russia religious processions were also held leading with the Veronika Icon. According to legend, St Veronika gave Christ, while on the way to Calvary, her handkerchief with which to wipe his face. His image was miraculously left on it; in 944, the Veronika Icon (in Greek, *eikon* means image) was purchased by Byzantine Emperor Konstantine and moved to Constantinople.

RUSSIAN LANGUAGE

CYRILLIC ALPHABET

CYRILLIC	APPROXIMATE PRONUNCIATION
Аа	*a* as in 'father'
Бб	*b* as in 'book'
Вв	*v* as in 'vote'
Гг	*g* as in 'good'
Дд	*d* as in 'day'
Ее	*ye* as in 'yes'
Ёё	*yo* as in 'yonder'
Жж	*s* as in 'pleasure'
Зз	*z* as in 'zone'
Ии	*ee* as in 'meet'
Йй	*y* as in 'boy'
Кк	*k* as in 'kind'
Лл	*l* as in 'lamp'
Мм	*m* as in 'man'
Нн	*n* as in 'note'
Оо	*o* as in 'pot'
Пп	*p* as in 'pet'
Рр	*r* as in 'red' (slightly rolled)
Сс	*s* as in 'speak'
Тт	*t* as in 'too'
Уу	*oo* as in 'fool'
Фф	*f* as in 'fire'
Хх	*kh* as in 'Bach'
Цц	*tz* as in 'quartz'
Чч	*ch* as in 'chair'
Шш	*sh* as in 'short'
Щщ	*shch* as in 'fresh'
Ъъ	hard sign (silent)
Ыы	no equivalent, but close to *ee*
Ьь	soft sign (silent)
Ээ	*e* as in 'men'
Юю	*u* as in 'university'
Яя	*ya* as in 'yard'

BASIC RUSSIAN VOCABULARY

ENGLISH	RUSSIAN PHONETIC TRANSLITERATION
Hello	*zdrahst'voitye*
Good morning	*do'broye oo'tro*
Good afternoon	*do'bree dyen*
Good evening	*do'bree vye'cher*
Good night	*spakoi'ne no'chee*
Goodbye	*da sveedahn'ya*
Yes	*da*
No	*nyet*
Please, You're welcome	*pozhal'sta*
Thank you	*spasee'bah*
Okay/good	*kharoshaw'*
Excuse me	*eezveenee'tye*
My name is ...	*menyah' zavoot' ...*
What is your name?	*kahk vahs zavoot'?*
Nice to meet you	*o'chin priyat'na svah'mee*
	pahz nahko'mitsa
How are you?	*kahk dyelah'?*
Do you speak ...?	*vii govoree'tye po ...?*
English	*ahnglee'ski*
German	*nemyet'ski*
French	*frantsooz'ski*
Russian	*roos'ski*
I speak English	*ya gavaryoo'po ahnglee'ski*
I don't speak Russian	*ya ne gavaryoo'po roos'ski*
I (don't) understand	*ya (ne) poneemah'yoo*
Speak slowly	*gavaree'tye myed'lenna*
Please repeat	*pazhal'sta paftaree'tye*
We (I) need a translator	*nam (menye) noo'zhen perevod'chik*
I'm a foreigner (male/female)	*ya eenastra'nets/eenastran'ka*
I'm from America/England	*ya eez Ahmer'eekee/ Ahn'glee ee*
I'm a tourist	*ya tooree'st*
Group	*groo'pa*
Tell me	*skazhee'tye menye'*
Show me	*pakazhee'tye menye'*
Help me	*pamaghee'tye menye'*

I (don't) want	*ya (ne) khahchoo'*
I want to rest/sleep	*ya khahchoo' ot dakhnoot'/spaht*
eat/drink	*yest/peet*
I can/can't	*ya magoo'/ne magoo'*
It (is) here/there	*e'to zdyes, tahm*
How old are you?	*skol'ka vahm lyet?*
Of course	*kahnyesh'na*
With pleasure	*soodavolst'veeyem*
Congratulations	*pazdrahvlah'yoo vahs*
where	*gedye'*
what	*shtoh*
who	*ktoh'*
when	*kagdah'*
how	*kahk*
why	*pachemoo'*
How much/many	*skol'ka*
How much does it cost?	*skol'ka stoi'eet?*
I	*ya*
he	*ohn*
she	*ahna'*
it	*ahno'*
you (informal)	*tii* (like German *du* and French *tu*)
we	*mii*
you (formal, plural)	*vii* (like German *sie* and French *vous*)
they	*ahnee'*
man	*moozhchee'na*
woman	*shchen'shcheena*
boy	*mahl'cheek*
girl	*dye'vooshka*
father	*otyets'*
mother	*maht*
brother	*braht*
sister	*sestrah'*
grandfather	*dye'dooshka*
grandmother	*ba'booshka*
husband	*moozh*
wife	*zhenah'*

AIRPORT

airplane	*samolyot'*
flight	*reys*
arrival	*prilyot'*
departure	*vylyet*
boarding	*pasad'ka*
baggage	*bagazh'*
my passport	*moy pas'port*
my visa	*maya' vee'za*
my ticket	*moy beelyet'*
suitcase(s)	*chemodahn' (ee)*
porter	*naseel'shchik*
I want to go to the airport	*ya khachoo' f aeroport'*

HOTEL

I want to go to the hotel	*ya khachoo' f gostee'neetsu*
Where is the hotel?	*gedye' gostee'neetsa?*
Where is Intourist?	*gedye' Intooreest'?*
floor lady	*dezhoor'naya*
maid	*gor'nichnaya*
key	*klyooch*
floor	*etazh'*
taxi	*tahksee'*
elevator	*leeft*
room	*kom'nata*
telephone	*telefon'*
lavatory	*tooalyet'*

TRANSPORT

map	*kar'ta*
street	*oo'leetsa*
crossing	*perekhot'*
Metro station	*stan'tseeya metro'*
bus stop	*astanof'ka afto'boosa*
tram stop	*astanof'ka tramva'ya*
taxi station	*stayahn'ka tahksee'*
train	*po'yezd*
station	*vokzahl'*
Must I transfer?	*na'do peresad'ku?*

Please tell me where/when	*skazheet'ye pazhal'sta gedye'/kagda'*
to get off	*na'da so' ytee*
I want to go to ...(by vehicle)	*ya khachoo' pahye'khat f ...*
Stop here	*astanavee'tyes zdyes*
Wait for me	*padazhdee'tye menyah'*
entrance	*vkhot*
exit	*vy'khot*
stop	*stoi'tye*
go (on foot)	*eedee'tye*
go (by vehicle)	*payezhai'tye*
Let's go (on foot)	*pashlee'*
Let's go (by vehicle)	*payekh'elee*
attention	*vneemahn'eeyah*
forbidden	*nelzya'*

THEATER

theater/ballet/opera	*teea'tr/balyet'/o'pira*
concert/cinema	*kantsert'/keeno'*
What is playing tonight?	*shto eedyot' sevod'nya vye'chiram?*
ticket office	*kas'sa*
Do you have tickets?	*oo vas yest bilye'tee?*
When does the show begin?	*kagda' nachinai'itsa predstavlyen'iye?*
museum/park/exhibition	*moozey'/Pahrk/Vees'tafka*

DAYS OF THE WEEK

Monday	*paneedyel'nik*
Tuesday	*ftor'nik*
Wednesday	*sreda'*
Thursday	*chetvyerk'*
Friday	*pyat'neetsa*
Saturday	*sooboh'ta*
Sunday	*vaskresyen'ye*
today	*sevod'nya*
yesterday	*fcherah'*
tomorrow	*zahf'tra*
morning	*oo'trom*
day	*dyen*
evening	*ve'cherom*
night	*noch*

week	*nedehl'ya*
month	*meh'syats*
What time is it?	*kator'ee chahs?*

CHARACTERISTICS

good/bad	*kharoshaw/plo'kha*
big/small	*ballshoy'/mal'enkee*
open/closed	*otkri'to/zakri'to*
cold/warm/hot	*kho'lodno/zhar'ko/gorya'chee*
left/right	*le'vo/prah'vo*
straight ahead	*preeyah'mo*
(not) beautiful	*(ne) krahsee'vo*
(not) interesting	*(ne) eenteres'no*
quick/slow	*bi'stra/med'lenna*
much (many)/few	*mino'ga/mah'lo*
early/late/now	*rah'no/poz'no/say chas'*
fun/boring	*ves'olo/skoosh'no*
(not) delicious	*(ne) fkoos'no*
possible/impossible	*mozh'no/nevozmozh'no*

NUMBERS

one	*adeen'*	nineteen	*devyatnaht'set*
two	*dvah*	twenty	*dvaht'set*
three	*tree*	thirty	*treet'set*
four	*chetir'ee*	forty	*so'rak*
five	*pyaht*	fifty	*peedesyaht'*
six	*shest*	sixty	*shestdesyat'*
seven	*syem*	seventy	*sem'desyet*
eight	*vo'syem*	eighty	*vo'semdesyet*
nine	*dye'vyet*	ninety	*dyevenos'ta*
ten	*dyes'yat*	one hundred	*sto*
eleven	*adeen'natset*	one thousand	*tee'syacha*
twelve	*dvenaht'set*		
thirteen	*treenaht'set*		
fourteen	*chetir'nahtset*		
fifteen	*pyatnaht'set*		
sixteen	*shesnaht'set*		
seventeen	*semnaht'set*		
eighteen	*vosemnaht'set*		

MAP GLOSSARY AND ABBREVIATIONS

big	*Bolshoi (Bol.)*
boulevard	*Bulvar (Bul.)*
small	*Maly/Malaya (Mal.)*
bridge	*Mahst*
embankment	*Naberezhnaya (Nab.)*
new	*Novy*
lane	*Pereulok (Per.)*
square	*Ploshchad (Pl.)*
passage	*Proyezd*
avenue	*Prospekt (Pr.)*
highway	*Shosse*
old	*Stary*
street	*Ulitsa (Ul.)*
rampart	*Val*

MENU VOCABULARY

APPETIZERS	*ZAKUS'KI*
mushrooms in sour cream sauce	*gribi'so smetan'oi*
caviar	*ikra'*
salmon	*lososin'a*
black olives	*maslin'i*
sardines	*sardin'i*
herring	*seld*
salad	*salat'*
crab salad in mayonnaise	*salat kra'bi pod*
cucumber salad	*salat iz ogurtsov'*
tomato salad	*salat iz pomidor'*
salad made with potatoes, mayo, small chunks of meat, pickles	*stolich'ni salat*

SOUP	*SUP*
borsch	*borshch*
bouillon	*bulyon*
meat and potato soup	*pokhlyob'ka*
cabbage soup	*shchi*
fish or meat soup	*solyan'ka-riibni* or *myas'ni*

MEAT	MYA'SO
mutton	bara'nina
steak	bifshteks'
meatballs	bitoch'ki
filet	file
beef	govya'dina
goulash	gulyash
sausage	kolbasa'
meat patties	kotle'ti
lamb patties/kebab-style	lyul'ya kebab
shish kebab	shashliik'
schnitzel	shnit'sel
wieners	sosis'ki
pork	svini'na
veal	telya'tina
ham	vetchi'na
tongue	yaziik'

FOWL	PTIITSA
chicken	kur'iitsa
duck	ut'ka

FISH	RII'BA
crab	kra'bi
flounder	kam'bala
carp	karp
shrimp	krevet'ki
salmon	lososi'na
perch	o'kun
sturgeon	osetri'na
pike	sudak'
cod	treska'

OTHER DISHES	
blintzes	blin'chiki
pancakes with fillings	blini'
fried meat pastries	chebur'eki
hot cereal	kash'a
boiled meat dumplings	pelmen'i

baked dough with fillings	*piro'gi*
small hot pastries with fillings	*pirozhki'*
rice	*ris*
cheese pancakes	*siir'niki*
fruit or cheese dumplings	*varen'iki*
cold cheese tarts	*vatrush'ki*

BREAD (BLACK/WHITE)

KHLEB (CHORNI/BELII)

rolls	*bu'lochki*
jam	*dzhem*
preserves	*varen'ye*

DAIRY PRODUCTS

MOLOCHNIYE BLYUDA

thick buttermilk-like yoghurt	*kefir'*
butter	*mas'lo*
yoghurt	*prostok'vasha*
cream	*sliv'ki*
sour cream	*smetan'a*
cheese	*siir*
cottage cheese	*tvorog'*
egg	*yait'so*

VEGETABLES

OVOSHCHI

peas	*goroshek'*
mushrooms	*griibi'*
cabbage	*kapus'ta*
potatoes	*kartofel/kartosh'ka*
onions	*luk*
carrots	*morkov'*
cucumbers	*ogurtsi'*
tomatoes	*pomidor'i*
beets	*svyok'la*

FRUIT

FRUKTI

oranges	*apelsi'ni*
watermelon	*arbuz'*
melon	*dii'nya*
pears	*grush'i*
strawberries	*klubnika'*

lemon	*limon'*
raspberries	*malin'a*
peaches	*per'siki*
grapes	*vinograd'*
cherries	*vish'nia*
apples	*yab'loki*

CONDIMENTS	*PREPRAVA*
garlic	*chesnok'*
mustard	*garchee'tsa*
ketchup	*ketsup*
honey	*myod*
pepper	*per'ets*
sugar	*sak'har*
salt	*sol*

DESSERT	*SLADKOYE*
candy	*konfeti*
ice cream	*morozh'noye*
nuts	*orek'hi*
small cake/cookie	*pirozh'noye*
ice cream with fruit topping	*plombir'*
chocolate	*shokolad'*
pretzels	*sukhari'*
cake	*tort*

BEVERAGES	*NAPITKI*
tea	*chai*
coffee	*kofe*
near-beer	*kvas*
seltzered soda	*limonad*
beer	*pee'vo*
wine	*veeno'*
vodka	*vodka*
water	*voda'*
- mineral	*mineralnaya*
- seltzered	*gaziro'vannaya*
milk	*moloko'*
cognac	*konyak'*

juice	sok
orange	apelsinovi
tomato	tomatni
grape	vinogradni
apple	yablochni

TERMS

TERMEN

hot	goryach'ee
cold	kho'lodno
too	slish'kom
sweet	slad'kee
dry	sukhoi'
fresh	svezh'ee
not fresh	he svezhee
tasty	vkus'no
it's very good/delicious	eto o'chen vkusno
not tasty	ne vkus'no
with sugar	s sak'harom
without sugar	biz sah'kara
with milk	s molokom'
without milk	biz moloka'
rare (meat)	s krov'yu
medium	sred'ne
well-done	prozhar'enye

RESTAURANT

RESTORAN'

self-service	samaapsloo'zhevaneye
open	otkri'to
closed	zakri'to
(lunch) break	(obyed) pereriv'
dinner	oo'zhin
breakfast	zaf'trak
no space available	mest nyet
plate	tarel'ka
napkin	salfet'ka
cup	chash'ka
glass	stakan'
knife	nozh
fork	vil'ka

spoon	*lozh'ka*
table	*stol*
chair	*stul*
cigarettes	*ceegare'tee*
matches	*speech'kee*
waiter/waitress	*ofit'siant/ka*
I want	*Ya khachu'*
I want tea	*Ya khachu' chai*
menu	*menyoo*
bill	*schot*
bring me a bottle of	*preenesee'te bootil'koo*
wine/beer	*veena'/pee'va*
give me	*dai'te menye'*
pass me	*peredai'tye menye*
please	*pozhal'sta*
thank you	*spasee'bo*

The apostrophes in the phonetic transliteration indicate that the stress falls on the preceeding syllable (eg. in *spasee'bo* the stress is on *ee*).

A village near Yaroslavl as seen by the Illustrated London News, 1861.

Recommended Reading

City Directories and Magazines

The Traveller's Yellow Pages for Moscow, and St Petersburg (also to **Novgorod and Vyborg**). Editor Michael R. Dohan. The first comprehensive business telephone book for these cities is now sold in many stores and hotels throughout Moscow and St Petersburg. Much of the information is also contained on their website: www.infoservices.com.

Russian Life Magazine: monthly, PO Box 567, Montpelier, VT 05601. tel. (800) 639-4301, fax. (802) 223-6105. www.russianlife.net.

Passport Magazine: Business, Politics and Culture of Russia and the CIS. Six issues per year. Worldwide sales office in New York, tel. (212) 725-6700; fax. (212) 725-6915. In Moscow, tel./fax. (095) 158-7583/7336.

Zephyr Press, 50 Kenwood St. Brookline, MA 02446, publishes many Russian-themed books, such as poetry by Akhmatova. tel./fax. (617) 713-2813. www.zephyrpress.org.

On-line Sites About Russia

Here are some of the most popular of the hundreds of Russian-related sites.

Russia Tourism: www.russia-tourism.com. Extensive travel and tourism links for Moscow and St Petersburg.

Russia Travel: www.gotorussia.com. Travel services, visas, etc.

Moscow: www.moscow-guide.ru. Official tourist site of Moscow government. Check out www.menu.ru for restaurant listings.

The Moscow Times: www.themoscowtimes.com. Latest news and events in and around Moscow (also has links to hotels, restaurants, etc.).

Gorbachev's Green Cross Intl: www.globalgreen.org.

The Exile Files: www.exile.ru. Hip takes on living in Moscow and St Petersburg with links to restaurants, entertainment, hotels etc.

St Petersburg Info: www.city-guide.spb.ru.

St Petersburg Times: www.sptimes.ru (or www.sptimesrussia.com). Information on the city, and the on-line version of St Petersburg Times.

Russia Today: www.russiatoday.com (select "Russia"). Russian news source.

Russian National Group: www.russia-travel.com. Travel, visas, hotels.

Russian National Tourist Site: www.whererussia.com. information on Moscow and St Petersburg.

Moskovskiye Novosti: www.mn.ru/english. "Moscow News" newspaper.

Gazeta: www.gazeta.ru/english. Moscow daily newspaper.

Russian National Tourist Office: www.interknowledge.com/russia.

Relcom Window on Russia: www.wtr.ru/. Moscow weather, business, travel info.

Music: www.realaudio.com. Tune into live broadcasts of Russian radio.

Orthodox Church in America: www.oca.org.

WayToRussia: www.waytorussia.net. Extensive travel, visa and tourist information.

RUSSIAN PRODUCTS IN THE USA

Hermitage Museum Gift Shop, www.hermitagemuseum.org/shop.

Kremlin Gifts, carries a wide selection of lacquer art. www.kremlingifts.com.

The Russian Shop (Maison Russe), offers a splendid array of Russian items. www. TheRussianShop.com. (Call 800-778-9404 for a free catalog.)

Musica Russica, specializes in Russian church and folk music. www.musicarussica.com. For Russian historic films, check www.ihffilm.com.

Russian Collection, has a large collection of Russian lacquer boxes, *Matryoshka* dolls and jewelry. In the US toll-free (800) 575-8049.

Russian Renaissance, has a wide variety of gifts from Eastern Europe. www.russianarts.com.

Russia Online, offers books and magazines for Russian speakers. www.russia-on-line.com.

Russian Sunbirds, offers everything from lacquer boxes to painted eggs. Tel. 619-220-7172. www.sunbirds.com, www.saint-petersburg.com/store.

Tolstoys, Russian souvenirs In US 1–888–849 TOYS, www.tolstoys.com.

To order a catalog of unique Russian products from Catherine the Great goblets to a Russian MIG pilot's high-altitude helmet set, contact the **Sovietsky Collection**, toll-free US (800) 442-0002; (619) 294-2000; www.sovietski.com.

GENERAL HISTORY AND CURRENT AFFAIRS

Applebaum, Anna, *Dark Side of the Moon. Gulag, A History* (Doubleday, 2003)

Aron, Leon, *Yeltsin: A Revolutionary Life* (St Martin's Press, 2000)

Brewster, Hugh, *Anastasia's Album* (1996)

Channon, John, *The Penguin Historical Atlas of Russia* (1995)

Conquest, Robert, *Reflections on a Ravaged Century* (2000)

Cronin, Vincent, *Catherine: Empress of All Russias* (1996)

de Jonge, Alex, *The Life and Times of Gregory Rasputin* (Dorset Press, 1987)

De Madariaga, Isabel, *Ivan the Terrible* (Yale University Press, 2005)

De Madariaga, Isabel, *Catherine the Great* (Yale University Press, 1990)

Dobbs, Michael, *Down with Big Brother: The Fall of the Soviet Empire* (1997)

Duffy, J P & Ricci, V L, *Czars: Russia's Rulers for Over One Thousand Years* (1995)

Feinstein, Elaine, *Pushkin: A Biography* (Ecco Press, 1999)

Figes, Orlando, *Natasha's Dance: A Cultural History of Russia* (Henry Holt, 2002); and *A People's Tragedy: The Russian Revolution 1891–1925*

Galy, Darya, *A Lifelong Passion: Nicholas and Alexandra, Their Own Story* (1997)

Harford, James, *Korolev: How One Man Masterminded the Soviet Drive to Beat America to the Moon* (1997)

Jack, Andrew, *Inside Putin's Russia* (2004)

Keenan George, *Tent Life in Siberia* (first published 1870, University Press of the Pacific, 2001)

Knight Amy, *Who Killed Kirov? The Kremlin's Greatest Mystery* (Hill and Wang, 1999)

Knobloch Edgar, *Russia and Asia—Nomadic and Oriental Traditions in Russian History* (Odyssey Publications, 2007)

Lenin, Vladimir, *What is To Be Done?* (Written 1902, published by Penguin, 1988)

Lincoln, W. Bruce, *Sunlight at Midnight: St Petersburg and the Rise of Modern Russia* (2001) and *The Conquest of a Continent* (Random House, 1994)

Massie, Robert, *Peter the Great* (Ballantine, 1980); *Nicholas and Alexandra* (Atheneum)

Massie, Suzanne, *Land of the Firebird: The Beauty of Old Russia* (Simon and Schuster, 1980); *Pavlovsk—The Life of a Russian Palace* (Little Brown, 1990)

McNeal, Shay, *The Secret Plot to Save the Tsar* (William Morrow, 2003).

Montefiore, Simon, *Stalin: The Court of the Red Tsar* (Alfred A. Knopf, 2003)

Montefiore Sebag, *Prince of Princes: The Life of Potemkin* (Thomas Dunne Books/St Martin's Press, 2001)

Morrison, John, *Boris Yeltsin: From Bolshevik to Democrat* (EP Dutton, 1991)

Lewin, Moshe, *The Soviet Century* (2005)

Oakley, Jane, *Rasputin: Rascal Master* (St Martin's Press, 1989)

Politkovskaya, Anna, *Putin's Russia*, (Metropolitan Books, 2006)

Radzhinsky, Edvard, *The Last Tsar: The Life and Death of Nicholas II* (Doubleday, 1991); *Stalin: The First In-Depth Biography* (1996)

Rasputina, Maria, *Rasputin: The Man Behind the Myth* (Prentice-Hall, 1977)

Reed, John, *Ten Days That Shook the World* (Written in 1919, published by International, 1967); *The Collected Works of John Reed* (The Modern Library, 1995)

Remnick, David, *Resurrection* (Random House, 1997); *Lenin's Tomb: The Last Days of the Soviet Empire* (Random House, 1993) (Winner of the 1993 Pulitzer Prize)

Richelson, Jeffrey, *A Century of Spies: Intelligence in the 20th Century* (1997)

Riehn, Richard, *1812: Napoleon's Russian Campaign* (McGraw Hill, 1990)

Salisbury, Harrison, *Nine Hundred Days: The Siege of Leningrad* (Avon, 1970)

Scott-Clark, Catherine & Levy, Adrian, *The Amber Room: The Untold Story of the Greatest Hoax of the Twentieth Century*, (Atlantic Books, 2004)

Service, Robert, *A History of Twentieth Century Russia* (1998); *The Russian Revolution 1900–1927* (Macmillan, 1986) and *Lenin: A Biography* (2000)

Shostakovich Reconsidered, edited by Allan Benedict Ho & Dmitri Feofanov (Toccato Press, 1998)

Smith, Hedrick, *The New Russians* (Random House, 1991); (also *The Russians*)

Ulam, Adam, *The Communists: The Story of Power and Lost Illusions 1948–1991*, (Charles Scribners Sons, 1992); *Stalin: The Man and His Era* (Beacon Press, 1989); *The Bolsheviks* (Macmillan)

Ure, John, *The Cossacks* (Overlook Press, 2003)

Volkogonov, Dmitri, *Lenin: A New Biography* (The Free Press, 1994); *Autopsy of an Empire: The Seven Leaders Who Built the Soviet Regime* (1998)

Warnes, David, *Chronicle of the Russian Tsars* (Thames and Hudson, 1999)

Yeltsin, Boris, *Against the Grain* (Summit Books, 1990); *The Struggle for Russia* (Time Books)

Yevtushenko, Yevgeny, *Don't Die Before You're Dead* (Random House) (about the 1991 coup attempt)

PICTURE BOOKS, ART AND CULTURE

Ardoin, John, *Valery Gergiev & The Kirov: A Story of Survival* (Amadeus Press, 2001)

Before the Revolution: St Petersburg in Photographs 1890–1914 (Harry Abrahms, 1991)

Berlin, Isaiah, *The Soviet Mind* (Brookings, 2004)

Bird, Alan, *A History of Russian Painting* (Oxford, London, 1987)

Botkin, Gleb, *Lost Tales: Stories for the Romanov Family* (1996)

Brumfield, William Craft, *Landmarks of Russian Architecture: A Photographic Survey*; *Lost Russia: Photographing the Ruins of Russian Architecture* (1995)

Ertl, Rett & Hibbern, *The Art of the Russian Matryoshka* (Vernissage Press, 2003)

Galitzine, Katya, *St Petersburg: The Hidden Interiors* (Vendome Press, 1999)

Gifts to the Tsars, 1500-1700 (Harry R Abrams, 2001)

Goldstein, Darra, *A Taste of Russia* (Russian recipes) (1999)

Gray, Camilla, *The Russian Experiment in Art 1863–1922* (Thames & Hudson, 1984)

Hamilton, George Heard, *The Art and Architecture of Russia* (Pelican, 1992)

Maxym, Lucy, *Russian Lacquer, Legends and Fairy Tales Vols I & II* (Coral Color Process, Ltd, 1986)

McPhee, John, *The Ransom of Russian Art* (Farrar, Straus & Giroux)

Moynahan, Brian, *A Russian Century: A Photographic History of Russia's 100 Years* (Random House, 1994); *Rasputin: The Saint Who Sinned* (1997)

Nice, David, *Prokofiev, A Biography: From Russia to the West* (Yale University Press, 2003)

Norman, Geraldine, *The Hermitage: Biography of a Great Museum* (Fromm, 1998)

Norman, Geraldine, *The Hermitage: The Biography of a Great Museum* (Pimloco, 1999)

Plisetskaya, Maya, *Maya Plisetskaya*, autobiography (2001)

Pokhlebkin, William, *A History of Vodka* (Verso, 1993)

Prince Michael of Greece, *Nicholas and Alexandra: The Family Albums* (Tauris Parke, 1992)

Riasanovsky, Nicholas, *A History of Russia* (5th edition, 1993)

Richmond, Yale, *From Nyet to Da* (1996, on the Russian character)

Rudnitsky, Konstantin, *Russian and Soviet Theater 1905–32* (Harry Abrahms, 1988)

Robinson, Harlow, *Sergei Prokofiev: A Biography* (Paragon, 1988)

Russian Fairy Tales (Pantheon, 1976; Collected by Alexander Afanasev)

Russian Masters: Glinka, Borodin, Balakirev, Mussorgsky, Tchaikovsky (W W Norton, 1986)

Saved for Humanity: The Hermitage During the Siege of Leningrad 1941–44 (Aurora, St Petersburg, 1985)

Shead, Richard, *Ballets Russes* (Wellfleet Press, 1989)

Shvidkovsky, Dmitri, *St Petersburg: Architecture of the Tsars* (1996)

Snowman, Kenneth, *Carl Fabergé: Goldsmith to the Imperial Court of Russia* (Crown, 1983)

Strizhenova, Tatiana, *Soviet Costume and Textiles 1917–45* (Flammarion, 1991)

Stuart, Otis, *Perpetual Motion: The Public and Private Lives of Rudolf Nureyev* (Simon & Schuster, 1995)

Sylvester, Richard, *Tchaikovsky's Complete Songs* (2002)

Thomas, D M, *Alexander Solzhenitsyn: A Century in his Life* (1998)

Townend, Carol, *Royal Russia: The Private Albums of the Russian Imperial Family* (1998)

Troitsky, Artemus, *Children of Glasnost* (1992); *Back in the USSR: The True Story of Rock in Russia* (Faber & Faber, 1987)

Vassiliev, Alexandre, *Beauty in Exile: The Artist's, Models and Nobility Who Fled the Russian Revolution and Influenced the World of Fashion* (Harry N Abrams, 2000)

Volkov, Solomon, *St Petersburg: A Cultural History* (Simon & Schuster, 1995)

Volkov, Solomon, *Shostakovich on Stalin* (Knopf, 2004)

von Solodkoff, Alexander, *Masterpieces from the House of Fabergé* (1996)

Yermikova, Larisa, *The Last Tsar* (1995)

York, Michael, *Are My Blinkers Showing?: Adventures in Filmmaking in the New Russia* (Da Capo Press [Member of Perseus Books Group], 2005)

NOVELS, POETRY AND TRAVEL WRITING

Andreyeva, Victorya, *Treasury of Russian Love Poems* (1995)

Aitken, Gillon, *Alexander Pushkin: The Complete Prose Tales* (W W Norton, 1996)

Akhmatova, Anna, *The Complete Poems of Anna Akhmatova*, expanded edition. Translated by Judith Hemschemeyer and edited by Roberta Reeder (Zephyr Press, 1997)

Akhmatova, Anna, *My Half Century, Selected Prose* (Ardis, 1992)

Akunin, Boris, *The Winter Queen* (2003); *Murder on the Leviathani* (Fandorin novels, 2005); *Pelagia and the White Bulldog* (Random House, 2006); *The Death of Achilles* (2006)

Arndt, Walter (transl), *Pushkin Threefold (poems, lyrics, narratives)* (1993)

Babel, Nathalie (ed), *The Complete Works of Isaac Babel* (W.W. Norton, 2001)

Bitov, Andrei, *Pushkin House* (Collins Harvill, 1990)

Brodsky, Joseph, *A Guide to a Renamed City* (essays from *Less Than One*, Farrar Straus Giroux, 1986)

Bulgakov, Mikhail, *The Master and Margarita; Heart of a Dog* (Penguin, 1993)

Bunin, Ivan, *Sunstroke* (Compiled works), 1933 winner Nobel Prize for Literature (2002)

Butov, Mikhail, *Svoboda*, winner of Booker Prize (Liberty, 1999)

Byron, Robert, *First Russia, Then Tibet* (Penguin, 1985)

Capote, Truman, *The Muses are Heard* (from A Capote Reader, Hamish Hamilton, 1987)

Chronicles Abroad: St Petersburg, Edited by John and Kirsten Miller (Chronicle Books, 1994)

The Portable Chekhov (Viking, Penguin); Rayfield, Donald, *Anton Chekhov: A Life* (1998)

de Custine, Marquis, *Letters from Russia* (Penguin, translated from French), first published in the 19th-century

Dostoevsky, Fyodor, *Crime and Punishment* (Bantam, 1982)

Eisler, Colin, *Paintings in the Hermitage* (1990)

Gerstein, Emma, *Moscow Memoirs* (The Harville Press, 2004)

Ginsburg, Evgenia, *Into the Whirlwind and Within the Whirlwind* (Collins Harvill, 1989)

Gogol, Nikolai, *Dead Souls* (Penguin)

Ilf & Petrov, *The Twelve Chairs* (Northwestern University Press, 1997)

Kalfus, Ken, *The Commissariat of Enlightenment* (Ecco, Harper Collins, 2003)

Kates, J (ed.), *In the Grip of Strange Thoughts: Russian Poetry in a New Era* (Zephyr Press, 1999)

Kelly, Laurence (ed.), *A Traveller's Companion to Moscow* (Interblink, 2005)

Mandelstam, Osip, *Journey to Armenia* (Redstone Press, 1989)

Mandelstam, Osip, *The Egyptian Stamp & Theodosia* (in *The Prose of Osip Mandelstam*, Princeton, 1965)

Mandelstam, Osip, *The Noise of Time* (in *The Prose of Osip Mandelstam*, Quartet Encounter, 1988)

Mandelstam, Nadezhda, *Hope Against Hope and Hope Abandoned: Memoirs* (Collins Harvill, London, 1989)

Marullo, Thomas Gaiton, *Cursed Days: Ivan Bunin* (Chicago, Ivan R. Dee, 1998)

Mochulsky, K, *Dostoevsky: His Life and Work* (Princeton University Press)

Morris, Mary, *Wall to Wall* (Penguin, 1989) (A trip from Beijing across Russia on the Trans-Siberian)

Nabokov, Vladimir, *Speak, Memory* (Capricorn, first published in 1947)

Pasternak, Boris, *Dr Zhivago* (Ballantine, 1988)

Pelevin, Victor, *Omon Ra (1998); Generation P (2000); Babylon (2001); Buddha's Little Finger (with Andrew Bromfield, 2001); A Werewolf Problem in Central Russia and Other Stories (2003)*

Reeder, Roberta, *Anna Akhmatova: Poet and Prophet* (1995)

Rybakov, Anatoly, *Fear* (Little, Brown & Co, 1992); *Children of the Arbat* (Dell, 1988)

Rzhevsky, Nicholas, *An Anthology of Russian Literature from Earliest Writings to Modern Fiction* (1996)

Solzhenitsyn, Alexander, *One Day in the Life of Ivan Denisovich* (Bantam); *The First Circle*, and *The Gulag Archipelago* (Harper and Row); *The Red Wheel* (1994).

Steinbeck, John & Capa, Robert, *A Russian Journal* (Paragon House, 1989), first published in 1948

Steinberg, Mark & Khrustalyov, Vladimir, *The Fall of the Romanovs* (Yale University Press, 1995)

Theroux, Paul, *The Great Railway Bazaar* (A trip across Russia on the Trans-Siberian)

Thubron, Colin, *Where Nights are Longest* (Atlantic Monthly Press, 1983); *Among the Russians* (Penguin, 1985); *In Siberia* (Harper Perennial, 2000)

Tolstoya, Tatyana, *On the Golden Porch* (1988); *Sleepwalker in a Fog* (1992); *You Love, You Love Not* (1997); *Sisters* (1998 with sister Natalya Tolstaya); *Kys* (2000); *Pushkin's Children: Writing on Russia and Russians*, 2003.

Topolski, Aleksander, *Without Vodka: Adventures in Wartime Russia* (Steerforth Press, 2001)

Trifonov, Yuri, *The Exchange & Other Stories* (1991)

Trifonov, Yuri, *The Old Man* (1999)

Tsvetaeva, Maria, *Milestones*, poems written in 1916 (2002)

Turgenev, Ivan, *Fathers and Sons* (Penguin)

Ustinov, Peter, *My Russia* (Little, Brown & Co, 1983)

Van Der Post, Laurens, *Journey in Russia* (Penguin, 1965)

Voinovich, Vladimir, *Moscow, 2042* (Harcourt Brace Jovanovich, 1987)

Wilson, A N, *Tolstoy Biography* (Ballantine, 1988)

Tolstoy reading list: The best English language translations of *Anna Karenina* and *War and Peace* are issued by Modern Library. W.W. Norton publishes *Tolstoy's Short Fiction*, *Confession*, and *Tolstoy*, a biography by A.N. Wilson. Northwestern University Press has issued *Tolstoy's Plays*, in three volumes. *Walk in the Light and 23 Tales* (collection of his short stories), 2000; *The Last Station*, by Jay Parini, reconstructs the last year of Tolstoy's life. For a fascinating glimpse of Tolstoy's marriage try *Love and Hatred: The Stormy Marriage of Leo and Sonya Tolstoy*, by William Shirer.

Trans-Siberian recommended reading: *In Siberia*, Colin Thubron (Harper Perennial, 2000); *Siberia, Siberia*, by Valentin Rasputin (Northwestern Univ Press, 1997); *Siberian Dawn*, Jeffrey Tayler (Ruminator, 2000); *Tent Life in Siberia*, George Kennan (first published 1870/Univ Press of the Pacific, 2001); *The Conquest of a Continent: Siberia and the Russians*, W. Bruce Lincoln (Random House, 1994); *The History of Siberia: From Russian Conquest to Revolution*, Alan Wood (Routledge, 1991); *The Trans-Siberian Handbook*, Bryn Thomas and the *Siberian BAM Book*, Yates & Zvegintzov (Trailblazer Guides, 2001/2002); and *Trans-Siberian Railway Guide*, (Lonely Planet), and *Through Siberia by Accident*, Dervia Murphy (paperback, 2006).

WEIGHTS AND MEASURES CONVERSIONS

LENGTH	MULTIPLY BY
Inches to centimeters	2.54
Centimeters to inches	0.39
Inches to millimeters	25.40
Millimeters to inches	0.04
Feet to meters	0.31
Meters to feet	3.28
Yards to meters	0.91
Meters to yards	1.09
Miles to kilometers	1.61
Kilometers to miles	0.62

AREA	
Square feet to square meters	0.09
Square meters to square feet	10.76
Square yards to square meters	0.84
Square meters to square yards	1.20
Square miles to square kilometers	2.59
Square kilometers to square miles	0.39
Acres to hectares	0.40
Hectares to acres	2.47

VOLUME	
Gallons to liters	4.55
Liters to gallons	0.22
US gallons to liters	3.79
Liters to US gallons	0.26
Fluid ounces to milliliters	30.77
Milliliters to fluid ounces	0.03

WEIGHT	
Ounces to grams	28.35
Grams to ounces	0.04
Pounds to kilograms	0.45
Kilograms to pounds	2.21
Long tons to metric tons	1.02
Metric tons to long tons	0.98
Short tons to metric tons	0.91
Metric tons to short tons	1.10

TEMPERATURE

°C	°F
-30	-22
-20	-4
-10	14
0	32
5	41
10	50
15	59
20	68
25	77
30	86
35	95
40	104
45	113
50	122
55	131
60	140
65	149
70	158
75	167
80	176
85	185
90	194
95	203
100	212

WOMEN'S CLOTHING & SHOE SIZES

CLOTHES				
American	6	8	10	12
British	8	10	12	14
Russian	34	36	38	40

SHOES				
American	6	7	8	9
British	4.5	5.5	6.5	7.5
Russian	37	38	39	40

Genealogy of the Imperial Family

This table is only a partial listing of dynastic relatives.

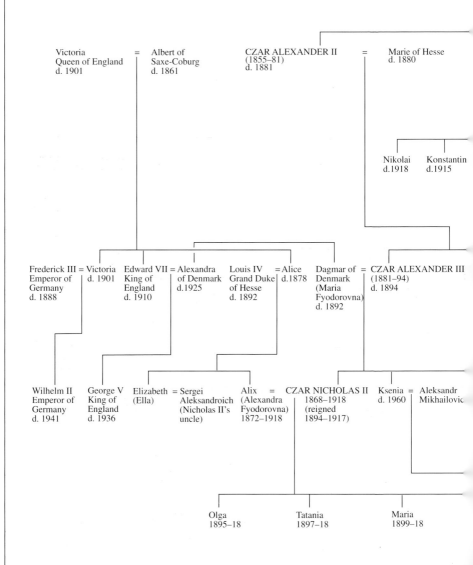

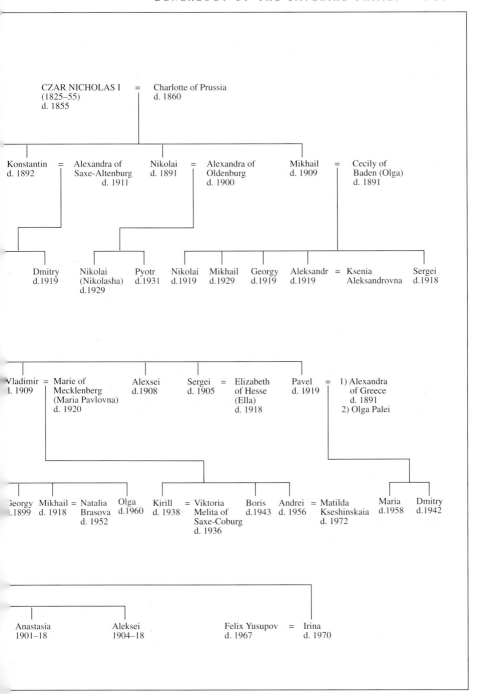

CZAR NICHOLAS I = Charlotte of Prussia
(1825–55) d. 1860
d. 1855

Konstantin = Alexandra of   Nikolai = Alexandra of   Mikhail = Cecily of
d. 1892   Saxe-Altenburg d. 1891   Oldenburg   d. 1909   Baden (Olga)
          d. 1911   d. 1900   d. 1891

Dmitry   Nikolai   Pyotr   Nikolai Mikhail Georgy   Aleksandr = Ksenia   Sergei
d.1919   (Nikolasha) d.1931 d.1919   d.1929   d.1919   d.1919   Aleksandrovna d.1918
         d.1929

Vladimir = Marie of   Alexsei   Sergei = Elizabeth   Pavel = 1) Alexandra
d. 1909   Mecklenburg   d.1908   d. 1905 of Hesse   d. 1919   of Greece
          (Maria Pavlovna)   (Ella)   d. 1891
          d. 1920   d. 1918   2) Olga Palei

Georgy Mikhail = Natalia   Olga   Kirill = Viktoria   Boris   Andrei = Matilda   Maria   Dmitry
d.1899 d. 1918   Brasova   d.1960   d. 1938   Melita of   d.1943   d.1956   Kseshinskaia   d.1958   d.1942
                  d. 1952   Saxe-Coburg   d. 1972
                                                d. 1936

Anastasia   Aleksei   Felix Yusupov = Irina
1901–18   1904–18   d. 1967   d. 1970

INDEX

User's Note

The order of index entries is word-by-word. Page references to the main text are in normal typeface.
Photographs and illustrations and their captions have also been indexed as appropriate. Page references to these entries are in italics.

A

Aalto, Alvar (architect), 586
Abramtsevo Estate Museum, 236
Academy of Agricultural Sciences, 510
Academy for Arts, Russian (*see also* Repin Institute of Painting, Sculpture and Architecture), 169
Academy of Sciences, *14–5*, 222, 487, 488, 514
accommodation (*see also* guesthouses, hotels, hostels, house rental, log-cabins), 362, 634
addresses, locating, 81
Admiralty, the, 501
air travel, internal, 72
airlines, 61, 360–1, 632–3, 676–7, 679–81
airports, 61, 70–1, 109, 224, 249, 359–60, 471, 632
Akhmatova, Anna, 437, 450, 529, 620–4
    burial place, 549, 585
    death of, 451
    monuments, 624
    museum, 172, 519–20
    quoted, 16, 485, 520, 557, 558, 585, 620, 621–4
    residences, 172, 252, 519
Aksakov, Sergei (writer), 237
alcoholic drinks (*see also* vodka), 93
Aleichem, Sholom (writer), 179
Aleksandrinsky Theatre, *see* Pushkin Drama Theater
Aleksandrovskaya Sloboda, 281–2
Aleksandrovsky Park, 477
Alexander I, Czar, 429–30, 491, 501
Alexander II, Czar, 21, 430, 525–6
Alexander III, Czar, 145, 348, 430, 476, 516
Alexander Column, 491

Alexander Fort, 583
Alexander Nevsky Bridge, 538
Alexander Nevsky Monastery, 426, 534
Alexander Palace, model of, *147*
Alexander Palace (Tsarskoye Selo), 595
Alexander Pushkin Museum, 168
Alexandria Park, 576
Alexandrov, Alexander (composer), 45
Alexandrov Gardens, 120
Alexandrovsky Garden, 501
Alexis, Czar, 89, 141
allergies, 70
All-Russian Exhibition Center, 212, 226–8
Amber Room, 589–90, *591*
ambulance service, 67
American Express offices, 66, 80
Amusement Palace (Moscow), 141
Amusement Park (St Petersburg), 477
Ananov, Andrei (jeweler), 147
Andreev, Nikolai (artist), 159
Andrei Rublyov Museum of Old Russian Art, 109, 225
Andropov Yuri, 24, 191
Angliisky Club, *see* English Club
Anhalt-Zerbst, Sophia Augusta Fredericka, *see* Catherine II (the Great)
Anichkov, Mikhail (engineer), 532
Anichkov Most (Bridge), 532
Anna Akhmatova Museum, 172, 519–20
Anna Ivanovna, Empress, 428
Anna's Fortress, 586
antiques, 189, 389, 653–4
    export of, 63, 95, 390
Apothecary Museum and Herbarium, 576
appartments (*see also* house rental), visiting, 81
applied and decorative art, museums
    Golden Ring, 280–1, 289, 345
    Moscow, 128, 183, 248, 249–50, 278
    St Petersburg, 484
Aptekarsky Botanical Gardens
    Moscow, 212
    St Petersburg, 479
Arbat district (*see also* Novy Arbat, Stary Arbat), 13
architects, *see* names of individual architects
Architectural Museum of St Petersburg, 477

architecture
  church, 265, 267
  skyscrapers, 214, 215
  styles, examples of
    art nouveau, 170, 478
    baroque, 200, 217, 218, 225, 245, 247,
      277, 487, 491, 526
    constructivist, 187
    Elizabethan rococo, 429
    Gothic, 201
    'Naryshkin', 195, 223, 276
    neo-Byzantine, 582
    neo-Empire, 187
    Old Russian, 122, 310, 322, 326, 335
    wooden, 243, *244*, 311, 336, 341, 345,
      346, 347, 619
architecture, museums of
  Kizhi Island, 619
  Kostroma, 311
  Moscow and vicinity, 154, 186, *243, 244*, 254
  Novgorod, 607
  Rostov Veliky, 292
  St Petersburg, 477
  Suzdal, 336, 345, 347
  Vladimir, 326
  Yaroslavl, 303, 304
archive collections, 31, 175, 311, 506
Arctic and Antarctic, Museum of the, 533
Argunov, Pavel (architect), 228, 249
Arkhangelskoye Estate Museum, 240–1
Armed Forces Central Museum, 211
Armenian Church, 526
Armenian community, 200
Armory Palace Museum, 142–3
arms and armor (*see also* cannons and guns),
  142, 304, 327, 477
Arsenal, the (Moscow), 124
art, 469–70
art galleries, 170, 172, 390–1, 655–6
Art Moderne Gallery, 172
Art Museum (Kostroma), 310
Art Museum (Trinity Monastery of St Sergius),
  278
art museums
  Golden Ring, 278–9, 292, 298, 303, 305, 312,
    314, 315, 324, 326
  Moscow, 109, 142–3, 154, 161, 165, 166,

  170, 172, 196, 212, 228 240–1, 249, 254
  St Petersburg and vicinity, 494–5, 498, 500,
    528–9, 598, 607, 619
art works (*see also* religious art)
  confiscated by Red Army, 498
  evacuation of, during World War II, 560
  export, 390
  fake, 69
artillery, *see* cannon and guns
Arts Square, 528
Assumption (Uspensky) Cathedral (Kremlin),
  56–7, 125, 131–5, *132–3*, 268, *270*
Assumption (Uspensky) Cathedral (Sergiyev
  Posad), 276
Assumption Cathedral (Vladimir), 327
Assumption, Church of the (Suzdal)
ATMs (automated teller machines), 65
Aurora (battleship), 423, 426, 431, 474, 479,
  539, 553
automobiles, Russian, 123, 158

B

bakeries and pastry shops, 175, 373
Bakhrushin, Alexei (merchant), 213
Bakhrushin Theater Museum, 213
Bakunin, Mikhail (anarchist), 430, 453
ballet, 456–7, *458*, 460–2
Ballets Russes, 462
Bank Bridge (Bankovski Most), *522–3*, 525
banks, 65, 66
bars, *see* pubs and bars
bas-reliefs, 326
bathhouses and saunas, 163, 413–4, 418–9, 533,
  673–4
Battle of Borodino Panorama Museum, 195
Bazhenov, Vasily (architect), 164, 253
bed and breakfast, 336, 370, 640
bell towers
  Golden Ring, 274, 277, 278, 282, 287, 291,
    296, 298, 306, 307, 335, 342, 344, 345
  Kizhi Island, 619
  Moscow, *125*, 131, 218, 229, 248, 260, 325
  St Petersburg, 474
bells, 224, *294–5, 296–7*
  Emperor, 130–1
Beloselsky-Belozersky Palace, 532, 535
Benois Museum, 576

Benois, Nikolai (architect), 250, 576, 580
Berdyayev, Nikolai (journalist), quoted, 33
Bergholts, Olga (poet), quoted, 559, 561, 577
Birzhevaya Ploshchad (Commerce Square), 486
bistros, origin of, 91
Bitov, Andrei (novelist), 452
Blair, Tony (British Prime Minister), 46
Blank, Karl (architect), 249, 250, 288, 573
Blok, Alexander (writer and poet), 450
Blue Bridge (St Petersburg), 510
Boat House (St Petersburg), 476
boats and boating (*see also* cruises), 179, 199,
    228, 252, 293, 306, 314
    excursions, 412, 671
    passenger docks, 672
Bobrinsky Mansion (Moscow), 182
Bogarevsky, Konstantin (artist), 180
Bogoliubovo village, 328
Bogoliubsky, Grand Prince Andrei, 134, 291,
    322, 324, 325, 328, 337
Bolshevik Party, 30, 431
Bolshevik Revolution (1917), 118, 423, 474,
    464, 479, 491, 517, 553
Bolshoi Gostiny Dvor (store), 527, 528
Bolshoi, Prince Andrei, 298
Bolshoi theater, 159, 160, *160*
Bondarchuk, Sergei (filmmaker), 242
books
    collections, 304
    display of, 182, 187, 225
    rare, 288
books, secondhand (*bukinisti*), 161
bookstores
    Moscow, 150, 187, 189, 391–2
    St Petersburg, 525, 656
Borisoglebsky Fortress Monastery, 296
Borisov, Grigory (architect), 296
Borodin, Alexander (composer), *538*
Borodino, 241–2
Borodino, Battle of, museums, 195, 241
Borodino Military History Museum, 242
Boroschchov Mansion, 310
Botanical Gardens, 212, 222, 479
Botanical Museum (St Petersburg), 479
botanical museums, 254, 479
Botik Museum (Pereslavl), 285
Boulevard Ring, 195–201

Bovet, Osip (architect), 159, 164, 172, 191, 223,
    224
Braunstein, Johann Friedrich (architect), 573, 588
Brezhnev, Leonid, 24, 43, 191, 542
Bridge of Kisses, 526
bridges
    Moscow and vicinity, 200, 254
    St Petersburg and vicinity, 471, 477, 484,
    485, 489–90, 510, 522–3, 525, 532, 538,
    568
Brodsky House Museum, 530
Brodsky, Joseph (writer), 434, 451–2
    quoted, 422, 434, 437, 452
Bronze Horseman, the, *see under* Peter I (the
    Great)
Bryullov, Alexander (architect), 516, 529
Buddhist Datsun (temple), 485
Bulgakov, Mikhail (writer), 168, 179
Bunin, Ivan (writer), 451
burial mounds (*sopki*), 615
burlaki (barge haulers), 302
buses and coaches, 75–6
    excursions, 412, 670–1
Bush, George H W (US President), 28, 46
Butov, Mikhail (writer), 453
Byelorussky Railway Station, *183*
Byron, Robert (English poet), 332
    quoted, 299

C
cafés and coffee shops
    Moscow, 189, 191, 374–5
    Golden Ring, 283, 285, 300, 321, 336
    St Petersburg and vicinity, 577, 604, 641
Cameron, Charles (architect), 588, 595, 599
camping, 285, 371, 641
Campioni (sculptor), 285
canals, *438*, 471, 485, 500, 517, 518–9, 522–3,
    555
cannons and guns
    displays,, 477
    Emperor Cannon, *129*, 130
car hire (*see also* driving), 77, 413, 672
carriages, 143, 347, 593
Casino Royale (Moscow), 184
Cathedral of the Annunciation, 137, 140
Cathedral of the Archangel Michael, 140–1

Cathedral of the Assumption (Moscow), 259–60
Cathedral of the Assumption (Pereslavl-Zalessky),
    288
Cathedral of the Assumption (Rostov-Veliky), 291
Cathedral of Bogoyavlensky, 150
Cathedral of Christ Our Savior, 13, 166–7, *166*,
    271
Cathedral of the Exaltation of the Holy Cross,
    316
Cathedral of the Holy Fathers of the Seven
    Ecumenical Councils, 224
Cathedral of the Nativity, 260
Cathedral of Our Lady of Kazan, 524–5
Cathedral of the Resurrection, 307
Cathedral of St Demetrius, 326, *326*
Cathedral of St George, 610
Cathedral of St Nicholas, 607
Cathedral of St Sampson-Host of Wanderers, 543
Cathedral of St Sophia, 607
Cathedral of the Transfiguration (Suzdal), 344
Cathedral of the Transfiguration of the Savior
    (Kizhi Island), 619
Cathedral of the Transfiguration of the Savior
    (Moscow), 229
Cathedral of the Virgin Nativity, 340
cathedrals (*see also* names of individual cathedrals),
    399
Catherine I, Empress, 20, 442
Catherine II (the Great), 21, 128, 141, 162, 197,
    201, 429, 502, 506, 511, 513–5, 578, 604
    coronation robe and crown, 142, 143
    estate (Tsaritsyno), 253–4
    Hermitage established by, 426, 494
    portrait, *512*
    social code, 504–5
    statue, 530
Catherine's Palace (Tsarskoye Selo), 588–98
    views of, *589–90, 594, 596–7*
caviar, 64, 69, 92, 95
cell phones, 79
cemeteries, 204, 210, 218, 220, 235, 538, 561
Central City Theater, 528
Central Lenin Museum, 516
Central Naval Museum, 486
Central Russian school (painting), 330
Central Telegraph Building, 174
Central Universal Store (TsUM), 161

Ceramics Museum, 250
Chakalov, Valeri (pilot), 212
Chancellor, Sir Richard (merchant), 151
Chapel-over-the-Well (Sergiyev Posad), *275*,
    276–7
Chechnya, 39, 40, 43, 46
Cheka police 155, 156, 157, 431, 501, 544
Chekhov, Anton (writer), 149, 161, 211, 260,
    448, 450
    museum, 211
    quoted, 89, 102, 187, 195
Chekhov House Museum, 211
Chemiakin, Mikhail (sculptor), 476
Chernyshevsky, Nikolai (writer), 430, 473
Chertogi Palace (Sergiyev Posad), 280
Chesme Church and Palace, 557
chess, 196
Children's Music Theater, 216
Children's Theater Museum, 211
Chinese Palace (Lomonosov), 580
Chistoprudny Bulvar, 199
chocolate factory, 213
Chorny, Daniil (artist), 267, 325
Church of the Archangel Gabriel, 199
Church of the Archangel Michael, 225
Churrh of the Assumption, 218
Church of the Deposition of the Lord's Robe, 223
Church of the Deposition of the Virgin's Robe,
    135
Church of Elijah Obdenny, 170
Church of Elijah the Prophet, 304
Church of the Emperor Constantine, 342
Church of the Grand Ascension, 182
Church of the Holy Trinity in Nikitniki, 154
Church of the Intercession in Fili, 195
Church of the Kazan Virgin, 247
Church of the Kazansky Icon of the Holy
    Mother, 558
Church of the Resurrection-on-the-Debre, 311
Church of the Resurrection of Lazarus, 619
Church of St Catherine, 526
Church of St George on Pskov Hill, *152, 153*
Church of St George the Victorious, 616
Church of St John the Baptist, 305–6
Church of St John upon Ishnya, 293
Church of St Maxim, 151
Church of St Nicholas (Moscow), 217, 268

Church of St Nicholas (Suzdal), 341
Church of St Nicholas-in-the-Field, 292
Church of St Varvara, 151
Church of Saints Cosmas and Damian, 199
Church of Saints Peter and Paul, 200
Church of the Savior on the Blood, 525, *526*
Church of the Savior-Not-Made-By-Hands, 237
Church of Sergius Radonezhsky, 162
Church of Simon Stylites, 189
Church of the Transfiguration (Suzdal), 347
Church of the Transfiguration of the Savior-on-
  Elijah-Street (Novgorod), 607
Church of the Virgin (Kostroma), 311, *313*
Church of the Virgin of All Sorrows (Moscow),
  172
churches (*see also* names of individual churches),
  399–400, 662–3
  architecture, 265, 267, *279*
  non-Orthodox denominations, 401–2, 663–4
  services held in, 151, 162, 172, 182, 189,
  216, 217, 218, 247, 260, 269, 273, 286,
  292, 342, 399, 525
cinema, Russian, 202–7
cinemas, 228, 405–6, 521, 673
circuses, 198, 216, 221, *230–1*, 232–5, *234*, 306,
  405, 519
  museums, 519
Ciniselli, Gaetano (equestrian entrepreneur), 232
Claudio, Antonio (painter), 223
climate, 55, 58
clinics, *see* medical services
clock towers, 6–7, *60*, 123, 516
clocks, 123, 248, 277, 511
coaches, *see* buses and coaches
coat of arms, Moscow, 104
Coffee House (St Petersburg), 518
Comedy Theater, 532
Commonwealth of Independent States (CIS), 12,
  104
Communist Party, 31, 35, 40, 47
  archives, 175
  membership, 30
complaints, 83
concert halls, 404–5
concerts, 250, 254, 488, 478, 494, 577
consulates (*see also* embassies)

foreign in Russia, 630–1
  Russian overseas, 676, 678, 679
convents, *see* monasteries and convents, *and*
  names of individual convents
Convent of the Deposition of the Robe, 342
Convent of the Nativity of the Virgin, 198–9
Convent of Saints Martha and Mary, 172
cooking
  monastic, 341
  Russian, 87–8, 241
Cosmonautic Memorial Museum, 226
Cosmos Museum, 299, 306, 307
Cottage Palace (Peterhof), 576
Cottage of Peter the Great, 478
country-club settlements, 236
courier services, 80, 191, 355, 628–9
credit cards, 55, 65, 74, 78, 95, 371
crime, 68–9
cruises, 62, 248, 306, 412, 671
cuisines, Georgian, 174
currency (*see also* money)
  counterfeit US, 65
  foreign, accepted, 78
  exchange, 65, 68
  Russian, 64
customs (behavior), 82
customs (government agency), 63, 95
Customs House (St Petersburg), 487
Cyrillic alphabet, 96, 98, 684
Czars (*see also* names of individual rulers)
  burial places, 140, 271, 474
  genealogy (from 1825), 706–7

D
dachas, 26–7, 110, 214, 236, 252, 286, 484, 593
Dalai Lama, 14th (Terzin Gyatso), 485
Damaskin, Abbot, 617, 618
Davilov Monastery, 287
Danilovsky Monastery, 224, 268
Davydov, Ivan (architect), 573
Decembrists (revolutionaries), 473, 477, 490–1,
  501–2
Decorative and Folk Art Museum, 183
Defense and Siege of Leningrad Museum, 518
demonstrations, *190*
dental services, 356, 630
department stores (*see also* GUM, Central

Universal Store), 161, 224, 392, 527, 656
departure tax, 72
Detsky Mir (Children's World department store), 156
Diaghilev, Sergei (artistic entrepreneur), 460, 464, 470
diamonds, 511
Diderot, Denis, 494, 502
dining (*see also* cafés and coffee shops, meals, menus, restaurants), 371–2, 641
disabled persons, 84, 111, 359
Dolgorukov, Vladimir (Moscow governor), 175
Dolgoruky, Prince Yuri (founder of Moscow), 122, 285, 286, 310, 322, 335, 337, 347
    statue, 175
dolls, Russian (*matryoshka*), 94, 96, 170, 280–1
Dom Knigi (House of Books), 189, 525
Dom Soyuzov (House of Trade Unions), 163
Donskoi Monastery, 150, 222–3
Donskoi, Prince Dmitri, 19, 122, 151, 153, 161
Dostoevsky Apartment Museum, 198
Dostoevsky, Fyodor (writer), 448, 534, 556
    quoted, 536–7, 626
    statue, 165
Dostoevsky Literary Museum, 533
drinking, 93–4
dress code, 273, 399
driving, 62
drugs, 63, 69
dual pricing, 66
Dubor, Yegor (builder), 316
Dumas, Alexandre (French novelist), quoted, 192–4, 486
Duncan, Isadora (ballet dancer), 169, 528
Dymov, Alexander (writer), quoted, 562–3
Dynamo Sports Complex, 109
Dzerzhinsky, Felix (revolutionary), 33, 155, 156, 164, 214, 501, 544, 556

E

economy, Russian, 16, 29, 34, 36–8, 48–50, 437–8
    crisis in, 42
Eisenstein, Sergei Mikhailovich (film director), 199, 202–4, 203, 248
elections, 28–9, 35–6, 40–1, 43, 47
electricity supply, 59

elektrichka (commuter trains), 75
Elizabeth I, Empress (Czarina), 429, 491, 535
Elizabeth II, Queen (Great Britain), 141, 476
embassies
    CIS, 358–9
    foreign, 356–8
    Russian overseas, 678, 679–81
embroidery
    collections, 128, 278, 341
    displays, 225
emergency services
    Moscow, 354
    St Petersburg, 628
enamels, 292–3
Engels
    archives, 175
    statue, 169
English (language), 17
English Club (Angliisky), 178, 197
Epiphany Cathedral, 293
ethnographic museums, 298, 487, 529
Ethnography Museum (Myushkin), 298
etiquette, 82
Exhibition of Economic Achievements (VDNKh), 226
Expedition Trophy Car Rally, 349

F

Fabergé, eggs and jewelry, 142, 145
Fabergé, Carl, 145, 147, 521
Fabergé, Gustav, 145
Fadeyev, Alexander (writer), 210
fakes (*see also* currency, icons, vodka), 95, 316
Falconet, Etienne (sculptor), 288, 429, 446, 502, 506, 521
farming, 336
fast food, 372
Federal Security Bureau, 44, 157
Fedorov, Ivan (printer), 149
    monument, 150
ferris wheels, 213, 227
ferry services, 62, 229, 671
festivals (*see also* Moscow International Film Festival), 336, 182, 187, 248
    church, 682–3
    music, 306
    poetry, 307

film locations, 225, 248, 260, 336
film, photographic, 59
film studios, 207, 216, 226, 478
Finland Railway Station, 539
Fioravante, Aristotele (architect), 131, 325
fires, in Moscow (1812), 102, 119, 164, 192, 209, 241, 304
fishing, 228, 252, 293, 347
    ice fishing, 253, 258
flea markets, 94, 200
floods, 477, 490, 518
Folk Arts Museum (Moscow), 176, 280
Fontana, Giovanni (architect), 578
food stores (see also Yeliseyev's), 175, 392, 641
foreign currency, see currency
fountains
    Moscow, 226
    St Petersburg, 501, 517, 568–73, 570–1, 575
    Tsarskoye Selo, 595
Freemasons, 253
frescoes
    locations
        Golden Ring, 286, 287, 291, 303, 304, 307, 311, 325, 327, 340, 344
        Moscow, 115, 131, 140, 154, 223
        Pskov, 612
        Staraya Ladoga, 616
    painting of, 134, 267, 316
    restoration, 266
friezes, 159, 326
Frunze, Mikhail (Bolshevik leader), 314
furs, 657
FyodorI, Czar, 222

G

Gagarin, Yuri (cosmonaut), 130, 141, 158, 227
    monument, 224
Gaidar, Yegor (architect), 36–7
Garden Ring (Sadovoye Koltso), 209–14
gardens, public
    Moscow, 120, 130, 153, 162, 198, 212, 228
    St Petersburg, 517–8, 544
Gatchina (village), 604–6
Gatchina Palace, 605, 605
Gatchina Park, 605
gates, city
    Moscow, 120, 148, 151, 186

St Petersburg, 558
    Vladimir, 324
Gay Rights Association, 84
gift shops, 393
gifts, custom of giving, 59
Gilyarovsky, Valdimir (writer), 174–5
glasnost, see perestroika and glasnost
Gliere, Reinhold (composer), 443
Glinka, Mikhail (composer), 45, 310, 549, 602
Glinka Music Museum, 183
Godunov, Boris, Czar, 137, 140, 195, 217, 222
Godunov family, 276, 311, 312
Gogol Memorial House, 196
Gogol, Nikolai (writer), 196, 237, 327, 446–7, 521
    monument, 186, 196
    quoted, 12, 87, 89, 208, 214, 477
Gogolevsky Bulvar, 196
Golden Palace of the Czarina (Moscow), 135
Golden Ring, 16
golf courses, 251–2, 415, 675
Golitsyn family, 150, 165, 223
Golitsyn, Mikhail (General), 223
Golitsyn, Prince Dmitri (governor of Moscow), 175, 494
Golivko, Ivan (folk artist), 315
Golovin, Alexander (artist), 159
Goncharov, Ivan (writer), 89, 170
Goncharova, Natalia (Pushkin's wife), 182, 188
Gorbachev, Mikhail Sergeyvich (President), 25, 28, 32–3, 40, 216, 268
    quoted, 30
Gorbachev, Raisa, 33, 88, 216, 220
Gorgovsky (poet), 434
Goritsky Monastery, 287–8
Gorky House Museum (Moscow), 180, 182
Gorky Library (Moscow), 216
Gorky Literary Museum (Moscow), 210
Gorky, Maxim (writer), 173, 180, 197, 221, 474
    monument, 183
    quoted, 233, 316
Gorky Park (Moscow), 213, 220–2, 222
Gorky Theater, 197
Gostiny Dvor (arcade), 151
graffiti, 29, 179, 181
Grand Hotel Europe, 527
Grand Palace (Moscow), 141

Great Palace (Peterhof), 575–6
Grebenshchikov, Boris (musician), 468
Green Belt of Glory, The, 557
Griboedov, Alexander (writer), statues of, 199, 534
Griboyedov Canal, 525, 526
Groot, Georg Christoph (court painter), 535
group tours, 51, 66, 124
guesthouses, 289, 312, 336, 369–70
GUM (State Universal Store), 6–7, 97, 114, 119
Gumilyov, Nikolai (poet), 450, 519, 529, 621

H
Hackert, Phiippe (artist), 575
Hall of the Glinka Maly Philharmonic, 526
handicrafts, 302, 391, 654–5
    collections, 183
health, see dental services, HIV, medical services, optical services
health clubs (see also bathhouses and saunas), 191, 413, 673
Hermitage Museum, 16, 426, 493–5, 498, 500
    views of, 424–5, 466–7, 496–7, 499
Hermitage Gardens (Moscow), 162, 198
Hermitage Pavilion (Peterhof), 573
Hermitage Theater, 494
Hero City of Moscow Obelisk, 191
Herzen, Alexander (revolutionary writer), 164, 188, 197, 502
Herzen Museum, 188
hippodromes (racecouses), 183–4
Historical Museum (Moscow), 6–7, 115, 118–9, 120, 610
History and Archives Institute, 149
History of Moscow Museum, 158
History Museum (Zvenigorod), 260
history museums
    Ivanovo, 314
    Moscow and vicinity, 153, 158, 178, 210, 254
    Novgorod, 607
    St Petersburg and vicinity, 476, 555, 568, 598
    Vladimir, 324
    Yaroslavl, 302, 305
History of Religion Museum, 525
hitch hiking, 77
HIV, status certificate, 52, 67

holidays, 84–5
    church, 682–3
Holy Trinity Cathedral, 535
homestays, 53, 370
homosexuals, 84, 410–1, 667–8
horse riding, 258, 347, 675
hostels, 638–9
Hotel Astoria (St Petersburg), 510
Hotel National (Moscow), 164
hotels, 77–8
    availability, 51
    Golden Ring, 274, 282, 283, 285, 289, 297, 300, 312, 315, 321, 336–7, 347
    Moscow and vicinity, 164, 174, 182, 191, 226, 256, 260, 362–9
    Novgorod, 611
    Pskov, 612
    St Petersburg and vicinity, 479, 490, 587, 616, 634–8
House of Boyars Romanov, 153
House of Friendship, 186
House Museum of the Ivanov-Voznesensk City Council, 314
House of Nikita Pustosviat, 344
house rental, 337, 370–1, 640
House of Trade Unions, 163
Huerne, Chevalier de (architect), 240
human rights, events on, 212
hunting, 247
hydrofoils, 229, 300, 567, 583

I
ice-skating
    Moscow and vicinity, 179, 199, 214, 221, 228, 254, 258, 415
    Suzdal, 347
    St Petersburg, 675
iconostases
    Golden Ring, 278, 304, 306, 311, 316, 325
    Moscow, 140, 154, 195, 201, 217, 218, 223, 247, 252, 260, 267
    St Petersburg, 474, 509
    stone, 291, 292
icon paintings, 329–33
    Apostle Paul, 171
    export, 95
    fakes, 200

location of
  Golden Ring, 286, 292, 303, 311, 325, 341
  Moscow, 115, 131, 134, 170, 175, 195,
    237, 245
  Novogorod, 607
  Kizhi Island, 619
  Our Lady of Vladimir, 322, *331*
  painting of, 224, 316, 329, 330, 340–1, 610
  restoration studio, 225
  return of, to Orthodox Church, 269
  for sale, 189, 223
  towers named after, 304
identity documents, 69
Ilyinsky Gardens, 153
Inber, Vera (poet), 560
  quoted, 510
independent travel, 51, 272
inflation, 32, 37, 49, 76
insurance, medical, 68
intelligence services, 157
Intercession Church, 201
Internet, 44
  cafés, 79, 164, 375, 647
Intourist, 77, 353
Ipatyevsky Monastery, 311
Iron Museum, 287
Isakov, Kiril (merchant), 311
Ivan III (Ivan the Great), 19, 122, 131
Ivan IV (Ivan the Terrible), 19, 89, 102, 137, 224
  residence, 281–2
  throne, 134, 142
Ivanov (serf architect), 240
Ivanovo (town), 314–5
Ivanovo Museums of Art and History, 314
ivory carvings, 341
Izmailovo (park), 200
Izmailovo Flea Market, 200

J
jaywalking, 70
jazz clubs, 191, 406–7, 667
jewelry, 142, 145, 189, 393, 511, 657
  collections, 128, 183, 278, 304
Jewish Committee, 168
Jones, Robert Trent Jr (golf course designer),
  251
journals, *see* newspapers and magazines

K
Kalashnikov family, 298
Kalinin, Mikhail (Party leader), 164, 186
Kalinin Museum, 164
Kalinin Prospekt, 184–6
Kamenny Island Theater, 484
Kavos, Albert (architect), 159
Kazakov, Matvei (architect), 128, 151, 164, 170,
  175, 197, 199, 253
Kazan Cathedral, 119, 269
Kazansky Bridge, 525
Kazansky Railway Station, 191
Kennedy, John F (US President), 159
Kent, Prince Michael of, 311
KGB, 156–7
  building, 156, *156*
Khodorkovsky, Mikhail (oil magnate), 47
Khrushchev, Nikita, 24, 156
Kideksha, village of, 347
Kievsky Railway Station, 191
Kiriyenko, Sergei (Prime Minister), 41, 42
Kirov Central Park of Culture and Rest, 484
Kirov Islands, 479, 484–5
Kirov Museum, 478
Kirov, Sergei (Party leader), 22, 478, 457, 545
Kirov Stadium, 485
Kirov Theater, 457
Kitai-Gorod ('China Town'), 148, 153–5
Kizhi Island, 619
Klin (town), 245
Klodt, Peter (sculptor), 159, 518, 532
  burial place
Kolomenskoye Museum Preserve, 246–8
Kolyvan Vase, *497*, 498
Komsomol (Communist Youth Organization), 30
Konenkov Memorial Studio, 176
Konenkov, Sergei (sculptor), 176
Konstantine Palace (Strelna), 567–8
Korin, Pavel (painter), 315
Kosmos Pavilion, 227
Kostroma (town), 310–2
"kottedzhi" (country homes) (*see also* dachas),
  236
Krasnaya Presnya Museum, 210
Kremlin (Moscow), 121–5, 128–37, 140–3, *261*,
  296, *417*
  walls, ashes interred in, 118, 180

kremlins, 121, 264, 275, 296, 303, 339, 344, 612, 615
Krestovsky (Island), 485
Kronstadt, 581–3
Kronverk Artillery, Engineers and Signals Museum, 477
Kropotkin, Prince Pyotr (revolutionary scholar), 168
    quoted, 262–3
Krupskaya, Nadezhda Konstantinovna (wife of Lenin), 551
    statue, 199
Krylov, Ivan (children's fabulist), monument, 179, 518
Kunstkammer (St Petersburg), 14–5, 487, 544
Kuskovo Palace Museum, 249–50, 249–50
Kustodiev, Boris (artist), 470
Kutuzov, Prince Mikhail, 191, 241, 242, 525
    statue, 195
Kutuzovvsky Prospekt, 191, 195
Kuzminki estate, 250
Kuznetsky Most (Bridge), 162

L

La Mothe, Vallin de (architect), 526, 527
lacquer boxes, 315–6
Lake Ladoga, 614
Lazarenko, Vitaly (clown), 233
Lazarevskoye Cemetery, 538
Lebed, General Alexander, 40, 41, 205
Leblond (architect), 517, 543
Lenin Library, see Russian State Library
Lenin Mausoleum, 6–7, 13, 60, 115, 118, 172, 554
    sarcophagus, 115, 187
Lenin, Vladimir Ilyich (see also Krupskaya, Nadezhda; Ulyanov, Alexander), 115, 158, 180, 423, 487, 583–4
    archives, 175
    decrees signed by, 123
    monuments, 286, 539, 543, 545
    museums, 516, 583, 584
    residences, 128, 164, 545
    return from exile to lead revolution, 431, 479, 539
    Russian revolution and, 551–4
    statues, 175, 281, 553

Leningrad (see also St Petersburg, Siege of Leningrad)
    naming of, 432
Leo Tolstoy Museum, 168–9
Lermontov Memorial House, 189
Lermontov, Mikhail (poet and playwright), 189, 212
lesbians, 84, 410–1, 667–8
Levitan House Museum, 312
Levitan, Isaac (landscape artist), 237, 312
libraries, 164–5, 303, 399, 471, 524, 530, 662
    church, 229
    literary, 182, 256
    public, 199, 291, 586
    science and technology, 158
Library of Russian Vodka, 298
Lidval, Fyodor (architect), 478, 510
lighthouses, 428, 486
Lights of Moscow Museum, 200
literature, market for, 453
literary awards, 453
Literary Institute (Moscow), 197
Literary Museum (Moscow), 161
literary museums
    Moscow and vicinity, 161, 168–9, 172, 173, 175, 180, 182, 188, 189, 198, 210, 211, 217, 236–7, 246
    Golden Ring, 252, 299
    St Petersburg and vicinity, 487, 511, 519–20, 533, 534, 606
log-cabins, 336
Lomonosov (Oranienbaum), 578, 580–1
    map, 579
Lomonosov, Mikhail (scientist), 98, 118, 214, 444, 514, 578
    statue, 164, 487
Lomonosov Museum, 14–5, 487
Lomonosov Porcelain Factory, 581
Lomonosov Univeristy, see Moscow University
Lubyanka prison, 156
Lubyanskaya Ploshchad (Square), 155–8
luggage, 55
    sightseeing check-in, 124, 500
Lumumba People's Friendship University, 224
Lunacharsky, Anatoly (writer), 517
Luzhkov, Yuri (Mayor of Moscow), 104, 105, 167, 168
Luzhniki Central Stadium, 217

M

McCartney, Sir Paul, 115, 469
McDonald's (fast-food outlet), 177–8
magazines, *see* newspapers and magazines
Malchish-Kibalchish (children's book character),
    statue, 216
Malevich, Kazimir (painter), 470
Mamontov, Savva (art patron), *28*, 209, 213,
    237, 469
Mandelstam, Osip (poet), 450–1
    quoted, 449, 624
Manezhnaya Ploshchad (Moscow), 173
manuscripts
    birch-bark, 267, 304, 607
    collections, 128, 182, 304, 326, 592, 610
    discovery of, 114
    writing, 275
Marble Palace, 511, 516
Maria Fyodorovna, Czarina, 476, 599
Mariinsky Theater, 457, 548, *550*
Marionette Theater, 532
marionettes, see puppet theaters
markets (*see also* flea markets)
    flower, 544
    Moscow and vicinity, 198, 211, 258, 341, 394
    St Petersburg, 657–8
Martos, Ivan (sculptor), 115
Marx, Karl, 551, 552
    archives, 175
    quoted, 268
    statue, 158
Marxism-Leninism Institute, Party archives of, 175
'Master Peter' (architect), 610
matryoshka dolls, 94, *96*, 170, 280
Matryoshka Museum, 280
Maxim's restaurant , 164
Mayakovsky Museum, 157
Mayakovsky Theater, 196
Mayakovsky, Vladimir (poet), 157, 182, 187, 451
    quoted, 121
meals, Russian, 90, 93
media, *see* newspapers and magazines, radio
    stations, television
medical insurance, 68
medical museums, 576
medical services, 58, 355–6, 629–30
Melnikov House, 187–8

Melnikov, Konstantin (architect), 187
Memorial to the Fighters of the Revolution (St
    Petersburg), 517
Memorial to the Heroes (Moscow), 109
Mendeleyev, Dmitri (scientist), 90
Menelaws, Adam (architect), 576
Menschikov Mansion, 197
Menschikov Palace, 488
Menschikov, Prince Alexander, 199, 488, 578
Menschikov, Prince Sergei: Mansion
menus, 91, 92
Merkurov, Sergei (sculptor), 175
Metro (Moscow), 76, 110–1
    map, 112–3
Metro Museum, 110
Metropol Hotel, 158–9
Mezhdunarodnaya (International) Hotel, 191
Michetti, Nicolo (architect), 567, 573, 575
Mikhailkov, Sergei (children's poet), 46
Mikhailov, Alexander (architect), 159
Mikhailovskoye estate (Pskov), 612
Mikhailovsky Castle, 518–20
Military Historical Museum (Vladimir), 324
military museums
    Moscow and vicinity, 142, 195, 211, 241, 242
    St Petersburg and vicinity, 477, 486, 495,
        518, 544, 557, 582
Minin, Kozma (and Dmitri Pozharsky),
    monument, 115
minorities, attitude to, 83
Mint, the (St Petersburg), 476
Minit, Old Royal (Moscow), 148, 476
Mironov, Alexei (serf architect), 249
Mirozhsky Monastery, 612
Mkhat Moscow Arts Theater, 174
mobile phones, 79
Modern History of Russia Museum, 178
Mokhovaya Ulitsa (street), 164–5
monasteries and convents (*see also* names of
    individual convents and monasteries)
    fortified, 217, 267, 275, 287, 296, 344
    Golden Ring, 298, 342
    Moscow, 229, 260, 273, 400
    Valaam Island, 617
Monastery of St Barlaam, 293
Monastery of St Nicholas the Miracle Worker, 616
Monastery of St Nicholas-on-the-Uleima, 297

money (*see also* currency)
  declaration of, 63
  safety of, 62, 67
  transfer of, 66
Mongols
  invasions, 19, 104, 122, 130, 153, 161, 223,
    247, 276, 293, 300, 322, 329, 335, 338, 606
  occupation by, 267, 274
Monomakh, Grand Prince Vladimir, 134, 142,
  322, 340
Montferrand, Auguste (architect), 130, 491, 509,
  510
Monument to the Defenders of Pavlovsk, 602
Monument to the Heroes of the Defense of
  Leningrad, 557
Monument to the Worker and Collective Farm
  Girl, 226
monuments
  Borodino, 242
  Golden Ring, 299, 327
  Moscow, 153, 162, 179, 183, 186, 191, 196,
    197, 224
  St Petersburg, 477, 506, 518, 549
Morozov, Arseny (merchant), 186, 209
Morozov family, 201
Morozov, Ivan (art collector), 165
Morozov Mansion, 179–80
Morozov, Savva (businessman), 179, 180
mosaic panels, 159
Moscow
  coat of arms, 104
  maps, 106–8, 116–7, 238–9
  population, 104
  rings, 109–10
Moscow Arts Museum, 174
Moscow Choral Synagogue, 153
Moscow Country Club, 251–2
Moscow Drama Theater, 179
Moscow Hippodrome (racecourse), 183, 184
Moscow International Film Festival, 85, 176,
  207
Moscow International Marathon, 85
Moscow Palace of Young Pioneers, 216
Moscow School (icon painting), 341
Moscow Stock Exchange (Birzha), 150
Moscow Triumphal Arch (St Petersburg), 556
Moscow University, 118, 164, 214, 216

Moscow Victory Park, 557
Moscow Zoo, 210
Moskovsky Vokzal (Moscow Railway Station)
  (St Petersburg), 533
Moskva Hotel (St Petersburg), 534
Moskva River, 229
Mouse Museum (Myushkin), 298
movie theaters, *see* cinemas
Mukhina, Vera (sculptor), 197, 226
murals, 340
Museum to Alexander Suvnov, 544
Museum of Anthropology and Ethnography,
  14–5, 487
Museum of the Arctic and Antarctic, 533
Museum of Art and Architecture (Vladimir), 326
Museum of Circus History and Variety Art, 519
Museum of Contemporary Art (Moscow), 161
Museum of Ethnography, 529
Museum of History, Architecture and Art
  (Novgorod), 607
Museum of History, Architecture and Nature
  (Moscow), 254
Museum of History and Art, 287, 288
Museum of the History of St Petersburg, 555
Museum of History of St Petersburg and
  Petrograd, 476
Museum of Local Art and History, 305
Museum of Musical Instruments, 510–1
Museum of Old Russian Art, 305
Museum of Old Wooden Architecture, 311
Museum of Palekh Art, 315
Museum of Political History, 478
Museum of Prison Art, 298
Museum of Private Collections, 165
Museum of Pyotr Smirnov, 299
Museum of Russian Art, 305
Museum of Russian Superstition, 298
Museum of Serf Art, 228
Museum of Soil Science, 486
Museum-Study of Mikhail Frunze, 314
Museum of Teapots, 287
Museum of Theatrical Art, 530
Museum of Urban Sculpture, 538
Museum of Wooden Architecture (Istra River),
  243, *244*
Museum of Wooden Architecture (Kizhi Island),
  619

museums (*see also* name of individual institution
    and type of museum), 176, 258, 394–9,
    658–62
    number of, 13, 471
Museums of Contemporary Artists and Ancient
    Town Life, 324
music (*see also* jazz clubs), 163, 463–5, 468–9
    festivals, 306
    museums, 183, 510–1
music schools (conservatories), 548
music shops, 393
musical instruments, colleçitons, 183, 510–1
Mussorgsky, Modest (musician), 524
Mussorgsky Maly Theater of Opera and Ballet,
    529
Myshkin (town), 298

N

Nabokov House Museum, 511
Nabokov, Vladimir (novelist and poet), 451
Nakhimov Naval School, 479
names, Russian, 82
Napoleon I, Emperor, 195
    attempted destruction of Moscow, 115, 123,
        131, 137, 217
    invasion of Russia (1812), 102, 124, 241
National Hotel, 174, 554
naval history, 427, 581–2
naval schools, 211, 479, 501
Neizvestny, Ernst (sculptor), 298
Nekrasov, Nikolai (writer), 307, 534
Nekrasov Estate Museum (Yaroslavl), 299, 307
Nekrasov House Museum (St Petersburg), 534
Nemirovich-Danchenko, Vladimir (playwright),
    149, 174, 176
Nevsky Banya Complex, 533
Nevsky, Prince Alexander, 285, 327, 344
    statue of, 286
Nevsky Prospekt (St Petersburg), 520–1,
    524–30, 532–5, 538
Nevzorov, Alexander (reporter), 437
New Arbat, *see* Novy Arbat
New Cathedral of the Donskaya Virgin, 223
New Circus, 216, 233
New Jerusalem Monastery, 243, 245
newspapers and magazines, 80, 355, 629, 696
    offices, 177, 183

Nicholas I, Czar, 21, 72, 348, 509
Nicholas II, Czar, 22, 430
    abdication, 461
    burial, 271, 474, 476
    coronation, 145, 202
    execution of, 423, 426, 431
    petition to, 454–5
nightlife, 408–11, 668–9
Nijinsky, Vaslav (ballet dancer), 460–1
Nikitin, Gury (artist), 287, 291, 304, 345
Nikitnikov, Grigory (merchant), 154
Nikitsky Bulvar, 196–7
Nikolayevsky Bridge, 489–90
Nikolo-Medvedsky Monastery, 616
Nikolskaya Ulitsa, 148–50
Nikolsky Old Believers' Commune, 201
Nikulin, Yuri (clown), 198, 218, 220, 235
    statue of, 162, 198
Nikulin's Circus, 198, 235
NKVD (People's Commissariat of Internal
    Affairs), 156, 157
Novgorod, 606–7, 610–1
    map, 608–9
Novgorod School (icon painting), 329, 332
Novinsky Bulvar, 209
Novodevichy Cemetery, 204, 210, 218, 220, 235
Novodevichy Convent, 109, 217–8, *219*, 220–1
Novy Arbat (New Arbat), 184, 189, 191

O

Obrazizov Puppet Theater, 211
October Revolution (1917), *see* Bolshevik
    Revolution
Okhotny Ryad (Hunter's Lane), 163–4
Okhotny Ryad Underground Shopping
    Complex, 163, 168
Okudzhava, Bulat (poet and singer), 188
Old Arbat, *see* Stary Arbat
Old Believers, 201, 225, 515
Old Cathedral of the Donskaya Virgin, 223
Old Circus, 198, 216, 233, 235
Old English Inn, 151
Olympic Sports Complex, 212, 217
Opekulin, Alexander (sculptor), 176
Open Air Museum Park of Wooden Architecture
    (Novgorod), 610
optical services, 356

Oriental Art Museum, 166, 196
Oranienbaum, *see* Lomonosov
Orlov, Count Grigory, 168, 511, 513, 516, 572, 575, 604
Orlova, Lyubov (film star), 178
Orlovsky, Boris (sculptor), 491
Orthodox Church, Russian (*see also* churches), 212, 268–9, 271–2, 289
  central library, 229
  holidays and festivals, 682–3
  Holy Synod, 134, 201, 442, 506
  leadership, 269
  Old Believers and, schism between, 201
  Patriarchs' burial places, 201, 223
Oruzheinaya Palata, *see* Armory Palace Museum
Ostankino Palace, 228–9
Ostankino TV Tower, 228–9
Ostrovsky, Alexander (playwright), 161, 173, 530
Ostrovsky House Museum, 173
Ostrovsky Humanitarian Museum, 175
Ostrovsky, Nikolai (writer), 175
Oswald, Lee Harvey (alleged assassin), 159
OVIR (Interior Ministry), 52, 53, 54

P
paintings, *see* icons, art museums, religious art
Palace of Congresses, 124
Palace of Curiosities, *see* Kunstkammer
Palace of Czarevich Dmitri, 298
Palace of Facets
  Moscow, 137
  Novgorod, 607
Palace of Peter III, 580
Palace Square (Dvortsovaya Ploshchad), 490–5, 492–3, 498, 500,
Palekh (town), 315–6
papier-mâché boxes, 315–6
Park of the Fallen Idols, 155, 214
parks
  Golden Ring, 293, 314
  Moscow, 200, 213, 228
  St Petersburg and vicinity, 477, 557, 576, 578, 593, 601, 606
Parland, Alfred (architect), 526
Pashkov Dom, *see* Russian State Library
passports, 53, 54, 55, 63, 362

Pasternak, Boris (writer), 252
  quoted, 17, 252
Pasternak House Museum, 252
pastry shops, *see* bakeries and pastry shops
Patriarch's Palace, 128, 130
Patriarch's Pond, 179–80, 182
patronymics, *see* names, Russian
Paul I, Czar, 599, 601, 604
Pavlova, Anna (ballet dancer), 459, 460–1
Pavlovsk, 599, 600, 601–2, 604
  map, 603
Pavlovsk Palace, 600, 601–2
Pavlovsk Park, 601
Pavlovsky Regiment, Barracks of, 517
Peredelkino (writers' and artists' colony), 252–3
Pereslavl-Zalessky, 283, 285–8
  map, 284
perestroika and glasnost, 25, 28–30, 437
performing arts museums, 174, 176, 197, 209, 211, 213
personal requisites, 58–9
Pertsov House, 170
Peshkov, Alexei Maximovich, *see*, Gorky, Maxim
Peter I (the Great), Czar (*see also* Peterhof), 16, 20, 137, 212, 217, 345, 439–40, 442, 474, 517, 581, 588
  boat and Boat House, 285, 476
  Bronze Horseman statue, 16, 426, 429, 442, 446, 502, 506, 521, 584, 625–6
  buildings initiated by, 124, 148, 427, 473, 487
  church reforms, 201, 338, 506
  Cyrillic alphabet simplified by, 96
  death of, 428, 584
  face mask, 288
  French cooking introduced by, 89
  monuments and statues, 105, 167, 214, 285, 476, 519, 568, 573
  museum, 478
  navy, development of, 211, 427
  portrait, 441
  residences, 248, 518
  thrones and throne room, 142, 495, 499, 575
  transfer of Russian capital, 102, 168, 422
Peter III, Czar, 572, 580
Peter and Paul Fortress, 427, 430, 473–7, 475, 601
Peter and Paul Lutheran Church, 524

Peterhof Palace (Petrodvorets), 16, 565, 567–9,
  572–7, *574*
  construction, 568
  map, 569
  in World War II, 576–7
Peter's Fortress (Petrokrepost), 614–5
Petipa, Marius (ballet dancer), 457
Petrograd, *see* St Petersburg
Petroskoye estate, 614
Petrovsky Bulvar, 198
photographic film, 59
photographs, display of, 187
photography, restrictions on, 59, 66, 118
Pirogov, Nilolai (surgeon), 209
Piskarevskoye Memorial Cemetery, 543
planetarium, 314, 477
Plekhanov, Georgi (Marxist), 525
Plios (town), 312
Plisetskaya, Maya (ballet dancer), 462
Pokrovsky (Intercession) Bulvar, 199–200
Poles, invasion by, 282, 297, 338, 344
police, 68–9, 83
political history museums, 164, 478, 501, 516,
  555, 583, 584
Polyakov, Valery (cosmonaut), 227
Polytechnical Museum, 158
Popov, Alexander (clown), *231*
Popov, Alexander (scientist), 511
Popov Central Communication Museum, 511
population, 12, 13, 29, 39, 50
  life expectancy, 37, 50
porcelain
  collections, 245, 605
  factory, 581
porters (at railway stations), 74
Posokhin, Mikhail (architect), 124, 165, 189
post office, 80
postage stamps, 80
potatoes, 88
Potemkin, Prince Grigory, 514, 532, 543
Poteshny Palace, *see* Amusement Palace
Pozharsky, Prince Dmitri, 119, 344
  monument (and Kozma Minin), 115
Presnya Banya (Bathhouse), 163
Primakov, Yevgeny (Prime Minister), 42, 43
printing, history, 149

prisons and prisoners, 156, 324, 345, 430,
  473–4, 614
Prokofiev, Sergei (composer), 464
Pskov, 611–2
  map, 613
public toilets, 69–70
pubs and bars, 384–7, 641–7
Pugo, Boris (Minister of the Interior), 31, 33
Pulkovo Astronomical Observatory, 555, 558
Puppet Museum (Uglich), 298
puppet theaters, 211, 314, 532
Pushkin (town), *see* Tsarskoye Selo
Pushkin, Alexander, 98, 182, 201, 443, 444,
  446, 593, 612, 614
  burial place, 446
  duel, 182, 446, 485, 524
  museums, 168, 188, 487, 500, *503*, 592
  portrait, 627
  quoted, 13, 87, 422, 426, 443, 446, 446,
  592–3, 614, 625–6
  statues, 176, 188, 197, *447*, 528, 558, 592
Pushkin Drama Theater, 530
Pushkin House Museum (Moscow), 188
Pushkin House Museum (St Petersburg), 500, *503*
Pushkin House Literary Museum (St
  Petersburg), 487
Pushkin Museum (Tsarskoye Selo), 592
Pushkin Museum of Fine Art, 109, 165
Putin, Vladimir Vladimirovich (President), 16,
  42, 43, 44–8, 426, 588

Q
Quarenghi, Giacomo (architect), 151, 487, 494,
  507, 527, 588, 595

R
Rabinovich, Sholom (writer), monument, 179
racecourses, *see* hippodromes
radio stations, 81
Radishchev, Alexander (writer), 148
Radonezhsky, Sergius, *see* St Sergius
Railway Museum, 556
railways (*see also* train services, Trans-Siberian
  Railway), 595, 602
  narrow guage, 285
Rasputin, Grigory, 159, 431, 550, 555
Rasputin Museum, 555

Rasputina, Maria Grigorievna, 555
Rastrelli, Bartolomeo (architect), 428, 429, 491, 524, 543, 544, 568, 572, 575, 588, 589
Rastrelli, Carlo (sculptor), 288, 428, 506
Razliv (village), 583–4
Reagan, Nancy, 88
Reagan, Ronald (US President), 28
receipts, 64
Red Guards, 553
Red Square (Krasnaya Ploshchad), 60, 114–5, 118–21
Reed, John (American journalist), quoted, 126–7, 491, 545
religion, 268, 271–2
    museum of, 525
religious art, 279, 326, 507
Repin, Ilya (artist), 282, 302, 469–70, 510, 585
Repin Institute of Painting, Sculpture and Architecture, 488–9
Repino (town), 585
Rerberg, Ilya (architect), 174
restaurants, 90–1
    Golden Ring, 273–4, 283, 289, 300, 321, 336, 337, 341
    Moscow and vicinity, 163, 164, 174, 178, 201, 220, 228, 229, 241, 253, 372–3, 375–84, 387–9
    Novogorod, 611
    St Petersburg and vicinity, 445, 587, 595, 598, 604, 647–53
    vicinity
Riabushinsky family (banking dynasty), 180, 201
Riabushingsky, Pavel, 150
Rimsky-Korsakov (composer), 549, 611
Rimsky-Korsakov Conservatory, 548
Rimsky-Korsakov Memorial House, 534
Rinaldi, Antonio (architect), 511, 578, 580, 588, 604
Roerich Museum, 165
Roerich, Nikolai (artist), 165–6, 196, 298
Rogozhskoye Cemetery, 201
Romanov family (see also House of Boyars Romanov), 172, 311
    genealogy, 706–7
Romanov, Nikita, 153
Romanov, Czar Mikhail, 20, 135, 223, 311, 340, 427

Romany Gypsy Theater, 184
Roosen, Jacob (architect), 588
Rossi, Carlo (architect), 484, 490, 495, 506, 509, 518, 521, 524, 530
Rostov Museum Preserve of Art and Architecture, 292
Rostov Veliky (town), 288–9, 291–3, 296–7
    map, 290
Rostral Columns (St Petersburg), 486
Rostropovich, Mstislav Leopoldovich (musician), 33, 159
royal family, Russian
    artefacts, 248
    execution of (1918), 172, 423, 431, 474
    genealogy, 706–7
    reburial, 426, 431–2, 474–5
    souvenirs of, 151
royal yacht, gold model of, 147
Rozhdestvensky Bulvar, 198–9
Rtishchev, Fyodor (advisor to Czar), 229
Rubinstein, Anton, 197, 549
Rubinstein, Nikolai, 197
Rublyov, Andrei (artist), 225, 267, 330, 332, 341
    film of, 260
    works by, 16, 171, 225, 260, 278, 325, 334
Ruffo (architect), 137
Rkavishnikv, Alexander, 220
Russia, chronology, 18–22, 24
Russian Federation, 13
Russian language, 59, 83
    alphabet, 96, 98, 684
    vocabulary, 685–95
Russian Museum, 519, 524, 528–9
Russian National Library, 530
Russian Orthodox Church, see Orthodox Church, Russian
Russian State Library (formerly Lenin Library), 164–5
Russians, character of, 82
Rutskoi, Alexander (politician), 191

S
Sabinsky, Walter, petition to Czar Nicholas II, 454–5
Sadovoye Koltso, see Garden Ring
St Andrew Monastery, 229
St Basil's Cathedral (Moscow), 6–7, 103, 114–5

St George, 104
    Order of, 141
St Isaac's Cathedral (St Petersburg), 442, 466–7,
    507, 508, 509
St Isaac's Square (Isaakiyevskaya Ploshchad),
    507, 509–11
St Jacob's Monastery of Our Savior, 293
St Nicholas Marine Cathedral, 546–7, 549, 549
St Peter and Paul Cathedral, 474
St Petersburg
    anniversary, 16
    ban on high-rise buildings, 434
    capital transferred to, 102, 422
    construction of, 422–8
    maps, 480–3, 566
    names of, 16, 22, 422, 431, 432, 554
    population, 429, 431, 434
St Petersburg Circus, 232–3, 519
St Petersburg Conservatory, 197
St Petersburg State Philharmonic, 528
St Petersburg Russian Museum, 341
St Petersburg University, 487, 488
St Petersburg Zoo, 477
St Sergius of Radonezh, 274, 275, 276, 278
saints, important Russian, 278
Sakharov, Andrei (human rights activist), 25
Sakharov Museum, 212
samovars, 87
Sanunovskiye Baths, 163
Sarai Museum (Razliv), 583
saunas, see bathhouses
Savin, Sila (artist), 287, 291, 345
Schlusselburg, 614
science and technology museums, 158, 200,
    212, 227, 299, 478, 486, 511, 544
sculptures, 159, 212, 220, 225, 288, 341, 517,
    538
Sculptures in the Park (Moscow), 250
Seaman's Cathedral, 582, 582
Seaside Victory Park, 485
security, personal, 62, 67, 74, 83
Senate building
    Moscow, 128
    St Petersburg, 506
Senate Square (Senatskaya Ploshchad), 501–2,
    506–7
Sennaya Square, 555

Serf Theater, 240
serfs and serfdom, 21, 250, 555
    abolition of, 510
    art, museum of, 228
Sergiyev Posad, 16, 273–81
    map, 277
Serov, Valentin (painter), 237
Shalash Museum (Razliv), 584
Shalyapin, Fyodor (singer), 209–10, 213
Shalyapin House Museum
    Moscow, 209
    St Petersburg, 479
Shaw, George Bernard (English playwright), 163
Shchukin, Sergei (art collector), 165
Shchusev, Alexei (architect), 172
Shchusev Architectural Museum, 186
Sheherbakov Literary Museum, 606
Shekhtel, Fedor (architect), 150, 179, 180
Sheremetyev family, 249, 520
Sheremetyev Palace, 519, 520
Sheremetyev, Prince Nikolai, 189, 228
Shevardnadze, Eduard (Foreign Minister), 32
Shevchenko, Taras (poet), statue of, 191
shopping, 94–5, 389
    districts and complexes, 161, 163–4, 185,
    187, 189, 228, 286, 304
Shostakovich, Dmitri (composer), 464–5, 528,
    560
Siege of Leningrad, 465, 474, 510, 528, 556,
    559–63
    commemoration day, 85, 543
    deaths during, 423, 434, 561
    monument to, 557
    museum, 518, 557
skiing, 214, 222, 252, 253, 254, 258, 415–6, 675
Skryabin (composer and pianist), 187
Skryabin Museum, 187
sledding (sledging), 214, 227
Smirnov, Pytor, 90
smoking, 70
Smolensky Bulvar, 209
Smolny complex, 544
Smolny Convent, 545
Smolny Institute, 545
snowmobiling, 252
Sobchak, Anatoly (law professor and mayor),
    437, 438

social history museums, 344
Sokolov, Yegor Konstantinovich (architect),
    541–2
Solario (architect), 137
Solzhenitsyn, Alexander (writer), 39, 104, 252
souvenirs, 94–5, 187, 200, 393
    royal family, 151
Soviet Union, fall of, 12, 33, 42, 191
Sovincenter office building, 191
Sovremennik (Contemporary) Theater, 199
space exploration, 227
Sparrow Hills, 214
Spas-Transfiguration Cathedral (Pskov), 612
Spaso-Andronikov Monastery (Moscow), 225
Spaso Borodinsky Convent (Borodino), 242
Spaso House (Moscow), 187
Spaso-Yevfimievsky Monastery (Suzdal), 344
sports (see also golf, ice-skating, skiing,
    swimming), 414–6, 674–5
Sphinxes, Egyptian, 489
Sputnik Rocket, 226
Sretensky Bulvar, 199
stained glass, 180, 509
Stalin, 22, 168, 204, 271, 434, 557
    dacha, 191
    destruction of buildings by, 13, 115, 119,
        120, 128, 167, 170, 271
    residences, 164
    wife of, 141
Stanislavsky Drama Theater, 178
Stanislavsky, Konstantin (actor), 149, 174
Stanislavsky Memorial Museum, 176
Staraya Ladoga, 615–6
Starov, Ivan (architect), 535
Stary Arbat (Old Arbat), 186–9,
    views of, 184–5, 188
Stary Tsirk, see Old Circus
Stasov, Vassily, 169, 209, 509, 544, 556
State History Museum (Zaryade Museum), 153
Statues of Atlas, 494
Steam Engine Museum, 287
Stevens, Thomas, quoted, 86
stock exchange, see Moscow Stock Exchange
Stock Exchange building (St Petersburg), 486
stone carvings, 260
stores, local, 95
Strasnoi Bulvar, 197–8

Stravinsky, Igor (composer), 464
street lighting, 200
Strelka, see Vasilyevsky Island
Strelna, 567–8
Streltsy (Musketeers), 303, 439
    revolt by, 137, 162, 218
Stroganov, Baron, 250
Stroganov family, 276, 524
Stroganov Palace, 524
student discounts, 66
Summer Garden (St Petersburg), 517
Summer Palace (St Petersburg), 518
Surikov, Vasily (artist), 169
Suvorov, Alexander (army commander), 196,
    516, 544
Suzdal (town), 16, 335–42, 344–5, 347
    map, 343
Suzdal Museum, 340, 342
Suzdal Museum of Wooden Architecture, 336,
    339, 345, 347
Sverdlov, Yakov (President), 158, 164
Sviritsa, village of, 616
Svyatogorsky Monastery, 614
Swedish wars, 581, 588, 606, 614, 615, 617
    defeated at Battle of Poltava, 137, 249, 427,
        543, 565
swimming, 229, 416, 675
synagogues, 155

T
Tarkovsky, Andrei (film director), 225, 260, 333
Tavarichesky Gardens (Children's Park), 544
taxis, 68, 71, 76–7
Tchaikovsky, Peter (Pyotr) (composer), 245,
    246, 464
    statue of, 197
Tchaikovsky Concert Hall, 182, 214
Tchaikovsky Conservatory Grand Hall (music
    school), 196–7
Tchaikovsky International Competition, 245–6
Tchaikovsky Memorial House, 246
Tchechulin, Dmitry (architect), 214
tea, 87–8, 93
telephone services, 78–80
    information and city codes
        Moscow, 354
        St Petersburg, 628

television, 34, 80–1
Temple to Catherine the Great, 240
Terebenyev, A (sculptor), 494
Terem Palace, 135, *136*
Tereshkova, Valentina (cosmonaut), 299, 306–7
Tetris Wax Museum, 176
textile industry, 314
Theater Square (Teatralnaya Ploshchad)
  (Moscow), 158–61
Theater Square (St Petersburg), 457, 548–50
theater museums, 530
theaters
  Golden Ring, 314
  Moscow, 174, 178, 179, 184, 187, 196, 197,
  199, 216, 228, 240, 402–4
  St Petersburg, 484, 494, 528, 529, 530, 532,
  664–7
Theophanes the Greek
  icons by, 140, 286, 332
  frescoes by, 607
Thon, Konstantin (architect), 141, 166, 533
Throne of the Monomakhs, 134
thrones and throne rooms, 142, 495, *499*, 575, 602
Thubron, Colin, quoted, 435–6
Tikhvinskoye Cemetery, 538
time zones, 12, 55
Timiryazev, Kliment (botanist), monument, 197
tipping, 65, 91
toilets, public, 69–70
  on trains, 74
Tolstoy Country Estate Museum (Moscow), 217
Tolstoy House Museum, Alexei, 182
Tolstoy House Museum, Leo, 256, 257, 258
Tolstoy, Leo (Lev) (novelist), 169, 242, 256,
  257, 345
  museums, 168, 169, 217, 256, 257, 258
  quoted, 102, 104, 255, 627
  statue, 210
tombs
  of czars and princes, 140, 340
  of Soviet notables, 118, 218, 538
  of the Unknown Soldier, 120, *561*
Tomsky, Nikolas (sculptor), 195
Tornagi, Iola (balerina, wife of Shalyapin), 209
tours, *see* group tours
towers (*see also* bell towers, clock towers, TV
  Tower)

Golden Ring, 280, 304
  Moscow, 123, 130, 141, 199
Town of Pushkin Regional Museum, 598
towns, Russian, 264–5
Toy Museum, 280–1
toys, wooden, carving of, 276
traffic, in Moscow, 214
train service, 61–2, 72–5, 361–2, 633–4
trains (*see also* Trans-Siberian railway)
  safety on, 62
trams, 75
Transfiguration of Our Savior Monastery
  (Yaroslav), 303
Transfiguration of the Savior Monastery (Valaam
  Island), 617
transport museums, 287, 556
transportation card (*talony*), 75
Trans-Siberian Highway, 349
Trans-Siberian Railway, 62, 348–53, *351*
  model of, 145
travel agencies, 53, 677–81
  Moscow, 411–2
  St Petersburg, 669–70
traveler's checks, 65, 66, 78
Treasury (Museum of Ancient Russian Art), 278
trees, 247
  Cosmos Oak, 130
Tretyakov Gallery, 109, 166, 170, 212, 213–4,
  223, 269, 322
Tretyakov, Pavel Mikailovich (art patron), 170,
  469
Tretyakov, Sergei (art patron), 170
Tretyakovsky Passage (Moscow's Fifth Avenue),
  99, 150
Trezzini, Domenico (architect), 474, 487, 543
Trinity Cathedral (Moscow), 224
Trinity Cathedral (Pskov), 612
Trinity Church (Moscow University), 216
Trinity Church (Silversmiths' Lane), 200
Trinity Monastery of St Sergius (Sergiyev Posad),
  275, 332
Trinity-Sergius Monastery (Strelna), 568
troikas, 149, 208, 228
Troitsky Most (formerly Kirov Bridge), 477
Tropinin Museum, 172
Tropinin, Vasily (artist), 172
Trotsky, Leon, quoted, 104, 268

Tsaritsyno Estate, 253–4
Tsarskoye Selo, 588–90, 592–3, 595, 598
    map, 592
Tsarskoye Selo Museum, 598
Tseretelli, Zurab (sculptor), 161, 167, 168, 188, 210
Tsiolkovsky, Konstantin (space pioneer), 227
Tuchkova, Margarita, 242
TsUM (Central Universal Store), 161
Tukhachesvsky, General, 582
Turgenev, Ivan (writer), 169, 223, 237, 447–8
    quoted, 40
Turkey, war against, 153, 575, 595
Tutayev (town), on the Volga, 307
TV Tower (St Petersburg), 479
Tver (town), 258
Tverskaya Ulitsa, 173–8
Tverskoi Bulvar, 197
Tyutchev, Fyodor (poet), quoted, 50

U

Uglich (town), on the Volga, 297–9
Ukraina Hotel (Moscow), 191
Ulanov, Kirill (artist), 195
Ulanova, Galina (ballet dancer), 462
Ulitsa Ilyinka (Ilyinka street), 150–1
Ulitsa Neglinnaya (Neglinka Street), 162–3
Ulitsa Petrovka, 161–2
Ulitsa Varvarka, 151, 153
Ulitsa Volkhonka, 165
Ulyanov, Alexander (Lenin's brother), 21, 474, 614
Ulyanov, Valdimir Ilyich, see Lenin, Vladimir Ilyich
Union of Journalists, 196
universities, see Lumumba People's Friendship University, Moscow University
Ushakov, Simon (artist), 218, 276
Uspensky Monastery, 616
USSR, see Soviet Union
Ustinov, Sir Peter (British actor), 576

V

Vagankovo Cemetery, 213
Vagonova, Agrippina (ballet dancer), 462, 530
Vagonova Ballet School, 462, 530, 532
    museum, 531

Vakhtangov Theater, 187
Valaam Island, 617–9
    map, 618
valuables
    declaration of, 63
    safety of, 62, 67, 74, 83
Vasily III, Grand Prince, 122, 217
Vasilyevsky Island, 428, 485–90
Vasnetsov, Apollinary (artist), 212
Vasnetsov, Viktor (artist), 28, 212
vegetarians, 67
Vekselberg, Viktor (oil and metals magnate), 147
Velten, Yuri (architect), 557
Viktor Vasnetsov Museum, 212
Virgin of Smolensk Cathedral, 218, 220–1
visas, 17, 52–4, 352, 362, 676
    business, 53–4
    tourist, 52–3
    visitors, 54
Vitali, Giovanni (sculptor), 155
Vladimir (town), 320, 321–2, 324–8
    map, 323
Vladimir, Prince, 94, 96, 265
vodka, 69, 89–90, 94, 298, 299
Voinovich, Vladimir, quoted, 138–9
Volga River, boat rides on, 306, 307
Volkov Drama Theater, 304
Volkov, Fyodor (theater pioneer), 304
Voronin House, 298
Voronikhin (architect), 524
Vozdvizhenka Street (Moscow), 184
Vrubel, Mikhail (artist), 159, 180
Vyborg, 586–7
    map, 587
Vysotsky Museum and Cultural Center, 213
Vysotsky, Vladimir (song writer), 213

W

Walrus Club, 477, 489
War of 1812 (see also fires, Napoleon I, Emperor)
    memorials, 121, 191, 490, 558
War and Peace (film), making of, 242
warehouses, 209
water
    drinking local, 67
    hot, supply, 70
water skiing, 258

Wax Museum, 532
  workshop, 580
weapons, *see* arms and armor
websites
  accommodation, 254, 258, 272–3, 283, 337,
    362–71, 634–41
  airlines, 61, 360–1, 632–3, 676–7, 679–81
  cafés and restaurants, 375
  car hire, 413, 672
  entertainment, 161, 241, 402–11, 548, 666–9
  health clubs and saunas, 413–4, 617–8
  mail and parcel services, 80, 355, 628–9
  media, 81, 355, 629, 696
  medical services, 356, 630
  museums and historical buildings, 123, 245,
    257, 289, 336, 395, 398, 486, 497, 500, 568,
    576, 658–62
  Russia, 696–7
  shopping, 147, 697
  taxis, 71
  train services, 61, 75, 350, 361–2
  travel services, 53, 68, 143, 353, 411–2, 619,
    669–72
weights and measures, 84, 705
White House (Beli Dom), 35, 189, 191, 216
Wigstrom, Henrik, 147
wind surfing, 258
Winter Palace (Saint Petersburg), 491–5
  storming of (1917), 491
Wit, Monument to (Moscow), 162
women, personal security of, 83
wood carving (*see also* toys), 280, 292
World War I, 431
World War II (*see also* Siege of Leningrad), 22,
    110, 434, 493, 557, 605
  monuments, 191, 242
Writers Club, 210
Writers' Union, 252

Y

Yakovlev, Vladimir (mayor), 438, 443
Yaroslavl, 299–300, 302–7
  map, 301
Yaroslavl Museums of Art, History and
    Architecture, 303

Yaroslavl the Wise, 300
  statue, 299
Yasnaya Polyana, 254, 256, 258
Yauzsky Bulvar, 200–1
Yekaterinburg, 172, 431
Yelagin Palace, 484
Yeliseyev, Grigory Grigoyevich, 540–1
Yeliseyev's (food store), 175, 532, 540–2, 542,
    641
Yellow Pages, 79–80
Yelokhovsky Cathedral, 201
Yeltsin, Boris, 28, 29, 31–5, 39–43, 191, 269
Yermolova House Museum, 197
Yermolova, Maria (actress), 174, 197
Yesenin Museum, 169
Yesenin, Segei (poet), 169, 187
Young Komsomol League, 216
Young Pioneers (communist Youty
    Organization), 216
youth hostels, 53
Yuryev-Polsky (town), 335
Yusupov Palace, 550
Yusupov, Prince, 550, 555

Z

Zakharov, Andreyan (architectural professor),
    501
Zaitsev, Vyacheslav (fashion designer), 212
Zavidovo resort, 258
Zemlyanoi Val, 212
Zhirinovsky, Valdimir (nationalist), 36, 41, 43
Zhuganov, Gennady (Communist Party leader),
    40, 47
Zhukov, Marshal Georgy, statue of, 120, 120
Zhukovsky (aviation pioneer), 223
Zhvanetsky, Mikhail (comedian), 37
Zolotarev, Karp (artist), 195
Zoological Museum
    Moscow, 197
    St Petersburg, 486
zoological museums, 197, 486
zoos, 210, 228, 477
Zubovsky Bulvar, 209
Zvenigorod, 259–60